Tune in Yesterday

Tune in Yesterday

The Ultimate Encyclopedia of Old-Time Radio 1925-1976

JOHN DUNNING

Prentice-Hall, Inc., Englewood Cliffs, N.J.

Art Director: Hal Siegel
Designer: Joan Ann Jacobus

Printed in the United States of America
Prentice-Hall International, Inc., London
Prentice-Hall of Australia, Pty. Ltd., Sydney
Prentice-Hall of Canada, Ltd., Toronto
Prentice-Hall of India Private Ltd., New Delhi
Prentice-Hall of Japan, Inc., Tokyo
Prentice-Hall of Southeast Asia Pte. Ltd., Singapore
Whitehall Books Limited, Wellington, New Zealand

10 9 8 7 6 5 4 3 2 1

Library of Congress Cataloging in Publication Data

Dunning, John
    Tune in yesterday.

    Includes index.
    1. Radio programs—United States—Dictionaries.
I. Title.
PN1991.3.U6D8   791.44′5   76-28369
ISBN 0-13-932616-2

This book is for Skip, who knows about friendship and old-time radio.

_____

Foreword

It all began November 15, 1926, with the opening of the National Broadcasting Company. It ended September 30, 1962, when the last two dramatic shows were canceled by CBS. The final struggle between radio and television for the affections of the American people ended with TV the total victor. There have been a few valiant, ill-fated attempts to revive dramatic radio, but there is little on the air today outside the music-and-news formula. There is no equivalent to *Jack Armstrong, The All-American Boy* on radio or TV.

Maybe this is what radio was all about: ultimately optimistic, undeniably innocent by today's standards, old-time radio conveyed noble myths: crime did not pay, goodness would always be rewarded, and evil would not go unpunished. *The Shadow* proved that weekly on another network.

But on the night of September 8, 1947, ABC set out to prove something far more difficult. The network had in its grasp a five-pound book, *America's Needs and Resources*, prepared by twenty-seven economists and written up as a deadly dull 1,000-page report. Normally this was the kind of thing the networks avoided like the plague, with good reason. The axiom that people wanted entertainment, not intellectual balderdash repeated itself every time the Hooper company released its ratings of top radio shows. The Neilsen company is still finding it true in TV three decades later: people best like shows that can be described as sheer escapism.

ABC took on the project anyway, dressing it up as semi-entertainment—a 60-minute documentary, *1960? Jiminy Cricket!* An orchestra was added and characters from Walt Disney Studios were employed to tell us the story. Jiminy Cricket was the host and narrator, describing the future for Donald Duck and the Seven Dwarfs. As always, the voices of Cliff Edwards and Clarence Nash were Jiminy and Donald, respectively; the whole thing was enormously upbeat, ending with the full orchestra-and-chorus number, "Can This Be Paradise?" It could be, we were promised, and it could all happen in just thirteen years.

Oh, sure, there were a few "ifs" thrown in. Jiminy, Donald, and company wanted our politicians to begin taking their mandates seriously. Some real planning would be necessary to handle the $51 billion a year the government would be spending by 1960. They were worried even then about the effects of the wartime baby boom, and the inevitable overpopulation that would result. Grumpy sounded an all-too-familiar note: "I guess you didn't read the newspapers," he complained to Jiminy. "Strikes, wars, inflation, vetoes, death, and destruction. A dollar of U.S. cash currency buys me nothing. I say we're on the downgrade; we're hittin' the skids. The whole dad-blamed country's goin' plumb to pot!"

Jiminy's sugar ultimately prevailed. Natural resources? "Why, this country's got more of that stuff than anybody." It said so right in Chapter 23. There could be no question that America had an over-abundance of almost everything, "enough to support an expanding American economy for decades to come." What we didn't have, other countries could produce for us. And if that ever wore thin, we always had that great intangible, inexhaustible quality, "American know-how," to pull us through.

Well, Jiminy's thirteen years have come and gone—twice. We have gone through two more wars, a lot of internal strife, and a presidential assassination. We still have slums, strikes, and inflation. Government spending has now topped $1 billion a day—six times Jiminy's "problem" budget for 1960.

But we'll never know what Grumpy thinks now, because somewhere along the way radio died and became simply an article of party-time conversation.

This book really began with a cheap Sony tapedeck and a few reels of tape. Six years were spent listening to those shows. Sonys are no longer cheap and the six reels have grown to a roomful. From the 12,000 shows contained on those reels comes the fact and folklore contained in this book. The writer wishes to take note of the friends who have contributed to this library, keeping in mind that any remaining flaws are solely the author's responsibility.

A great debt of gratitude is due the entire fraternity of radio-show collectors. Without them, the sounds would surely have perished.

Dave Amaral, Fremont, California
Karl Amundsen, Brooklyn, New York
Ralph Becker, Denver, Colorado
Terry Black (*Cinnamon Bear* research), Springfield, Illinois
Al Block, San Bruno, California
Barry and Richard Brooks (*Lux Radio Theatre* log), Winthrop, Massachusetts
Howard Brenner, Mar-Bren Sound, P.O. Box 4099, Rochester, New York 14610
Fred Dickey, Sequim, Washington
Albert Ellis, Denver, Colorado
George Fowler, Great Radio Shows, Box 254, Woodinville, Washington 98072
Don Frey, Jr., Topeka, Kansas
Charles Gibson, Evergreen, Colorado
Joe Hehn, Allentown, Pennsylvania
Jay Hickerson, Orange, Connecticut
Joe McGoey, Don Zucker, KFML Radio, Denver, Colorado
Jack Miller, Hamden, Connecticut
John R. Olsen, Jr., Box 321, Baker, Oregon 97814
Bob Proctor, Adrian, Michigan
Pat Rispole, Schenectady, New York
Jay K. Springman, Xavier University, New Orleans, Louisiana
Ray Stanich (various program logs), Brooklyn, New York
Bill Thoennes, Denver, Colorado
Bob Wallenberg, Seattle, Washington
Marion Wedin (*One Man's Family* log), College Station, Texas

The quote from "A Final Fiance For Helen Trent" is excerpted from a *Life* article by Peter Bunzel, © 1960 Time Inc., and is used by permission.

Thanks also to the Denver Public Library, for help in digging out some 2,000 magazine articles from the "golden age"; to Roy Bright, Wyoming, Illinois, who supplied some 900 issues of *Radio Life*, a highly factual weekly review of radio when it was happening; and to Skip Craig, truly one of the outstanding collectors in America.

Most of the other material came from my personal collection of some 3,000 magazine articles, written when radio was going strong, and from my library. With radio dead but not quite forgotten, the "nostalgia boom" swept in and books appeared "remembering when." Though the bulk of the research for *Tune In Yesterday* came from other sources, these books provided overall scope. Such autobiographies as Meredith Willson's *And There I Stood With My*

Piccolo, Fred Allen's *Treadmill to Oblivion*, Eddie Cantor's *My Life Is in Your Hands*, Jessica Dragonette's *Faith Is a Song*, and Mary Jane Higby's *Tune in Tomorrow* still make entertaining reading. A debt is also owed the nostalgia volumes, Richard Lamparski's *Whatever Became of. . .?* series, and Jim Harmon's *Great Radio Heroes* and *Great Radio Comedians*. James Thurber's fine 1948 series of *New Yorker* articles, later assembled in book form, gave a listener's perspective of the best "washboard weepers" of that era, and Hadley Cantril's *Invasion From Mars* summarized the Orson Welles Martian scare. The *New York Times Directory of the Film* helped date shows containing movie stars, and Harrison Summers' *Thirty-Year History of Radio Programs, 1926–1956* was an invaluable source in tracking shows to their starting dates. Two final book sources were *The Serials*, Raymond William Stedman's survey of movie and radio serial drama, and *The Big Broadcast* by Frank Buxton and Bill Owen, the first extensive compilation of radio-show casts.

This book uses the Buxton and Owen alphabetical approach. Shows are listed alphabetically, by *full* title. For example, *Jack Armstrong, The All-American Boy* and *The Jack Benny Program* will both be found under the letter J. You won't find *Ozzie and Harriet* or *Sam Spade* under O or S, however, because the full title of both shows throughout their runs began with *The Adventures of. . ."*. Similarly, *The Romance of Helen Trent* and *Meet Corliss Archer* are listed under R and M respectively, though listeners might well remember them best as *Helen* and *Corliss*. For cross reference of stars and staff, see the index.

Quite unlike any previous books, this is also an historical reference, a nostalgia reader, and (because tapes of the shows can now easily be obtained by everyone) an entertainment review. Each show is covered in narrative form, giving such vital information as dates, networks, sponsors, time changes, and personnel. The interrelationships of important characters in serials, situation comedies, and running dramas are explored in some detail, and full biographical data is included on many of the stars who played those roles.

Scores of shows are discussed here for the first time, but this book doesn't pretend to include every series from radio history. A twelve-volume set would be needed for that. The scope has been limited to drama, comedy, and variety. Band remotes, straight newscasts, and documentaries are books in themselves. Newscasters are covered only when they were billed regularly as semi-entertainment (Walter Winchell, Hedda Hopper), bandleaders only when they had a regularly sustained variety show (*Kay Kyser's Kollege of Musical Knowledge*). Show casts were carefully checked in closing credits and in cross-indexed magazine articles, then were double-checked against Stedman, Buxton, Owen, Harmon, et al.

To describe the compiling of this book as work would be an injustice. It was fun. I hope the reading is as much fun. Remember *The Shadow?* . . . Remember *The Lone Ranger?* Return with us now to those thrilling days of yesteryear. This is how it was.

John Dunning
Denver, Colorado

Note...

Casual readers will note an apparent discrepancy in references to the NBC Blue Network. When NBC was formed, it was organized into two separate and independently operated networks, Red and Blue (at one time there was even an Orange Network for the Pacific Coast). In the late 1930s, the Federal Communications Commission recommended that no single corporation be allowed to own more than one network, and the result was the sale in 1943 of the Blue Network to Edward J. Noble. The Red Network then became simply NBC, and the Blue Network was renamed the American Broadcasting Company.

For a time during this transition, it was simply called the Blue. Then it was called "The Blue Network of the American Broadcasting Company." Finally the change was complete, in mid-1945 it became simply ABC. This is why some of the early references are to NBC Blue and some later references are to Blue or, during the transition, Blue-ABC.

Tune in Yesterday

The Abbott and Costello Show

The Abbott and Costello Show. Bud Abbott and Lou Costello, remembered primarily as a movie team, got their first shove toward stardom in radio and stayed with the medium through the 1940's when their fame as film comics was at its height.

Their personal lives almost contradicted their screen and radio images. William Abbott was born October 2, 1895—it is said in a circus tent—to a family of veteran circus performers. Born March 6, 1908 in Paterson, N.J., Costello would become known in show business circles as "Hard Luck Lou." They met in 1929, when Costello was booked with a vaudeville act into a neighborhood Brooklyn theatre. Abbott worked in the theatre's box office, and soon found himself onstage serving as Costello's straight man. The men seemed to fit together from the beginning, and before long they were hitting the boards as a regular team. They played burlesque and vaudeville through the Depression and in 1938 signed for an appearance at Loew's in New York. Ted Collins, then riding high as the architect of Kate Smith's career, saw their show and asked them to come on the air with Kate.

They brought an old-style vaudeville slapstick style to radio, a standup comedy that consisted mainly of short skits involving clever plays on words. Costello's shrill shrieks mixed well with Abbott's flat sarcasm, and the team was an instant radio hit. For more than a year they were regulars on *The Kate Smith Hour*, and the exposure there led to Hollywood, to films, and to frequent guest appearances with

Edgar Bergen on *The Chase and Sanborn Hour.* Their first starring radio roles came in 1940, when they filled in for a summer in Fred Allen's NBC slot, beginning July 3.

Together they made and lost a fortune. Signed by Universal Pictures in 1939, they almost single-handedly bailed the financially troubled studio out of the red. Their own regular airshow was first heard October 8, 1942, running for five years on NBC as a Thursday night feature for Camel Cigarettes. For the 1947–48 season they switched to ABC, sustained for two years on Wednesdays and later on Thursdays. Their *Abbott and Costello Children's Show* was heard Saturday mornings at 11 on ABC from 1947 through 1949, awarding $1,000 savings bonds to "outstanding youngsters of the week" and featuring top juvenile talent.

But their nighttime *Abbott and Costello Show* became the backbone of their success. Consistently heard by more than 20 million listeners, it supplemented such films as *Buck Privates, In the Navy,* and *Hold That Ghost* to keep their names constantly at the top of the zany comic heap. Their air skits were often extensions of the routines they had used on stage. The famous baseball spoof, "Who's On First?" was developed for a live audience, but was especially adaptable for radio. The skits developed their images: Abbott became the stern taskmaster, while Costello fumbled his way through life and shrugged off his bumbling with "I'm a baaaad boy!"

They opened with fanfare. Leith Stevens was tapped for musical arrangement; Marty Gosch became their longtime producer-director, and early writers included Hal Fimberg, Don Prindle, and Joe Kirk. Connie Haines did the vocals, and later Marilyn Maxwell was brought aboard to sing and be ogled by Lou. Skits were also built around the home life of announcer Ken Niles, with Elvia Allman playing Mrs. Niles.

Costello's life was marked by numerous tragedies, and he became known in the trade as "hard luck Lou." In March 1943, with the radio show at its peak, he was stricken with rheumatic fever and forced off the air. Abbott refused to carry on alone, so the new team of Jimmy Durante and Garry Moore was hastily assembled to replace them. Costello returned in the fall, but fate wasn't finished with him yet. In dress rehearsal for his first show, he was called to the phone to learn that his year-old son had fallen into the family swimming pool and drowned.

Costello rushed home, and the news spread through the film city. Mickey Rooney was brought in to read Costello's lines; calls offering to help came in from Durante, Bob Hope, and Red Skelton. But around 6 P.M., Costello called Abbott and said he was returning for the show. For 30 minutes he fought back tears and wisecracked with Abbott on the air. Just after Ken Niles had read the sign-off he broke down before the studio audience. Abbott then stepped forward and explained to the audience what had happened.

The team survived into the 1950's, but by then their peak had passed. Then the tax people descended, and nothing was ever again the same. Costello died March 3, 1959. In his old-age, Abbott thought about comebacks with new partners, but it didn't work. He had earned millions in his film and air career, but both he and Lou were "always broke." He died a pauper April 24, 1974, after an eight-year audit of his back taxes left him penniless.

Abbott Mysteries

Abbott Mysteries was a spinoff of the *Mr. and Mrs. North* and *Thin Man* success formula, featuring Charles Webster and Julie Stevens as Pat and Jean Abbott, a San Francisco couple whose particular penchant was stumbling over bodies in hallways or wherever. Although the series got good reviews and capitalized well on the breezy detective format, it never enjoyed the success of the big two, and was relegated to irregular summertime runs of the late 1940's. Adapted by Ed Adamson from stories by Frances Crane, *Abbott Mysteries* was heard on Mutual in the summers of 1945, 1946 and 1947. Webster and Miss Stevens carried the roles for most of the run, but the parts were played for a time by Les Tremayne and Alice Reinheart.

The Abe Burrows Show

The Abe Burrows Show premièred in its Saturday night quarter-hour format on July 26, 1947, over CBS. Manhattan born and reared, Burrows journeyed to Hollywood in the late 1930's and found work writing for radio. He was the life of any party and soon gained a reputation among the town's superstars as the nation's greatest satirist. He made his name satirizing the songs of Tin Pan Alley, rambling to the accompaniment of his own piano and belting out such beauties as "I Looked Under A Rock And Found You," and "Walking Down Memory Lane Without A Goddamn Thing On My Mind." Burrows helped Ed Gardner create Archie, the sloppy barkeep at "Duffy's Tavern." When *Duffy* became a regular series March 1, 1941, Burrows became head writer, a job he held for four years. He worked on a serial of his own creation, *Holiday and Company*, which ran on CBS in 1946. But *The Abe Burrows Show* was his first stab at performing before the mike. The show ran 29 weeks and was dropped, despite winning a Radio Critics Award as best comedy of the year. Burrows returned to the CBS microphone July 4, 1949 in a show called *Breakfast With Burrows*. Explaining to *Newsweek* why a breakfast show was scheduled at 9 P.M., he said simply, "I get up late." Ahead were brighter days in other fields: a successful TV series, writing of the hit musical *Guys and Dolls* and co-authorship of *How to Succeed in Business Without Really Trying*. Today *The Abe Burrows Show* is just another little audio curiosity.

Abie's Irish Rose

Abie's Irish Rose was first heard January 24, 1942, as part of NBC's *Knickerbocker Playhouse. Knickerbocker* had been running two years then, offering lighthearted comedies à la *First Nighter*. Then the sponsor, Procter & Gamble, bought *Abie's Irish Rose*, which had been one of the great hits of Broadway, having had more than 2,000 performances before closing in 1927. *Knickerbocker* was gradually phased out, and *Abie's Irish Rose* became part of the NBC Saturday night lineup as a show of its own. It was one of the very early theatrical thrusts into the "marriage of two cultures" theme. Author Anne Nichols intended it as a "true love conquers all" statement, pitting Catholic and Jewish families against each other as in-laws. Abie Levy was played in the first year by Sydney Smith; his young bride Rosemary Murphy was Betty Winkler. The marriage set family against family until twins were born to Abie and Rosemary on Christmas Day and the families decided to patch up their differences. Still, fights between the crusty old fathers were just beneath the surface. Alan Reed played Solomon Levy and Walter Kinsella was Patrick Joseph Murphy. The start of the second year brought Richard Coogan and Mercedes McCambridge to the mikes as Abie and Rosemary.

Sponsored by P&G's Drene Shampoo, this program was "dedicated to the spirit of freedom and equality which gives to this nation the greatness that is America," and came packaged to the organ theme, "My Wild Irish Rose." It ran until September 1944.

Academy Award

Academy Award, although on the air for just one season, reached a high point in audio drama. Probably as much because of the stature of its stars as the slickness of its production, it stands the test of time well and remains historically an important piece of radio.

It is one of the great "forgotten programs" of the air. Broadcast weekly in half-hour episodes, *Academy Award* dramatized many famous stories of the movies, using the original film casts wherever possible. When the stars weren't available, other big names were tapped to fill in. Each play had one thing in common: either the players or the movie on which it was based must have won or been nominated for an Academy Award.

It opened March 30, 1946, with Bette Davis in *Jezebel*. Ginger Rogers starred in *Kitty Foyle* for the second offering. It was a Saturday-night show through June, when it moved to Wednesdays and continued until December 18, when it left the air. Sponsored by The House of Squibb, a drug manufacturing firm, *Academy Award* offered such standout productions through the year as *Stagecoach* with Randolph Scott and Claire Trevor; *The Maltese Falcon* with Humphrey Bogart, Sydney Greenstreet, and Mary Astor; *Young Mr. Lincoln* with Henry Fonda, and *Keys of the Kingdom* with Gregory Peck. But movie stars were expensive, often getting $4,000 and more for a single appearance. The sponsor also had to pay $1,600 a week to the Academy of Motion Picture Arts and Sciences for use of the name, but perhaps the most serious problem was the shortage of suitable scripts because of constant repetition on similar shows, and after nine months the show was scrapped.

While it lasted, Dee Engelbach was producer-director, and the plays were adapted from the screen by Frank Wilson. Original musical scores and themes were composed and conducted by Leith Stevens, and the production had all the appeal of *The Lux Radio Theatre*, *The Screen Guild Theatre*, or any of the other major screen theatres of the air.

Adopted Daughter

Adopted Daughter was developed from a series of regional skits and played on a regional NBC hookup for several years beginning in the summer of 1939. Jettabee Ann Hopkins wrote the script for this soap opera, and played the part of Jerry Jangles, the "courageous young wife who fights for home and happiness." Miss Hopkins had developed *The Jangles* as a radio play in 1934, and had produced it locally at various radio stations where she worked. It told the story of the Jangles family and their adopted daughter Jennie, and soon attracted a following wherever it played. In 1937, Miss Hopkins joined WOW, Omaha, and after a trial run, *The Jangles* was picked up by a very rich sponsor, J. C. Penney. That made the network sit up, and in April 1939 NBC brought Miss Hopkins to New York for a transcribed run, immediately changing the name to *Adopted Daughter*.

Adult Education Series

Adult Education Series, one of the early experiments with adult education on the air, came to CBS April 28, 1938, under the direction of Sterling Fisher, and was divided into three areas of learning: "Americans at Work," "Living History," and "Adventures in Science." The "Americans at Work" segments were especially popular, recording interviews with blue-collar workers and executives in their jobs. The show followed Walt Disney through a typical day, but built most of its format around the "common man."

Adventure Parade

Adventure Parade came to Mutual in 1946, running for three years as a 15-minute daily serialization of the classics. John Drake was first host-storyteller, doing all the voices for such plays as *Moby Dick, Last of the Mohicans,* and *Swiss Family Robinson.* Later the shows were more fully dramatized, and the stories usually lasted about a week. Announcer George Hogan called the club to order with "Adventurers, atten-shun! Fall in for Adventure Parade!"

Adventures by Morse

Adventures by Morse, a syndicated series, was produced by writer Carlton E. Morse in 1944 after his *I Love a Mystery* was dropped from the networks. Morse was one of radio's most prolific, versatile writers and directors, doing soap opera (*Woman in My House, Family Skeleton*), evening drama (the long-running *One Man's Family*, a radio legend), and hair-raising adventure shows.

Adventures by Morse picked up the same high adventure themes Morse had been using in *I Love a Mystery* since 1939. Hero of the series was a San Francisco detective named Captain Bart Friday. With his sidekick Skip Turner, Friday roamed the world solving mysteries and seeking out dangerous adventure. The stories often bordered on the supernatural, though in the Morse tradition there was usually a logical explanation.

It was produced in serial form, each chapter 30 minutes long and programmed once a week. A full year of *Adventures by Morse* was produced for syndication, with the major stories done in ten chapters. Breather stories of three chapters were sandwiched between the longer runs. These terror-thrillers were the kind of radio writing Morse did better than anyone. He sent Friday in the first show to a graveyard in northern California where corpses walked, wolfmen prowled, and ghouls roamed at will. In subsequent shows, Friday and Skip headed for Cambodia, in the heart of French Indo-China, and had a confrontation inside a great hollow mountain with an ancient order of vampire priests. Another adventure found them in the quiet California town of Holman, where dead men prowled the night and a skeleton dragged people out of their windows into the sea. And if Friday and Turner couldn't quite replace Jack, Doc, and Reggie in radio's Hall of Fame, they still gave a good account of themselves when the chips were down.

Even the characters were developed along *I Love a Mystery* lines. Captain Friday, as the strong-voiced leader figure, was played by Elliott Lewis, David Ellis, and Russell Thorson over the run. The character of Skip Turner had—probably not without reason—a strong Texas accent, and was more than a little reminiscent of ILAM's Doc Long. A fine adventure show, almost Grade-A Morse.

The Adventures of Christopher Wells

The Adventures of Christopher Wells was a brief adventure show created by Ed (*Mr. District Attorney*) Byron, premiering on CBS September 28, 1947, and running for one season. Wells was played early in the run by Myron McCormick and later by Les Damon. He was a tough New York newsman with a flare for globe-trotting and an eye for a shapely leg. He was aided in his adventures by Stacy McGill, the inevitable beauteous girl Friday, played by another *Mr. D.A.* refugee, Vicki Vola. Robert Shaw wrote the scripts and music was by Peter Van Steeden. In short, just another action show. Some programs might have survived against *Fibber McGee and Molly, Christopher Wells* didn't. Neither did its sponsor, the DeSoto automobile.

The Adventures of Frank Merriwell

The Adventures of Frank Merriwell, "beloved hero of American fiction," had its roots in the dime novels of the late nineteenth century. On radio, Frank goes back to the mid-1930's, to a three-a-week serial for Dr. West's Toothpaste. That show, announced by Harlow Wilcox, has been virtually obliterated by time. The "new" *Adventures of Frank Merriwell* came to NBC as a Saturday-morning half-hour October 5, 1946, featuring Lawson Zerbe as Frank. Co-starred were Hal

Studer as Frank's pal Bart Hodge and Elaine Rost as girlfriend Inza Burrage. Other regulars were Pat Hosley, Lamont Johnson, Brad Barker, and Grace Keddy. The show was directed by Ed King, later by Joseph Mansfield and Harry Junkin. Frank Merriwell was a student at turn-of-the-century Yale, a super athlete who always kept his wits. The show opened to the clip-clop of a trotting horse as announcer Mel Brandt set the stage: "There it is, an echo of the past, an exciting past, a romantic past—the era of the horse and carriage, gas-lit streets and free-for-all football games; the era of one of the most beloved characters in American fiction, Frank Merriwell. Merriwell is loved as much today as ever he was, and so the National Broadcasting Company brings him to radio, in a new series of books written by Gilbert Patton under the pen name Burt L. Standish." Scripting actually was done by Ruth and Gilbert Brann and William Welch, but the series contained much of the original flavor, and lasted until 1949.

The Adventures of Frank Race

The Adventures of Frank Race was an adventure series, beginning syndication May 1,1949. The chief protagonist, Race, was an attorney who took up a life of intrigue after the war. When the war was over, his former life was over too; adventure had become his business. The shows were written and directed by Joel Murcott and Buckley Angel for Bruce Eells Productions. Eells had a cute trick of producing the early episodes of his shows with a "name" star, then dropping the star once the series had been sold. So it was with *The Adventures of Frank Race*. Tom Collins, fresh from his distinctive performance in *Chandu, the Magician*, was signed as Race, but was dropped after the first few months in favor of Paul Dubov. The series was run of the mill, though it did have a creative musical score, written and played by Ivan Ditmars.

The Adventures of Nero Wolfe

The Adventures of Nero Wolfe, "detective genius who rates the knife and fork the greatest tools ever invented by man," came to the Blue Network July 5, 1943, as a Monday- and later a Friday-night mystery show for Elgin watches. Wolfe, first seen in the mystery novels of Rex Stout was a "gargantuan gourmet" and orchid fancier first class, the fat genius whose eye for detail solved many a "perfect" murder. To watch over his personal and financial affairs, Wolfe had a secretary, Archie Goodwin, who goaded him into taking a case whenever the bankbook got too low, and Archie's appreciation for female curves gave the show an occasional shot of romance. Santos Ortega and Luis Van Rooten were among the early Wolfes. The 1943 series soon disappeared, but Wolfe was resurrected in late 1945, starring Francis X. Bushman with Elliott Lewis as Archie. Louis Vittes wrote the scripts. The show ran Sundays for Jergens Lotion and ended December 15, 1946. In 1950, still another *Nero Wolfe* was brought to the air, sustained by NBC on Fridays. It featured Sydney Greenstreet as Wolfe, and rotated so many actors into the role of Archie that listeners must still be confused. Among those playing Goodwin in this last series were Gerald Mohr, Wally Maher, Harry Bartell, Herb Ellis, and Lawrence Dobkin, who also played other roles in other weeks. Produced by Edwin Fadiman, directed by J. Donald Wilson, and announced by Don Stanley, the show was last heard April 27, 1951.

The Adventures of Ozzie and Harriet

The Adventures of Ozzie and Harriet premièred on CBS on the Nelson's ninth wedding anniversary, October 8, 1944. A New Jersey native, Ozzie had formed his first orchestra at 14, and had worked his way through college and law school playing proms and balls. He graduated from Rutgers and emerged from academia with a law degree, but soon found his band doing so well that he postponed hanging out his legal shingle.

Harriet came out of Iowa, playing her first stage role at the age of six weeks in the arms of her actress mother. Her name was Peggy Lou Snyder then; her parents were part of a traveling stock company, and by the time she was 5, Harriet was a veteran performer. After school she continued her career, traveling the old Orpheum vaudeville circuit with Ken Murray, Bert Lahr, and others. Her stage work led inevitably to Hollywood, where as Harriet Hilliard she signed a contract with Paramount and appeared as a dancer in the 1932 short film, *Musical Justice*.

By that time, Ozzie Nelson was leading one of the best-known dance bands of the time, and was packing them in at the old Glen Island Casino. He had an idea that a girl singer might go well with his band (rather a novel thought in those early days), and one day he caught Harriet's act in *Musical Justice*. He liked her and arranged a meeting. She liked him, and agreed to give up her current job—singer in a New York restaurant—and join the band. Together they worked out the patter-and-song routine that became their trademark. While the band played lightly, Ozzie and Harriet would toss songs back and forth between them in lighthearted, lyrical banter, developing a style distinctive for its time.

For Ozzie, though he didn't know it then, it was the final stroke of fate that pushed him irrevocably away from the practice of law and cemented him into show business.

After three years together in the band, Ozzie and Harriet were married on October 8, 1935. In the meantime, they had signed as melodians of Joe Penner's *Baker's Broadcast*, an engagement they continued after Penner left the show and Robert "Believe-It-Or-Not" Ripley took over. Their son David was born October 24, 1936; another son, Eric, arrived on May 8, 1940. After the birth of Eric, who became widely known and later famous as Ricky, the Nelsons forsook the East Coast and moved to Hollywood, where they joined *The Red Skelton Show* in 1941.

Here Ozzie's natural talent for comedy began to emerge, and the Nelsons found themselves acting as well as singing. The Skelton job lasted three years, folding suddenly when Skelton was drafted. Then Ozzie and Harriet began the second phase of their joint career, in a new radio situation comedy. *The Adventures of Ozzie and Harriet* would portray the Nelsons at home, living the good life, but constantly entangled in amusing situations of their own making. They were billed as "America's favorite young couple," and the plots were as simple as a Walt Disney movie: setup, complication (always by Ozzie), deeper complication, and resolution (usually by Harriet). Ozzie was the pivotal character, and his tangents were the vehicles to confusion. Once Ozzie got his mind set on something, nothing could sway him from the path of disaster. This week it might be a "men are superior" kick; the next week he might suddenly get the idea that the boys were being neglected. Whatever the cause, Ozzie was sure to muff it by taking it to ridiculous lengths, Harriet tried to gently guide him away from the newest crusade, David and Ricky would get in a few wisecracks, and there would be some well-intended (but usually ill-advised) advice from the neighbor, Thornberry (Thorny for short).

Naturally, nobody on Radio Row thought it would fly, but *The Adventures of Ozzie and Harriet* became one of the long-running comedy hits of the air. Ozzie wrote much of the finished material himself, and employed numerous rough-draft scripters. At first he refused to allow the boys to portray themselves, feeling that the experience of big-time radio was a bit too much for youngsters of 8 and 4 to handle. As he later put it, he wanted no inflated egos at the dinner table. Initially the roles of David and Ricky were handled by Tommy Bernard and Henry Blair.

For its first three seasons, 1944–47, *Ozzie and Harriet* was a Sunday night show for International Silver on CBS. The same sponsor followed the show to Fridays in 1947, and to Sunday night NBC in 1948.

In March 1949, Ozzie relented and let David and Ricky play themselves. John Brown gave a fine supporting performance as Thorny; Lurene Tuttle was Harriet's mother (usually on the phone); Janet Waldo was Corliss Archer all over again as Emmy Lou, the breathless teenager who gave Ozzie poor advice as freely as Thorny did; Bea Benaderet played the Nelsons' maid, Glorie, in the early run. Original music, composed and conducted by Billy May, became one of radio's best-known themes. The longtime announcer was Verne Smith, who also narrated the weekly adventures at 1847 Rogers Road (rather an insidious plug for the 1847 Rogers Brothers Silver sold by the sponsor).

Ozzie and Harriet moved to ABC for Heinz Foods in 1949, and were heard on Friday nights there until they left radio for TV in 1954. Heinz dropped sponsorship in 1952, and the show was picked up by a variety of interests.

The show made almost a painless transition to television and became one of that medium's early success stories. The characters were as homey and consistent on TV as they had been on radio. The voices were the same, the shows were in good taste, and the Nelsons didn't even *look* radically different than we expected.

It's still surprising that the Nelsons were able to shift gears so often and with such flexibility. They couldn't go on forever, of course. Ricky was about to emerge as one of the early superstars of rock and roll; David was a family man with a career of his own. They were truly big-time with everything they touched, until they tried a twilight comeback on TV in the 1970's, with an ill-fated series called *Ozzie's Girls*. It wasn't even up to their radio standards of 25 years before, and soon vanished from the air.

On June 3, 1975, Ozzie Nelson died at his California home of cancer.

The Adventures of Phillip Marlowe

The Adventures of Phillip Marlowe, the tough private detective created by Raymond Chandler, came to NBC in 1947 as a summertime replacement for *The Bob Hope Show*. It starred Van Heflin as Marlowe, a hardboiled gumshoe whose antics had first been told in such Chandler stories as *Farewell, My Lovely*, and *The Lady in the Lake*. The character had also survived a leap to the screen and subsequently turned up in the *Lux Radio Theatre* dramatization of "Murder, My Sweet," with Dick Powell. So why not a regular series? Heflin's Marlowe was adapted from the original Chandler by Milton Geiger, and the music was scored by Lyn Murray. Wendell Niles announced, and the show provided a nice summertime contrast to Hope. But then it was gone until September 26, 1948 when the new *Adventures of Philip Marlowe* came to CBS, running Sundays, then Saturdays into 1949 and 1950. Gerald Mohr was starred as Marlowe in a fine show produced and directed by Norman Macdonnell. Mohr was the toughest Marlowe yet, heavier of voice than any of the thugs who opposed him. "Get this and get it straight," he barked, opening the show; "crime is a sucker's road, and those who travel it wind up in the gutter, the prison, or an early grave." Mohr's scripts were written by Gene Levitt, Robert Mitchell, and Mel Dinelli; special music was by Richard Aurandt. Macdonnell drew support from radio's finest, employing many actors who had worked with him on *Escape*. Among them: Edgar Barrier, Vivi Janniss, Gloria Blondell, Lou Krugman, David Ellis, Wilms Herbert, Virginia Gregg, John Dehner, Lawrence Dobkin, Jack Moyles, Laurette Fillbrandt, Parley Baer, and Howard McNear. Lieutenant Abar was played by Jeff Corey; Roy Rowan announced. Despite the obvious quality, *The Adventures of Philip Marlowe* was sustained for most of its run, picking up the Ford Motor Company as sponsor for a time in 1950.

The Adventures of Sam Spade

The Adventures of Sam Spade was first heard on CBS July 12, 1946, as a Friday-night summer series. The show clicked at once, and went into regular fall lineup September 29, 1946. From then until 1949, *Sam Spade* was a Sunday-night thriller for Wildroot Cream Oil, starring Howard Duff in the title role. With Duff's departure, NBC took the series, leaving it on Sundays for Wildroot and starring Stephen Dunne as Spade. This version lasted until 1951, the last year running as a Friday sustainer.

Spade's appearance on the air marked an almost literal transition from Dashiell Hammett's 1930 crime classic, *The Maltese Falcon*, where he first appeared. Spade was a San Francisco detective, one of the most distinctive of the hardboiled school. His jump to radio was wrought by William Spier, who had already carved out a reputation as a master of mystery in his direction of another highly rated CBS thriller, *Suspense*.

Spier was editor, producer, director. A lifelong radio man, he had broken in during the primitive days of 1929 and earned his stripes serving on such pioneering shows as *The March of Time*. Spier assembled the writing team of Bob Tallman and Ann Lorraine and began putting Spade together. He was impressed by the deep, cynical, tough qualities in Howard Duff's voice. Duff had had long experience as an actor, a career that traced back to his high school days in Seattle. He had originally wanted to be a cartoonist, but the sound of applause in a senior-year play at Roosevelt High changed all that. Suddenly stagestruck, Duff began hitting the boards. He worked in local theatre groups and cracked radio as an announcer on a local station. When the war came, Duff went with Armed Forces Radio as a correspondent, a job he held for more than four years. He emerged in Hollywood in 1945, a seasoned but unsung microphone veteran. With his perfect voice and polished delivery, it wasn't long before Duff was playing supporting parts in top dramas of the air.

Sam Spade shot him to national fame. The character, as Spier saw it, would have many easily identifiable traits. The first thing Spade usually wanted to know was, "How much money you got on you?"

Two hundred? Okay, I'll take that and you can pay me the rest later." But Spade wasn't a spendthrift—he never threw silver-dollar tips à la Johnny Dollar, even if he could have put it on his expense account. Spade's favorite way to travel was by streetcar; it took him almost anywhere for a dime. He disliked cabs and liked cheap booze. You didn't need more than an occasional, subtle reminder; those glasses clinking every week as Sam opened his desk drawer and began dictating were enough. We knew Sam and Effie weren't toasting each other with Sal Hepatica. Sam was a man who worked out of his desk, and the thing closest at hand in that top drawer just might be a half-empty bottle of Old Granddad.

His clients got bumped off with startling regularity. Then Sam sent his report (and presumably his bill) to the widows. He dictated his cases to his faithful secretary, Effie Perrine, a babbling, man-hungry female who might have been the adult Corliss Archer. Each case came out as a report, dated, signed, and delivered. Spade's license number—137596—was always included in the report. The cases unfolded in chronological order, the scenes shifting between Sam and Effie and the dramatization of Sam's dictation. Effie, who always seemed on the verge of tears whenever Sam became involved (as he did weekly) with a curvy client, was beautifully played by Lurene Tuttle. Jerry Hausner played Sam's lawyer, Sid Weiss. Lud Gluskin directed the music and Dick Joy announced. Soon after the series began, Ann Lorraine dropped her writing duties, and Gil Doud became Bob Tallman's writing partner.

By the summer of 1949, congressional Un-American Activities probers were beginning to toss Dashiell Hammett's name around. CBS dropped the show, even though Hammett wasn't linked to any Communist activity. Sam Spade was snapped up by NBC, but Duff had moved on to other things. NBC ran the show as though nothing had happened, using Steve Dunne as a boyish-sounding Spade. Spier and Miss Tuttle followed the series over, and for a time so did Wild-root. Wildroot and the listeners all got wise around the same time. Dunne was a good radio man, but he sounded like Sam in knee pants.

Duff once said that Hammett had done such a great job in *The Maltese Falcon* that any actor could have played Sam and become a radio hero. He saw that theory proved wrong. In spades.

The Adventures of Superman

The Adventures of Superman was on the air within a few months of its 1938 debut in Action Comics in a series of crudely done syndications. The comics have always adapted well to juvenile radio, and what better radio subject than a man of steel, complete with X-ray vision, dependent comrades, and a distinctive swishing sound effect that carried us along in flight? In reality, he was a "strange visitor from another planet, who came to earth with powers and abilities far beyond those of mortal men, and who—disguised as Clark Kent, mild-mannered reporter for a great metropolitan newspaper—leads a never-ending battle for truth, justice and the American way."

He came to earth as a child from the planet Krypton, which had been destroyed by violent earthquakes. On earth, he found that his ordinary Kryptonese powers were extraordinary; he could fly to heights never achieved by planes in those years of propeller-driven aircraft. He could bend steel in his bare hands, change the course of mighty rivers. He was

> faster than a speeding bullet . . .
>> more powerful than a locomotive . . .
>>> able to leap tall buildings at a single bound . . .
>>> Look! Up in the sky!
>>> It's a bird!
>>> It's a plane!
>>> It's . . . *Superman!*

That ingenious opening set the stage perfectly for those 15-minute fantasies, which one month found Superman fighting train robbers, another battling Nazis and "Japs" at the North Pole. During the war, Superman was juvenile radio's best fighter for the cause. Only two things stopped him: his X-ray vision couldn't penetrate lead and, when confronted with the element Kryptonite, he was rendered helpless. Kent, who wore glasses in his disguise as a *Daily Planet* reporter, was bullied by his boss and was barely tolerated by Lois Lane, the *Planet's* star female reporter (who adored Superman). If only Lois had known that in the twinkling of an eye Kent could dash into that empty janitor's closet, rip off his clothes, and dart to the window as SUPERMAN!

In the comics by Jerry Siegel and Joe Shuster, we could see Superman fly out of that window. On radio, we had to visualize it. So we got "up, up, and away!" whenever Superman took off. Admittedly, it's difficult to imagine a grown man perched on a window ledge shouting "Up, up, and away!" but Superman could get away with a lot. The character was soon brought to Mutual, starting on February 12, 1940, as a three-a-week 15-minute sustained serial. *Superman* was dropped in 1942, but the clamor of young listeners led to its return August 31, 1942, this time as a five-a-week show. Kellogg's Pep picked it up in 1943, remaining sponsor until 1946.

Writer Jack Johnstone and director Robert Maxwell went to great lengths to protect Superman's identity, onstage and off. In the scripts, anyone who discovered this well-kept secret was a dead duck. Superman didn't kill them; the writer simply polished them off. No matter; they were always the bad people anyway (good guys wouldn't go messing around in Superman's affairs like that). At the same time, the producers insisted that the identity of Clayton (Bud) Collyer, the actor who gave voice to the man of steel, be stamped TOP SECRET. For six years, Collyer kept his name out of the limelight, finally stepping forward in a 1946 *Time* interview to promote a Superman campaign against racial and religious intolerance. The serial became the first of its kind to tackle such heavy themes. Thus Superman added bigots to his list of people to fight.

In 1945, another Action Comics hero, Batman, was introduced on Superman's show. Batman and his young sidekick Robin joined Superman frequently during those middle years, bounding out of Gotham City to tackle Metropolis scandal. But the inevitable comparison with Superman left Batman a second-rate hero. Batman couldn't fly; he couldn't even bend steel in his bare hands. Batman never did break away for a radio show of his own.

Supporting Collyer in the serial were Joan Alexander as the cynical Lois Lane, Julian Noa as crabby Perry White, editor of the *Planet*, and Jackie Kelk as Jimmy Olsen, energetic cub reporter. As in the comics, it was often Jimmy Olsen's curiosity that led Superman into action. One of the trademarks of the serial was Collyer's ability to change characters in mid-sentence, from the mousy Kent ("this looks like a job for . . .") to the barrel-chested ("SUPERMAN!") man of steel.

Jackson Beck gave a gusty delivery as announcer, too. The show is best-remembered from its wartime days, under sponsorship of "that super-delicious cereal," Kellogg's Pep. Mutual again sustained it until 1949. In 1949, *Superman* crossed over to ABC for a 30-minute Saturday show. Michael Fitzmaurice played the title role. This sustained version was extended to two a week in 1950, and went off in 1951.

The Adventures of the Thin Man

The Adventures of the Thin Man was first heard on NBC July 2, 1941, as a summer replacement.

It was a long jump from *Inner Sanctum Mysteries* to the sophistication of Dashiell Hammett's *Thin Man*, but radio people were flexible. Himan Brown produced and directed both those thrillers, and even managed to dabble a bit in soap opera.

The Thin Man was actually as much comedy as thriller. Based on the 1934 film, itself based on the Hammett novel of the same year, it chronicled the adventures of Nick Charles, a retired private eye who just couldn't stay away from murder. During his decade on the air, Nick happened upon as many bodies per show as did Mr. and Mrs. North. Like Mr. North, Nick was assisted in his spadework by an eccentric, lovely woman—his wife Nora. Billed for a time as "the happiest, merriest married couple in radio," Nick and Nora had without question the lightest, sexiest thriller on the air. They came virtually unspoiled from the screen, cast in the images of William Powell and Myrna Loy. Brown couldn't get Powell and Loy, so he settled for Les Damon and Claudia Morgan, two radio pros who learned to talk like the screen stars and like it. They were chosen specifically for their abilities at simulating the movie sound—and so successful were they that, despite the credits, many listeners thought that Powell and Loy really *were* doing the radio roles. As Nora, Miss Morgan cooed invitingly into the microphone, mouthing long, drawn-out kisses that threatened to blow the radio tubes. Between the cooing and the cadavers, she kidded Nicky-darling mercilessly about his outlandish pajamas.

Nick, ever the deductive genius, literally purred at his wife's fantastic figure, became the top sleuth of the martini set, and kept up a running acquaintance with such underworld characters as Dippy Danny the Pickpocket, Charlie the Creep, and Big-Ears Benny.

The show was an audio version of the film, with Nick and Nora breezing through the half-hour in the most painless manner allowed by their thriller format (and the censors). When *The Thin Man* first came to NBC in 1941, Nick and Nora were the only two regular characters—if you don't count their wire-haired terrier, Asta.

By fall, the show was so popular that it had become part of the regular NBC schedule, under Wednesday-night sponsorship of Woodbury Soap. In 1942, it moved to CBS for Post Toasties, where in 1943 it ran Sundays, in 1944 Fridays, and then Sundays until 1946. Parker Fennelly was added as Nick's old friend and partner, Sheriff Ebenezer Williams of Crabtree County. Fennelly played basically the same Titus Moody part he always played—a country cynic from New England whose observations were laced with dry wit and humor. He added greatly to the lighthearted mood.

When Damon went into the service in 1944, he was replaced by David Gothard, erstwhile Gil Whitney from *The Romance of Helen Trent*. Gothard was replaced by Les Tremayne in 1945. Then Damon returned, carrying the role in 1946–47. In 1947, it became a Friday-night CBS show, still for Post. A *New Adventures of the Thin Man* series ran on NBC during the summer of 1948. Tremayne again starred as Nick in NBC's 1948 summer series, sponsored by Pabst Blue Ribbon. Claudia Morgan played Nora throughout. Scripting was by Milton Lewis and assorted freelancers.

Throughout the run, *The Thin Man* got generally good reviews. One exception was *Radio Life*, the weekly trade magazine based in Hollywood. Its critic objected strongly to the overly suggestive sexiness of the scripts, the "oooohs" and "mmms" during the "squeaky" kisses and love scenes. *The Thin Man*, the critic suggested, should be thankful that TV hadn't yet arrived. "No censor on earth would allow scenes enacted that would tie in with the noises that come out of our radio on *Thin Man* night."

A final series began on ABC in the fall of 1948 and was heard Fridays until September 1, 1950. Joseph Curtin was the last Nick.

The Adventures of Topper

The Adventures of Topper will be instantly familiar to connoisseurs of early television, who will remember Leo G. Carroll's portrayal of Cosmo Topper, the character from the Thorne Smith novel whose life was complicated by two friendly ghosts. The TV series was a milestone, so memorable that few people remember *Topper* as a radio show. About a decade before the TV show hit full stride, *Topper* turned up June 7, 1945, as an NBC summer series sponsored by Post Toasties. As in the pictured version, the Kerbys were Cosmo's private ghosts; no one could see or hear them but Topper. He always seemed to be talking to himself, because the ghosts created much the same embarrassing situations that Francis the Talking Mule caused for Donald O'Connor and friends. Roland Young, who played the character in the movies, was the radio Topper, Paul Mann and Frances

Chaney originated the roles of George and Marion, and Mrs. Topper was played by Hope Emerson. This was an interesting series, if not quite up to television's standards.

The Affairs of Ann Scotland

The Affairs of Ann Scotland told the story of a girl private eye, and was heard on an ABC West Coast hookup in 1946 and 1947. Arlene Francis starred as the female gumshoe, quite a departure from the glamor-girl reputation she had previously built. Miss Francis had been the announcer for Phil Spitalny's all-girl orchestra in the Hour of Charm, and had served as the sultry-voiced femcee on the audience shows What's My Name? and Blind Date. In her first jump into the down-and-dirty game, she was directed by Helen Mack, and played a satin-tongued cutie, quick on the uptake. Del Castillo provided music on the organ.

The Affairs of Peter Salem

The Affairs of Peter Salem was a Mutual detective offering, premièring in mid-1949 as a Thursday and later a Monday night sustainer. It starred Santos Ortega as Salem, a small-town detective matching wits with big-time criminals from the metropolis. Himan Brown, director of Inner Sanctum, brought this to the air as a contrast to Ortega's Nero Wolfe, which had been one of radio's detective favorites of the early 1940's. Everett Sloane and Ann Shepherd were featured players. It moved to Sundays in 1950, and was heard as a sustaining feature until 1953.

African Trek

African Trek was an interesting series of folklore from the African veldt, performed on the Blue Network Sundays by Josef Marais and three companions. Marais, long a collector of Boer campfire songs and a former musician with the symphony orchestra in his native Cape Town, brought the show to radio in 1939. It was like a 15-minute whiff of his homeland, and was so popular that the network soon expanded it to 30 minutes. Later it was shortwaved to Africa. Opened each week to the theme "Sarie Marais," it was built around stories and songs Marais had been collecting since childhood.

Against the Storm

Against the Storm was one of the most unusual soap operas of the air, a serial with a message. Written by Sandra Michael, it premièred on NBC October 16, 1939 to the growing tempo of war, and quickly established in its theme a resistance to that war, and to all war. Its central characters were the Allen family: Professor Jason Allen, his wife Margaret, their children Christy and Siri, and Christy's husband Philip Cameron. Professor Allen taught at a college campus, and was an outspoken opponent of Hitler and of warfare. Some shows contained nothing but this philosophy, as on Memorial Day 1941, when he and his wife sat alone and pondered the past. Professor Allen then remembered walking through a cemetery with a childhood pal in 1894, looking at the tombstones of those who had died so young in the Civil War, and arguing about the inevitability and necessity for wars to continue. Twenty-three years later, his friend was killed in World War I. And now, again, the world was on the brink of insanity...

From the outset, *Against the Storm* won laurels for originality and treatment. Edgar Lee Masters appeared on the show, and in 1942 it became the only daytime serial ever to win radio's highest award, the Peabody. Even President Roosevelt accepted a speaking appearance on *Against the Storm*. (Ironically, his appearance was canceled by the bombing of Pearl Harbor.) Despite *Newsweek's* contention that *Against the Storm* "didn't click with the listening housewives," it held highly respectable ratings through most of its run. Roger De Koven played Professor Allen, with Gertrude Warner and Claudia Morgan as Christy. Miss Michael was consistently at odds with sponsor Procter & Gamble over what kind of show *Against the Storm* should be, however, and it was dropped in 1942, just seven months after winning "radio's Pulitzer." Attempts to revive it by Mutual in 1949 and by ABC in 1952 were not successful. Under Miss Michael, it promoted an optimistic "this too shall pass" subtitle: "Against the storm, keep thy head bowed, for the greatest storm the world has ever known came to an end one sunny morning."

The Air Adventures of Jimmy Allen

The Air Adventures of Jimmy Allen, first heard by syndication in 1933, followed the life of a young daredevil pilot in the sometimes shaky days of early aviation. It was produced in Chicago, where the real Jimmy Allen (also known as Murray McLean) beat out twenty-five adolescents for the role. Jimmy was 16 then, and sponsor Richfield Oil liked him so much that the hero was made over in his image. Originally slated for another title, the show was called *Jimmy Allen* after the star. It became very popular, attracting more than three million kids into Jimmy Allen Flying Clubs. Jimmy's popularity led to a movie, *The Sky Parade*, released by Paramount in 1936. Like the fictional character, the real Jimmy was a pilot. But the Jimmy of the airwaves flew on dangerous missions around the world and competed in great intercontinental air races for pride and glory, accompanied on his fictional trips by his close friend, veteran pilot Speed Robertson. The scripts were written by Robert M. Burtt and Wilfred G. Moore, who six years later would hit big-time ether with *Captain Midnight*. In the early 1940's, the original transcriptions were re-released, but the heyday of Jimmy Allen was 1933 to 1936, when boys from coast to coast had great dreams of piloting one of those double-winged beauties themselves someday.

Al Pearce and His Gang

Al Pearce and His Gang represented a long-running network formula that was used throughout the 1930's and 40's. Pearce, one of radio's early comedians, played a long string of local engagements before landing on the Blue Network with a Saturday-night show in early 1934. He started collecting his "gang" in California, and gradually worked into his easy-going format. A native of San Jose, he developed the show from his own experiences, beginning his entertaining in barbershops with banjo songs and silly impersonations.

Pearce moved into radio when things got tough. With his brother Cal, he had operated a dairy business, using their one cow for sole supply, when their father died and left them the responsibilities of providing for the family. Later Pearce took up the thankless life of a salesman, selling insurance door to door. Eventually he and Cal entered the real estate business in San Francisco.

At the same time, Pearce began moonlighting as a singer at KFRC, bringing in an extra $35 a week and enjoying it to boot. One day Jack Hasty, a jack of all trades and sometime writer, asked Pearce to play the part of Elmer Blurp in a skit he had written. Pearce found no problem identifying with the character; Blurp was a self-conscious salesman who'd rather miss a sale than confront a customer, and Pearce had been in that spot once or twice himself. He played the role, and initiated Elmer as the first member of his "gang."

The gang began to grow in 1929. Pearce found Blurt easier to say than Blurp, so Elmer got a new surname. Other San Franciscans joined him, and the station gave him a show, billed for four years as *The Happy-Go-Lucky Hour*. In 1929, the original Al Pearce "Gang" included brother Cal, Jean Clarimoux, Norman Nielsen, Hazel Warner, Abe Bloom, Monroe Upton as "Lord Bilgewater," Tommy Harris, Charles Carter, Edna Fisher, and Cecil Wright. That was a good year for radio, and a bad year for real estate. When the bottom fell out of the market Pearce began to consider the new medium as a potential source of permanent employment.

Radio was good to Pearce. His show, once established as a network headliner in 1934, was on the air continuously for a decade.

In 1935, Pearce took the show to New York, beginning with a Pepsodent-sponsored format on NBC. In January 1937, Ford Motors picked up the show and it moved to CBS Fridays. In October 1938, he went back to NBC for Grape Nuts; in October 1939 back to CBS for Dole Pineapple; in May 1940 the Friday night CBS series was picked up by Camel Cigarettes. That ran until 1942. As best remembered, in the late 1930's and 40's, the show was a mixture of heavy comedy and variety. Backed by the music of Carl Hoff, Pearce often conducted talent hunts in his audience. His skits as Elmer Blurt are especially memorable, with Elmer going door to door, selling insurance for a quarter-a-week premium, knocking distinctly with his bump bump-bump bump bump, bump bump and muttering, "Nobody home, I hope-I hope-I hope." For a time, that catchy phrase was a national slogan.

In those years the "gang" included Arlene Harris, "the human chatterbox" who could almost out-talk Walter Winchell; Kitty O'Neil, "the laughing lady"; Arthur Q. Bryan; Artie Auerbach; and "Tizzie Lish," the show's expert in cooking and health. Tizzie, who read weird recipes, was developed and played by Bill Comstock, a former drummer in vaudeville who had picked up the character by mimicking a women's recipe show on a station he had once worked.

The Pearce show, though it never gained the almost fanatical following that built around some comedies, was a solid part of radio during its formative years. But many of the shows are dated and do not stand the test of time.

Pearce was carried by ABC-Blue for one season as *Fun Valley* in 1943. In 1945–46 he returned to ABC with a variety show, which lasted one season. After that brief run on ABC daytime, Pearce slipped out of radio. He turned up briefly in TV appearances during the early 1950's, then dropped into oblivion. He died June 3, 1961 of complications from an ulcer.

The Alan Young Show

The Alan Young Show was first heard on NBC June 28, 1944, as a summer substitute for The Eddie Cantor Show. Young, an English-born comic had learned the radio ropes through the Canadian Broadcasting Corporation, and and had graduated from office boy in local radio to master of ceremonies of a network variety hour based in Toronto. He brought a mixture of situation comedy and straight gags to the summer show, and was promptly hailed by critics as the up-and-coming comedy find of 1944. His success in Cantor's slot led, on October 3, 1944, to the opening of The Alan Young Show for Bristol Myers on the Blue Network. Young took his style from Charlie Chaplin, Harold Lloyd, and others of the silent screen, and usually played an underdog named Alan Young, who was forever taken advantage of by others. Jean Gillespie joined the show in March 1945, playing Young's girl friend Betty. Ed Begley was her father, crusty Papa Dittenfeffer and Jim Backus played friend Hubert Updike. In 1946, the series was picked up by NBC, where it ran Friday nights —still for Bristol Myers—for one season, when comic Charlie Cantor became a regular. After a season on the shelf, Young's show was reactivated by NBC for its Tuesday night lineup, bringing back Backus and Nicodemus Stewart in support. The series premièred for Tums January 11, 1949, while Young was a regular with The Jimmy Durante Show. Louise Erickson played girlfriend Betty in the Tums run, and songs were by the Regulaires (Sue Allen, Faye Reiter, Ginny Reese and Ginni Young, the star's wife). Ken Christy and Hal March appeared in support, and Helen Mack directed. Young finished out the year on his and Durante's shows. But fate blew hot and cold on Young's career throughout his radio years; he was always the man about to make it big, but never quite grabbed the brass ring. He made some movies, which also were received with mixed enthusiasm, then went into TV, where his humor seemed better placed.

The Aldrich Family

The Aldrich Family is one of the best-remembered of all radio comedies, primarily because of its unforgettable format. In sheer nostalgia value, the opening ranks with The Shadow's laugh and creaking door of Inner Sanctum Mysteries. Every week for fourteen years,

Henry Aldrich was summoned into 20 million living rooms by his frustrated mother's forlorn wail: "Hen-Reee! Henry Aldrich!" The cracking voice of adolescence that answered "Coming, Mother!" was your validated ticket to mayhem.

Henry was the creation of Clifford Goldsmith, a rags-to-riches playwright who had tried vainly to crack show business on several levels. He created the Aldrich family in the play, *What a Life!* and hit upon a formula that would adapt to the air, to the screen, and finally to TV as one of the pioneering series of the tube.

Goldsmith was virtually penniless and making his living on the high school lecture circuit when he wrote the play. Developed from material Goldsmith had collected on his lectures, the plot was set entirely in the office of Henry's high school superintendent. It came to Rudy Vallee's attention in 1938; Vallee asked Goldsmith to write some radio skits about his characters, and the Aldrich family came to radio with the original cast. Within a few years, Goldsmith was hauling in $3,000 a week as one of radio's highest-paid writers.

One of the Vallee skits was heard by Ted Collins, man Friday and all-around boss of *The Kate Smith Hour.* Collins signed Goldsmith for Miss Smith, getting *The Aldrich Family* for some forty weeks. That led directly to the long-running series when Jack Benny took his summer vacation, and a limited engagement opened on NBC Sunday nights. *The Aldrich Family* premièred July 2, 1939.

By fall, it was a solid hit. Bought by Jell-O, it was inserted into the Blue Network's Tuesday lineup and in 1940 went to Thursday on NBC. Soon the commercial jingle sung by the cast was almost as famous as Henry's opening croak:

Oh, the big red letters stand for the Jell-O family;
Oh, the big red letters stand for the Jell-O family;
That's Jell-O!
Yum-yum-yum!
Jell-O Pudding!
Yum-yum-yum!
Jell-O Tap-i-oca pudding, yes sir-eee!"

. . . *And now for* The Aldrich Family.

What unfolded then was sheer lunacy, by any of today's standards. Goldsmith used the trials and tribulations of adolescence only as a starting point; then embellished them with snowballing complications that now seem ridiculous. The shows turned on situations involving the generation gap, teenage love, or that vital something that gets lost (such as Henry's pants) and must somehow (golly-jeepers!) be retrieved. Henry Aldrich could make a crisis out of the simple act of going to the store. If the show began with tying up the family telephone, you just knew that within the half-hour, he would somehow manage to have every phone in town snarled up, with calls coming into the Aldrich home for everything from taxis to plumbers.

Early in the run, Henry must have sipped the same magic potion that kept Helen Trent 35 years old for three decades. He had been just 16 in 1937, when he leaped full-blown into Broadway and he was 16 years old in 1953, when he left the air forever. The show opened its regular run October 17, 1939, with Ezra Stone as Henry, House Jameson as his father, lawyer Sam Aldrich, Katherine Raht as the ever-patient Mrs. Alice Aldrich, and Ann Lincoln as sister Mary.

Henry was played to perfection by Stone, who originated the role on stage and badly wanted the film part that went to Jimmy Lydon. Jackie Kelk played Henry's companion in mischief, Homer Brown. House Jameson continued as Henry's father; Regina Wallace would later play Mrs. Aldrich, and Mary Shipp took turns as Henry's meddlesome sister Mary and as his girlfriend Kathleen.

They were merely the best-remembered players. The Aldrich Family had one of the highest turnover rates in the business. With the exception of Jackie Kelk, who remained with the show for most of the run, every part in the show was recast many times. By 1943, there wasn't one member of the original cast left. The radio magazine Tune In reported that the show had gone through five fathers, four mothers, at least a dozen Marys, and two Henrys. Ezra Stone had joined a traveling Army variety show in June 1942, and was on tour. He was replaced by his understudy, Norman Tokar. A month later, Tokar was called to active duty with the Army Signal Corps. His departure at the end of the 1942 season sent scouts on a frantic search for yet another replacement; by one account, more than 700 young actors were tested before the role went to Dickie Jones. Jones, really 16 years old, had first appeared before the microphones at age 5. Among his screen credits were two films destined to become radio shows: Stella Dallas and Renfrew of the Mounted. His biggest part was the voice of Pinocchio in the 1940 Walt Disney feature cartoon. In July 1945, with Stone, Tokar, and Jones all in the Army, Raymond Ives became the newest Henry.

Stone resumed the part in October 1945, playing the eternal teenager into his thirties. He became a television director when the show folded in 1953. Even as a middle-aged man, twenty years later, he could still get his voice "up" on demand for a facsimile of that long-lost croak: "Coming, mother!"

Alec Templeton Time

Alec Templeton Time was first heard July 4, 1939, as a summer replacement for *Fibber McGee and Molly*. Templeton, a brilliant young pianist blind from birth, came to the United States from his native Britain in 1935 and created a mild sensation with his offbeat, often comic interpretations of the classics. His show was built around satire, and kept enough audience during its first summer to carry it over as a fall regular on Monday nights. It ran on NBC for Alka Seltzer for two years, moving to Fridays in 1940–41. Templeton had been composing since age 4; his musical education included study at London's Royal Academy of Music. His initial appearances on American radio were on *The Rudy Vallee Show*, *The Chase and Sanborn Hour*, *The Kraft Music Hall*, and on the unusual *Magic Key*, a show that blended classical music with interviews. Templeton loved to dip in and out of classical interpretations, mixing them, blending with new arrangements of old masters. He often played popular songs of the day in the styles of such composers as Strauss and Mozart. He was directed on the air by his manager Stanley North, who used a system of touch cues (finger across the back, hand squeezing the shoulder). Templeton's show included a full orchestra and chorus, directed by Daniel Saidenberg, and featured songs by Irishman Pat O'Malley. Templeton was also heard on the Blue Network three times a week in 1943, and was featured with Morton Gould in a 1944 CBS series, *Carnival*. In 1947, Templeton was starred in a Sunday afternoon NBC show, directed by Ezra McIntosh, and featuring his wife, the former concert singer Juliette Vaiani. He died in 1963.

Amanda of Honeymoon Hill

Amanda of Honeymoon Hill, one of the many afternoon soap operas developed by Frank and Anne Hummert, told the story of a common girl who married into a rich, aristocratic Southern family. It came to the Blue Network February 5, 1940 and ran until May 1, 1946, for Phillips Milk of Magnesia and other drug products.

Like other Hummert soaps, *Amanda of Honeymoon Hill* was high camp. Accompanied by mellifluous organ music, the show opened like this:

And now, *Amanda of Honeymoon Hill*, the story of a young man who married a girl who had nothing in life except her own beauty—neither education nor background nor any real contact with the world. Her name was Amanda Dyke until Edward Leighton, a handsome young Southerner who lived in a mansion on the hill, married her and took her away from her strict father, who kept her close to their Virginia valley. This is the story of Edward and Amanda who now, in spite of the hatred of both their families, seek happiness on Honeymoon Hill in Virginia, in a world that few Americans know . . .

Played by Joy Hathaway, Amanda was portrayed as a "beauty of flaming red hair" whose great life struggle was to blend into Edward's crusty family and still preserve her common valley heritage. Edward, played by Boyd Crawford and later by George Lambert, was a patient blueblood who might have been interchangeable with Lord Henry Brinthrope of *Our Gal Sunday*. He was an artist whose time before the war was mainly filled making portraits of lovely Amanda. The war changed that bliss. Suddenly, Edward was away much of the time in Abbeyville, overseeing his factory, converted to war production. Amanda was busy on the hill, helping in the day nursery she had established for the children of war workers.

Complicating things was that neither Amanda's father nor Edward's mother had ever accepted the marriage. Sparks flew whenever they met. The father was Joseph Dyke, common baker of bricks, played by Jack MacBryde; the mother was Susan Leighton, a snooty women's clubber, played by Muriel Starr.

Father thought Amanda had lost her humility and her sense of common tradition; mother thought Edward had lost his mind for marrying beneath him. The overriding factor was a son, Robert Elijah, born to Amanda and Edward and dearly loved by all. When life became truly unbearable, Amanda had the shoulder of kindly old Aunt Maizie to turn to. The wise old woman of the valley, played by Cecil Roy, shared her wisdom between puffs on her corncob pipe and even took an active role in the in-fighting when Joseph Dyke became too much to handle.

The Amazing Mr. Tutt

The Amazing Mr. Tutt, based on the *Saturday Evening Post* stories by Arthur Train, came to CBS in a summertime format July 5, 1948, starring Will Wright as the crafty old New England lawyer Tutt, whose intimate knowledge of law became the focal point of most plot complications. Rather a melodramatic series, *The Amazing Mr. Tutt* featured John Beal as Bonnie Doon, Tutt's "legal helper" and accomplice; Norman Field as Judge Babson; Joe Granby as D.A. O'Brian; and Herb Rawlinson as Edgar the courthouse guard. Arnold Perl wrote the scripts, music was by Lud Gluskin, and Anton M. Leader was producer-director.

American Agent

American Agent was a farfetched ABC series of 1950–51 depicting the fictional life of Bob Barclay, globe-trotting soldier of fortune who led two lives. In real life, he was a foreign correspondent for *Amalgamated News*, but under cover, he was a spy for the government. The series was one of the lesser lights of producer George W. Trendle, whose greater shows included *The Lone Ranger* and *The Green Hornet*. But while *Lone Ranger* and *Green Hornet* were harmless juvenile operas, *American Agent* was viewed by the press as a dangerous attack on the profession. The idea of a newsman working as a government spy was offensive to the press at large, and reporters protested to ABC in droves. Their major complaint: that the series was hurting the case of real-life newsman William Oatis, imprisoned in Czechoslovakia on a charge of espionage. For whatever reason, *American Agent*, sponsored by Mars Candy on Wednesday nights, was dropped after one season.

The American Album of Familiar Music
and Waltz Time

The American Album of Familiar Music and *Waltz Time* were both early, long-running programs on NBC, produced by Hummert Radio Features Company, a creation of Frank and Anne Hummert. The Hummerts, who became better known for their soap operas, brought *The American Album of Familiar Music* to NBC Red in 1931; *Waltz Time* followed two years later, on September 27, 1933. *Album* featured "supremely lovely" songs and music, mostly familiar tunes of long popular standing, sung by a cast of regular and guest stars and headed by Frank Munn. Munn, one of radio's pioneers, also sang on *Waltz Time*, a Friday-night NBC show that brought tantalizingly familiar, floating melodies from Abe Lyman's Orchestra. Both shows were durable: *Album* ran twenty seasons and was last heard in 1951; *Waltz Time* expired in 1948 after a fifteen-year run.

The American Forum of the Air

The American Forum of the Air was first heard on Mutual in 1937, an outgrowth of the network's three-year-old Sunday Forum Hour. Under its American Forum banner, it was moderated by Theodore Granik, a prominent Washington attorney, former assistant district attorney for New York County, former counsel for the United States Housing Authority, and special counsel for the Bank of America. Granik, long an advocate of free speech, developed an interest in radio as a most effective tool; he did his earliest broadcasts—readings from the Bible—in the pioneering days of 1926, and was active in the medium for some thirty years. The American Forum of the Air was for most of its run a Sunday show, heard in various lengths (30, 45 and 60 minutes over the years) and featuring unbridled, often heated discussions from leaders of opposing schools of thought. Though the series drew such guests as Dorothy Thompson, Donald Nelson, and William Allen White, no one was paid to appear. Granik kept most of his own political leanings under wraps, remaining neutral but always, in the opinion of Radio Mirror, "firm, hard-headed and diplomatic." Much of his time was spent maneuvering the guests away from personal barbs and back to the issues. Usually he had to change shirts after the broadcast, because his original shirt had become thoroughly sweat-soaked. In 1943, The American Forum of the Air was moved into a 45-minute Tuesday slot. In 1949, the show was picked up by NBC, where it was reestablished as a Sunday feature, and could still be heard in the mid-1950's.

The American School of the Air

The American School of the Air was a novelty when it opened on CBS February 4, 1930. So new was the concept of education by radio that few teachers were interested. Many openly predicted the show's early demise. But within a few years, this program was required listening in classrooms across the nation. Half a dozen states blended it into their formal curricula; some 6 million children cheerfully put down their books for a half-hour of fun. The show was carried to Hawaii, Alaska, Canada, and Puerto Rico. Network executives prepared a teaching manual to help teachers blend the show into their classwork. The American School of the Air was broadcast Monday through Friday for 30 minutes each day. Each show was the equivalent of a half-hour course, often presented in dramatic form by radio's top acting talent.

On Mondays, *School* would carry "Frontiers of Democracy," true accounts of happenings in industry and agriculture; on Tuesdays the class was "Folk Music of America"; on Wednesdays, "New Horizons," telling of the feats of American explorers; Thursdays, "Tales From Far and Near"; and Fridays, "This Living World," dramas and discussions of contemporary life. Under the supervision of various CBS education chiefs, including Sterling Fisher and Dr. Lyman Bryson, the show helped stamp the network as a leader in the field. It became required listening in some 200,000 classrooms, and ran eighteen years before expiring in 1948. As an added mark of prestige, CBS refused all offers of sponsorship for the show, sustaining it throughout its long run.

America's Hour

America's Hour was the first real attempt by a national network to cross into the no-man's-land of editorial comment. First heard July 14, 1935, it was created by CBS president William S. Paley as an unabashed attempt to boost the American way. Coming when the Depression was at its worst, *America's Hour* offered kudos to the man who worked and slaps to the radical. In a large sense, it was a roving thumb on the pulse of the nation, moving in documentary style from the railroad roundhouse to the college campus, tied together on Sunday nights in a slick package with an orchestra conducted by Howard Barlow.

America's Town Meeting of the Air

America's Town Meeting of the Air was an outgrowth of a Manhattan forum for public debate. It was hosted by George V. Denny, Jr., who had given up acting aspirations to take up lecturing and debating. The show grew out of Denny's meeting with Mrs. Richard Patterson, wife of an NBC vice-president. Denny asked about the chances of a national forum on the air. He related his dismay at the closed mind of a neighbor, who refused to consider any political view that didn't mesh with his own, and had never listened to any of President Roosevelt's "Fireside Chats." Denny had a sympathetic audience; Mrs. Patterson was associate director of the League for Political Education, an outgrowth of the suffrage movement that had been going strong since November 1894.

The League's offices were in the Town Hall, a building near 43rd and Broadway that had long been identified with public debate. Public affairs programs, lectures, and panel discussions were booked regularly into the Town Hall. Denny thought the addition of a microphone could pep up such programs and expand their scope to include a national audience.

On May 30, 1935, the first of *America's Town Meetings* was launched experimentally on NBC as a 60-minute show. Denny established the format quickly: no holds barred, keeping only within the bounds of good taste. He ran the show with an iron hand, but allowed enough spontaneity and flexibility to keep the suspense high and the pace fast. No one would ever be asked to speak who didn't have "America's interest at heart," but that interest could be expressed in any kind of political theory. It opened with a crier ringing a bell and shouting "Hear ye! hear ye! town meetin' tonight," and the first show tackled the sensitive topic, "Which Way America—Fascism, Communism, Socialism or Democracy?" The speakers: Lawrence Dennis, A. J. Muste, Norman Thomas, and Raymond Moley.

Each guest was clocked and required to stay within his allotted time. Afterward, the floor was opened to the audience in a verbal brawl that became the backbone of the series.

The experimental status ended six weeks later; *Town Meeting* had by then shown enough promise to be booked regularly. Its following over the years was almost fanatical. More than 1,000 debate and discussion clubs were formed to listen to the broadcasts and hotly continue the debate afterward. In 1936, *Radio Mirror* termed the show "a stupendous innovation for radio."

Its sucess was due in no small measure to Denny, who handpicked the guests, moderated each discussion, and kept the talk on track. His showmanship, directly traceable to his early career on stage, kept *Town Meeting* lively and provocative long after other debate shows had vanished from the air.

Sometimes it was all George Denny could do to keep his guests from physically assaulting each other. That was probably to be expected; the guests were usually political and philosophical opposites. Tempers ran high; the constant verbal brickbats—combined with open hissing and booing from the audience—often drew quick emotional retaliation, occasionally violating Denny's rule against personal attacks. At least one libel suit was filed against one guest by another.

Uninhibited heckling was permitted from guests and audience alike. In 1936, Denny announced a new "remote control" feature, which allowed *Town Meeting* to bring in people from all parts of the country. By 1938 he was getting 1,000 letters a week and was soon drawing such top guests as Eleanor Roosevelt, Carl Sandburg, Mayor Fiorello La Guardia, and Wendell Willkie. The high point of the 1938 season was Willkie's debate with Robert H. Jackson, assistant U.S.

Attorney General, on the topic: "How Can Government and Business Work Together?"

Denny was named president of the League in 1937, and promptly changed its name to Town Hall, Inc. He screened all offers of sponsorship, but rejected them to avoid even the subtlest restraint on open speech. For the first seven years, the program was sustained by NBC; by 1943, it had moved to ABC, where only briefly, in the mid-1940's, *Reader's Digest* was allowed in as sponsor. It ran on various nights and in various lengths for twenty-one years as radio's top forum of debate, closing in 1956.

The Amos and Andy Show

The Amos and Andy Show was an outgrowth of a pre-network show, *Sam and Henry*, which evolved from a blackface act at Chicago's WGN. Amos was Freeman F. Gosden, who abandoned sales and electronics to crash show business in the early 1920's. Born in Richmond, Virginia, May 5, 1899, Gosden had deep Southern roots. His Virginia family sent its sons into battle for the Confederates during the Civil War; Gosden himself sold cars and tobacco, and served in the Navy as a World War I radio operator.

Charles J. Correll, who played Andy, was born February 2, 1890 in Peoria, Illinois. As a young man he was a bricklayer and a stenographer; then he pursued a piano-plunking hobby into show business, becoming a traveling producer of small-city stage shows. In Durham, North Carolina, he met Gosden, who had just come to work for the same road company. They became great friends, forming professional and personal bonds that lasted until Correll's death on September 26, 1972.

The men spent the early summers of their friendship in Chicago, home base of their parent company. There they planned the road seasons, when they would travel—sometimes together, sometimes alone—and stage their amateur productions for small stage groups, providing everything but the acting talent.

In 1920 they were introduced to radio on a New Orleans station that was just beginning to experiment with the medium. They cut some talking records for Victor, which a national magazine would describe years later as "terrible." And in the summers, sharing an apartment in Chicago, they worked on a song-and-joke routine, employing some of the black dialect that would serve as their entrée to radio when the time was right.

Gosden and Correll had begun the black dialect in 1925, and on January 12, 1926, they went on WGN as Sam and Henry. *Sam and*

Henry was a solid hit in Chicago, so well-received that, when Gosden and Correll left WGN two years later, the station decided to keep the name. On March 19, 1928, Gosden and Correll went to WMAQ, which was to become the CBS outlet for the Chicago area. Unable to obtain the rights to *Sam and Henry*, they began putting together a new show, *Amos and Andy*. Legend has it that they decided on the names while riding up on an elevator at WMAQ for their first broadcast. Actually, the decision followed some three months of hard thought. Everything about *Amos and Andy* was done meticulously, and with Gosden and Correll's personal touches. They wrote the scripts and, for the first decade played all the parts.

When *Amos and Andy* first went on NBC Red for Pepsodent August 19, 1929, the blackface gags of *Sam and Henry* were continued, with deepening characterization. Amos Jones and Andrew H. Brown were played as Harlem blacks who owned the Fresh Air Taxi Company, so called because its one asset—a rattletrap cab—had no windshield. Amos was the solid, hard-working half of the partnership. A church-goin' man who played life straight and believed in the basic goodness of his fellow beings, he had a fine wife, Ruby, and two children. So straight was Amos that his dramatic and comic appeal declined as the show took on new sophistication and depth. Eventually he was all but written out of the scripts, and by the time the half-hour version premièred in 1943, Amos was reduced to infrequent walk-ons.

In his place, Gosden played the conniving George Stevens, the "Kingfish" of the "Mystic Knights of the Sea" lodge hall. The plots began to revolve around the double-dealings of the Kingfish, with Andy the usual victim. If Kingfish wasn't selling Andy a piece of the moon, it was the Brooklyn Bridge, the Washington Monument, or a car with no motor. So slick was the Kingfish that Louisiana's most famous politician, Huey P. Long, was nicknamed after the Gosden character.

Andy, meanwhile, was the perfect fool, thick of voice and more than a little dense. Single and pudgy, he wore a derby, smoked old stogies (whenever he could find them), and made his lifework chasing women. He never worked, but usually had a little change in his pocket that made him ripe for the Kingfish's latest scheme. Early in the series, Andy berated Amos loudly for being dumb. Later it was painfully obvious that Andy was no match for the quick-witted Kingfish, so he sometimes took to lecturing other dense members of the cast, like Lightnin', the slow-moving janitor of the lodge.

In Lightnin', Gosden created a shuffling character with a high-pitched drawl. "Yazzah," he would say to the Kingfish, "Ah'll jus' whiz right on ovah deah," but listeners knew it might take him days to arrive. Correll played the stodgy Henry Van Porter.

In the program's early years, Gosden and Correll did more than 100 separate voice characterizations, though the bulk of the action was centered on Amos and Andy. Later new people were brought in. Lou Lubin played the stuttering Shorty the barber; Eddie Green was Stonewall the lawyer; Ernestine Wade was Sapphire, the battle-axe wife of the Kingfish; and Amanda Randolph was her formidable Mama, who went even Sapphire one better on battle-axmanship. Other characters, such as Amos' wife Ruby (Elinor Harriot) and the hard-charging Madame Queen (Harriette Widmer) were used sparingly.

Radio itself was a national toy then, and *Amos and Andy* is generally regarded as the first great radio show. The Depression had settled into America's gut, leaving a sour taste. For a little while each night, the bitterness was relieved by the plights of two commonest of common men. We were all in this together, and Amos Jones and Andrew H. Brown epitomized the men with no money, no job, and no future. At first it was a late-night show, running at 11 P.M. Eastern Time; later it was scheduled at 7 P.M., where it ran as a 15-minute nightly serial until 1943.

Ratings were unreliable then, but *Amos and Andy* at its peak may well have been the most popular show ever broadcast. People who lived through the early 1930's still remember the marquees on movie houses, announcing that the film would be stopped at 7 o'clock, so *Amos and Andy* could be piped in. That was the only way a theatre could hold an audience. In 1931, when the *Amos and Andy* craze was just coming to its peak, everyone listened, from J. Edgar Hoover to Herbert Hoover, from street vendors to elevator operators. The listening audience may have exceeded 40 million a night.

Some newspapers published daily accounts of Amos' trial for murder; no trial in fact or fiction ever interested the people more. Bus lines and taxis had no passengers; if records can be believed, people didn't run water or flush toilets at *Amos and Andy* time. Public utility use was down; auto theft was up. Thieves well knew that, from 7 to 7:15, everyone in almost any house you wanted to pick would be at the radio set. In big-city neighborhoods and small Midwestern towns, people could walk down the streets on warm spring nights and listen to the show as they walked. Every window was open and every radio tuned to *Amos and Andy*.

People who couldn't afford the vaudeville acts of Jack Benny, Fred Allen, and Eddie Cantor got *Amos and Andy* free. Later, Cantor, Benny, Allen, and a host of vaudeville comics invaded the air and changed the shape of radio comedy. But the first few years belonged to the pioneers, and *Amos and Andy* led the way.

On December 31, 1937, Pepsodent sponsorship ended; Campbell Soups picked up the show on January 3, 1938. The 15-minute shows were simple in concept and production, combining the best elements of situation comedy and soap opera. Many episodes had cliff-hanger endings; tension was developed over two- and three-week story lines, sometimes building to a shattering climax that left listeners exhausted. One such sequence occurred in 1939, when Andy got down to the final "I do" in an elaborate wedding ceremony. Just as the minister was about to pronounce him married, a shot rang out and Andy fell wounded to the floor.

Before the show, Gosden and Correll had researched the legalities of marriage, to get as much tension into the scene as possible. How far could a wedding ceremony be dragged out before it became legally binding? Did the preacher have to say those final words, "man and wife," for it to be a valid ceremony? They were assured by lawyers and clergymen that, yes, the ceremony had to conclude, the minister must pronounce them man and wife or there was no marriage. With that information, they constructed a scene with the gunshots coming just after the words, "I now pronounce you . . ."

The entire show was devoted to the wedding. On and on droned the voice of the preacher, while Andy squirmed and Amos fished through his pockets for the ring. Then it happened: Shots were fired! Andy fell wounded to the altar. Excited voices blend together, while above it all rings Amos' renowned wail of distress, "Ow-wah! ow-wah! ow-wah!"

The next day, controversy erupted in the press. Was Andy married or not? No one seemed to know for certain. Lawyers jumped into the fray, bickering over fine points of law. One attorney cited New York statutes, claiming that the marriage was valid even though the ceremony hadn't finished. Another divorce lawyer submitted a four-page brief on Andy's behalf, opting for no marriage. *Time* collected opinions from jurists in New York, Iowa, and California. As for Gosden and Correll, they let it drop, and Andy continued on his single way. The painstaking attention to detail paid off, in money and fame alike. By 1939, their weekly salary had soared to more than $7,000.

Such techniques assured a steady audience through the 1930's. But with the beginning of a new decade, the audience began to trickle away. Times were better now, and the air had been invaded by a host of slick vaudevillians, who came equipped with bands, announcers with charisma, and studio audiences that laughed out loud over the air. *Amos and Andy* fell victim to the new era; the show slipped to sixtieth on the rating charts. The writing was on the wall; Gosden and Correll knew they must change or die.

In February 1943, the 15-minute version ended forever. But on October 8, 1943, *Amos and Andy* returned as a half-hour weekly variety show for Rinso, broadcast on Fridays and from 1945 through 1948, on Tuesdays. Now they were backed by a full staff, including Jeff Alexander's orchestra and chorus. Gone was Bill Hay's traditional introduction ("Heah they ah . . ."), and in his place was the peppy Harlow Wilcox of *Fibber McGee and Molly* fame. Lubin, Green, and other cast members were added. Bob Connolly and Bill Moser helped with the production and writing, and the careers of Freeman Gosden and Charles Correll set sail in a new direction.

It worked. Again, *Amos and Andy* vaulted into the top ten, a place they occupied throughout the 1940's. A dramatic departure from the original, the new show saved them from certain oblivion. When CBS began to raid NBC's shows in 1948, Gosden and Correll made the jump along with Jack Benny, pocketing $2.5 million and giving CBS ownership of the show and its characters for twenty years. Meanwhile, they continued to draw healthy salaries as stars of the show. From 1948 through 1954 it was heard on CBS Sundays, the first year for Rinso, the last five for Rexall.

But hard times again fell on *Amos and Andy*—and on radio as a whole—in the 1950's. Ratings slipped again; Rexall canceled the show in 1954, and most of the radio stars were frantically trying to get aboard the TV bandwagon. Obviously Gosden and Correll couldn't play the roles on TV, so real blacks were hired and the show began filming, with Gosden and Correll supervising. Conflicts erupted between the cast and the creators. No one, it seemed, was happy with the TV show. Blacks charged that it was a disgrace to their race, and official protests by the National Association for the Advancement of Colored People helped force it off the air. Gosden and Correll were personally stung by the controversy, refusing to comment on any questions regarding race. Later, Gosden especially became a very private man, refusing even to discuss the show or comment on the occasion of his partner's death.

They were the products of a dead era whose humor couldn't stand the sensitive scrutiny of the emerging black movement. Perhaps Gosden sensed that as early as 1948, when he told *Newsweek* that "what we've tried to do over the years is mirror the trials and tribulations of Negroes, of whom we're very fond." Their characters might be earthy and uneducated, even lovably conniving. But they could never be malicious or evil. If there had to be a villain in *Amos and Andy*, he had to be white.

By 1954 the characters were just glorified disc jockeys in a new show called *The Amos and Andy Music Hall*. Here, they played popular records on CBS and did short *Amos and Andy* skits between cuts. Even in this watered-down format, they survived until November 25, 1960.

They had come a long way from Chicago and the *Sam and Henry* days and from the time when their audience ranged from presidents to George Bernard Shaw. It was Shaw who gave them their finest tribute. "There are three things I'll never forget about America: The Rocky Mountains, Niagara Falls, and *Amos and Andy*."

The Andrews Sisters

The Andrews Sisters, the singing trio, appeared often on the air, in their own shows and in guest spots. Eleven years separated them (LaVerne was born in 1915, Maxine two years later, Patti in 1926), but the Andrews Sisters took to the entertainment circuits as a trio as early as 1932, beginning an intense effort to grab off a little of the fame and glory that the other big sister acts—the Boswells and the Pickens —were enjoying. From their native Minneapolis they went on tour with a small band entertaining throughout the south and midwest; they sang in hotels and vaudeville-style in theatres.

After six years of it, they were broke and discouraged and ready to give it up. Then Lou Levy, a promoter who would become their manager and eventually Maxine's husband, put over a deal with Decca Records. The sisters sang "Bei Mir Bist Du Schön" with pheno- menal sucess; the record swept the country, earning a fortune for Decca but—because it was only a test record and there was no royalty arrangement—enriching the Andrews coffers by only $50. Little mat- ter; the record had established them with the public. It led to their great hits of the late 1930's and early 1940's: "Well, All Right," "Rhumboogie," "Beer Barrel Polka," "Hold Tight," "Rum And Coca Cola." The Andrews Sisters were soon riding a $400,000 annual windfall.

Naturally, radio beckoned. They were signed by CBS for appear- ances on the Dole Pineapple show, and later costarred with Glenn Miller on the Chesterfield broadcasts. Though they were big-name guests with Fred Allen, Bing Crosby, and other headliners, their own show was short-lived and sporadic. On December 24, 1944, their *Andrews Sisters Eight-to-the-Bar Ranch* premiered on ABC. It was heard for Kelvinator; George "Gabby" Hayes, the perennial sidekick of western thriller movies, was a regular, and the music was by Vic Schoen.

In 1946, they were heard on CBS Wednesday nights. The

Eight-to-the-Bar Ranch had by then become the *N-K Musical Show-room*, named for sponsor Nash-Kelvinator. It featured music by Schoen, songs by Curt Massey and, as a special feature, "The N-K Green Room." Out of the Green Room each week stepped a celebrity to do the act most associated with his name. In Green Room slots, Abbott and Costello did their "Who's On First?" skit, Ethel Merman sang "I've Got Rythm," and Morton Downey sang "Carolina Moon." The sisters' singing act disolved in the late 1940's. LaVerne died of cancer in 1967.

The Answer Man

The Answer Man was a radio show on which the listeners submitted the questions and the "Answer Man" provided the answers—that was all there was to this syndicated show. Still, it proved a popular 15-minute entry, supporting star Albert Mitchell, producer Bruce Chapman, and their staff of up to forty workers for more than fifteen years. First heard in 1937, *The Answer Man* took all questions on all subjects, answered them by mail and read the best ones on the air. At the height of the show's popularity, some 900,000 letters a year went out to the curious public. "Is it true that only the male cricket chirps?" "Did the Pilgrims have snow the first Thanksgiving?" The show was marked by Mitchell's rapid-fire answers, creating the illusion that he had the answer to anything at his fingertips. This was almost true —the headquarters of *The Answer Man* were just across the street from the New York Public Library.

Arch Oboler's Plays

Arch Oboler's Plays was a series of original dramas by the medium's newest wonder boy. The late 1930's was a golden age of experimental drama on radio. At the top of the heap was *The Columbia Workshop,* a CBS training ground for such writers as Norman Corwin and William Saroyan. NBC had its long-running *Radio Guild* and on March 25, 1939, added *Arch Oboler's Plays.*

Arch Oboler was a short man with a liking for informal dress and a flair for words. He grew up in Chicago, one of the busiest centers of radio drama in the 1930's. Almost a prodigy, he sold his first script to NBC while he was still in school, and made a substantial living from radio for more than a decade. After his initial success at NBC, Oboler began writing mini-dramas for the network's *Grand Hotel,* went from there to *The Rudy Vallee Show,* and landed in 1936 in an eerie little midnight brew called *Lights Out.*

Oboler is best remembered for his *Lights Out* work, but even then he wanted to try straight experimental drama. After two years, he left *Lights Out* because, as he explained it then, he tried to top each show and just couldn't top himself any longer. Actually, he had inherited *Lights Out* from Wyllis Cooper, and he wanted his own show—an Oboler production from writing to casting to directing. It was an ambitious goal for a man not yet 30, but Oboler had made his name and earned his stripes. NBC gave him the slot, and in the spring of 1939, *Plays* came to the air.

It had a sporadic run, heard for a year on Saturday nights and lasted until March 23, 1940. The show ran the gamut from tragedy and fantasy to the same kind of horror he had done on *Lights Out*. Oboler employed techniques that had seldom been used on the air. He wrote in a rambling stream-of-consciousness style, sometimes blending voices into an audio collage, other times using filters to create the effects he wanted. His fame spread, and top-flight stars began to ask for roles in his *Plays*. Everyone wanted to work with genius.

Bette Davis, Edmond O'Brien, Frank Lovejoy, and James Cagney appeared on Oboler's show. Because of his short frame, he climbed on a table to direct them, earphones strapped to his head as if he were the conductor of some private symphony.

His productions were critically acclaimed. "Alter Ego" won a 1938 award as best original drama of the year. Dalton Trumbo's "Johnny Got His Gun" was strong stuff by 1940 standards, but Oboler and James Cagney did it on March 9. Perhaps the highest tribute to Oboler's work came on August 26, 1939, when the NBC Symphony Orchestra appeared on *Plays*, the first time it had ever been used as backup for a drama. NBC gave it 60 minutes instead of the usual 30, and Oboler produced a strange dramatization of the love between the great Russian composer Piotr Tchaikovsky and his rich patroness, Mme. Nadezhda von Meck. Titled "This Lonely Heart," it starred the Russian actress Alla Nazimova, who appeared with Oboler often.

Plays closed March 23, 1940, and Oboler turned his attention to propaganda dramas for the government. Hitler was on the move, and it was obvious that sooner or later, the big fight would involve America too. Oboler turned out scores of anti-German skits for such government productions as *Treasury Star Parade*. He donated his time to the cause, giving up $3,000 a week, and by 1942 he was feeling the financial pinch. He went to CBS with a revival of *Lights Out*.

But experimental drama was still close to his heart. On April 5, 1945, he turned up on Mutual with a new version of *Plays*. By then Norman Corwin had become poet-in-residence at CBS, and a master of the form Oboler had helped create in the late 1930's. Many of Oboler's dramas strongly resembled Corwin's in style and content.

Plays ran through the summer on Mutual, and ended October 11, 1945.

Archie Andrews

Archie Andrews. The characters of Bob Montana's popular comic strip were first dramatized by Mutual in a daily 15-minute form May 31, 1943. But the show is best remembered as a 30-minute Saturday morning comedy. That version ran on NBC from 1946 through 1953, mostly sustained by the network, but sponsored by Swift and Company in 1947–48.

As developed on radio, Archie was almost as zany as that other notorious teenager of the air, Henry Aldrich. But nobody could out-Henry Henry, and Archie at best was still second-string. Although Betty, Veronica, Jughead, Reggie, and all the rest of Montana's cast made the transition, the radio show lost the flavor of the strip and reflected Archie as just another insane teenager. The plots were virtually copies of *The Aldrich Family* (family locked out of the house; family trying to retire early, bothered by everyone in town). Had this show gone on first, it might have been the hit, but it didn't and wasn't. Most familiar were Archie's inane giggle and his father's frantic "Quiet! . . . QUIET! . . . QUI-I-ETT!" over the babble of everyone talking at once. There were several casts. Jack Grimes played Archie in the five-a-week shows of 1943 and '44. Best remembered is the cast of the late 1940's. Bob Hastings was Archie; Harlan Stone was his pal Jughead Jones. Mom and Dad Andrews (Fred and Mary to each other) were Alice Yourman and Arthur Kohl. Veronica Lodge, Archie's girlfriend, was Gloria Mann; Rosemary Rice played Betty Cooper. It was produced and directed by Kenneth MacGregor.

The Armstrong Theatre of Today

The Armstrong Theatre of Today, following strongly in the footsteps of *Lincoln Highway* and *Stars Over Hollywood*, soon developed into one of the pacemakers of Saturday morning drama. Before 1940, Saturday was considered by network people as "the ghetto of the schedule." Then came *Lincoln Highway*, luring top stars for strong Saturday dramas, and everything changed. *Stars Over Hollywood* followed in 1941 and, later that year, on October 4, 1941, *Armstrong Theatre of Today*. The back-to-back programming of these two shows gave CBS the edge in the Saturday dramatic derby for thirteen years. *The Theatre of Today*, slotted for the noon half-hour, opened with a few minutes of straight news by "Armstrong's news reporter," and then went straightaway into the dramas. The stories, following the pattern established by Stars Over Hollywood, were generally light; few "heavies" were considered suitable for Saturday programming. Generally, the actors were not of the "super-name" variety that Stars Over Hollywood used, but the ratings of both shows hovered near 10 and occasionally jumped to 12. Ira Avery was producer-director; the sponsor for twelve years was the Armstrong Cork Company, whose commercials were read by "The Armstrong Quaker Girl," generally Elizabeth Reller or Julie Conway. Tom Shirley was announcer; George Bryan was Armstrong's news reporter. Armstrong dropped the show in 1953, and it was picked up for a final season by Cream of Wheat.

The Army Hour

The Army Hour, a giant wartime extravaganza first heard on NBC April 5, 1942, gave Americans their first in-depth look at the war and how it was being fought. This 60-minute variety show, broadcast Sunday afternoons, replaced a low-key Army show This Is the Army, that had been heard from camps since 1940. Developed from an idea by Lt. Col. Edward M. Kirby of the War Department, it was put together with an unusual mixture of professional and military talent. Wyllis Cooper, creator of horror tales on Lights Out a few years earlier, was brought in as writer-producer-director. NBC sportscaster Bill Stern was among those tapped to interview troops and experts in the fine art of warfare. Interviews ranged from Chiang Kai-shek to the private struggling through the muck. The format was sweeping; the canvas as large as the world. When the Army took a village, Army Hour correspondents were there; listeners heard the sniper fire and machine guns in the background. But the show was also equipped, in its premier offering, to dramatize the plight of the World War I veteran sending his boy to fight in a new conflict. By the time the show was a year old, it was heard in 3 million homes. It ran until 1945.

Arnold Grimm's Daughter

Arnold Grimm's Daughter premièred on CBS July 5, 1937, but moved to NBC for General Mills within a year. Although it enjoyed a brief flurry of popularity around 1940, it was dropped in 1942 and today remains just a fading memory. Set to the theme of a "Modern Cinderella," the serial featured the romantic misadventures of one Connie Tremaine, proprietress extraordinaire of a shop dealing in ladies' unmentionables. Connie, the daughter of Arnold Grimm, had married young Dal Tremaine, but his death left her with no other choice but to work for a living. Betty Lou Gerson was starred as Connie, and the part was also played by Luise Barclay and Margarette Shanna. Don Merrifield played Arnold Grimm, and husband Dal was handled by Ed Prentiss and Robert Ellis.

Art Baker's Notebook

Art Baker's Notebook. Quizmaster, commentator and interviewer, Art Baker's radio career began in 1936, when he was asked to announce a show called Tapestries of Life. He decided to stay in the medium, gradually worked up to $15 a week and became host of Reunion of the States, an audience participation show which later became his specialty. Baker went to CBS for Hollywood in Person, a celebrity interview show running in 1937 and 1938. In 1938, he became master of ceremonies of Pull Over Neighbor, the forerunner of People Are Funny, which he also hosted until producer John Guedel dropped him for Art Linkletter. Baker got his first national network job hosting The Bob Hope Show. He worked Hedda Hopper's Sunkist shows from 1939 through 1941. Such obscure numbers as Paging John Doe, Don't Be Personal, and Traffic Tribunal followed. Then Baker was tapped as the West Coast announcer for the giveaway series, Pot O' Gold. In 1943–44, he hosted the CBS audience show, Meet Joe Public. But perhaps Baker was best known for a series that wasn't on the networks. In Art Baker's Notebook, he syndicated his musings, his philosophies and tidbits on the ways of the world. It was first aired September 8, 1938, at KFI, Los Angeles, and ran for more than a decade.

Arthur Godfrey Time

Arthur Godfrey Time was first heard on a network (CBS) April 30, 1945, but as a radio personality Godfrey goes back to 1929 and can be traced through a variety of freelance appearances.

Born in New York City on August 31, 1903, Godfrey led a colorful, nomadic life as a young man. He ran away from home at 15 and worked at a variety of jobs on both coasts. He drove a truck, worked in a coal mine, worked as an office boy for an architect, cleared tables in restaurants. His formal education was almost nil. But ambition and hard work often made a difference in those days. Godfrey took some courses from the International Correspondence School and learned the rest of what he knew in the "school of hard knocks." By 1921 he had joined the Navy and accumulated enough general knowledge to pass the rugged admissions test for Annapolis. But Godfrey spurned the famed school, preferring sea duty as a radio operator.

By the middle of the decade, he still hadn't decided his future. He left the Navy in 1924, resuming his drifting, job-hopping ways. In Detroit, he took a job selling cemetery lots, and began to see that selling came naturally. Soon he had accumulated $10,000, a small fortune in those days of the nickle subway ride. By then he was strongly attracted to show business; he had learned to play banjo in the Navy, and the ham in him demanded some form of release. He sank his bankroll into a traveling vaudeville act originating in Chicago and pushing west to California. The show went broke in Los Angeles, and Godfrey was hustling again.

He rode the rails back to Chicago and took a job driving a cab. A former shipmate who happened to be riding in Godfrey's cab talked him into another hitch—this time in the Coast Guard—and in 1927 Godfrey again became a man of the sea.

He was in Baltimore in 1929, when his real career began. While listening to *Saturday Night Function,* an amateur show on Station WFBR, Godfrey and some buddies decided to storm the station and thrust their talent upon the unsuspecting world. The station manager, who was having trouble getting enough talent to fill his program, put Godfrey on the air as "Red Godfrey, the Warbling Banjoist." Coincidentally, Godfrey was doing some legwork for the governor of Maryland at that time; legend has it that the chief executive helped him gain his release from the Coast Guard to pursue his new career in broadcasting.

WFBR first offered him a $5-per-show plunking-singing-talking format for its Triangle Pet Shop account. Later, they offered a full-time job. In 1930, he was added to the NBC staff as an announcer in the network's Washington outlet. In 1931, he was involved in an automobile accident which he often pinpointed as the turning point of his life. His car hit a truck head-on and left him immobilized for five months. During that time there was little to do but listen to the radio. Godfrey decided that most of it, especially where the advertising was concerned, was slop.

Announcers drooled into the microphone. Their sales technique didn't ring true because it wasn't true; they tried to appeal to groups of people instead of the one person who was all people. Godfrey had understood a principle that is still in use today.

He had decided that his pitch would be to "one guy" in an imaginary audience. It would be as though two people—Godfrey and his "guy"—had sat down for an informal chat. If there were more than two people in a room, Godfrey figured that "they'd have something better to do than listen to the radio."

But when he tried out the technique, he had an immediate run-in with station hierarchy. His off-the-cuff remarks, especially when they put down the advertising, were strongly discouraged. Godfrey kept at it, and finally split with NBC in late 1933. In January he was refused reinstatement, and a few weeks later he was hired by the competition, station WJSV, which later became WTOP of CBS in Washington.

That was the beginning of an association with CBS that would last for almost four decades. He was put into an all-night slot, playing records and chatting away with his "one guy" to his heart's content. Soon it was apparent that the one guy was at least several guys—sales on Godfrey-advertised products began to pick up. The idea had passed its first test. But Godfrey was struggling to get to New York and break out of the local mold. CBS still considered him primarily a "local boy" whose appeal on a nationwide hookup was questionable. He got a brief shot on a network show called *Manhattan Pee-rade*, after Walter Winchell gave the Washington show a rave notice in his column. But *Manhattan Pee-rade* bombed badly. Suspicions confirmed.

In April 1941, his fortunes began to change. WABC, the affiliate in New York that would later become WCBS, began carrying his Washington show in greater New York. On October 4, 1942, Godfrey began announcing for the new Fred Allen show, *The Texaco Star Theatre*. In his eighteen months in New York, Godfrey had become a popular man. When he read his name over the network, the audience responded with a loud round of applause. Six weeks later, Allen dropped him from the show, but Godfrey continued doing his morning stints for Washington and New York. Still yearning for a national slot, he appeared as a freelancer on various CBS programs, and in April 1945 he was assigned as the network's special reporter for the funeral of President Franklin D. Roosevelt. Godfrey wept at the microphone in a broadcast that has become classic. A few weeks later, after a serious threat to quit and join NBC, Godfrey was booked into the morning CBS lineup.

He opened April 30, to the theme "Beautiful Dreamer," in a format that differed from his other shows in several respects. Instead of playing records, he now used live talent. Thus were born the "Little Godfreys," that tight little group that over the years continued and included Frank Parker, Marion Marlowe, the McGuire Sisters, Pat Boone, the Chordettes, Janette Davis, Bill Lawrence, and Julius La Rosa. Tony ("Here's that man himself") Marvin was the announcer and Archie Bleyer conducted the orchestra.

Godfrey's CBS show was sustained for almost two years, possibly because by then he had gained a reputation for chiding sponsors on the air. Morning time wasn't very popular with sponsors, but soon Chesterfield Cigarettes picked up the show, and by 1948 Godfrey was becoming a listening institution. He was doing three daily shows: an early-morning disc jockey show for WCBS New York, a repeat for WTOP Washington, and the network show.

The stories of his commercial appeal have taken on the characteristics of legends. Once he was given some copy for a local department store that was running a sale on ladies' black lace panties. "Man, is my face red," Godfrey said into the microphone. "Why do they give me junk like this to read?" But the department store people didn't mind. The next day they were mobbed by women anxious to buy the panties "that made Godfrey's face red."

Once, ordered by station management to play the "William Tell Overture" for his breakfast audience, he retaliated by breaking the record on the air, and followed that up with a sputtering Bronx cheer for the boss. He probably got away with such irreverence because of the early-morning format. Few of his bosses listened, and by the time they caught on, it was too late. Godfrey's following was too large for any executive tampering. Sponsors bit their tongues and allowed him free reign, then reaped the benefit in increased sales.

Contrary to popular belief, Godfrey never criticized a product directly. That was a big difference between Godfrey and Henry Morgan, another notorious sponsor-drubber. While Morgan blasted his sponsors directly, Godfrey concentrated on the "jerks" who wrote the advertising copy. He screened his sponsors carefully, ever mindful of his reputation for telling it straight, and no sponsor got into the show without his approval. By then he could afford to be choosy; as many as sixty-three sponsors carried his morning shows, and there was a long waiting list of prospects.

Godfrey was fantastically popular with his listeners. On one all-night broadcast, he talked at length about being marooned in a suburban Virginia "swamp." He longed for some coffee, and perhaps a bit of breakfast. How many listeners filled their thermos bottles and brought sandwiches to the studio still isn't reliably known, but the number has been estimated as high as 8,000 in national news magazines.

His sucess on the air is still an enigma. He couldn't sing; he couldn't dance or act; he wasn't even the cleverest ad-libber on the air. The charm of the Godfrey show came from its spontaneity. He conveyed a "don't give a damn" attitude that was cherished by his "guy"; he ate breakfast between records, often talking about products that had never been his sponsors. Sometimes he threw away the script, asking the orchestra to blunder through numbers that hadn't been rehearsed. Sitting with him at the table was the ever-popular Margaret

("Mug") Richardson, a former North Carolina beauty queen who became his girl Friday. It was "Mug" who handled the writers and the endless stream of salesmen wanting to get to Godfrey. Little matter; Godfrey never used their stuff anyway.

People trusted Arthur Godfrey, and his sucess along Radio Row was as simple as that. Godfrey might rib his sponsors' advertising copy; he might throw it away and "wing" the commercial on his own, ending with "Boy, the stuff they ask me to read!" The sponsors cringed, but the listeners loved it. More important, the listeners bought the products. And that made Godfrey, during the heyday of his radio career, the hottest salesman and the most valuable single property at CBS.

Sales of Godfrey-advertised products soared, and Godfrey's income soared along with them. He was fond of saying that he made $400,000 before the average man started his office day, and there was a lot of truth in that. Fred Allen, in his immortal parody of breakfast shows, once barked into the microphone, "Six o'clock in the morning! Who's up to listen to us? A couple of burglars and Arthur Godfrey!"

Allen's spoof, funny as it was, took a few liberties. One was the fact that, on any typical day, a lot of people were up—listening to Arthur Godfrey. It was once estimated by CBS that the red-headed star was heard by 40 million people a week. Nobody argued with the figures. Godfrey's weekly stint before the microphone was usually more than fifteen hours, a feat that would have floored Fred Allen or any other master of the half-hour format.

On July 2, 1946, CBS signed him to a weekly nighttime show, Arthur Godfrey's Talent Scouts, which was soon nestled among the top twenty shows. Still another program, Arthur Godfrey's Digest, began on Saturday January 1, 1950. Later, he would broadcast remotes from his farm, an 800-acre estate in Virginia that became almost as well-known to listeners as the house in the next block. CBS installed a mini-studio at the farm, and listeners often didn't realize that Godfrey was in Virginia and the rest of the crew was in New York.

Godfrey was especially interested in young talent. His Talent Scouts, carried by Lipton Tea, the sponsor most associated with Godfrey, was broadcast each Monday night, after an initial season on Tuesdays. The winners by audience vote were invited to perform on Godfrey's morning show Tuesday through Thursday. Those few Godfrey liked best stayed indefinitely. Godfrey's attitude toward them grew almost paternal. "I have so much trouble with these kids," he told Time in 1950. "They don't know when they're well off." It was an attitude that would cause him trouble and pain. The showdown came one October night in 1953, in a controversial on-the-air dismissal of Julius La Rosa, and the subsequent firing of bandleader Archie Bleyer.

Even as he brought La Rosa to the microphone for his number, Godfrey seemed in good spirits. "It pleases me mightily whenever I see the reception you give these kids, particularly Julius here," he said.

Then he began to recap La Rosa's career, beginning with "Julie's" first Godfrey show. He told the audience he had picked La Rosa while Julius was still in the Navy. La Rosa, he said, had had a humble streak that could be found in all the "Little Godfreys."

"I pick them all that way," Godfrey said.

His tone was still warm as he discussed La Rosa's awe of "stars" on the show. "I said, 'Julie, you don't know it, but I don't have any stars on my show. We're all just a nice, big family of very nice people like yourself. You hold onto that quality and you'll never have to worry about a thing.' "

But in two years on the show, Godfrey continued, La Rosa had built a great following. "He and Archie have their own recording company now, and he's gotten to be a great big name."

Godfrey spoke the last three words slowly and deliberately. Then he asked La Rosa to sing "I'll Take Manhattan." At the end of the song, Godfrey said, "Thanks ever so much, Julie. That was Julie's swan song with us. He goes now out on his own, as his own star, soon to be seen in his own programs, and I know you wish him godspeed the same as I do. This is CBS, the Columbia Broadcasting System."

After the show, Godfrey called Bleyer into his office and asked about a rumor that his recording company had just finished a Chicago recording featuring Don McNeill, the host of The Breakfast Club. When Bleyer confirmed the report,, Godfrey said, "Well, I just fired Julie, and it was like tearing my eyeballs out. I guess you're next."

He relayed the conversation the next day at a news conference, called to head off growing criticism of the La Rosa firing. Godfrey told the press that La Rosa had "lost his humility" and had created a morale problem among the other members of the cast. Bleyer, he said, would be retained on one of his nighttime TV shows. He said he loved both men, and again wished them well.

Neither La Rosa nor Bleyer would comment. La Rosa signed for highly publicized appearances on Ed Sullivan's Toast of the Town TV show, and soon sank into obscurity. In 1969, he turned up as a disc jockey at Station WNEW, New York.

Whatever the effect on La Rosa, the firing also marked the beginning of the end for Godfrey. His popularity dipped sharply; he was rebuked by media critics for his brash handling of the La Rosa affair. Godfrey made a successful transition to TV with Talent Scouts and with another weekly show, *Arthur Godfrey and His Friends*. But he continued his morning radio for years after the TV shows had folded. Then he got lung cancer and devoted most of his time to that fight. He emerged in the 1960's, pronounced fully cured and pulling at the bit for a new TV show.

But TV had changed and so had his image. CBS had no spot for him. He continued his network radio show until he took it off the air himself, broadcasting an emotional farewell April 30, 1972—twenty-seven years to the day after his CBS show began.

Godfrey took up a new cause, that of the ecologist/conservationist, and did occasional commercials for Axion, a Procter & Gamble laundry product. But he was still conscious of his standing reputation for honesty, and when he learned from congressional hearings that Axion had as much polluting power as washing power, he publicly rebuked it. "How can I preach ecology and sell this stuff?" he said.

It was almost like the old days. Only the smile was gone.

Asher and Little Jimmy

Asher and Little Jimmy was a highly popular early show, beginning syndication out of WSM, Nashville around 1931. Asher was Asher Sizemore, singer of mountain ballads; Little Jimmy was his son. During their 15-minute show, they sang five songs—sometimes solo and sometimes as a duo. Little Jimmy closed each night with his prayer, "Now I lay me down to sleep . . ." They also did numbers for WSM's *Grand Ole Opry*.

Auction Gallery

Auction Gallery was a 1945 Mutual show, created and moderated by Dave Elman of *Hobby Lobby* fame. Elman, who had been parading unusual hobbies past the microphones for eight years, now brought unique items to the audio auction block, giving people all over America the chance to bid against the experts. The small and select audience for *Auction Gallery*, brought in by invitation only, consisted of gallery hounds and established antique collectors who well knew the cash value of old, intriguing items. Each item was described by Elman, who then opened the bidding to the studio audience. After the bids were in, Elman "threw open the bidding to the nation," giving the listening audience two weeks to submit bids by mail. Highest total bid won the item. Among the artifacts auctioned by Elman were Mark

Twain's writing desk, documents containing signatures of Declaration of Independence signers, Dolly Madison's will, Adolph Hitler's personal set of dice, the notebook of Robert Burns, and Lincoln's draft of the Thirteenth Amendment. Elman was assisted in his search for interesting items by twelve staffers. Bernet Hershey assisted as bidder.

Aunt Jenny's True-Life Stories

Aunt Jenny's True-Life Stories, unlike most soap operas of the era, told its tales in brief, five-chapter, complete-each-week productions, providing the format for constantly shifting casts and themes. It was first heard January 18, 1937, and ran for almost twenty years on CBS, finally bowing out in 1956. Aunt Jenny, a widow, was played through the run by Edith Spencer and Agnes Young. Each day she invited listeners into her homey kitchen for a bit of home cooking, a piece of positive philosophy, and the latest installment in her story of the week. The stories were all set in the tiny town of Littleton, where Aunt Jenny was well established as the philosopher of record. Friends and neighbors flowed through her kitchen in great numbers, pausing long enough to share some grief from their troubled lives. Aunt Jenny used these problems as vehicles for her tales, which inevitably contained some barely concealed correlation to the visitor's problem. With the episode of the day concluded, Aunt Jenny turned to cooking, usually dispensing one tip each day from her well of menu magic. The tips were often simple, and were shamelessly linked to her longtime sponsor, Spry ("The secret of boiling fish fillets—brush with lemon juice, then with melted Spry, and boil to a golden brown"). The talk of Spry brought in announcer Dan Seymour ("Danny" to Aunt Jenny), who then delivered an informal commercial. The show closed with Aunt Jenny's "golden thought of the day."

Author, Author

Author, Author was a Mutual quiz derivative, beginning April 7, 1939, and running through the summer. Sidney Joseph Perelman was quizmaster, and the idea behind the program was simple: assemble a panel of fiction writers and let them work out mystery plots from raw material sent in by listeners. Regular panelists were Frederic Dannay and Manfred Lee, who combined their talents to write the Ellery Queen stories. With such guests as commentator Dorothy Parker and newsman Heywood Broun on hand, the panel tackled plot situations that bordered on the ridiculous, and sometimes came up blank.

Author Meets the Critics

Author Meets the Critics, a lively show of confrontation, was based on an idea created by producer Martin Stone in the mid-1940's. When he was asked to do a book review show on local radio, Stone thought a more interesting program would grow out of face-to-face meetings between authors and their critics. It premiered on Mutual June 12, 1946, after a local New York run, and was heard on Wednesdays. Two "critics of unquestionable stature"—often from *The New York Times*, the Book-of-the-Month Club, or other literary backgrounds, were brought in to dissect a book page by page. This took up the first 15 minutes of the half-hour show, one critic taking the book's defense while the other tore it apart. The author was given a bell, which he could ring whenever he disagreed with either critic or with moderator Barry Gray. In the second half of the show, the author was given his shot at the critics. Often the discussions were quite heated, centering on the finer points of character and style, and even on the writer's integrity. The show was dropped after one season, but was revived in the summer of 1947 as a Sunday-night NBC show. *Author Meets the Critics* turned up on ABC as a Thursday-night offering in 1949. In 1950, the show moved to Sundays for a final season. John McCaffery, editor of *American Mercury*, was the moderator for NBC and ABC.

The Avenger

The Avenger was syndicated in 1945; it was a blatant copy of the popular *Shadow*. The Avenger was Jim Brandon, famous biochemist. Through his numerous scientific experiments, Brandon had perfected two inventions that aided him in his fight against crime: the telepathic indicator, by which he was able to pick up thought flashes; and the secret diffusion capsule, which cloaked him in the black light of invisibility. Brandon's assistant, the beautiful Fern Collier, was the only one who shared his secrets and knew that he was the man the underworld feared as "The Avenger."

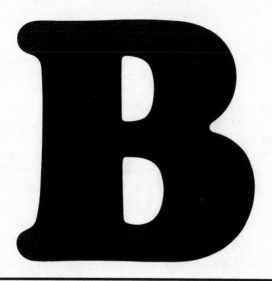

Baby Rose Marie

Baby Rose Marie was one of the first great child stars of the air, first singing on NBC in 1926, at the age of 3. She was born Rose Marie Curley in New York's lower East Side on August 15, 1923, and the adult sound of her child voice amazed the nation. Soon she was appearing on *The Rudy Vallee Show*, and in 1932 her 15-minute Sunday show became a Blue Network regular; the following year it was picked up by Tastyeast for a twice-a-week run. Rose Marie faded for a time, then emerged in 1938 with another twice-weekly song show for NBC. She eventually became a highly accomplished comedienne, appearing as the wisecracking script-writer of television's *Dick Van Dyke Show.*

Baby Snooks

Baby Snooks was the impish little-girl character developed by Fanny Brice of *Ziegfeld Follies* fame and introduced on radio on the *Follies* show of February 29, 1936.

In truth, Snooks was born on October 29, 1891, with Fannie Borach in New York's lower East Side. Snooks and Borach grew together, playing in the streets near Harlem, running away from school, mooching nickles and dimes at Coney Island. But Snooks lay dormant; Fannie was imp enough for one girl. She entertained whenever she could find an audience with a few pennies. She picked up the earthy accents of European families who had settled into

Manhattan a generation before, and learned how to do dialect comedy. By her mid-teens, the pennies had grown to dollars; she was scratching out a slim living playing amateur nights in neighborhood saloons.

Her break came in 1910. She met Irving Berlin, then a struggling young song-writer. Berlin had written a piece called "Sadie Salome"; he suggested that she sing it in a dialect at the Columbia Burlesque House, where she was working. Her performance, utilizing the combined tongues of her street people, was seen by Florenz Ziegfeld, who offered her a job in the *Follies*. Money and acclaim began to pour in, and Fannie successfully played a *Follies* girl for the next thirteen years.

A preview of Snooks came in 1912, when Miss Brice began doing a baby routine in vaudeville. But her main interest then was concentrated on other facets of her career, and she didn't need Snooks yet anyway. She was belting out songs like "Second Hand Rose," lively ditties that worked well with her semi-comic image. Magazine writers have pinpointed the birth of Snooks to a party in 1921, when Fannie was asked to entertain and trotted out her impersonation of a 7-year-old brat.

But Ziegfeld asked her for a change of pace in 1921. That was when she first sang "My Man," a haunting love song that became closely identified with her own life. For those were the years of Nicky Arnstein, the gambler she married in 1918, divorced after nine stormy years, but remembered with great affection even two decades later.

Her peak came during the crazy 1920's. She changed the spelling of her first name to "Fanny" and began to think about movies. She made three films, and in 1932 joined George Olsen's orchestra for an ill-fated radio series, nothing more than a brief showcase for her musical talent. On February 29, 1936, Snooks was to emerge as a person in her own right. Fanny Brice was almost 45 years old; the days of vaudeville and *Follies* glory were past. But on this Saturday night a new *Follies* began, *The Ziegfeld Follies of the Air* on the young Columbia network. Miss Brice uncorked Snooks for the nation, then sang "My Man" by request of the theatre audience.

That radio show, like her first, ended after a brief run. But in December 1937 she joined NBC in another musical-comedy extravaganza, *Good News of 1938*. Snooks became a regular part of that hour-long show, and was a major part of radio continuously for the next fourteen years.

A notable change occurred in Fanny Brice. Her personality slipped into the background as Snooks emerged. Once Baby Snooks was established as a radio star, Miss Brice all but abandoned her natural voice in public. Seldom was she out of character; even in interviews she often referred to "Schnooks" almost as a living person. A new generation grew to maturity without knowing Fanny Brice as anything but Baby Snooks.

The *Good News* show continued through 1939, and in March 1940 was streamlined to 30 minutes. It became known as *Maxwell House Coffee Time*, and was split into 15-minute routines by comedian Frank Morgan and 15-minute Snooks skits.

Regular supporting players were added. Hanley Stafford, who rivaled Gale Gordon and Hans Conried as one of the best stackblowers in radio, became Snooks' long-suffering "Daddy," Lancelot Higgins. Arlene Harris, "the human chatterbox" of the *Al Pearce Show*, took the part of "Mommy" Higgins, in a family situation comedy that set the pace for such later efforts as *The Bickersons* and Jackie Gleason's *Honeymooners*. John Conte announced; music was by Meredith Willson and Mann Holiner produced. Daddy and Mommy were always fighting about something, be it Lancelot's old girlfriends of Mommy's burnt toast. Snooks, playing one perfectly against the other, added fuel to the weekly fires. If Lancelot came home with lipstick on his collar, Snooks would find a way to bring it to Mommy's attention. She was a shameless blackmailer, sometimes even a double-crosser, leaving the shirt ("by accident," of course) precisely where Mommy would find it, even after she had collected her quarter bribe to drop it in the wash and keep her mouth shut.

Miss Brice seldom ad-libbed. She relied heavily on Stafford, and on the talents of her writers. Dave Freedman and Phil Rapp wrote the *Snooks* material in the *Good News* and *Maxwell House Coffee Time* years. Later writers included Jess Oppenheimer, who went on to write many of the big-name television series. Her brother Robespierre was played by Leone Ledoux.

Snooks was compared with Charlie McCarthy and Junior, Red Skelton's "mean widdle kid," as one of the three "bad kids" of the air. But Snooks had neither the sophistication of Bergen's dummy nor the crudeness of Skelton's Junior. Confronted, she was the soul of little-girl innocence. Even on radio, you could almost see her batting her eyes and looking at her feet and saying softly, "Whyyyy, Daddy. . . ."

Snooks worked in a variety of formats. Her unusual partnership with monologuist Frank Morgan through the early 1940's was marked by intense competition, with Morgan and Miss Brice each striving to top the other. It wasn't until 1944 that she emerged on CBS with her own half-hour *Baby Snooks Show*. She was heard Sunday nights for Post cereals in 1944–45, and for Sanka Coffee in 1945–46. In 1946, the show was moved to Friday, still for Sanka. It ran until 1948, when many of the big names jumped from NBC to CBS in the famous talent raids. Miss Brice went the other way, bringing Snooks to NBC Tuesday nights in 1949. The show was still going strong in 1951. But on May 24, Fanny Brice suffered a cerebral hemorrhage. Five days later, she was dead at 59, and Baby Snooks was dead at the ripe old age of 7.

Bachelor's Children

Bachelor's Children was first heard on CBS September 28, 1936, and enjoyed a ten-year run for Old Dutch and Wonder Bread. It was the story of Dr. Bob Graham, whose promise to his dying sergeant in the Great War brought him two nearly grown girls to raise. One of the daughters, Ruth Ann, eventually became his wife; the other, Janet, married his best friend, Sam Ryder. Written by Bess Flynn and billed as "radio's beloved serial," *Bachelor's Children* won awards for its "realistic" portrait of American life. The story followed Ruth and "Doctor Bob" through their relationships with each other, the Ryders, and other people in the small town where they lived. Hugh Studebaker played Doctor Bob, except for a five-month period in 1940, when a throat illness forced him off the air. Art Kohl carried the part from May until December, when Studebaker returned. Ruth Ann was played by Marjorie Hannan and Janet was Patricia Dunlap. Olan Soule played Sam Ryder. The serial, one of the most popular of its kind in the late 1930's, was introduced to the organ theme, "Ah, Sweet Mystery of Life."

Backstage Wife

Backstage Wife had a perfect theme for an afternoon serial. Mary, a lovely girl from the Iowa sticks, became a lowly stenographer in New York, but reached for the heights by falling in love with Larry Noble, a "handsome matinee idol of a million other women." When they were married, that made her name Mary Noble and consigned her forever to the backstage wings, watching nervously as dozens of glamorous starlets drooled over her incredibly handsome, sometimes fickle man.

Backstage Wife premièred on Mutual, August 5, 1935. It ran for almost seven months there, closing March 27, 1936. The following Monday it was picked up by NBC, where it enjoyed a run of some twenty-three years, holding put until January 2, 1959.

This program was one of the earliest, most successful efforts of Frank and Anne Hummert, the phenomenal couple who rose from obscurity to become virtual rulers of daytime radio. Both came from journalistic backgrounds. As a young man, Frank Hummert worked for the *St. Louis Post-Dispatch*. He gave that up for the better pay of advertising, joining Chicago's Blackett and Sample agency in 1927. After a year as chief copy writer, Hummert began toying with an idea that would eventually explode on the air as soap opera.

From the beginning, Hummert was involved with radio copy, but not until the agency hired Anne Ashenhurst as his assistant did the soap formulas begin to jell. Anne had written advice to the lovelorn for the old *Baltimore News*, and more recently had worked for the *Baltimore Sun* and the *Paris Herald*. Her addition to the Blackett-Sample staff in 1930, combined with radio's growing influence as an entertainment medium, sent Hummert's stock soaring. Their first two serials were *Just Plain Bill* and *Betty and Bob*. The success of those led to others. By 1935, both Hummert and Ashenhurst had become high-ranking company officers; that same year the name Hummert was added to the company logo.

Hummert's first wife had died, and he and Anne were married in 1935. Their fortunes continued to expand, with the Hummert-radio end of the agency taking on the characteristics of an empire. On January 1, 1944, the Hummerts split with Blackett and Sample and formed their own Hummert Radio Productions, Inc. It became the largest operation of its kind, a veritable assembly line of soap operas. In their peak years, the Hummerts bought more than $8 million worth of air time annually, an amazing 8 percent of all time sold on the networks.

Hummert Radio Productions handled the business end, while a subsidiary called Air Features, Inc., took care of production. Up to sixteen writers and editors were employed by Air Features to flesh out the sudsy outlines created by Anne. Anne dictated most of the plot lines from her home in Connecticut, concentrating her time on the soaps while Frank handled their mystery shows (*Mr. Keen, Mr. Chameleon*) and the long-running musical programs (*Manhattan Merry-Go-Round, American Album of Familiar Music,* and *Waltz Time*). Mrs. Hummert dictated very thin plots, for often they had fifteen or more serials going at once. Her outlines would then be sent to Air Features, where one or more of the staff writers would whip up the dialogue. Hummert writers were paid the union minimum, $200 per show at best, and they worked on each serial a month to six weeks in advance. The finished scripts were read over by Anne and sent to the Air Features studios for production. They were usually signed with the tagline, "Dialogue by Anne Hummert." The Hummerts then sold the serials to sponsors and came to the networks with complete packages. All the networks provided was the air time.

Over the years their agency produced such classics and forgottens as *Kitty Keene, The Carters of Elm Street, Judy and Jane, Our Gal Sunday, The Romance of Helen Trent, John's Other Wife, Lorenzo*

*Jones, Arnold Grimm's Daughter, Valiant Lady, Young Widder
Brown, Stella Dallas, Amanda of Honeymoon Hill, David Harum,
Light of the World, Lone Journey, Front Page Farrell, Ma Perkins,
Those Happy Gilmans* (NBC, 1938–39), *Doc Barclay's Daughters*
(CBS, 1939–40), *Central City* (NBC, 1938–41), *Caroline's Golden
Store* (NBC/CBS, 1939–40), *The Man I Married* (NBC/CBS, 1939–42),
Orphans of Divorce (Blue Network, 1939–42), *The Trouble With
Marriage* (Blue, late 1939), *Beyond These Valleys* (CBS, 1939–40),
Helpmate (NBC, 1941–44), *Marie, The Little French Princess* (CBS,
1933–35), *Mrs. Wiggs of the Cabbage Patch* (CBS/NBC, 1935–38),
Molly of the Movies (Mutual, 1935–37), *Five Star Jones* (CBS/Blue,
1935–37), *Love Song* (Mutual, 1936–37), *Houseboat Hannah*
(Syndicated/NBC, 1936–41), *Second Husband* (CBS, 1937–46, the
first five years as a weekly nighttime show starring Helen Menken)
and *Modern Cinderella* (CBS, 1936–37).

Backstage Wife was more melodramatic than most, far closer in
theme to *The Romance of Helen Trent* than to the softer, homier *Ma
Perkins.* Mary Noble found her life with the handsome matinee idol
anything but smooth. Evil sirens were forever luring Larry to the brink
of infidelity, and Mary herself was pursued through her twenty-
three-year air run by the usual Hummert host of maniacs. The villains
were so deliciously evil that murder, blackmail, and double-dealing
were Mary's constant companions. Her most formidable rival: the evil
adventuress Regina Rawlings, whose plotting against Mary and Larry
eventually included her equally evil cousin Arnold. Regina's motive:
to spoil Mary's happiness, of course. Did anyone need a better reason
than that?

Mary's hold was a strong one; bolstered by their son, Larry Jr., and
by such staunch friends as Maude Marlowe (well-known character
actress in the scripts), Old Pop, the stage doorman, and Tom Bryson,
Larry's longtime theatrical manager, she battled the Reginas and the
Virginia Lansings from the stage door to the footlights. Once, in a
dazzling display of her own acting ability, she humbled the great
Larry Noble himself.

Vivian Fridell, a Milwaukee girl who broke into radio on her
college station, originated the role of Mary. She played the part well
into the 1940's, when Claire Niesen took over for the last fifteen years.
Larry was played by Ken Griffin, and later by James Meighan and Guy
Sorel. Charles Webster was Tom Bryson; the role was also played by
Frank Dane and Mandel Kramer. Ethel Wilson and Henrietta Tedro
were heard as Maude Marlowe; Anne Burr was Regina Rawlings, and
Helen Claire was Virginia Lansing. Wilda Hinkel played Larry Jr.
Alan MacAteer was Pop. Heavy on organ music, the show opened in

1935 to the haunting melody, "Stay as Sweet as You Are," and was billed as "the true-life story of Mary Noble, a sweet young girl from Iowa, who marries Broadway's most handsome actor Larry Noble, dream sweetheart of a million other women, and the struggle she has to hold the love of her husband in the complicated web of backstage life." Later the theme was changed to "Rose of Tralee," and the wordy epigraph was trimmed.

Beat the Band

Beat the Band was an interesting musical quiz, with strong audience participation. First heard on NBC January 28, 1940, the show starred the fourteen-piece Ted Weems orchestra, including Elmo ("The Whistling Troubador") Tanner, "Country" Washburn, and vocalists Marvel Maxwell and Perry Como. Master of ceremonies was young, energetic Thomas Garrison Morfit, who had just changed his name for professional reasons to Garry Moore. Moore solicited musical questions from listeners and used them to quiz the band. Listeners whose questions were used received $10; those who "beat the band" got a $20 minimum and a case of Kix Cereal, which sponsored the show. The questions were usually posed as riddles (Q: What song title tells you what Cinderella might have said if she awoke one morning and found that her foot had grown too large for the glass slipper? A: "Where, Oh Where Has My Little Dog Gone?"). As an interesting sidelight to the main contest, band members who missed questions had to "feed the kitty" by tossing half-dollars into a big bass drum. The musician who scored the most points by the end of the show took home the "kitty." The show was heard Sundays for a season from Chicago. In 1943 it was revived in New York as a Wednesday-night show for Raleigh cigarettes. That one starred "The Incomparable Hildegarde" as hostess and ran one season.

Believe-It-Or-Not

Believe-It-Or-Not was a collection of audio oddities, developed from the newspaper cartoon of the same name. Cartoonist Robert L. Ripley had begun the newspaper feature in December 1918 in the *New York Globe*. Ripley threw together a cartoon of two athletes who had set track records running backward, and called it "Believe-It-Or-Not." He devoted his life to such oddities, employing a staff of more than sixty by the end of the 1930's. Ripley was host for the show, which first came to NBC in a variety format April 14, 1930. For the next two decades, Ripley was on the air in many formats, on different networks and at different times. His show had become a 15-minute twice-a-week Blue offering by 1932, and he returned to a 30-minute Blue Network Sunday variety show in 1935. During the 1935–38 run, it was part of *The Baker's Broadcast*, which had starred Joe Penner. Ozzie Nelson's orchestra continued providing the music and Harriet Hilliard the vocals. In 1937, B. A. Rolfe took the baton and the show ran one more season on NBC. But Ripley was back on January 17, 1942, a Saturday-night Blue program that ran one season. In 1943, Ripley had a five-a-week 15-minute show for Mutual; in 1945, he became part of the CBS variety show, *Romance, Rhythm and Ripley*. Ripley returned to NBC in May 1947 for a daily afternoon show. It seemed that people never tired of the strange and inexplicable, and Ripley was usually there to give it to them. Throughout his career, his radio shows were extremely popular, bolstered by cartoons that appeared in up to 300 newspapers.

His show was one of the first to use remote pickups; Ripley liked to talk with his record-breakers from the scenes of their exploits. He often touched on the occult (the curse that comes true), and once presented a woman billed as "the world's fastest-talking human," who could recite the Gettysburg address in 26 seconds. Including radio, newspapers, books and fair exhibits, Ripley's oddities became a multimillion dollar business. He died May 27, 1949.

The Bell Telephone Hour

The Bell Telephone Hour and its Monday-night sister shows addressed an audience that had been vastly underestimated by network commercialism. These were the people who attended concerts, who loved good music and plenty of it. On NBC Monday nights, they got what they wanted.

One of the great long-running shows of radio, *The Bell Telephone Hour* consisted of concert music performed by the Bell Telephone Orchestra and various guest artists. The show was first heard April 29, 1940, and ran for eighteen years with few changes in format.

By 1950, it was linked with *The Railroad Hour*, *The Voice of Firestone*, and the NBC Symphony in a solid block of musical programming known as "NBC's Monday Night of Music." It took courage to schedule such shows back to back while other networks were offering *Inner Sanctum Mysteries* and *My Friend Irma* as competition. But the *Monday Night of Music* tapped into that hidden audience, some 7 million strong, and roped in a good share of the general population too. Each show had its own special flavor. *The Telephone*

Hour was medium-heavy, especially in comparison with the much lighter Railroad Hour. Each week The Telephone Hour offered some great artist in concert, backed by the fifty-seven-piece Bell Orchestra under the direction of pencil-waving Donald Voorhees.

Voorhees, a musical prodigy, had first tried conducting on radio in the mid-1920's, after a fling at Broadway and musical revues. His earliest efforts, like all of that era, were experimental, but they led to one of network radio's great early variety shows, The Atwater Kent Hour. Voorhees worked for CBS out of WABC, New York, during the first year of the network's existence. He was in radio almost continuously thereafter.

He conducted orchestras for many of radio's biggest shows of the early 1930's—headliners like Ed Wynn's Fire Chief program and The Maxwell House Showboat. He joined Bell for its first broadcast over NBC, and became one of the driving forces behind the show's success. The highly memorable "Bell Waltz," durable theme of the series, was written by Voorhees.

For the first two years, The Telephone Hour featured regular solsists James Melton and Francia White. But with the appearance of violinist Jascha Heifetz on the show of April 27, 1942, Bell initiated its "Great Artists" series. Over the years stars like Ezio Pinza, Nelson Eddy, Maggie Teyte, Helen Traubel, Lily Pons, Gregor Piatigorsky, Grace Moore, Lawrence Tibbett, Fritz Kreisler, and Marian Anderson were featured, and brought back for encores. But The Telephone Hour wasn't limited to the highbrow. Benny Goodman appeared; so did Bing Crosby. One entire show was devoted to music from South Pacific, performed by the original stars, Ezio Pinza and Mary Martin. And on December 14, 1953, Voorhees lured Fred Allen out of semi-retirement for a memorable reading of Prokofiev's Peter and the Wolf. Wallace Magill was longtime producer; announcers were Floyd Mack and Tom Shirley.

In 1946, The Telephone Hour began its annual presentation of young talent, the winners of the Walter W. Naumburg prize. In 1949, it won the Peabody Award, radio's highest honor. The shows were always fairly loose, rehearsing fully on Monday afternoon before the broadcast. But the guest artists were booked almost a year ahead. It survived until 1958, when the clamor for more local time by affiliates began to squeeze even the last few shows off the air.

Ben Bernie, The Old Maestro

Ben Bernie, The Old Maestro, built his reputation around a slow delivery of sweet music and suave, intimate chatter and gags.

Throughout his career, Bernie had one of the air's most popular variety shows. Born Bernard Anzelevitz in 1891, he developed early in life a smooth tongue and a sense of showmanship that almost rivaled Walter Winchell's. At one time he wanted to be a concert violinist. He was selling violins when he decided to hit the vaudeville boards around 1910. Later, Bernie played vaudeville with Phil Baker, doing serious violin-accordion routines and later adding comic undertones. In the early 1920's, Bernie took over a band that had been assembled by Don Juelle, and began his unique show that would eventually prove ideal for radio. The show was built around Bernie as a "personality." He wasn't a smashing comic; he didn't even conduct the orchestra much of the time, leaving that job to first violinist Mickey Garlock. What Bernie did was talk. He blended words like "s'elp me," and his voice suggested the influences of Europe, Brooklyn, and the Old South. Bernie referred to his listeners as "youse guys and youse gals"; he called the musicians "all the lads"; his trademarks were the fat cigars which he chain-smoked, the phrases "Au revoir" and "Yowsah, yowsah, yowsah," and the traditional closing, "Pleasant dreeeams." Featured soloists with Bernie over the years included Dick Stabile, Jane Pickens, Buddy Clark, Lew Lehr, and Gracie Barrie.

Bernie was one of the true pioneers, doing his first broadcast on local New York radio in 1923, in a remote from the Roosevelt Hotel. He was booked into New York's WJZ January 24, 1930, for a Friday-night series for Mennen shave cream, and began his Tuesday-night run on CBS in 1931. He was well-known in New York even before radio, but it took Walter Winchell and their famous "feud" of the early 1930's to make his name familiar to America's heartland.

Bernie's show moved to NBC, still on Tuesdays, in 1932. It was sponsored by Pabst Blue Ribbon until 1935, when American Can began paying the bills on the Blue Network. U.S. Rubber sponsored a Wednesday Bernie show on CBS in 1937 and 1938. The "old maestro" signed with Half & Half tobacco in 1938, in a variety show that also had Bernie conducting a quiz game. He disliked that format and moved back to his old Blue Network Tuesday slot for Bromo Seltzer in 1940. By 1941, CBS was offering Bernie's band and songs by the Bailey Sisters in a five-a-week, fifteen-minute early evening show for Wrigley's Gum. Soon thereafter he became ill. Bernie died on October 20, 1943.

The Better Half

The Better Half was a lively Mutual quiz show, first heard January 10, 1943, a creation of WOR sound man Jack Byrne. The idea grew out of

Byrne's fascination with how well women on the home front were adapting in munitions factories, aircraft plants, and other tradition-ally male jobs. He wondered how husbands and wives would do in competition with each other on a radio show; *The Better Half* resulted in scores so close that neither side could claim clear victory. But it did make for an entertaining 30 minutes. Four married couples were brought onstage and subjected to various stunts involving traditional concepts of "manhood" and "womanhood." Stunts were built around old prejudices and concepts—do women take longer to dress? Is a woman's place in the home? In one stunt, a husband was blindfolded and kissed by his wife, a French poodle, and a sound effects man. While he struggled to guess which had been his wife, the audience roared. Tom Slater was the emcee when *The Better Half* went on as a Sunday-nighter in 1943. The show was heard intermittently through the 1940's, and in mid-1944, Tiny Ruffner became host.

Betty and Bob

Betty and Bob, one of the first true soap operas of the air, premièred on NBC Blue October 10, 1932, and promptly set the standard for all the washboard weepers that would follow. This was the very first day-time serial of Frank and Anne Hummert, whose organization would grow into one of radio's giants. Although the Hummerts had *Just Plain Bill* on the air, that serial was then a nighttime drama; *Betty and Bob* truly cast the mold, employing in its eight-year network run all the elements that would come to be so well-indentified with the soap. Betty was a girl of humble origins, a simple-but-beautiful secretary who worked for the dashing heir to the Drake fortune. But when Bob Drake fell in love with her, his father cut him off without a dime, forcing him into Betty's workaday world and the frightening prospect of making a living. They had a son, Bobby, whose presence in the serial served mainly to drag it down.

The pre-Bobby shows exploited typical Hummert themes: Bob's dashing nature, irresistible to the Depression-era molls, vamps, and countesses who always lurked nearby; Betty's jealousy; various schemings against their happiness by strangers of both sexes. Even murder played a part. This was a new kind of daytime fare, and early ratings were spectacular. With the marriage of Betty and Bob and the subsequent birth of their son, listener interest began to lag. Raymond William Stedman, in his book *The Serials*, speculates that the demise of *Betty and Bob* in the ratings wars might be traced to their son. Listeners would no longer accept marital bickering and petty jealousies, Stedman points out, when a child was involved. For whatever reason, the producers killed Bobby off with a case of pneumonia in the late 1930's. At the same time, Bob and Betty were going through a painful divorce (they were later to remarry), Bob had broken away from the evil Countess Velvaine only to be swept in by the lovely socialite Pamela Talmadge. Betty, forsaken by Bob in her hour of need, had opened a dress shop with the help of Harvey Drew, the elderly man who was secretly in love with her. Bobby's death drew the couple together again, but by then few listeners cared.

Throughout the run, Bob teetered on the verge of emotional and physical breakdowns. He was forever "recuperating at the country home" near the little town of Walton. At one point, late in the run, Betty and Bob took over management of *The Trumpet*, crusading newspaper in the city (pop. 250,000) of Monroe. Don Ameche played Bob in the early network run, when the serial was produced in Chicago. His departure for Hollywood in the mid-1930's is blamed by Stedman and others for part of the loss of popularity. The role was subsequently played by Les Tremayne, Van Heflin, Onslow Stevens, Spencer Bentley, and J. Anthony Hughes. Betty was played by an equally long line of actresses: Elizabeth Reller, Beatrice Churchill, Alice Hill, Mercedes McCambridge, and Arlene Francis. Edith Davis played Bob's mother May Drake, and also served as Gardenia, the black ("sho is good to have you back, Mistah Bob") servant. Ethel Kuhn played Pamela Talmadge; Bill Bouchey was Harvey Drew and Frankie Pacelli was little Bobby. The serial was carried through most of its run by General Mills, in the interests of Bisquick, Wheaties, and other products. It crossed to CBS in 1936, moved to NBC in 1938, and was canceled on March 18, 1940, when General Mills moved its support to *The Light of the World*. A new *Betty and Bob* series, starring Arlene Francis and Carl Frank, was transcribed that year and sold to NBC. Everett Sloane, Ray Collins, Agnes Moorehead, and Edmond O'Brien appeared in support, but the new *Betty and Bob* died a quick death.

Between the Bookends

Between the Bookends began, like so many shows of early radio, when an act failed to show up, and eventually became the air's top series of sentiment and poetry readings. Alden Russell, a recent college graduate, had just gone to work with KMBC, the CBS affiliate in Kansas City, as a ukelele player, announcer, and general man Friday. The time was the late 1920's. When a hillbilly act failed to arrive for a scheduled slot, Russell was thrown into the breach, told to read poetry and somehow fill the next ten minutes. Embarrassed at the assignment, he agreed with the condition that his name not be used. Announcer Hugh Studebaker, also working spontaneously, introduced him as "Ted Malone," and a new personality was born. Russell read William Cullen Bryant's "Thanatopsis" with such feeling that letters began pouring in. Russell broadcast ever after as Ted Malone, filling the air with heartbreaking poems for more than twenty years. His show was picked up by CBS in 1935, and was still going strong on ABC in 1956. Like Tony Wons, Malone used contributions of listeners and drew upon a huge personal library of tidbits and poems. His show drew 15,000 letters a month, and varied between two-a-week and five-a-week 15-minute doses. Malone went to the Blue Network in 1938. He returned (it had then become ABC) in 1945, after a stint with the network as a war correspondent. Westinghouse carried his show from 1945 through 1949; various sponsors thereafter.

Beulah

Beulah, Radio Row's most famous black maid, came to prominence in a January 25, 1944, episode of Fibber McGee and Molly. Played by Marlin Hurt, a white man, the character became a mild sensation, and for more than a year was a Fibber McGee regular. Then Hurt was offered his own show, and on July 2, 1945, The Marlin Hurt and Beulah Show arrived for Tums.

For Hurt, it meant arrival at the top of Radio Row, a goal that had eluded him for fifteen years. He had broken into radio in 1929, forming a trio with Bud and Gordon Vandover, singing as the second-liners "Tom, Dick and Harry." Hurt was Dick. For a time they were part of NBC's Plantation Party, but few people putside the cast knew Marlin Hurt by name. Hurt had something other than a singing voice; he also had a sense of comic timing and a high-pitched falsetto female characterization, developed as a child from his real-life black nursemaid in Illinois. When one of his singing partners died in 1943, Hurt was thrust into radio as a single.

Don Quinn, the writer of Fibber McGee and Molly, heard him doing Beulah on The Fred Brady Show in Los Angeles. The war had taken many of Fibber's best-known voices; Quinn had lost "The Old Timer," "Horatio K. Boomer," "Nick Depopolous," and "Wallace Wimple" all at once when Bill Thompson joined the Navy, so Beulah became the McGees' maid for the duration.

Listeners couldn't believe that Beulah was actually a man. Hurt set the country on its ear with such phrases as "Love dat man" and "Somebody bawl fo' Beulah?" When Hurt broke away for his own series, Phil Leslie went along to write the scripts. Leslie had been Quinn's assistant, and was familiar by then with Hurt's strong points. Hurt was written into the new show, as master of the house where Beulah worked. In addition to playing Beulah and talking in his natural voice, Hurt also played Bill Jackson, Beulah's shiftless boyfriend. John Brown played the obnoxious neighbor Mr. Jenkins; Carol Stewart was vocalist, and music was by Albert Sack. Ken Niles was announcer; Helen Mack was producer and director.

The show was less than a year old on March 21, 1946, when Marlin Hurt collapsed and died in his wife's arms. He was only 40. The following Sunday, his time slot was devoted to a memorial program, and Beulah the maid slipped from the air.

It was a tailor-made role that might have died with Hurt, but Beulah was revived on April 2, 1947, on ABC. Ironically, the lead was again played by a white man, young Bob Corley. In the fall of 1947, Beulah went into a nightly 15-minute serialized show that ran on CBS for Procter & Gamble until 1954. At the height of Hurt's popularity, Beulah had been described by *Newsweek* as a "big, black and good-natured radio version of the screen's Hattie McDaniel," and it was Hattie McDaniel who got the serial role. Now Beulah worked for a family known as the Hendersons, Harry and Alice and their son Donnie. Harry Henderson was played by Hugh Studebaker and Jess Kirkpatrick, Alice by Mary Jane Croft and Lois Corbett. Beulah's boyfriend Bill was Ernest Whitman. Louise Beavers and Lillian Randolph also played Beulah before the show closed shop in 1954.

The Bickersons

The Bickersons, as portrayed by Don Ameche and Frances Langford, had enjoyed great popularity as a skit on *The Charlie McCarthy Show*. So, in 1946, NBC brought the pair into its Sunday-night schedule, added Pinky Lee and later Danny Thomas just for laughs, backed them with the music of Carmen Dragon's orchestra, and called it *Drene Time* as a courtesy to the sponsor. But to the listeners it was still *The Bickersons*, and the heart of the show still revolved around the squabbling couple first heard on *Charlie McCarthy*. Ameche played John Bickerson and Langford was his wife Blanche. The Bickersons fought about everything from menus to Blanche's driving, but most often they fought because John was devoted to his sleep, Blanche, an insomniac, hated to be up alone.

Although the show was on for only two seasons, it has become a mini-classic in the minds of many people who don't even remember the specifics or format. For its 1947 season, the show moved to CBS Friday nights for Old Gold. It featured *Bickersons* skits and short monologues by Frank Morgan. A summertime *Bickersons* show was also heard on CBS in 1951, featuring Frances Langford and Lew Parker as the battling pair. It was one of the most memorable husband-wife fighting formats, and Ameche was still heard in 1970's commercials as John Bickersoh.

Big Jon and Sparkie

Big Jon and Sparkie. Jon Arthur brought two memorable children's shows to ABC in 1950: the Saturday-morning *No School Today* and the daily *Big Jon and Sparkie*. *No School Today* started as a two-hour show and eventually was tightened to 90 minutes. *Big Jon and Sparkie* began as a 30-minute daily shot and ran 15 minutes a day after its first year. The shows revolved around one "normal" adult (Big Jon) and a supporting cast of fantasy characters, also played by Arthur. Star of the show was Sparkie, "the little elf from the land of make-believe, who wants more than anything else in the world to be a real boy." It was billed as a show "for the younger generation and the young at heart," and featured stories and songs to the theme of "Teddy Bears' Picnic."

Arthur, son of a Pennsylvania minister, held jobs in theatre and journalism before a course in radio announcing changed his life. In 1939, he landed on a West Virginia station, and took his first step in children's entertainment. When an act failed to show, Arthur offered his version of "The Three Little Pigs." He created Sparkie and *No School Today* at WSAL, Cincinnati, and later expanded into ABC. For the first two years Sparkie was merely an invisible voice. But so many fans wondered what he looked like that Arthur decided to create a picture. He threw the question back to his listeners and got 25,000 responses. From those letters Leon Jason, a comic book artist, was commissioned to draw a composite character. Other Arthur devices included a "magic spyglass," which he used to see into listeners' homes and check up on their hygiene habits; a continuing "movietime serial," and adaptations of such classics as *Treasure Island*. Riddles from listeners were also used, and they were predictably corny. Example: What is no larger when it weighs five pounds than when it weighs one pound? Answer: A set of scales. The shows were among radio's last offerings for children, running into the late 1950's.

The Big Show

The Big Show was radio's last major gasp in the face of growing TV encroachment. It was also a coup for NBC, still smarting from the loss of most of its Sunday night stars to CBS in the talent raids of 1948–49. Armed with big guns, the network prepared to go all-out with its 90-minute Big Show.

More than $100,000 was budgeted for a single show. It was, Newsweek noted, "real television money," spent on a dying medium in an almost desperate attempt to shoot in a booster, to keep the heart beating for a while longer. Tallulah Bankhead, one of the legendary lights of Broadway and London theatre, was coaxed into the limelight as "mistress of ceremonies," and Fred Allen was brought out of retirement as a regular supporting star. Jimmy Durante, Ethel Merman, Frankie Laine, Jose Ferrer, Paul Lukas, and Danny Thomas were lined up for the opener. Dee Engelbach was producer-director, Jimmy Wallington announcer. Meredith Willson assembled his music makers, and a team of writers including Selma Diamond, George Foster, and Frank Wilson was headed by Goodman Ace of Easy Aces fame.

The show premièred November 5, 1950. "This is radio, 1950," Miss Bankhead said, opening the first show. "The greatest stars of our time on one big program. And the most fabulous part about this, dah-lings, is that every Sunday we will present other stars of the same magnitude. Pardon me if I sound like a name dropper, but just listen to three or four of the names we've lined up for next week's show . . . Groucho Marx . . . Fanny Brice . . . Jane Powell, and Ezio Pinnnn-zah!

"Well, now, don't just sit there with your mouths open, dah-lings. I know what you're thinking. You think such a radio show every week is impossible . . . but NBC says nothing is impossible. All it takes is courage, vision and a king-size bundle of dough."

King-size was right. For the start of its second season, NBC flew the entire Big Show cast and crew to London to join British stars Robb Wilton, Vera Lynn, and Beatrice Lillie. After one broadcast in London, it was off to Paris, with William Gargan and Gracie Fields. The American press was ecstatic. Again from Newsweek came the opinion that The Big Show was "the biggest bang to hit radio since TV started."

The show had a piece of everything, and the time to do it right. Durante was at his word-twisting best; Merman belted out numbers like old times on Broadway. Scenes from top Broadway plays were dramatized with the actual stars. But the program made only a small dent in the ratings of *The Jack Benny Program* and *Charlie McCarthy*, both recently "stolen" by CBS. What smashed them all was TV. The doomsters, who had been predicting radio's death since the late 1930's, were ultimately right. Within a few years Benny and Bergen would be gone too, but first to fall was the biggest. After two years on the air NBC had lost $1 million on the *The Big Show*, and it succumbed in 1952.

Big Sister

Big Sister was one of the most popular and durable of radio's soap operas, the story of Ruth Evans, and her troubles guiding her younger sister and brother through the trials of life.

This heartthrobber was first heard on CBS September 14, 1936, and sold Rinso for ten years. In an abrupt change, sponsorship then went to Procter & Gamble, Lever Brothers' top competitor, which carried it for another six years. It was last heard December 26, 1952.

In the beginning, Ruth Evans was a swinging single. Jim Ameche introduced her strife, to the show's opening gong of four bells from the Glens Falls town hall clock. By 1939 she had settled down as the wife of Dr. John Wayne, a physician working with Dr. Duncan Carvell. She was "big sister" to Sue Evans (Dorothy McGuire) and Little Neddie Evans (Michael O'Day), a cripple who had been cured by Dr. Wayne. But to Reed Bannister, her husband's best friend, she was womanhood perfected, the impossible, unattainable love. The noonday serial focused on Ruth's relationship with her husband and friends, and was filled with all the stock heartaches.

There were bouts with amnesia, a rare malady that became almost commonplace between the hours of noon and five. There was John's eye for a pretty leg, finally manifested in an affair with Hope Evans, wife of Ruth's little brother Ned. There was a long separation during the war, when John was held in a Japanese prison camp, and a hundred and one other troubles that could only happen in a radio soap opera.

Problems came early to Ruth and John. Even before they were married, John was getting plenty of trouble from his first wife Norma. Consider this early episode, retold in a 1939 issue of *Radio Mirror*:

Norma has trapped Ruth and John in a secret cabin rendezvous to cause a scandal that will wreck John's career. She rushes back to town in triumph, with John and Ruth in hot pursuit. Norma's automobile is wrecked, leaving her on the verge of death. John and Ruth carry her to a farmhouse, and there must face a terrible decision. Without an immediate operation, Norma will surely die.

If Norma dies under the knife, John will surely face a murder charge. If she lives, she will ruin his career. What should they do?

Being good people, they hesitate but an instant. With Ruth shakily holding a flickering lamp, John performs the operation and saves Norma's life. But the operation leaves Norma's mind impaired, and John must face disciplinary action from a hospital review board. When "allowed to resign" gracefully, he opts for the coward's way out. He signs as a crewman on a freighter and ships out in the middle of the night. The freighter is reported lost at sea, with all hands drowned. Ruth is heartbroken until she learns that John may indeed have survived. She traces him to his remote farm (the one place he might go), where she learns that he was blinded in the explosion aboard ship. John, mistaking her true devotion for pity, sends her away in anger.

This art of snowballing complication, of misery piled upon disaster, could keep a single story line alive indefinitely.

The part of Ruth was initiated by Alice Frost, who met her future husband Wilson Tuttle when he was director of the serial. Nancy Marshall took the part in 1942; Marjorie Anderson, and Mercedes McCambridge also played Ruth before the role finally passed to Grace Matthews in 1946.

Martin Gabel originated the part of Dr. John Wayne. In later years John was played by Paul McGrath, one of the creepy hosts of *Inner Sanctum Mysteries*, and Staats Cotsworth, best known as Casey, in *Casey, Crime Photographer*. The show was created by Lillian Lauferty and for a time was written by Julian Funt, well known in the trade for his ability with medical material.

Big Sister always got respectable ratings and, in an unusual experiment, one of the characters on the show was lifted and placed in his own format. This was Michael West, played by Richard Kollmar, and the new serial was *Bright Horizon*, first heard on CBS in 1941. Alice Frost played Ruth briefly until *Bright Horizon* was established on its own. But this show never attained the prominence of its *Big Sister*, and faded from the air after a few seasons.

The Big Story

The Big Story grew out of a real-life crime case.

On October 10, 1944, City Editor Karin Walsh of the Chicago *Times* handed a classified ad clipped from the *Times* to James McGuire, ex-private investigator turned reporter. "Might be a feature in this," Walsh said . . . McGuire read the ad: "$5,000 reward offered for the killers of Officer Lundy on December 9, 1932. . . ."

That was how *Newsweek* summed it up in 1946. Bernard J. Prockter, an independent producer of radio shows, read the article, and a new idea for a radio show popped into his mind.

The story told how Reporter McGuire interviewed Mrs. Tillie Majczek, who had placed the ad. Her husband Joseph had served eleven years of a 99-year sentence for the murder of a policeman in a 1932 holdup. Mrs. Majczek was convinced that her husband was innocent, and McGuire became convinced too. He and another *Times* reporter, Jack McPhaul, worked on the case for ten months, writing more than thirty stories before uncovering evidence that led to Majczek's full pardon in August 1945.

Prockter took the case beyond its surface and began exploring it with the active mind of a radio man. How about a series built around reporters and their "big stories"? Would it work?

It worked. First heard April 2, 1947, *The Big Story* ran eight years on Wednesday-night NBC, and was also seen on early television.

In its first year, it leaped into a surprising nip-and-tuck ratings battle with Bing Crosby's popular *Philco Radio Time. The Big Story* actually topped Crosby in several alarming ratings reports, before the crooner changed formats and shifted into the time slot thirty minutes earlier.

In Prockter's eyes, "big stories" were crime thrillers, so that's what kind of show *The Big Story* was. Supposedly devised to honor reporters overlooked by Pulitzer committees, it concentrated upon old murder cases or other violent crimes against society. The material was culled from old newspaper files or by referral, and always involved closed cases to avoid charges of pretrial publicity.

Narrator was Bob Sloane, directors included Tom Vietor and Harry Ingram. Among the cast regulars were Robert Dryden, Bill Quinn, Bernard Grant, Betty Garde and Alice Frost. Ernest Chappell announced, calling the real reporters on stage after the play for the $500 "Big Story Award" from the makers of Pall Mall cigarettes, longtime sponsor.

Big Town

Big Town came to CBS October 19, 1937, yet another series about reporters and their never-ending fight against racketeers and criminals. For its early years, *Big Town* lured a power-packed cast of Hollywood film stars, and soon it jumped into radio's top ten shows. Its hero: Steve Wilson, crusading editor of *The Illustrated Press*.

Edward G. Robinson, then at the crest of his popularity for the gangsters he had played, beginning with the film *Little Caesar* in 1931, originated the role of Wilson. Claire Trevor, then a young starlet with her best film roles ahead of her, played Lorelei Kilbourne, society editor at the *Press,* whose curiosity and nose for news almost matched that of her boss.

The *Press* was the tough-as-nails newspaper in *Big Town,* which might have been any town in America, and Robinson was well-suited to the tough projection that Wilson's character demanded. Jerry McGill, who wrote and directed the early shows, had been a newspaperman himself and should have known that managing editors and society editors just don't get personally involved with gangsters and racket-busting. But *Big Town* took itelf seriously; McGill portrayed reporters as diligent, sober champions of justice. The show zealously pushed freedom of the press, creating a memorable slogan for Steve's paper: "Freedom of the press is a flaming sword. Use it justly; hold it high; guard it well."

Robinson and Trevor, aided by a sharp company of supporting actors, waded in with four fists every week. Jack Smart appeared in many of the early shows usually in small comic parts that were added for color. District Attorney Miller, the semi-pompous prosecutor who was too often too anxious to convict an innocent man, was given the proper pomp by Gale Gordon. Helen Brown played Miss Foster, Steve's secretary. Among the other regulars: Paula Winslowe, Tommy Hughes, and Lou Merrill. A behind-the-scenes romance culminated when Miss Trevor was wooed and wed by Clark Andrews, one of the early producers. By 1940 the show was directed by William N. Robson, who went on to become "the master of mystery and adventure" on *Suspense.*

Robinson played Wilson until 1942. With his departure, McGill brought in Edward Pawley, a stage actor who had substituted for E. G. a few times and knew the character. Claire Trevor had also left by then, turning over Lorelei to Ona Munson, who later bequeathed it to Fran Carlon. It was Pawley, with Carlon in support, who carried the show for most of its fourteen-year run. *Big Town* was consistently good, if slightly melodramatic, fare.

The show was heard on CBS for eleven years: from 1937 through 1940 on Tuesdays and until 1942 on Wednesdays for Rinso, from 1943 to 1945 on Tuesdays for Ironized Yeast, 1945–48 Tuesdays for Bayer Aspirin. In 1948 it moved to NBC for Lifebuoy, running Tuesday nights until 1951, when it moved to Wednesday for a final season. The *Illustrated Press* printed its final edition in 1952, but did turn up in early TV.

The Billie Burke Show

The Billie Burke Show was a lighthearted Saturday-morning effort, built around Miss Burke's image as a scatterbrain with a heart of gold. Best known for a time as the widow of Florenz Ziegfeld, Miss Burke came to CBS in 1944 in a morning show called *Fashions in Rations*. By fall of that year, her *Billie Burke Show* had taken root in its Saturday slot. Aided by Earle Ross, Lillian Randolph, and Marvin Miller, she offered a solid half-hour of situation comedy, portraying Billie Burke as a woman of unknown age who would go out of her way to aid a bum in distress or help the neighborhood kids get a playground. After her show folded in 1946, she played the same basic character with Eddie Cantor, who had gotten his start in her husband's *Follies* years before. She was also featured in a Wednesday night NBC comedy series *Chicken Every Sunday* in 1949.

Bill Lance

Bill Lance was a Sunday-night mystery-thriller, heard on West Coast CBS stations in 1944 and 1945. It starred John McIntire as a daring criminologist whose exploits had earned him the nickname "Fer de Lance" in the underworld. Flanked by friend Ulysses Higgins (Howard McNear), Lance used his deductive mind to bring criminals to justice. Glen Heisch produced; the series was created by J. Donald Wilson, who had worked on the original *Whistler* series. *Bill Lance* was written by Stewart Sterling, and drew support from such accomplished stars as Cathy Lewis, Joseph Kearns, and Mercedes McCambridge.

The Bing Crosby Show

The Bing Crosby Show took several distinct forms on the air, but always had the same flavor. That was due to the nature of the star. Born Harry Lillis Crosby (May 2, 1904) in Tacoma, Washington, he abandoned the study of law to become a drum-beating, singing vaudevillian of the late 1920's. In his autobiography, *Call Me Lucky*, Crosby pinned his nickname on a comic strip he once read and liked called *Bingville Bugle*. In NBC publicity material, the name was traced to his early childhood, when he played cowboys and Indians with the kids and shouted "bing" instead of "bang." For whatever reason, "Harry Lillis" was left in Spokane, where his family had moved in his childhood, and he became "Bing" for the road and forever after. The lighthearted sound of it, combined with boyish good looks that he would retain, became part of a Crosby image that still exists.

He often referred jokingly to his real name on the air, especially in his verbal duels with Bob Hope. He also talked of the old days in Spokane, and of his brother Everett, who had become his business manager in the early days. The early days—those of struggle and obscurity—were 1925 to 1931.

Crosby first hit the road in 1925, traveling to Los Angeles with Al Rinker, a musical pal from Gonzaga University. At Gonzaga, the two had organized a seven-piece band, entertaining at parties and high school dances. Crosby found that entertaining was more fun than law, so he dropped out of school and headed for Los Angeles. There they had a contact—Rinker's sister Mildred Bailey, who then was singing swing numbers on the new medium called radio. Mildred got them a job at the Tent Cafe, then owned by Abe Lyman's brother Mike. Crosby played traps and Rinker pounded the piano. Both sang. They booked into the Boulevard Theatre, toured with revues, and played movie houses as "Two Boys And A Piano." In 1927, Paul Whiteman saw them at the Metropolitan Theatre in Los Ageles, and signed them to tour with his band.

Soon they were playing Chicago and New York. In New York, Whiteman hired Harry Barris to accompany them; the trio was a hit as The Rhythm Boys. They sang with Whiteman until 1930, then went to Los Angeles and worked with Gus Arnheim out of the Coconut Grove.

Bing Crosby first sang on the air while performing with Gus Arnheim's orchestra at the Coconut Grove, Los Angeles, in 1930. It was there that he met Dixie Lee (born Wilma Winifred Wyatt), a beautiful starlet whose career had begun the year before with *The William Fox Movietone Follies of 1929*. Dixie played hard to get. It is said that Crosby's famous recording, "I Surrender, Dear," was done for her. If so, it won him both fame and the lady. Dixie became his wife and—when brother Everett sent the record to the networks—Crosby was asked to audition for both NBC and CBS.

Offered jobs at both, he opted for CBS. His première was to be in late August 1931, but he was stricken with laryngitis and was unable to go on. By September 2, he had recovered, and a young Harry Von Zell introduced him on a nationwide CBS hookup, *Fifteen Minutes With Bing Crosby*. Crooning had come alive. For 15 minutes, Crosby buh-buh-booed his way through such numbers as "Just One More Chance" and "I'm Through with Love."

Everything broke at once. With his first nationwide radio hookup, his star rose as fast as any in show business, and he became almost overnight the super-hot property eagerly sought by hucksters in three distinct show business entities.

Crosby made *The Big Broadcast of 1932*, and settled into a hectic pace of two to three films a year. He began recording for Decca, and the following year he picked up Chesterfield as sponsor of a twice-a-week songfest. In 1933 the show landed in prime time as a weekly half-hour for Woodbury Soap.

Crosby's best radio shot came in 1935, when he left CBS to host NBC's popular 60-minute variety show, *The Kraft Music Hall*. The hour-long format suited his casual style just fine. It suited his audience, too. His show—though never the blockbuster of the Jack Benny calibre—always got the major share of Thursday-night listeners, usually finishing the year with a Hooper average in the low to mid 20's.

He stayed with Kraft for ten years. As it developed under Bing, *The Kraft Music Hall* featured relaxed conversation, jokes, and music. Bob Burns, "The Arkansas Traveler," joined the regulars, and established himself as a tall-tale-teller about life back home. Victor Borge, who escaped the Nazi invasion of his native Denmark, was booked as a comedian in 1942, and served as a *Music Hall* regular for a year. Borge's professional reputation as the "devilish Dane" who might or might not be able to play the piano started (after a boost from Rudy Vallee) on *The Kraft Music Hall*.

In January 1942, Kraft lured Mary Martin from Broadway to sing in the *Music Hall* for about a year. Crosby also featured singer Peggy Lee, who would rejoin him on *Philco Radio Time*. Connie Boswell (who sometimes spelled it Connee) and Ginny Simms appeared often; so did great names from the world of jazz: Duke Ellington, Artie Shaw, the Dorsey Brothers, Jack Teagarden, Joe Venuti. Crosby brought Lionel Barrymore to the microphone. Humphrey Bogart, still in the early stages of his career, made an appearance; other shows featured Frank Sinatra, Johnny Mercer, and Spike Jones and the City Slickers.

The top headliner was Bob Hope. Whenever Hope and Crosby appeared together, ratings were high. Since *The Road to Singapore*, their first "Road" film together, Hope and Crosby had established themselves as a loosely formed team. They appeared together a few times a year, just enough to rekindle the flame, then each returned to his own enterprises. Whenever Hope was around, Crosby's low-key humor came off almost straight, and Bing's best shots were with his sometimes remarkable use of the King's English.

By 1943, Crosby was firmly established as one of radio's best-loved performers. His "When the Blue of the Night Meets the Gold of the Day" had become one of the medium's classic themes. When his home was destroyed in a fire, thousands of listeners responded with gifts. Some offered pipes, a Crosby trademark in his films. Others sent complete collections of his records. Some offered to replace the family dog, which had been lost in the blaze. Crosby had one quality everyone liked in those wartime days; an image of honesty and integrity. In some of his offstage, secretly recorded performances, he also proved he could be difficult and moody, but that was the private man that America seldom saw.

Regulars surrounded Crosby, and stayed with him for years. Carroll Carroll was a longtime writer during the Kraft years, serving as lone script writer from 1936 to 1938 and as head writer thereafter. Ken Carpenter became his announcer of long standing, sticking through format changes from Kraft to Philco to Chesterfield to General Electric. John Scott Trotter was orchestra leader through most of the Kraft years, and through the end of Crosby's 30-minute General Electric show. Bill Morrow and Murdo MacKenzie produced and directed. In 1946, when he wanted to prerecord his shows he ran up against stiff NBC and Kraft resistance, so he quit *The Kraft Music Hall*, which later returned as a vehicle for Al Jolson. Crosby moved to ABC for *Philco Radio Time.*

The Philco-sponsored show was the first major transcribed network show, and many people in the trade were apprehensive about its chances. There was a general prejudice against "canned" entertainment in radio; producers and many performers felt that the public just wouldn't buy it. Crosby believed that the public didn't care either way. If something was good, who would care if it was live or coming from a disc? Recording allowed him to edit out flat sections and produce a smooth 30-minute package. Rehearsals and recording sessions could be scheduled at everyone's convience. That was what Crosby wanted to do and that was that.

A clause was inserted into his contract, stipulating that he would return to live shows immediately if his Hooper fell below 12 for any four consecutive weeks. *Philco Radio Time* started with a bang on October 16, 1946, finishing high in the top ten its first week. Crosby had opened with Bob Hope, but followed with a string of lesser-known guests. His ratings started to sag. By the end of the month, his Hooper had dropped to 12.2, and the doomsters were coming out of the woodwork. But it bottomed out there; more attention was given to scheduling, and *Philco Radio Time* finished out the year with a respectable 16. The program ran Wednesdays until June 1, 1949. Crosby's Chesterfield show was heard on CBS Wednesday nights from 1949 through 1952. In 1952, General Electric picked up the show, as a Thursday nighter and in 1953 it went to Sundays; the show went into a 15-minute daily format for various sponsors in 1954, and ran until 1956.

On radio, Bing Crosby could do what he did best—simply be Bing Crosby. He didn't have to worry about neckties and pressed pants. If he was recreating the role of Father O'Malley for The Screen Guild Theatre, he didn't even need a priest's collar. The listening audience "saw" him in black, projecting the dignity of the church as he broke the news to a tearful Ingrid Bergman that she had tuberculosis. In fact, Crosby might have been wearing baggy pants with the tail of a Hawaiian shirt sticking out over his belt. But that was one of the joys of the medium.

It was also one of the reasons why Crosby held out against television until the bitter end. General Electric, sponsor of his show in the waning days, recognized the TV appeal of its star and finally added a clause to his contract, in effect penalizing him for every week he shunned the TV cameras. Crosby finally gave in, appearing on a series of TV specials. But he kept his radio show until slipping ratings caught up with everyone.

Crosby's career reached the heights on all fronts of entertainment. In films he was top box office; his records sold in the millions. But radio first spread his name far and wide, as he developed that smooth, easy-going, conversational style that (once his initial mike fright wore off) was described by friends as an extension of his real personality. It was radio that kept Crosby synonymous with top show business for three decades.

Crosby was still doing some radio work into the 1960's, but The Bing Crosby Show of old ended in 1954. He missed the broadcast of October 30, 1952, for his wife Dixie Lee died of cancer two days later, leaving him four sons. Crosby later remarried and continued making films at a one-a-year rate until the mid-1960's, when he eased into semi-retirement, to be seen thereafter in television specials and annual Christmas shows.

Biography in Sound

Biography in Sound was an NBC series heard from 1955 through 1957, offering portraits of famous people seen through the eyes of friends who knew them best. The shows were hour-long snatches of life, told in interviews and remembrances. The subjects most often were people of the past (Fiorello La Guardia, Ernie Pyle, W. C. Fields), but the series also did living subjects, as in its "Danny Kaye, Prince of Clowns" show of September 10, 1957. On May 29, 1956, shortly after his death, *Biography* offered a "Portrait of Fred Allen." Two weeks earlier, the May 15 show was a biography of radio, appropriately called "Recollections at 30." Joseph O. Meyers was producer. In all, this was a solid, respectable series, but it came too late in radio's history to attract many listeners.

The Black Castle

The Black Castle was an early evening mystery-terror show, running on Mutual in 1943 and 1944. Broadcast Tuesdays and Thursdays, the 15-minute program offered mini-dramas of the weird and occult. All the voices and characterizations were done by one man, Don Douglas, who also served as announcer. The opening made good use of imagery, with the tolling of a churchbell in the distance. The creepy voice of the host welcomed his listeners: "Come, follow me, please, for again we visit the wizard who dwells yonder in the great hall . . . Now, up these steps to the iron-studded oaken door, which yawns wide on rusted hinges, bidding us enter . . . Follow softly . . . down this long stone-wall corridor . . . [the sound turns hollow in mid-sentence; organ music is heard in the distance] Music! do you hear it? . . . Yes, it is he, sitting before the organ, clutching the keys in his ancient, bony fingers . . . There, perched on his shoulder is his pet raven . . . Wait! it is well to stop, for here is the wizard of the Black Castle!" Then the cackling wizard took over, sending his raven Diablo to its perch in the rafters while he told us his story—which was generally trite, hardly a match for the terrific opening. When the story ended, we retraced our steps, following the host back through the corridor to "our place of rendezvous, on the hillside overlooking the peaceful valley." Churchbells fade, and out.

The Black Hood

The Black Hood was about the corniest of old-time radio. This 15-minute wartime serial for kids was an adaptation of a comic strip, and was one of the endless "secret identity" shows that came in the wake of *The Shadow*. This time the hero was Kip Burland, rookie cop, who—unknown to all except beautiful newspaperwoman Barbara Sutton—was really "The Black Hood," masked fighter of crime. There was one new twist in this show—the mask itself was mystical, and wearing it gave Burland extraordinary powers. The show, premièring on Mutual July 5, 1943, opened with the ringing of a gong, and Burland's ominous challenge to criminals: "Criminals, beware . . . The Black Hood is ev-ery-where." Then a howling wind and Burland's staccato voice again: "I—The Black Hood—do solemnly swear—that neither *threats*—nor bribes—nor bullets—nor death itself—shall keep me from fulfilling my vow: *To erase crime—from the face of the earth!*" Scott Douglas starred, and it was hokey-plus.

The Black Museum

The Black Museum was a fine series, produced by the BBC and brought to Mutual for a year-long run beginning January 1, 1952. Hosted by Orson Welles, the show dramatized incidents from Scotland Yard's Black Museum, a gruesome assemblage of murder artifacts. Each week Welles opened the show with a walk through the Black Museum, where some ordinary object would prompt him to tell a tale. Sometimes a straight razor, sometimes an old trunk, all the objects had been used in some way in a celebrated murder case. The shows were historically and dramatically fascinating, and Welles added greatly to their artistic success. But they didn't last long, bowing out December 30, 1952.

Blackstone, the Magic Detective

Blackstone, the Magic Detective was a combination mystery-trick show, tied together in a neat 15-minute syndicated package of the late 1940's. The show opened with Blackstone, "the world's greatest living magician," telling friends John and Rhoda about a case he had solved some time ago. Through dramatic flashback, the listener could "see" the story develop. There was always a magical ending to the stories, which Blackstone explained after a commercial pause. After the story, Blackstone offered a trick, which kids could practice to "mystify" their friends. Tricks included such things as balancing a glass on the edge of a dollar bill, balancing an egg, a walking hairpin, and a disappearing half-dollar. Almost eighty shows were produced, with Ed Jerome as Blackstone, under such intriguing titles as "The Riddle of the Other Eightball," "The Knife in the Dark," and "Footsteps in the Night."

Blackstone Plantation

Blackstone Plantation featured Frank Crumit and Julia Sanderson, generally considered the first husband-wife team to rise to radio stardom. Both came out of vaudeville, meeting around 1922 in the New York musical comedy *Tangerine*. Crumit was then a ukulele-playing leading man; Julia had been dancing since her fifteenth birthday. After their marriage, they became well-known as a musical comedy team, and Crumit's reputation was enhanced through his many phonograph records. The recording business led naturally to radio, and in 1929 he introduced his wife to the air audience and the beginning of a fifteen-year joint career. Their first regular airshow was *Blackstone Plantation*, a Tuesday night entry in the 1929 CBS lineup; it was sponsored by Blackstone Cigars. In 1930, the *Plantation* moved to NBC, where it was heard on both the Red and Blue networks for a time before expiring in 1933. *Blackstone* set the style for Crumit and Sanderson: light, gay patter and cheerful music, punctuated often by Julia's girlish giggle. In 1933 they returned to CBS for Bond Bread, in a late afternoon Sunday show that lasted until 1936. Intermittently, they appeared on such popular shows of the time as *The Norge Musical Kitchen* and Harry Richman's *It's Florida's Treat*. In 1938, they were engaged for the leading roles in the spirited NBC quiz show, *The Battle of the Sexes*, which later starred Walter O'Keefe. They stayed with *Battle* for two years, and emerged in 1942 with *The Crumit and Sanderson Quiz*, a Saturday night CBS series for TUMS. In 1943, they began their noontime *Singing Sweethearts* broadcasts, heard Monday through Friday on CBS West to the theme, "Sweet Lady." Crumit died September 7, 1943, having attained a repertoire of 7,000 to 10,000 songs. After his death, Julia went on Mutual with the 1943–44 ladies' show, *Let's Be Charming*.

Blind Date

Blind Date, a merry show of conversation and imagination, starred sexy "femcee" Arlene Francis and was first heard on NBC July 8, 1943 as a summer replacement for *Maxwell House Coffee Time*. Miss Francis arranged dates between people who had never met until the moment of selection. Maxwell House carried the show through the summer, and by then it had shown enough promise to be picked up by ABC for its fall schedule. *Blind Date* ran on ABC for three seasons, two years on Monday for Lehn and Fink, one year on Friday for Hinds Cream. Tom Wallace created, owned, and directed: he selected the six men and the three dates they competed for. The early summer shows were built around servicemen, and their "blind dates" were usually popular actresses. The men tried to sell themselves to prospective dates, who were screened from view behind a large partition. Couples selected had a night on the town, with Maxwell House picking up the Stork Club tab until 3:30 A.M. Maxwell House also picked up the tab for a chaperone who guided the lucky couple about town and left them in the wee hours, when they presumably went their separate ways and the sponsor's responsibility ended.

Blondie

Blondie, Chic Young's popular character, was first seen on the comic pages in 1930, graduated to movies in 1938, and came to CBS on July 3, 1939. A zany situation comedy, this show ran on Mondays for five years, under sponsorship of Camel cigarettes. To concoct it, the creators took an actor who once described his own life as "bum-steady," added a blonde refugee from movie bit parts, stirred in a little *Great Gildersleeve*, and seasoned heavily with Hanley Stafford. Then—Uhh-uhh-uhh—don't touch that dial! Listen to . . . Blonnnnndie!

Dagwood and his wife Blondie formed the nucleus of the Bumstead home, center of radio chaos through the 1940's. Cartoonist Chic Young, who brought the Bumsteads into the world, believed that even comic strip characters should grow and change over the years, and so it was with Blondie and Dagwood. There were no eternal infants like Popeye's Sweet Pea in the Bumstead home. "Baby Dumpling" eventually grew into a copy of Dagwood and became known as Alexander. A daughter born during the war became Cookie. The family owned a dog, Daisy, which became as much a part of the family as its human members.

The stage was already well set, through a decade of comics and two feature films, by the time *Blondie* premièred on CBS. For the radio show, the film stars were lured to the microphone, in a team effort that would remain essentially intact for the first seven years of the run.

Arthur Lake needed little coaxing. He enjoyed the part of Dagwood, and sometimes remarked how nice it would be if the show could just go on forever. Lake was the son of Arthur Silverlake, a circus strongman, and Edith Goodwin, legitimate stage actress. Greasepaint got into his blood early, as he toured small-time tent shows in the South with his family. It is said that Lake got his first taste of footlights at the age of one year, serving as the infant in the ice-jumping scene for a backwoods production of *Uncle Tom's Cabin*. By 1930 he was a movie veteran; nine years later a radio star.

Penny Singleton captured the part of Blondie well. Her portrayal transferred some of the logical insanity from comic page to audio—no small feat. She had been a Broadway songstress before her Hollywood days; though she had come West in the early 1930's, starring roles eluded her until Columbia filmed *Blondie* in 1938. The films followed in sequence: *Blondie Meets the Boss* (1939), *Blondie Goes Latin* (1941), *Blondie Hits the Jackpot* (1949), and so on. They were popular B-films, and the radio show might well be classified the same way.

As in the strip, Dagwood worked for the J. C. Dithers Construction Company as an accountant. His mind worked literally like an adding machine. Sometimes in the radio shows we could hear him adding; computerlike sound effects were employed to suggest the Great Brain at work. Dithers, his foul-tempered boss, was well done by Hanley Stafford, better known as "Daddy" to "Baby Snooks." Herb Woodley, the Bumsteads' neighbor, was played by Harold Peary, "The Great Gildersleeve," and later by Frank Nelson. Various performers carried the roles of Alexander and Cookie.

Tommy Cook introduced the Alexander role in May 1943; in the summer of 1946, Larry Simms took the part, and Bobby Ellis began playing it in 1947. Jeffrey Silver became the fourth Alexander around 1949. Leone Ledoux was the first Cookie, and also played Alexander during his cooing Baby Dumpling years. The first Cookie speaking role was handled by Marlene Aames, who played it in 1946–1947. Norma Jean Nilsson played the part in 1947–1948, and Joan Rae took over in 1949. John L. Greene wrote the scripts.

Sadly, Lake's wish didn't come true. The show didn't last forever, but it did have a respectable run of about eleven years.

In 1944, *Blondie* moved to Sunday, where it was heard for four years for Super Suds. In 1948 it moved to Wednesdays, NBC, for Colgate. It was last heard on ABC in 1949–50, as a Thursday-night sustaining show. Not unexpectedly, Lake went all the way as Dagwood. Penny Singleton dropped out in the mid-1940's, and "Blondie" was played by Patricia Van Cleve, Mrs. Lake in real life. Although Penny Singleton returned to the show briefly in 1948–1949, she didn't stay, and the final season in 1949 and 1950 starred Ann Rutherford.

Blue Ribbon Town

Blue Ribbon Town, another variety show that took its name from the sponsor, must have warmed the hearts of promotion men at the Pabst Brewing Company. It was first heard on CBS March 27, 1943, and ran for one season. Written and directed by Dick Mack, it served chiefly as a vehicle for Groucho Marx. After a film career as the kingpin of the zany Marx Brothers, Groucho still hadn't found his radio legs. He hadn't developed the bite, the verbal sting that would mark his most successful show, *You Bet Your Life*. Aided and abetted by Kenny Baker, Virginia O'Brien, announcers Dick Joy and Ken Niles, the Blue Ribbon Blenders, and Robert Armbruster's orchestra, Marx relied heavily on such guest stars as Charles Laughton, and Barbara Stanwyck. Leo Gorcey, who played Mugs in the *Dead End Kids* film series, had become a regular by 1944 and was used mainly to needle Groucho. But it was an interesting 30-minute show, and especially interesting as early Groucho.

The Bob and Ray Show

The Bob and Ray Show was the creation of Robert Brackett Elliott and Raymond Walter Goulding, now a middle-aged pair of comics who each—at least when performing professionally—seem to know the other's mind. Bob and Ray aren't new to comedy; they've been around for almost three decades, entertaining radio audiences with outrageous parodies and satires on everything from eating habits to stuffy American institutions. But what passes between them when they're working does seem to border on the psychic, and those who have seen it describe it as phenomenal.

Using no script whatever, Bob and Ray manage to produce their funnies spontaneously, with a single often flawless sense of timing. They could do it in five minutes for the now-defunct *Monitor* and they can do it in a four-hour daily marathon between records on local radio. Without putting it into words, each seems to understand where the other is heading. A single word or phrase might send them down new paths, with only instinct and a keen understanding of each other to guide them. They don't worry too much about fluffs; even when they happen, Bob and Ray will often find some way to twist them into the plot of their skit, to make the fluff more than just a dropped sound effect.

They've been working together since both were young veterans just home from the service after World War II. Bob, born in Boston, Massachusetts on March 26, 1923, had landed a job as an announcer at WHDH during the war, and returned there in 1946 after his release from the military. He was doing a morning disc jockey stint when the station hired Ray, another New Englander, born March 20, 1922, in Lowell. Ray read news on the hour, but soon he and Bob began goofing around together on the air, creating mini-skits just after the newscast. When listeners reacted favorably, Bob and Ray went to work on the characters who would become the heart of their best-known routines.

They created Wally Ballou, Mary McGoon and Charles the Poet. Ray, with his deep baritone voice, still does all the very low, gruff voices and all the falsetto females. Bob handles the adenoids department, making Wally Ballou a pinched-nosed scatterbrain slightly under the influence of New England. Bob also handles most of the European accents that surface on the show. Ray does the roars, Bob the flat dullards, of which there are many on *The Bob and Ray Show*.

Wally Ballou has become the epitome of the bumbling radio reporter. He interrupts his guests, constantly mumbles over their voices, and asks dozens of questions that have just been answered. He introduces himself as "the highly regarded Wally Ballou, winner of over seven international diction awards." Usually his microphone is off for the first seconds of his newscast, and almost always he is cut off in the middle of a word.

Ray, meanwhile, is Mary McGoon and Charles the Poet. Mary has had a recipe and menu show; Charles still reads drippy poetry to the accompaniment of faint, sentimental music and chirping birds. But he never makes it to the end of a poem without bursting into fits of uncontrollable laughter.

When WHDH got rights to broadcast games between the Braves and the Red Sox in 1946, Bob and Ray were asked to do a 25-minute show before each game, to be called *Matinee with Bob and Ray*. The scope of their jesting was suddenly expanded. Now they concentrated on skits with continuing story lines, outrageous takeoffs on such radio serials as *One Man's Family* and *Backstage Wife*. In the hands of Bob and Ray, these shows became *One Feller's Family* and *Mary Backstayge, Noble Wife*. The serials moved ahead at a snail's pace that almost equals the originals, and bear some resemblance to the same subject matter. *Backstayge* is the story of Mary and Harry Backstayge, a middle-aged husband-wife acting team who live in Skunkhaven, Long Island. Supporting characters are Calvin L. Hoogevin, a neighbor; Pop Beloved, a stage doorman; Greg Marlowe, "a young playwright secretly in love with Mary"; and Fielding Backstayge, Harry's "long-lost blacksheep brother." With the success of these, new serials flowed from *The Bob and Ray Show: Linda Lovely; Lawrence Fechtenberger, Interstellar Officer Candidate; Mr. Trace, Keener Than Most Persons; Jack Headstrong, The All-American American; Wayside Doctor, Hawaiian Ear, Eye, Nose and Throat Man; Kindly Mother McGee, The Best Cook in the Neighborhood;* and *The Gather-*

ing Dusk, a "heartwarming story of a girl who's found unhappiness by leaving no stone unturned in her efforts to locate it." At one point, Dusk was sponsored by "the Whippet Motor Car Company, observing the forty-fifth anniversary of its disappearance."

Scores of characters have been added to the cast. They spoof sportcasters with Steve Bosco, whose reporting is usually somewhat under the influence. They kid Arthur Godfrey with the character Arthur Sturdley, red-headed talent scout described as "just a jerk." They rib commercial premium offers with their "Little Jim Dandy Burglar Kit" and "The Bob and Ray Home Surgery Kit." Their Tex Blaisdell does rope tricks on the air, and Natalie Attired, the "song sayer," speaks the words of songs to the accompaniment of drums.

After five years at WHDH, they were ready for national exposure. The chance came in 1951, when an agent took their audition record to Bud Barry, an NBC vice-president. Barry liked it; Bob and Ray were brought to New York for a 15-minute early evening show which premièred July 2, 1951, on NBC.

Soon they were also doing a weekly 60-minute prime-time show, with full orchestra and guest stars. That series was short-lived, but the basic idea was revived in 1952 as a Saturday-night half-hour. At the same time, Elliott and Goulding were doing a two-hour and forty-five-minute morning show, carried locally in New York, in direct competition with Gene Rayburn and Dee Finch. Rayburn and Finch had had a corner on the local fun market for more than four years. Within weeks their rating began to drop. A new kind of comedy was on the air.

For two years Bob and Ray played Bert and Harry, the Piel brothers, in a riotous series of commercials for Piels Beer. They made the full cycle of network radio, leaving NBC in 1953, and doing a TV show on ABC. In 1954 they returned to local radio; the following year they began their five-minute live routines on NBC's Monitor. By 1956 they had signed as disc jockeys with Mutual. In June 1959 they opened in a 15-minute, five-a-week show for CBS. That lasted for a year, then they dropped out of radio for two years to do commercials. In 1962, they went to WHN for a four-hour late-afternoon show. In 1965, they again left radio. Their Broadway show, The Two and Only, opened in 1970. Bob and Ray resurfaced on the air in 1973, broadcasting for WOR, home station of the Mutual Network. Until their departure from radio in 1976, they were still reminding their faithful:

"This is Ray Goulding, reminding you to write if you get work . . ."

"And Bob Elliott, reminding you to hang by your thumbs."

The Bob Burns Show

The Bob Burns Show started out as *The Arkansas Traveler,* a comedy-variety show that premièred on CBS September 16, 1941, for Campbell Soups. After a short run under that name, it settled into a Tuesday-night format and became simply *The Bob Burns Show.*

Burns really was an Arkansas traveler of sorts. He wandered far from his hometown of Van Buren, drifting around the state gathering the folk songs and tales that would later make him famous.

His nickname came from the legendary Col. Sanford C. Faulkner, who roamed the ante-bellum South, fiddling and singing wherever people gathered. Whether he was the traveler the legend suggests, Faulkner did write a tale to be related with fiddle music. The Colonel's story was of an Arkansas traveler who met a hillbilly toiling away on a fiddle in a desperate effort to capture a haunting tune. The traveler knew the tune; when he played it, the hillbilly welcomed him as a brother. Burns came along about a century later, when radio could instantly spread a man's tales to every part of the country. But before he became a radio man, Burns was in for some tall traveling himself, gathering the legends, embellishments, and just plain tall tales that would form the backbone of his act.

One of the earliest ingredients was a new musical instrument created by Burns from two gas pipes and a whiskey funnel. He was playing mandolin in the Van Buren "Silvertone Cornet Band," and one night when the band was practicing in a plumbing shop, Burns slapped the pipes together—trombone style—and blew out a bassy tune. The tone seemed to suggest the word "ba-zoo-ka," and "bazooka" became its name then and there. Armed with his new device, Burns took off across the Southern low country, playing carnivals and backwoods vaudeville, sometimes for as little as $3 a week. It was a long apprenticeship. He skirted around the edges of the big time, but never quite made it until 1935, when, after a borderline career in films, he packed up his family and went to New York with the single purpose, he told a *Radio Mirror* reporter, of getting on Rudy Vallee's *Fleischmann Hour.*

In those days, Vallee was a known maker of stars, responsible for the start of many top radio acts. Burns arranged an audition with J. Walter Thompson, the ad agency handling the Vallee show. The Thompson people liked his homey, country approach; more importantly, they saw in Burns a solid competitor for Will Rogers, whose *Gulf Show* was giving Vallee a run for his rating.

In his first appearance with Vallee, Burns talked politics in the best Rogers style. But on August 15, Rogers and pilot Wiley Post were killed in an Alaskan plane crash. Rogers became an instant legend, and Burns had to do some radical changing overnight to avoid being washed away as a second-rate imitator. He went hillbilly, and was brought back to the Vallee stage for several more appearances. His voice reached Hollywood, where Bing Crosby had just taken over *The Kraft Music Hall*. Burns was invited to join Kraft for a twenty-six-week engagement. The twenty-six weeks became six years.

Several times during his Kraft years, Burns tried to break away for a show of his own. He didn't succeed until 1941, when he interested Campbell Soups in a format of folksy comedy and song, surrounded by the same rural monologues he had done with Crosby. His comedy skits played on the "Arkansas Traveler" theme, featuring Burns as a guy from the sticks who wandered the countryside doing good deeds.

He often used his real first name—Robin—on the air, and was supported by regulars Ginny Simms and Edna May Oliver, and such guests as Ann Rutherford. His early show was produced by Thomas Freebairn-Smith, with orchestra by Billy Artzt. Burns moved to NBC in 1942, broadcasting Wednesday nights for Lever Brothers. Shirley Ross was a regular songstress during the middle years, and in 1944–1945 his show featured comic routines by the black duo Mantan Moreland and Ben Carter.

From 1943 through 1946 his show was on Thursdays; in 1946 it moved to Sundays, still on NBC, for American Foods. It ran until 1947.

As for the bazooka, it went on to immortality of its own. In World War II, the Army developed an over-shoulder weapon to launch armor-piercing rockets. It was christened bazooka, after Bob Burns' gas pipes and whiskey funnel.

The Bob Hawk Show

The Bob Hawk Show was the brain-child of a man who started on radio in 1927, reading poetry in Chicago. During the next decade, he worked in all kinds of radio jobs, from acting to announcing. But Hawk was to make his mark as a quizmaster. Some of his early quiz shows, such as *Foolish Questions* and *Fuz Quiz* (1936) are now happily forgotten, but they helped set the trend for later man-on-the-street question shows. In 1938, Hawk worked on two more obscure quizzes: *Quixie Doodles* and *Name Three*. He finally hit the big-time quiz trail April 21, 1940, with *Take It or Leave It* on CBS for Eversharp.

Hawk left that show in 1941 in a salary dispute with the sponsor, and the choice job was taken by Phil Baker. Hawk opened a new show,

How'm I Doin'? in January 1942 for Camel cigarettes. That was dropped after a brief run, and Hawk created another show for Camel, Thanks to the Yanks, which premièred on CBS October 31, 1942. In this program, Hawk stood in a pulpit at the end of a runway jutting out from the stage, and asked questions of audience contestants. The contestants, answering from their seats, chose "three-carton," "five-carton" or "ten-carton" questions; if they answered correctly, the free Camels were sent to servicemen of their choice.

Thanks to the Yanks became very popular, a fact due in no small measure to Hawk's skill at choosing provocative questions. The questions, though trivial, often could be answered two ways and were open to interpretation. Hawk's decisions were sometimes violently protested by listeners. But he used such questions as "Does a bull really get angry at red, or just the waving of a flag?" only after satisfying himself that scientific evidence clearly pointed one way or the other. Supporting him was a research staff, headed by his sister Betty. Thanks to the Yanks ran for the duration of the war, becoming simply The Bob Hawk Show in 1945. During the latter era, Hawk initiated his memorable "Lemac" quiz, bestowing upon winners the title "Lemac" to the singing of "You're a Lemac now." It was fine advertising, for "Lemac" spelled backward was—guess what. Camel carried the show as a CBS Monday night feature until 1953, with one year (1947–48) at NBC.

The Bob Hope Show

The Bob Hope Show had its roots in vaudeville. Like his friend Bing Crosby, Hope worked up to first-class radio stardom from the stage. Like Crosby, Hope began as a singer. Like Crosby, he performed in road shows until at last he got a toehold in the big time. Like Bing, he rose swiftly.

Born Leslie Townes Hope in England on May 29, 1903, Hope was taught to sing by his mother, who had been a concert performer on the Welsh stage. His father, a stone mason, brought the family of eight to the United States in 1907, and soon young Hope changed his name to Bob to avoid ribbings from other kids. As a child, he held many jobs to help his family; after school he decided to become a boxer. He entered the ring as "Packy East," but fistic glory had a sudden end in the Golden Gloves finals. For a while he taught dancing, then he worked with a car company and finally decided to try vaudeville. Hope teamed up with another young hoofer, one George Byrne, and the men played small towns in the Midwest under the billing, "Two

Diamonds in the Rough." Gradually they worked their way to New York where they were hired to fill out an act featuring Siamese twins. They were working up a new act for Chicago when Hope began considering a change.

Friends had told him that his real talent was with monologue. In a Newcastle, Indiana, stopover, Hope abandoned the blackface and soft shoe, and tried out a standup act. There, on the spot, the new Bob Hope was born.

In Chicago, it was a different story; there were few jobs of any kind, and Hope went through a long period of unemployment. Eventually he got booked into a few neighborhood theatres, and gradually expanded into the entire Midwestern vaudeville circuit. Based in Chicago, Hope did so well that he was able to form his own company, employing as one of his acts the young Edgar Bergen and his ageless dummy, Charlie McCarthy. But Hope had his eye on New York. He crashed the RKO vaudeville circuit and moved up to bigger stage parts. Radio beckoned. Despite an initial dislike of the new medium, Hope did three brief radio series.

Hope came to radio in a ready-made show, premièring on the Blue Network January 4, 1935, in a format that already starred James Melton and Jane Froman. It was called *The Intimate Revue*, and continued—with Melton, Miss Froman, and the Al Goodman Bromo Seltzer Orchestra—into the spring of 1935. That same year he was heard in the equally brief *Atlantic Family* for Atlantic Oil, with Red Nichols waving the baton. His third radio show, *Rippling Rhythm Revue* was sponsored by Jergens-Woodbury in 1936; it soon went the way of the others.

Movies beckoned. Hope was featured in *The Big Broadcast of 1938*, and one of the songs from that film—"Thanks for the Memory"—would become famous as his theme when his *Pepsodent Show* opened on NBC September 27, 1938.

Pepsodent became the pacemaker of all radio during the next decade. In its first year, the show carved out a huge share of the total Tuesday audience. By 1940, it had moved into a solid fourth place, behind Bergen, Benny, and *Fibber McGee and Molly*. In 1943 Hope's program topped all shows with a whopping Hooper of 40-plus. It became a long-running Tuesday night program on NBC, holding very high ratings until about 1950.

His format was simple enough, totally dependent on his skill as a gag man. Like other comedians, Hope used a small company of regular stooges. He booked guest stars constantly. Al Jolson, Dorothy Lamour, Frank Sinatra, Judy Garland, Fred Allen, Eddie Cantor, and Bing Crosby were among the many who helped boost Hope's ratings.

But most of the work was done by Hope and his regular cast: Skinnay Ennis, Barbara Jo Allen, Blanche Stewart, Elvia Allman, Frances Langford, and Jerry Colonna.

Colonna, a wild-eyed trumpet player from Boston, was hired by Hope before the first show. During the next decade, he became the comedian's right-hand man, traveling with Hope to camps, hospitals, and naval bases around the world as an integral part of The Bob Hope Show. Colonna sported a sweeping walrus moustache which many listeners—after seeing his picture in radio fan magazines —erroneously suspected was a prop. His contribution to the show was on the zany side; when Colonna was on, Hope became the stooge and fed him the straight lines. Colonna would suddenly appear, playing a variety of characters from carpenter to U.S. Senator, but most often referred to simply as "Professor." Listeners found Colonna's booming voice hilarious, especially when he sang serious songs, beginning softly and finishing with a great roar. His famous opening line was "Greetings, Gate." Nobody knew what it meant, but for a short time "Greetings, Gate" became a national salutation. Colonna also created Yehudi, a character who existed in name only. Frequently, in conversation with Hope, he would launch into a Yehudi scenario, and Hope would scream "Who's Yehudi?" That too, for a little while, became part of America's language.

Skinnay Ennis was the longtime director of music for The Pepsodent Show. Les Brown led the band beginning in 1947. Frances Langford was the singer most often associated with Hope. It was on Pepsodent that Barbara Jo Allen created her squeaky man-crazed old maid, Vera Vague. Blanche Stewart and Elvia Allman played Brenda and Cobina, scatterbrained socialites. Many top announcers worked for Hope, including Wendell Niles, Bill Goodwin, Hy Averback and Art Baker. But it was Hope who carried the show. Unlike Crosby, whose style was slow and relaxed, Hope came at his listeners like a machine gun. If one joke didn't grab you, the next one was already on the way. Hope was one of the quickest ad-libbers on the air, rivaled only by Fred Allen. But Allen's quips were intellectually based, while Hope's were rooted in the lingo of the common man. It was the common man who built his Pepsodent Show into the biggest radio powerhouse of the early 1940's.

Those were the years when he was nip and tuck with Edgar Bergen, Jack Benny and Fibber McGee and Molly for the ratings championship. His was a formidable show, the nucleus of NBC's Tuesday-night schedule for some fifteen years. His opening monologues, then as now, were crisp and topical. When entertaining in Palm Springs, he joked about Palm Springs weather. At Army camps, he jabbed fun at military police. His jokes came from the front pages of newspapers; they concerned pompous politicians and egomaniacal entertainers, names familiar to all America. No one was safe from Hope's pointed jabs but the pope. To work up this brew, Hope employed up to eight writers at once. But the final decisions on what to use were made by Hope. His jokes often bordered on the risqué, but he seldom crossed swords with the NBC censor. Still, his reputation as a dirty jokester was rampant, possibly because—with just the right inflection of voice—he could put insinuations into gags that words themselves might not convey.

Even bigger was his reputation as a humanitarian. Even before America's entry into World War II, Hope had given more than 500 free performances for servicemen. By the end of the war, Newsweek was reporting that Hope had "appeared at almost every camp, naval base and hospital in the country." He had made half a dozen trips overseas, entertaining GI's on the front lines in Europe, Africa, and the Pacific. It was, Newsweek said, "probably the biggest entertainment giveaway in history." When Hope went on the road, he took his Pepsodent cast with him and put the Tuesday-night show together wherever they happened to be.

For producer Al Capstaff, that was a special problem: booking the 42-member Hope entourage into trains and hotels across the country. In Hollywood, Hope usually broadcast from Ken Murray's Blackouts Theatre. By one account Hope put on only one studio show between Pearl Harbor day and the end of the war. For his service, he received more than 100 special awards and citations, and two special Oscars. One year he was the only entertainer voted a place in the Smithsonian Institution Living Hall of Fame.

With the end of the war, gradual erosion set in. Hope, still hyperactive and ready to go, took The Pepsodent Show to college campuses. He found the reception somewhat chilly after the warm response of GI's and sailors. By 1950 he had slipped badly, but most of radio had slipped along with him. His was one of the first of the big four comedies to sag under the encroachment of TV. Hope made his first television appearance in The Star Spangled Revue in 1950. But by 1951, two-thirds of his radio audience had vanished. Hope broke with Lever Brothers in 1950, and was sponsored successively by Camel, Chesterfield, General Foods, and American Dairy. In 1952, he was asked to serve as NBC's comedy commentator in its coverage of the Democratic and Republican national conventions. The same year saw the debut of his 15-minute NBC daytime show, a straight, toned-down monologue heard by housewives five times a week.

But the writing was on the wall. The Pepsodent Show had died, and new sponsors were trying to pick up the pieces. What they wouldn't admit was that radio too had died, and there just weren't any pieces left. That folded after two years. His regular show ran until 1958, though the last four four years consisted of repeats.

Bobby Benson and the B-Bar-B Riders

Bobby Benson and the B-Bar-B Riders premièred on Mutual in the fall of 1949, ostensibly a new show but actually a throwback to a serial of the early 1930's. As *Bobby Benson's Adventures*, it was heard on CBS in three-a-week, then five-a-week installments between 1932 and 1936. It was sponsored by Heckers H-O Cereals and, as was often the case then, the sponsor got a finger in the dramatic pie and got Bobby's ranch named after its product. Bobby was just a kid, but he was owner of the H-Bar-O Ranch in the Big Bend country of south Texas. Supported by a cast of regulars that included Tex Mason, foreman, Harka the Indian ranch hand, and Windy Wales, ranch handyman and teller of tall tales, Bobby was so convincing that, in a 10-year-old's vivid imagination, it seemed as if he might ride right out of the console and stampede across the living room. Bobby was played by, among others, Billy Halop of the "Dead End Kids." Noted cowboy star Tex Ritter played several parts, notably Tex Mason and Diogenes Dodwaddle, another yarn-spinner. When Heckers canceled sponsorship in 1936, Bobby changed ranch brands, and his spread became the "B-Bar-B." But the show itself was soon dropped, and it wasn't revived until *Bobby Benson and the B-Bar-B Riders* went to Mutual in 1949. It alternated between twice-a-week and Sunday time slots, finally settling in as a daily 25-minute show and running until 1955. Most memorable was the thundering opening: Here they come! They're riding fast and they're riding hard! It's time for action and adventure in the modern west with BOBBY BENSON AND THE B-BAR-B RIDERS! And out in front, astride his golden palomino Amigo, it's the cowboy kid himself, Bobby Benson! BEEEEE-BAR-BEEEEE!

Bold Venture

Bold Venture had two things going for it from the beginning: Humphrey Bogart and Lauren Bacall. Set in Havana, the show was produced by Bogart's Santana Productions and syndicated by the Frederic W. Ziv Company during the winter of 1950 and 1951. By spring 1951, it was playing in more than 400 markets and bringing in more than $4,000 a week for the Bogarts. Bogie played Slate Shannon, owner of a Cuban hotel; Bacall played Sailor Duval, whose father had died, leaving her under Slate's supervision. Sailor sounded well able

BOX 13   91

to take care of herself, and spent most of her time trying to get beneath the patented Bogart brushoff. The title came from Shannon's boat, *Bold Venture*, which was often employed in their tales of adventure and modern piracy. The run-down hotel setting was perfect for the widest assortment of drifters and causes, becoming a crossroads of treasure hunters and revolutionaries. A calypso singer named King Moses provided musical bridges, incorporating story developments within his songs. Backup and theme music was by David Rose. The scripts were by Morton Fine and David Friedkin. It was an interesting canned series with bigger names and a bigger budget than most network offerings, but it lacked the bang it should have had.

Boston Blackie

Boston Blackie, one of the most memorable names of radio and early TV, was radio's answer to the B-movie. In fact, the character started in a B-movie, Columbia's *Meet Boston Blackie*, in 1941. In 1944 Chester Morris (the screen Blackie) came to NBC with a *Boston Blackie* airshow, sponsored by Rinso and announced by Harlow Wilcox as a summer replacement for *Amos and Andy*. The series had a spotty radio history, running for a short time under Morris, and revived by 1945 as a syndicated show with Richard Kollmar as Blackie. Boston Blackie, in any case, was a private detective with a flair for the smart comment. Billed as "enemy to those who make him an enemy, friend to those who have no friends," Blackie liked nothing better than making the cops look stupid. With Inspector Faraday heading the local police effort, that was a snap. Richard Lane played Faraday in the NBC Morris version; the role was played under Kollmar by Maurice Tarplin. Lesley Woods played Blackie's girlfriend, Mary. The show was high in corn content, but hardly one of radio's schedule stoppers.

Box 13

Box 13, was far above most detective thrillers in production, acting, and suspense. Like *Bold Venture*, it was independently produced and syndicated, and featured a "name" movie star, Alan Ladd. His role: Dan Holiday, a former newsman who had "made it" as a writer of mystery novels. Holiday sought adventurous material for his books; to find it, he ran this ad in the *Star-Times*: "Adventure wanted; will go anywhere, do anything—Box 13." Then he employed a scatterbrain named Suzy to screen the mail and run his office. The ad brought in mail from screwballs of all kinds—one week a racketeer's victim, the next a psychopathic killer looking for fun. It all added up to danger for Holiday and a fine piece of radio for the listener. It was syndicated by Mayfair Productions, a partnership between Ladd and Bernie Joslin of Mayfair Restaurant fame, and was bought by Mutual, premièring August 22, 1948. It featured Sylvia Picker as Suzy, who was just a little too well-baked and the show's weakest link. Betty Lou Gerson, Lurene Tuttle, Alan Reed, Luis Van Rooten, and John Beal formed the company that produced most of the supporting voices. Richard Sanville produced and Verne Carstensen directed; music was by Rudy Schrager. Russell Hughes wrote the scripts.

Brave New World

Brave New World was first heard in November 1937; it was a CBS series with a dual purpose: to counter the distorted newscasts coming out of Europe and to help Americans learn about their neighbors. Billed by *Time Magazine* as "the most elaborate educational radio program ever attempted by the government," *Brave New World* was produced by the U.S. Office of Education and offered dramatized accounts of the history of other lands. The WPA pumped in $1,000 a week for the show; CBS matched that with $3,000 from its coffers, and offered *Brave New World* on a sustaining basis.

Break the Bank

Break the Bank was spawned during the postwar quiz boom, when radio giveaways were the hottest things on the air. Originally a wartime summer show, it had used a different master of ceremonies every week. One of them was Bert Parks, a young soldier just returned. Parks displayed such vigor and enthusiasm on the air that when Mutual decided to book the show in 1945, he was tapped as permanent emcee.

It became one of the biggest cash giveaways on Radio Row. *Bank* jackpots of four figures were common. The "bank" started at $1,000 and was enriched weekly until someone won. On Christmas Eve 1948, Mr. and Mrs. Clifton Powers walked out of the ABC Ritz Theatre $9,000 richer—then an all-time record for radio. And Mrs. Powers got on the air only because her 3-year-old son Michael squirmed out of her arms and ran up on the stage during the broadcast.

Break the Bank ran on Mutual for a year, then moved to ABC where it ran Fridays for Bristol-Myers until 1949. It moved to NBC for a final season on Wednesdays in 1949–50. The show was designed for people in the know; the questions were definitely tougher than average, but the rewards were greater. *Break the Bank* was built around different category questions, each category containing eight queries worth $10 to $500. The contestant who got that far was asked one final question to "break the bank." One miss was allowed; when a contestant missed twice, the "bank" was enriched by the total of his or her winnings.

One of the most interesting sidelights was the selection process for contestants. Co-host Bud Collyer scanned the audience for potentials, and directed men with portable microphones to the people in their seats. The potentials were brought onstage before the show and were interviewed briefly by producer Ed Wolfe. Wolfe would then select the order of their appearance, giving $5 to those who didn't make it.

In its salad days, *Break the Bank* was telecast simultaneously. The most visual thing about it was the table piled high with fresh greenbacks. *Break the Bank* paid its smaller winners—in cash and on the spot. Winners of large "bank" jackpots were paid with checks that were being processed even before the applause had died away. The questions were written by Joseph Nathan Kane, author of *Famous First Facts*, and the show was tied together with the music of Peter Van Steeden.

Breakfast at Sardi's

Breakfast at Sardi's featured Tom Breneman as host. This early-morning interview show had its roots in an advertisement for Sardi's Hollywood restaurant. By August 1941, the show had become so popular that it went on a nationwide Blue Network hookup. Breneman, a longtime radio personality, moved among the tables at Sardi's, interviewing people, asking silly questions, poking fun at himself and others, and always drawing the women out with silly hat contests and "wishing ring ceremonies." One of the early gimmicks was Joe the railway express boy who delivered orchids to women whose community work had earned them the title "good neighbors."

In its early years, *Breakfast at Sardi's* was designed as a break from the wartime pressures on the home front. Nell Olson was hostess. Ladies were given corsages as they entered the restaurant and were served juice and coffee before the show. By the mid-1940's, Breneman's show was one of the hottest things on the morning air. In 1945 he bought his own restaurant and moved out of Sardi's. The new location was Sunset and Vine. The show became *Tom Breneman's*

Hollywood and soon simply *Breakfast in Hollywood.* Mail was heavy—predominantly female, though men listened too. In 1942, *Newsweek* reported that convicts at Folsom Prison had voted it their favorite daytime program. It was still running strong the morning of April 28, 1948, when Breneman died suddenly just before the broadcast. After a frantic search for a new host, the producers settled on Garry Moore. The show ran until 1949.

The Breakfast Club

The Breakfast Club was a show that couldn't give away a commercial spot during its first six years, but it left an undeniable imprint on the development of morning broadcasting. Born in the depths of the Depression, the show combined just the proper amounts of Midwestern corn, unabashed sentiment, audience participation, and old-fashioned music and song to please the eardrums of middle America. As many entertainers discovered, that was a sure-fire road to overnight fame and fortune.

For Don McNeill, the fame arrived somewhat later than overnight, but the fortune—when it came—was well worth the wait. During the three-and-a-half-decade run of his *Breakfast Club,* McNeill watched his salary soar from $50 a week to more than $200,000 a year. He saw the show develop from a white elephant that the network kissed off as hopeless into one of the great blockbusters of the morning air, costing each of its four regular sponsors $1 million a year.

And yet, the show that bowed out on December 27, 1968, didn't differ radically from the première of June 23, 1933. The main difference was that McNeill wanted to take a fond look backward.

The corn element always ran rampant through the fabric of the show. Perhaps that was its greatest charm, and the secret of its long success. McNeill made no bones of the fact that he was just a country boy at heart. Born December 23, 1907, in Galena, Illinois, he had abandoned early ambitions to be an editorial cartoonist, and had leaped into radio during the wild 1920's. He teamed with Van Fleming, a singer he met while working in Louisville, and the two sang at West Coast stations under the name "Don and Van, the Two Professors." They split up the act when money ran out and bookings looked slim. McNeill headed east. In 1931, he married Kay Bennett, a college classmate, and they went to New York together to chase a career in big-time radio.

But New York could be a frustrating town, and eventually the McNeills returned to Chicago. He auditioned for a job opening at NBC

Blue, as master of ceremonies of a sagging early morning show called *The Pepper Pot*. It paid $50 a week, and the main fringe benefit was that McNeill could run it any way he wanted. Network executives were still writing off the early hours as dead time, so it really didn't matter much what McNeill did with it. It turned out that he transformed a sagging Blue Network show into one of the most dynamic offerings of the early-morning air.

The first change McNeill made was in the title. *The Pepper Pot* became *The Breakfast Club*, and the show was envisioned as developing in four stages. These were termed "the four calls to breakfast."

The program was broadcast from Chicago. First heard on June 23, 1933, it became one of the longest-running shows in network history. McNeill personally wrote the scripts for about two months. After that he began using short pieces of folksy humor sent in by his listeners. His wife—one of his most important critics—thought the show went better that way. McNeill asked for permission to run *The Breakfast Club* without a script. Network brass still didn't care, and the show eased into the spontaneous, unrehearsed format that would serve it for the next thirty-four years.

McNeill's gang of Breakfast Clubbers changed with the times, but several members lasted almost as long as the host. In the early months, Jim and Marian Jordan (later famous as Fibber McGee and Molly) played a couple called Toots and Chickie. Bill Thompson first tried out his "Wallace Wimple" voice on *The Breakfast Club*. Other people passing through on their way to new careers were Jan Davis (later of *Arthur Godfrey Time*) and Alice Lon, who would make her mark as one of Lawrence Welk's Champagne Ladies. Homer and Jethro practiced their corn, Johnny Desmond was a singing Johnny-on-the-spot, and Patsy Lee talked wistfully of her hope chest on McNeill's show. Gale Page and the Merry Macs also used *The Breakfast Club* as a stepping stone to bigger things: semi-regulars over the years included Mildred Stanley, Jack Baker ("The Louisiana Lark"), Jack Owens, Nancy Martin, Marion Mann, Betty Olson and Floyd Holm.

But to others the show became a career. Cliff Petersen joined the cast in 1936 as part of a singing trio called The Escorts and Betty. He graduated to the role of producer-director. Eddie Ballantine, a trumpet player with the original Walter Blaufuss orchestra, eventually took over the baton himself. Sam Cowling, a paunchy, durable comedian, joined the show in 1936 and became master of the one-liner. His "fiction and fact from Sam's Almanac" was an established part of the show. Finally there was Fran Allison, who played the gossipy spinster Aunt Fanny. As a "Clubber," Miss Allison relayed tales of her countrified neighbors (Ott Ort, Bert and Bertie Beerbower, the

Smelsers), but she became best known outside *The Breakfast Club*, as Fran on the TV show *Kukla, Fran and Ollie*.

The show opened with a bang, to this snappy theme from the salad days of 1944:

> Good morning, Breakfast Club-bers
> It's time to sing ya
> Another cheery greeting,
> So may we bring ya:
> Four—calls—for break-fast!
> Kel-logg's—call—to break-fast!
> So every Breakfast Club-ber
> Young and old,
> Come and join our hap-py
> Care-free fold;
> Yes, wake up, Breakfast Club-bers,
> And smile a-while;
> A day begun with Kellogg's
> Makes life worth-while!

Every 15 minutes, there was a "call to breakfast," done with a drum roll, whooping, and a trumpet fanfare. The cast joined McNeill for a "march around the breakfast table," which sometimes continued up the aisles of the broadcast studio. Later in the show came "Memory Time," when McNeill dipped into the mailbag for a piece of nostalgic poetry contributed by a listener. Other well-remembered features were "The Sunshine Shower" (requests by McNeill for listeners to write to people confined in nursing homes, hospitals, and orphanages); and "Prayer Time," a nonsectarian appeal to the Maker, culminated by McNeill's 15 seconds of silent prayer:

> All over the nation,
> Each in his own words,
> Each in his own way;
> For a world united in peace,
> Bow your heads and let us pray.

"Prayer Time" was first heard during the broadcast of October 28, 1944, and was conceived as a comfort for families with sons serving in the war. But it became such an established part of the show that McNeill kept it even after the war ended. He was especially responsive to such requests from listeners, and was fond of saying that *The Breakfast Club* was really written by the audience. "I just found that the folks who listen in can write this show a whole lot better than I can," he said in a 1950 Colliers article. More than one million pieces of mail came in each year, and the heart of The Breakfast Club developed right out of the mailbag. Gags, verse, and regional anecdotes were all grist for McNeill's mill. Interspersed with songs and interviews, the mail filled out the hour, and kept the show moving at a comfortable pace.

Guest stars were used, though sparingly, and they soon joined the spontaneous mood. Breakfast Clubbers still remember the morning when Jerry Lewis set fire to a commercial script as McNeill was reading it, creating such pandemonium that announcers nationwide missed their regular station cues. Just as unpredictable were the people from the studio audience, chosen by McNeill from the interview cards passed out before the show. One morning in 1949, he brought an 11-year-old boy to the microphone. After the interview, young Bernie Christianson asked McNeill's permission to sing a few bars of "Galway Bay" for his grandparents. The boy's voice was electrifying, stirring the audience to a two-minute ovation. Bernie was brought back as a "Breakfast Club" regular during the next year.

Best-known of the show's regulars were the members of McNeill's own family. Wife Kay appeared often; sons Tom, Don, and Bobby also turned up occasionally. For many years the family participated in a Christmas-season holiday show. Once a year McNeill took The Breakfast Club on tour for a month. By then his closing line—"be good to yourself"—had become nationally familiar.

The Breakfast Club was brought to TV in a simulcast on February 22, 1954. But McNeill wasn't able to cope with the camera, and it bombed. There would still be radio, for a little while yet, and The Breakfast Club would hang in there till the end, establishing a long-distance record that few shows of any kind could equal. With few changes in style of format, it ran for more than thirty-four years, broadcasting its finale December 27, 1968.

Breakfast with Dorothy and Dick

Breakfast with Dorothy and Dick was purely local radio, originating from WOR, New York, in 1945 and continuing for more than five years. Local or not, the fame of early-morning breakfast shows had spread throughout the land. The format was so well-known that Fred Allen developed an immortal parody for his huge NBC audience, complete with canary and Tallulah Bankhead. The canary came directly from Breakfast With Dorothy and Dick, being their ever-chirping pest, Robin. The husband-wife breakfast shows had begun in 1942 with Ed and Pegeen Fitzgerald, and there was no stopping them after that. When the Fitzgeralds jumped from WOR to WJZ, *Dorothy and Dick* were brought in as replacements. Dorothy was Dorothy Kilgallen, famous columnist for the *New York Journal*. Dick was Richard Kollmar, sometime radio actor and Broadway producer. They had married in 1940 and now had a cozy little love nest to share with the world. Every morning their sixteen-room Park Avenue penthouse came alive for all New York; Dorothy pushed aside the breakfast dishes to make room for the WOR microphones, and they chatted away on subjects ranging from family life to the Great White Way. Their breakfast show was thrust into direct competition with that of the Fitzgeralds, and an intense competition developed. Dorothy and Dick considered the Fitzgeralds crude and uncouth; Ed and Pegeen thought the Kollmars aloof and snooty. Above it all was the third husband-wife team, Tex (McCrary) and Jinx (Falkenburg).

Bride and Groom

Bride and Groom came to ABC November 26, 1945. Before its demise in 1950, almost 1,000 new couples were interviewed hot from the altar. Though the actual ceremony was performed privately in a small chapel just off the ABC studio, the on-the-air nationwide interview was conducted immediately afterward. Host John Nelson quizzed the couples on their meetings and courtships, spotlighting the funny, offbeat things that happen in any human relationship. Jack McElroy doubled as singer-announcer; John Reddy and John Masterson coproduced with Nelson. Couples qualified by writing about themselves; a panel of three judges then selected the most interesting, and they were invited. The interviews were spontaneous and unrehearsed; afterward, the couple was showered with expensive gifts from luggage to appliances. And Nelson—the cad—never failed to take advantage of the gaiety. He always stole a kiss from the bride.

Bright Star

Bright Star was a syndicated series heard on some NBC stations in 1952. It starred Irene Dunne as Susan, owner of the financially troubled *Hillsdale Morning Star*, and Fred MacMurray as George, her star reporter. The story line often found George struggling with the realities of running the paper while Susan indulged in philanthropy—the endless cynic-idealist theme. With names like

Dunne and MacMurray, it should have been much better, but the stories often sagged somewhat in the writing department.Harry Von Zell announced. In the end, just another of radio's frantic attempts to save itself with big names, in the face of the inevitable.

The Brighter Day

The Brighter Day was the story of the Dennis family—the kind, gentle Reverend Richard Dennis and his daughters Elizabeth, Althea, Barbara, and Patsy. This Irna Phillips serial was first heard on NBC for Procter & Gamble October 11, 1948. It evolved from Joyce Jordan, M.D.; in the fall of 1948, Joyce introduced the character of Liz Dennis (Margaret Draper), and by early October Joyce was merely a hostess; Liz then launched into her own story. On October 8, 1948, Joyce Jordan was dropped altogether. As The Brighter Day, it ran on radio for eight years and was also seen on television. The setting was the little town of Three Rivers, where widower Reverend Dennis ran his parish and tried to be both mother and father to his brood. But Elizabeth, the eldest daughter, became the show's dominant female character, taking almost a mother role in the practicalities of family life. Liz helped keep the family spirit together while Mrs. Kennedy, "their faithful Irish housekeeper," did the dirty work. Liz had little time for housekeeping, being forever worried by the doings of the tempestuous Althea or planning her wedding to Dr. Jerry Forrester. In short, this was a typical, solid Phillips serial, coming a bit too late in radio to be much of a force. Margaret Draper played Liz, and the role was also taken by Grace Matthews. Bill Smith was Reverend Dennis; Lorna Lynn played Barbara, known as "Bobby" through the run; Jay Meredith was Althea; and Pat Hosley was Patsy. John Raby played Dr. Jerry Forrester. Typical of Phillips soaps, The Brighter Day opened with a short piece of philosophy "Our years are as the falling leaves; we live, we love, we dream, and then we go. But somehow we keep hoping, don't we, that our dreams come true on that brighter day."

Bringing Up Father

Bringing Up Father was another adaptation from the comics. It dramatized the weekly hassles of Maggie and Jiggs. Jiggs, the rolypoly Irish husband, was forever trying to get away for an evening with the boys; Maggie thwarted him at every turn. Agnes Moorehead wore her best sourpuss voice as Maggie. Mark Smith, a veteran of Broadway and radio, took Jiggs to heart, sharing his round profile and his love of corned beef and cabbage. Based on the comic strip by George McManus, this version of *Bringing Up Father* was heard Tuesdays on NBC in 1941.

Broadway Is My Beat

Broadway Is My Beat was the story of Danny Clover, detective of New York Police. Clover's beat was Broadway—"from Times Square to Columbus Circle—the grandest, the most violent, the lonesomest mile in the world." A better-than-average police show, *Broadway Is My Beat* came to CBS in 1949 and ran for more than four seasons. Larry Thor played Danny Clover as a tough cop of the Jack Webb school. Charles Calvert was the semi-humorous Detective Tartaglia. Produced and directed by Elliott Lewis, and written by Morton Fine and David Friedkin, with a downbeat theme of "I'll Take Manhattan," this show rated as good entertainment in the old radio Hall of Fame.

Brownstone Theatre

Brownstone Theatre. On February 21, 1945, Mutual aired "The Lion and the Mouse," the first show in its new *Brownstone Theatre* series. It was billed as "a theatre of memories—your own memories, perhaps—for here we present plays that you may have enjoyed once upon a time; plays that have entertained and thrilled many an audience in many a theatre; plays you will still enjoy." The format was slightly reminiscent of the famous *First Nighter Program,* with an announcer telling the listener that "you are in your seat at the Brownstone Theatre now," although the show really originated at WOR, New York. It was on the air for one season, offering such classic plays as "The Man Without a Country," "The Prisoner of Zenda," and "Cyrano de Bergerac." Jackson Beck was male lead from February through May 1945, then it passed to Les Tremayne. Gertrude Warner was the female lead. Jock MacGregor directed and Sylvan Levin provided the music. Host was the drama critic and writer, Clayton Hamilton.

Buck Rogers in the Twenty-Fifth Century

Buck Rogers in the Twenty-Fifth Century was first heard on CBS November 7, 1932, as a 15-minute daily serial. Buck Rogers was a young adventurer who got trapped in suspended animation and woke up in the wonderful world of the twenty-fifth century. The radio show was another successful adaptation from the comics, and became one of the first great children's serials of the air.

Buck's adventures in the twenty-fifth century were naturally space-oriented. He made friends with a beautiful young lady named Wilma Deering and the brilliant scientist, Dr. Huer, master inventor of such marvels as the "Mechanical Mole" for burrowing to the center of the earth, and the "Gyrocosmic Relativator." Sometimes Buck's adventures took him to the depths of the solar system to recover a stolen Huer invention. The safety of the universe was usually at stake.

Often the thief was a black-hearted bum named Killer Kane. Kane and Buck became arch rivals; Kane's accomplice in crime was the equally evil adventuress, Ardala Valmar. On Buck's side, in addition to Wilma and Dr. Huer, was a friendly but stupid Martian named Black Barney. A former space pirate, Barney had realized the errors of his old ways and became the air's first Martian with a heart of gold.

Buck Rogers was one of the important early links in the development of the juvenile adventure serial. It was based on the comics by Dick Calkins and Phil Nowlan, and was set in Niagara, capital of twenty-fifth-century society. The series was brought to the air, adapted and directed by Jack Johnstone, with Adele Ronson as Wilma and Curtis Arnall as Buck.

In 1932–33 the show was sponsored by Kellogg; in 1933 Cocomalt became sponsor; in 1935 Cream of Wheat began paying the bills. The serial was dropped in May, 1936, but returned in April 1939, still adapted and directed by Johnstone, as a three-a-week show for Popsicle. By the summer of 1940 it was heard in a Saturday half-hour format. The actors changed over the various runs, but the format remained the same. John Larkin, the last Buck Rogers, eventually went on to the starring role in television's *Edge of Night*. His voice had just the right qualities for Buck—strong and forceful—and he took the show out with a bang.

The final run opened on Mutual September 30, 1946. To support Larkin, Edgar Stehli returned as Dr. Huer and Virginia Vass played Wilma. The last adventure was heard March 28, 1947, when Buck finally caught up with Killer Kane and the two decided to fight it out to the finish. It was one of the wildest episodes of all radio, with a fight scene that consumed most of the show.

And afterward, as Buck and Wilma brought the imprisoned Kane back to earth for trial, there was a strong hint of serious man-woman business afoot. Time for a little vacation, Buck said wistfully, and what better place than Niagara? After all, Niagara was quite popular with honeymooners in twentieth-century America. . .

Bulldog Drummond

Bulldog Drummond was developed from the Paramount films of the 1930's, following the cases of the British inspector who weekly stepped "out of the fog, out of the night and into his American adventures." The show premiered September 28, 1941, on WOR, New York. Mutual carried it for six years, and again in 1953. Most notable about *Bulldog Drummond* was its opening: hollow footsteps and the intermingling blast of a foghorn; then—two shots!—three sharp blasts of a cop's whistle!—and again Drummond was ready to step out of the fog. With his sidekick Denny, Captain Hugh Drummond solved the usual run of murders, collected the usual run of bumps on the head, and ran afoul of underworld characters ranging from radium thieves to counterfeiters. Another well-remembered piece of radio, *Bulldog Drummond* ranks higher today for nostalgia value than as entertainment. Now it's just another example of how hackneyed radio could be at times. Interesting were the frequent appearances of such *Mercury Theatre* alumni as Ray Collins (once described by Orson Welles as the medium's best actor) and Agnes Moorehead. George Coulouris, another old *Mercury* player, was the first Drummond, playing the role in 1941 and 1942, while Everett Sloane played assistant Denny. But through most of the run, Drummond was played by those old pros Santos Ortega and Ned Wever. Luis Van Rooten played Denny. The series was produced and directed by Himan Brown, best known as the creator of *Inner Sanctum Mysteries*. When it returned in 1953, the title role was played by Sir Cedric Hardwicke.

Burns and Allen

Burns and Allen was another pioneering radio act. Like Jack Benny, Fred Allen, Eddie Cantor, and others who eventually found their way into the airwaves George Burns and Gracie Allen came from vaudeville, one temporary booking after another, with standup patter and song. Both had long apprenticeships.

Gracie was born in San Francisco, July 26, 1905, daughter of Edward Allen, who toured with a song and dance act. At 3 she had already appeared on stage with her father, and by her early teens she was ready to quit school and take up the life of footlights and greasepaint. She joined her three sisters in a dance routine under bookings of the Larry Reilly Company, but quit in frustration because

Reilly wouldn't give her feature billing. Then Gracie decided to drop out of show business. Around 1922 she enrolled in a New York secretarial school and roomed with friends while attending classes. One of her roommates, Rena Arnold, was appearing in small-time vaudeville at Union Hill, New Jersey. Gracie was invited to see the show, and there she was introduced to George Burns, a young comic with a sandpaper voice.

Burns was the male half of an act known as Burns and Lorraine. The girl, Billy Lorraine, played the straight part, feeding Burns setups for his punchlines. But Burns and Lorraine were parting company and George needed a replacement. On the spot, he persuaded Gracie to give up her steno career and take another fling at vaudeville.

Burns was Nathan Birnbaum, born January 20, 1898, in New York. His first professional appearance, also in childhood, was with a group of half-pint singers known as the Peewee Quartet. Burns sang for a time in saloons, then took off on his own, holding a variety of jobs, always close to theatre. With the departure of Billy Lorraine and the addition of Gracie Allen, Burns discovered a different texture in his act.

Gracie wasn't always as dumb as she seemed on the air. Early in her career with Burns, she played the straight part and George gave out with the funnies. But even a dummy could see that she was getting the laughs. George Burns was no dummy, he quickly switched the parts, deciding that Gracie, with her natural sense of humor, should become the comedian. And that was how they played it, for more than thirty years. In later life, George Burns would become widely known as the world's foremost straight man.

George and Gracie were married by a Cleveland justice of the peace on January 7, 1926. They returned to New York and a long string of stage performances. By 1930, they were doing so well that they decided to take off for the summer and vacation in Europe. They were in London only two days when they accepted a vaudeville stage engagement, and first performed their comedy act on radio for the BBC. It was the beginning of a long seige of mike fright for Gracie. Like so many stage performers, she had trouble adjusting to radio, to the concept of addressing that terrifying little box in a sealed room. After that first show, they always insisted on a live audience, finding people easier to play for than electronic gadgetry.

The following year, back in New York, they opened at the Palace on a bill with Eddie Cantor and George Jessel. Cantor, impressed by Gracie's wit, asked her to appear on his Sunday-night NBC hour. She created a minor sensation and was booked—this time with her husband—into Rudy Vallee's *Fleischmann Hour.* Vallee was known as a maker of stars, but Burns and Allen were well on the way anyway. By early 1932, they were signed by CBS for their own show.

Their first broadcast in a regular format was on CBS, February 15, 1932, for Robert Burns Cigars, when they were inserted as regulars on The Guy Lombardo Show. They were on the air continuously for the next eighteen years.

One of their earliest gags was also their most famous. It began innocently enough, with Gracie barging into Eddie Cantor's show claiming to have lost her brother. Later she repeated the story for Jack Benny's audience. She and George talked about her missing brother on their own show, adding more fuel to the fire. In the days that followed, Gracie chased her mythical lost brother all over the airwaves, breaking into shows on all networks in the alleged search. Delighted listeners never knew where she might turn up next.

Meanwhile, out in San Francisco, Gracie's real brother was leading a life of quiet anonymity. He was George Allen, a shy accountant with Standard Oil, who wanted nothing in the world more than to simply be let alone. All that privacy vanished one day when a reporter discovered who he was. News articles and pictures of George Allen erupted into the press; he was hounded by people wherever he went. The "Gracie Allen's brother" jokes became as common as elephant and Polish jokes would become three decades later. George Allen was ridiculed everywhere. He thought of changing his name. In desperation, he sent a terse wire to Gracie ("Can't you make a living any other way?") and disappeared until the gag had run its course.

Whatever effect the "lost brother" jokes had on George Allen's private life, they worked wonders for the new show. White Owl Cigars carried the show from 1933 through 1935 on Wednesday nights; from 1935 to 1937, Campbell's Soups were sponsors. George and Gracie went to NBC as a Monday-night team for Grape Nuts in 1937.

Gracie kidded George about everything, from his singing to his manliness. Burns never failed to bristle whenever Gracie mentioned her latest screen idol; Charles Boyer seemed to rankle him longest and most often. Especially in their later years, they were backed by a cast of radio's best actors and musicians. Mel Blanc created his memorable "Happy Postman" on the *Burns and Allen Show.* Announcers and orchestra leaders had large speaking parts. Ray Noble, Paul Whiteman, and Meredith Willson were all good microphone men in addition to being top musicians. All appeared with Burns and Allen. Elvia Allman played Gracie's friend Tootsie Sagwell, and Gale Gordon and Hans Conried were frequently employed as miscellaneous stuffed shirts. In 1937, one of their stars was singing cowboy Dick Foran.

Harry Von Zell became a regular *Burns and Allen* announcer, following them into TV. And Bill Goodwin, their announcer of the middle years, was often played against Meredith Willson for comic contrast. Willson was cast as a bashful bachelor, while Goodwin was the girl-chasing wolf. The *Burns and Allen* theme, "Love Nest," became one of the best-known on the air.

By 1938, George and Gracie were among the established performers of the air; back in the CBS lineup that year, the show was carried one season each by Chesterfield (1938, Friday), Hinds Cream (1939, Wednesday), and Hormel Packing (1940, Monday, NBC) before beginning a long association with Lever Brothers in 1941. They continued using running gags, sure-fire audience pleasers. In 1940, Gracie announced her candidacy for president on the Surprise Party ticket. They pushed that one to extraordinary lengths, even scheduling a political convention in Omaha. George helped write a platform and Gracie wrote an article, "America's Next President Should Be a Woman" for *Liberty Magazine*. She also wrote a presidential campaign booklet, published by the Gracie Allen Self-Delusion Institute. That same year, she proved offstage that she was no dumb blonde. During the summer she appeared as a guest panelist on the intellectually based quiz, *Information Please*, and held her own with the highly touted experts. Onstage, she became the model for such later dummies as Marie Wilson's *My Friend Irma*, following each crazy notion full-circle to its illogical conclusion. When Gracie talked about Mrs. Tenderleaf spending all those hours filling up her husband's teabags, she really seemed to believe it, and that made it funnier.

Eventually, George and Gracie's show began to move out of its standup vaudeville phase. In 1942, they appeared on the air as a married couple, and the shows became rooted in situation comedy. For four years they pushed Swan Soap on CBS—on Tuesdays from 1941 through 1944, on Mondays in 1944–45. In 1945, Burns and Allen jumped networks again, taking over NBC's *Maxwell House Coffee Time* for four years on Thursdays. Their final jump—back to CBS —came in 1949, their last full season on radio. In October 1950, George Burns and Gracie Allen made a successful move into TV.

Gracie was truly the star of the show. Alongside her, Burns seemed flat and unimaginative. He purposely built the show that way. In private life, he was highly respected by Hollywood's best comedians as an extraordinary humorist. For four decades he played stooge to his wife's antics. When Gracie died in 1964 Burns slipped into retirement. He tried a brief TV show, which failed. Burns without Allen was like a car without gas. It just wouldn't go. But at age 78, Burns proved himself still an able actor and sharp wit, winning a 1976 Academy Award for his performance in the film, *The Sunshine Boys*.

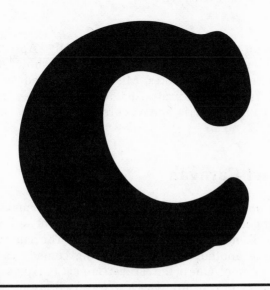

Café Istanbul

Café Istanbul was a show of international intrigue and high adventure, first heard on ABC January 6, 1952. It starred Marlene Dietrich as the manager of an Istanbul café that became a haunt of spies and agents of many lands. The most notable thing about the series was the regular appearance of the famed sultry singer from Berlin. In its review, *Time Magazine* called the early plots "chaotic," and termed Dietrich's character "the same romantic Weltschmerz role, with whispered snatches of French and German songs," that she had been playing for a professional lifetime. In essence, it was the same atmosphere moviegoers found in her 1930 film classic, *The Blue Angel*. Dietrich played Mademoiselle Madou, who ran the cafe for Steve Lacey, a hot-tempered American who was also the show's romantic interest. Arnold Moss played the third regular, Colonel Maurice Lesko of the local police. Dietrich, in line with her image as the hard-working pro, did the final script rewrites herself. *Cafe Istanbul* was produced by Leonard Blair. In 1953, Miss Dietrich took the show to CBS, changed a few names and settings, and emerged with a carbon copy called *Time for Love.*

Call for Music

Call for Music was a short-lived show of music and song featuring Dinah Shore and Johnny Mercer's popular vocal solos and duets, with

Harry James on the trumpet. First heard on NBC April 20, 1948, it filled the time vacated by Milton Berle when his show left the air. In addition to her singing chores, Miss Shore served as mistress of ceremonies. As the title indicates, in its own veiled way, the show was sponsored by Philip Morris, and was produced by Jerry Lawrence and Bob Lee.

The Camel Caravan

The Camel Caravan was a name dearly loved by the makers of Camel Cigarettes. It got the product's name right out front and conveyed an image of mixed entertainment. And that it was. The name was applied at one time or another to most of the big comedy-variety shows sponsored by Camel. One of the earliest Camel Caravan series was the Walter O'Keefe show, heard twice a week on CBS from 1934 through 1936. It featured singer Deane Janis and the music of the Glen Gray Orchestra. In 1937 the Caravan image was revived as Benny Goodman's Swing School, a Tuesday-night CBS entry featuring Johnny Mercer and Martha Tilton. Bob Crosby was the next Caravan master, setting up shop on NBC Saturday nights on January 6, 1940, and moving over to Thursdays later that year, for an encore season. Xavier Cougat took up the baton for Camels in 1941, holding down the same Thursday-night NBC slot just vacated by Crosby. By 1942 Herb Shriner, an Indiana comedian with a Will Rogers–Bob Burns style, had become the star. With the illness of Lou Costello in March 1943, a new Camel Comedy Caravan was formed to fill the breach (Camel also sponsored The Abbott and Costello Show, which was cancelled for the duration of the season). Some of the old Caravan alumni were brought in for the new show. It starred Jack Carson as master of ceremonies, and was built around the antics of a cast of regulars and special guests, including Shriner, Connie Haines, and Ken Niles; music was by the Freddie Rich Orchestra. Elvia Allman played Mrs. Ken Niles and Mel Blanc did as many as a dozen characters per show. Guests included Diana Barrymore, Frank Morgan, Mickey Rooney, Linda Darnell, and the like.

The show ran Fridays on CBS, first as a 45-minute, and later as a 60-minute variety headliner. It brought Jimmy Durante out of inactivity and made him a radio personality, teaming him with Garry Moore for yet another Camel Caravan format. The Durante and Moore partnership ran in 30-minute form on CBS Thursday and later Friday nights during the mid-1940's. In 1945, Camel applied the Caravan moniker for a time to The Bob Hawk Show, a CBS quiz carried by Camel until 1953. In 1946, the cigarette company also took on The

Vaughn Monroe Show, a Saturday-night CBS variety show that ran until 1954. Monroe was more in line with the *Caravan* image than Hawk, and his show soon assumed the title, keeping it until the end.

The Camel Quarter-Hour

The Camel Quarter-Hour was one of the earliest major 15-minute variety shows, first heard on CBS in 1931. It immediately established the fact that top variety acts didn't have to come in lavish 60-minute doses. *The Camel Quarter Hour* featured songs by Morton Downey, the music of Jacques Renard's orchestra, and two minutes of poetry and philosophy by Tony Wons, who then was riding a tide of popularity as "America's heartthrob." With the exception of Wons' part, the show offered a faster pace than the established longer shows, and forced many of them to pep up.

Campana Serenade

Campana Serenade. Dick Powell was desperately trying to change his glamor-boy image in the early 1940's, but all he could get were shows like this. *Campana Serenade,* in the end, was just another song show, and Powell was at his glamor-boy best with songs like "Blue Skies," "You'll Never Know," and "In My Arms." The Saturday songfest, sponsored by Campana makeup, graced the NBC airwaves in 1943, and switched to CBS in the fall of that year. Powell was backed by Lud Gluskin's orchestra and occasionally by the sweet voice of Benny Goodman's old singer, Martha Tilton. Just ahead was precisely the tough-guy role Powell wanted—lead detective in the film version of Raymond Chandler's *Murder, My Sweet*—and that would lead ultimately to several memorable private-eye roles on the air. But Powell didn't know it then. All he could do was flinch a bit, and croon the sticky Campana theme:

> Love-ly to look at
> De-lightful to knowww
> And hea-ven to kissss . . .
> A com-bee-nation like thissss . . .
> Is quite my most impossible scheme come true,
> Imagine finding a dream like you . . .

In all, this was a pleasing musical interlude for those who enjoy the melodies of that era. But Powell must have blanched every time he faced that mike.

Can You Top This?

Can You Top This? was a panel show of jokes and toppers, first heard on New York's WOR December 9, 1940. The premise was simple enough. The listening audience was solicited to send in jokes—old or new, and based on any subject but religion, politics, or arson. They would be given a reading on the air by Peter Donald, and a panel of humor experts would try to top them with jokes on the same subject. The panel was never told in advance what the jokes would be about; its three members relied on their expert knowledge of humor, and became as well-known in their field as the *Information Please* panel was on matters intellectual.

The show grew out of joke-swapping sessions at New York's Lambs Club, where "Senator" Ed Ford ("good evening"), cartoonist Harry Hershfield ("howdy"), and comedian Joe Laurie Jr. ("hel-lo") often entertained each other for hours. "Senator" Ford developed the impromptu joke sessions for the air, and actually got the show booked into the WOR schedule. Peter Donald, who later served as Fred Allen's Ajax Cassidy was brought in to stump the experts, and Ward Wilson was the moderator.

Ford actually was no senator at all. The title was added strictly for show-business charisma. His ties to vaudeville went back to the early years of the century; he was once described by the fan magazine *Tune In* as "dour and sullen offstage as well as on."

Harry Hershfield was a talented cartoonist, creator of "Abe Kabibble" in the comic strips and known as New York's best after-dinner speaker. Before his radio days he was a photographer and reporter. At his peak he made some 200 dinner speeches a year.

Joe Laurie, Jr. got his start at a fireman's benefit, and graduated to vaudeville bookings in the 1920's. By the time *Can You Top This?* came to the air, Laurie had done everything from dramatic parts to musicals. His radio work included gag writing for Eddie Cantor and Al Jolson, and there were frequent references to his "pint-sized" appearance, both on his show and in trade journals.

Among them, they knew more than 15,000 jokes, many of which could be changed around to fit multiple situations. The jokes were constantly sorted and were alphabetically categorized for easy reference. They might not have heard every joke in their eleven years on the air, but Ford once said that he had never seen a completely new joke cross his desk.

The listeners tried anyway. They sent in 6,000 letters a week, each with a snatch of humor to test the experts. The jokes were sorted by

Betty North, and the few good ones were passed on for Donald to read. A huge "laugh meter" was set up onstage. It was shaped like a smiling man's face, and the gauge was in the center of the smile. A direct hookup to a special microphone measured audience reaction on a scale from 0 to 1,000. If a listener's joke was read on the air, he got $5. He got $2 extra for each panelist who couldn't top his joke, giving him a maximum prize of $11. If all panelists topped the joke (which happened 75 percent of the time), the listener was sent a joke book.

By 1942, the show had gained enough popularity to go on the network. It was picked up by NBC, where it ran as a Saturday-night feature for Colgate until 1947; by 1948, it had moved to Friday. The show continued locally on WOR, which ironically was the home station of the Mutual Network. It was dropped by NBC in 1948, and picked up by Mutual, where it ran Wednesday nights until 1950 (the last year for Ford Motors). In 1950, *Can You Top This?* was bought by Mars Candy, and ran for a year on ABC Tuesdays. In 1953 the show was brought back by NBC for a one-year sustaining daily shot.

The Candid Microphone

The Candid Microphone, although on radio briefly, created a new form of entertainment that is still with us. Years later, this idea would be resurrected as the highly successful TV show, *Candid Camera,* and would form the nucleus for the first respectable X-rated movie, *What Do You Say to a Naked Lady?* It premiered July 6, 1947; it folded in 1948, partly because of the widespread belief that it was rigged. But *Candid Mike* would return for a summer run in June 1950.

Allen Funt made a national reputation as an eavesdropper, and he was letter-perfect for the part. He asked people the *dumbest* questions, always in that flat deadpan voice. He asked strangers for favors as though imposing was his right, then badgered them mercilessly until the inevitable flare of temper or grunt of disgust rose to the surface.

And when tempers blew, Funt had it all recorded for posterity and the American Broadcasting System. "You're on *Candid Microphone,*" he said, joking quickly about being a good sport and how much fun it is to laugh at yourself. Funt had an uncanny instinct for the foibles of human nature; he seemed to know exactly how far to push. Knowing that probably saved him more than once from a well-earned punch in the nose.

Candid Microphone grew out of Funt's wartime experiences, when he was stationed with the army in Oklahoma. One day, reading the "gripe column" in the army newspaper *Yank,* he thought of recording the gripes of servicemen for broadcast. The original idea didn't work. The servicemen were too self-conscious at the microphone, and the format was flat and colorless. Funt devised a new idea—recording their spontaneous gripes with a hidden microphone. The result was hilarious, and that provided the spark for a new radio idea when the war ended.

Funt had had some radio experience before his army days. He had been an independent producer, once worked with Eleanor Roosevelt on her radio commentaries, and had been a gag man on *Truth or Consequences*. After the war, he became producer of *Ladies Be Seated*, and independently began putting *Candid Microphone* together. Early in 1947, he rented an office and went to work. Because there were no portable recorders in those days, "victims" had to be lured inside. Funt posed as a businessman named Lester Kannon, and devised all kinds of devilment for unsuspecting insurance salesmen, bill collectors, and locksmiths, then recorded their reactions for the air. One early stunt involved a locksmith who was brought in to release Funt's secretary, who had been chained to her desk. The man's startled, then indignant reaction provided one of Funt's first airable interviews.

With his ABC contract in hand, Funt's operations began to expand. Soon after his show went on, a portable recorder was developed, allowing him to roam the world at large. Occasionally he got good material by simply planting the mike and letting people be themselves, but more often, some goading was necessary. No one could out-goad Funt. With his microphone carefully hidden in his lapel or as part of his hearing aid, Funt roamed the streets and parks looking for victims. He tried to pick up girls, bothered people in restaurants, and hassled walkers for directions to places he didn't want to go. And when it was over, he retreated to his editing room, where with six assistants he put *The Candid Microphone* together, editing, chopping out dull spots, and dubbing in a soft, feminine "censored, censored, censored" over the profanity. Funt seldom used the names of his victims, and never broadcast the segments without signed permission. Permission was almost always obtained by appealing to sportsmanship and slipping the victim $15.

Candy Matson

Candy Matson, undoubtedly one of the brightest, most unusual detective shows of the air, originated at KNBC, San Francisco, and was first heard on Pacific Coast NBC stations June 29, 1949. It starred Natalie Masters as the chic, beautiful girl detective Candy, whose crisp voice meant business. She operated out of her San Francisco apartment (telephone YUkon 2-8209) and managed to scare up as many murders as most male gumshoes. The murder element was always prevalent in *Candy Matson*, though character was developed to a degree not always found in series detectives. Candy was portrayed as an extremely feminine heroine, but without a trace of squeamishness. Somewhere along the line, she usually dragged in her friend Rembrandt Watson, played by Jack Thomas. Watson wasn't much in the down-and-dirty department, being something of a creampuff, so he usually handled record-checking and other legwork. Candy's male idol was San Francisco policeman Ray Mallard, well-played by Henry Leff. Eloise Rowan provided organ music and Dudley Manlove was announcer. The shows were written and produced by Natalie's husband, Monte Masters, and were heard until May 21, 1951. That was the grand day when Mallard finally popped the question. Candy didn't give him an instant answer, but Mallard announced with grand authority that it would be her last case. And it was.

Captain Flagg and Sergeant Quirt

Captain Flagg and Sergeant Quirt, based on the Laurence Stallings–Maxwell Anderson play *What Price Glory?*, came to the Blue Network September 28, 1941. It starred Victor McLaglen (Flagg) and Edmund Lowe (Quirt) as the rough-and-tumble Marines who were forever feuding. McLaglen and Lowe had starred in the 1926 film, but *Captain Flagg and Sergeant Quirt* was their first joint appearance before the microphone. It ran for one season on Monday nights for Mennen, and was marked by the arrogant catch phrases of the forever feuding comrades: "Sez who?" "Sez me!" John P. Medbury wrote the scripts.

Captain Midnight

Captain Midnight, one of the best remembered serials of old radio, was developed at Station WGN, Chicago, and was on the air regionally in 1939 for the Skelly Oil Company. When Ovaltine dropped *Little Orphan Annie* in 1940, *Captain Midnight* became its replacement on Mutual, first heard September 30, 1940.

By the time *Captain Midnight* came to Mutual, the adventure serial was firmly established as an early-evening must for millions of Midwestern kids. The show developed the themes they liked best: action, mystery, a master villain, and plenty of peer identification.

Like the ever-popular *Jack Armstrong, Captain Midnight* even had a girl along for the ride.

The show was developed by Robert Burtt and Wilfred Moore, and was based on many of Burtt's World War I adventures. Burtt had served with the Lafayette Escadrille and, according to *Radio Life*, had once engaged eight enemy planes in a dogfight. Even Captain Midnight couldn't withstand those odds; Burtt's plane was shot down, and he brought it in in a belly-flop squarely between the two great armies. With machine-gun bullets ripping the ground around him, Burtt crawled back to his trenches. There, in the crater-marked fields of Europe, Captain Midnight was born.

Burtt conceived Midnight as a man of mystery, whose job in the war was so important that not even his superiors knew his identity. But kids who had been listening from Denver to Chicago to those pre-network Skelly episodes already knew that. He was Captain Red Albright, super-pilot who traveled the world battling evil. In this serial, evil manifested in the person of Ivan Shark, who with his daughter Fury and a pack of henchmen one day planned to rule the world. Captain Midnight's sidekicks were the youthful Chuck Ramsey and Patsy Donovan, who helped Red chase the evil bunch from the wilds of Mexico to the Canada wastelands.

Some changes were made when the show went to Mutual in 1940. Chuck Ramsey survived the network cuts, but Patsy lost her starring role to a new Secret Squadron member, Joyce Ryan. Chuck, played on the network by Billy Rose, became as accomplished a pilot as his mentor, and was known in Secret Squadron circles as "SS-2." Joyce, played by Angeline Orr, was "SS-3." The other regular "SS" member was Ichabod "Ichy" Mudd, the squadron mechanic.

Captain Midnight was played in the regional run by Bill Bouchey and on Mutual by Ed Prentiss; Ivan Shark was brought to evil (heh-heh-heh) perfection by Boris Aplon. With the Mutual première, the story of the great pilot was begun anew, playing up the man of mystery theme almost to the point of secret identity. In the opening chapter, we learned that he was a captain of the Allied armies in the Great War, and was sent on a not-too-specific mission "to save France." The mission never was fully explained, but its importance was underlined by the fact that the chances against its success were "about 100-to-one."

But the young captain came roaring back triumphantly at midnight, and forever after bore the name "Captain Midnight." For twenty years, strange stories were whispered about "a shadowy plane and a mysterious pilot who, whenever trouble started in any part of the world, was certain to come diving furiously from the night sky."

Soon Captain Midnight and his young partners were involved

with new enemies—the insidious Japs, enemies of all the free world. Later they went back to the battle against Ivan Shark, and the show became one of the greatest premium-givers of the air. For an Ovaltine seal and a dime, a kid could get a wide variety of premium toys; better yet, he or she could then gain membership in Secret Squadrons around the nation. Members received decoder badges, allowing them to decipher secret messages from Captain Midnight, which were usually transmitted by number-code at the end of the day's chapter. Pierre André, who had replaced Don Gordon as announcer when the show went nationwide, introduced the serial to the midnight gong of a churchbell and the furious diving sound of Captain Midnight's airplane . . .

> *Capppp———tainnnMidnight!*
> *Broughttoyoueveryday . . . MondaythroughFriday . . .*
> *By the makers of O-val-tine!*

Five times a week, André and company came roaring out of the early evening sky, luring thousands of boys and girls into its Secret Squadron before folding on December 15, 1949. The show eventually turned up on TV, but even a 21-inch screen was too small for *Captain Midnight*. For two generations of kids, nothing less than broad imagination would do.

Carefree Carnival

Carefree Carnival was an interesting early variety show, heard on NBC from 1933 through 1935. It featured comics, songs, and occasionally heavier "thought" material. Master of ceremonies was Ray Tollinger, and later Gene Arnold; music was by Meredith Willson. The show featured Elmore Vincent as Senator Fishface, Ben Klassen and Myron Niesley as sometimes singers and sometimes comic philosophers, Charlie Marshall as "hillbilly and cowboy warbler," and a very young Pinky Lee. This was thirty minutes of sheer nonsense, sponsored by Blue Jay Corn Plasters.

The Carnation Contented Hour

The Carnation Contented Hour was a very successful, though low-key show of popular music, first heard on NBC Blue January 4, 1932. The following year the show moved to NBC Red, where it ran for more than fifteen years, most of the time on Mondays. In the late 1940's, it was part of NBC's "Monday Night of Music." Dropped in 1949, it was picked up by CBS, where it ran for two years on Sunday. Over the years, The Carnation Contented Hour offered an impressive lineup of singers and musicians, including Gladys Swarthout, Richard Bonelli, Buddy Clark, and Dinah Shore. Orchestras over the years included those of Dr. Frank Black, Josef A. Pasternak, Percy Faith, and Ted Dale. The Contented Hour was sponsored for its entire nineteen-year run by Carnation.

The Carters of Elm Street

The Carters of Elm Street, the "story of a second wife and her fight for happiness," was heard on NBC during the 1939–40 season. It premièred February 13, 1939, another of the dozens of Hummert Features soaps. As Mrs. Carter, the Hummerts cast Virginia Payne, better known as "Ma Perkins." Vic Smith was featured as Mr. Carter. With their children, the Carters formed a trouble-plagued family in the town of Galesville. Sponsored by Ovaltine, this show was nothing special, and vanished from the air on January 19, 1940.

The Casebook of Gregory Hood

The Casebook of Gregory Hood was an imaginative piece of mystery-adventure, coming to Mutual on June 3, 1946, as a summer replacement for Sherlock Holmes, and graduating into the fall schedule under sponsorship of Petri Wines. Initially it ran only one season, but it resurfaced periodically in summer slots and eventually had another full season as a 1949–50 ABC sustainer. Casebook grew out of the long-distance collaboration of writers Anthony Boucher and Denis Green, who had also written Sherlock Holmes for Petri Wines. Green lived in Los Angeles, Boucher in San Francisco. Boucher worked out the plot lines for their radio scripts; Green then wrote the dialogue. They conceived Gregory Hood as a San Francisco importer dealing in rare items. With his sidekick Sanderson ("Sandy") Taylor, Hood traveled the world seeking artifacts for his import house. Each item found by Hood had an intriguing history and was inevitably linked to some present-day mystery. Ned Tollinger produced and Gale Gordon starred as Hood when the show opened on Mutual. Another show, heard on Mutual in the summer of 1948, featured Elliott Lewis as Hood and Howard McNear as Sandy. The lead was also handled at various times by Jackson Beck, Paul McGrath, Martin Gabel, and George Petrie.

Casey, Crime Photographer

Casey, Crime Photographer first came to the air as Flashgun Casey on July 7, 1943. Soon the name was changed to Casey, Press Photographer, then Casey, Crime Photographer, and finally simply Crime Photographer. Based on the character created by George Harmon Coxe in his Casey novels, he was a detective-reporter of a different cut. Casey did his reporting with a camera. He operated out of the Blue Note Café and, with girlfriend Annie Williams, got into the usual run of trouble. Casey's newspaper was The Morning Express; his show contained several stock characters. Among them were Ethelbert the bartender at the Blue Note (John Gibson) and police Inspector Logan (Jackson Beck), who naturally hated Casey's guts. Casey was played by Staats Cotsworth; Annie by Lesley Woods, Jan Miner, and others. It had a sporadic run with its best years 1946 to 1950. It was revived on CBS in 1953 as a 30-minute sustaining Wednesday show and ended in 1955 as a 25-minute five-a-week show. Sponsors over the years included the Anchor-Hocking Glass Company (1946–48, Thursday); Toni Home Permanent (1948–49, Thursday); and Philip Morris (1949–50, Thursday). Announcers were Tony Marvin, during the Anchor-Hocking run, and Bill Cullen for Toni. The show was directed by John Dietz and written by Alonzo Deen Cole. Casey was a decent entry in the whodunit handicap, not quite up to Sam Spade or Johnny Dollar, but definitely a few cuts above Mr. Keen, Boston Blackie, and Bulldog Drummond.

The Cavalcade of America

The Cavalcade of America, one of the most intelligent and longest-running of all prestige shows, was first heard on CBS October 9, 1935. In 1939 it became a regular in the NBC lineup. It dramatized incidents from American history and literature, using top talent from Broadway and Hollywood. It had to be accurate, anthentic to the finest detail, and still have wide common appeal. The series told stories of the famous (Abe Lincoln) and the not-so-famous (Roger Williams), but always kept its audio foundations set deeply in the roots of fact.

Soon after it moved from CBS to NBC, a network press release said the show would combine "authentic history with the appeal of best-sellers." A board of "historical advisers" was established to choose material and to authenticate each facet of the broadcast. Headed by Dr. Frank Monaghan of Yale, the board, which included Carl Carmer,

historical writer, and Marquis James, two-time Pulitzer Prize biog-
rapher, conducted painstaking research and, to make sure the show
wasn't bogged down under the sheer weight of historical detail, hired
some of America's best writers to cut away the fat.

In addition to a staff of house writers, special Cavalcade projects
were put together by such as Carl Sandburg, Stephen Vincent Benét,
Maxwell Anderson, and Robert Sherwood. Sandburg even appeared
as narrator for the 1941 production of his own Native Land. The leads
of Cavalcade shows were played by stars like Raymond Massey
(whose Abe Lincoln would become critically acclaimed), Charles
Laughton, Lionel Barrymore, Dick Powell, Tyrone Power, and Edward G. Robinson. Alfred Lunt and Lynn Fontanne made their first
radio appearances—separately—on Cavalcade. Clark Gable's first air
appearance was on a Cavalcade show. Orson Welles and several of his
Mercury Theatre stars got early experience before the Cavalcade of
America microphone. Roger Pryor and later Paul Stewart and Jack
Zoller produced. Donald Voorhees, who would go on to direct The
Bell Telephone Hour, was musical director, and later Robert
Armbruster waved the baton.

It was a big prestige show in the truest sense, carving out an area
of expertise and competence that went unchallenged in all radio.
With its high budget (some $7,500 a week, even in 1943), the show
paid top rates for its work, and the directors demanded excellence.
Homer Fickett, original producer of The March of Time, took over
directorship in the late 1930's, just before the show went through one
of its few phases of transition. Before World War II, Cavalcade had
concentrated on straight history. Later modern themes and historical
correlations were developed; the historical framework was used to
illuminate some aspect of modern life. The committee, working about
four months and twenty stories ahead of broadcast, now accepted and
produced such stories as the life of Babe Ruth, in addition to time-
honored heroes like Ben Franklin.

But even with its vast historical references and authorities,
Cavalcade wasn't infallible. The difference between a Cavalcade
mistake and mistakes on other shows was that Cavalcade's audience
itself had a high degree of expertise. Fickett, in a 1943 Radio Life
interview, recalled one blooper on the production, "Abe Lincoln in
Illinois." The sound effects men, creating the sound of a train starting
and stopping, used recent recordings of locomotives. Three letters of
protest came in. Trains of 1860, the producers were told, didn't have
air brakes. Humbly, Fickett admitted that they were right.

Throughout its eighteen-year run, Cavalcade was sponsored by
duPont, which first promoted its "Better things for better living
through chemistry" slogan on the show. Initially heard on Wednes-

days, it moved to Mondays in 1938, to Tuesdays in 1939, to Wednesdays in 1940, Mondays in 1941, and finally back to Tuesdays in 1949. It was last heard March 31, 1953.

The CBS Radio Mystery Theatre

The CBS Radio Mystery Theatre is the most ambitious plan yet to revitalize the dead art of audio drama. Created by Himan Brown (yes, the same H. Brown of Inner Sanctum, Joyce Jordan, and so many shows of the "golden age,") The CBS Radio Mystery Theatre premiered January 6, 1974, with full-hour dramas of the macabre. It has been running seven days a week, 365 days a year, using new scripts, old formula rehashes, and classics ("Dracula," "The Horla" and "The Black Cat" were among early shows). The first drama starred Agnes Moorehead, and subsequent shows have featured such old-timers as Mandel Kramer, Larry Haines, Santos Ortega, Bret Morrison, Ian Martin, and such new-to-radio stars as Kim Hunter and Lois Nettleton. E. G. Marshall is host. Marshall, best known for his work in the TV series The Defenders, greets listeners in much the same manner that Raymond Edward Johnson used to do on the old Inner Sanctum. The show is still running strongly in 1976, offering several new dramas and an intermingling of repeat broadcasts each week. Critics have pegged the shows very good to very bad; the good ones approach the best of "golden age" series, while the bad ones come quickly apart at the seams. Another major problem: in these days of canned radio, many CBS affiliates refuse to carry the 60-minute shows. Sometimes they have been picked up by independent stations and other affiliates, sometimes not. Often they are run at ungodly hours. In Denver, The CBS Radio Mystery Theatre was heard on KOA, long the NBC affiliate, at 11 P.M.

The CBS Radio Workshop

The CBS Radio Workshop, one of the most ingenious pieces of radio ever aired, was a revival of the old Columbia Workshop of the 1930's and 1940's, but done with even greater flair and imagination than the original. Sadly, it premièred in the waning days of the medium, on January 27, 1956, and ended about twenty months later, September 22, 1957.

But it began with a bang. In a great coup, CBS had persuaded Aldous Huxley to narrate an ambitious two-part adaptation of his modern classic, Brave New World. Huxley opened the show with a warning: We had moved much closer to the terrifying world he had described than even he had imagined. "If I were writing today, I would date my story not 600 years in the future, but at the most 200."

And then the sounds of the "brave new world" blended in. Huxley took us into the hatchery, where human beings were breeded and cultivated artificially. "These are the sounds of test tube and decanter." The sound was only 30 seconds long, but it had taken three sound men and an engineer more than five hours to create. Through the ingenious use of sound, Time noted in review, the producers of the experimental theatre "hope to catch the mind's eye with the ear."

The review described the creation of the baby hatchery for radio. It had consisted of a ticking metronome, the beat of a tom-tom (heartbeats), bubbling water, an air hose, the mooing of a cow, repeated "boings," and three different glasses clinking against each other. The sounds were blended and recorded, then played backward on the air with a slight echo effect. Sound effects were always addressed carefully on The CBS Radio Workshop. Creativity of production always took priority over writing, casting, or pace.

The series was "dedicated to man's imagination—the theatre of the mind." Some of the best professionals of the old days—probably interested but not hopeful for a revival of their dead medium—were on hand for the opener. William Conrad was announcer. Bernard Herrmann composed and conducted. In the cast were Lurene Tuttle, Jack Kruschen, Joseph Kearns, Parley Baer, Vic Perrin, Sam Edwards, Charlotte Lawrence, and Gloria Henry. All through its run, the Workshop drew the likes of John Dehner, Raymond Burr, Stan Freberg, Edward R. Murrow, Howard McNear, Vincent Price, Herbert Marshall, Robert Young, and then-Senator John F. Kennedy. Musical directors included Amerigo Moreno and Leith Stevens. Producers-directors, usually booked on a guest, or rotating, basis, included William Froug, William N. Robson, Jack Johnstone, Paul Roberts, Dee Engelbach, and Elliott Lewis.

It was big-time, ambitious, creative radio at its best. As CBS vice-president Howard Barnes told Time, "We'll never get a sponsor anyway, so we might as well try anything."

The point was well-taken. The CBS Radio Workshop was sustained, and did try anything good that came along. It dramatized the science fiction of Ray Bradbury and conducted an "interview with Shakespeare." One of the great early shows was "The Legend Of Jimmy Blue Eyes," with Conrad narrating the poetry and prose against a backdrop of 1920's New Orleans blues. "Report on the We'Uns," based on the Harper's Magazine story by Robert Nathan, poked not-so-gentle fun at the archaeologists and anthropologists who tell us with such great authority where we came from. "King of the Cats" was a fantasy about an orchestra leader who conducted with his tail. In "1,489 Words," Conrad reminded us that one picture is not always worth a thousand words. Perhaps the most unusual of all *Workshops* was "Nightmare," about the terrible dreams of a man in a coma, written, directed by, and starring Elliott Lewis.

The CBS Radio Workshop was one of the great shows of the air. Its life was far too short.

Ceiling Unlimited

Ceiling Unlimited, a series of patriotic, informative dramas about aviation, was first heard in its 15-minute Monday-evening format on CBS November 9, 1942. Orson Welles wrote, directed, produced, and narrated the opener, and served as producer-director for several months. Carried by such guests as Marlene Dietrich, Ronald Colman, Cary Grant, and William Powell, *Ceiling Unlimited* was considered a prime contribution to the war effort. Its sponsor, the Lockheed-Vega Corporation, took great pain not to overdo commercial mention; in fact, Lockheed was mentioned only briefly during the show, and often the planes of rival companies were featured. *Ceiling* sometimes offered straight dramas, other times brought personal messages from movie stars. Narrator was Patrick McGeehan, who emphasized the weekly theme: "Man has always looked to the heavens for help and inspiration, and from the skies too will come his victory and his future." In its second year, *Ceiling Unlimited* moved to Sundays and was expanded to 30 minutes. It was last heard in 1944. Each guest star was asked to sign a miniature P-38 Lightning plane, which eventually was to be auctioned off at a war bond sale. Anyone know what became of it?

The Chamber Music Society of Lower Basin Street

The Chamber Music Society of Lower Basin Street, first heard on the Blue Network February 11, 1940, served as a notable springboard for several performers who later went on to attain star status. Dinah Shore was the show's earliest "diva," billed as a singer "who lights a fire by rubbing two notes together." Zero Mostel first came to public attention on *Basin Street*. Mostel was a small-time artist who occasionally performed on local radio. He was booked into a New York café in the spring of 1942, and there several officials of the network caught his act. They signed him immediately, and he was introduced on the show in April 1942. Mostel was an overnight sensation, and the radio show led directly to his career on Broadway and in films.

The show itself was a combination of satire and hot-and-cool blues and jazz. It was built around the "three B's"—barrelhouse, boogie-woogie, and the blues—and was under the "chairmanship" of Milton Cross. Cross seldom let the opportunity pass for some terrible jokes ("A Bostonian looks like he's smelling for something; a New Yorker looks like he's found it."). Director was Tom Bennett. Among the stars spotlighted on the show were Diane Courtney, Kay Lorraine, and Jane Pickens. Music was under direction of Paul Lavalle and Charles "Corn Horn" Marlowe. In all, this was an interesting, unusual show, which held its own against big-time comedians through the war years. *The Chamber Music Society of Lower Basin Street* was sustained for three years, picking up Woodbury Soap as sponsor in 1943 and 1944, its final regular season. It was revived as a summer series in 1950 with Jane Pickens, and featuring Henry "Hot Lips" Levine as conductor.

Chandu the Magician

Chandu the Magician, an important piece of juvenile radio, was one of the first and last shows of its kind. First heard on KHJ, Los Angeles, in 1932, *Chandu* soon spread into most of the Don Lee Network, a West Coast network that later merged with Mutual. It was sold independently to some stations and carried in the East and Midwest by Mutual. White King Soap sponsored the show in the West; Beech Nut in the East. Running as a nightly serial in 15-minute installments, *Chandu* was on the air until 1936.

The hero, Frank Chandler, was an American-born mystic who learned the secrets of the East from a yogi in India. Using his occult powers and a far-reaching crystal ball, Chandler combated evil throughout the world, and became widely known as "Chandu the Magician." Chandler, along with his sister Dorothy and her children Betty and Bob Regent, was forever off to some strange and wonderful corner of the world in his quest for dangerous adventure and exotic intrigue.

The original show was created by Raymond R. Morgan and Harry A. Earnshaw. Vera Oldham, an office girl who worked for the partners, tried out as writer and won the job, turning out several hundred *Chandu* episodes over the next four years. The first sixty-eight episodes were devoted to the search for Robert Regent, Dorothy's husband, who had vanished in a shipwreck ten years before. Through his occult powers, Chandler learned that Regent might be alive, held prisoner by the evil, malignant Roxor, a master criminal with fiendish plans for world domination.

Off went the audience to Egypt, for a long series of confrontations with Roxor and his cronies. There were several subplots: Chandler's low-key romance with Nadji, the Egyptian princess; Betty's ill-fated romance with a bedouin beggar; Dorothy's fight against mounting fear. Chandler's magic was useless in the face of blind fear, and therein was his weakness.

In this early 1932–36 version, Gayne Whitman played Chandu; Margaret MacDonald was Dorothy; Bob Bixby was young Bob Regent and Betty Webb played his sister Betty. Cyril Armbrister was director and music was by Felix Mills and later Raymond Paige.

The original Chandu had been off the air for twelve years when Morgan, searching around for a new radio show, decided to try a revival. On June 28, 1948, the series was revived, based on the original scripts, for broadcast on the West Coast over the Mutual-Don Lee Network. Armbrister was brought in from the East Coast to direct; Vera Oldham was reactivated for a light rewrite of the original scripts; the show was resold to the original sponsor, White King Soap, and Chandu 1948 was ready to roll. Even the old gong for the first series was brought out of mothballs and used on the new show.

This time Tom Collins, whose suave delivery made him perfect for the part, played Chandu. Irene Tedrow played Dorothy; Lee Millar was son Bob and Joy Terry was daughter Betty. Veola Vonn played Nadji and Luis Van Rooten was Roxor. Music was by Juan Rolando, who played under his Hindu name, Korla Pandit, on the organ. The messages of White King were read over a souped-down version of the original Chandu music. In 1949, Chandu became a 30-minute weekly show, running for a final season on coast-to-coast ABC. It was last heard in 1950.

Chaplain Jim

Chaplain Jim was a War Department exercise in dramatic propaganda, first hitting the Blue Network air in 1942 and starring John Lund in the title role. War Department officials produced the show, employing a serial tie to get across the not-too-subtle messages from the European and Pacific war zones. Chaplain Jim was a kindly young man of God who served both war fronts and occasionally had time, during a home leave, to help out families of the fighting men with personal problems. The show lasted one season, but returned to Mutual in the closing months of the war with basically the same approach. Don MacLaughlin played Jim, and the show was "dedicated to the mothers, wives, sweethearts and families of the men who wear the khaki of the United States Army." Jim was usually around after the show to remind his listeners to send that "daily, cheerful letter" to a soldier overseas.

Charlie Chan

Charlie Chan, the famous Chinese detective, was given better treatment and a kinder reception in the Sidney Toler movies than he found on the air, but *Chan* did emerge in several respectable runs, complete with Number One Son and a variety of corpses. Based on the stories by Earl Derr Biggers, *Charlie Chan* first came to NBC Blue December 2, 1932, in a Friday-night series sponsored by Esso and starring Walter Connolly in the title role. The half-hour series folded May 20, 1933, but the character was revived in October 1937 for a nightly 15-minute serialized program on Mutual. That one ended in April 1938. Like a corpse that just wouldn't stay dead, *Chan* resurfaced on ABC June 6, 1944, with Ed Begley as the wiry Oriental police inspector and Leon Janney as Number One Son. In 1945, Begley began a 15-minute daily series on ABC which was heard regionally for two years. On August 11, 1947, *Chan* went to Mutual, in a 30-minute Monday series for Pharmaco. Santos Ortega played Charlie in the final run and Janney returned as Number One Son. The series ended June 21, 1948. Although nostalgia hounds remember the character with much fondness, Charlie's heyday was 1937 to 1940, on the silver screen.

The Charlie McCarthy Show

The Charlie McCarthy Show was the first major variety hour to use ventriloquism on the air. Edgar Bergen was born in Chicago, February 16, 1903. Charlie McCarthy was born of a block of white pine about seventeen years later. During those seventeen years, Bergen took his first steps on the million-dollar road that would lead to his life's work. The first step was a developing interest in magic and ventriloquism when he wasn't yet out of grammar school. The second step was a 25-cent investment for a booklet that contained instructions for "throwing your voice." It was the best quarter Bergen ever spent. By the time he was 11, Bergen was using ventriloquism for household jokes. He especially loved sending his parents to the door when there was no one there. It was a riot, and all grist for the mill, practical experience that he would use over the next half-century.

Nobody knew it then. Bergen was thinking of becoming a doctor, but by his second year in high school the Charlie McCarthy part of his personality was clamoring to get out. One day in school, Bergen sketched the face that would launch a thousand radio shows. He patterned Charlie's features after a kid who sold newspapers in the neighborhood. Later he paid $35 to a carpenter named Theodore Mack, and had the face carved in pine. The dummy's name was derived from the combined monikers of Mack and the newsboy, whose name was Charlie. Charlie McCarthy was born.

Bergen was still pursuing medicine; he entered Northwestern as a pre-med student. To help pay his way, he and Charlie entertained in back-room parties and in semi-pro theatre engagements. During the summers he followed Chautauqua. In the mid-1920's, he decided that medicine wasn't for him. He hit the road with Charlie to entertain full-time. For ten years man and dummy traveled together, often scaring up just enough bookings for food and shelter. They played all over Europe and North and South America. It was the lean time that all vaudeville comics went through.

Most of the big names of the air came out of obscurity much sooner than Bergen, but none came any faster. Edgar Bergen and his dummy Charlie McCarthy were first heard on radio on Rudy Vallee's *Royal Gelatin Hour*, December 17, 1936. Vallee had caught Bergen's act at a party, and invited him to appear on the Thursday-night NBC variety hour. Bergen knew that Vallee's invitations had made many a star. He accepted. Then both he and Vallee had second thoughts. The idea of a ventriloquist doing radio frightened both of them. In the end, Vallee insisted that they give it a try.

People will still argue that ventriloquism isn't—and never has been—a suitable occupation for a radio comedian. Ventriloquists need visual contact with the audience. The principle is still sound; exactly why it worked in reverse for Edgar Bergen is still something of a mystery.

Charlie was sensational, and Bergen wasn't half bad himself. They were so popular with Vallee's huge audience that they were brought back again and again. Chase & Sanborn finally decided to cash in on the act's sudden fame by bankrolling Bergen in his own show beginning May 9, 1937.

The move wasn't cheap, but big acts seldom are. A star-studded cast was assembled for the new program. Bergen was flanked by W. C. Fields, then America's top comedian; Don Ameche, who had made great inroads as leading man of *The First Nighter Program* a few seasons earlier; and Dorothy Lamour, then riding the crest of the sarong craze. Soon after the première, *The Chase & Sanborn Hour* had leaped ahead of such established front-runners as *The Jack Benny Program*, *The Eddie Cantor Show*, *Town Hall Tonight*, and *The Kraft*

Music Hall. Bergen finished that year with a strong lead, and held the top spot for almost three years. After almost fifteen years of playing parties, night clubs, vaudeville, and the Chautauqua circuit, Bergen was the hottest thing on the air.

Much of the credit for the early showing goes to W. C. Fields, who started an immediate feud with Charlie McCarthy and kept the show moving at a fast pace. Fields developed a deep personal hatred of the dummy, which consistently topped him on the air. When Fields drew laughs by threatening to carve Charlie into a venetian blind, the dummy got a bigger laugh with, "That makes me shudder." When Fields insulted Charlie's pine cone ancestry with talk of "the little woodpecker's snack bar," Charlie came back with jabs at Fields' drinking or his big red nose. One of Charlie's best lines from the classic feud was, "Pink elephants take aspirin to get rid of W. C. Fields."

Ventriloquism is a visual art. But in Charlie McCarthy, Bergen had something going for him that transcended those restrictions. In the minds of millions of Americans, Charlie McCarthy became a real person. His character took on three-dimensional qualities and adapted itself with peculiar zest to the audio format. Whether he was mercilessly roasting W. C. Fields or cuddling up to Dorothy Lamour, Charlie was America's most lovable bad boy.

He came to us fully decked out in formal dress, with tails and top hat, though he had a $1,000 wardrobe that included a cowboy suit, a Foreign Legion outfit, and a Sherlock Holmes detective suit. The formality of his dress clashed with the down-to-earth manner of his speech, but that was just another thing that made Charlie Charlie. Few comedians got away with more inconsistencies than Edgar Bergen. Always—thanks to Charlie—they came out smelling like a couple of roses. In 1937, Charlie McCarthy received an honorary degree from Northwestern, as Master of Innuendo and the Snappy Comeback. He had become a person in his own right. He was even included, to the tune of $10,000, in Bergen's will.

Fields left the show after about five months as a regular, but his departure hardly dented the rating. In December 1937, Bergen brought in Mae West for her infamous "Adam and Eve" skit. The skit was passed by the NBC censor, but Miss West read her part with such a strong sexual drawl that it created a storm of protest. Her dialogue with the snake in the Garden of Eden was wild by 1937 standards, containing bald references to the "palpitatin' python" getting stuck while sliding through the Garden fence. "Oh, shake your hips," Miss West cooed in her most sultry voice. "Yeah, you're doin' all right now. Get me a big one; I feel like doin' a big apple." There were more references to "swivel hips" and "original applesauce." Before the show was off the air, the NBC phones were ringing off the hooks.

More than 1,000 letters of protest came in, many from church groups and "leagues for decency." Some of the letters were funny. One wasn't. It was an ominous note from the Federal Communications Commission.

The FCC wanted a full electrical transcription of the show, a copy of the network's contract with the sponsor, and the call letters of all stations that had carried the skit. The result was a slap on the wrist and a network ban against Mae West that would last for fifteen years. On NBC, it was taboo even to mention her name.

In 1939, Bergen created his second dummy, the dopey, slow-talking Mortimer Snerd. By 1940, Chase and Sanborn decided that Bergen was the best part of the show. In January Ameche and Miss Lamour were dropped and the show was condensed from 60 to 30 minutes. It ran with this format, which provided just enough time for a band number by Ray Noble, a brief guest shot, and Bergen's witty monologues with Charlie and Mortimer, until December 26, 1948, when Bergen parted with Chase & Sanborn.

Charlie usually chatted about his schooltime adventures with his pal, Skinny Dugan; Mortimer talked about how stupid he was in a voice that sounded strongly like Walt Disney's Goofy. Bud Abbott and Lou Costello became regulars, and were heard until their own show opened in 1942. Don Ameche later returned with Frances Langford to begin their memorable *Bickersons* skits on the Bergen show. Pat Patrick played the blubbering Ercil Twing in shows of the late 1940's. Bergen was a master of the running gag; he was perhaps the most accomplished of all radio comedians at milking a joke for all it was worth. In 1942, to promote enlistments in the armed forces, he entered Charlie in the Army Air Corps as a master sergeant. The following week, Charlie tried to obtain another commission by joining the Marines. It culminated in a highly publicized "military trial," on location at the Stockton, California, army base. Lieutenant James Stewart was brought in to defend Charlie, who, in the end, was found as guilty as he was.

In 1944, Bergen created a third dummy, the man-crazy old maid Effie Klinker. Later he made still another, Podine Puffington. But they never went over like Charlie and Mortimer. In Bergen's heart, even Mortimer could never be another Charlie. There was only one real Charlie McCarthy, and Bergen had that original block of white pine insured for $10,000.

By 1945, Bergen was knocking down $10,000 a week from the radio show alone. That wasn't to mention another $100,000 a year from royalities on the sale of Charlie McCarthy mementos, which ranged from dolls to mugs and spoons. Bergen was in. He left NBC in 1948, and after sitting out a year, he returned in 1949 with a CBS show sponsored by Coca-Cola. With startling speed, he again captured a major share of his old Sunday-night audience. Coke carried the show until 1952, when sponsorship went to Hudnut. Bergen's show was again changed in 1954, becoming a 60-minute Kraft Cheese offering. The show was sustained by the network in 1956, its final year. Bergen's daughter Candice, still a child and years away from film stardom in her own right, frequently appeared on his 1956 shows.

The Chase

The Chase was an obscure suspense series that ran on NBC in 1952–53. It told stories of people caught in traps and people on the run. The theme was caught up in clever opening sound effects —walking footsteps, then frantic running and panting. "There is always the hunter and the hunted, the pursuer and the pursued. It may be the voice of authority, or a race with death and destruction, most relentless of the hunters. There are times when laughter is heard as counterpoint and moments when sheer terror is the theme!" (Gunshots, and the feet begin to drag; then a body falls)—"but always there is the chase!" It was created by Lawrence Klee, a refugee from the *Mr. Keen* writing ranks, and faded after one season.

Cheerio

Cheerio was a long-running series of daily "good cheer" messages, first heard June 22, 1925, at KGO, San Francisco. On March 14, 1927, the show moved to NBC and a coast-to-coast audience. Charles K. Field, a second cousin of poet Eugene Field, was Cheerio, though he took great pains to preserve his anonymity. Field felt that his mission in life was to spread cheer and good will, and for fifteen years he did his radio show for little or no fee. Even after the Sonotone hearing aid company picked up the program in 1936, most of Field's fee was donated to charity. He began his show with the British greeting, "Cheerio," and the name stuck. His mother's favorite storybook provided much of his material; Field also played cheerful music to the accompaniment of four chirping canaries. He was a former magazine editor who closely resembled Calvin Coolidge, and never let his fame go to his head. He never allowed photos to be taken, seldom granted interviews, and preferred that each listener form his own impression of what "Cheerio" looked like. After a decade in his six-a-week 30-minute morning format, "Cheerio" cut back to one evening broadcast a week. This lasted from 1937 through 1940 on the Blue network Sunday nights, after which he faded from the air.

Chesterfield Supper Club

Chesterfield Supper Club was first heard on NBC December 11, 1944, as an unusual five-a-week 15-minute musical springboard for Perry Como and Jo Stafford. Como sang three nights a week; Miss Stafford filled in for the remaining two nights. Announcer was Martin Block. In 1949, it became a 30-minute Thursday-night offering, with hostess Peggy Lee, the Dave Barbour Orchestra, announcer Tom Reddy, and such guests as Buddy Clark, Frankie Laine, and Dick Haymes. It was decidedly different from the earlier Chesterfield Time.

Chesterfield Time

Chesterfield Time, first heard on NBC in 1939, was simply The Fred Waring Show under sponsorship of Chesterfield Cigarettes. It was straight music with one interesting deviation: announcer Bill Bivens' nightly readings (in season) of the day's baseball scores, to great fanfare by the orchestra. Waring's theme during the Chesterfield years was "A Cigarette, Sweet Music, and You." His closing theme was the orchestra's famed "Sleep." Chesterfield dropped the show in 1944, in favor of its new Supper Club, which ran until 1950.

The Chicago Theatre of the Air

The Chicago Theatre of the Air grew out of a listener survey conducted by Station WGN in 1940, and became one of radio's greatest popular offerings of condensed grand opera and dramatic operettas. The survey revealed that a huge block of Chicago's listening audience wanted the music of opera; another large segment wanted the escapism of heavy drama. WGN combined the two, and The Chicago Theatre of the Air went into the entire Mutual Saturday-night hookup October 5, 1940. It ran until 1955, and succeeded in bridging the gap between traditional opera and the mass market. In this highly selective field, only The Railroad Hour managed to find a more receptive audience.

The success was due in large part to the group's dedication to popular entertainment. The operas, long beyond the understanding of many Americans, were carefully translated into English by George Mead and Thomas P. Martin, assuring that even the uninitiated could follow them without difficulty. The melodies, already hauntingly familiar to most listeners, now were backed up by strong story lines. Jack LaFrandre, program director, wrote a dramatic script, fitting the story into the 60-minute format with slots for all the major music. A team of arrangers, headed by choral director Robert Trendler, then linked the dramatic scenes with musical bridgework. For his casts, LaFrandre chose from the best dramatic radio talent in Chicago. Bret Morrison, Betty Winkler, Marvin Miller, Willard Waterman, Barbara Luddy, Les Tremayne, Betty Lou Gerson, and Rita Ascot were among the dozens tapped for dramatic readings. Soloists came from the stages of the Metropolitan Opera, the San Carlo Opera Company and the Chicago Civic Opera Company. For the first seven years, Marion Claire was the show's prima donna, while her husband Henry Weber conducted the orchestra. Miss Claire retired from singing in 1947, but remained as the show's production supervisor. Her leading men during her reign included James Melton, Richard Tucker, and Thomas L. Thomas. Leading musical roles also were handled by Graciela Rivera, Ann Ayars, Jane Lawrence, Selma Kaye, Winifred Heidt, Morton Bowe, Thomas Hayward, Andzia Kuzak, George Tozzi, Dorothy Staiger, Attilio Baggiore, Ruth Slater, Bruce Foote, Earl Willkie, and others.

Among the hundreds of operas offered were *Carmen, Tales of Hoffman, The Girl of the Golden West, Maytime, La Boheme, Rigoletto, Faust, Die Fledermaus, The Student Prince, The Barber of Seville* and *The Countess Maritza.* The cast went through a week of rehearsals, blending all elements of the show into a smooth-running whole; some 100 artists assembled for the complete broadcast, the soloists occupied center stage, the dramatic cast was on the left, and the thirty-voice chorus was on the right. The orchestra was drawn from the Chicago Philharmonic.

Chick Carter, Boy Detective

Chick Carter, Boy Detective, premiered on Mutual July 5, 1943, offering late afternoon serial lovers an unusual link with a popular Sunday show. For Chick was billed as the adopted son of Nick Carter, Master Detective, whose Sunday show was then only three months old. Writers Walter Gibson and Ed Gruskin—who also worked up the early scripts for *Nick Carter*—promised a strong inter-relation between the shows. But for the most part, Nick had his hands full with murderers of the adult school, while Chick was in a constant tangle with an evil one known as The Rattler. Bill Lipton originated the role of Chick; later that summer he bequeathed it to Leon Janney. Stefan Schnabel was The Rattler and Gilbert Mack played Chick's pal Tex. Chick lacked the staying power of his famous father, and disappeared from the matinee air after a single season.

Child's World

Child's World was the Candid Microphone of the young set, but done for a different purpose. While Candid Mike brought out the funny and unusual, Child's World served as an educational tool showing the problems of kids. There was no attempt to hide the microphone but to promote spontaneity the sound engineer was hidden away in another room. The show was recorded on wire in the New York apartment of Helen Parkhurst, its originator. Miss Parkhurst, a noted educator, had founded Dalton School, one of the largest private schools in New York State. Her experiences had convinced her that adults needed insights into a child's world to understand that children aren't always carefree and without troubles. During the half-hour, she interviewed kids from 4 to 15 about such subjects as teachers, playing hookey, God, jealousy, death, babies, and being Negro. The children were brought in from every part of New York, from every economic and racial background. Not bad for October 26, 1947, when it premièred on ABC. It ran for two years.

A Christmas Carol

A Christmas Carol was brought to CBS by Lionel Barrymore, on December 25, 1934, and each year the Charles Dickens' classic became a listening must for millions. Barrymore's portrayal of the miserly Scrooge was as flawless as anything radio ever produced. For his first performance he was supported by Beatrice Lillie, while Alexander Woollcott served as master of ceremonies. In 1936, with the death of Barrymore's wife, his brother John took the part. Orson Welles played Scrooge in 1938, when Lionel became ill. But the following year he was back, in Welles' own Mercury Theatre, for a full 60-minute production with Welles as narrator. On December 23, 1944, Barrymore did the story in 30 minutes as part of his regular Mayor of the Town show. Many listeners and critics considered A Christmas Carol the greatest Yule story ever done on the air. Until his death on November 15, 1954, Barrymore, with almost clockwork regularity, captured the very essense of "that grasping, clutching, conniving, covetous old sinner, Ebenezer Scrooge."

Cimarron Tavern

Cimarron Tavern was a very brief entry in the log of the juvenile serial, beginning April 9, 1945, on CBS and barely finishing out the year. It was billed as "the gateway to the old west," the story of a pioneer family that moved west and opened a tavern in Oklahoma Territory. It also told of the fictional exploits of Star Travis, federal scout, and Randy Martin his young sidekick, "on the trails of adventure." Randy came under Travis' wing when his parents were murdered in the opening episode. Paul Conrad played Travis; Felix Holt wrote the show and John Dietz directed.

The Cinnamon Bear

The Cinnamon Bear was a Christmas story, syndicated to stations around the country in twenty-six chapters, usually beginning just before Thanksgiving and ending just before Christmas.

First heard in 1937, the show was repeated yearly in many markets because of its universal appeal to children. *The Cinnamon Bear* took them to a world of fantasy, where giants, pirates, dragons, and witches lived. It began in the home of Judy and Jimmy Barton, two normal, healthy kids anxiously awaiting Christmas. When their mother sends them into the attic for the Silver Star, traditional ornament for the top of the tree, the adventure begins. There, they meet Patty O'Cinnamon, a stuffed bear come to life. The cinnamon bear tells them that the star has been stolen by the Crazy Quilt Dragon, who has escaped with it to Maybeland. If the kids are ever to see the silver star again, they must follow the dragon.

The Cinnamon Bear teaches them to "de-grow," and they shrink to the height of four inches. Off they go through a crack in the wall, into the world of make-believe. The quest takes them through the land of ink-blotter soldiers, across the Root Beer Ocean, and into confrontations with such characters as the Wintergreen Witch, Fe Fo the Giant and Captain Taffy the Pirate.

The show was written by Glen Heisch and directed by Lindsay MacHarrie, with music by Felix Mills. Songs were by the Paul Taylor Quartet. The entire serial was unearthed by Terry Black, an Illinois collector. With the help of Frank Nelson, he came up with most of the names of the cast members:

Judy Barton: Barbara Jean Wong
Jimmy Barton: Unknown
Mother Barton: Verna Felton
The Cinnamon Bear: Buddy Duncan
The Crazy Quilt Dragon: Joseph Kearns
Snapper Snitch, The Crocodile: Hanley Stafford
Samuel the Seal: Slim Pickens
The Cowboy: Howard McNear
Penelope the Pelican: Elvia Allman
Mr. Presto the Magician: Elliott Lewis
Santa Claus: Lou Merrill
Captain Tin Top: Frank Nelson
Captain Taffy the Pirate: Cy Kendall
Indian Chief: Cy Kendall
Weary Willie the Stork: Gale Gordon
Ostrich: Gale Gordon
Professor Whiz the Owl: Ted Osborne
Fe Fo the Giant: Joe DuVal
The Wintergreen Witch: Martha Wentworth
Fraidy Cat: Dorothy Scott
Assistant Blotto Executioner: Ed Max
Narrator: Bud Heistand
Queen Melissa: Unknown
Wesley the Whale, others: Lindsay MacHarrie

The Circle

The Circle was the radio belly-flop of 1939. The first great star-spiked talk program, it premièred January 15, 1939, on NBC. Despite a glittering cast from Hollywood, it was removed from the air even before its first season ended.

It was an hour-long Sunday night show, sponsored by Kellogg's Corn Flakes and featuring uninhibited talk from the upper crust of the entertainment world. The idea was sound, as Jack Paar and Johnny Carson would prove on TV decades later. But dropping as it did into the prewar jitters of 1939, *The Circle* never really got off the ground. Some of the best-loved performers in America were tapped for the round-table discussions, but it didn't matter. America wasn't listening.

The table, especially designed for the show, was modeled after a Universal newsroom copy desk, circular with a small slot. The microphone stood in the slot and the stars sat around the table. Ronald Colman, ending a long holdout against series radio, was president;

Carole Lombard was secretary. Cary Grant took the position of devil's advocate and Groucho and Chico Marx provided touches of insanity. Others in the circle were Lawrence Tibbett of the Metropolitan Opera and later, Basil Rathbone. The Circle was the result of a trend toward spontaneity, giving the regulars a go at anything they wanted to discuss. Carole Lombard told why women could run the world better than men. Colman struck out against oppression, telling a timeless tale that happened to be set in ancient Greece. There was lively reaction back and forth, broken by the music of Robert Emmett Dolan's orchestra, songs by The Foursome and appearances of such guests as Noel Coward and pianist José Iturbi. Anything from war and death to the arts was fair game. In other words, The Circle was a highbrow show.

The Marx brothers were probably included to keep it from getting too highbrow, but it attracted little of the mass audience. Some $25,000 a week was split between the Circle members. Even the good pay wasn't enough to keep Ronald Colman from quitting five weeks into the series. Despite his subsequent appearances as a guest, The Circle went downhill from there, but not before costing the sponsor an estimated $2 million—a phenomenal sum for radio.

The Cisco Kid

The Cisco Kid, one of radio's most memorable Westerns, came to WOR-Mutual October 2, 1942. At that time, Cisco was played by Jackson Beck, his fat and funny sidekick Pancho was Louis Sorin, and the series was billed as a story of "O. Henry's beloved badman who rides the romantic trail that leads sometimes to adventure, often to danger, but always to beautiful señoritas." Cisco was a Mexican adventurer, promoted as an outlaw who victimized the rich and greedy. This early series, directed by Jock MacGregor, lasted little more than a season, but the characters were revived in a Mutual-Don Lee version of about 1946. This time Jack Mather played Cisco and Harry Lang was Pancho. Virtually gone were references to Cisco's badman nature. What little remained was crammed into the show's famous opening: "Ceesco! The shereef, he ees getting closer!"

"This way, Pancho, vamanos!"

Mather and Lang made a solid juvenile adventure team. They developed their characters well, using familiar slang and affectionate nicknames. To Cisco, Pancho became "Chico." Despite his bulk, Pancho was a handyman with a bullwhip and showed courage in fights. Cisco inevitably triumphed over evil; his reward was always a kiss from the señorita. The kissing effect was achieved with dreamy

organ music, the señorita would breathe, "Ohhh, Cisco," and Cisco would answer, "Oooooooh, señorita." Then he and Pancho were off to new adventures. There was always a closing punchline—a terrible pun by Pancho and feigned disgust by Cisco: "OH, PAN-CHO!"
"Oooo, Ceesco!"
"Up, Diablo!"
"Up, Loco!"
Whooping laughter, horses galloping into the sunset, and out.

Cities Service Concerts

Cities Service Concerts, one of the great early shows of concert music, was first heard on NBC February 18, 1927, after several trial broadcasts in 1925 and 1926. The premise behind this program never changed: it aimed to present the best in music, whether it was Beethoven or Berlin. The only thing that changed was the cast that delivered it. And the personnel changes that occurred in the *Cities* shows, especially in the first decade, made radio history.

The show was one of the first musical productions of network radio. An NBC log of February 18, 1927, reveals that a blown fuse cut three minutes out of the first show. But that was horse-and-buggy radio for you. The network was a scant three months old when *Cities Service Concerts* premièred. Graham McNamee did the announcing and the band, heavy with cornets, was under the direction of Edwin Franko Goldman. In June 1927, Goldman passed the baton to Rosario Bourdon, and the semi-classical/popular theme was established.

Jessica Dragonette was aboard by December 27, 1929, bringing with her long years of voice training and a huge repertoire. Miss Dragonette sang her way into radio immortality on the *Cities* show, flanked by Frank Parker and the Cavaliers Quartet. Behind the scenes, discontent festered and grew as Miss Dragonette sought slight format changes without any encouragement from the sponsor or its officers. She wanted to do operettas, with dramatizations as well as song; the sponsor refused to consider any change in the show, which called for her to do up to eight numbers—solos and duets with Parker. With startling suddenness, she quit in the winter of 1937, jumping to CBS and Palmolive's *Beauty Box Theatre*. Into her shoes on February 5, 1937, stepped Lucille Manners, a 1936 summertime replacement for Jessica who would build a name of her own during her decade with the show. In another format change, the Cavaliers were replaced by the Revelers quartet.

Cities Service Concerts became one of the first major shows to blend music and talk in generous doses of each. The talk segments began May 19, 1933, with the appearance of Amelia Earhart on the anniversary of her flight across the Atlantic. On December 8, 1933, Colonel Louis McHenry Howe, President Roosevelt's secretary, came to the microphones to discuss the government's plans for Depression America. Announcer Ford Bond began his baseball commentaries during the summer of 1933, and they were so well-received that Grantland Rice was brought in that fall for football talk. Bond and Rice returned to sports year after year, adding an unusual twist to a concert program.

The show ran for thirteen years without changing its 60-minute format or its Friday night time slot. In 1938, the baton went to Dr. Frank Black, NBC director of music. In 1940, the show was trimmed to 30 minutes; in 1944 its title was changed to *Highways in Melody*. Paul Lavalle, a clarinetist with the original Goldman band, took over the orchestra that year. In 1948 it became *The Cities Service Band of America*, still broadcasting from the old Friday-night time slot. That too changed in 1949, when the show was shifted into NBC's "Monday Night of Music." In the mid-1950's, after three decades on the air, the show was still going strong. In 1956, listeners could still catch *The Cities Service Band of America*. By then most were unaware that they were listening to a little piece of history whose roots ran deep.

Clara, Lu and Em

Clara, Lu and Em was created from a sorority sisters' skit at Northwestern University in the mid-1920's. It was first broadcast on the Blue Network, after a brief run on local radio, in 1931. This was a low-key comic soap opera about three gossipy women who lived in the same apartment building. Each had strong characteristics: Clara was a compulsive housekeeper, Lu a widow who lived upstairs, and Em the slow-talking mother of five children. The parts were played by Louise Starkey (Clara), Isabel Carothers (Lu), and Helen King (Em). The women had created the characters at Northwestern for school parties, with no thought of radio. They graduated in 1927 and separated. Two went into teaching, but Helen King decided to try radio. During a reunion years later, they revived the gossipy characters and sold a skit locally. It was well-received, and NBC brought them to Chicago. The show folded suddenly with Miss Carothers' death in 1936, but was revived briefly by CBS June 8, 1942, when Pillsbury Flour went looking for a new serial. Starkey and King returned for the new version, while the part of Lu was played by Harriet Allyn. The new version disappeared after a short run.

The Clock

The Clock, a series of suspense and adventure, told of races against time, narrated by a deep-voiced fellow with a Father Time image. "In England they call me Ben, and I have a large and extremely showy flat in Westminster Tower. Just between the two of us, I feel more comfortable at the end of a chain. And there's the quiet old lady who keeps a favored place for me in the corner of her room; to her, I'm known as grandfather." These stories were carried for two seasons on ABC, beginning in 1946. The program was written by Lawrence Klee, directed by Clark Andrews, with music composed by Bernard Green. Gene Kirby was announcer.

Club Matinee

Club Matinee, a 60-minute daily variety show, marked Garry Moore's debut on the air. This is where he learned the basics from an old pro named Ransom Sherman. Sherman would go on to a series of short-running jobs and Moore's career as a professional master of ceremonies would span thirty years. But Garry Moore was just a skinny, crew-cut kid when he joined *Club Matinee* in 1939. He was still going by his given name—Thomas Garrison Morfit—and one listener won $50 in a rename-the-Morfit contest by cutting the last name, dropping Thomas, and respelling Garrison. *Club Matinee* began on NBC Blue in 1937. It was really Sherman's show; he took young Morfit under his professional wing and taught him a few things about radio comedy. Moore came to share the writing duties and the emcee mike with Sherman before departing Chicago in 1942, for the greener pastures of New York. *Club Matinee* expired the same year.

The Clyde Beatty Show

The Clyde Beatty Show brought the circus roaring into living rooms in a series of late 1940's syndications by Commodore Productions. It was produced by Shirley Thomas, whose husband Walter White, Jr., was president of Commodore and also produced the *Hopalong Cassidy* series. The stories were "based upon incidents in the career of world-famous Clyde Beatty and the Clyde Beatty Circus." Beatty, whose wife Harriet was included in the fictionalized accounts, told domestic tales of circus life and wilderness tales of tracking wild beasts. In 1950, the show was brought to Mutual in a three-a-week show for Kellogg; it ran there one season.

Coast-to-Coast on a Bus

Coast-to-Coast on a Bus began in the pre-network days of 1924, when it was established on WJZ. At first it was called *The Children's Hour*, becoming part of the early-morning Sunday lineup with the establishment of NBC. It served as the air's outstanding amateur hour for children from 1927 through the 1930's, and became widely known as "The White Rabbit Line," from the name of the bus it was supposed to represent. Milton Cross was conductor of the bus—general host for the show from its inception. It was arranged and conducted by Madge Tucker, billed as "the lady next door." Many children who later became well-established show business personalities got their start on "The White Rabbit Line." For several years in the late 1930's, Walter Tetley—later Leroy on *The Great Gildersleeve* and a variety of smart-aleck kids on other network shows—was part of Cross' company. Art Scanlon was the Negro porter, and other members of the 1939 cast included Jackie Kelk (Homer to Ezra Stone's Henry Aldrich) and Estelle Levy, also of *Let's Pretend*. Others who rode the White Rabbit included Eddie Wragge, Jimmy McCallion, and Billy Halop, who went on to *Dead End Kids* fame. Few children were too young to appear on the White Rabbit Line: Diana Donnenwirth was a prima donna at three; Ronald Liss sang and read stories at four; and Joyce Walsh was a regular at six. Among the passengers were Renee and Joy Terry, Jimmy Burke, Audrey Egan, Marie Skinner, Vivian Smolen (who would go on to play *Our Gal Sunday* and Lolly-Baby on *Stella Dallas*), Florence Halop (Billy's sister and a future Miss Duffy on *Duffy's Tavern*), Eleanor Glantz, Peggy Zinke, Billy and Bobby Mauch, Mildred Schneider, Nancy Peterson, Mary Oldham, Winifred Toomey, Thomas Brady, Mary Baune, Patsy and Dotty Dowd, Anne Heather, Edna Roebling, Dabby Lewis, Walter Scott, Bob Hastings (one of four actors who later played *Archie Andrews*), Michael O'Day, and Andy, Jimmy, and Tommy Donnelly. The show was introduced by the blowing of a bus horn and the White Rabbit theme: "Coast-to-coast on a bus, the White Rabbit Line, jumps anywhere, anytime!" The kids, ranging in age from 3 to 16, then let fly with the theme song:

> Oh, we just roll-along,
> Havin' our ups, havin' our downs,
> Havin' our ups and downs,
> All day loonng!

The show itself was mostly music, beginning at 9 A.M. each
Sunday with the morning hymn. "Ronald the Bunny" and "Peter and
Mumsy Pig" skits somehow got sandwiched between songs.

The Coke Club

The Coke Club featured Morton Downey, tenor, known as "The Irish
Thrush," "The Irish Troubador" and other blarney names. Actually
Downey was born in Connecticut in 1902; he got his earliest taste of
show business in Wallingford, his home town, where he sang at
church socials and Elks Club meetings. Downey's first big-time break
came in 1919, when he was discovered by a Paul Whiteman talent
scout while singing at the Sheridan Square Theatre in New York. His
rise was swift; soon he was getting equal billing with the band; his
name was splashed on marquees from Hollywood to Florida,where he
appeared in a Ziegfeld show. In the mid-1920's, Downey made a tour
of Europe, becoming widely known to audiences in Paris, Vienna and
Berlin. He first sang on the air in a BBC broadcast around 1928. When
he returned to the United States the following year, CBS signed him
immediately for a four-a-week quarter-hour sustainer. Soon Downey
was the featured star in "The Camel Quarter Hour," where he received
up to 90,000 letters a week. In 1932, he moved into a 30-minute slot on
the Blue Network for Woodbury Soap; by 1936, he was one of the top
musical stars of the air, earning an estimated $250,000 a year. In the
early 1940's, Downey signed a five-year contract, at a reported $4,000
a week, to sing for Coca–Cola. His formats for Coke spanned various
networks, and were usually offered in daily 15-minute doses known
as "The Coke Club."

The Colgate Sports Newsreel

The Colgate Sports Newsreel featured Bill Stern, whose interest early
in life had been split between sports and theatre. Born July 1, 1907, he
went to work in the mid-1920's as a sportscaster in Rochester, N.Y.
His hometown radio station wasn't big enough for his ambition, and by 1932 he had become stage director of Radio City Music
Hall. After a few seasons he tired of that, and went to pioneer sports
announcer Graham McNamee for another announcing job. Stern
joined McNamee in 1934, covering football part-time while keeping
his Radio City job. He was so popular with the fans that he was signed
as a regular by NBC in 1937.

Bill Stern was first heard nationally in a special "sportstalk" format, *The Bill Stern Sports Review,* on the Blue Network December 5, 1937. For four years he broadcast the Friday-night fights on NBC Blue for Adam Hats, and in 1938 he began a long association with MGM's *News of the Day* newsreel, which he plugged weekly on his sportsreel shows.

His famous *Colgate Sports Newsreel* was first heard October 8, 1939. On this program Stern eulogized the great, near-great, and obscure with fantastic yarns that would have made Ripley jealous. He used wild coincidence, twists of fate that bordered on the supernatural. He told tales of horse races won by dead jockeys, of limbless baseball players, of any thread-thin influences sport had had on the lives of the great. Stern never let the facts get in the way of a good story—occasionally he told the same story twice (allowing for a decent time span between the tellings), using conflicting facts and passing both versions off as true.

Stern covered his tracks by reminding listeners that some of his tales were hearsay, some legend, "but all so interesting we'd like to pass them along to you." His manner of telling suggested gospel. Backed by a melodramatic organ, full dramatizations, and sound effects, Stern's voice contained so much pent-up emotion that the listener was swept along by the tempo. One tended to overlook the fact that time—especially in Stern's hands—had a way of coloring things. After all, Bill used real names, often names of people still living.

Stern's shows were among the most entertaining 15-minute shots ever done on the air. Always more showman than newsman, Stern got the scores right—but sometimes rival announcers in the press booth, overhearing snatches of Stern's colorful commentary, wondered if they were watching the same game. He did his shows on location, wherever he happened to be in his pursuit of sports news, and often he persuaded top stars—Orson Welles, Jack Benny, Frank Sinatra, and skater Sonja Henie were just a few—to do guest spots. Each star had a personal tale that related in some way, however small, to sports.

His theme ("Bill Stern the Colgate shave-cream man is on the air—Bill Stern the Colgate shave-cream man with stories rare") was sung in barbershop quartet style to the tune of "Mademoiselle from Armentières." He ended his show with "That's the three-o mark for tonight," a reference to the traditional newsman's "30" code for ending a story.

Stern's show would become one of NBC's best-remembered, most popular 15-minute features, running until June 29, 1951. He continued doing nightly shows until 1956, finishing on ABC with a *Sports Today* show. Stern died in 1971. His shows were vivid examples of a zesty man giving his listeners their money's worth.

The Collier Hour

The Collier Hour was radio's first significant dramatic offering, running on NBC Blue from 1927 through 1932. The 60-minute show was divided into plays of 15 minutes each, dramatized from the pages of Collier's magazine, the sponsor. Initially heard on Wednesdays before publication, the show soon switched to Sundays after publication to avoid damaging readership of the stories, which were running concurrently. Complete stories and serials were done on The Collier Hour; the serials were usually of the thriller type. Thus the show has the distinction of being a forerunner of the adventure serial as well as the earliest important showcase for straight drama. The stories were introduced by the Collier "editor," played by Jack Arthur and later by Arthur Hughes and Phil Barrison. Best-known of the Collier Hour serials was Fu Manchu, the insidious Oriental criminal created by British writer Sax Rohmer. At least three twelve-chapter Fu Manchu serials were done on The Collier Hour, and Rohmer himself appeared for a 1931 installment of "Yu'an Hee See Laughs." In 1930, The Collier Hour took on variety airs, bringing more guests to the microphone and giving Ernest LaPrade's orchestra a bit more to do.

Columbia Presents Corwin

Columbia Presents Corwin was a special series of 30-minute plays by Norman Corwin, CBS resident poet, beginning March 7, 1944, and running each Tuesday through the summer and into 1945. Corwin, one of the big guns of American radio, had had many other specials, one-shots, and mini-series before and after Columbia Presents Corwin came to the air. That was simply his best, most sustained showing. In Columbia he refined and polished the artistic touches he had been learning since the late 1930's. Backed by the music of Lyn Murray, Corwin's peculiarly vocal style reached its peak and produced some of the most memorable radio of the era.

Born May 3, 1910, in Boston, Corwin had come to radio through the newspaper business, first doing a nightly newscast for the Springfield Republican, where he worked as a feature writer. The paper, in agreement with a local radio station, furnished Corwin for its commentaries and evening news wrap-ups. Eventually he moved on to New York radio and a guest appearance on NBC's Magic Key. In the spring of 1938, he was signed by CBS, and spent most of his radio days there.

Corwin directed such early CBS shows as Americans at Work and

Living History before getting his own show late that year. It was called *Words Without Music*, and was just that—dramatizations of his own work, intermingled with modern classics. He used Walt Whitman's "Leaves of Grass," Edgar Lee Masters' "Spoon River Anthology," and Carl Sandburg's "The People, Yes," which he repeated in 1941. For Christmas 1938, Corwin aired what many people have come to regard as his masterpiece, the charming drama of Satan's "Plot to Overthrow Christmas," with dialogue in verse. His reputation was growing quickly; it took another leap with "They Fly Through the Air with the Greatest of Ease" in January 1939. In this play, Corwin began his attack on Fascism, a worthy opponent that would serve as his audio punching bag throughout the 1940's.

He returned to a light mood with "The Undecided Molecule," a classic verse play that starred Vincent Price, Robert Benchley, and Groucho Marx. On December 15, 1941, all networks aired "We Hold These Truths," an emotional endorsement of the Bill of Rights, featuring James Stewart, Lionel Barrymore, and an all-star cast, and including a personal message from the president. Three years later, Corwin wrote the script for a star-studded endorsement of Roosevelt's fourth term, carried on all networks on November 6, 1944, the night before election. So strong was this show that both NBC and CBS adopted policies prohibiting such last-minute blitz tactics in future elections.

In the meantime, Corwin had collaborated with *The Columbia Workshop* for a six-month series called *Twenty-Six by Corwin*. This was first heard May 4, 1941, and ran through the fall. He wrote and directed a series of government propaganda programs, *This Is War*, carried on all networks beginning February 14, 1942. On August 17, 1943, a new Corwin series, *Passport for Adams*, began on CBS. It starred Robert Young as a small-town editor on a good-will mission to countries favoring the Allied cause. The initial *Passport* script was later redone on the 1945 *Columbia Presents Corwin* series.

Corwin's imagination knew no bounds. His series led off with "Movie Primer," a thorough ribbing of the film industry, told in music and poem through the ABC's of the movies. The following week, he took us to Czechoslovakia for "The Long Name None Could Spell," a compassionate drama of the agony and helplessness of the little nation when Hitler invaded in 1939. His third offering, "The Lonesome Train," described the bleak journey of the train bearing the body of Abraham Lincoln; it featured Raymond Massey as Lincoln, with folk music by Burl Ives. Throughout the year, Corwin displayed his versatility with dramas like "Savage Encounter" (a fantasy of a lost race, living in peace on a small island) and "The Odyssey of Runyon Jones" (a little boy's journey to heaven to find his dead dog).

Most of the shows were personally written; all were done under Corwin's supervision. They ran from documentaries to comedies, and were exactly the kind of radio that had made Corwin famous.

In 1945, Corwin cut short the scheduled run of his *Columbia* series to produce a special documentary for V-E Day. The show, "On a Note of Triumph," was heard on CBS May 13, 1945, just after the collapse of Germany. With the fall of Japan, Corwin wrote "Fourteen August," a 15-minute documentary heard August 14, 1945. Orson Welles gave "Fourteen August" a fiery, almost melodramatic reading ("God and uranium were on our side . . . The wrath of the atom fell like a commandment, and the very planet quivered with implications . . ."). But it was, he noted, a fitting end to "the father of great anniversaries."

Corwin's style was distinctive, employing staccato narration, strong sound effects, and speech that sounds rather purple today. His favorite theme was the magnificence of the "common man," the injustices he suffered, and the tyrants he overcame. For this, Corwin was widely, though not universally acclaimed. *Harper's Magazine* panned "On a Note of Triumph," terming it "very bad writing" and lashing Corwin's "pretentious" style for four scorching pages. But the V-Day documentary earned Corwin several prizes for excellence, among them the 1946 Wendell Willkie One World Award. That award included a trip around the world, which Corwin began with CBS sound engineer Lee Bland in June 1946. The trip covered more than 40,000 miles through sixteen countries, and Corwin came home bearing wire-recorded interviews with princes and commoners alike. The result was a thirteen-part documentary series, *One World Flight*, which began on CBS January 14, 1947.

One of Corwin's very best plays came late in radio's history. Produced in 1950 for United Nations Radio, "Document A/777" was his strongest plea yet for an International Bill of Human Rights. The scene was set during a roll-call of the United Nations. As the roll progressed, the nations voted on the bill. Occasionally the narrator froze the action on one country. Incidents from that country's history were then dramatized—stark, raw incidents emphasizing in brutal detail man's inhumanity to his fellows. The show worked on three levels, with the action being carried by a great international cast. Playing the major roles in "Document A/777" were Richard Basehart, Charles Boyer, Lee J. Cobb, Ronald Colman, Joan Crawford, Maurice Evans, José Ferrer, Reginald Gardiner, Van Heflin, Jean Hersholt, Lena Horne, Marsha Hunt, Alexander Knox, Charles Laughton, Sir Laurence Olivier, Vincent Price, Edward G. Robinson, Robert Ryan, Hilda Vaughn, Emlyn Williams, and Robert Young.

The Columbia Workshop

The Columbia Workshop, one of the great early experimental theatres of the air, came to CBS July 18, 1936, with many innovations in sound effects and production. This program was unusual radio fare. The art was still in a fairly primitive state; many of the sound techniques that later would become common hadn't yet been developed. For Irving Reis, young playwright whose St. Louis Blues had cought the eye of CBS, it became a stiff challenge.

Reis was brought in as first producer-director of The Columbia Workshop, a Saturday-night sustaining series that the network wrote off for many years as its contribution to the arts. He was given a free hand, lots of cheap talent, and a "laboratory" for use in developing new sound techniques. Here, filters and echo chambers were brought into use. The Columbia Workshop was one of the first shows to use a parabolic microphone, allowing an engineer to zero in on one voice in a crowd. In announcing the Workshop, Reis pledged to "do almost anything that lends itself to unique treatment and interesting experiments with sound effects and voices."

From the beginning, Workshop was seen as a showcase for young writers and actors, and for the first ten months it was exclusively that. Paying a mere $100 per script, the show couldn't afford the work of the great. But it used the work of the potentially great; much of the young talent that first saw action on The Columbia Workshop went on to become the big names of the medium just a few years later.

The emphasis changed, but only slightly, with the April 11, 1937, production of "The Fall of the City" by Archibald MacLeish. Now writers who had done little if any radio work began to see the potential of the new show. William Saroyan, Dorothy Parker, Alfred Kreymborg, Lord Dunsany, Pare Lorentz, Stephen Vincent Benét, and other talented writers offered plays. The plays were first produced under Reis and later under his protégé, William N. Robson, and always with the idea that production—not "story"—came first.

That was a principle that guided Workshop through three separate formats. Despite the infusion of well-known talent after MacLeish's play the series still offered experience to the young and a chance to be heard with something unconventional. Norman Corwin came out of the Workshop, as did Orson Welles. Bernard Herrmann, CBS composer-conductor, was assigned musical chores. The Workshop offered shows ranging from the simple "Sound Demonstration" in the lean days of October 1936 to Edwin Granberry's controversial "A Trip to Czardis" in August 1939.

Many of the plays, such as Benét's adaptation of his *John Brown's Body*, became classics of the medium. But none drew more acclaim than the works of MacLeish. When it was first heard, "The Fall of the City" was electrifying, so effectively capturing the emotions of the conquered city awaiting the appearance of the arrogant conquerer. MacLeish followed that in 1938 with the anti-war drama, "Air Raid." In its own way, "Air Raid" gave off the same kind of sound and emotion that would mark the Orson Welles' "War of the Worlds" panic broadcast later in the year. It may have contributed in a small way to cancellation of the series in 1941. *Newsweek*, welcoming the *Workshop* back to the air in 1946, noted that its cancellation five years earlier had been the result of a network decision that it "was just a little too frolicsome for wartime consumption." The show was revived February 2, 1946, but after an uneventful 1946–47 season, it folded again. The basic idea was revived again in 1956, with the new *CBS Radio Workshop*.

Command Performance

Command Performance was described by *Time* as "the best wartime program in radio," but few Americans at home ever got to hear it. The show was produced by the War Department, beginning early in 1942, for direct shortwave transmission to troops fighting overseas. It was once estimated that a show like *Command Performance* might cost $75,000 a week, yet it had no budget and paid no money to anyone. All talent was donated. Both CBS and NBC donated their studios for production. The result was an unprecedented extravaganza. Such stars as Bing Crosby, Bob Hope, the Andrews Sisters, Red Skelton, Edgar Bergen and Charlie McCarthy, Ethel Waters, Spike Jones, Dinah Shore, Kay Kyser, and Charles Laughton appeared on a single show. People like Lum and Abner, Fibber McGee and Molly, Rudy Vallee, George Raft, George Burns and Gracie Allen, Judy Garland, and Bob Burns stood in line to appear gratis. The series was conceived and written by Glenn Wheaton of the War Department. It was directed by Vick Knight, who gave up a $1,000-a-week salary on *The Fred Allen Show* to work for nothing on *Command Performance*. The show was written to the specifications of homesick fighting men. By request, listeners heard Carole Landis sigh, the sounds of Fifth Avenue, a slot machine hitting the jackpot, and other personal oddities, sandwiched among songs by Dinah, Bing, or Frankie. The stars considered *Command Performance* part of their contribution to the war effort, and the show was booked solid through the war. On Christmas Eve, 1942—a *Command Performance* was played in the United States, on all four networks. In 1945, an all-star cast assembled for an off-the-cuff piece of insanity called "Dick Tracy In B-Flat," or "For Goodness Sakes, Isn't He Ever Going to Marry Tess Trueheart?" The cast:

Dick Tracy: Bing Crosby
Tess Trueheart: Dinah Shore
Old Judge Hooper: Harry Von Zell
Chief of Police: Jerry Colonna
Flat Top: Bob Hope
Gravel Gertie: Cass Daley
Vitamin Flintheart: Frank Morgan
The Mole: Jimmy Durante
Snowflake: Judy Garland
The Summer Sisters: The Andrews Sisters
Shaky: Frank Sinatra

After the war, CBS tried to produce a peacetime version, for home consumption, titled *Request Performance*, and sponsored by Campbell Soups, which premiered October 7, 1945. But the vitality of *Command Performance* was strictly a wartime phenomenon, and in April 1946, this mini-version faded from the air and was forgotten. *Command Performance* continued on AFRS until December 1949.

The Count of Monte Cristo

The Count of Monte Cristo brought the intrigue of Paris of the 1830's into 1944 living rooms when Alexandre Dumas' novel was dramatized weekly on the West Coast's Don Lee Network. Carleton Young was tapped as Edmond Dantes, the legendary Count who battled personal enemies and foes of the Crown with instinctive cunning and a quick sword. Anne Stone played Dantes' friend and co-conspirator, the lovely Marie Duchene, who spent many pleasant evenings being entertained by the Count's spinet and wishing for a great deal more. Ferdinand Munier was René, the Count's faithful manservant and ardent admirer. This early version was directed by Thomas Freebairn-Smith. On December 19, 1946, the drama was carried to the entire Mutual Network, still starring Young as Dantes, but with Parley Baer as René and direction by Jaime Del Valle. The Mutual show ran for a year on Thursdays, and from 1949 through 1951 on Tuesdays. William Conrad, Jay Novello, Virginia Gregg, Howard McNear, and John Dehner took many supporting roles.

Counterspy

Counterspy was one of radio's long-running adventure shows; it was first heard on the Blue Network May 18, 1942. It remained with Blue-ABC under various sponsors until 1950: Monday nights, 1942–44; Wednesdays 1944–45; Sundays 1945–48; and twice a week, Tuesdays and Thursdays for Pepsi Cola in 1948–50. Counterspy was then heard on NBC for three years: Sundays, sustained, 1950–51; Thursdays for Gulf Oil, 1951–52; and Sundays for Gulf, 1952–53. In 1954, it went to Mutual, where it ran for multiple sponsors until 1957. The plots revolved around the United States counterspies, who were "especially appointed to investigate and combat the enemies of our country, both at home and abroad." That meant, at least in the beginning, counter-espionage against Germany's Gestapo and Japan's Black Dragon. Later the counterspy activity became more general, but always revolved around threats to the nation's security, with the agents functioning as sort of a super-FBI. Head counterspy was David Harding, a stout-voiced anthoritarian played by Don MacLaughlin. Harding's assistant Peters was played by Mandel Kramer. The show was created by Phillips H. Lord, who had brought Gang Busters to the air a few years earlier. For years the opening remained basically the same: "WASHINGTON CALLING DAVID HARDING, COUNTER-SPY! WASHINGTON CALLING DAVID HARDING, COUNTERSPY!" And, after a frantic burst of teletype activity: "HARDING, COUN-TERSPY, CALLING WASHINGTON." The program was just above average as a juvenile cop show.

County Seat

County Seat was notable primarily for the early experience it gave Norman Corwin and Ray Collins at CBS, beginning as a five-a-week early-evening serial in 1938. By 1940, this lighthearted show had disappeared, and both Corwin and Collins had gone on to other things. Corwin directed the show and Collins played the lead. Collins was Doc Will Hackett, a town philosopher with feet of clay, who owned a drugstore in the little hamlet of Northbury. In a large sense, this was a drama of high school life, revolving around the doings of Doc's nephew Jerry Whipple, his loves, and his feuds with classmate Billy Moorehead. The cast included Cliff Carpenter as Jerry, Charme Allen as his mother Sarah, Elaine Kent as Lois Johnson (Jerry's flame), Jackie Jordan as Billy Moorehead, Guy Repp as Dr. Abernathy the town physician, and Luis Van Rooten as Dr. George Priestly, the high school chemistry teacher with a mysterious past.

The Court of Missing Heirs

The Court of Missing Heirs was created by James Waters, a young lawyer whose hobby was collecting stories of missing heirs and unclaimed estates. Waters thought the idea might be good for radio, but the networks didn't agree until Skelly Oil agreed to pay the bills. The Court of Missing Heirs opened on CBS in October 1937, broadcasting for twenty-nine stations in the Midwestern area served by Skelly. Within weeks, Waters had found his first heir. Other heirs trickled in as new shows were aired, and in 1939 the show was expanded into the entire CBS network. Waters hired a staff of probate investigators to find his stories. Two cases were done each week, with the stories told in dramatic machine-gun style. This show ran until 1942, and was revived for a season on ABC in 1946. During its run, Waters found more than 150 heirs worth nearly $1 million. Most had no idea they were anyone's heir, and many were rescued from the clutches of poverty.

Crime Classics

Crime Classics was a neat little series of "true crime stories from the records and newspapers of every land from every time." It came to CBS September 30, 1953. Host was the fictitious Thomas Hyland, played by Lou Merrill and described as "a connoisseur of crime, a student of violence and a teller of murders." The production crew was among radio's finest: Elliott Lewis, producer-director, created the show from his large personal library of crime cases; Bernard Herrmann, composer, who duplicated authentic music of the era being dramatized; Morton Fine and David Friedkin, writers. Cases ranged from seventeenth-century murder to the assassination of Abraham Lincoln.

The Crime Club

The Crime Club's host was Raymond Edward Johnson, the original Raymond from Inner Sanctum Mysteries. This half-hour Mutual crime series, premiering December 2, 1946, had as producer-director Roger Bower, who seemed a bit anxious to cash in on the Inner

Sanctum format, using Raymond as the Club librarian. Listeners were invited into the library (as in "through the creaking door") for the week's tale. Unlike Inner Sanctum, the Crime Club opening was so low-key that it almost put a listener to sleep. The stories were just average, done in single-shot anthology style. Crime Club was a front for Crime Club Books, a series of whodunits that came out of the postwar years faster than you could read them. The show ran through the 1947 season.

Crime Doctor

Crime Doctor was the long-running saga of Dr. Benjamin Ordway, criminal psychiatrist extraordinaire, who operated out of a Sunday-night CBS slot for Philip Morris from August 4, 1940, through 1947. Dr. Ordway became one of radio's classic cases of amnesia. Originally a criminal himself, he got zapped on the head and lost his memory. With the help of a kind doctor, he began to build a new life and identity, studying medicine and eventually going into psychiatry. When Ordway regained his memory, his new life was complete. He decided to specialize in criminal psychiatry because of his intense interest in, and understanding of, the criminal mind. Early in the series, Ordway became head of the parole board, listening to the pleas of convicts who wanted out. Each show explored a different case.

John McIntire played the lead, and supporting roles were handled by his wife, Jeanette Nolan. After the McIntires retired to the wilds of Montana (they retired frequently, returning to radio only long enough to earn another grubstake), the emphasis of Crime Doctor changed. Now Ordway retired from public service; he operated out of his home, working with ex-convicts and helping them keep out of trouble, while at the same time aiding the local police in the unending fight against crime. By June 1942, Hugh Marlowe and Elspeth Eric were playing the leads, under direction of Jack Johnstone. Everett Sloane took the role in January 1943. Ordway was also played by House Jameson and Ray Collins. Max Marcin produced and wrote the scripts. Edith Arnold, a Marcin discovery, played hundreds of gun molls over the run, and once calculated for Radio Life that she had "bumped off" at least 200 people on the show. One interesting facet of the early run (around 1942) was the "jury" that was assembled from the studio audience to decide if a prisoner in question should be granted a parole. Voting ran two-to-one in the prisoners' favor, with female jurors almost always voting to release handsome male prisoners. However, in those long ago days before the women's movement, such sexist reactions from the male viewpoint were seldom recorded.

Crime Does Not Pay

Crime Does Not Pay was a syndicated show produced by Metro-Goldwyn-Mayer. It was based on the famous short films of the same name and first heard on WMGM, New York October 10, 1949, with Donald Buka as star. The show told of perpetrators of crime, often innocent kids who just got in too deep. It ran through 1951 as a WMGM show, and was picked up by Mutual beginning January 7, 1952, and ending December 22, 1952. Ira Marion wrote the scripts, and Marx B. Loeb directed.

Crime Fighters

Crime Fighters was rather a hokey Mutual series, heard from 1949 through 1956. Directed by Wynn Wright, it told in 30-minute anthology fashion of crime-fighting methods from coast to coast. "Crime fighters: they are all kinds—master manhunters to match master criminals, shrewd experts in a thousand rackets or simple men who study human nature, the city dicks who work in teams, the country sheriffs covering lonely regions, federal men with a nation to police or the scientists whose weapon is the laboratory."

The Croupier

The Croupier was another of those programs, like Whistler and Mysterious Traveler,whose tales of fate bordered on the supernatural. According to Webster, a croupier is an attendant who collects and pays debts at a gambling table; radio's "Croupier" collected and paid the debts of life. Each week he would spin a tale about people caught in a web, of man against fate. Milton Geiger wrote and directed, and Vincent Price was lured to the microphone for the opener. But by then TV had turned the corner. The Croupier premièred on ABC September 21, 1949, and ran only one season on Wednesday nights.

The Cuckoo Hour

The Cuckoo Hour, one of radio's earliest comedy-variety shows, was originated by Raymond Knight. Knight was born in Salem, Massachusetts; he studied law at Boston University and passed the bar in his home state. But drama was more appealing than law, so he returned to college, this time to study acting and writing at Harvard. He became a member of the 47 Workshop, a famous dramatic group directed by George Pierce Baker, and in 1927 he won a Drama League award for best one-act play of the year. It was called *Strings*, and in 1928 it was adapted for radio and broadcast via shortwave to England. Knight hit the big-time radio trail with the January 1, 1930, inauguration of *The Cuckoo Hour* on NBC Blue; it was a zany mix of situations and one-liners, heavy on satire, and starring Knight as Ambrose J. Weems, who ran the mythical radio station KUKU. His accomplice was Adelina Thomason, a former Shakespearian actress who played the role of Mrs. George T. Pennyfeather, delivering absurd hints for the home through her "Personal Service for Perturbed People." *The Cuckoo Hour* was sustained, first, 30-minutes on Wednesdays, and later in 15-minute Saturday morning doses, until 1932. Then Knight brought two new shows to the NBC air: his *Wheatenaville Sketches* ran on the Red from 1932 through 1935, while *Making the Movies* was heard on the Blue around 1932. *Wheatenaville Sketches* featured Knight as Billy Bachelor, editor of a small-town newspaper; it was heard 15 minutes each evening at 7:15, sponsored, naturally, by Wheatena. *Making the Movies* gave listeners Knight's backstage view of such early film runs as *Kelly Komedies*, *The Hazards of Helen*, and *Kelly News Reels*. It was sponsored by Kelly-Springfield Tires. In 1934, a new *Cuckoo Hour* was produced for NBC, sponsored by A.C. Spark Plugs, again starring and written by Knight, with assists from James Stanley, Wilfred Pelletier, and the Robert Armbruster Orchestra. Knight was a major comic influence on Bob Elliott, of *Bob and Ray* fame, and in the 1950's he worked on the *Bob and Ray* show as a writer of skits and situations. Elliott and Knight became close personal friends. When Knight died, Elliott married his widow and adopted his children.

Curtain Time

Curtain Time, a series of romantic dramas, was heard on Mutual for a season in 1938, broadcasting out of Chicago for Kix. Under the direction of Blair Walliser, it was rather a heavy *First Nighter* copy, complete with a theatre setting, a warning for first act, and an announcer's reminder that "again a gay and fashionable audience crowds every seat of our theatre." Arch Oboler was among the young writers who worked for this show. It folded after a year, but on July 4, 1945, a new *Curtain Time* with a similar theme opened on ABC for Mars Candy. This one starred Harry Elders in a regular leading man role, with Beverly Younger as the heroine of the week. Directed by Norman Felton, this version moved to NBC in 1946 and ran until 1950.

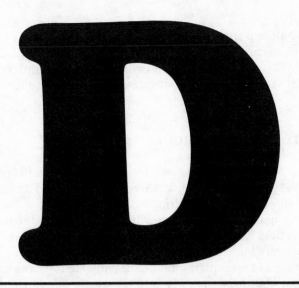

The Damon Runyon Theatre

The Damon Runyon Theatre was a good series, syndicated by Alan Ladd's Mayfair Productions, premièring on the West Coast in January 1949, and later in the East. It brought to life the people of Damon Runyon's New York. The stories were told through the eyes of a hood with a heart of gold. His name: Broadway; his accent: Brooklyn, and you could cut it with a knife. Unlike some dialect humor, Broadway's stories had warmth and appeal. John Brown did a fine job as lead, using a present-tense narration that moved the action well. Brown, a solid radio actor with a diverse background in comedy, had previously done Thorny on *Ozzie and Harriet*, Al in *My Friend Irma*, and Digger O'Dell on *The Life of Riley*. Assisting Brown were Alan Reed, Frank Lovejoy, Eddie Marr, Luis Van Rooten, Joe DuVal, Gerald Mohr, and William Conrad. Runyon's hoods weren't real, but they were interesting and funny. The shows were directed by Richard Sanville and written by Russell Hughes.

Danger, Dr. Danfield

Danger, Dr. Danfield, notable as one of the worst detective shows ever to curse the ABC airwaves, hit with a thud in 1946, starring Michael Dunn as Dr. Daniel Danfield, brilliant authority on criminal psychology, with JoAnne Johnson as his secretary Rusty Fairfax. What made Rusty especially obnoxious was her penchant for telling everybody off and sticking her foot squarely into her mouth. Danfield couldn't have cared less. Rusty was allegedly beautiful, and in 1946 maybe that was enough qualification for a steno job. Ralph Wilkinson, writer, and Wally Ramsey, producer, shared the blame for this one.

Dangerous Assignment

Dangerous Assignment was just another spy show, starting on NBC February 6, 1950, and running for three years. It starred Brian Donlevy as Steve Mitchell, globe-trotting troubleshooter for a Big Brother agency with tentacles everywhere. Mitchell got his assignments from a nameless boss known only as "The Commissioner." As Mitchell, Donlevy narrated the show, striving for a sense of listener identification by doing it in present (it's happening now) tense. Even that didn't save it from sinking frequently into the audio muck. Donlevy was flanked by Herb Butterfield as the commissioner, and by a regular cast of rotating characters including Dan O'Herlihy, Betty Lou Gerson, Paul Frees, GeGe Pearson, and Ken Peters. Betty Moran was the commissioner's secretary. Mitchell's theme: "Yeah, danger is my assignment—I get sent to a lot of places I can't even pronounce. They all spell the same thing, though—trouble." Another version of this show was syndicated, starring Lloyd Burrell as Mitchell. That one began with the theme: "Bagdad! Martinique! Singapore! And all the places of the world where danger and intrigue walk hand in hand —there you will find Steve Mitchell on another dangerous assignment!"

The Danny Kaye Show

The Danny Kaye Show premièred on CBS January 6, 1945. If judgment is reflected by popularity poll rather than Hooper rating, Kay's show was one of the most popular in the land. At least *Radio Daily* thought so. The magazine ranked him in fifth place among all shows. His Hooper of 12-plus wasn't a disgrace either, though writer Goodman Ace later described the show as a bomb. Kaye was on for just over a calendar year, broadcasting for Pabst Blue Ribbon. A veteran of vaudeville, Broadway, and movies, Kaye's stage training made him a superb radio comedian, a master of tongue-twisters and double-talk, at home with any dialect. Kaye could (and did) say "geet get gettle de de be basah da gat gat gettle de de be basah da gat gat gettle de de BEEP" week after week without missing a "gat gat gettle" or a "be basah." His company included Eve Arden, Lionel Stander, and Harry

James and his Music Makers. Ken Niles announced; Dick Mack directed. Writing for the series was Ace, Abe Burrows, and Sylvia Fine, who was Mrs. Kaye in private life. This was a solid variety show.

A Date with Judy

A Date with Judy demonstrated that radio was the medium for rampaging teenagers. The shows came in two forms: teenage boys and their troubles with girlfriends, and teenage girls and their troubles with boyfriends. *A Date with Judy* and its CBS counterpart *Meet Corliss Archer* were the female counterparts of *The Aldrich Family,* and *Archie Andrews.*

Of the four, *Corliss* was strongest; there was little to distinguish Judy from Henry, and Archie was beyond all hope. "Judy" was Judy Foster, and she first came to NBC June 24, 1941, as a summer replacement for Bob Hope's *Pepsodent Show.* While filming at Paramount, Hope had met a child star, 14-year-old Ann Gillis. He introduced her to his radio producers, she auditioned and won the title role for their new summertime situation comedy.

On that early version, Paul McGrath played her harried father, Melvin Foster; Margaret Brayton was her mother Dora; and 14-year-old Tommy Bond was brother Randolph. Lurene Tuttle played Judy's best friend Gloria.

Judy—hyperactive, intense, and unpredictable—created the usual adolescent chaos, keeping her father forever on the verge. Judy's favorite piece of furniture was the telephone; her favorite pastime, dating; her biggest problem, three consecutive nights at home when she didn't "rate a date." Boys who measured up became "super-dates." Eventually Judy settled down with a semi-steady oaf named Oogie Pringle.

By the summer of 1942, Ann Gillis had departed and 14-year-old Dellie Ellis had taken her place. Gloria had been deposed as "best friend" by a character named Mitzi, played by Louise Erickson. When *Judy* came back for its third replacement season in 1943, Miss Erickson took the title role and held it for the duration. Joe Kearns and Bea Benaderet were her parents. Eventually, the parental roles were taken by John Brown and Lois Corbett (Myra Marsh played Mom in 1945). Judy's pesty brother Randolph was played by Dix Davis, only 12 when he came to the show in 1942. Oogie Pringle was Richard Crenna, whose best radio role was Walter Denton on *Our Miss Brooks.* Sandra Gould was ultimately tapped as Mitzi. The production crew in the mid-1940's was virtually all female, with Aleen Leslie writing the scripts, Helen Mack directing, and Clara Groves providing sound effects.

A *Date with Judy* finally broke out of the replacement status in 1943, going into the Tuesday-night NBC schedule for Tums. In 1946, sponsorship went to Lewis and Howe. *Judy* moved to ABC for a final season in 1949–50, for Revere Cameras. She was a heroine in the breathless mold, like *Corliss Archer*. But the show falls somewhere below *Corliss* in the radio Hall of Fame, probably because of the nature of the boyfriends. Oogie Pringle was no Dexter.

A Day in the Life of Dennis Day

A *Day in the Life of Dennis Day* came to NBC October 3, 1946, when Colgate-Palmolive backed a series built around Jack Benny's singer-stooge. Day was a man of great vocal and comic talent; in the new format he was to play a character named Dennis Day—not quite the same Dennis who played on the air with Benny, but with the same screwball characteristics. This Dennis was a poor man, a lowly soda jerk at Willoughby's store who occasionally referred sarcastically to "that singer on the *Jack Benny Program*." His problems revolved around his low salary and his relationship with his girlfriend Mildred Anderson (Sharon Douglas and later Barbara Eiler) and her feisty parents. Dennis usually sang a couple of numbers, proving that he could sing at least as well as Jack Benny's Dennis Day. Scripts were prepared by Frank Galen. Frank O'Connor directed and music was by Charles "Bud" Dant. John Brown, always a pro, was Willoughby, Bea Benaderet was Mildred's mom, and Francis "Dink" Trout played her father, a henpecked creampuff who called his wife "Poopsie." The show ran for five years, finally bowing out in 1951.

Deadline Dramas

Deadline Dramas was an interesting Blue Network show of 1944, based on a fifteenth-century practice of Italian court players. Bob White, lifelong actor and prolific writer of radio and movie scripts, had read about the medieval improvisional theatre and developed it as a parlor game for his houseguests—mostly actors and actresses of the early 1930's. A decade later, White decided that the format would make good radio, and the framework was developed: listeners submitted a plot situation of no more than twenty words. White and his cast then retired to the soundproof control room, where they had two minutes to work out a fully developed plot. While they picked each other's brains, a sound man listened in via earphones, improvising his own effects and devising cues for organist Rosa Rio. When the trio emerged, they delivered a polished 7-minute playlet, to the amazement of the studio audience and those listening at home. White, the "plotmaster" of the group, was well qualified to build his situations on the spot. He had written some 1,500 radio shows and more than a dozen movies, and was currently writing *The Sea Hound* and directing *Dick Tracy*. His accomplices when the show opened were Joan Banks and Elsie Mae Gordon, who was known as "the girl with 100 voices." When Miss Gordon left, her spot was taken by Ireene Wicker, radio's famous "Singing Story Lady," who had been among White's original guests of the early 1930's. Three plots were used each week from the 1,200 submitted, and the contributors were awarded $25 war bonds.

Death Valley Days

Death Valley Days, a series of true dramas of the old West, was one of radio's earliest and longest-running adventure shows. First heard on NBC Blue September 30, 1930, the show was a regular fixture until 1941, when it switched to CBS.

Ruth Cornwall Woodman was an advertising copysmith in 1930 when the idea came along. Asked to create the format and write the scripts, Mrs. Woodman first ran into a problem of geography. For *Death Valley Days* was just what its name implies—a rugged Western, set in the remote Death Valley regions of California. And Mrs. Woodman, a banker's wife, Vassar graduate and longtime New Yorker, was well-rooted in an Eastern lifestyle. Before *Death Valley Days*, she had had little more than a passing interest in the desert, its history, or its people.

But within months, Mrs. Woodman was writing one of the most respected dramas of early, primitive radio. Through her annual story-gathering pilgrimages to the region, she quickly became a self-made expert in the habits of desert rats, prospectors, and saloon girls.

Because all *Death Valley Days* stories were rooted in fact, Mrs. Woodman had to spend up to two months a year on location, grubbing through ghost towns, interviewing old-timers, sifting through museums, and reading yellowed newsprint. Accompanied by acknowledged desert rat W. Wash Cahill, she scaled the mountains west of Death Valley to reach Panamint City, a tough mining town of the 1870's. She talked with small-town newspaper editors, old men who ran gas stations, proprietors of general stores, and—when she could get into saloons—bartenders. Then she returned to New York to write the stories she had gathered, and the following year she did it all again.

To tell her tales, Mrs. Woodman created the Old Ranger, a composite character who had known the bushwhackers, desperados, and lawmen of the old days by first name. The Ranger, introduced by Dresser Dahlstead to a fading, forlorn bugle call, reminded children not to miss upcoming stories. Teachers reminded them too. By 1940, the show's reputation for historical accuracy was well-established.

One of the early features of the show was the Lonesome Cowboy, John White, whose ballads were sung as an opening signature. That was soon dropped in favor of simpler openings. Dahlstead's introduction was straight and free of fanfare: "As the early morning bugle call of covered wagon trains fades away among the echoes, another true *Death Valley Days* story is presented for your entertainment by the Pacific Coast Borax Company, producers of that famous family of products—20 Mule Team Borax, 20 Mule Team Borax Soap Chips, and Boraxo. Well, Old Ranger, what's your story about tonight?"

Longest-running of the Old Rangers was Jack MacBryde, who joined the show in 1931. Jean King, also a much-heard regular, joined the company in 1932, mastering western dialect for scores of roles. Other veteran members of the cast were Frank Butler and Geoffrey Bryant. *Death Valley Days* was dropped in 1945, when the Pacific Borax Company, its longtime sponsor, switched to a new show, *The Sheriff.*

Detectives Black and Blue

Detectives Black and Blue, a very early comedy-mystery show, was syndicated about 1931. It followed the careers of two unlikely adventurers named (you guessed it) Black and Blue. They were shipping clerks in a Duluth market, but they yearned for action and adventure. Opportunity came in the form of a criminology correspondence course. Using the motto, "Detec-a-tives Black and Blue, good men tried and true," they opened an agency and helped set criminology back forty years. The shows were very primitive, using virtually no sound effects. The bulk of the "action" was carried in dialogue between Black and Blue.

Dick Cole

Dick Cole was another juvenile adventure series; syndicated in 1942, it was developed from a character in Blue Bolt Comics. Dick Cole, a modern Frank Merriwell, was a cadet at Farr Military Academy; with his friends Ted and Simba, he won football games, tracked down crooks, and brought new glory to the legend of Farr. The show opened each week with a rousing, sickish singing dedication to the academy:

We'll always be near to Farrrrr,
We'll praise her where'ere we arrrrre!
We'll cheer her each day
With a hip! hip! hooray!
It's a rule there's no school like Farrrr!

. . . and on and on and on ad nauseum.

The Dick Haymes Show

The Dick Haymes Show, built around the vocals of radio's wartime heartthrob, came to NBC June 20, 1944, as a Tuesday-night Autolite variety program. It was heard on CBS Saturdays in 1945–46 and Thursdays, still for Autolite, in 1946–47. Haymes came out of the old Harry James band, and for a time was seriously considered a staunch rival to Bing Crosby and Frank Sinatra for the nation's crooning crown. But his popularity waned after the war, and his final radio fling, the melodramatic *I Fly Anything* of the early 1950's, made no use whatever of his previously touted singing ability.

Haymes first starred on the air in *Here's to Romance*, a 1943 CBS Thursday-night show, with another old alumnus of the James band, singer Helen Forrest. Both left *Here's to Romance* to others when the Autolite slot opened on NBC. Miss Forrest co-starred with Haymes through the 1946 season. Her departure ushered in two new characters, Lina Romay and Mrs. Wilson, owner of a flower stand, played by Cliff Arquette. Mrs. Wilson, who wandered into the show at various times and never knew the time of day, was the singer's comic relief. Gordon Jenkins went all the way with Haymes as orchestra director.

Dick Tracy

Dick Tracy, protector of law and order, was developed from Chester Gould's comic strip and was heard in two respectable runs on the air. On September 30, 1935, the first *Tracy* serial opened on Mutual; it moved to NBC in 1937 and went off the air in 1939. The second run began and ended on the Blue Network (which became ABC in 1945), and spanned the years 1943–48. The radio show was complete with

Gould's supporting characters: Pat Patton, Tracy's detective sidekick; Junior, Tracy's adopted son; Tess Trueheart; Vitamin Flintheart; Flat Top. It opened with a burst of radio code and Tracy's terse summary of action, on wrist radio, naturally: "This is Dick Tracy, leading a search party on a hunt for Junior and Moccasin Joe, in 'The Case of the Hooting Owl.' " In 1946, ABC brought the characters into a short-lived Saturday-evening format, somewhat cornier and less intense than the serial, which was still running during the week. The Saturday shows were enacted to the unlikely theme, "Toot-Toot Tootsie," a low-key bow to the sponsor, Tootsie Rolls. Sidney Slon wrote the Saturday shows; John Wray and Everett S. Crosby did the serials. Tracy was played during the ABC run by Ned Wever.

Dimension X

Dimension X was first heard on NBC April 8, 1950, and ran until September 29, 1951.

Strange that so little good science fiction came out of radio; they seem ideally compatible, both relying heavily on imagination. Some fine isolated science fiction stories were developed on the great anthology shows, *Suspense* and *Escape*. But until the première of *Dimension X*–a full two decades after network radio was established—there were no major science fiction series of broad appeal to adults. This show dramatized the work of such young writers as Ray Bradbury, Robert (*Psycho*) Bloch, Robert Heinlein, Isaac Asimov, and Kurt Vonnegut. In-house script writer was Ernest Kinoy, who adapted the master works and contributed occasional stories of his own.

Dimension X was a very effective demonstration of what could be done with science fiction on the air. It came so late that nobody cared, but some of the stories stand as classics of the medium. Bradbury's "Mars Is Heaven" is as gripping today as when first heard. His "Martian Chronicles" was one of the series' most impressive offerings. *Dimension X* played heavily on an "adventures in time and space, told in future tense" theme. Actors who worked regularly on the show included Joe Di Santis, Wendell Holmes, Santos Ortega, Joseph Julian, Jan Miner, Roger De Koven, John Gibson, Ralph Bell, John Larkin, Les Damon, and Mason Adams. It was directed by Fred Weihe and Edward King. The deep-voiced narrator was Norman Rose.

The series played heavily on the "X" factor in the title, as did *X-Minus One* a few years later. The signature was boomed out of an echo chamber as "DIMENSION X X X X X x x x x x . . ."

The Dinah Shore Show

The Dinah Shore Show featured a young woman who left her Nash-ville home and set out to crack into radio. It was the summer of 1938, a good time to be alive, but big-time network radio wasn't easy to crack. Still, the 22-year-old brunette singer had broken into a CBS show with "Maestro" Ben Bernie by the spring of 1939. Five months later, on August 6, her own show premièred on the Blue Network as an early evening Sunday songfest. Fifteen minutes long, it ran through 1942, before expanding to 30 minutes and making a jump to CBS. Dinah's half-hour ran Thursday nights for Birdseye Foods, moved to NBC in 1944 and continued in the Thursday Birdseye format until 1946. She was heard Wednesday nights for Ford on CBS in 1946 and 1947. The soundtrack of her TV show was played on NBC for Chevrolet in a twice-a-week 1953–55 format. But Dinah's name as a 1940's star was made on The Chamber Music Society of Lower Basin Street and on The Eddie Cantor Show. She was most effective under "guest" billing—a refreshing personality, but not quite strong enough at that time to carry a full show alone. She appeared often with Bing Crosby, Bob Hope, and even with Archie of Duffy's Tavern. She signed with Cantor in the fall of 1940, after enjoying great success as Basin Street star, and was hostess for the 1943 NBC summer show, Paul Whiteman Presents.

Dr. Christian

Dr. Christian premiered on CBS November 7, 1937, as Dr. Christian of River's End. The format, like the good doctor himself, was simple and without gimmickry. Nurse Judy Price lifted the telephone and, in a cheery voice, said, "Dr. Christian's office." Nothing special—yet there are still many people who remember the opening, even though they can't recall a single specific story situation. If they're prodded vigorously, they might remember that it was also called "The Vas-eline Program—the only show in radio where the audience writes the script."

Quite literally, the audience did. Beginning in 1941, the show phased out the work of professional writers and turned for material to the listeners. That was the year the Dr. Christian Award was initiated, bringing the producers up to 10,000 manuscripts a year for consideration. The contest was climaxed by an award of $2,000 for the best script of the year, though other audience-written scripts were used and paid for in amounts up to $500. By the mid-1940's, the audience was writing virtually the entire show.

Dr. Christian was played by Jean Hersholt, who came to America from Denmark in 1912, headed for silent Hollywood, and liked it enough to become a citizen six years later. Longtime president of the Motion Picture Relief Fund, Hersholt became well-known for his "Dr. Christian" image offstage and on. Dr. Christian grew out of a 1936 Hersholt film, The Country Doctor, being the story of Dr. Allan Roy DaFoe, who became a sudden celebrity when he delivered the Dionne quintuplets. Hersholt wanted to bring his film character to the air. When he couldn't get the air rights, he decided to go ahead with a doctor series anyway. He mulled over names, and up popped Hans Christian Andersen, his favorite author. The name "Christian" was strong; it had a religious connotation that Hersholt liked. The name clicked with the people too, and the classic novel-to-movie-to-radio formula worked in reverse. RKO's Dr. Christian films began in 1939, with Hersholt in the title role. Finally, in 1944, the character came to literature, with publication of the novel Dr. Christian's Office.

Hersholt's name was linked with many charities, and his personal philosophy was locked into a "help others" theme. That was the way of Dr. Paul Christian, too—helping others so much that at least one reviewer wondered in print how the doctor found time to thump chests and push pills. Dr. Christian was forever involved in someone's life, and his involvement took many forms. One week he was the kindly town philosopher; the next week he was cupid. On at least one occasion Dr. Christian even became involved in a murder plot, and had to turn gumshoe with a stethoscope for a week.

Developing in that way, the show was borderline anthology. The only other regular character of note was Judy Price, the doctor's secretary. Judy was played for most of the run by Rosemary De Camp, who had broken into radio on One Man's Family a few seasons before. She had played on the brief Atlantic Family, and served in minor roles with The Goldbergs and The Columbia Workshop before winning the part of Judy.

Simplicity made Dr. Christian the great light drama of the air, and kept it around until 1953. The entire sixteen years was served on CBS, thirteen of them on Wednesday night, and all for the same sponsor. Hersholt went all the way in the lead, with the part played by Claude Rains for a brief run in 1945, when Hersholt went home to Denmark to survey needs for the National War Fund.

The Doctor Fights

The Doctor Fights came to CBS June 6, 1944, as a high-quality summertime salute to America's war doctors. It starred Raymond Massey in a new portrayal each week of some doctor on a far-flung battlefield, and was sponsored by the makers of the new wonder drug, penicillin. Produced and directed by Dee Engelbach, The Doctor Fights gained an immediate and enthusiastic audience, and was returned to the air for the summer of 1945. This time, instead of using one actor for the entire run, a guest-star system was initiated. Doctor roles were assumed by, among others, Robert Cummings, Gene Lockhart, Ronald Colman, Cary Grant, Robert Young, Van Heflin, and Robert Montgomery. The real doctor on whose experiences the play was based was then brought out for an informal chat. Jimmy Wallington announced; music was by Leith Stevens.

Dr. I.Q., The Mental Banker

Dr. I.Q., The Mental Banker came to NBC June 10, 1939; a dog and pony show that traveled to cities around the nation, playing vaudeville style on the stages of movie houses everywhere, spending a month in each location and using nine microphones to achieve its effect. Two of the mikes were simply for audience applause and laughter. Six were for roving assistants who were stationed throughout the theatre looking for contestants. And the last was for the man himself, Dr. I.Q.

Standing at center stage, Dr. I.Q. showered silver dollars upon anyone who could answer his questions. "I have a gentleman in the balcony, doctor," an assistant would offer. And immediately Dr. I.Q. would bark: "Six silver dollars to that gentleman if he can answer this question!" The questions were tough—even the cheapies. Why are a cat's whiskers the same length as the width of his body? What's the difference between jam and preserves? On what date does Easter fall this year?

The contestants did all right; even in its first year, sponsor Mars Candy was budgeting $700 a week for silver-dollar winners. By the end of its run, Dr. I.Q. had become a moderately large prize show. One contestant in Denver won $3,100 by identifying the Gettysburg Address as the source of a famous quotation. The "right or wrong" portion of the show—in which Dr. I.Q. read six rapid-fire questions and asked for "right or wrong" answers—had grown to $1,000 for the right answers to all six. Other well-remembered features included the "biographical sketch" (six clues to the identity of a famous person, submitted by listeners whose prize increased as the listener missed the clues), and the "thought twister," read "one time and one time only" by Dr. I.Q., with the contestant being required to repeat it verbatim. A typical twister: *Boxes can be opened when they're closed; boxes when they're opened can be closed.*

But in the early years, the jackpots were small and the pace fast. Contestants either won or lost on the spot. When they lost, the "Doctor" would offer sincere-sounding condolences, crowing "I'm sooo sorry—but a box of Dr. I.Q. candy to that gentleman!" and moving quickly along to the next person.

The first Dr. I.Q. was Lew Valentine, who started in radio as a singer-announcer with Station WOAI, San Antonio. Valentine gave up his "Doctor" role in 1942 for a three-year hitch in the army, and the job was taken by Jimmy McClain, a young theology student with his eye on the Episcopal ministry. McClain was Dr. I.Q. until May 27, 1946, when Valentine returned. For that show there were two "Doctors" onstage, as McClain and Valentine shared the job. Then McClain dropped out, announcing his intention to retire from radio and devote full time to the church. But McClain would return as *Dr. I.Q.*, taking a leave of absence from the ministry to host ABC's television version in 1954. Valentine continued as Dr. I.Q. until December 8, 1947, when he left to prepare a format for the new *Dr. I.Q. Jr.* show. During his ten-week absence, the "mental banker" was played by Stanley Vainrib. Allen C. Anthony, the genial, longtime announcer, made the candy in the commercials sound as appealing as the silver dollars on stage.

Dr. I.Q. ran on NBC for Mars from 1939 through 1949, a Monday-night mainstay. In 1949, the show was picked up by ABC for a final year, on Wednesdays.

Dr. I.Q. Jr.

Dr. I.Q. Jr. was often described as *Dr. I.Q.* in knee pants. It was a Saturday-afternoon children's show, premiering March 6, 1948, and running for one season. Actually, *Jr.* had its beginning May 11, 1941, starring Jimmy McClain in a brief show that failed, and then the idea lay dormant for seven years. The 1948 show was a copy of *Dr. I.Q.*, complete with Lew Valentine and sponsorship by Mars Candy. The difference was that the silver dollars to winners were replaced by silver dimes, and the questions were slightly easier. Features included the "tongue twister" (a variation of "I.Q.'s" "thought twister") and "history in headlines," in which great historical events were retold in newspaper language, with a 100-dime award to the contestant who pegged it. In this show, Mars announcer Allen C. Anthony appeared as Bugs Beagle in a weekly storytelling stint containing three factual errors. Prizes were given to contestants who pointed out the errors.

Dr. Kildare

Dr. Kildare was produced for syndication in 1949 at WMGM, New York. It was based on the popular Dr. Kildare movies of the late 1930's and early 1940's, and brought to the microphone the stars of that series, Lew Ayres and Lionel Barrymore. Ayres played the young, idealistic Dr. James Kildare; Barrymore, ever in character, was the crusty, lovable diagnostician, Dr. Leonard Gillespie. The men worked at Blair General Hospital, "one of the great citadels of American medicine—a clump of gray-white buildings planted deep in the heart of New York—where life begins, where life ends, where life goes on." The opening was moderately memorable—announcer Dick Joy shouting "The Story of Dr. Kildare!" then fading away to an echo-chamber reading of the medical oath by Ayres. "Whatsoever house I enter, there will I go for the benefit of the sick, and whatsoever things I see or hear concerning the life of men, I will keep silence thereon, counting such things to be held as sacred trusts." Kildare really believed that oath, and that's what this series was all about. His battles with hospital administration, stupid patients, and stupid parents made this the Marcus Welby of the 1940's. The chief problem, both for Kildare and the listener, was that Blair Hospital was peopled by too many eccentrics. Gillespie, played to the limit by Barrymore, was enough for any show. But Dr. Carew, head of hospital administration, was a nut of the first order. Nurse Parker was a totally unbelievable old maid. Ted Osborne did what he could with Carew, and Virginia Gragg's fine talent was hopelessly lost in the chattering role of Parker. In the end, Ayres and Barrymore saved this series, providing some solid stories, especially when they ventured into the real world and got away from the dummies at Blair. Writing and directing were done on a freelance basis; music was by Walter Schumann. Actors contributing to Dr. Kildare included Stacy Harris, Isabel Jewell, Jay Novello, Georgia Ellis, Paul Frees, Raymond Burr, and Jack Webb.

Dr. Sixgun

Dr. Sixgun was an NBC Western sustained by the network during the 1954–55 season. It told of a "guntoting frontier doctor who roamed the length and breadth of the old Indian territory, friend and physician to white man and Indian alike, the symbol of justice and mercy in the lawless west of the 1870's." It was a solid show, but again came too late to matter. The stories were told by Pablo, one of the doctor's sidekicks, played by William Griffis. Karl Weber was Dr. Sixgun. Harry Frazee directed and Fred Collins announced.

Don Winslow of the Navy

Don Winslow of the Navy, based on the Frank Martinek comic strip, premiered on NBC Blue October 19, 1937, and ran for two seasons. It followed the young naval intelligence commander in his pursuit of the evil mastermind, The Scorpion, the evil one's daughter Tasmia, and their worldwide organization of corruption and sin. Don, played by Bob Guilbert, was backed by his pal, Lieutenant Red Pennington, and best girl Mercedes Colby. Winslow was dragged out again on October 5, 1942, for another Blue run. This time, Red Pennington said in announcing the series, the enemies were Japs and Germans; the action was global. And they weren't kidding: Winslow and Pennington started the new series with a submarine battle and promised to give orders in future episodes on how the kids at home could keep the home front going. Under Post Toasties' sponsorship, this Don was played by Raymond Edward Johnson.

Doorway to Life

Doorway to Life entered the sensitive world of childhood psychological problems with dramatizations of actual case histories. The cases were combed by an advisory board, with senses tuned to the common mistakes made by parents and the likely result for their kids. Cases that seemed especially common were then referred to writers Virginia Mullen and Bill Alland for dramatization. The finished scripts were checked by psychologists for accuracy, and the goal of the show was to present "message" drama in such a simple way that no listener could miss the point. Problems explored included adoption, school, and dating. Hassles with parents became the backbone of the series. It was heard Thursdays on CBS in 1948, and became a showcase for such prime juvenile talent as Marlene Aames, Norma Jean Nilsson, Anne Whitfield, Henry Blair, and Johnny McGovern. William N. Robson created the series, and served as producer-director.

Dorothy Gordon

Dorothy Gordon was the name of the show and the name of the star. It was a three-a-week Mutual offering of folk tales, songs, and classics for children beginning on December 16, 1938, and running for one season. Miss Gordon had a long background in children's programming; she had served as musical director of *The American School of the Air* from 1931 to 1938, and with other children's shows going back to the mid-1920's. Her *Dorothy Gordon* shows were seen as an alternative to the thrillers that dominated the air at suppertime. It was a low-key production—so low-key that Miss Gordon persuaded her sponsor, Wheatena, not to put too much superlative balderdash in its spots, and to refrain completely from the frantic premium offers ("just one boxtop and ten cents") then rampant in children's radio.

Double or Nothing

Double or Nothing, more durable than most quiz shows, was heard on Mutual from September 29, 1940, through 1947 for Fennamint and other drug products; then on CBS as a five-a-week daytime show for Campbell Soups in 1947. The format was simple: an easy question for $2, a slightly harder one for $4, and so on to $10. When the $10 plateau was reached, contestants were eligible to play "Double or Nothing," to a "grand slam" question of $80. Higher prizes were awarded in the "Double or Nothing Sweepstakes." It was a pretty dull quiz. Walter Compton was host until 1943; John Reed King became emcee in 1943. He was followed in 1945 by Todd Russell. Walter O'Keefe, its best-known master of ceremonies, took over when the show went from Mutual to CBS in 1947. During the show of October 15, 1948, O'Keefe got quite a shock—while interviewing a waitress contestant, she began to talk in a matter-of-fact monotone about the psychological problems of a male friend. Ultimately, she said, a mutual friend had recommended that he "get a good-looking girl like you and take her home and just have a big screwing party." O'Keefe almost swallowed the microphone in his frantic effort to change the subject, but the damage had been done. The show had been carried live on the East Coast, and the CBS switchboard was jammed with indignant calls.

The network ordered all its West Coast affiliates (which transcribed the show for broadcast in different time slots) to cancel it and destroy the transcriptions. For whatever reason, *Double or Nothing* was dropped by CBS in 1947; it was picked up by NBC, still in daily form, for Campbell, until 1952.

Dragnet

Dragnet, offering police dramas of unprecedented realism, came to NBC July 7, 1949. For its first two years it was heard Thursdays for Fatima Cigarettes. Jack Webb had been active in radio for about four years before finding the series that finally shot him to fame. *Dragnet* did that, but it also stereotyped Webb, stamped him indelibly into his hardboiled role, Sergeant Joe Friday of the Los Angeles Police Department.

But if the stamp has been bad for Webb, it doesn't show. In the 1970's, a middle-aged Webb could still be seen cavorting with Harry Morgan in a revamped, modern version of *Dragnet* on television. Yeah, still Joe Friday. Still a cop, after more than twenty years.

With its first broadcast, *Dragnet* was a trend-setter. Friday was a cop's cop; his world unfolded every week in painstaking detail. Designed to show the cop's day-by-day routine and the tedious double-checking that leads to an arrest, *Dragnet* still managed to come alive and grab listener interest in its first five minutes. The listeners were totally in the dark; they didn't know any more than the cops. There is a crime. A woman is missing and her husband suspects foul play. Your job: find her.

The cases developed clue by clue. Suspects were identified only after careful questioning and checking. The evidence had to be strong, not merely circumstantial. Strong enough, perhaps, to convince a real jury of the suspect's guilt. Slowly it is gathered by listener and cop alike, as Friday takes us minute by minute through his day:

> It was Tuesday, June 17th. It was warm in Los Angeles. We were working the day watch out of burglary. My partner's Ben Romero. The boss is Ed Backstrand, chief of detectives. My name's Friday. I was on my way to work that morning, and it was 7:53 A.M. when I got to Room 45. Burglary Detail.

From that first immortal DUM-DE-DUM-DUM of Walter Schumann's theme, *Dragnet* was something special. Announcer Hal Gibney virtually commanded attention when—after those opening bars—he said, "Ladies and gentlemen, the story you are about to hear is true. Only the names have been changed to protect the innocent."

That phrase in itself would become a classic. The voices of Gibney and George Fenneman, tossed back and forth between story and commercial, kept the show moving at an intense pace.

For the next thirty minutes, in cooperation with the Los Angeles Police Department, you will travel step by step on the side of the law, through an actual case, transcribed from official police cases. From beginning to end, from crime to punishment, *Dragnet* is the story of your police force in action.

Dragnet became one of the first radio shows to effectively break the unwritten taboo against dramatizing sex crimes. It was the first show to effectively introduce the jargon of cops to the world. Through *Dragnet*, such terms as "MO" (method of operation) and "R and I" (records and identification) became known to people who had never seen the inside of a police station. Webb and company were helped by W. H. Parker, Los Angeles chief of police, who provided up to three cops as technical advisors and got a credit on the show. As director, (Bill Rousseau directed early episodes) Webb followed the paths of journalist and dramatist; his demand for detail and accuracy called for as many as 300 sound effects by five sound men in a single episode.

As *Dragnet* developed, the characters of Friday and partner Romero were expanded. Character-building quirks were incorporated into story lines. Friday was a bachelor who lived at home with his mother; his partner was a family man with family problems. Ben Romero was played by Barton Yarborough, well known to radio addicts as Cliff in *One Man's Family* and Doc Long on the original *I Love a Mystery*. When Yarborough died in 1951 the character Joe Friday went through a succession of partners before settling on Frank Smith.

Frank, a genial worrywart, was played to perfection both on radio and TV by Ben Alexander. Alexander was a veteran entertainer by the time his *Dragnet* slot opened, having learned the ropes as a child working in films under Cecil B. DeMille and D. W. Griffith. As Frank, he brought the show decided comic relief. When he wasn't playing cupid for Joe, he was fretting over some minor problem with his wife Fay, or worrying over the fact that she had packed his brown bag with tuna sandwiches for the third day in a row. Frank became the most human member of the small cast.

But it was Webb's show all the way. *Dragnet* bore the strong Webb stamp that would follow him through his professional life. When the banter with Frank was finished, there were still criminals to catch, still justice to be met. And they were. And it was. The *Dragnet* closing was pure Webb. Trial and punishment, summarized in a few brief sentences. DUMMMM-DE-DUM-DUM, and out. In 1951–52 Chesterfield sponsored the show on Thursdays, on Sundays from 1952 until 1953, Tuesdays 1953 to 1956. *Dragnet* ran until 1956, was televised with great success, and was the basis for a full-length *Dragnet* movie in 1954.

Dramas of Youth

Dramas of Youth was a Mutual show, starting in 1933 with dramatizations of the lives of famous people when they were young. It also employed the talents of the young, using teenage actors and actresses for its Saturday shows. A regular company of young talent worked on *Dramas of Youth*, including Louise Erickson, Rolland Morris, Peter Rankin, Barbara Eiler, Helen Thomas, Geraldine Nolan, Jean Lang, Don Chapman, and Charles West. It was produced and directed by Marion Ward until her death in 1940. Then the emphasis was changed slightly to include adaptations of classics and original plays.

The Dreft Star Playhouse

The Dreft Star Playhouse came to NBC June 28,1943, as an experiment to see if daytime radio could support a show of nighttime quality. It was first called *Hollywood Theatre of the Air,* but the name was changed in October 1943 to avoid confusion with other shows using the "Hollywood" angle. *The Dreft Star Playhouse* was an ambitious undertaking, spending up to $3,000 a week for "name" talent. It adapted romantic movies for the air, using the 15-minute serial format, broadcasting five times a week for Procter & Gamble. Producer was Les Mitchel; musical director was Dick Aurandt. The show's opener was "Bachelor Mother" with Jane Wyman. Among the other productions were "The Magnificent Ambersons" with Agnes Moorehead, "Hold Back The Dawn" with Maureen O'Sullivan, "Take a Letter, Darling" with Mary Astor, and "Suspicion" with Margo. The stories were usually wrapped up in five or ten episodes, but "Dark Victory" with Gail Patrick ran for about two months. A noble experiment, *Dreft Star Playhouse* nevertheless vanished from the air after the show of March 30, 1945.

Duffy's Tavern

Duffy's Tavern really began when Ed Gardner created the voice of Archie, the Brooklyn barkeep, for an obscure CBS show *This Is New York* in 1939.

Archie was the making of Gardner. Before the show came along, Gardner was strictly a third-string actor, though he had had long experience writing, directing, and producing for some of the networks' biggest shows.

For Gardner, success hadn't come without a struggle. Born Edward Poggenberg June 29, 1905, in Astoria, Long Island, he had dropped out of school at 16 to begin a wild decade of odd jobs. Ironically, his first job was playing piano in a saloon of the early 1920's. By 1929, he was selling pianos. That was the year he met Shirley Booth. She too had dropped out of school, striking out at 14 for New York's theatre district and a distinguished career behind the footlights. Late that year—on November 23, 1929—she and Gardner were married.

Miss Booth had already achieved a toehold for herself in the theatre, having appeared on Broadway as early as 1925. Her star rose much faster than Gardner's. Gradually he worked into radio as a writer-director. By 1940, he had done *Believe-It-or-Not*, *The Rudy Vallee Show*, *Burns and Allen*, and *Good News of 1939*.

He was in Hollywood, working on *The Texaco Star Theatre* when he began putting *Duffy's Tavern* together as a viable package. Gardner had created Archie while he was director of the CBS sustaining show, *This Is New York*. In one segment, Gardner wanted the voice of a "typical New York mug," and he couldn't find an actor to fill the bill. Twenty-eight minutes before air time, he was still auditioning actors for the part. In frustration, he took the microphone himself, to demonstrate how the lines should be read. Out of his mouth popped Archie. Archie was first heard in full dress July 29, 1940, on the CBS audition series *Forecast*. Then all the obscurity melted into ether when Gardner donned his apron and battered fedora and welcomed Colonel Lemuel Q. Stoopnagle and Gertrude Niesen as the first guests of *Duffy's Tavern*.

Duffy's Tavern was a fly-infested dive on New York's Third Avenue. The food was horrible, the service lousy, and the atmosphere dank. The one thing that was kept at a consistently high level at Duffy's was the insanity. When the format premièred on *Forecast*, it was quickly stamped as the most original new comedy of the year.

On March 1, 1941, *Duffy's Tavern* became part of the regular CBS lineup. It ran on CBS for Schick, Thursday nights through 1941. As a regular part of the 1941 lineup, Gardner surrounded himself with a small group of talented regulars, each a zany character in his own right. *Duffy's* was simply a state of mind, a showcase for the talents of Ed Gardner, Shirley Booth, Eddie Green, Charlie Cantor, and anyone who wanted to drop in. That's the illusion the show promoted—that anyone could (and probably would) drop in within the next half-hour—though the guest list was prepared as carefully as that on any high-powered variety show. Archie the barkeep made lampooning such guests as Roland Young, Deems Taylor, Bing Crosby, and Clifton Fadiman the specialty of the house. They came each week to the piano theme "When Irish Eyes Are Smiling." Charlie Cantor, an old vaudevillian and radio bit player who had once done criminal parts on *The Shadow* and *Dick Tracy* became Clifton Finnegan, the super-stupid customer whose every remark began with "Duh . . ." Eddie Green, who would find greater fame as Stonewall the Lawyer on *Amos and Andy,* played Eddie Green, the waiter. Alan Reed, whose best role on the air was Pasquale on *Life with Luigi,* became Clancy the Cop on *Duffy's.* And Shirley Booth was Miss Duffy, man-hungry daughter of the proprietor. Duffy himself never was heard, but he called every five minutes during the show to tell Archie how bad it was.

In 1942, *Duffy's* went to the Blue Network as a Tuesday-night feature for Ipana. The part of Miss Duffy had been especially written for Miss Booth,and was ideally tailored to her comic Brooklynese. The role was so completely hers that when she left the show in 1943 (the year after she and Gardner were divorced), the part never was satisfactorily filled on a permanent basis. Gardner had become expert in the finer points of New York dialect, and was convinced that only a true refugee from Flatbush could master it. A nationwide search was conducted for a new Miss Duffy. Gardner offered auditions to girls named Duffy as a promotional gimmick; he took the contests to the local level, with appeals in large cities across the country. He even resorted to mass auditions by telephone and transcription. The show was only a few weeks away from the fall première when Gardner signed Florence Halop, sister of Dead End Kid Billy Halop and a radio veteran at 20. Miss Halop, who had appeared on dozens of serials since her debut as a child on Milton Cross' *Coast-to-Coast on a Bus,* sounded more like Shirley Booth than Shirley Booth.

But Gardner was never fully satisfied with the part after Miss Booth's departure. More than a dozen girls were tried over the years, including Helen Lynd, Doris Singleton, Sara Berner, Connie Manning, Florence Robinson, Helen Eley, Margie Liszt, and Sandra Gould. But Shirley Booth continued to do a better characterization in guest appearances on other shows. She simply changed the name to Dottie Mahoney, but the Brooklynese was Miss Duffy all over. The only Miss Duffy ever to approach the quality of Miss Booth's was Florence Halop, who returned to the role in 1948 after an absence of several years.

In 1944, Ipana followed the show to NBC, where it was booked Friday nights until 1946 and Wednesday nights until 1949. In 1949, Blatz Beer took the show for a season on Thursdays. *Duffy's* finished on NBC as a Friday-night show in 1950–51.

Duffy's was good radio comedy, personally written by Gardner after Abe Burrows and a staff of top writers submitted a rough draft. Much of it holds up even after thirty years. "Duffy's Tavern, where the elite meet to eat, Archie the manager speakin', Duffy ain't here—oh, hello, Duffy," became one of America's best-known radio introductions. And Gardner became America's best-known butcher of the king's English. Nobody but Archie would say, "I tink you've given me da mucous of an idea." Who but Archie would say, "Listen, Eddie, wit good management, dis place could show a nice overhead?"

As Archie might say, Ed Gardner was one actor with plenty of "poi-sonal maggotism."

Dunninger the Mentalist

Dunninger the Mentalist featured Joseph Dunninger, master magician, hypnotist, and—it was claimed—a reader of minds. His ability as a "mentalist" developed during his youth, and he reportedly was able to tell his parents who was at the door or on the phone before receiver was lifted or door opened. Dunninger became a close friend of magician Harry Houdini and, by the early 1920's, was entertaining in vaudeville with a magic act of his own. His fame grew, and he was asked to perform before Presidents Theodore Roosevelt, Calvin Coolidge, and Franklin D. Roosevelt. His act amazed Thomas A. Edison, and Dunninger—ever on the alert for publicity—began to capitalize on his popularity with the famous. The result was a Blue Network show, which premièred September 12, 1943, and in January 1944 found as sponsor the Sherwin-Williams Company. In the show, Dunninger surrounded himself with a panel of "unimpeachable" judges—famous or well-known people who participated in the mind-reading stunts and swore to their authenticity. The judges included entertainers, politicians, editors, and once a justice of the New York Supreme Court. The show began with random readings from the audience—birthdays, names, addresses—and included more elaborate stunts as the evening wore on. Often he dismissed people briefly with "I thank you very much," after "reading" a brief snatch of thought. Dunninger emphasized that he was correct "only 90 percent of the time," but throughout his career there was much speculation on the possibilities of trickery. Still, no one ever collected the $10,000 standing award that Dunninger offered for proof that he used accomplices. His radio debut created a minor sensation, but his act soon became repetitious and rather boring. The show was dropped December 27, 1944, to be heard occasionally as a replacement and in early TV.

The Easy Aces

The Easy Aces, "Radio's laugh novelty," was created around 1930 on station KMBC, Kansas City. And, like many of the best radio shows, it came about by accident.

Goodman Ace was a movie and drama critic for the old *Kansas City Journal-Post* in 1928. Two events that year changed his life. He married Jane Sherwood (like himself a native of Kansas City), and he began doing his first primitive radio shows.

He began reading the comics on Sunday for $10 a show. His station was Kansas City's KMBC, an affiliate of the newly formed CBS. Later he began doing *The Movie Man*, based on his newspaper reviews, also at $10 a shot. Ace was finishing his *Movie Man* stint one night in the late 1920's when the program director frantically motioned him to stay on the air. The performers for the next 15-minute program hadn't arrived (and they never did, but radio in those days was like that), and the station was in a pickle.

Ace was in a pickle too. His material exhausted, he began to ad-lib. Jane, standing nearby, jumped into the breach, and they started an on-the-air dialogue. They talked about "last night's bridge game," and about a gruesome murder that had been committed a few days before. Ace talked about justifiable homicide. The experience left them slightly breathless, but delighted the audience. Favorable reaction poured in, and KMBC put *The Easy Aces* on as a regular feature.

It was soon so popular that it attracted network attention. A Chicago advertising man heard the show, and dangled $500 a week and a thirteen-week network contract before them. The Aces were brought to Chicago for a trial run on CBS; the show opened in October 1931. Eleven weeks later, their contract was up in the air, and they were facing cancellation. The network suggested that they test listener response by appealing for their show on the air. More than 100,000 letters swamped the station, and The Easy Aces was a solid network fixture for the next fifteen years.

By 1935, the show was done out of New York for NBC Blue, in three-a-week early evening format for Anacin. It was heard for ten years, moving to CBS November 24, 1943, where it ran Wednesdays as a half-hour. It was last heard there on January 10, 1945. The broadcasts were informal, the principals sitting around an old card table with a built-in, concealed microphone. NBC built the table to Ace's specifications early in the run, an effective remedy against mike fright, and they used it throughout the serial version.

Jane Ace was radio's mistress of misinformation. More openended double meanings flowed through her lips in 15 minutes than passed through the minds of Gracie Allen and Marie Wilson in a week. Jane brought the "Malapropian principal" to radio. Originated by the eighteenth-century British playwright, Richard Brinsley Sheridan, Mrs. Malaprop was a character whose sentences were filled with wrong words; because they strongly resembled proper speech, they had great comic effect. A century and a half after Sheridan, Goodman Ace—with the help of his wife's nimble tongue—was doing the same thing for radio.

To Jane, a problem became "the fly in the oatmeal." Her "time wounds all heels" and "Congress is still in season" were to become radio classics. When Jane had a tough day, her usual comment was, "I've been working my head to the bone." Delivered in a dry, Midwestern nasal twang, and accompanied by sparse sound effects and no audience reaction (the Aces never used an audience in the 15-minute shows), the result was a comedy serial that other comedians loved.

Ace wrote all his material. To keep the cast fresh, he permitted only one quick rehearsal reading just before broadcast. In the scripts, he never used his first name, referring to himself only as "Ace." Jane was simply Jane. Most of the early scripts, following the pattern set in that first accidental show, revolved around their talk over bridge. Later the "stories" branched out, but the story element was always incidental to the lines. It came to the accordion theme, "Manhattan Serenade," and featured four main characters: the Aces, Jane's "insufferable" friend Marge, and stuffy old Mrs. Benton. Mary Hunter, a receptionist in the studio, was tapped by Ace for the role of Marge, whose chief asset was an asinine giggle. Peggy Allenby played Mrs. Benton.

Ace was a highly original, fiercely independent writer who ran his show and tolerated no sponsor interference. For years he avoided personal contact with his sponsors, believing that personal meetings would ruin their working relationship. And Anacin—*Easy Aces'* longtime sponsor—kept its corporate finger out of Goodman's pie until late 1944. But then one day Ace got a sharp criticism from an Anacin officer of a musical bridge he was using. He replied in kind: he said he didn't like the way Anacin was packaged either—the company's practice of using cardboard boxes instead of tin was a gyp. Infuriated, Anacin canceled the show in January 1945.

The producers of *The Danny Kaye Show* signed Ace as chief writer at $3,500 a week. The show bombed, but by then Ace had left anyway. Out of work, he and Jane dusted off some old transcriptions of the originals and let ZIV syndicate them, turning a profit of some $75,000 a year. In August 1946, Ace was coaxed back to CBS as "supervisor of comedy and variety," where he worked on Robert Q. Lewis' *Little Show* and on *CBS Is There*.

In February 1948, the show was revived in half-hour format under the title, *mr. ace & Jane*, (exotic lower case is his) on CBS. In this version, Ace played an advertising man who lived next door to a radio announcer, giving him plenty of opportunity to satirize his two favorite targets. Jane was simply Jane.

CBS insisted that they do it up with orchestra and audience, and Ace grudgingly agreed. But he refused to ham it up à la Milton Berle, and they never did fully adapt to the audience format. So they passed from the radio scene in 1949. Ace continued working in the media, writing for a variety of TV shows. Jane died in 1974, writing finis to another of radio's most memorable chapters.

The Ed Sullivan Show

The Ed Sullivan Show came over the airwaves long before Sullivan became America's toastmaster on the pioneering TV show, *Toast of the Town*. The first *Ed Sullivan Show* premièred January 12, 1932, when CBS brought the New York newspaper columnist to the Tuesday-night air for a series of gossipy talk-and-interview shows. It ran one season and later became well-known as the launching vehicle for Jack ("Baron Munchausen") Pearl and Jack Benny. Both first spoke on the air in interviews with Sullivan, and turned up in shows of their own in 1932. Benny, after his appearance of March 29, 1932, seemed to know with showman's instinct that the new medium was for him, and gave up a lucrative stage contract to take his chances in radio. As for Sullivan, he signed years later with CBS for a Monday-night variety show, *Ed Sullivan Entertains*. That short-lived show ran in the fall of 1942.

The Eddie Bracken Show

The Eddie Bracken Show was basically an extension of the characterizations and situations developed by Bracken and William Demarest in their comedy films *The Miracle Of Morgan's Creek* and *Hail The Conquering Hero*. Bracken played the same sadsack bumpkin, the "eternal helper" who always manages to leave things more muddled than he found them. The show premièred on NBC February 4, 1945, in a Sunday format that featured Ann Rutherford as girlfriend Connie Monahan and Demarest as her crusty father. Janet Waldo was featured as another of Eddie's girlfriends, and the writing was by Robert Riley Crutcher. Though it got generally favorable reviews, ratings sagged and the show lasted only through the summer. It returned in the fall of 1946 as a CBS Sunday entry for Texaco. The same basic cast was assembled, with help from Cathy Lewis, Wally Maher, Irene Ryan, and orchestra director director Paul Smith. Bracken co-scripted with writer George Hope, putting more meat into his part in an effort to make the movie magic work on the air. It didn't, and *The Eddie Bracken Show* faded after the 1946–47 season.

The Eddie Cantor Show

The Eddie Cantor Show was the biggest blockbuster of early radio. Cantor had made several isolated appearances in primitive 1920's radio, one coming as early as 1921. But with his appearance on Rudy Vallee's *Fleischmann Hour* on February 5, 1931, his radio career began in earnest. Born Edward Israel Iskowitz on January 31, 1892, he was a product of New York's East Side. His Russian parents died when he was still a toddler, and Cantor was raised by a grandmother. As he grew, he learned the ways and language of neighborhood New York. He quit school at an early age, sang for change on a street corner, and eventually got a job as a singing waiter in a Coney Island beer garden where Jimmy Durante played piano. In 1908, he won $5 first prize in an amateur-night contest at Miner's Bowery Theatre, and soon after changed his name for professional purposes to Edward Cantor. He played vaudeville and joined a juggling act, where he was introduced in blackface, a straw hat, and horn-rimmed glasses. That characterization followed him through his vaudeville years, and began to fade only when Chase & Sanborn made him a radio star.

Cantor played in blackface with Gus Edwards, whose renowned ensemble of juvenile talent included Walter Winchell, George Jessel, and Bert Gordon. Gordon would later become famous working for Cantor, but they were all kids then. From vaudeville, Cantor's reputation grew quickly as he played Ziegfeld's *Follies*, Broadway, and in 1926, embarked on a career in films. But his greatest success came on the air.

He was the first of the great stars of vaudeville and burlesque to make it big in radio—almost a year ahead of Jolson, Wynn, Fred Allen, and Jack Benny, three years ahead of Crosby, seven years ahead of Hope. He trailed Rudy Vallee by a couple of seasons, but Vallee was cut from a different log. In fact, Eddie Cantor would later go down as a Rudy Vallee "discovery."

In a way, it was true. Cantor's first big radio break came, as it did for so many others, on Vallee's *Fleischmann Hour*. But stars like Cantor were easy discoveries. Already a vaudeville headliner when he first appeared with Vallee, Cantor's own show was a foregone conclusion.

By September 13, 1931, Cantor was on the air with *The Chase & Sanborn Hour*, which ran on NBC Sunday nights until 1934. It drew phenomenally high ratings and became one of the biggest shows of the early 1930's, soaring past Vallee's ever-popular Thursday show within weeks of its arrival. Cantor brought with him a cheering, laughing studio audience—one of the great taboos in the experimental days of the 1920's, when audiences were either banned outright or warned that the program was ON THE AIR, and they should utter not a peep. Cantor changed all that. He believed laughter was contagious, that it would reach out and grab the listeners at home. First he encouraged, then urged his audience to laugh, cheer, and applaud loudly. In a real sense, his audience became the final testing ground for his material. Six hours before each broadcast, Cantor would hold a full dress rehearsal in front of another studio audience. The reaction of the audience often dictated broad last-minute cuts and changes.

In his early days, he was promoted as "the king of clowns," a brash little comic with bulging eyes and a flair for irreverence. "The keynote of his capers is impudence," *Radio Stars* said in 1933; "a flip defiance of powers or persons stronger than himself." Listeners could dig that. When Cantor ran up against a bone-crushing osteopath in one of his early shows, the audience pulled for Eddie. The people loved the defiant "pfurttt" sound he made into the microphone. If the primitive rating system of those early days can be believed, Cantor's audience was colossal, topping even the peak years of *Amos and Andy*. By the middle 1930's, he was hauling in about $10,000 a show.

Cantor dropped out of radio briefly, touring overseas in 1935. His streamlined, 30-minute program opened on CBS for Pebeco Toothpaste in the fall of 1935, again as a Sunday-night feature. In 1936, sponsorship went to Texaco Oil; in 1937, the show moved to Wednesdays; in 1938 it went Mondays for Camel Cigarettes.

His show changed little from the mid-1930's on. In 1935, he hired Bert Gordon as stooge. Gordon (Barney Gorodetsky) stayed with him to the end. In 1936 Gordon created The Mad Russian, a harebrained character with a thick Slavic accent, who was soon one of the most popular features of Cantor's show. Gordon's standard "Russian" salutation, "How dooo you dooo?" never failed to click with the audience. Harry Einstein first introduced his idiotic Parkyakarkas on Cantor's show.

Following Vallee's example, Cantor had a continuing interest in young talent. He claimed among his discoveries George Burns and Gracie Allen, Bobby Breen, and Deanna Durbin. Billie Burke and Margaret Whiting appeared on his later shows. Longtime announcer was Harry Von Zell; Jimmy Wallington announced in earlier days. Cantor's longstanding trademark was his family life—wife Ida, who had married him in the uncertain days of 1914, and their five daughters. Cantor joked about his daughters throughout his later career. They weren't as sensational, but it is said that the five Cantor girls were as well-known as the Dionne quintuplets.

Cantor's show opened in 1931 to the music of Rubinoff and his musicians. Cantor's 1937 troupe included vocalist Pinky Tomlin, "telephone comedian" Saymore Saymore, Deanna Durbin, and Jacques Renard's orchestra. By 1938, Cookie Fairchild was leading the orchestra.

Cantor was off the air again in 1939; for a year he was virtually blacklisted after branding some U.S. officials as Fascists at the 1939 New York World's Fair. But NBC brought him back in the fall of 1940 with a show called *Time to Smile* for Sal Hepatica.

In 1942, Cantor signed Dinah Shore as a regular; she returned in 1943, and rejoined him in 1948. The 1942 season also saw the first appearance of 16-year-old ventriloquist Shirley Dinsdale and her dummy, Judy Splinters. Shirley and Judy first appeared with Cantor November 11, 1942, creating a sensation in radio circles as "Bergen's rival." Edgar Bergen, reacting to that in *Time* Magazine, termed Shirley "the best natural ventriloquist I ever saw." She was one of the few ventriloquists who could make her puppet really sing, and not just in a screechy falsetto. But in the end Judy Splinters was no match for Charlie McCarthy.

Cantor was one of the air's best-known pushers of charity; his special cause was the March of Dimes. Frequently with his celebrated signoff—"I Love to Spend Each Sunday with You"—he gave a free pitch for charity, treasury bonds, or some service organization. In 1944, broadcasting out of KPO, San Francisco, Cantor did a 24-hour marathon for war bonds, raising more than $28,000 a minute, for a grand total of $40 million. His show was heard Wednesdays until 1946, when Cantor went to Pabst Blue Ribbon. His Pabst show was heard on NBC on Thursdays in 1946–48, and on Fridays in 1948–49. Thereafter, Cantor moved into TV, with *The Colgate Comedy Hour* of 1950.

Cantor's last year in radio was little more than disc-jockeyism. On September 10, 1950, he leaped into TV and never looked back. Two years later, he was stricken with a heart attack. Cantor never really recovered the old bounce after that. He died on October 10, 1964.

Eleanor and Anna Roosevelt

Eleanor and Anna Roosevelt came to ABC in 1948, but the former first lady was no stranger to radio. Mrs. Roosevelt did a number of special broadcasts for both NBC and CBS during the 1930's; some were sponsored, with the fee going to charity. On February 15, 1935, her Friday-night CBS series, *It's a Woman's World*, brought issues of women to the air. In 1940, her NBC show was heard Tuesdays and Thursdays for Sweetheart Soap. Her commentaries were delivered in a hesitant, nervous voice, and she soon became widely mimicked at private parties. But by the late 1940's, she had emerged from her late husband's shadow to become a forceful, almost dynamic commentator. Her show, *Eleanor and Anna Roosevelt*, done with her daughter Anna Boettiger on ABC in 1948 and 1949, displayed these qualities and made coast-to-coast news. The first broadcast, November 8, 1948, was covered by both *Time* and *Newsweek*. Mrs. Roosevelt commented from Paris by transcription while Anna handled the rest of the show live. She blasted the "Dixiecrat" elements of the Democratic Party, calling on the party bosses to throw the boll weevil out for good. While Washington buzzed in reaction, *Variety* raved over Mrs. Roosevelt's courage and termed her "one of the standout commentators on the air." Anna provided a homey influence, discussing sports, apparel, and her memories of life in the White House, while Mother handled the weighty problems of the world. In a 1949 show, Mrs. Roosevelt discussed the plight of station KMPC, whose license was being challenged because of an alleged policy of slanting the news to a specific racial and religious bent. The shows were produced by John Masterson, John Reddy, and John Nelson. Nelson also served as announcer.

Ellery Queen

Ellery Queen was first heard on CBS June 18, 1939. It was based on the detective character created by Frederic Dannay and Manfred Lee, but the radio show was an unusual format, created and produced by George Zachary. Dannay and Lee also wrote for the radio show, turning out original mini-mysteries at $350 each. Near the end of each mystery drama, the action was stopped and a panel of "armchair detectives" tried to guess the solution. The "armchair" panel was generally drawn from the ranks of entertainment, literature, journalism, or politics (Deems Taylor, Ed Gardner, Lillian Hellman, and Margaret Bourke-White appeared), but their track record at guessing the killer was so dismal that the producers began soliciting its "experts" from the listening audience. That was even worse. The listeners were not only wrong most of the time, they were lifeless and dull *all* the time. Finally, Zachary arrived at the right formula: a panel of mystery writers imported from Hollywood. The "armchair detective" formula was modified over the years, as the show changed stars, times, and networks. The original Ellery Queen was Hugh Marlowe; Marion Shockley played his adventurous secretary Nikki. The show was heard for a season on CBS Sundays; ran Saturdays on NBC in 1941–44, the last two years for Bromo Seltzer; returned to CBS for a Wednesday-night run in 1945–47 for Anacin; and finished on ABC Thursdays in 1947–48. Queen was portrayed throughout as a modern-day Sherlock with a fine eye for clues. He usually entered the cases at the request of his father, the Inspector. Carleton Young played Queen during the early NBC run; Sydney Smith took part in the fall of 1943. As for authors Dannay and Lee, they were cousins who created Ellery over lunch one day in 1929. They also served on the radio show, *Author, Author,* another audio literary puzzler.

Elsa Maxwell's Party Line

Elsa Maxwell's Party Line premièred on the Blue Network January 2, 1942 with Elsa, the world's greatest party-giver, telling real-life stories about the great people she had known. It was Miss Maxwell's first regular radio stint, so the network brought in veteran announcer Graham McNamee to help her along. McNamee's job was to draw her out and serve as stooge for her gags and yarns. Elsa, who had been

giving parties on the grand scale since 1912, gave a weekly account-
ing of her battle of the bulge. Tipping the scale at 190 for the first
broadcast, she conducted an on-the-air war against flab, using a scale
built especially by the network and operated by McNamee. Sponsor of
the Friday show was Ry-Krisp, which was promoted as a great aid in
the fight against fat. By 1943, the show had disappeared from the
Blue, but a version could be heard as late as 1945 via Mutual and
transcriptions.

The Eno Crime Club

The Eno Crime Club came to CBS on February 9, 1931, as a 15-minute,
five-a-week thriller show. By the end of its first season the show had
undergone several transfusions: it had been revamped as a Wednesday half-hour, and finally offered as a twice-a-week (Tuesday and
Wednesday) inter-connecting drama, done in two 30-minute parts on
the Blue Network. That format carried The Eno Crime Club through
1934 and another change. That year it became Eno Crime Clues; in
1935 the format again reverted to 30 minutes, once a week (Tuesdays).
It was sponsored by Eno "Effervescent" Salt, and featured stories of
Spencer Dean, known to one and all as "The Manhunter." Written by
Stewart Sterling, who got unusual up-front billing, each Eno Crime
Club tale was billed as "another Manhunter mystery." It was a primitive bit of radio by later standards; its mysteries in the classic tradition
told of locked rooms and clues dropped hither and yon, with the
listener challenged to "match wits with the Manhunter." Edward
Reese and Clyde North served stints as Dean; Jack MacBryde played
his partner, Danny Cassidy. Eno Crime Clues was last heard in 1936.

Escape

Escape, radio's greatest series of high adventure, began an irregular
run on CBS July 7, 1947, with Rudyard Kipling's "The Man Who
Would Be King."

Week in and week out, Escape was one of the best shows on the
air. Yet it never was a major continuing series in its own right. Shifted
here and there, used often as a summer replacement for such shows as
Suspense, Escape never was able to attract a permanent sponsor and
establish a steady time slot of its own. The Richfield Oil Company
came aboard briefly in the summer of 1950, but for most of its run
Escape was sustained by the network. With its small, sustaining
budget, Escape didn't have the higher-priced film stars who often
appeared on Suspense. Instead, a steady group of radio's old pros put

the series together. Luis Van Rooten, Jay Novello, Jack Webb, Sam Edwards, Virginia Gregg, Georgia Ellis, Parley Baer, Ben Wright, Lawrence Dobkin, John Dehner, Vivi Janniss, Edgar Barrier, Berry Kroeger, Byron Kane, Wilms Herbert, Frank Lovejoy, and Jack Kruschen worked often on *Escape*. William Conrad and Paul Frees were the shining lights. Frees did the announcing in the early days; Conrad took over later. With his million-dollar radio voice, Conrad's opening was letter-perfect:

Tired of the every day grind?
Ever dream of a life of . . . romantic adventure?
Want to get away from it all?
We offer you—ESCAPE!
Conrad's voice blended into a drum roll, and a fiery rendition of "Night On Bald Mountain," the show's theme. *"Escape! Designed to free you from the four walls of today for a half-hour of high adventure!"*

Listeners came to expect gripping tales of high adventure, often better than what they heard regularly on *Suspense*. *Escape* employed tighter writing, leaner, more intense plots, and acting that was at least as good. The main difference between *Suspense* and *Escape* was one of emphasis. *Suspense*—though it too had stories of adventure—concentrated more on mystery and crime. *Escape* was concerned with life-or-death situations, with violent twists of fate, delving more into the supernatural, into the blood-and-guts world of the jungle, into war and the old West. Never on radio was the action formula better utilized. Within five minutes, *Escape* listeners were literally up to their earlobes in alligators.

In its early days, *Escape* took its stories from the classics of adventure—from Joseph Conrad and H. Ryder Haggard and Edgar Allan Poe. Later, original scripts were used, but *Escape* was still doing such well-known adaptations as Daphne Du Maurier's "The Birds" and Jack London's "The Scarlet Plague" in its last year.

Many of the stories dramatized on *Escape* became radio classics and were later redone on *Suspense*. Listeners were first subjected to the horrors of man-eating ants ("Leinengen vs. the Ants," January 14, 1948) and to the plight of three men trapped in a lonely lighthouse overrun by rats ("Three Skeleton Key," November 15, 1949) on *Escape*. The series offered such imaginative plays as "The Time Machine" and "The Country of the Blind," by H. G. Wells, and "A Diamond as Big as the Ritz," by F. Scott Fitzgerald. In "Evening Primrose," a disgruntled poet took shelter in a department store, and there found a world of night dwellers and unimaginable horror.

"Present Tense" was a tricky tale exploring the inconsistencies of a condemned man's mind, while "Poison" delivered a tense commentary on the poisons of racial prejudice. One of the best dramas ever done was "Earth Abides," based on the end-of-the-world novel by George Stewart, and heard on *Escape* in two parts, November 5 and 12, 1950.

Producer-director for much of the run was the talented Norman Macdonnell, who seemed to get a rock-hard performance almost every time out. William N. Robson, "the master of mystery and adventure" on the waning days of *Suspense*, also had a directional hand in *Escape*.

Stories were adapted by Les Crutchfield, with editorial supervision by John Dunkel. Organ music was played by Ivan Ditmars. The musical score was conceived by Cy Feuer; later arrangements were by Del Castillo, Wilbur Hatch, and Leith Stevens. Writers included John and Gwen Bagni, Kathleen Hite, Joel Murcott, Antony Ellis, Morton Fine, and David Friedkin. Sound men were Bill Gould and Cliff Thorsness, who termed the sound of rat hordes on "Three Skeleton Key" their most difficult assignment. Roy Rowan worked with Frees as a second announcer; the program ended September 25, 1954, with the science fiction drama, "Heart of Kali."

The Eternal Light

The Eternal Light was first heard on New York's WEAF October 8, 1944, went on a nationwide NBC hookup in 1946, and could still be heard in the mid-1950's. It was a joint project of the network and the Jewish Theological Seminary, offering dramatized incidents of the ancient Judaic past and other Biblical dramas. The Seminary, under the direction of Dr. Moshe Davis, did the research; the network provided the air time and shared the production expenses. Frank Papp directed; Morton Wishengrad wrote the scripts, and original music was by Morris Mamorsky under the direction of Milton Katims.

Ethel and Albert

Ethel and Albert, following in the pattern set by Paul Rhymer's *Vic and Sade*, was a daily 15-minute comedy show built around an average couple and their lives in the little town of Sandy Harbor. Further following in the Rhymer pattern, Ethel and Albert were generally the only two characters who appeared, fleshing out other townspeople with their dialogue. But where Rhymer's comedy was deliberately absurd, Peg Lynch, writer of *Ethel and Albert,* cast her serial in a more realistic vein. "The big events in one's life occur only now and then, but there are some smaller events in everyday life that are familiar to every family," the announcer said. "And it's these daily incidents that make up the private lives of Ethel and Albert."

Ethel and Albert were the Arbuckles. They had one daughter, Susy, and Albert was manager of an office in Sandy Harbor. Each day for a dozen minutes they chatted about these everyday incidents: their troubles with the new babysitter; the fact that Ethel had made a $5 bet with a neighboring housewife on the heavyweight championship fight, to cancel out Albert's bet with the neighbor's husband; Albert's hassles exchanging a lighter for a cigarette case for his brother-in-law's Christmas present, only to learn that said brother-in-law had quit smoking. The result was an afternoon bright spot that, though it never rivaled Rhymer's show for inspired lunacy, had a certain charm all its own.

Miss Lynch began the show at Station KATE, Albert Lea, Minnesota, in 1938; it opened on ABC in 1944, with the author playing Ethel and Richard Widmark cast as Albert. When Widmark left for movie stardom, Alan Bunce got the job, and held it until the show left the air in 1950. Bunce had never heard of *Ethel and Albert* when he auditioned for the role, and was generally considered the worst actor who tried out for the part. But as Miss Lynch recalled years later, he had certain Albertish qualities and was kept over the protests of 800 letter-writing fans. Robert Cotton was producer-director through most of the network run; the show was billed for a time as *The Private Lives of Ethel and Albert,* and was introduced to chimes playing "There's No Place Like Home."

The Ethel Merman Show

The Ethel Merman Show was proof that success on stage was no guarantee of success on the air. Miss Merman was a star at 24 when on May 5, 1935, she first tried a musical-variety series. It was called *Rhythm at Eight,* and was plugged into the CBS Sunday schedule for Lysol. *Rhythm* had a thin story line built into its fabric, but mainly it served as a showcase for Ethel's "knock 'em down" voice. Unfortunately for Miss Merman, she was scheduled against *Major Bowes' Amateurs,* then at the peak of its popularity. She never made a dent, and *Rhythm at Eight* was yanked off the air after thirteen weeks. Undaunted, Miss Merman returned to Broadway. Fourteen years later, she came back for another try, this time on NBC. The format was much like the first—flimsy comic story line and Merman musical cutups. It went on the air, again on Sunday, on July 31, 1949. The story revolved around the attempts of Merman and her pianist-friend, Eddie McCoy (Leon Janney), to stage a musical revue. Allen Drake played Homer Tubbs, the floormop king and "angel" of the new Broadway show. It was written by Will Glickman and Joe Stein, produced and directed by Kenneth MacGregor, and, like the earlier show, it failed to last out the year.

The Eveready Hour

The Eveready Hour was the first major variety show of the air, premièring on WEAF, New York, December 4, 1923. For much of its first year, the program was heard irregularly—sometimes once a week, occasionally as many as three times. It was produced by George C. Furness, manager of the radio division of the National Carbon Company, which sponsored it. Without doubt one of the great ground-breakers of radio history, The Eveready Hour offered everything from opera to jazz, comedy to straight drama, minstrel shows to lectures. Furness conceived the show after hearing a stirring dramatization of Ida Tarbell's "He Knew Lincoln" on WJZ; he used this same drama often on The Eveready Hour, repeating it each year on Lincoln's birthday. Throughout the early weeks, the show featured minstrels, poems by Edwin Markham, and the skit, "The Governor's Lady," starring Emma Dunn. Other shows featured Cissie Loftus, Ernest Thompson Seton, and Yap's Hawaiian Ensemble. In September 1924, the battery company arranged with WEAF for a continuous weekly hour, which continued until 1930. In 1926, with the formation of NBC, The Eveready Hour was instituted as a network variety show, running for three years on Tuesdays. Paul Stacey directed the early shows. He left in 1927, and Douglas Coulter took over. Nathaniel Shilkret directed the orchestra. One of the most popular early shows was "Galapagos," telling of explorer William Beebe's trip to the Galapagos in the words of Martin "Red" Christianson, who had once been marooned there. Among the great early entertainers who appeared at The Eveready Hour microphones were George Moran and Charlie Mack (the Two Black Crows), Joe Weber and Lew Fields, Will Rogers, the Revelers, John Drew, Eddie Cantor, Ignaz Friedman, Richard Dix, Pablo Casals, Julia Marlowe, George Gershwin, Lionel Atwill, D. W. Griffith, Belle Baker, Beatrice Herford, and the Flonzaley String Quartet.

Everyman's Theatre

Everyman's Theatre was a mixture of Arch Oboler dramas and adaptations, that was heard on NBC from October 4, 1940, through March 28, 1941. It continued the techniques (offbeat plotting, realistic sound effects, and stream-of-consciousness narration) that had won Oboler national acclaim in Lights Out and Arch Oboler's Plays. In fact, it used some of the same dramas from each of those earlier series. The show opened with "This Lonely Heart," starring Russian actress Alla Nazimova, a miniature version of a 1939 Plays show. The third offering, "Cat Wife," was one of Oboler's most successful shows on Lights Out. Many Hollywood stars, such as Joan Crawford and Ronald Colman, were avid admirers of Oboler's talent and sought out opportunities to appear in his plays. Among the Everyman's offerings were "Mr. and Mrs. Chump" with Walter Huston, "I'll Tell My Husband" with Mary Astor, "Flying Yorkshireman" with Charles Laughton and Elsa Lanchester, "Of Human Bondage" with Bette Davis, and "Madame Affamee" with Marlene Dietrich. As usual, Oboler directed as well as wrote. The show was sponsored by Oxydol.

Everything for the Boys

Everything for the Boys was a unique collaboration between actor Ronald Colman and writer Arch Oboler to provide servicemen on Allied fighting fronts whatever they wanted in the way of dramatic entertainment. The half-hour series, sponsored by the Electric Auto-Lite Company, was first heard on NBC January 18, 1944. It was a natural outgrowth of Oboler's devotion to the war cause and his friendship with Colman. That friendship began when Oboler moved to Hollywood in 1939. One of the welcoming calls he received was from Colman, who had been deeply impressed by Arch Oboler's Plays, an NBC series which until then had been produced in Chicago. Colman wanted to work with Oboler, and said so. Oboler was honored; for years Colman had shunned radio, and now he offered to do the Plays show, "The Most Dangerous Game," for nothing. Colman was adamant; he accepted only the $17.50 union minimum for his performance. Their collaboration in Everything for the Boys was a study in contrasts, with the suave Colman and the sweat-shirted Oboler strangely complementing each other's abilities. It resulted in 20-minute dramas by Oboler, starring Colman or a famous guest. Much of Oboler's work in this show consisted of adapting classics for radio, a chore he insisted was impossible to do well in 20-minute doses. *Everything for the Boys* produced such modern dramas as "The Petrified Forest" with Ginger Rogers, "Lost Horizon" with Mercedes McCambridge, "Of Human Bondage" with Bette Davis, and "This Above All" with Olivia de Havilland. The remaining ten minutes of the half-hour shows consisted of shortwave interviews with fighting men everywhere, from Algiers to the invasion bunkers off the coast of Europe. Gordon Jenkins provided the music. After Colman and Oboler left, the show was revamped with Dick Haymes as star.

Exploring the Unknown

Exploring the Unknown featured stories of "science at work, searching for knowledge that will shape your future." It was produced by Sherman H. Dryer Productions for broadcast on Mutual. Sponsored by the Revere Copper and Brass Company, *Exploring the Unknown* ran on Mutual from December 2, 1945, through 1947, taking its science theme to its broadest aspects. The stories moved from entomology to sociology to psychology, telling of man's battles against disease one week, denouncing race hatred the next. Such stars as Orson Welles, Veronica Lake and Paul Lukas appeared. After the 1947 season, *Exploring the Unknown* moved to ABC for one season (1947–48) as a sustained offering.

Exploring Tomorrow

Exploring Tomorrow, rather an obscure science fiction show, was heard on Mutual in 1957–58; it invited listeners to "step into the incredible, amazing future." John Campbell, Jr., late editor of *Analog Magazine*, was the "guide" to this futuristic world, Sanford Marshall was producer-director. Radio was well over the hill by the time this series appeared; some of the stories had been better handled on *X-Minus One* a season or so earlier, anyway. Mandel Kramer, Bryna Raeburn, Lawson Zerbe, Lon Clark, and other old pros from the acting ranks helped save the program. Campbell returned at the end of each show, with a few words of philosophy set against the unlikely string theme, "As Time Goes By."

Eyes Aloft

Eyes Aloft, first heard on NBC Pacific Coast stations in July 1942, was the result of an army appeal to the network to help bolster its sagging aircraft warning system. The initial heat of Pearl Harbor had worn off, and the army was having trouble getting skywatch volunteers. *Eyes Aloft* offered dramas of aircraft warning system people and the work they did. It was written and directed by Robert L. Redd of *Point Sublime*, and was aired on the West Coast, where fear of Japanese attack was rampant in the months after December 7, 1941.

The Fabulous Dr. Tweedy

The Fabulous Dr. Tweedy premièred June 2, 1946, as a summertime replacement for *The Jack Benny Program*. It starred Frank Morgan in an NBC situation comedy format that gave rise to the absent-minded professor and exposed another facet of Morgan's ability. Until then, he had been known chiefly as a teller of tall tales, through the 30-minute comedy show he shared with Fanny Brice. When they split up, Morgan went into situation comedies, and *The Fabulous Dr. Tweedy* was the result. Morgan played Thaddeus Q. Tweedy, dean of men at a small college called Pots. Here he lived with his adopted son Sidney and an ex-hobo manservant named Welby. Nana Bryant co-starred as Miss Tilsey, head of the school, and Barbara Eiler was also a regular. Scripting was by Robert Riley Crutcher; Harry Von Zell co-starred.

The Falcon

The Falcon, Drexel Drake's suave detective, came first to the screen in a slick series of RKO Radio Pictures. From there, it was one step to radio with Berry Kroeger playing the role on ABC in the fall of 1943. On July 3, 1945, *The Falcon* emerged on the Mutual network as a Tuesday-night mystery series. James Meighan starred as Michael Waring, "that freelance detective who's always ready with a hand for oppressed men and an eye for repressed women." Waring, for reasons

more dramatic than practical, was known to friend and foe alike as the
Falcon. The format was built around the telephone. The show began
with the phone ringing; inevitably there was some gorgeous dish on
the other end. Waring's greeting was smooth, laced with a slight trace
of British put-on, and very identifiable. Always addressing women as
"Angel," he begged out of a date each week, with such excuses as,
"I've got to teach some gangsters that you can't get away with
murder—especially since the murder they want to get away with is
mine!" That was our entrée, as the bouncy *Falcon* theme blended into
an opening signature. Waring's style was somewhere between *Ellery
Queen* and *Richard Diamond*. He had a fine eye for detail, but was
usually on the outs with the cops. Little matter; in this show, as in
many detective thrillers of the air, the cops were stupid anyway. The
Mutual series was sponsored by Gem Razors and Blades, and contained one of the most memorable commercials of the era. In a whispering voice, the announcer spoke against the ticking and tolling of a
clock, dropping each word between the clock's chimes:

> Avoid . . .
> > . . . five . . . o'clock . . .
> > > shadow! . . .

Use Gem Blades! . . . Use Gem Blades! . . . Use Gem Blades!
The show was produced by Bernard L. Schubert. Meighan played the
title role for several seasons, then passed it to a succession of actors,
most notably Les Damon. The Gem Razor Tuesday-night series ran on
Mutual from 1945 through the spring of 1947. Then Mutual moved it
to Monday in 1947 and Sunday in 1948, where it was sustained until
1949. Anahist picked up sponsorship of the show in 1949. In the fall
of 1950, announcer Ed Herlihy came aboard for Kraft Cheese, which
sponsored the show on NBC Sunday nights until 1951. It was again
sustained in 1951–52, returning to Mutual as a Monday-night General
Mills series in 1952–53. *The Falcon* was last heard on Mutual in 1954.
The part of Waring was also played by Les Tremayne.

Family Skeleton

Family Skeleton, a Carlton E. Morse creation, ran on CBS from June 8,
1953, until March 5, 1954. The format, if not the content, was patterned after his highly successful *One Man's Family*. Morse developed *Family Skeleton* in episodes and phases (he wrote *One Man's
Family* in chapters and books), but *Skeleton* just didn't measure up. It
was the story of Sarah Ann Spencer (played by old Morse alumnus
Mercedes McCambridge) and her fight for happiness. A look at a

typical chapter gives a clue to the nature of this one. Episode 20, Phase 2 is titled, "Sarah, Have You Come Home to Cry Over Spilled Milk?" Sarah, pregnant and worried, brings a scandal with her when she returns home. She says she's married. Her growing abdomen says she'd better be married. But is she really? The town is ready to believe the worst, and Sarah's certificate has been obliterated by bloodstains. Interesting, as something less than first-rate Morse. The cast also included Herb Vigran and old Morse favorite Russell Thorson.

Family Theatre

Family Theatre premièred on Mutual February 13, 1947, with strong dramas of family life. It was broadcast from Hollywood, using the talents of top movie stars. The first show was "Flight From Home," starring Loretta Young and Jim Ameche. That established the high standards that marked the show through its ten-year life. *Family Theatre* was presented by Father Patrick Peyton of the Holy Cross Fathers, and throughout the run only one commercial was heard—the continuous plea for family prayer in America.

Most *Family Theatre* shows were upbeat, but the series also produced tragedies, war stories, classics, and even some Westerns and science fiction. The only requirement was that the story illustrate—without obvious moralizing or preaching—the value of family love and group prayer.

Several memorable slogans came out of *Family Theatre*. Week after week, guest stars reminded us that "the family that prays together stays together." Then announcer Tony La Frano, using an echo chamber for greater effect, drove the point home: "More things are wrought by prayer than this world dreams of." After the play, we were gently reminded that "a world at prayer is a world at peace," and La Frano signed off with the traditional *Family Theatre* hope—"That the blessing of God may be upon you and your home."

But *Family Theatre* wasn't a religious show. Even stories of brutality were used, when they served the theme. Ironically, the worst shows were the sticky family comedies that contained too-obvious morals. The best offerings were those that got outside the theme of family life. When the series offered "Moby Dick" or "Robin Hood" or "The Gold Bug," it was on solid ground. And it can probably safely be stated that *Family Theatre* assembled as many superstars as any 30-minute show ever.

Within its first two months, *Family Theatre* had presented Walter Brennan, Beulah Bondi, Bing Crosby, Irene Dunne, Van Heflin, Margaret Sullavan, J. Carrol Naish, Pat O'Brien, and Ethel Barrymore.

Miss Barrymore's "Passion, Death and Resurrection" became, for a time, a traditional Easter offering. Others who appeared in early *Family Theatre* shows were Gary Cooper, Gregory Peck, Chester Morris, Charlie Ruggles, Ozzie and Harriet Nelson, Vincent Price, William Holden, Robert Young, Jimmy Durante, and Dennis Day.

The host was usually a name star, and often the play itself contained one of more stars of equal stature. Many directors worked on the show. Those who put in the most time were Jaime Del Valle, Joseph Mansfield, John Kelley, and Robert O'Sullivan. For a time in the 1950's, Henry Mancini scored the music. The program stayed on the air until 1957.

Famous Jury Trials

Famous Jury Trials, a collection of great moments in American jurisprudence, came to Mutual September 28, 1936, as a Monday-night show for Mennen Aftershave. After one year for Mennen it was heard as a sustaining program before moving to the Blue Network in 1940 and a six-year run for O. Henry candy bars. It was heard on Mondays in 1940–41; on Tuesdays in 1941–44, and on Fridays in 1944–46. In 1946, the show moved to Saturdays, still on the Blue (which by then had become ABC). General Mills carried it in 1947 and 1948. It ran one final season as a Saturday ABC sustainer in 1948–49. The early shows were dramatized and produced by Don Becker, after long research through court records. By the time they got on the air, they were almost entirely fictionalized anyway. It was billed as "the dramatic story of our courts, where rich and poor alike, guilty and innocent, stand before the bar of justice." That said, we entered the court, where a judge was instructing his jury: "Gentlemen of the jury, you are the judges of the evidence to be laid before you. Be just, and fear not, for the true administration of justice is the foundation of good government." Among the techniques used on *Famous Jury Trials* was that of transporting a radio announcer back in history to report a great trial of the past "as it happened." This was used some fifteen years before *You Are There* adopted it as a general format.

The Fat Man

The Fat Man was created by Dashiell Hammett especially for radio. The show was first heard on ABC January 21, 1946. The opening of the program was packed with contrasts, a sure-fire attention-getter and perfect for radio. It started with the sweet sound of a harp, which blended into that first immortal mention of Pepto Bismol by announcer Charles Irving:

> When your stomach's upset . . .
> Don't add to the upset . . .
> Take sooooooooooothing Pepto Bismol . . .
> And feel—goooood again!

Again the harp came up, and we did the drugstore scene with Runyon.

> His name: Brad Runyon. There he goes now, into that drugstore.
> He's stepping on the scale.
> Weight? Two hundred thirty-nine pounds. Fortune—danger!
> Whooooooooo is it?
>
> *The Fat Man!*

The sound of that penny dropping into the scale was amplified, adding to the already firm illusion of the hero's weight. Then, that music—marvelously low and bassy, created especially for *The Fat Man.* Eight notes blown squat and fat out of a bass horn. Then Runyon himself came in, with a short "crime does not pay" prologue, delivered in that unique style:

> With the possible exception of a ticket for parking or passing a red light, most people go through life without a brush with the law. But there is a very small minority who seem to devote their entire careers to hating cops and statute books. They usually matriculate at San Quen-nnnn-tin and take a postgraduate course in Leavennnn-worrrth. And some of them end up in the death house, due to a slight case of murrrrr-derrrrr!

After the commercial, the announcer inevitably launched into the show with, "Now let's catch up with *The Fat Man.*"

Runyon was the one gumshoe of the air who couldn't be copied. It wasn't only his Rock-of-Gibraltar appearance that chief scripter Richard Ellington built into our minds; a lot of it had to do with the way Runyon handled himself—that hardboiled, tough way he had of dealing with difficult people. That was a direct gift from the master of the hardboiled school, Hammett himself. And the way Runyon talked. The Fat Man didn't mess around. When he said murrrr-derrrr, brother, murder it was.

Stepping into those oversized shoes was J. Scott Smart, who

weighed 270 pounds himself and filled them nicely. Runyon's size 58 belt fit Smart too, and his voice was just right. He had had a lot of practice in front of a microphone, starting with *The March of Time* in the early 1930's. Smart had worked on such top network shows as *Theatre Guild on the Air, Blondie, The Fred Allen Show,* and *The Jack Benny Program;* he had done stints in films and on stage. A squat man who often appeared in bow tie and suspenders, Smart gave a witty, tongue-in-cheek performance, and soon made *The Fat Man* one of the top detective thrillers of the air.

Though he created the character and gave his name to the series, Dashiell Hammett left the writing to Ellington, Lawrence Klee, and others. But Hammett cast the mold for Runyon, using many of the same characteristics of Nick Charles, the hero of his 1934 novel, *The Thin Man.* Despite their obvious physical differences, both Charles and Runyon were urbane and slick, with a sense of humor that was rooted deeply in the school of the grotesque. Both bore striking similarities to Hammett's third great detective of literature and the air, the redoubtable Sam Spade. While each developed a distinct, sharp image through dialogue and description, all bore the unmistakable Hammett influence. It came through even on radio, and Hammett had as little to do with the radio shows as possible.

Ed Begley co-starred as Lieutenant MacKenzie, and regular support was received from Betty Garde, Paul Stewart, Linda Watkins, Mary Patton, and Vicki Vola. When the series premiered, Amzie Strickland played the "girl friend" and Nell Harrison was the Fat Man's mother. The eleven-man orchestra was directed by Bernard Green. The show ran for more than a year as an ABC sustainer, and was picked up in 1947 by the Norwich Company for Pepto-Bismol. It ran three years on Fridays for Norwich, then moved to Wednesdays for a final season sustained by ABC.

Father Brown

Father Brown, based on the stories by G. K. Chesterton, came to Mutual as a summer series on June 10, 1945. Directed by William Sweets, it starred Karl Swenson in the title role, as Chesterton's famous detective priest, "the best-loved detective of them all."

Father Coughlin

Father Coughlin, known as "The Fighting Priest," rose to power quickly after his first CBS broadcast October 5, 1930, and was soon one of the most influential voices in the nation. Born Charles Edward

Coughlin October 25, 1891, in Hamilton, Ontario, Coughlin was ordained a priest in 1916, and in 1926 became a pastor of the Shrine of the Little Flower in Royal Oak, Michigan. He first took to the air locally, broadcasting over Detroit's WJR in 1926—a sermon that brought five letters from his listeners. It was a far cry from the 1,000,000 letters that sometimes deluged Royal Oak in a single week of the mid-1930's when the priest's influence was at its peak. But Coughlin's style was polished even in those early local talks; soon he was being carried by WMAQ Chicago, then WLW Cincinnati. With his acceptance into a national network, Coughlin's sermons grew increasingly political; he attacked President Herbert Hoover vehemently, then turned his wrath upon bankers, socialism, and the uneven distribution of wealth. He established an early rapport with Franklin D. Roosevelt, strongly supporting his candidacy in the 1932 presidential race. With Roosevelt's election, rumors spread that Coughlin was in line for a high administrative post, that he would soon quit the church in favor of government service. The priest's comment that Roosevelt was "about 20 years ahead of the thought that is current in the country today" seemed to bolster such claims. But Coughlin became disenchanted with Roosevelt too; his first public break with the President came in 1934, when he urged payment of a soldier's bonus and Roosevelt publicly threatened to veto it. By 1935, his break with Roosevelt was complete, by 1937 his attacks on the president had become so violent that they led ultimately to a rebuke from the Pope. Roosevelt found Coughlin a formidable enemy. The priest had a staff of confidential investigators in Washington, headed by a former Hearst journalist, and his advisors in financial matters consisted of bankers and brokers in New York. His themes centered more and more on money; his constant charge was that Roosevelt had betrayed the people by failing to "drive the moneychangers from the temple," and that Congress had delegated its lawmaking powers to the President. By then Coughlin had formed his own radio chain. Temporarily dropped from the air in April 1931 after a dispute with CBS (the network tried to censor a speech and Coughlin abandoned the talk and instead used his hour to loudly berate CBS), Coughlin tried to go on NBC. NBC hid behind a policy of not accepting "commercial religious broadcasting." So, using WOR New York and WJR Detroit as his flagstations, Father Coughlin gradually increased the scope of his broadcasts, buying time on stations, until he could be heard virtually anywhere in the nation. He paid for the time through voluntary contributions estimated at $500,000 a year. Coughlin was proud that he never asked his listeners for money, but his announcer always closed with the gentle reminder that "this hour has been made possible by the outstanding financial support of the radio audience." His magazine *Social Justice* amplified his political views, and by

1939 he was buying his time in 60-minute blocks. Coughlin's attacks eventually broadened to include Jews, and in the early 1940's his influence began to decline. In 1942 his magazine was banned from the mails by the Espionage Act. It soon folded, and church leaders began applying pressure to have the priest silenced as well. Coughlin yielded to the pressure and dropped abruptly from the political scene in 1942. He retired as pastor of the Shrine of the Little Flower in 1966.

Father Knows Best

Father Knows Best, one of the bright spots of late radio, was first heard August 25, 1949, on NBC. It lasted until 1954, carried all the way on Thursday night by General Foods, for such products as Post Toasties and Maxwell House Coffee. It told the story of the Andersons, an average family who lived on an average street (Maple) in an average town (Springfield), where the father was an insurance man and the mother and kids were so lovably American.

Over the years, the family had plenty of growing room, and by the time *Father Knows Best* was ready for TV, Jim Anderson had become the patient, loving, all-wise father figure of the air. Jim liked to give his three children, Betty, Bud, and Kathy, plenty of freedom while maintaining some degree of control. His wife, Margaret, almost always yielded to his judgment—thus the title, *Father Knows Best*.

As originally proposed by author Ed James in a 1948 audition record, the family was named Henderson, and Jim hadn't begun to develop the wisdom-in-depth that was his on television. In the audition, and even in many of the regular radio shows, he bordered on the scatterbrained, occasionally meddling in the kids' affairs and constantly putting his foot in his mouth. Margaret was a trifle too sweet, and the kids acted like holdovers from a *Henry Aldrich* reject. But the audition contained the basic elements.

Stepping into the role of Jim was Robert Young, whose acting credits went back to 1931 and the first Charlie Chan movie, *The Black Camel*. Young had since made more than 100 films and had appeared in enough radio to qualify as a veteran first-class. He first addressed a microphone on August 6, 1936, and did his first regular series with Fanny Brice and Frank Morgan on *Good News of 1938*. Young had made many dramatic air appearances, playing leads on *The Lux Radio Theatre*, *Hollywood Startime*, *The Screen Guild Theatre*, and *Suspense*. In 1943, he teamed with Norman Corwin for a series of globe-trotting adventure, *Passport for Adams*, and in 1944 he again appeared with Frank Morgan. So Young was no stranger to broadcasting. But *Father Knows Best* would become his best-known radio role, setting the stage for his jump into television, where twenty years later he was peering into eyeballs as Marcus Welby, M.D.

Appearing as Margaret in the audition was June Whitley; the part was later played by Jean Vander Pyl. Rhoda Williams went all the way as Betty; Ted Donaldson was Bud, and Kathy was played by Norma Jean Nilsson and later Helen Strong. Bill Forman was announcer, and the scripts were written by Ed James, Paul West, and Roz Rogers.

Theme for the radio series was a variation of "Just Around the Corner There's A Rainbow in the Sky," blending into a "let's have another cup of coffee" melody for Maxwell House. The stories almost always revolved around the problems of Betty, the eldest, or Bud, whose exasperation at life's tricks manifested in the catch phrase, "Ho-ly cow."

In January 1950, Robert Young began a staunch *Father Knows Best* campaign to educate teenagers in the habits of safe driving. It became an intensely personal cause, and was promoted heavily on the program. Young was the only original Anderson to survive the jump from radio to TV. On the tube, Margaret was played by Jane Wyatt, Betty by Elinore Donahue, Bud by Billy Gray, and Kathy by Lauren Chapin.

Favorite Story

Favorite Story, a series of classics syndicated from 1946 through 1949, contained a triple-pronged appeal: a well-known host, an immortal play, and selection of the play by a famous personality as his or her "favorite story." Host was Ronald Colman, who often assumed the lead. The plays were adapted from such novels as *Vanity Fair, Wuthering Heights, Frankenstein, The Moonstone, The Adventures of Tom Sawyer, The Time Machine,* and *Treasure Island.* Sinclair Lewis, Alfred Hitchcock, Eleanor Roosevelt, Fred Allen, and Irving Berlin were among the celebrities who selected them. The show was written and directed by the team of Jerry Lawrence and Bob Lee, who had been working together since 1942 and would move from here to the Monday-night *Railroad Hour* on NBC. Claude Sweeten provided the music, and *Favorite Story* came off as one of Radio Row's better pieces of "canned" entertainment.

The FBI in Peace and War

The FBI in Peace and War, one of radio's best-remembered crime shows, was also one of the longest-running. The entire run came on

CBS, spanning the years from November 25, 1944, to 1958. Though the stories were rather flat by today's standards, this program created such a classy format that it still stands the test of time. The theme was a rousing, fully orchestrated rendition of Sergei Prokofiev's "Love For Three Oranges" march. For the first ten years, the sponsor, in whole or in part, was Lava Soap. The commercials were as memorable as the format, with a male voice accompanied by a bass drum booming "L-A-V-A—L-A-V-A!" out of an echo chamber. The soap's identification with the show was unusually strong. Other sponsors included Wildroot Cream Oil (1951–52), Lucky Strike (1952), Nescafé (1953), and Wrigley's Gum (1954–56). Scripts were by Louis Pelletier and Jacques Finke, and the show was introduced as "Another great story, based on Frederick L. Collins' copyrighted book, *The FBI In Peace And War!—Drama!* Thrills! Action!!" Max Marcin was producer-director through the mid-1940's; by 1949 Betty Mandeville had taken the helm becoming, for a time, the only female director of a nighttime crime series in network radio. Warren Sweeney was longtime announcer, but André Baruch announced briefly during Lucky Strike sponsorship.

Variations of the show's tagline ("All names and characters used on the program are fictitious; any similarity to persons living or dead is purely coincidental") became widely used on other shows as well. Although Collins had attended FBI classes before writing his book, listeners were reminded weekly that "this is not an official program of the FBI." But the Bureau was always presented in a favorable light. *The FBI in Peace and War* was an anthology, bound only by the sometimes-thin FBI story line. The main characters were the criminals, and the stories usually unfolded from their viewpoints. Occasionally the scene shifted to the pursuing FBI, against the busy clatter of teletype machines. The FBI was personified as Agent Sheppard (Martin Blaine), though a true character never formed around the name. Some of radio's best old pros worked on the acting end of this show. Among them: Ed Begley, Elspeth Eric, Frank Readick, Rosemary Rice, Harold Huber, Charita Bauer, and Grant Richards.

Fibber McGee and Molly

Fibber McGee and Molly was developed from an earlier daytime show, *Smackout*, which ran on Chicago radio from 1931 until 1935, and on the Blue Network in 1931–33.

The story of Jim and Marian Jordan was one of childhood sweethearts from the Peoria sticks, making it big in Hollywood against the slickest competition of the time. Jim Jordan was a farm boy, born near Peoria in 1896. He had a lot of ham in him. Early in life, he wanted to be a singer; he was singing in a church choir when he met Marian Driscoll, a coal miner's daughter who wanted to be a music teacher. They were married in 1918, when Jordan marched triumphantly back to Peoria after a year of glory with a traveling vaudeville act at $35 a week.

Over the next few years, there were a lot of odd jobs. Jordan was a mailman when he was drafted into World War I—just long enough to lose the job. They had a daughter, Kathryn, and a son, Jim, Jr. After the birth of their daughter, the idea of musical careers seemed remote, so they fed the ham with a local act, singing in lodge halls and churches. In 1922, they saved some money, left the baby with Jordan's parents, and took their act on the road. Now they booked into opera houses and theatres; the tempo of the Chautauqua life carried them for four months. When their second child was born, Jordan took the show on the road alone. That didn't work; he went broke and came home to Peoria to find work in a department sore.

They got into radio on a bet in 1924. "We could do better than that," said Jordan, after hearing a singer on the air. "Ten bucks says you can't," said his brother. Jim and Marian breezed into WIBO and were hired as the O'Henry Twins at $10 a week. It wasn't a fortune even in those days, and eventually they returned to vaudeville to earn enough money to pay their bills.

But by 1927, they had begun to carve out a niche for themselves in radio. Never again, as long as radio was alive and well, would they find themselves without work. At WENR, Chicago, they were heard three times a week as The Air Scouts, and it was here that Marian first began experimenting with the little-girl voice that would emerge a few years later as Teeny, the impish character who drove McGee nuts.

Undoubtedly the turning point for the Jordans was their introduction to Don Quinn, a Grand Rapids cartoonist who wanted to write for radio. Their collaboration in 1931 with Quinn was to last a professional lifetime. But in those economically troubled times, the Jordans were struggling to keep body and soul together, and Quinn couldn't buy a writing job anywhere. Writers were in disfavor then; comedians were supposed to be totally original, not dependent on someone else's material for laughs. Quinn didn't buy that idea, and within a year he could point to Paul Rhymer, writer of *Vic and Sade*, as the perfect example of his argument. But then nobody was in the market.

Finally Quinn hooked up with the Jordans at $20 a week. One of his first acts was to create a new show called *Smackout*, in which Jim would play a Fibber-like grocer who was always "smackout of everything but tall tales." That show ran for four years in Chicago before an advertising agency executive handling the Johnson's Wax account heard the show, bought it for his client and in the spring of 1935, the Jordans prepared to go coast to coast. On April 16, 1935, the show first went on NBC Blue as *Fibber McGee and Molly* for Johnson's Wax. For a time it was broadcast on Monday nights, in direct competition with the formidable *Lux Radio Theatre*. But by 1939, *Fibber* had settled into its permanent slot on the Red Network, Tuesday nights at 9:30, Eastern Time.

When it did come, the success of *Fibber McGee and Molly* must have surprised a lot of people. The mark of vaudeville was all over the show, from the cornball jokes that twisted words without mercy to the imaginative opening of Fibber McGee's closet. It wasn't slapstick, but it was a close cousin—a slapstick of the tongue, with Fibber hurling insults as fast as Jordan's creative mind could handle them.

Some changes had to be made for a national audience. The grocery store man from *Smackout* became Fibber McGee; the show became *Fibber McGee and Molly*. In those early days, Fibber was envisioned as just an extension of his *Smackout* character, mainly a teller of tall tales. The show started slowly and built its huge audience gradually over six years.And there were some drastic refinements along the way.

The shows of the mid-1930's really lacked polish. In many places they were stiff, jerky, and unbelievable. Even in 1939, as the Jordans prepared to desert Chicago for a new life in Hollywood, the show lacked the sparkle it would attain on the Coast. But refinements were being made all the time. Quinn, who had become a full partner, began adding new dimensions to the McGee characters. Marian insisted that the show get closer to reality. What couldn't happen back home in Peoria, she said, shouldn't happen on *Fibber McGee and Molly*. The Jordans were already at the doorstep of the big time when they moved to Hollywood. They came west in a trailer from Chicago, their home base for more than eight years, and never quite fit into the pasteboard world of Hollywood society.

For a time, McGee would retain the whopper-telling image that had earned him his name. "Pretty Please McGee, I was known as in those days," he would crow, referring to his prowess long ago as a prosecuting attorney. "Pretty Please McGee, proclaimed by the press and public the peerless prosecutor of pilfering pickpockets, political parasites and persons performing petty peccadilloes, putting prison pajamas on poker players preyin' on poor punks with peculiar pasteboards, pleadin' with passion and pathos for poor people in pretty pickles—a peppy personality with a capital P!"

By then the McGees had moved to their famous address, 79 Wistful Vista. As the 1940's dawned, the whopper-telling receded into the background. Now Quinn used this device at most once or twice a season, letting McGee's considerable ability as a windbag carry the action. Fibber became the hard-headed, lovable blunderer—the kind of guy who would, and did, blunder through the night to change a $100 bill to pay a parking lot attendant, when the quarter he thought he'd lost had actually fallen into his pants cuff. Fibber's best-intentioned gestures always turned into disasters, things like fixing breakfast in bed for Molly on Mother's Day, making ice cream at home, sewing a dress on a dare. Dares and challenges were big things to Fibber. He was the eternal crusader of Wistful Vista. If he got it in his mind, as he did in the winter of 1942, that women were taking over, that might lead directly to another Fibber crusade.

Fibber and Molly were always hustling for the war cause, pleading with their audience to save gas and rubber, to pitch into the soap drive with a little more elbow grease, to keep away from black market meat. But it was always developed as entertainment, well within the context of the story. The meat episode was pure Fibber. McGee had a great chance to buy some beef without ration points by going to the black market. Molly fussed and scolded, but McGee was convinced that everyone else was doing it, so why not? True to poetic justice, the meat turned out to be spoiled. We learn our lesson along with the McGees: "Never buy beef from the black market."

Marian played Molly perfectly. She was long-suffering, faithful, and strong, a woman of rugged pioneer stock. Molly had a voice that was forever middle-aged and always suggested kindness. Maybe that was why, when she really put her foot down, McGee jumped. Often, when Jordan would fluff a line, Marian would laugh loudly into the microphone, and her guffawing drew out the audience, making a laugh out of a disaster. Her "Goodnight, all" always closed the show. As Teeny, her "Whatcha doin', huh, mister, whatcha?" drove McGee to tears. Teeny existed to help McGee into his inevitable corner.

But so did all the characters. *Fibber McGee and Molly* was really only a series of skits; there were no "stories" as such, just general themes to be developed by McGee and friends. Several supporting characters became so well-known that they outgrew Wistful Vista and emerged in shows of their own. Harold Peary created his man of great pomp, Throckmorton P. Gildersleeve, on *Fibber McGee and Molly*. Peary emerged in 1939 in a succession of loud roles, all characters named Gildersleeve. By 1940, he had become *the* Gildersleeve, and had settled down in the house next door to the McGees. Gildersleeve and McGee were forever on the brink of mortal combat, and did once fight it out with hoses while watering the lawns.

In April 1941, *Fibber McGee and Molly* topped Jack Benny and Bob Hope to lead all the shows in the ratings wars. They were hauling in more than $3,500 a week, a far cry from the peanuts their characters—the McGees—had to live on. And a far cry from the early days, when they first sang and talked on Chicago radio for $10 a week.

Then in the summer of 1941, Gildy moved bag and baggage from Wistful Vista to the town of Summerfield, where he became water commissioner in his own show, *The Great Gildersleeve*, and set about raising his nephew and niece. When the McGees returned from vacation on September 30, 1941, it was to bid a sad farewell to their old friendly enemy.

Actually, it was the beginning of a character crisis for the show. Soon Bill Thompson entered the Navy, and with him went four of the show's best-known character voices. With great flexibility, Thompson played the Old Timer, Wallace Wimple, Horatio K. Boomer, the hustler who sounded more like W. C. Fields than W. C. Fields, and Nick Depopolous, a Greek restaurant owner whose talent was twisting words so that they came out logically illogical. By then Boomer had all but vanished from the show, and Nick the Greek never was a great Thompson creation anyway. But Wallace Wimple and the Old Timer would be missed.

Thompson first began experimenting with his Wimple voice on the *Breakfast Club* shows of the 1930's. By April 1940, he was using it regularly—though it still had no name—on *Fibber McGee and Molly*. Wimple emerged as a character in 1941. Thompson somehow managed to arrange his mouth with just the right combination of tongue and air to bring off Wallace as the perfect creampuff. His weekly adventures with his "big old wife," the rough and tough Sweetie Face, were always interrupted by McGee's goading. "I predict you gotta have it out with that woman one of these days, Wimp," McGee said. "Show her who's boss." To which Wimple would reply, "Oh, she already knows that, Mr. McGee—*she* is."

The Old Timer, another throwback to Chicago, lasted for the duration of the show. He tried to match Fibber in the tall tales department, and his weekly line—"That's purty good, Johnny, but that ain't the way I heerd it"—never failed to get a laugh from the audience and a groan from McGee. The void created by Thompson's exit grew wider when Gale Gordon joined the Coast Guard in 1942. Gordon also had dual roles on *Fibber McGee*, playing Mayor La Trivia and Foggy Williams, the weatherman. Foggy never was a major character; his "Good day—probably" was funny for a while, but didn't wear well. But Mayor La Trivia became very popular, proving a solid rival for McGee in the windbag department. Inevitably he got himself so tongue-tied in his arguments with the McGees that he blew his top as only Gordon could do it.

To fill the void, the talents of Arthur Q. Bryan, Shirley Mitchell, Isabel Randolph, and later, Marlin Hurt were brought into the spotlight. Bryan, who had been appearing as Floyd the barber on *The Great Gildersleeve*, became Doc Gamble on April 6, 1943. Gamble plugged the gap left by Harold Peary when Gildersleeve moved to

Summerfield; he became McGee's friendly enemy, hurling and getting verbal brickbats whenever they met. Isabel Randolph was snooty old Abigail Uppington ("Uppy " to Fibber), who had been around for some time, but now was given better exposure. Shirley Mitchell, the conniving Leila Ransom of *The Great Gildersleeve*, came over to do an entirely different kind of character for *Fibber McGee*. She played Alice Darling, the scatterbrained, man-crazy war plant worker, who rented out the McGees' spare room starting with the show of October 5, 1943. Alice was a charming character who would have been a continuing asset to the show, but she was dropped abruptly when Bill Thompson returned January 15, 1946.

Finally, there was Beulah the black maid, played by Marlin Hurt, a white man. The audience never failed to respond hysterically when Hurt blurted, "Somebody bawl fo' Beulah?" Beulah was the only character on the show who appreciated McGee's cornball humor. She would laugh riotously at his worst jokes, pausing just long enough to sigh, "Love that man!" between giggles. Beulah first appeared in the show of January 25, 1944, and the character became so popular that Hurt departed for his own show the following year.

Even Harlow Wilcox, the genial Johnson's Wax salesman, had a major comic role. Borrowing a technique started by Ed Wynn, Quinn created the "integrated commercial," a device later used with great success by Jack Benny. There was simply no commercial break in the middle of the show; the salesman would suddenly appear within the story context, and would frantically try to promote the product over the action. Wilcox was especially good, priding himself on his ability to turn any discussion to Johnson's Wax. The Johnson people must have loved it, because they saved some ten years of *Fibber* transcriptions in their Racine, Wisconsin office long after their sponsorship ended in 1950. Johnson's Wax sponsored the show until the summer of 1950. Pet milk took over when it returned in the fall. Reynolds Aluminum became the sponsor in 1952.

There were numerous characters in *Fibber McGee and Molly* whose voices we seldom, if ever, heard: Molly's drunken Uncle Dennis; Fred Nitny, Fibber's much-discussed old buddy; Myrt, the telephone operator. Of all the speechless characters, Myrt is most memorable. Whenever McGee picked up the phone, Myrt came on the line. "Oh, is that you, Myrt?" he would say. "How's every little thing, Myrt? . . . Your uncle? . . . smashed his face and broke one of his hands?" At this point, the gullible Molly would usually say, "Oh, dear, poor man! What happened, McGee, did he fall down the stairs?" And Fibber would come through with the inevitable, "Naw, he dropped his watch."

Quinn's humor played heavily on such familiar gags. He established patterns, then varied or broke them often enough that the audience never knew quite what to expect. Even the famed closet was occasionally straightened out by Fibber, and the audience laughed as hard at the silence as they had at the prospect of McGee buried under all that junk. For a time the junk—books, skates, empty cans, trays, old shoes, dumbbells, and tin pie pans—stacked precariously on a tier of steps and climaxed by the tinkle of a tiny bell, was the responsibility of Frank Pittman. Pittman joined the show as sound effects man in 1941, and eventually became producer-director. Quinn tried to establish the mythical Wistful Vista intersection of 14th and Oak as a comic town catchall, but that never caught on. Whenever McGee went anywhere—to a baker, to the drug store, to the local dry goods store —it was always located at 14th and Oak. Quinn thought it one of the show's funniest subtleties, but it was so subtle that few listeners noticed.

Quinn eventually hired another writer, Phil Leslie, to help put the scripts together. Later Leslie and Keith Fowler did the writing. Donald Novis was the show's singer in the early Chicago days; the King's Men (Ken Darby, Bud Linn, Jon Dodson, and Rad Robinson) sang novelty numbers throughout the show's "golden" era. Billy Mills was *Fibber's* longtime bandleader.

Fibber McGee and Molly was dropped as a weekly half-hour feature after the show of June 30, 1953. It returned in October as a five-a-week 15-minute show, which lasted until 1957. The McGees could still be heard in the late 1950's, as a five-minute sketch on NBC's *Monitor.*

Marian Jordan died April 7, 1961. And *Fibber McGee and Molly* passed into history, a small but important part of a medium whose own life was far too short.

The Fire Chief

The Fire Chief was Ed Wynn, the first performer to bring an entire comedy show before the microphones.Wynn played *The Perfect Fool* in 1922 on WJZ, Newark. More than a decade later, his *Fire Chief* program opened as one of the early comedy offerings of NBC.

A stage headliner since 1904, Wynn had played in two *Ziegfeld Follies* and more than a dozen Broadway shows before he came to radio. He created The Perfect Fool character for the stage in 1921, and continued playing the part until 1924.

Wynn never was a true radio comedian. His act was rooted in greasepaint and footlights; his appeal was to an earlier age of innocence and naiveté. Out trouping when the century turned, Wynn was still practicing techniques that came out of Victorian theatre when radio bloomed as a serious entertainment form in the 1920's.

That isn't to say that Wynn's part in radio wasn't important. His Perfect Fool, performed at the very dawn of radio, became the first true comic demonstration of the air. It was Wynn who first introduced the technique—so successfully copied later by Jack Benny and Fibber McGee—of breaking into commercial messages with comedy lines. But Wynn was essentially a stage man. Legend has it that when no laughter erupted at his Perfect Fool antics, Wynn instantly created the first makeshift studio audience, assembling janitors and studio hands to watch him play. He was the first radio comedian to appear in full costume and makeup. But that was another gimmick rooted in his stage career, a boost to help Wynn past his periodic bouts of mike fright.

The Fire Chief developed when a Texaco official caught Wynn's performance in The Laugh Parade, a show saved from critical and financial disaster by Wynn's meticulous rewrite. Wynn first refused the radio offer, correctly sensing that his act depended too much on visual material. He never told even a borderline risqué joke: his effect was achieved, he pointed out, by such vaudeville props as silly hats, bell-bottomed coats, and lots of pancake.

But Texaco persisted, and finally got Wynn for a reported $5,000 a week. It was a high salary in those Depression days, but Wynn was worth it. Sponsored by Texaco, The Fire Chief premièred April 26, 1932. The show finished a strong third in the ratings that year, topped only by Eddie Cantor and Jack Pearl, and ran until 1935 on Tuesday nights.

Wynn was an important but brief link between very early radio and the polished medium of the 1940's. His Fire Chief, highly popular when it appeared in 1932, caught America still mired in the old ways. Within a few years, the old would be swept away in a tide of slick new radio comics. Many came out of vaudeville and Chautauqua, but they were younger people with more inclination to change. The people were ready for slick entertainment packages, and no one could ever accuse Ed Wynn of being slick.

Wynn's mike fright began immediately, and subsided only after long experience on the air. He was terrified at the thought of entertaining 30 million people; his voice came out as a frantic, high-pitched wail that was so well-received he decided to keep it. His cracking "S-o-o-o-o" was one of the early catch phrases of the air. The show featured the great early announcer, Graham McNamee, with music by Donald Voorhees (Eddie Duchin in the final season). It was built largely around banter between McNamee and Wynn. Often, near the end of the show, Wynn read letters from his listeners.

Wynn did a brief show on the Blue Network in 1936–37, playing Gulliver and The Perfect Fool. Then he dropped out of radio until September 8, 1944, when his Happy Island was launched on the Blue.

Happy Island, a fantasy show, featured Ed Wynn as King Bubbles, ruler of the mythical kingdom of happiness. Here Wynn went to even greater staging lengths than he had used on The Fire Chief, establishing elaborate sets and exotic lighting and decking out his entire cast in gay costumes—all for a radio show! Happy Island featured Evelyn Knight and Jerry Wayne as vocalists and as the lovers Princess Elaine and Prince Richard. Ralph Sedan was Blotto, the king's adviser, and Winfield Hoeny was King Nasty of Castor Isle. For the Borden's Milk commercials, Wynn featured Hope Emerson as Elsie the Cow, Lorna Lynn as Beulah the Calf, and Craig McDonnell as Elmer the Bull. Mark Warnow conducted the orchestra and Ray Knight assisted with the writing.

Wynn played the golden-hearted king, who wandered through the Worry Park helping people solve their problems. But the show opened to dismal reviews, and ran only a few months as a variety show for Borden's Milk; it was dropped early in 1945. Wynn found new life in the late 1950's as a character actor in movies and TV, but the demise of Happy Island in 1945 left him—temporarily at least —just another actor whose time had gone. He died June 19, 1966.

The Firestone Voice of the Farm

The Firestone Voice of the Farm was a 1938 farm-variety show with songs by the Firestone Quartet and interviews with champion farmers by Everett Mitchell. Traveling to RFD America and whistle stops everywhere, Mitchell talked with top apple growers and hog farmers, men who knew tractors and trucks. The quartet offered "darky" songs in the Stephen Foster tradition, such as "A Cornfield Medley," from Show 17:

Some folks say that a darky won't steal
(chorus) Way down yonder in the corn field
But I caught a couple in my corn field (chorus)
One had a shovel and the other had a hoe (chorus)
If that ain't stealin', then I don't know (chorus)

The First Nighter Program

The First Nighter Program was the earliest, and one of the last, of the significant dramatic playhouses of the air. Coming to NBC for Campana Balm on December 4, 1930, the show kept its sponsor through three changes of network. An elaborate format and an American fascination with theatre can be credited for much of the early success of The First Nighter Program. In Depression America, Broadway was far too expensive for the average pocketbook. Little matter—The First Nighter took us there, in a clever audio sleight of hand. Had the listeners only known that those great plays from "the Little Theatre off Times Square" actually came from NBC's Merchandise Mart studios in Chicago, things might have been different.

But probably not. First Nighter was an idea whose time had come. Built around the concept of an opening night on Broadway, the format was one of the greatest ever devised. The opening of the March 26, 1944 First Nighter took 135 seconds to deliver, during which we met out host—"the genial First Nighter"—and somehow got to the "theatre" in time for first act curtain. The First Nighter walked along Broadway (couldn't get a cab in those wartime days), and all around us as we walked with him were the noises of the Great White Way —cars and horns, police whistles, people buzzing around like bees. The host picked up the bee analogy: "Broadway's buzzing with excitement, and eagerly waiting to welcome an opening night performance in the Little Theatre off Times Square. There'll be a crowd of onlookers and autograph fans on hand at the entrance to greet the celebrities who always attend a premier on the Great White Way, so let's not miss a minute of the excitement."

Up Broadway to 42nd Street. There, an attendant shouted, "Have your tickets ready, please; have your tickets ready, please! . . . Good evening, Mr. First Nighter, the usher will show you to your box."

Inside, at our "fourth-row center" seats, the First Nighter gave us a quick reading of the program—title, cast, and author. Then the "famous First Nighter orchestra" played a few bars of music, until an usher came down the aisle shouting "Curtain! Curtain!" Buzzers sounded to announce the curtains, and ushers reminded the people to smoke in the lobbies only. After the play, the effect was reversed, in briefer form. The First Nighter went out into the crowded street and melted into the crowd.

The show was done in typical theatre fashion, in three acts, with commercials for Campana between the curtains. The format, unique when The First Nighter premièred, was soon copied by such shows as Curtain Time and Knickerbocker Playhouse. Even the hardy Lux Radio Theatre shows some First Nighter influence.

As for the stories, First Nighter fare tended to be light, romantic comedy. Occasionally such heavier material as Arch Oboler's "The Chinese Gong" was used, but most First Nighter shows bordered on situation comedy, employing the boy-gets-loses-gets-girl theme like an audio version of the old Saturday Evening Post. "The Little Town of Bethlehem" became the annual Christmas offering after its first broadcast in 1936.

A company of regulars was established for The First Nighter from the beginning. Best-known of the "famous First Nighter orchestras" was that of Eric Sagerquist, who waved the baton over the opening show in 1930 and continued as musical director for fourteen years. Frank Worth was later orchestra leader. The theme was a slow rendition of "Neapolitan Nights," played with heavy violin emphasis. The sounds of Broadway were reproduced in part by sound man Robert Opper.

Dashing Don Ameche became the first star, playing opposite June Meredith and Betty Lou Gerson until Hollywood lured him away in 1936. That was the year Barbara Luddy opened as long-running female lead, a position she held until the show folded. Playing opposite Miss Luddy for six years was Les Tremayne.

In 1930–31, The First Nighter was heard Thursday nights on the Blue; in 1931, it moved to Tuesdays. The show moved to Fridays in 1932, and in 1933 went to NBC for six years. In 1938, it moved to CBS, remaining a Friday-night show until 1940, when it moved for a season to Tuesday.

The genial host was seldom identified in the credits. Charles Hughes was an early First Nighter, Macdonald Carey had the part for a time around 1938; it was also played briefly by Bret Morrison and Marvin Miller. By the mid-1940's, Rye Billsbury had become the First Nighter.

In 1941, the show returned to CBS on Fridays. Mutual picked it up in 1942, running it as a Sunday show until 1944; in 1945–46 it was heard on CBS Saturdays. Olan Soule took the lead in 1943; he and Miss Luddy finished the series in 1949. When NBC revived it three years later, Luddy and Soule again were tapped as stars. The final two years for Campana (1947–49), First Nighter was a Thursday CBS show.

The later shows were directed by Joseph T. Ainley. Supporting casts over the years read like a Who's Who of broadcasting. Among them: Hugh Studebaker, Willard Waterman, Herb Butterfield, Sidney Ellstrom, William Conrad, Parley Baer, Sarah Selby, Ben Wright, and Verna Felton.

In 1952, the show was revived for a season on NBC, Tuesday nights for Miller High Life Beer, and it was Billsbury who revived the character of the host—this time with billing.

The Fitch Bandwagon

The Fitch Bandwagon was first heard on NBC in 1937, featuring vaudeville-type acts and bands. Gradually it assumed more comic properties, and emerged in 1946 as the well-developed forerunner to *The Phil Harris–Alice Faye Show*. Under Harris and Miss Faye, it featured Elliott Lewis and Walter Tetley, and was written by Ray Singer and Dick Chevillat. In short, Harris used *The Fitch Bandwagon* as a launching platform for his new show. For most of its run, *Bandwagon* was comprised of guest orchestras (Freddy Martin, Jan Savitt, Glen Gray and the Casa Loma Orchestra, etc.) and assorted guest stars, under supervision of producer Ward Byron. Bill Lawrence had become producer by 1944, the year that Dick Powell signed as *Bandwagon* master of ceremonies, and Andy Devine came aboard as gravel-voiced comic. Wendell Niles was announcer. Cass Daley became head comedienne in 1945, changing the emphasis from musical variety to comedy-music. Her rendition of the *Bandwagon* theme is still remembered:

> Laugh a-while, let a song be your style,
> Use Fitch Shammmmmmm-poooo!
> Don't despair, use your head, save your hair,
> Use Fitch Shammmmmmmm-pooo!

Miss Daley departed in mid-1946. The first Phil Harris show was on September 29. Harris continued the *Bandwagon* theme through the spring of 1948, when the show closed shop. The following fall, *The Phil Harris–Alice Faye Show* opened on NBC for Rexall.

The Fitzgeralds

The Fitzgeralds, Ed and Pegeen, started the early-morning husband-wife shows parodied so successfully by Fred Allen. Their show began on New York's WOR in 1940. It grew out of two separate formats, Ed's *Book Talk, Back Talk and Small Talk*, and Pegeen's show, *Pegeen Prefers*. Ed reviewed books while Pegeen discussed beauty and fashion. But Pegeen wasn't satisfied: she wanted to do an intimate home conversation show with her husband, done on location from their East 36th Street house. Eventually she wore down Ed's reluctance, and the result was *The Fitzgeralds*.

For a time the program was done out of the WOR studio. Then Pegeen (whose real name was Margaret) became ill, and a remote system was established at the house. The Fitzgeralds used no script, preferring to let the talk flow spontaneously out of the news, mail, and their interests in fashion, books, and people. By 1945, *The Fitzgeralds* was big business locally. Their defection to WJZ and the ABC Network left WOR without a replacement, so Dorothy Kilgallen and Richard Kollmar were persuaded to do a similar show, *Breakfast with*

Dorothy and Dick, on the Mutual station. The shows were fierce competitors. The Fitzgeralds, who sometimes disagreed heatedly on the air, were decidedly livelier than the prim, proper Dorothy and Dick. Ed didn't hesitate to tell Pegeen and all New York when she began getting slightly plump. Once he stalked off in a huff during a show, after one of their famous "spats." The success of the Fitzgeralds and Kollmars led to a third breakfast show, *Hi, Jinx!* featuring Tex McCrary and Jinx Falkenburg. But Ed and Pegeen were the first. By 1947, they were doing—in addition to their daily breakfast show—a three-a-week evening show, *Dinner with the Fitzgeralds,* and a half-hour program on Sundays. They now have a mid-day five-a-week show on WOR.

Five Minute Mysteries

Five Minute Mysteries were syndicated shows offered to stations well into the 1950's, in which full mystery cases were dramatized in a five-minute format. Clues, victims, suspects, and resolution were all sandwiched into a five-minute show! The action was carried exclusively through dialogue, and the listener was asked to figure out which clues led to the murderer's undoing. It was terrible stuff, used mainly for fillers. Usually the clues were so obvious that a first-grader could handle them, or were so vague that they didn't make sense even after the answer was revealed.

The Five Mysteries Program

The Five Mysteries Program was another series of five-minute mysteries, using the syndications to stump a panel of "armchair experts." Five mysteries were squeezed into a 30-minute show, heard on Mutual Sunday afternoons in the late 1940's. Five "mystery minds" were chosen from the audience; listeners who wanted to be on the panel submitted their names, and the panel was made up from the cards received. After each mystery, the panel tried to guess the solution and give reasons for their answers. Then, back to the drama for the real solution. For each correct answer, a panelist received $5.

For Your Approval *and* Forecast

For Your Approval and *Forecast* were shows that asked the audience to be the critics. Both solicited listener comments on pilots, ideas, and proposed series. They were sounding boards for many different kinds of shows, from drama to comedy to musical to quiz. *Forecast,* earlier of the two, was first heard July 15, 1940, on CBS Monday nights, and was also heard in 1941. A regular promotion was its "Double Feature," two contrasting 15-minute plays within the same half-hour. *Duffy's Tavern* was first heard on *Forecast,* premièring July 29, 1940, and eventually becoming the most successful offering of either show. *For Your Approval* ran on Mutual Saturday afternoons in 1947, with Jock MacGregor as host.

The Ford Sunday Evening Hour

The Ford Sunday Evening Hour was a long-running, highly respected hour of music. The fare ran from popular ballads and hymns to grand opera, and featured a variety of singers and performers. John Barbirolli and Fritz Reiner were among the conductors; Gladys Swarthout and Helen Jepson the singers. The show was first heard in 1934. After a shaky start, it became part of the regular CBS lineup and ran on that network until March 1, 1942. As the show evolved, it featured different soloists and conductors each week. John Charles Thomas was a regular during 1936–37. *The Ford Sunday Evening Hour* became a great platform for young artists, and had a sizable audience in the mid-1930's. Henry Ford himself took a great interest in the show, hiring the Detroit Symphony Orchestra and personally suggesting the "Children's Prayer" (from *Hansel and Gretel*) theme that served as opening and closing. The show was dropped in 1942, when Ford cut its advertising budget, but it returned in the fall of 1945 for a season on ABC. William Reddick was longtime producer.

The Ford Theatre

The Ford Theatre premièred on NBC October 5, 1947. After one season, the 60-minute Sunday show was completely revamped, returning on CBS with a new format and crew. The last NBC show was June 27, 1948; the first show for CBS was October 8, 1948. Despite the jazzed-up format, the new version also expired after one season, leaving the air July 1, 1949.

So different were the two seasons of *The Ford Theatre* that they might have been separate shows. Sponsored by the Ford Motor Company, the show was billed in preseason press releases as the highest-budgeted program of its kind.

Despite its big budget, *The Ford Theatre* began almost timidly. There was little ballyhoo and few guest stars from Hollywood and the stage. The show offered 60 minutes of modern and time-tested classics. Instead of chasing *The Lux Radio Theatre* down the yellow brick road of Hollywood, *The Ford Theatre* used the top professionals of radio for leads and character roles alike. Karl Swenson, Mason Adams, Anne Seymour, Vicki Vola, Wendell Holmes, Santos Ortega, Lauren Gilbert, Les Tremayne, John Larkin, and Everett Sloane were among the leads in the first year. The plays covered the entire spectrum of popular entertainment, from Twain's *Connecticut Yankee* to O'Neill's *Ah, Wilderness!* Host was Howard Lindsay, co-author of *Life with Father*. Musical score was by Lyn Murray, and the show was directed by George Zachary. The producers offered $2,000 for scripts in an effort to attract big-name novelists and playwrights. They got few, though *The Ford Theatre* in its first year set as its goal two original plays each 13 weeks.

High-calibre productions didn't offset low ratings, and *The Ford Theatre* was completely reorganized for its second season under the direction of Fletcher Markle. It was booked Friday nights on CBS. Even the theme music was different, and Markle began to take his leads from the forefront of Hollywood stardom. The new series led off with *Madame Bovary*, with Claude Rains, Marlene Dietrich, and Van Heflin. The second show brought Burt Lancaster to the microphone for a rare radio appearance in James M. Cain's *Double Indemnity*. In the following weeks, such stars as Lucille Ball, Ingrid Bergman, Douglas Fairbanks, Jr., Ronald Colman, Jean Arthur, Edward G. Robinson, Claudette Colbert, Vincent Price, Bob Hope, Jack Benny, Bing Crosby, Charles Laughton, Montgomery Clift, Bette Davis, and Helen Hayes appeared for Ford. It was clear by then that Markle had decided on the yellow brick road after all. It was well and good—it just wasn't the same show any more.

Foreign Assignment

Foreign Assignment came to Mutual July 24, 1943, following the fictitious trail of Brian Barry, correspondent for *The American Press*. With his lovely assistant Carol Manning, Barry was neck-deep in wartime espionage, fighting the Gestapo in occupied France. It opened to the rhythmic beat of teletypes: "And one of those machines you hear—listen—[*clatter, click*]—that machine is beating out a story written especially for you; a story unfolded against the screen of actual events that are making the news." Jay Jostyn and Vicki Vola, the hard-hitting team from *Mr. District Attorney*, were brought in as Brian and Carol. The show was created and written by Frank H. Phares, and directed by Chick Vincent.

Fort Laramie

Fort Laramie was brought to CBS on January 22,1956, by Norman Macdonnell, who had four years of Gunsmoke experience behind him. But Fort Laramie was much lower-key than Gunsmoke, built around situations that were far less tense. Macdonnell intended Fort Laramie to be "a monument to ordinary men who lived in extraordinary times." Their enemies were "the rugged, uncharted country, the heat, the cold, disease, boredom and, perhaps last of all, hostile Indians." Men died at Fort Laramie—some of drowning, some of freezing, others of typhoid and smallpox. "But it's a matter of record that in all the years the cavalry was stationed at Fort Laramie, only four troopers died of gunshot wounds." This, then, is what this show was about: everyday life on the Wyoming frontier. It wasn't Gunsmoke, to be sure, but then, few shows were. Macdonnell told the story of Captain Lee Quince and the men who served him. Quince was well-played by Raymond Burr. Vic Perrin was Sergeant Goerss, Harry Bartell was Lieutenant Seiberts, and Jack Moyles was Major Daggett. Music was by Amerigo Moreno; sound effects were by those Gunsmoke perfectionists, Ray Kemper, Bill James and Tom Hanley. This was another of the solid shows that came along after taps had blown for radio.

The Four Star Playhouse

The Four Star Playhouse was a 1949 NBC effort, first heard July 3, and quickly put together as part of the network's barrage against CBS. During the previous summer, CBS had raided the top of NBC's comedy line, luring Jack Benny, "Amos and Andy," and others into a network jump. NBC's reaction was almost frantic: a battery of new shows like this one, featuring glamor and lots of big names. The Four Star Playhouse was an audio repertory, using four famous movie stars, with each playing one part a month. The stories were adapted from Cosmopolitan; the stars were Fred MacMurray, Loretta Young, Rosalind Russell, and Robert Cummings. The productions, directed by Warren Lewis, were entertaining and well done, but the new NBC lineup just couldn't compete against the old, which CBS stacked into the same time slots on Sunday. Most of the new shows vanished from the air within months, and The Four Star Playhouse was one of them.

The Frank Morgan Show

The Frank Morgan Show was, in the end, a misnomer of sorts, because Morgan spent most of his radio career sharing a format with someone else. Those shows, covered elsewhere, are recapped as follows: in 1937, Morgan became a regular with Fanny Brice on NBC's Good News of 1938. That show evolved in 1940 into Maxwell House Coffee Time, slimming down from 60 to 30 minutes but keeping the same sponsor and Thursday-night time slot. Maxwell House Coffee Time was divided equally between Morgan and Brice; she used 15 minutes for a "Baby Snooks" skit, he used the remaining 15 for a monologue—usually a tall tale about his exploits in younger days. This joint format ran for four years. In 1944, Fanny Brice pulled away for her own Baby Snooks Show, and Morgan began his Frank Morgan Show. This was essentially a variety hour, featuring more tall tales and backed by Robert Young and Cass Daley. It too was carried by Maxwell House in the old Thursday time slot. But Morgan without Snooks lost a huge piece of rating. This show lasted only a year. Morgan came back in 1946 for another season of situation comedy, as The Fabulous Dr. Tweedy.

The Frank Sinatra Show

The Frank Sinatra Show was an outgrowth of the Sinatra mania that had gripped the nation's bobby-soxers in the early 1940's. Sinatra first came to radio in 1937, as a member of the singing quartet, The Hoboken Four. For a time, the group appeared on Major Bowes' Amateur Hour. Later, Sinatra sang with the orchestras of Harry James and Tommy Dorsey; still later, he appeared on NBC's Your Hit Parade.

Sinatra came up through the ranks of the big swing era, graduating from news reporting to entertaining. For a time in his youth, he worked for a small New Jersey paper, but decided to get out of journalism after seeing the adoration lavished upon Bing Crosby at a live appearance. After a brief apprenticeship as one of The Hoboken Four, Sinatra struck out on his own. For six months he traveled with Harry James, and in December 1939, he joined Tommy Dorsey. It was his first giant step on the road to fame and glory.

By September 1942, Sinatra had learned the finer points of radio, film, and live performing. He left Dorsey and began to freelance. He was ripe for radio and radio was ready for him. His own Frank Sinatra Show came to CBS on January 5, 1944, for Lever Brothers and later Max Factor.

If any of Sinatra's radio shows had significance, it was his war-time show for CBS. When this Wednesday series opened in 1944, Sinatra was the hottest property on Radio Row. Girls stood in line for more than ten hours, then packed into CBS' Vine Street Theatre for a 30-minute glimpse of the crooner in action. *Radio Life*, covering a Sinatra broadcast early in 1944, found fans gathering on the street outside the theatre at the "unbelievably early" hour of 6:45 A.M. They camped all day on the sidewalks, bringing brown-bag lunches and fat Sinatra scrapbooks. Some drifted away for lunch at a nearby hot dog stand, then scampered back to the line before the real crowds came. They were the bobbysox crowd, long rows of sweaters and skirts and white socks rolled down over saddle shoes. By 3 P.M.—still three hours before the show—the street was packed tight with them.

The theatre opened to an overflow crowd. Those who couldn't get in often tried to bluff their way past guards. They claimed to be Sinatra's kin; some passed bogus tickets and tried to brush past before the guards could stop them. Others found hiding places in the theatre, crouching in the shadows until the audience from the previous broadcast had left.

The show itself was just another variety hour. Sinatra brought on such high-powered guests as Gene Kelly, Jane Powell, Lawrence Tibbett, Fred Allen, and his old maestro Tommy Dorsey. But to the studio audience, "Frankie" was the only attraction. They burst into wild shrieking, screaming, and sighing as he "ooo-ahhed" his way through his number. So fanatic were Sinatra's fans that some critics openly branded them "morons." Some even suggested that the gasps, screams, and swooning by Sinatriacs was staged by the singer's promoters. George Evans, Sinatra's press agent, offered $1,000 to anyone who could prove that. Maybe the "moron" explanation stands the test of time. Anyway, nobody collected.

When the show arrived on CBS, Sinatra imported an old friend from the Dorsey years, Axel Stordahl, to arrange the music. Sponsor-ship switched to Old Gold in 1945, and the title became *Songs by Sinatra*, but the show continued its basic musical variety format. The Pied Pipers—another act from the Dorsey days—were brought in to handle novelty numbers between his acts. And when, in October 1945, the "sentimental gentleman of swing" himself appeared as guest, it was almost like old home week.

The show ran on Wednesday nights until 1947. Sinatra's five-a-week 15-minute show, *Light Up Time*, featuring Dorothy Kirsten began on NBC in 1949, running one season for Lucky Strike. Sinatra also had shows in 1950–51 (CBS, Sunday); 1953–55 (NBC, two a week); and 1956–58 (ABC).

The Fred Allen Show

The Fred Allen Show starred the king of the snarling whine, born John Florence Sullivan on May 31, 1894, in Cambridge, Massachusetts. He worked his way from a 20-cent-an-hour library aide to a million-dollar-a-year radio comic, and along the way added a solid corner-stone to the growing medium of radio entertainment.

Allen entered radio through the vaudeville stage door, parlaying an ability to juggle four balls into first, a cornball comic routine and later, a sophisticated act that didn't need the visual boost of juggling to carry it. He became one of the nation's best authorities on humor, accumulating 4,000 books on comedy. But even Allen was sometimes puzzled at the things that made people laugh. He knew what they were and how to use them. Just why they worked was something the analysts could figure out.

Allen was a lifelong entertainer, starting on the amateur night circuit around Boston in 1912 for 50 cents a night and supper. For his first appearance, he was billed as Paul Huckle, European Entertainer. Later he became Fred St. James, juggling for $25 a week in small New England theatres. As his sense of timing grew and his instinct for comedy broadened, he began to downplay the juggling and bring out his funny side. He underwent another name change, becoming Fred-die James, the World's Worst Juggler. In 1914, he saved $100 and went to New York to try big-time vaudeville.

What Allen found in the city was big-time poverty. He ate 10-cent meals and lived in a $4-a-week hotel. He worked when his agent could place him, but lived always on the edge of starvation. In 1916, he took a booking in Australia, coming home the following year more polished and better equipped to search for the success that had eluded him before.

He booked into the New England road circuit at $175 a week. Poverty was a thing of the past now. By 1920, Allen was an estab-lished vaudeville headliner, moving into the new decade with a new name.

He was Fred Allen now, taking the name from an agent named Allen. He came to Broadway in The Passing Show of 1922, and there met a young chorus girl, Portland Hoffa, who became Mrs. Allen in 1928. Portland shared his career in an active way, becoming his squeaky-voiced co-star when he opened on CBS October 23, 1932, in The Linit Bath Club Revue, a Sunday-night 30-minute comedy pro-gram for Linit Bath Oil.

It must have been sheer fright, Allen sometimes suggested later, that made her use that high-pitched squeal on the air. Actually, her voice was quite gentle, but the squeak took hold and the softer tones were saved for the real Portland that listeners of the radio never heard. Offstage, the Allens were a strange couple by stardom standards. They lived quietly and modestly, renting their Manhattan apartment, never owning such luxury items as cars, and usually shunning large gatherings and loud parties. They were known as one of radio's most devoted couples, seldom seen apart, filling their spare moments with long walks around New York late at night, when the workday was finished. At the height of his career, Allen had little time for anything else.

He griped incessantly about his daily grind, swearing often to give it up for a more sane existence. He was working twelve to sixteen hours a day, and the "grind" followed a prescribed routine. Once a week he met with his writers, for an impromptu give-and-take session of joke-swapping. When the show ran Sundays nights, the session took place on Wednesday; when the show moved to Wednesday, the staff met on Friday. Allen took notes in the meetings, scribbling in his own cryptic shorthand, then retired to a small room in his apartment to write the script. His scripts were usually highly topical; he constantly scribbled tidbits of talk from friends, and he read and clipped nine newspapers a day. All weekend long he worked on the script, breaking only for Sunday Mass. He emerged on Monday with a rough draft, still far from complete. Improvisions continued through the week, through two rehearsals and sometimes right up to air time.

Even with the show in progress, Allen might toss away pages of script for long sessions of ad-libbing. He was the undisputed master of the ad-lib, a craftsman who thought on his feet with the pressure of a nationwide audience on his back. In an immortal tribute, his friendly enemy Jack Benny once said, "You wouldn't dare talk to me that way if my writers were here."

Like most vaudeville comics, Allen made a slow transition from the stage to the air. His *Linit* shows, backed by the music of Lou Katzman, still showed heavy influences of standup patter and stiff stage comedy. In 1933, Allen was heard in *The Salad Bowl Revue* for Hellman's Mayonnaise. Later that year he opened to Ferde Grofe's music on NBC for Sal Hepatica, *The Sal Hepatica Revue*, which became *Hour of Smiles* and finally, in 1934, his famous *Town Hall Tonight*.

Town Hall Tonight, by then a full 60-minute Wednesday night production, served as a vehicle for young Walter Tetley, who on *The Great Gildersleeve* and *The Phil Harris–Alice Faye Show* more than a decade later became one of the great obnoxious brats of the air.

It was on the *Town Hall* program in 1936 that Allen started his well-remembered feud with Benny. He began to wisecrack about Benny's violin, saying that the strings of that fabled instrument would have been better off left in the cat. Benny bristled on his Sunday show; Allen came back the following Wednesday. So it went, all through that year, until there was little left but to fight it out.

The "battle of the century" was slated before a nationwide radio audience in the ballroom of the Hotel Pierre. After a long buildup, the boys squared off on March 14, 1937, bludgeoning each other with torrid insults and finally, stepping out into an alley to have it out. The fight was on, with staggered commentary by Mary Livingstone and announcer Don Wilson. And the winner? We may never know. When Benny and Allen returned to the ballroom, they were backslapping and talking as warm friends, remembering the old days in vaudeville. But the "feud" was to continue for another twelve years, until Allen left the air forever.

Both men changed their formats, from the stiff vaudeville acts of the 1930's into the polished comic routines of the 1940's. After a six-year Wednesday-night romp through the old *Town Hall*, the program closed its doors in 1939, becoming simply *The Fred Allen Show*, but sticking to the 60-minute format into 1940. Within that hour, Allen presented some song and music, the "News of the Day Newsreel," and a feature skit performed by the Mighty Allen Art Players. The newsreel feature usually was devoted to some obscure news event, carefully culled from Allen's critical reading of the papers. Often in the middle of the show, he would interview someone with an unusual occupation, such as a glass blower, or the owner-proprietor of a lunchwagon. Harry Von Zell was his announcer; Peter Van Steeden who had taken the baton from Lennie Hayton in April 1935, conducted the orchestra. Fred's Oriental detective character, One Long Pan, was created in the *Town Hall* era, often serving as star of the Mighty Allen Art Players skit.

The 1940's brought new demands from the radio audience. The hackneyed vaudeville comedy was out. The people wanted sophistication, flow, and polish. In the fall of 1940, Allen returned to CBS and the half-hour format running Wednesdays as *The Texaco Star Theatre*. That show went to 60 minutes again in 1941, was trimmed to 30 minutes and inserted in the CBS Sunday schedule in 1942. Arthur Godfrey served briefly as Allen's announcer, and such big-name guests as Charles Laughton and the Andrews Sisters helped fill the bill. The mid-1940's also featured the singing of the DeMarco Sisters (Ann, Gene, Gloria, Marie and Arlene). Vick Knight was Allen's director, quitting for *Command Performance* in the early 1940's; Howard Reiley was director through the mid- and late-1940's. Al Goodman was orchestra leader after 1945. But what set his show apart was uniquely Allen's; a wit that was totally original and always sharp.

During the early 1940's, Allen began experimenting with an idea that would eventually emerge as Allen's Alley. The alley, as it developed, was the most unlikely street in the world—it was never described, but left strictly to the listener's imagination. It was sheer radio, with Fred visiting, in order, the Brooklyn tenement of Mrs. Nussbaum, the farmhouse of Titus Moody, the shack where Ajax Cassidy lived, and the ante-bellum mansion of Senator Claghorn.

Mrs. Nussbaum, played by Minerva Pious, was always relating the problem of the week to her troubles with her husband Pierre. Her thick Jewish accent initially bothered some network executives, for even in those innocent days the networks were wary of offending certain minority groups. But Mrs. Nussbaum worked fine, and became one of the long-running stars of Allen's Alley. Parker Fennelly, an ageless character actor, played Titus Moody to perfection. Fennelly, who always greeted Allen with, "Howdy, Bub," was one of the funniest characters on the show. Once he described himself as so anemic that his cut finger didn't bleed—it just puckered and hissed.

The character who doesn't really stand the test of time is Ajax Cassidy, the loudmouth Irishman who lived near the end of the Alley. That spot formerly had been reserved for Falstaff Openshaw, the Alley poet, played by Alan Reed. Allen never was completely happy with that spot, dropping Falstaff-Reed and taking on Peter Donald as Ajax. In the end, Ajax Cassidy proved as difficult to write for as his poetic predecessor.

Star of the Alley was Senator Beauregard Claghorn, who bloomed into a national sensation early in 1946. Claghorn was Kenny Delmar, Fred's announcer, who was also doing the announcing for *Your Hit Parade* and four other shows at the same time. Delmar modeled the Claghorn character after a Texas rancher who gave him a ride in a Model-T Ford in the early years of the Depression. Delmar never forgot the man, or the deep Southern drawl, or the repetitious sentences that were frequently followed by, "That's a joke, son!"

Delmar's impersonation of the rancher was first noticed by Minerva Pious, who brought it to Allen's attention. Allen liked the character at once; it was dubbed Senator Claghorn, Delmar was rushed to Allen's Alley and he became literally an overnight success. By the end of his first month on the air—a total of about five minutes air time—people across the country were mimicking the voice. Senator Claghorn became a brief national sensation. Commercial firms turned out Claghorn shirts and compasses (the needles always pointed South, son). And Delmar cut two Claghorn records, "I Love You, That Is," and "That's a Joke, Son."

High blood pressure forced Allen off the air in 1944, but he returned to NBC in the fall of 1945 for Tenderleaf Tea on Sunday-night. Fred Allen was a show business junkie, an addict who couldn't stay away even after warnings from his doctor that his 80-hour week was wreaking havoc on his blood pressure.

Allen perfected the running gag; his feud with Benny was probably the longest-running gag in radio. It culminated on May 26, 1946, when Benny appeared in the famous "King for a Day" skit on Fred's show. Allen, getting in some digs at giveaway shows, had prepared a skit in which Benny was to pose as a contestant. Benny won the "grand prize," which included a pressing job on his baggy suit. A pressing machine was set up onstage, and the struggling Benny was stripped to his shorts (really) in one of the wildest finishes ever heard. The show ran long, and was cut off the air as Kenny Delmar desperately tried to get in a final word for Tenderleaf Tea above the pandemonium.

It wasn't the first time he had been cut off the air. Allen's show often ran late, but beyond that, he waged war with a group of overly sensitive NBC executives through the middle 1940's. Frequently, when he went to the attack on the air, he was simply blipped out by the network. Allen enjoyed nothing better than jabbing away at network vice-presidents; many of his funniest skits were built around the insanities of the radio business. He was blipped, and came back for more. Finally an angry public forced the network's hand off the button, but still his scripts were subjected to careful network scrutiny.

Allen was never finer than when he was spoofing musicals. His Gilbert and Sullivan material was among the best comedy ever done on the air. For the show of November 25, 1945, he lured Leo (The Lip) Durocher out of the dugout for a wild singing performance as "The Brooklyn Pinafore," complete with Shirley Booth as Dottie Mahoney. In February 1946, Beatrice Lillie helped him destroy *Oklahoma!* with a great skit called "Picadilly!" which also marked the beginning of another running gag—Rodgers and Hammerstein appeared in a subsequent show with a threat to sue Fred for copyright violations.

In the show of October 13, 1946, Allen did another of his famous ripoffs of Gilbert and Sullivan in a skit called "The Radio Mikado." As originally written, the "Mikado" took some hard digs at the "jerks" who ran radio, but Allen never got it past the NBC censor. He had to do a frantic rewrite just before the show went on. It was still funny, and stands today as vintage Allen.

Sponsorship went to Ford Motors in 1947. By then his Alley was firmly entrenched. The long hours began again, leading Allen to gripe that agents "get 10 percent of everything but my blinding headaches." The show was in its last days then, still producing some of the best sounds on the air. But radio was changing again, in an ominous way that wouldn't leave room for the original comedy that Fred Allen practiced. Week by week, TV was cutting into the radio audience. The byword now was gimmickry. Allen's rating dropped 17 points when *Stop the Music,* a first-class gimmick show, was scheduled against him by ABC.

Allen did his final show on June 26, 1949. Appropriately, along with Henry Morgan, his last guest was Jack Benny. Then Allen faded into the woodwork, confining himself mainly to guest spots. He did a TV special, which bombed. In 1952, he was to begin a TV series when his first heart attack forced him into semi-retirement.

But Fred Allen was the kind of man who couldn't stay retired. He took a spot as a panelist on the TV show *What's My Line?,* a job he was holding at his death. That came on the night of March 17, 1956. In one of the few walks he had taken without his wife, Allen collapsed and died just outside the West 75th Street home of a friend.

His show was a pacemaker of radio comedy. His greatest appeal was always to a thinking audience, but his biting wit and Boston twang touched the masses as well. Three decades later, in recordings of his old shows, he still touches them.

The Fred Waring Show

The Fred Waring Show was heard for twenty years, in a wide variety of times and formats. Waring's band grew from a Penn State quartet into a dynamic organization of more than "half a hundred Pennsylvanians," and at one time numbered about seventy. All had to be paid, and that made Waring's show one of radio's most expensive. But his sound became an audio trademark, and few were the years between 1930 and 1950 when Waring's orchestra and chorus wasn't found on some network. It all started in 1920 when Waring organized his first band and began touring. In 1932, Waring was signed for a CBS series of Sunday night Roxy Theatre shows, where the band was a six-month hit. By 1933, he was heard on CBS Wednesday nights for Old Gold Cigarettes. In 1934, Waring's Pennsylvanians were taken in by Ford Motors and were set up in New York's renovated Hudson Theatre for their Blue Network series, first heard Thursdays and in 1935 Tuesdays and Fridays over two networks. One of the themes in those days was "Breezing Along with the Breeze," which fit well with the "Watch the Fords Go By" messages from the sponsor. NBC signed Waring in 1938; that was the beginning of an association with that network that would last for the rest of his radio years. In the 1938–39 season, his show was sponsored by Bromo Quinine. On June 19, 1939, he began *Chesterfield Time;* it ran until 1944. In June 1945, Waring became part of an NBC experiment, an effort to bring nighttime quality to daytime radio. His show, starting at 11 A.M. (EST), was heard five times a week, and was sustained by the network. At $18,000 for the orchestra alone, it was rumored to be the highest-priced daytime show ever. It soon picked up partial sponsorship of the American Meat Company, and ran until 1949. From 1947 through 1949, Waring also did a weekly nighttime NBC series for General Electric. In 1950, he was on the air Saturdays.

Waring's long, successful career was the result of a distinctive sound. His huge orchestra projected a sense of depth not found elsewhere. The Pennsylvanians sang the numbers they played. Waring's organization contained many vocal groups, a renowned glee club, and scores of soloists, composers, and arrangers. Some of them were Jane Wilson, Joan Wheatley, Gordon Goodman, Jimmy Atkins, Gordon Berger, Don Craig, Daisy Bernier, Three Bees and a Honey, Donna Dae and Ruth Cottingham. Drummer Poley McClintock and Fred's brother, Tom, were with Waring from his high school days.

The Free Company

The Free Company was formed on CBS on February 23, 1941, as a unique group of distinguished American writers who had joined forces to combat foreign propaganda. The writers, through their most effective tool, would try to "interpret the true spirit of the Bill of Rights." Their interpretations were designed to prove that "in the spring of 1941, with all our flaws and all our problems, the American way is still the best way of life on earth."

Joining hands in the venture were Orson Welles, Robert Sherwood, Sherwood Anderson, George M. Cohan, Ernest Hemingway, Stephen Vincent Benét, Archibald MacLeish, Maxwell Anderson, Marc Connelly, Paul Green, William Saroyan, Norman Corwin, and Elmer Rice. James Boyd, distinguished writer of American historical novels, was chairman. The group would, he said, be "unpaid, unsponsored and uncontrolled—just a group of Americans saying what they think about this country and about freedom."

Less than two months after its opener, *The Free Company* itself was on the carpet—accused in the pages of William Randolph Hearst's newspapers of promoting the same subversive propaganda it was trying to blunt. Hearst quoted American Legion officials and members of the California Sons of the American Revolution, who objected to the shows. The following week, the story broke nationally, with a column in *Time.* One of the Legion's objections concerned the show, "The Mole On Lincoln's Cheek," a plea for "freedom to teach" and a plug for "honest textbooks." But *Time* pointed out that Hearst's campaign seemed particularly geared against Orson Welles. Most of the negative comment concerned the April 6 Welles-written contribution, "His Honor, the Mayor," about freedom of assembly and a group of fascist "white crusaders."

Time also noted that Hearst's blast seemed especially timed with the release date of the Welles film, *Citizen Kane*. Hearst had previously sought to have the film suppressed, the magazine said, "on the grounds that it looked too much like an unflattering portrait of Citizen Hearst."

The Free Company took the defense, sending Burgess Meredith before the microphone for the April 20 show to read a long-winded explanation—not once, but twice—of the group's purpose, problems and philosophy. *The Free Company*, he said, had the endorsement of the attorney general and the solicitor general of the United States. Meredith recapped the careers of the writers, throwing in their past military and literary service to America. He told of the "thousands of letters of appreciation" received from the listening public. None of it mattered much. Soon *The Free Company* slipped from the air and was forgotten.

As a group, its writers were too strong for American radio. They were just a few years ahead of their time.

Free World Theatre

Free World Theatre was produced and directed by Arch Oboler for the Blue Network. It premièred February 21, 1943, and ran about four months, bowing out on June 27. The show was conceived by Oboler as a dramatization of ideas, offered by world leaders, for handling the war and the coming peace. Oboler spent a month just writing to the leaders. Among them: Thomas Mann, Aldous Huxley, Winston Churchill, President Roosevelt, Henry Wallace, George Bernard Shaw, Joseph Stalin, and Chiang Kai-shek. Answers began coming in almost immediately. Since this was a government show, Oboler had the top actors and writers in America at his disposal. He wrote the first show, "The People March," then did about one a month, leaving the bulk of the writing to others. Musical score was by Gordon Jenkins. As for the quality of the statements from world leaders, Oboler received only one negative reply, a grumbling statement from George Bernard Shaw. He even used that, in a play about the negative side. The big trouble with the statements, Oboler confided in *Newsweek*, was that "some of these gentlemen don't understand what a drama is. We got some important statements, but some very dull ones."

Friendly Five Footnotes

Friendly Five Footnotes, a delightful Blue Network show of 1930–31, featured an enjoyable blend of music and news from the primitive world of aviation. Master of ceremonies was a character identified only as Friendly Fred who tap-danced to the theme, "I've Got Five Dollars." The orchestra, known as the Friendly Five Orchestra, was called to attention this way: "Gentlemen! On your toes! The Friendly Five Footnotes are on the air!" Aviation news was delivered by Casey Jones, vice-president of the Curtis-Wright Corporation. Sponsor was Friendly Five Shoes, whose outlets offered a premium booklet, *It's Easy to Learn to Fly*.

Front Page Farrell

Front Page Farrell, an unusual cross between soap opera and nighttime thriller drama, took to the Mutual air June 23, 1941. In 1942, it moved to NBC, where it ran for twelve years. It was the story of a "crack newspaperman and his wife, the story of David and Sally Farrell." With dozens of its peers, it came from the production studios of Frank and Anne Hummert.

Murder usually was involved in *Front Page Farrell*, but that didn't stop the Hummerts from miring the action in afternoon goo. In its early days on Mutual (when young Richard Widmark played David), it was known as "the unforgettable story of marriage and a newspaper office—the story of a handsome, dashing young star reporter on one of New York's greatest newspapers, and the girl he marries on impulse, to save her from throwing herself away on a rich man twice her age."

David was the star of the *New York Eagle*, and the corny epigraph was discarded as the show moved to NBC. Staats Cotsworth, best known for his lead in *Casey, Crime Photographer*, played David for most of the run, and it was also played by Carleton Young. Florence Williams and Virginia Dwyer were featured over the years as Sally. Sponsors for the Mutual series were Anacin and later Kolynos Toothpaste. In short, this was just another Hummert soap, though the reporter-crime angle was unusual for afternoon listening. During its earliest, corniest period, David was often sent to cover war production work. Once, to demonstrate his manhood to listeners, he enlisted in the army and prepared to go to war. Just before he was scheduled to report, he and Sally stood gazing dreamily at the stars and pondering their future:

SALLY: All my life I've wished on that star. And tonight I'm going to make the most important wish of all.

DAVID: What is it, dear?

SALLY: It's almost a prayer, David. I wish that in dedicating our future and our lives to our country and our God, you and I will be adding one tiny spark to bring back the light of peace and security to our darkened world . . . and that, when victory has come, we'll start here again, at the door of our home together, and live out the rest of our lives in contentment.

DAVID: Yes, darling—it'll come true. It's got to come true!

SALLY: Yes, David.

DAVID: I know it so well. Even though you and I will be apart—I in the Army, and you working here in New York, we'll never really be apart. Your hand will be in mine—like this. We'll be together in our love, darling. We'll be together *always*! No matter what happens, nothing can—nothing *will* ever change that. *Nothing!*

Organ Music Up

ANNOUNCER: And so David and Sally Farrell stand on the doorstep of their little home, facing the future, not knowing what it will bring them, but knowing in their hearts that they have kept faith with themselves, their country and their God. They stand there beneath the stars, ready to do their part to bring back to this world the everlasting right which belongs to each and every one of us—the right to live in love, security and peace!

Frontier Gentleman

Frontier Gentleman began with these words: "Herewith, an Englishman's account of life and death in the West. As a reporter for *The London Times*, he writes his colorful and unusual accounts. But as a man with a gun, he lives and becomes a part of the violent years in the new territories. Now, starring John Dehner, this is the story of J. B. Kendall, Frontier Gentleman . . ."

That was the beginning of as fine a series of Western drama as ever graced the air. *Frontier Gentleman* was the last important show to première on radio. It was heard on CBS for a brief run premiering February 9, 1958, and stands as the only serious rival to *Gunsmoke* in the radio Hall of Fame.

The producers could do no better with the part of Kendall than John Dehner. Dehner, who also played Paladin in the better-known but inferior *Have Gun, Will Travel,* was always convincing in these parts that called for dry wit and subdued sophistication. His handling of J. B. Kendall was letter-perfect, and he got fine support from such old pros as.John McIntire, Jeanette Nolan, Lawrence Dobkin, Stacy Harris, Harry Bartell, Virginia Gregg, Jack Moyles, Joe Kearns, and Jack Kruschen. The series was created by Antony Ellis, the writer-director whose work on *Gunsmoke*, *Escape*, and other top shows stamped him as one of radio's outstanding talents. Wilbur Hatch and Jerry Goldsmith, both composers and conductors, were responsible for the beautiful trumpet theme that introduced the show.

Kendall's adventures through the new territories came in all forms. There was tragedy, brutality, pathos, and earthy humor. Kendall met nameless drifters, bushwackers, and real people from history. Ellis asked his listeners to believe that when Jack McCall shot Wild Bill Hickok during a poker game, J. B. Kendall was one of the players. Kendall met Calamity Jane, Jesse James, and "the richest man in the West." He won a slave girl, Gentle Virtue, in a card game, and became friends with a gambling queen. He defended an unpopular man against a murder charge, and one night on the wild Kansas prairie, he even had a brush with the supernatural.

.Perhaps the best of all *Frontier Gentleman* shows was "Random Notes." It wasn't even a story in the strict sense—rather a loosely woven collection of vignettes. On a long stage trip, Kendall jotted down some of the funny, touching things he had seen in Western America; little snatches of life that might really have happened. A condemned killer asked Kendall to write his story; a hick-town production of Shakespeare turned to shambles. That detail, cumbersome on other shows, was what made this series go. Too bad Kendall's great performance was for a condemned medium.

Fu Manchu

Fu Manchu, the prince of darkness, master scientist and evil genius created by Sax Rohmer, had several hearings on radio. The first was on the old *Collier Hour* in a series of twelve-chapter serials, running around 1929–30. Arthur Hughes played the title role. A new series of *Fu Manchu* dramas was launched on CBS on September 26, 1932, and ran until April 24, 1933. These were half-hour stories, each complete in itself, sponsored by Campana Balm Monday evenings at 8:45. They were produced at the CBS studio in Chicago, and Rohmer himself was on hand for the opener. Fred Ibbett directed, and John C. Daly played the evil Dr. Fu. The heroes, Nayland Smith and Dr. James Petrie, were played by Charles Warburton and Bob White. Sunda Love was the beautiful Karameneh, slave to the evil scientist's powers. Half way through the production, John C. Daly and Sunda Love dropped out, and were replaced by Harold Huber and Charlotte Manson.

The third series was *The Shadow of Fu Manchu;* it began syndication as a three-a-week 15-minute serial in 1939. This one featured Hanley Stafford and Gale Gordon, funnymen-to-be, as Nayland Smith and Dr. Petrie. The shows were faithful to Rohmer's books, and admirably captured the creeping yellow fog of London at midnight. Nayland Smith was Dr. Fu's sworn enemy, relentlessly tracking him around the world. Fu Manchu was depicted as one of those ingenious people, "born once every three or four generations," who had the ability to change the course of the world. He might have revolutionized science, but chose the path of evil instead. His arsenal of weapons ranged from the snake in the cane handle to a green mist, delivered in letters, which filled a room and killed instantly. In one episode, police were attacked and killed by a fungus growing in Dr. Fu's basement. Smith and Petrie were drugged, threatened, and tortured. They encountered a paralyzing "flower of silence," a strange force that could bring horrible, coughing death, a "fiery hand," a sacred white peacock, and poisoned claws. These elements made Fu Manchu one of the most effective villains to come out of juvenile radio. The final series was produced in seventy-seven chapters, and was broadcast in New York from March till September 1940.

Furlough Fun

Furlough Fun, first heard on NBC West Coast stations in 1943–44, featured music, comedy, and interviews with servicemen who had seen action on the war fronts. "Femmcee" Beryl Wallace chatted informally with the men, who came from hospitals, redistribution centers, flying fields, and camps. A comic routine was developed by George Riley; music was by Spike Jones and the City Slickers. The interviews were of the "most thrilling moment" type, and the show was heard on Friday nights. Bradford Brown produced; Larry Keating announced.

Gang Busters

Gang Busters grew out of an earlier show called *G-Men*, which was first heard on NBC for Chevrolet July 20, 1935, with a dramatization of the death of John Dillinger. Born in violence, the show featured the sounds of mayhem: The sharp blast of a policeman's whistle. Shuffling feet. Shots. A broken window. The metallic voice of a burglar alarm. The forlorn answer of a police siren. Machine guns spraying bullets like Flit. Tires screeching, glass breaking. The war on the underworld has begun anew. *Gang Busters* is on the air.

This best-remembered of all police shows was done "in cooperation with police and federal law enforcement departments throughout the United States." It was billed as "the only national program that brings you authentic police case histories."

It came about in the summer of 1935, when Phillips H. Lord talked NBC into developing a "thoroughly authoritative" pilot series about the government's war against crime. The G-Men were hot stuff in those days. The FBI shootout with Dillinger outside the Biograph Theatre had made headlines the year before, and was still fresh in the minds of the people. It was the golden age of gangsters; "Pretty Boy" Floyd, "Baby Face" Nelson, and Clyde Barrow helped glamorize the underworld. Radio needed a show glamorizing the other side, and Phillips H. Lord was the guy to give it to them.

Lord, recognized as one of the great idea men of radio, had played *Seth Parker* since 1929, and was ready for a change of pace. He sold his idea to Chevrolet, then flew to Washington to gather the official blessing of J. Edgar Hoover, head of all the G-Men. Hoover agreed to let Lord use FBI files on "closed" cases (provided the Bureau could review the scripts), and the new series was off and running. On January 15, 1936, the show began its Wednesday night run on CBS for Palmolive Soap, under the title *Gang Busters*.

The format was interview style. It began with Lord interviewing, "by proxy," a local lawman or federal agent who figured prominently in the story. Later, Colonel H. Norman Schwarzkopf of the U.S. Army was brought in as interviewer. "Now picture our setting as a special office, turned over to *Gang Busters* by Lewis J. Valentine of the New York City police," the announcer said. Valentine's name was thus associated with the show even when he didn't appear, and the "office" setting gave the connotation of official blessing. Lord, and later Schwarzkopf, would chat informally in this "office," which actually wasn't at police headquarters at all. They reviewed the case chronologically. The voices of Lord and his "proxy" cop faded slowly and the dramatization began.

The dramatists took some liberties with the cases. Instead of sticking with the documented investigative aspects, they usually told the stories from the criminal's viewpoint. They related in detail his mad, violent, and always hopeless flight to avoid justice. Seen through the lawbreaker's eyes, the road of crime looked scary indeed. There were mad dogs in *Gang Busters*, to be sure, but many others were ordinary people trapped by time and circumstance. No matter. The message of *Gang Busters* rang loud and clear: *Crime isn't the way. Crime doesn't pay.*

The sound effects for the opening were the loudest, most elaborate ever devised for radio. Cutting into the opening was a filtered voice, giving descriptions of men in "calling all cars" fashion. "More to follow on *Gang Busters'* Clues!" the announcer shouted, and the story began.

The "clues" element became one of the most successful aspects of the show. After each play, nationwide alarms were broadcast for actual criminals wanted by police or FBI agents. Fine details of the criminal's appearance—with special emphasis on scars and distinguishing marks—helped capture 110 wanted men in the first three years of the run.

Sponsorship shifted to *Cue Magazine* in 1939, and the show was heard Saturday nights. *Gang Busters* moved to the Blue in 1940, was heard until 1944 on Fridays for Sloan's Liniment; by then the Blue had become ABC. By 1943, more than 1,500 clues had been broadcast, often as many as six per show. The tally that year showed that 286 real criminals, always described as "armed and extremely dangerous," had been brought to justice by *Gang Busters*.

From 1945 through 1948, *Gang Busters* was heard Saturdays on ABC for Waterman Pens. Adding another "authoritative" element was Lewis J. Valentine, crime-busting commissioner of New York police. Valentine advised Lord on technical matters and wrote brief introductions for the early shows. His association with Lord was long-lasting and cordial. In 1945, after forty-two years as a cop, Valentine retired from the force to become full-time *Gang Busters* narrator. He left the show in 1946 to reorganize the Japanese police force for General Douglas MacArthur.

In 1948, the show switched to CBS for General Foods, which carried it on Saturdays until 1953. It was sustained on Saturdays by CBS from 1953 till 1955. *Gang Busters* was last heard on Mutual in 1955–57, as a Wednesday-night show for various sponsors.

Interestingly, *Gang Busters* was among several old shows syndicated and rebroadcast during the current nostalgia craze. The show was not well-received, and one station took it off after a barrage of complaints. The most intriguing complaint was that *Gang Busters* conveyed an image that was far too "pro-police."

The Garry Moore Show

The Garry Moore Show officially opened on CBS in 1949, but by then Moore had been on the air for more than ten years in a variety of formats with many co-stars. He graduated from doing small-time comedy on local radio in Baltimore, St. Louis, and Chicago to become co-star in 1939 of Ransom Sherman's Blue Network *Club Matinee*, a six-a-week affair that gave him his first national exposure. Moore was still going by his given name, Thomas Garrison Morfit, and a lady from Pittsburgh won $50 in a *Club Matinee* "Name the Morfit" contest. By 1940, Moore was hosting NBC's *Beat the Band;* on August 17, 1942, he took the helm of a Monday-through-Saturday morning show, NBC's first attempt to crack into the early-morning bonanza created by Arthur Godfrey and Don McNeill's *Breakfast Club.* Moore's morning show was called *The Show without a Name* until a listener won a $500 contest by naming it *Everything Goes.* It featured the usual early-morning chatter, songs by Brad Reynolds and Marie Greene, the Merry Men Quartet, Irving Miller's Orchestra, and announcer Howard Petrie. Moore picked Petrie as announcer-straight man because of his size. Petrie towered over Moore, and they referred to this fact frequently in their gags. Moore's morning show caught the attention of R. J. Reynolds Tobacco Company, and he was booked into the nighttime *Camel Comedy Caravan* as host. Here he was backed by Ginny Simms, Xavier Cougat's Orchestra, and, again, Petrie. This show led to his meeting with Jimmy Durante and their joint stint, for four years, on CBS. Moore left the *Durante-Moore Show* in 1947, becoming host of NBC's *Take It or Leave It*. He hosted *Breakfast in Hollywood* after the death of Tom Breneman in April 1948. His *Garry Moore Show* of 1949–50 was the same basic formula he had used on *Everything Goes* in the early 1940's: jokes with Petrie, music by Irving Miller and Billy Wardell, banter by Durward Kirby, and songs by Ken Carson and Eileen Woods. It was heard on CBS for 60 minutes each weekday afternoon, giving Moore his push into TV and such game shows as *I've Got a Secret*. His trademarks were zany radio comedy, a crewcut, and a bow tie.

The Gay Nineties Review

The Gay Nineties Revue reflected the nostalgia of the 1940's, showing what America had been singing, saying, and dancing to in the era of gaslights and horse-drawn carriages. Produced by Al Rinker, the show came to CBS in the fall of 1940 after a couple of seasons as a summer replacement, and ran for four years. In a stroke of genius, Rinker hired as master of ceremonies an old-time hoofer named Joe Howard, whose career actually did go back to the "Gay Nineties" and beyond. Howard, at 73 one of the oldest men ever to host a major network show, had begun as a St. Louis trouper in the late 1870's. In the 1880's, he played *Uncle Tom's Cabin* and sang with one of his many wives in the rough-and-tumble Colorado mining camps. By the turn of the century, Howard was a professional song-writer; he wrote some two dozen musicals and 500 songs, including "What's The Use of Dreaming?" and the famed "I Wonder Who's Kissing Her Now." His "Somewhere in France Is the Lily" became one of the most popular songs of World War I. Billed with Howard was Beatrice Kay, playful songstress who delivered Howard's sacred music (in the opinion of a *Radio Life* reviewer) with "burlesque overtones and mock melodramatic touches. She kids them constantly, but Joe still considers them the most serious, sentimental music of our time." Howard was especially attracted to Gay Nineties songs, the reviewer noted, because their themes were "broken hearts, trusts betrayed, weeping women under weeping willows and faded floral wreaths on forgotten graves."

The show had some comedy, some talk, but mainly *The Gay Nineties Revue* offered soft renditions of such old favorites as "After the Ball," "The Band Played On," and "Sweet Adeline." Comic Billy Greene was along for relief, and the rousing numbers were done by a barbership quartet (Philip Reed, Claude Reese, Hubert Hendrie, and Darrel Woodyard). Ray Bloch conducted the music. By 1943, Miss Kay had gone on to Hollywood; her spot was filled by Lillian Leonard, a singer with ancestral ties to Lillian Russell. During this period, a female singing group was billed as The Floradora Girls. The show was sustained on Saturday nights in 1940–41, and ran Mondays for the Model Smoking Tobacco Company in 1941–44. A board of advisors kept material authentic to the period, and *The Gay Nineties Revue* was one of the rare radio shows that dressed its cast to fit the theme. On November 11, 1944, Miss Kay returned on NBC with a new Gay 90's show. This one, *Gaslight Gaieties,* ran Saturday nights and featured Michael O'Shea, singing emcee; Sally Sweetland; the Rockaway Four, Bill Days, Art Davies, Frank Holliday, and Harry Stanton; announcer Perry Ward; and maestro Charles "Bud" Dant.

Gene and Glenn

Gene and Glenn was another comedy-team show that came out of radio's very early days and gained enormous popularity in the Depression era. The men were Gene Carroll and Glenn Rowell, who teamed up in a piano-records-chatter-and-situation format that landed them on NBC for Quaker Oats on December 29, 1930. Broadcasting as *The Quaker Early Birds Program*, Gene and Glenn were heard 15 minutes a day, six days a week. Glenn fed the straight lines and Gene did the comedy. Gene played himself, and was also featured as both Lena and Jake. Lena was owner and Jake was handyman of a boarding house where Gene and Glenn lived. Gene had created these voices before he teamed up with Glenn, tracing the origin to a Tony Wons broadcast at WLS, Chicago, in the late 1920's. Wons was dramatizing *Rip Van Winkle,* playing all the roles himself. But he couldn't get his voice "up" for Rip's wife, so he asked Gene to play that part. An announcer, overhearing the show, said later that Carroll sounded "just like Jake"—whatever that meant. Still joking, the announcer invited Gene on the air again and this time, he said, "bring your girl Lena with you." Gene's portrayal of Lena and Jake always got tremendous response from the audience. Listeners argued constantly over how many people actually were on the air, and some people expressed dismay that Lena would live in a boarding house with three men. Carroll's partnership with Glenn Rowell lasted on various network and local radio slots until 1943. They were playing in Hartford, Connecticut when Glenn decided to quit show business and settle there. Carroll returned to local radio in Cleveland, and in 1947 was signed for *Fibber McGee and Molly* as Lena, the McGees' maid.

Gene Autry's Melody Ranch

Gene Autry's Melody Ranch enjoyed one of the longest, steadiest runs of the air. Beginning on CBS January 7, 1940, Autry's show spanned sixteen years, always on the same network, always for the same sponsor—Wrigley's Gum. The show was always heard either Saturday or Sunday.

Autry had many odd jobs as a boy and young man; he liked to tell how his singing cost him many jobs, and about the time Will Rogers stopped in at the telegraph office where he was working and advised him to keep at it. Job or no job, Autry never did stop singing, and his voice eventually led him into radio. In 1929, he broke in with Station KVOO, Tulsa, singing and telling cowboy yarns gratis. The following year, he emerged on WLS, Chicago, appearing frequently on *The National Barn Dance* and *The National Farm and Home Hour*. By the late 1930's, his screen reputation was established, and Autry was doing guest shots on top nighttime shows. His own show changed little over the years. It featured a slightly sophisticated version of his 1929 act—Autry stories and songs, projected in a campfire atmosphere. Autry told his listeners that his broadcasts were coming directly from his home, Melody Ranch, in the San Fernando Mountains. He surrounded himself with a cast of regular foot-stompers, including Pat Buttram, the Cass County Boys, the Gene Autry Blue Jeans, Johnny Bond, the Pinafores, Alvino Rey, and Carl Cotner's Melody Ranch Six. Announcer was Charlie ("Now, here's the boss man himself, America's favorite cowboy, Gene Autry") Lyon. The music was decidedly Western, with heavy accordion emphasis. There was usually one "Cowboy Classic" by Autry. Buttram's acts were inserted for comic relief, and consisted mainly of back-and-forth banter with Autry (who Buttram always called "Mister Artery") in that croaking frog voice. The jokes were simple—AUTRY: Patrick, how can you be so stupid? BUTTRAM: Well, it ain't easy when you ain't got no brains!—and were greeted by howls from the campfire gang.

The highlight of each show, at least for the juvenile listeners, came when Autry told a 10- to 15-minute story, fully dramatized, of some recent adventure. Then, a few more words about "healthful, refreshin' Doublemint gum, and it was time to be "Back in the saaddle a-again!"

The only break in Autry's long radio career came during the war years, when he joined the Army Air Corps. His oath of office was given on the air in July 1942. In September 1945, he returned to CBS with a 15-minute Western variety show. By 1946, Autry had picked up where he had left off, in his old 30-minute Sunday slot for Wrigley's. There he stayed until 1948, when his show moved to Saturday nights. In 1953, it returned to Sundays, where it ran until 1956.

Gentleman Adventurer

Gentleman Adventurer was a forgettable Mutual adventure that ran in 1948 and starred James Meighan as Allan Drake, insurance investigator. The slant on this was somewhat different. Drake worked for his father, owner of an insurance company specializing in marine policies. His cases found him fighting pirates and hijackers from Burma to the Indies.

Glamor Manor

Glamor Manor premièred July 3, 1944, with Cliff Arguette. It was heard on ABC five times a week at noon, EST, running from 1944 through 1947 as part of the trend—started on NBC—to bring nighttime sounds to daytime radio. *Glamor Manor,* was a situation comedy-variety show, later starring Kenny Baker with Arguette in support.

Baker got his start by winning a 1933 radio contest, did some movies, and was "discovered" by Jack Benny while singing at the Coconut Grove in October 1935. The following month, he began a long association with Benny, as the dumb singer later perfected by Dennis Day. *Glamor Manor* presented Baker as the greatly addled proprietor of the Glamor Manor Hotel. He was forever a day late and a dollar short in business and in his romance with girlfriend Barbara Dilley, played by Barbara Eiler. There was a village idiot named Schlepperman (Sam Hearn), and such well-known guests as Jack Benny helped pep up the noonday hour. Elvia Allman played man-crazy Mrs. Biddle and Don Wilson was the hotel's star boarder. Harry Lubin provided the music, and the show was sponsored by Crisco and Ivory Snow. Kenny's theme was "There's a small hotel . . . . "

The Goldbergs

The Goldbergs had its roots in a 1929 Gertrude Berg serial, *Effie and Laura,* which lasted only one broadcast on CBS. Undaunted, Mrs. Berg took her idea to NBC, where in November, her comedy-serial, top-heavy with rough Jewish dialect, was accepted and scheduled for broadcast.

Mrs. Berg had always wanted to write. Born in Harlem October 3, 1899, she married Lewis Berg at 19 and spent the next ten years raising her family. In the late 1920's, she returned to her writing. She tried magazines with no success, and started seriously writing for radio at the suggestion of a friend. Hers was the first major Jewish comedy of the air, an innovation when Phillips Carlin, chief of NBC sustaining shows, decided to try it in 1929. *The Rise of the Goldbergs* went on the NBC air November 20, 1929, as a weekly 15-minute sustaining show. Even though it was heard most often in soap opera time, *The Goldbergs* cut across radio lines and became something unique in broadcast history.

Gertrude Berg was one of those rare people who could create an image of herself and find it nationally acceptable as a true way of life for millions of others. She wrote her early NBC shows for $75 a week. For this fee, she was also asked to play Molly, after she read the scripts for NBC officers to show how the inflections should be done. Soon she became so closely identified with Molly Goldberg that fans forgot her real name. Even studio hands called her Molly, and acquaintances addressed her husband as Mr. Goldberg. Her Molly Goldberg became one of the great characters of the air, possessing the very breath of the Jewish ghetto.

It was a world Mrs. Berg knew first-hand, even though she didn't live there. During the early years of the show, she often went shopping, socializing, or browsing among the rat-infested tenements, vegetable stands, and pushcarts of New York's lower East side. Here were gathered thousands of Jewish immigrants, hard-working common people, peddlers, panhandlers. Their language was pure Yiddish, a tongue Mrs. Berg had learned from her grandmother. Their frustrations were universal. Basically, they were family people who worried about life's earthy values and carried on a quiet, timeless struggle with outsiders and each other. Mrs. Berg went among them incognito, to avoid upsetting the routine. Then she captured that struggle on paper and shared it with a radio audience numbering millions.

The show revolved around Molly's relationship with her vigorous husband Jake, their children Sammy and Rosalie, and Molly's Uncle David on her father's side. The Goldbergs lived at the mythical address, 1038 East Tremont Avenue, which Mrs. Goldberg later confessed was an intersection in the Bronx. It may have been the lowest-key of all daytime shows. Molly was a tender, kindly, homespun philosopher, who "Yoo-hooed" her way through life; Jake was a family man, a poor tailor of quick temper. James R. Waters played Jake all the way; Roslyn Siber was Rosalie and Alfred Ryder was Sammy.

In 1931, the show was picked up by Pepsodent as a nightly serial. It ran on NBC until Pepsodent dropped it in 1934. In 1937, the show was revived on CBS for Oxydol and was heard concurrently on Mutual for a short time. It ran continuously in that CBS daily format for eight years. In June 1941, *The Goldbergs* was picked up again by NBC, again giving it brief rare exposure on two networks. At the same time, it was heard in New York on WOR, home station of the Mutual network.

Uncle David, added to the family after the show was under way, was created by Menasha Skulnik, who played the part through the war years. But it was Mrs. Berg who ran the show. By then she was getting $5,000 a week for writing, producing, directing, and starring in *The Goldbergs*. As sole owner, she became a benevolent dictator, insisting on control even over such fine points as sound effects. She insisted on authenticity; few sounds were simulated on *The Goldbergs*. When a scene was set in the Goldberg kitchen, Mrs. Berg broke real eggs into a real frying pan, and each member of the cast rattled his own china. Once she gave Roslyn Siber an on-the-air shampoo, when the script called for Molly to wash Rosalie's hair. Her ear for dialect was critically tuned for each broadcast. "I've watched her make Waters, who has played Jake for ten years, repeat a simple line like, 'Sammy, you're breaking your father's heart,' seventeen or eighteen times, until she feels it will register with the unseen audience," William Birnie wrote in a 1941 *American Magazine* article.

Birnie also had great respect for Mrs. Berg's writing abilities. "Once when an important character failed to show up at the last moment, she turned out an entirely new script in eight minutes flat." Those were the days when Mrs. Berg was doing two *Goldbergs* broadcasts, writing her scripts three weeks in advance, and churning out the soap opera *Kate Hopkins* at the same time.

The Goldbergs might be described as the Jewish version of *One Man's Family*. The kids grew up, changed, got married. The parents got plump and old and fretful. Through it all Molly was the stalwart, the wise mother figure whose best lines ("Better a crust of bread and enjoy it than a cake that gives you indigestion") were often ad-libbed. Her one-way conversations up the dumbwaiter shaft with the unseen, unheard Mrs. Bloom ("Yoo-hoo, Mrs. Bloo-oomm!"), her worries over the premature loves of Sammy and Rosalie, and her efforts to keep Jake's blood pressure down contributed to some of radio's biggest moments.

The Goldbergs was discontinued in 1945. It led to Broadway (where the play, *Molly and Me* ran from February to July 1948), and to TV (*The Goldbergs* was one of the smash hits of early television). It returned to CBS in 1949, for one season as a Friday-night half-hour for

General Foods. This show was based on the TV series, which had begun on CBS January 17, 1949. For the 1949 season, Uncle David was played by Eli Mintz. A feature-length Goldbergs movie, *Molly,* was released in 1951. But despite its later success, *The Goldbergs* really died when those 15-minute daily snatches were phased out in 1945. Seldom thereafter would Mrs. Berg have the time for her visits to the ghetto, where so much simple life was hers for the taking. "It's hard, darling," she told a *Newsweek* reporter in 1949. "Everybody now is getting to know what I look like." Gertrude Berg died September 14, 1966.

Good News of 1938

Good News of 1938 was to have been the most spectacular radio show ever launched. But with all its "name" talent, *Good News* couldn't quite live up to its preshow press releases. It did fill nicely the time slot just vacated by the old *Maxwell House Show Boat,* and it marked the first time that a national network joined hands with a major film studio to create a show for sale to a commercial sponsor.

The result cost Maxwell House $25,000 a week, and *Good News of 1938* appeared on NBC for the first time on November 4, 1937. The idea was simple and flashy. Metro-Goldwyn-Mayer would produce the show, making available every star in its fold ("except Garbo"). There would be stories and songs, musical comedy and intimate glimpses of Hollywood with its hair down. Each week a new MGM film would be previewed in a fully dramatized mini-version, using the original stars for the radio roles. Casts would be gigantic and would change constantly. One of the features, "Backstage at the Movies," would let listeners in on executive conferences at MGM. Films would be discussed in the planning stage, even before the casts were chosen, and listeners would get audio tours of their favorite stars' dressing rooms.

Hosts included Hollywood's elite, from James Stewart to Robert Young, and in 1938 Robert Taylor was signed as emcee. Jeanette MacDonald, Sophie Tucker, Gus Edwards and Eva Tanguay helped kick off the series. And it was all done to the opening and closing of MGM's famed trademark—the roar of Leo the Lion.

The concept alone created a minor panic in Hollywood, where Paramount and Warner Brothers immediately began laying plans to follow suit. But by the time the show was a month old, it was apparent that something was wrong. Critics were lukewarm or downright cold. *Newsweek* said its listeners "couldn't decide whether Metro-Goldwyn-Mayer was trying to sell Maxwell House, or if the coffeemakers were putting out Metro-Goldwyn-Mayer in airtight containers."

It was a classic case of too many fingers in the pie. There was too much control by the studio, and MGM's prime interest seemed to be self-promotion. After a few weeks on the air, Fanny Brice was added as a regular member of the cast. That was the beginning of her long association with Frank Morgan, who did *Good News* monologues. Both were back the following fall for the new edition, *Good News of 1939*. The final *Good News* year was 1940. In March of that year the show was "streamlined" to 30 minutes, and Mary Martin was brought in as a regular. By fall it had become simply *Maxwell House Coffee Time*. The extravaganza disappeared as suddenly as it had come, and what was left was a 30-minute program split between Morgan and Brice.

But while it lasted, *Good News* was interesting. It brought together superstars who might never have worked in radio, and whipped up a glamorous audio potpourri for listeners who cared. Meredith Willson provided the melodies, offering original arrangements of classical music, written especially for *Good News* by such noted composers as Peter de Rose, Morton Gould, and Dana Suesse. Roland Young, Walter Huston, Alice Faye, Spencer Tracy, and Mickey Rooney were just a few of the stars presented. Robert Young was master of ceremonies for *Good News of 1939*. Bill Bacher produced, and for a time the show was directed by Ed Gardner, who even then was preparing to launch *Duffy's Tavern* upon the unsuspecting world.

Goodwill Court

Goodwill Court offered free legal help to the poor long before legal aid societies and public defenders became fashionable. There was one hitch: the people had to come before the NBC microphones and tell their stories to the world. Their identities were protected, and they were ever under the eyes of mediator A. L. Alexander, lest some profanity or the name of an actual person slip out over the air. Once over their initial mike fright, the people poured out their troubles. Caught up in the emotions of their personal troubles, they told of marital problems and troubles with loan sharks; of garnisheed wages, failure to meet monthly installments; of all the trials and tragedies shared by millions of listeners. It made compelling radio. Shortly after its September 20, 1936, premièr, the program rocketed into the top ten among all the country's radio shows.

Alexander had created the show in 1935, while working as staff announcer at WMCA, New York. But the roots of *Goodwill Court* went far back to Alexander's early days, when as a young police reporter he had seen first-hand the inequities of the legal system. With his radio show, he proposed to do something about it. His first WMCA show was aired March 31, 1935. It drew no response whatever, so Alexander began visiting the courts, asking defendants if they would air their problems anonymously. The next step was to acquire a panel of judges to give out the legal advice. Jonah J. Goldstein and Pelham St. George Bissell, two New York jurists, finally agreed. The show became a sensation, airing as many as fifteen cases per session. Alexander's staff answered all mail, giving free advice even to those who weren't invited to appear; some 6,000 people were helped in the first year alone. More than forty judges appeared over the two-year run.

When *Goodwill Court* went nationwide and became a powerful legal influence, such groups as the New York County Lawyers' Association rose up against it. In December 1936, two months after its network première, the New York Supreme Court barred lawyers and judges from appearing, and Chase and Sanborn promptly dropped it. Alexander returned to national radio on Mutual in 1943 with a similar show, *A. L. Alexander's Mediation Board.* Instead of lawyers, this show used sociologists and educators for its panel. Although not the spectacular success of its predecessor, *Mediation Board* ran in various lengths and formats until 1950. It was heard for most of the run on Sundays.

The Goodwill Hour

The Goodwill Hour was a far cry from *The Goodwill Court,* but the concepts were similar and there was a connecting link. When *Goodwill Court* was knocked off the air by a New York Supreme Court ruling, a Bronx hustler named John J. Anthony saw his golden opportunity. Anthony persuaded WMCA, A. L. Alexander's old station, to give him a format patterned after *Goodwill Court* in 1937. Anthony would avoid the lawyers and judges who had become such a problem for Alexander; he, himself, would give advice to the miserable. Anthony set himself up as an expert in all areas of human relationships. He claimed to have three university degrees, and at least once said he studied under Sigmund Freud in Europe. Actually, he was a high school dropout who had become bored with the structured ways of formal education. Anthony never failed to jab away at the institutions of education and social sciences, and his show contained a good deal more P. T. Barnum than had Alexander's program.

The Goodwill Hour made its Mutual première August 1, 1937, though Anthony himself had had microphone experience dating back to 1932. In 1938, Ironized Yeast became sponsor, carrying him through one change of network, in April 1940, to NBC Blue. The show remained on the Blue until 1943, moving back to Mutual for Clark Gum. By 1945 the show had disappeared from the network, but Anthony returned four years later in a TV version. Throughout its radio run, it was heard on Sunday nights, and the slogan, "Ask Mr. Anthony" became a household joke. Anthony, whose real name was Lester Kroll, was under constant attack from judges, social organizations, and radio critics, many of whom openly branded him a charlatan. He also founded a Marital Relations Institute, getting the idea for that while serving a jail term for nonpayment of alimony. In his "Institute," Anthony would bestow his wisdom upon the unfortunate for a $5 fee. He upped the fee to $25 after The Goodwill Hour had made him famous.

Roland Winters was the longtime announcer of this show, opening with, "You have a friend and advisor in John J. Anthony, and thousands are happier and more successful today because of John J. Anthony." Then Anthony would hear his first guest, opening with, "What is your problem, madame?" (The majority were women). Only initials were used, and even they were fictitious; frequently he reminded people, "no names, please." His answers to even the most difficult questions were brief and simple; his philosophy was based on fidelity and the Golden Rule. Sometimes, when a guest confessed infidelity, Anthony scolded him sternly on the air.

The Gracie Fields Show

The Gracie Fields Show featured the prewar British songstress-comedienne, well-known for her rousing concerts, which often contained songs that bordered on the bawdy. Gracie brought a toned-down version of the same to the Blue Network on October 12, 1942, in a 5-minute nightly mini-show for Pall Mall, hitting the air with one story and one song at 9:55 P.M., Eastern War Time. The format was expanded to 30 minutes weekly in 1944, and it was wrapped up in a Tuesday-night ABC package for Bristol-Myers. Miss Fields was also heard on Mutual in 1951–52, a sustained Friday-nighter. Her unforgettable voice, heavily laced with Manchester influence, was equally at home with such serious music as "Ave Maria" and comic ditties like "Walter, Walter, Lead Me to the Altar."

Granby's Green Acres

Granby's Green Acres was a CBS situation comedy premiering July 3, 1950; it ran during the summer and was inspired by characters heard on the Lucille Ball show, *My Favorite Husband*. The Granbys, a city family moved to the farm, were played by Gale Gordon and Bea Benaderet, who had also played the Atterburys on *Husband*. Like Rudolph Atterbury, John Granby had been a clerk in a bank. His wife Martha, like Miss Benaderet's earlier portrayal of Iris Atterbury, was somewhat addled and impractical. Louise Erickson played their breathless teenage daughter and Parley Baer was the hired hand Eb. Jay Sommers wrote, produced, and directed.

Grand Central Station

Grand Central Station was an anthology of the air, best remembered in its midday Saturday run on CBS. But the show actually had a long run on several networks beginning in 1937 on Friday nights on the Blue for Listerine. In 1938 it moved to CBS, still Fridays for Listerine; 1940 to the Blue, Tuesday nights for Rinso; 1941, NBC, Friday nights for Procter & Gamble; 1944, CBS, Saturday noontime for Pillsbury (sponsor changes: Toni, 1951–52; Cream of Wheat, 1952–53); 1953, ABC, for a final season as a midday 25-minute five-a-week show for Campbell Soups.

    Grand Central Station was always far better remembered for its format than its stories. The blast of that train whistle grabbed us at once, setting up emotions for a barrage of words and rushing train effects:

> As a bullet seeks its target, shining rails in every part of our great country are aimed at Grand Central Station, heart of the nation's greatest city. Drawn by the magnetic force of the fantastic metropolis, day and night great trains rush toward the Hudson River, sweep down its eastern bank for 140 miles, flash briefly by the long red row of tenement houses south of 125th Street, dive with a roar into the two-and-one-half-mile tunnel which burrows beneath the glitter and swank of Park Avenue, and then . . . EEEEEESSSSSSHHHHHHSSssss . . . GRAND CENTRAL STATION! Crossroads of a million private lives! Gigantic stage on which are played a thousand dramas daily!

That train came in on time without fail, with bells clanging and steam hissing and people talking as they got off. The stories were about the passengers—just everyday people who had come to New York to live, play, love, work, what have you. There was no binding theme beyond that. Once the Grand Central element was done, the people moved out of the terminal for their little dramas of human life. We went along with one of them for 30 minutes of eavesdropping. Jack Arthur was longtime narrator; others included Stuart Metz and Alexander Scourby. The stars came from the second and third ranks of Broadway and from the first ranks of radio. Announcers included George Baxter, Tom Shirley, and others.

Grand Hotel

Grand Hotel was another light dramatic anthology, geared to the same formulas that were used on First Nighter and Grand Central Station. But the format wasn't quite as elaborate. This one revolved around people staying at the Grand Hotel, opening with a hotel-switchboard setting and an operator (Betty Winkler) connecting calls to rooms. The show was heard on the Blue Network for Campana Balm premièring October 1, 1933, and running through 1938, with a one-year stay at NBC Red in 1936–37. It was dropped in 1938, but returned for a brief season on CBS January 7, 1940, again for Campana. The early stars were Don Ameche and Anne Seymour; later the leads were played by Jim Ameche (Don's brother) and Betty Lou Gerson. Joseph Ainley directed, and Les Tremayne was featured during the 1936–37 season.

Grand Marquee

Grand Marquee was another light dramatic offering, first heard on NBC July 9, 1946 and running through 1947. It was strictly situation comedy, heavy on the boy-meets-girl theme, but employing witty, imaginative situations and good talent. Jim Ameche and Beryl Vaughn were the stars when the show opened. Soon Olan Soule took Ameche's part as the leading man. The story situations ran from the couple in a haunted house to the beautiful girl who inherited a baseball team (complete with superstitious pitcher). Broadcast from NBC's Chicago studios, the opening described a grand marquee, "lighted by stars—twinkling, glowing, blazing with myriad lights and colors against the night sky—Rayve Cream Shampoo's mammoth billboard announces another exciting evening in the world of make-believe!" The shows were produced and directed by Norman Felton.

Grand Ole Opry

Grand Ole Opry king of all hillbilly shows, originated from a spur-of-the-moment change of programming on November 28, 1925, at Station WSM, Nashville. It really began before there was such a thing as radio, when George Dewey Hay packed into the Ozarks on a mule expedition. There he found a simple life, almost unchanged since the days of Valley Forge, and he soon became a connoisseur of the primitive mountain music enjoyed by the people at dances and socials.

Years later, George Hay became station manager at WSM. He found that radio had a deep fascination for mountain people; some came from far back in the hills just to see the station. One day an old-timer named Uncle Jimmy Thompson showed up, fiddle in hand, and asked for a tour. Instead, Hay decided to put him on the air.

Thompson was amazed at the idea that his fiddle could be heard by people hundreds of miles away. He fiddled for an hour, and Hay asked him to come back and bring some of his banjo-picking friends. Soon the mountain folk began to swarm into the studio, bringing with them unwritten songs that had been passed from generation to generation. Some walked down; some came on mules and in wagons. They brought earthy American ballads of unknown age and origin—songs like "Greenback Dollar" and "Brown's Ferry Blues" and "Rabbit in the Flea Patch." None could read music; they just scraped and sawed away by ear, turning out the closest thing to pure Americana ever heard on the air. WSM was a powerful station that, even on those prewar Saturday nights, could reach into thirty states. People wrote fan letters from as far away as Alaska, making it clear that—with the possible exception of a kissin' cousin called The National Barn Dance—there was nothing on the air quite like Grand Ole Opry.

Relatives and neighbors began to swarm the WSM studios on Saturday nights. So popular was the show that it soon moved to a nearby auditorium with several hundred seats. It was to outgrow two more theaters before moving to Nashville's War Memorial Stadium (2,000 seats), then Ryman Auditorium (4,000 seats), and finally moving in 1974 to a 4,000-plus-seat opry house built especially for the show. Musicians were drawn from the hills and woods of six states. Most were lifelong farmers, people of the earth whose entertainment was built around fiddles, dulcimers, banjos, mouth harps, and washboards. Until 1925, the entertainment of the hills had been carried on in isolated pockets. Then came Grand Ole Opry; the people put aside their plows and hoes, picked up their banjos, and headed for the biggest shoutin', whoopin', whistlin', foot-stompin' hoedown in the land. And even serious students of American music began to listen.

The name "Opry" was acquired early in the run. WSM, an NBC affiliate, had just carried the National Symphony Orchestra, a network program of grand opera. Dr. Walter Damrosch, conductor, introduced a piece with this brief speech: "While we do not believe there is a place in the classics for realism, this work so depicts the onrush of the locomotive that I have decided to include it in the program of grand opera."

Hay, whose show immediately followed Damrosch's, opened like this: "From here on out, folks, it will be nothing but realism of the realest kind. You've been up in the clouds with grand opera; now get down to earth with us in a shindig of grand ole opry!"

The name stuck, and has carried for fifty years. Opry began as an hour show, but participants complained that an hour wasn't even a fittin' warmin'-up time, so Hay extended it gradually until it consumed the entire evening. From 8:00 until midnight, the hillbillies fiddled and stomped, frequently going long after the show was off the air.

George Hay became the Solemn Ole Judge, another name for master of ceremonies, through most of the long radio run. Until his death, Uncle Jimmy Thompson, an 80-year-old who had served in the Civil War, was the grand patriarch. That role eventually was passed to Uncle Dave Macon, a youngster of 70 and another of the early Opry performers.

After the program had been broadcast as a local show for more than fourteen years, NBC in 1939 picked up a 30-minute segment of the Saturday-night marathons for its coast-to-coast audience. When the network came aboard, Whitey ("Duke of Paducah") Ford became master of ceremonies for the 30-minute national segment. For many years the network run was sponsored by Prince Albert Tobacco. A script was prepared for the network, but as always it was followed only loosely. Grand Ole Opry continues as a spontaneous, unrehearsed show to this day.

The roster of Opry stars contains both the famous and the obscure. There were people who made show business a way of life; others who hung up their dulcimers on Sunday morning and went back to the soil on Monday. Sid Hark Reader was a clothing salesman; Claude Lampley, a floor finisher; Tommy Lefew, a barber; George Wilkerson, an iron molder. On Saturday nights they dropped their scissors, buffers, and other tools to become members of the Gully Jumpers and the Fruit Jar Drinkers. As many as 137 people gathered on the Grand Ole Opry stage for the Saturday-night shindigs. Wilkerson and the Fruit Jar Drinkers, it was said, used to pass around a jar of moonshine between numbers. Others included the Possum Hunters (a fiddle band comprised of farmers), Rachel and her Golden West Cowboys, Smiling

Jack and his Missouri Mountaineers, "Cousin" Minnie Pearl (standup comedienne who told stories of the simple life in Grinders Switch, Tennessee), DeFord Bailey (black harmonica player who for a time was billed as the show's "mascot"), Bill Monroe and His Bluegrass Boys, The Gully Jumpers (musical auto mechanics), Zeke Clements ("The Dixie Yodeler"), Sam and Kirk McGhee (guitar-banjo team), Kay Carlisle, the Williams Sisters, Ernest Tubb, Little Jimmy Dickens, Red Foley, Tommy Jackson, Jimmy Selph, Hank Williams, George Morgan, Carl Smith, the Carter Sisters, Hank Snow, Eddy Arnold, and Roy Acuff and His Smoky Mountain Boys.

As it slipped into the big-time of the country music world, the Opry virtually closed its doors to newcomers. Roy Acuff tried for three years before getting on in 1939, and then became one of the show's brightest stars. Each year, thousands of would-be performers made the journey—sometimes hundreds of miles—to Nashville, only to be told politely that the show was "all filled up." Hillbilly music had come far since the "Solemn Ole Judge" had ridden a mule into the hill country.

The NBC portion of this program was dropped in 1957, but even today the *Grand Ole Opry* is alive and well in Nashville.

Grand Slam

Grand Slam was a long-running daytime quiz show that began in 1943 as a late-afternoon CBS Wesson Oil feature and eventually settled into a five-a-week morning slot for Continental Baking. It ran on CBS until 1953, and its motivating force, producer, and singing emcee was Irene Beasley. She had broken into radio with a Memphis station in 1928 and had been signed by CBS the following year. She conceived *Grand Slam* as a spirited competition between the listeners and the studio audience; when she pitched the idea to an ad agency executive, he told her he could sell the show *if* she could cut an audition disc within two days. Unable to obtain either an emcee or a singer on such short notice, she handled both jobs herself, and continued to do so after the show was sold. *Grand Slam* was a musical quiz in which listeners submitted five-part questions. The music was sung by Miss Beasley to the accompaniment of pianist Bob Downey and organist Abe Goldman. Each part of the question was called a "trick." If a studio contestant won a trick, he won a prize; if he missed the trick, the listener who had submitted the question got the prize. Five tricks on either side was a "grand slam," bringing the winner a $100 savings bond. Dwight Weist announced, and Miss Beasley was assisted in writing by Lillian Schoen.

Grapevine Rancho

Grapevine Rancho was the 1943 version of The Ransom Sherman Show, with Sherman as host of a half-hour variety act built around an Old West format. It ran on Thursday nights on CBS for Roma Wine. As with all Sherman's shows, this one had imagination and creativity, but for some reason never made it. Sherman played the owner of the Grapevine Rancho, where the comedy and song took place; guest stars were brought in and backed by Lud Gluskin's orchestra, and skits were performed by a cast of regulars. Leo Carillo was featured as Pedro, the Mexican hired hand; Lionel Stander was Hoolihan, the Irish ranch foreman; and Ann O'Neill was Cynthia Veryberry, a paying guest at Sherman's ranch. Songs were by Carlos Ramirez, South American baritone; Fred Shields read the commercials for Roma. In the main, this was just another showcase for Sherman's zany talent, which should have made much bigger noises on radio than it did.

The Great Gildersleeve

The Great Gildersleeve was created by Harold Peary while he was working on Fibber McGee and Molly in Chicago. The basic ingredients of the character began to fall together in 1937, and by 1939 Gildersleeve was turning up in almost every McGee script. The character became so popular that, on August 31, 1941, Gildersleeve broke away for his own Sunday-night NBC slot.

Peary was the son of a Portuguese immigrant; christened Harrold Jose Pereira de Faria, he had been active in radio for nine years before he hooked up with the Fibber McGee and Molly show. He had first worked in San Francisco radio, performing on an NBC show called The Spanish Serenader, around 1928. Peary had a natural singing voice, and occasionally he sang in his Gildersleeve role as part of his infamous Jolly Boys' Club, or for an occasional holiday solo. The audience always asked for more, and Peary's singing became one of the charms of the show. He was also an accomplished character actor, at home with dialect and very flexible in voice changes. Peary played many roles before coming to Chicago for the big time in 1935. In Chicago, he made the rounds of many network shows, sometimes playing half a dozen parts in a single program. He saw Gildersleeve (though the character hadn't yet been named) as the perfect rival for McGee—a blundering windbag whose heart of gold was well-concealed beneath the second biggest bluff in Wistful Vista. He originated the character, and then presented the idea of a foil for McGee—a stuffed-shirt in his own right—to writer Don Quinn. Quinn liked it, and he christened the character "Gildersleeve"—the most pompous name he could think of.

The rivalry clicked at once. After playing a series of floating characters named Gildersleeve, Peary became Throckmorton P. Gildersleeve and settled down next door to the McGees. There they glared at each other across the fence, played their little-boy tricks, and once engaged in an outrageous water fight. Gildersleeve's most famous line, repeated in almost every show, was "You're a haaarrrd man, McGee!" Peary developed his "dirty laugh" especially for Gildy; he played the part with all the menace of a grizzly bear. Forever on the verge of "tearing McGee limb from limb." Gildersleeve in the end was McGee's only radio match in the hot-air department.

All that changed when Kraft bought The Great Gildersleeve. On a summer day in 1941, a train pulled out of the mythical town of Wistful Vista with 42-year-old Throckmorton P. Gildersleeve on board. Ostensibly, he left for a short business trip to Summerfield, a town at the end of the line, telling his tearful employees at the Gildersleeve Girdle Works that he might be gone "as long as three days."

In fact, he was gone a lot longer than that. Except for occasional visits, Throckmorton P. Gildersleeve would not return to Wistful Vista. His new home would be in Summerfield, where he set about raising his nephew Leroy and his niece Marjorie, became the town water commissioner, and spread his reputation as a windbag, a most eligible bachelor, and a ladies' man extraordinaire.

The Great Gildersleeve is thought to be the first radio show based on a supporting character from another radio show. It was also the most successful. Gildersleeve became a character in his own right, grew into his specialized radio format, and soon made the McGees and Wistful Vista part of the distant, nostalgic past. Though it never quite ranked with Fibber McGee and Molly in overall popularity, The Great Gildersleeve did pull a respectable share of the audience through the 1940's, and in fact Gildy outlasted McGee by almost two years.

Gildersleeve's long-running feud with crusty old Judge Horace Hooker began on that first day of his new show, on the long train ride from Wistful Vista to Summerfield. The judge (or "the old goat," as he was called by Gildersleeve) was perfectly played by Earle Ross. Stepping into the role of 12-year-old Leroy Forrester, Gildy's nephew, was Walter Tetley, at 18 a radio veteran of The Children's Hour, The Fred Allen Show, Raising Junior, and many assorted serials. Tetley was without doubt the best of all radio wiseguys. His Leroy role didn't have quite the bite of Julius Abbruzio, the delivery boy of The Phil

Harris–Alice Fay Show, but he was still the perfect deflator of Gildersleeve's ego. Leroy always addressed the pompous great one as "Unk," and loved catching Gildersleeve in some blatant transgression or fib. "What a character!" he would shout, letting Gildy know that he wasn't putting anything over on anyone. To which Gildersleeve inevitably replied, "Lee-ee-ee-ee-roy!"

Marjorie, Leroy's sister, was an energetic teenager who gave her uncle trouble of another kind. Marjorie went through all the fads of the forties, and seemed to Gildersleeve overly boy-crazy. But eventually she settled down, marrying her boyfriend Bronco Thompson in May 1950 and making Gildy the proud grand-uncle of twins—a boy and a girl. Lurene Tuttle originated the role; Louise Erickson took it in 1944, and Marylee Robb became Marjorie in 1948. Dick Crenna played Bronco.

Two of the show's most memorable characters were Peavey, the henpecked druggist, and Birdie Lee Coggins, the Gildersleeve cook. Peavey, whose voice was a dry Midwestern nasal twang, was Gildersleeve's sounding board for advice on new plots. Gildersleeve seldom bought anything in Peavey's drug store, but he spent many hours pouring out his troubles over the counter. Mr. Peavy's inevitable reaction was, "Well, now, I wouldn't say that." It became the best-known line of the show. Peavey was played by Richard LeGrand, an old trouper from the turn-of-the-century Bijou Theatre. LeGrand, a twenty-seven-year veteran of vaudeville, had worked in early radio in his own show, *Ole and the Girls,* and had later done various parts for Carlton E. Morse on both *One Man's Family* and *I Love a Mystery.*

Birdie was probably the best of all the stereotyped black maids of old-time radio. She had far more charm and wit than Marlin Hurt's Beulah; like Leroy, she was capable of punching Gildersleeve full of holes, but her jabs were softer and, in line with the times, always delivered with courtesy and respect. Lillian Randolph did a fine long-running job as Birdie.

As for the others, Shirley Mitchell was conniving widow Leila Ransom, and Bea Benaderet played Eve Goodwin, the school principal dated by Gildersleeve in the early years. Una Merkel played Leila's cousin, Adeline Fairchild, who set out hooks of her own for Summerfield's water commissioner when the Widow Ransom left town. Cathy Lewis was Nurse Kathryn Milford, another Gildersleeve heartthrob of the early 1950's, always sweet and slightly unattainable. Arthur Q. Bryan played Floyd Munson the barber, Gildersleeve's sometime friend whose loyalty was usually open to the highest bidder. Gale Gordon was Rumson Bullard, the rich, super-obnoxious neighbor across the street who was ever feuding with Gildersleeve. Pauline Drake and later Gloria Holliday played Bessie, Gildy's dense secretary. And Ken Christy was Police Chief Gates, the cop with the heart of gold whose mournful stock phrase—"Fellas, fellas, let's all be Jolly Boys!"—could usually be heard whenever Gildy and Hooker began feuding again.

Cecil Underwood was producer; Frank Pittman directed; Jim Bannon announced. The scripts were written by Leonard L. Levinson. These men comprised the production staff when The Great Gildersleeve first came to the air. Fran Van Hartesveldt later produced the show. John Whedon and Sam Moore took over the writing in the second year, later relinquishing to John Elliotte and Andy White. Music through the mid-1940's (after an initial season by Billy Mills) was by Claude Sweeten; later Jack Meakin waved the baton, and by 1951 Robert Armbruster was the maestro. Announcer in the mid-1940's was Ken Carpenter; later John Wald took over; still later Jay Stewart and John Hiestand announced.

Writers Whedon and Moore developed The Great Gildersleeve almost in serial form. The great one's campaign for mayor took up most of the 1944 season; his love affairs sometimes spanned weeks or months. Gildersleeve once found himself engaged to both Leila Ransom and Eve Goodwin. Leila—a drawlin' Southern belle who called him "Throck-mahhhtin"—actually got him to the steps of the altar. The romance took on characteristics of a soap opera in 1942 when members of a California women's club picketed NBC, urging Gildy with placards not to go through with it.

For thirteen years the show was sponsored by Kraft Foods, switching to Wednesday nights in 1946 and continuing there until 1954. As the program approached its tenth birthday, Harold Peary tired of the role and eventually dropped it. He went into a new, short-lived comedy, Honest Harold, which he owned and directed. By all odds, Gildersleeve should have been doomed then and there, but into Peary's shoes came Willard Waterman, whose interpretation was so much like the original it was startling. Waterman's career had run along the same tracks as Peary's. He had come to Chicago in 1936, and had played many of the same bit parts that Peary would play in the following year. But Peary went into Fibber McGee and Molly, Waterman freelanced for such shows as The First Nighter, Ma Perkins, and Mary Marlin. He was a prolific actor, doing as many as forty radio parts a week. In 1945, he took the lead in Those Websters, a zany situation comedy that eventually moved to Hollywood. Waterman went with it, playing such big-time shows as Escape, The Lux Radio Theatre, and The Screen Guild Theatre.

Peary's last show was June 14, 1950; when the show returned

from vacation on September 6, Waterman was Gildersleeve. So well did he blend into The Great Gildersleeve that, from one year to the next, the voice is almost indistinguishable. The show was lucky that way. Forrest Lewis eventually replaced Richard LeGrand as Peavey, and carried on with no appreciable loss of quality. Most shows never have a break like that. In the end, that luck made The Great Gildersleeve one of the last great comedies of the air. For its 1954–55 season, the program was a daily 15-minute offering, with each episode loosely connected. The show returned to 30 minutes in 1955, and ran on Thursdays until 1958.

The Greatest Story Ever Told

The Greatest Story Ever Told, was based on the book of the same name by Fulton Oursler, and came to ABC for Goodyear Tires on January 26, 1947. It was an ambitious show, with a full orchestra and a sixteen-voice chorus, dramatizing the life and times of Jesus Christ, "the greatest life ever lived." So highly regarded was The Greatest Sory Ever Told that in 1948, a rival tire company took out nationwide newspaper ads praising the Goodyear show. Goodyear used no commercials, just a simple tagline reminding listeners—in accordance with Federal Communications Commission requirements—of its sponsorship.

The Greatest Story Ever Told was the first radio series to simulate the voice of Christ as a continuing character. Warren Parker played the part, though none of the show's actors were ever promoted as "stars." Oursler, then religious editor of Reader's Digest, kept a strong interest in the show, meeting weekly with writer Henry Denker before scripts were prepared. Oursler and Denker often discussed ideas in terms of modern problems, then found a corollary in the life of Christ and emerged with a theme. Denker, a longtime student of the Bible, held additional meetings with clergy of all faiths. The show was additionally guided by an interdenominational advisory board. The stories quite effectively captured the essence of Oursler's book, a beautifully simple, popular dramatization of Christ's life as set down by four apostles. Marx Loeb directed it; Leonard Blair was assistant director and Wadill Catchings was producer. William Stoess composed the music; the orchestra and chorus were directed by Williard Young. In many areas, The Greatest Story Ever Told was an integrated part of school and church work; it was heard on ABC as an early-evening Sunday show until 1956.

The Green Hornet

The Green Hornet appeared first on WXYZ, Detroit, January 31, 1936. And it was no mere coincidence that a fearless crusader for justice named "The Green Hornet" bore a striking resemblance to another well-established radio hero. Both *The Green Hornet* and *The Lone Ranger* were creations of George W. Trendle. Both were largely written, at least in their early years, by Fran Striker.

This show came roaring our way in a gust of smoke and on the lively strings of "The Flight of the Bumble Bee." Trendle had learned his lesson well with *The Lone Ranger*—classical music and juvenile adventure *did* go together.

The opening was sheer radio. The Hornet buzz, "Bumble Bee" up, and opening epigraph: "He hunts the biggest of all game, public enemies who try to destroy our America!" An interesting variation of that was tried during the 1939 NBC run: "He hunts the biggest of all game, public enemies that even the G-Men cannot reach!" Reportedly, J. Edgar Hoover objected to that, and it soon vanished.

The remainder of the opening was a direct lift from *The Lone Ranger;* "With his faithful valet Kato, Britt Reid, daring young publisher, matches wits with the underworld, risking his life that criminals and racketeers within the law may feel its weight by the sting of *The Green Hornet! . . .* [car sounds as "Black Beauty" starts] . . . Ride with Britt Reid in the thrilling adventure, 'Polarized Glasses!' The Green Hornet strikes again!" By the time *The Green Hornet* arrived on Mutual in April 1938 as a twice-a-week sustaining juvenile feature, *The Lone Ranger* had had several years of fighting badmen of the Old West under his belt. The Green Hornet not only borrowed his crime-fighting abilities from The Lone Ranger, he literally *inherited* them.

Trendle created Britt Reid as a son of Dan Reid, who faithful listeners immediately recognize as the Lone Ranger's nephew. In other words, Britt followed in the footsteps of his colorful grand-uncle, who rode masked across the plains of the early Western United States. Britt Reid had a mask too, and also a cape and a jazzy outfit. His criminals were mobsters and swindlers and corrupt cops—all the blights of a modern 1936 society—and he fought them with an arsenal of tools that included gas guns and smokescreens and the fastest car (the unforgettable, whirring Black Beauty) on earth. The Hornet's car had to be fast. Like his grand-uncle, he constantly had trouble with unreasonable cops. Cops just never understood why good men sometimes have to wear masks!

On the surface, Britt Reid was a normal, slightly flamboyant newspaperman. As owner of the *Daily Sentinel,* he assigned his reporters to crusading causes and when the going got too tough for them—about twice a week—he slipped into cape and mask and became the Green Hornet. Naturally, nobody on the *Sentinel* staff knew who he was. That honor was reserved solely for Britt's Filipino valet Kato who, like Tonto before him, was true-blue and faithful.

Kato was probably the most underestimated character on the show. Anyone who thought of him as just another Oriental soon got his thinking changed around. Kato knew the secrets of Oriental infighting, and he was smart. He had graduated from college. A master chemist, he could cook and care for a house, and drive like hell besides—and no one of lesser skills would do for the Hornet's sleek Black Beauty.

Completing the cast of regulars were three *Sentinel* staffers: Mike Axford, Lenore Case, and Ed Lowry. As ace reporter, Lowry was a little on the dull side; the show had room for only one ace, and Reid was it. Axford, on the other hand, may have been the dumbest character ever to grace the air, at least a solid rival for *Mr. Keen's* Mike Clancy in that department. Even his fellow *Hornet* characters realized that Axford would never become radio's all-time deep thinker. Once a cop, later Reid's bodyguard, Axford finally became *Sentinel* police reporter. He was the epitome of the stereotyped dumb Irishman. Through the series, his chief goal was to "captuuure the Haarnet" and bring glory to himself and the *Sentinel.*

Lenore Case ("Casey" to Axford but ever "Miss Case" to Reid) was the love interest. But the love was so subdued that it virtually smothered from inattention. That was the way Trendle handled all his superheroes—no mush or goo for the kids—but Casey never lost hope. She worked late, tried hard, and once or twice she dropped her steno pencil and even got to help cover a good story. But she never got to cover Britt.

Many of the WXYZ actors who worked on *The Green Hornet* also played character roles in *The Lone Ranger* and in Trendle's other juvenile adventure, *Sergeant Preston of the Yukon.* The part of Reid was played by Al Hodge for the first seven years, and successively by Donovan Faust, Robert Hall, and Jack McCarthy. Kato was originated by Tokutaro Hayashi (Raymond Toyo) and later played by Rollon Parker and Mickey Tolan. Casey was Lenore Allman; Axford was played by Jim Irwin and Gilly O'Shea. Ed Lowry was Jack Petruzzi. It went to NBC in 1939, was heard twice a week on the Blue Network in 1940, and later that year was placed in the Blue's Saturday lineup. *The Green Hornet* ran on the Blue (ABC) for more than eight years, heard variously on Sundays, Saturdays, Tuesdays, and Thursdays.

General Mills sponsored the show on Tuesdays in 1948; it was sustained twice a week in 1949 and was heard in various timeslots in 1950. The *Hornet* returned in a brief Mutual two-a-week show for Orange Crush in 1952.

The shows always ended with a newsboy (Rollon Parker) chanting in read-all-about-it fashion about the Hornet's latest bust. Fran Striker wrote the early shows. Other writers included Dan Beattie, Steve McCarthy, Tom Dougall, and Leo Boulette. The show was directed by James Jewell and Charles Livingstone. The final broadcast was December 5, 1952.

The Green Lama

The Green Lama was a summertime CBS adventure show, heard in 1949 and featuring Paul Frees in the title role. Frees played a New York adventurer named Jethro Dumont, known as the Green Lama because of his study in a monastery of lamas in Tibet. From his headquarters in New York, the Green Lama roamed the world, meting out justice with the help of his faithful Tibetan servant, Tulku (Ben Wright). His chant of justice: "Om mani padme hum!" It was produced and written by William Froug and Richard Foster, with music by Dick Aurandt.

The Guiding Light

The Guiding Light, Irna Phillips' long-running drama of clerics and doctors, was first heard on NBC January 25, 1937, from Chicago. Over its forty-year run, characters died, moved away, got married, disappeared, drifted out of the story line. Leads changed. Even the central focus of the story changed drastically. When it first came to NBC Red, *The Guiding Light* told the story of the Rev. John Ruthledge, minister of a nonsectarian church in the little town of Five Points.

Miss Phillips, the show's creator, was a young teacher when she broke into radio at Chicago's WGN in 1930; there, the 27-year-old writer got her first major writing exposure with a serial called *Painted Dreams*. With Frank and Anne Hummert, Miss Phillips was one of radio's most prolific producers of soap opera. The main difference between the Hummerts and Miss Phillips—aside from the Hummerts' stronger tendency toward melodrama—was that Phillips actually wrote much of her material, some two million words of it each year. Using a large month-by-month work chart, Miss Phillips plotted and wrote up to half a dozen soaps at once, dictating the action in lengthy stints with her secretary. Mentally juggling the plights of scores of characters, she belted out 15-minute snatches of life in dramatic form, acting the parts in changing voices while the steno hurriedly scribbled the dialogue that flowed from her lips.

Soap operas (and radio itself) were in the primitive stages of development, and there was plenty of room for growth if a person had ideas. Miss Phillips certainly had ideas. She thought cliff-hanger serials were sure-fire audience builders, and that organ bridges between the scenes would create a smooth flow and contribute to the sense of drama. She became a pioneer with these and other widely used techniques. She was the first to effectively use the same characters between serials. When she took her highly popular *Today's Children* off the air in 1938, she initiated a new serial, *Woman in White*, which called for some interrelated scenes with the old *Today's Children* cast. In 1943, three of her soaps were scheduled consecutively and billed as *The General Mills Hour*. Thus, characters from the resurrected *Today's Children* drifted through *The Guiding Light* and *Woman in White*, which followed. Ed Prentiss, who as Ned Holden had become one of the major characters of *The Guiding Light*, was master of ceremonies for the entire 45-minute block. Prentiss served as a guide through the complex framework of the three soaps, blending the shows with narrative bridgework. Then he stepped back into his own world when *The Guiding Light* came on.

Miss Phillips believed that these devices added to listener enjoyment, and created the greater illusion of life that all good soaps strived for. At one time, she seriously considered scheduling her three "block" serials in offbeat lengths. Each show would run between 10 and 20 minutes, depending on plot developments and the demands of the story, instead of the traditional 15-minute segments. She abandoned the plan the following year. Meanwhile, her serial, *The Right to Happiness*, was running strong on NBC. It had evolved directly out of *The Guiding Light* when in 1939 the fictitious Kransky family was transplanted into a new setting. Along with the jump went Ruth Bailey as Rose Kransky, Seymour Young as Jacob Kransky, and Mignon Schreiber as Mrs. Kransky. But like the Rev. Mr. Ruthledge, the Kranskys were eventually swallowed by time, as *The Right to Happiness* became the continuing saga of Carolyn Kramer Nelson.

The Guiding Light, meanwhile, continued as one of the most popular daytime shows of the air. When the serial was dropped briefly in 1941, some 75,000 letters of protest forced its reinstatement. Its good reverend, pastor of the Little Church of Five Points, had become a symbol of the worthwhile life, despite the endless run of sudsy problems that made it a soap opera. The show moved with the speed of life itself; it was almost agonizing in its postponement of even the most vital problems. Most of the chapters contained only one scene, peopled usually by only two characters. That was another Phillips trademark—sparse, lean stage setting and long, slow discussions. It was another contrast with the melodrama of the Hummerts, who jumbled character and development together in a collage of jerky action.

Running through the fabric of the early *Guiding Light* was the philosophy of Reverend Ruthledge and his church—the goodness of life, the inspiration of the American way. Sometimes Miss Phillips even devoted the entire 15 minutes to a Ruthledge sermon.

The cast of 1942 included Prentiss as Ned Holden, the orphan taken in by Ruthledge at age eight; Sarajane Wells as Mary Ruthledge Holden, the pastor's daughter and ultimately Ned's wife; Ruth Bailey as Rose Kransky, the Jewish girl whose father, Abe Kransky, ran a Five Points second-hand store, and who formed a close friendship with Mary Ruthledge; Reese Taylor as Edward Greenman; Eloise Kummer as Mrs. Greenman; Norma Jean Ross as the Greenmans' daughter Ronnie; Laurette Fillbrandt as Nancy Stewart, and Gladys Heen as the vibrant Torchy Reynolds.

Other memorable characters played through the prewar run: Rose Kransky's brother Jacob; Fredrika Lang, Ned Holden's real mother, who shot and killed her husband Paul and reached the threshold of the electric chair before a governor's pardon saved her; Charles Cunningham, head of the large publishing house where Rose Kransky worked, whose involvement with Rose resulted in a scandalous divorce action by his wife; and Ellis Smith, "Mr. Nobody from Nowhere," the mysterious stranger who wandered into Five Points and took the apartment below the Kranskys.

Arthur Peterson played Ruthledge, "The Good Samaritan of Five Points," from the beginning. When he went to war in 1944, Miss Phillips sent Ruthledge with him, as chaplain in the armed forces overseas. She brought in a new character to replace him, one Dr. Richard Gaylord, played by John Barclay. Ruthledge would return in 1946, but never again would *The Guiding Light* be as much under his influence as before the war years.

Bernice Yanocek was Miss Phillips' organist; in *The Guiding Light* she got a good workout, for the show opened to a thunderous rendition of "Aphrodite." Carl Wester produced the Phillips shows. They were sold to sponsors independently and offered to networks as complete packages. Fort Pearson, Bud Collyer, and Herb Allen were among the announcers on *The Guiding Light*. And as for Irna Phillips, after paying casts, announcers, production crews, and advisors (two doctors and a lawyer on retainer), she was still pulling in $5,000 a week. Not bad, even at two million words a year.

Even the good reverend couldn't survive forever as a star of afternoon drama. Somewhere in the late 1940's, *The Guiding Light* stopped being *his* story, as new characters and situations proved more interesting. By 1947, Dr. Charles Matthews (played by Hugh Studebaker) was running things from his Church of the Good Samaritan. Willard Waterman was playing prison parolee Roger Barton, who went by the alias Ray Brandon; Betty Lou Gerson was Charlotte Wilson, who later married Brandon; and Ned LeFevre was playing Ned Holden.

CBS acquired the show in 1947, and began televising concurrent episodes July 30, 1952. By the time the program went to TV, Meta Bauer and her family had come to the forefront of the story line. *The Guiding Light* was dropped from radio four years later, but the television serial is still going strong on CBS. Today's TV show is filled with people named Bauer, young doctors and lawyers in the mythical town of Springfield. But even now it bears the personal stamp of Irna Phillips, whose career in afternoon drama has been marked by a devoted fascination with professional people (doctors, lawyers, and ministers) as heroes.

The Gulf Show

The Gulf Show came to the Blue Network April 30, 1933, featuring "music by the Al Goodman Orchestra, the singing of the Revelers Quartet and a few words from Will Rogers." The bulk of the show consisted of Rogers' lengthy monologues, his earthy jabs at Roosevelt and Congress, Democrats and Republicans. It was a Sunday-night show, sponsored by Gulf Oil and running on CBS in its second season. Rogers was just hitting his stride as a radio humorist when he was killed in a plane crash on August 15, 1935.

Gunsmoke

Gunsmoke, the first of radio's "adult Westerns," was first heard on CBS April 26, 1952. For its first two seasons it was sustained on Saturday nights. Norman Macdonnell was 35 years old when *Gunsmoke* became a radio series. As producer-director, he strived for a sense of realism seldom achieved on radio or TV, surrounding himself with many of the same professionals who had worked with him on *Escape*. His *Gunsmoke* was one of the great shows.

Everything about Gunsmoke was first-class, from the music and the acting to the writing and the sound effects. Gunsmoke offered a listener total radio, complete involvement, from the opening scene to that last spot for L&M filters. When Marshal Dillon went out on the plains, you didn't need a narrator to know what was happening. You heard the faraway prairie wind and the dry squeak of Matt's pants against saddle leather. You could almost hear the bit moving in the horse's mouth, count the hoofbeats on the parched earth.

Tom Hanley, Ray Kemper and Bill James were audio magicians. They were the men responsible for the amazing sound effects on Gunsmoke. When Matt opened his jail-cell door, you heard every key drop on the ring. When he walked the streets of Dodge, his spurs rang with a dull clink-clink, missing occasionally, and the hollow boardwalk echoed back as the nails creaked in the worn wood around them. Buckboards passed, and you heard them behind the dialogue, along with muted shouts of kids playing in an alley, and the farther sounds from the next block, where the inevitable dog was barking.

Dodge City, Kansas, 85 years ago.

Into the role of Dillon came William Conrad. He received fine support from Georgia Ellis as the saloon girl Kitty Russell, from Parley Baer as the deputy Chester Proudfoot, and from Howard McNear as grizzled old Doc Adams. Conrad brought to the part a depth never quite achieved by James Arness on TV. Conrad's Dillon was a tough man, hard as nails, and on the Kansas frontier there are only two ways for a man like that to go. Dillon, bound by his own personal code of the West, had decided his destiny.

There would be no just-in-time cavalry rescues on Gunsmoke. Happy endings would be the exception, and once in a while the Marshal would get the hell kicked out of him—just to keep him honest. In a 1953 Time interview, Macdonnell described Dillon as "a lonely, sad, tragic man." Kitty, he said, "is just someone Matt has to visit every once in a while. We never say it, but Kitty is a prostitute, plain and simple."

The Gunsmoke stories were among the most violent of radio. The famed horror shows of radio's salad days never killed their victims as brutally as did Macdonnell and company. Mutilated bodies left by Indians to rot on the plains, gunmen split open by axes or knives, families burned out and slaughtered—this was standard Gunsmoke fare. But that's one thing you learned quickly in this series—violence breeds violence. And around Dodge City and territories on west, there was just one way to handle the killers and the spoilers—that's with a U.S. Marshal, and the smell of gunsmoke.

Macdonnell's pros were writer John Meston, conductor-composer Rex Koury, and a stable of supporting actors that included

Harry Bartell, Lou Krugman, Vic Perrin, Sam Edwards, Jeanette Nolan, Lawrence Dobkin, and John Dehner. Dobkin and Dehner were especially effective as the countless mad-dog characters who drifted through Dodge, spreading misery and death in their wake.

Through the mid 1950's, *Gunsmoke* was sponsored by Chesterfield and L&M. Roy Rowan announced the early shows; announcer through most of the run was George Walsh, and George Fenneman was backup announcer during the L&M years. *Gunsmoke* alternated between Saturday and Sunday time slots until its demise on June 18, 1961.

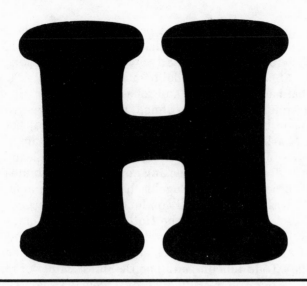

The Hall of Fantasy

The Hall of Fantasy came out of Chicago and was carried on Mutual for a season beginning in January 1953. Produced and written by Richard Thorne, who also played some of the character roles, it concerned man's struggle against the black forces of the unexplainable. The difference between this program and its competitors was that here, man was usually the loser. The supernatural was offered as something respectable, awesome, sometimes devastating and always frightening. *The Hall of Fantasy* specialized in shock endings, with the vampire's teeth sinking into the hero's throat or the hands of the rotted corpse clutching at the screaming girl. Eloise Kummer played many of the female leads; original music was by Harold Turner, and Leroy Olliger directed.

Hallmark Playhouse

Hallmark Playhouse was first heard for Hallmark Cards in the Thursday-night CBS lineup, June 10, 1948, and ran until 1953, when the format was reorganized as *The Hallmark Hall of Fame*. That version ran on CBS Sunday nights until 1955, and can still be seen in occasional television specials.

The first show produced in 1948 was "The Devil and Daniel Webster." Soon the series established its formula: well-known works of contemporary and classic literature, often enacted by the top stars of Hollywood.

The stories were selected by best-selling novelist James Hilton, who also hosted the series through its early years. Hilton picked yarns like Edna Ferber's *Cimarron*, Carl Sandburg's *Prairie Years*, and Ring Lardner's *Elmer the Great*, deliberately trying to stay away from stories that had been filmed and rehashed on the air. He did select liberally from his own much-filmed, much dramatized work in the initial season, but *Goodbye, Mr. Chips* (Ronald Colman), *Lost Horizon* (Herbert Marshall), and *Random Harvest* (Joan Fontaine) were just good stories, and always made enjoyable radio. To Jean Holloway went the difficult job of condensing novels into 30-minute programs. Producer-director was Dee Engelbach. Frank Goss announced, and the music was composed and conducted by Lyn Murray.

With the changeover to the *Hallmark Hall of Fame* format in 1953, the literary slant disappeared. Now the show produced true stories of Americana and world history. The lives of Madame Marie Curie, Mary Todd Lincoln, and Lee De Forest, father of radio, were among those done on the *Hall of Fame*. Freeman (Amos) Gosden and Charles (Andy) Correll appeared on the De Forest show. Frank Goss stayed aboard as announcer, and William Gay directed. Host for *The Hallmark Hall of Fame* was the distinguished Lionel Barrymore, who bellowed "Goood eeevvening, ladies and gentlemen!" as though he really meant it. In its occasionally seen TV format, *The Hallmark Hall of Fame* has become the ultimate prestige show, and a sure-fire promotion for the slogan that was the standard even in 1948: "Remember—a Hallmark Card, when you care enough to send the very best."

The Halls of Ivy

The Halls of Ivy starred Ronald Colman who, for the first decade of radio's life, had avoided microphones with a passion. He was a top movie star through the 1930's, and radio was a crude, often bumbling form of entertainment that had developed its biggest names from burlesque and vaudeville. That formula began to change in the 1940's; the golden age of movies was slipping away, and radio began to develop into a smooth, often memorable, sometimes great medium. So Colman began appearing more frequently. He worked with Arch Oboler and Norman Corwin. He starred on *Suspense* and *The Lux Radio Theatre*, and hosted the syndicated series, *Favorite Story*. Colman even proved himself a superior comedian with his frequent guest shots on *The Jack Benny Program*.

When the right series came along, Coleman took it hook, bait and sinker. *The Halls of Ivy* was first heard on NBC January 6, 1950. It ran, under sponsorship of the Joseph Schlitz Brewing Company, on Fridays and later Wednesday nights, until 1952.

With Colman came his wife Benita Hume, who had accompanied him on *The Jack Benny Program* and had been equally charming as a light comedienne. *The Halls of Ivy* was tailor-made for the Colmans; it suited their style and timing perfectly. Colman played William Todhunter Hall, president of Ivy College in the "town of Ivy, U.S.A.," and Benita was Vicky, "the former Victoria Cromwell of the English theatre." Dr. Hall belied the sterotyped college head by taking a personal hand in the problems of his students. He met with them individually as friend and counselor, and invited them to his home. Vicky, his wife, had been a star of musical comedy shows before her marriage. She had an air of earthy wit, referring to her husband by the pet name "Toddy-dear," and counterbalancing in a pleasant way his four-syllable words with proper diction.

The show was created by Don Quinn, 49 years old and a veteran of almost two decades with *Fibber McGee and Molly* when he began to put *The Halls of Ivy* together. It was as radical a change of pace as he could have asked for, without turning to suspense or Western melodrama. Nat Wolff directed, and, with apprentice Walter Newman, helped Quinn with the writing. Announcer was Ken Carpenter. The theme, "Halls of Ivy," was sung in hallowed Ivy League fashion, by a group of soft males voices in an echo chamber: We love the Halls of Ivy / That surround us here today . . .

Quinn's writing, as always, was first-rate. But the success of *The Halls of Ivy* rested mainly with the Colmans. Their warmth and comfort with the characters, combined with the distinctive campus flavor, made the show one that appealed greatly to listeners.

Hap Hazard

Hap Hazard was first heard on NBC July 1, 1941, as a thirteen-week summer replacement for *Fibber McGee and Molly*. It starred Ransom Sherman as Hap Hazard, harried proprietor of the Crestfallen Manor, a ramshackle hotel in the Stop and Flop chain. Sherman, who also wrote the show, had built a solid reputation as host-writer of *Club Matinee*, a Chicago-based variety series of a few years earlier. Johnson's Wax, impressed by the reviews on *Hap Hazard*, bought it for the regular fall lineup. But Sherman's career on the air was hot and cold; he was one of the "in" comedians whose abilities were respected by those in the business, but never really made it big with the general public.

Hap Hazard was no exception. It disappeared soon after its fall première. The situations revolved around Hap's hotel and money. The floors creaked, the doors wouldn't shut, the water taps dripped, and the hotel slipped forever toward bankruptcy. Hap spent most of his time rescuing guests from problem situations. Billy Mills stayed through the summer as orchestra leader, then Felix Mills was brought in to wave the stick. Edna Odell was vocalist, Harlow Wilcox announcer.

The Happiness Boys

The Happiness Boys were Billy Jones and Ernie Hare, singers and comedians heard throughout radio's first decade in a light format of patter and music; they sang together on the air as early as 1921 and were featured regularly on NBC until the death of Hare in 1939. They went on the network soon after its formation in 1926, in a Friday-at-eight, 30-minute show for Happiness Candy, from which they took their best-known nickname. As "The Happiness Boys," they were introduced with this bouncy song, the words being altered with their changing sponsors through the years:

> How do you do, every-body, how do you do?
> Gee it's great to say hell-o to all of you;
> I'm Billy Jones
> I'm Ernie Hare,
> And we're a silly-lookin' pair;
> How do you doodle-doodle-doodle-doodle-do?

In 1929, Jones and Hare went on the Blue Network for Interwoven Sox, and were known during this association as "The Interwoven Pair." In 1931, they became affiliated with Tastyeast Bakers in a series called, alternately, "The Tastyeast Jesters" and The Tasty Breadwinner." But their first moniker—"The Happiness Boys"—followed them through their careers and after. Hare died March 9, 1939; Jones, November 23, 1940.

The Hardy Family

The Hardy Family was a Metro-Goldwyn-Mayer syndication produced around 1950 and starring the original cast from the Andy Hardy movies. Mickey Rooney was Andy, Lewis Stone was his father,

Judge James Hardy, and Fay Holden was Mrs. Hardy, Emily to the judge. The series supposedly reflected "the common joys and tribulations of the average American family"; in reality, Andy Hardy was a cross between Archie Andrews and Henry Aldrich—two parts pandemonium to one part chaos. The show was just another comedy about an insane teenager, and much better remembered as a film series. The scripts were by Jack Rubin. Music was by Jerry Fielding. Thomas McAvity directed.

Harvest of Stars

Harvest of Stars was a program of concert music first heard on NBC October 7, 1945. It opened under the baton of Howard Barlow, with Lyn Murray's 20-member choir and Raymond Massey as host; it was sponsored by the International Harvester Company and produced by Russ Johnson. In the second year, Dr. Frank Black became musical director and James Melton, Metropolitan opera star, was soloist. The show also featured light dramatic skits by the Harvester Players. Glen Heisch produced, booking such guests as the original Revelers (for a reunion with their old tenor Melton) and Jane Powell. It was heard until 1950, all the way on NBC, with the exception of a brief CBS fling in the 1948–49 season.

The Haunting Hour

The Haunting Hour was a series of murder thrillers syndicated to local stations in 1946. The opening reeked of fog, darkened streets, and movements in the shadows; a churchbell tolled ominously, there was a click-click of footsteps. The announcer tried desperately to keep us: "No! No, stay where you are! Do not break the stillness of this moment! For this is a time of mystery, a time when imagination is free and moves forward swiftly. This is The Haunting Hour!" The mystery-crime anthology that followed used and abused most of the cliché plots of the time; many sounded like fast Inner Sanctum rewrites.

Have Gun, Will Travel

Have Gun, Will Travel was an audio oddity—one of the few radio shows that originated on television. Beginning in the mid-1950's as a Richard Boone TV series, Have Gun reversed the trend a few years later and migrated to radio. Like the TV version, it ran on CBS and attracted a fine star for the lead.

The lead was simply Paladin, a Western soldier of fortune with an even temper and a fast gun. Paladin did the dirty work others wouldn't do—for a hefty price. He operated by the same code of the West that made Marshal Dillon tick; often he stepped up to the line, but rarely crossed it.

The role went to John Dehner. Nobody could duplicate Boone, and Dehner didn't even try. His interpretation of Paladin was an interesting contrast. Dehner comes across as a new Paladin, slighter of build perhaps, but still dressed in black, still a deadly foe.

The show premièred on CBS November 23, 1958 and ran until November 27, 1960, thus becoming one of the last radio dramas. The scripts closely followed the TV format, using the same staccato music and the technique of opening with a small snatch of Paladin dialogue. The dialogue was usually a threat, and Paladin didn't mince words: "If the girl who's being held prisoner has been harmed in any way, I'll flip a coin to see which one I gun down first," he said, opening one show.

Paladin was a loner, a man of few friends with a wide reputation. His relationship with Heyboy, the Oriental who worked at San Francisco's Carlton Hotel where Paladin made his headquarters, was cordial but cool. More than once Paladin saved Heyboy's neck from the Western toughs who were always itching for trouble, but their friendship remained almost businesslike. It never got within shouting distance of the "kemo sabe" stage. Paladin was always "Meestah Paladin" and Heyboy was always Heyboy. Dehner was supported by Ben Wright as Heyboy and Virginia Gregg as Heyboy's girlfriend, Miss Wong. The series was created by Herb Meadow and Sam Rolfe, announced by Hugh Douglas, and directed by, among others, Norman Macdonnell.

When last heard, Paladin was heading back to Boston to claim a $100,000 inheritance. It was an unusual finish to an unusual series —the cowboy riding east into the sunrise. It turned one of the last remaining pages of old-time radio.

Hawaii Calls

Hawaii Calls, first heard on the Pacific Coast in July 1935, was created, produced, and directed by Webley Edwards, who got the idea while listening to a shortwave transmission from Hawaii in 1934. In the classic tradition, Edwards reckoned he could do better. His show of islander music was broadcast each Saturday from the shores of

Waikiki Beach, before a live audience of some 2,000 people. It featured Hawaii's best singers and musicians, the swish of wahine skirts, the roar of the Pacific (one sound man was assigned to the oceanfront with a microphone, to add to the mood that listeners back home loved). The group used no brass—only drums, guitars, and ukeleles. They performed ten songs a week, three purely native Hawaiian and the rest in English or novelty style. Edwards made great use of the campfire atmosphere, emphasizing that his show was produced "right under the banyan trees" with the famous Diamond Head in the background. Al Kealoha Perry, Harry Owens, Hilo Hattie, and Alfred Apaka were among the performers. Jim Wahl was assistant director. The show as picked up by the entire Mutual network in 1945 for a long run; it could still be heard locally into the 1970's.

Hawk Larabee

Hawk Larabee, an unusual Western, came to CBS in 1946 and was heard in two disjointed seasons. It told the story of the Black Mesa Ranch and its owner, Hawk Larabee. Barton Yarborough was Hawk, and Barney Phillips played his sidekick, Sombre Jones. The stories, all told from Hawk's viewpoint, were accompanied by singing bridges between the acts. The lyrics suggested story developments to come and were done to the tune of "The Old Chisholm Trail." A combo comprised of Rod May, Fran Mahoney, Bob Crawford, and Tookie Cronenbold did the singing, a job that later fell to Andy Parker and the Plainsmen. The musical bridges clashed somewhat with the show's adventure themes, but were used through two distinct versions of the show. In the other version, Yarborough was relegated to the role of sidekick Brazos John, while the title role went to Elliott Lewis. William N. Robson was producer-director. The show opened to "the Hawk's whistle," and the announcer's cry, "The hawk is on the wing!"

Hawthorne House

Hawthorne House was broadcast to NBC's West Coast stations from the San Francisco studios Monday nights at 9:30. First heard in 1935, *Hawthorne House* mixed elements of heavy drama, situation comedy, and soap opera in the *One Man's Family* tradition. It followed the adventures of Mother Sherwood and her family—son Mel, daughter Marietta, and adopted son Billy—in their struggle in Depression America after the unexpected death of wealthy Mr. Sherwood. The market crash had left them destitute and Mother Sherwood, in order to pay the bills, turned their Oakland mansion into a guest home, taking in anyone who could pay (and many who couldn't). Her home became a catchall of worldly trouble and strife—a melting pot of mixed talents, emotions, and desires. Mrs. Sherwood's first guest, Lois Liston, was a lovely young lady seeking shelter for herself and her grandmother. Son Mel promptly fell in love with Lois—unrequited love, for Lois had eyes only for Jerry Tremaine, a writer (also penniless) who had moved in under the Sherwood roof. Over a span of time, Lois and Jerry became engaged and were married, and Mel began a love affair with Miriam Bracefield; they also were married.

The cast was headed by Pearl King Tanner as Mother Sherwood. Mel was played by Jack Moyles for much of the run; Miriam was played by Billie Byers. Daughter Marietta was Florida Edwards, and the part was later played by Natalie Park, who originated the role of Lois Liston. Sam Edwards, still years away from his *Corliss Archer* role of Dexter Franklin, played adopted son Billy. David Drummond wrote the series, a job assumed by Ray Buffum around 1942. The family was complete with its black cook, Martha. She was played by Dixie Marsh, a white woman billed in *Radio Life* as "famed colored impersonator and singer of darky songs."

Heart's Desire

Heart's Desire was a Mutual giveaway show, heard from September 9, 1946 through 1948 in a five-a-week daytime format. Ben Alexander, still a light-year away from his *Dragnet* role, was master of ceremonies, known to his matinee audience as Uncle Ben. The format of *Heart's Desire* was dangerously simple: people wrote in asking for things, and the better the cause, the better the chance of getting their "heart's desire." Of course, the chances never were very good to begin with. Up to 50,000 letters a week poured in from people everywhere. They were read and judged by hospitalized veterans, people in the studio audience and the show's staff; out of that giant pot a few were picked for each show.

Alexander, former child movie star, was enjoying a busy radio career in those days. In addition to *Heart's Desire*, he was doing *The Ben Alexander Show* (informal chatter and yarn-spinning on Mutual in the morning), sharing a Mutual news analysis, show and occasionally playing Marjorie's boyfriend, Bashful Ben, on *The Great Gildersleeve*. Alexander once estimated to *Radio Mirror* that 60 percent of the *Heart's Desire* mail came from people wanting things for others.

The Hedda Hopper Show

The Hedda Hopper Show was one of the best-known of the Hollywood gossip reports. Hedda of the bizarre hats had several full careers behind her when she broke into radio around 1938, with local fashion reports. By 1939, manager Dema Harshbarger had landed her a spot on *Brenthouse*, an NBC serial, in which she played a working housewife. But even then it was obvious to Miss Harshbarger that Hopper's real forte was Hollywood reporting.

Hedda had been on the scene forever and knew everyone. She first came to Hollywood in the silent days of World War I, a runaway from her Pennsylvania Quaker home. Still in her teens, she set about finding work in films and on stage. She played many supporting film roles in the pioneering days, but eventually saw that her star would never rise, and turned her energies elsewhere. By the time she came to radio, she knew personally of skeletons in famous closets, or knew who did know and how to get to them. Her attendance at every Hollywood function was taken for granted; she gathered her tips from every corner of town. Unlike Walter Winchell, who frequently tried to hide his mistakes, Hedda gave herself the bird on the air, tweeting away with a gold-plated mechanical canary whenever she flubbed. Hopper had landed several times as a guest on *The Rudy Vallee Show*, and her gossip show began on CBS for Sunkist fruits in 1939. It was a three-a-week, 15-minute affair, in which Hopper dissected the famous with behind-the-scenes accounts of their transgressions. The show ran until 1942, and was resurrected in 1944 as a weekly Monday-night feature for Armour & Company. That lasted until 1946, when Hedda began syndicating 5-minute interview shows. She snared such notables as Lew Ayres, Bing Crosby, and Mickey Rooney for these spots. A final Hedda Hopper number was heard in a 30-minute Sunday variety format during the 1950–51 NBC season.

The Heinz Magazine of the Air

The Heinz Magazine of the Air was an ambitious undertaking by CBS and the Heinz Foods Company, first hitting the air September 2, 1936. It was an expensive serial-variety show, offering 15 minutes of chatter, interviews, and music and a 15-minute continuing drama, "Trouble House," by Elaine Carrington. *The Heinz Magazine of the Air* was broadcast on Mondays, Wednesdays, and Fridays at 11 A.M., EST, and followed the magazine formula to audio perfection. The "editor" was

Delmar Edmondson; music was by Leith Stevens. The interviews were with famous people from all walks of life—literature, entertainment, sports, aviation. The opening show featured Grand Duchess Marie of Russia.

The serial, sandwiched between the variety acts, had a short life, and never built up the following that unadorned soaps had. "Trouble House" had the additional problem of being heard only three times a week, losing its continuity every Tuesday and Thursday. In 1937, it was replaced by a new drama, "Carol Kennedy's Romance." By the middle of that season, Heinz had thrown in the towel on the "magazine" format, leaving "Carol Kennedy's Romance" to fill the 11:15 to 11:30 time slot alone. That show too was destined for a short life; It went off the air in 1938.

The Helen Hayes Theatre

The Helen Hayes Theatre was billed as prestige drama, but the series was so sporadic that it never really built the reputation of the great theatres of the air. Miss Hayes, "the first lady of the theatre," had appeared on radio as early as 1930. On October 1, 1935, she brought her first Theatre to the Blue Network for Sanka Coffee, dramatizing such plays as The New Penny in serial form. The New Penny, written by Sherlock Holmes producer Edith Meiser, starred Miss Hayes as a small-town rebel. The series expired two years later, and Miss Hayes did not accept another Theatre until 1940. Her new show began on CBS September 29, 1940 for Lipton Tea; it was an elaborate Sunday-night theatre of contemporary drama. She became the first radio casualty of World War II when, on December 28, 1941, Lipton dropped the show in anticipation of tea shortages from India. Of all her shows, this one became best known.

Miss Hayes selected her own material, choosing from the most popular stories and best-selling novels of the time. She supervised the entire production, from casting to special effects; the series offered such standbys as Let the Hurricane Roar by Rose Wilder Lane, and Kitty Foyle by Christopher Morley. Miss Hayes played the female leads, and guests served as her leading men. George Bryan was announcer and music was by Mark Warnow. In 1945, a third Helen Hayes Theatre came to CBS under sponsorship of Textron. Broadcast Saturday nights, this one lasted one season. In 1948 Miss Hayes starred on Electric Theatre for CBS Sundays. In 1963 she headed a repertory that made a noble but futile attempt to bring back radio drama. Titled The General Electric Theatre, it was syndicated in stereo to FM stations by the QXR Stereo Network, out of WQXR, New

York. In the company were Cyril Richard, Peter Ustinov, Joseph Cotten, Agnes Moorehead, and Dina Merrill. The group performed such plays as Gore Vidal's *Visit to a Strange Planet*, Herman Melville's *Billy Budd* and Henry James *Turn of the Screw*.

The Henry Morgan Show

The Henry Morgan Show starred "the bad boy of radio." Morgan got his start as a page boy at WMCA, New York in 1931; two years later, he began announcing there and moved through a succession of announcing jobs at stations in Philadelphia, Duluth, Boston, and New York. He was born Henry Lerner von Ost, Jr., March 31, 1915; the Lerner von Ost, Jr. was dropped around 1932, and he became simply Henry Morgan. From the beginning of his radio career, he was galled by the reverent tones required in the reading of commercials, and soon he began to throw in a few barbs. When both he and the world survived those barbs, Morgan gradually took more liberties with the copy. In 1940, he turned up at WOR, New York.

His first WOR shows ran Saturday mornings under the title, *Meet Mr. Morgan*; By October 1940, *Meet Mr. Morgan* was a nightly show; it soon evolved into the notorious *Here's Morgan*, a six-a-week 15-minute corner of insanity, where it remained until Morgan entered the war in 1943.

It was in this nightly format that Morgan did his most devastating work and built his reputation. He was good with dialect, creating many zany characters for sketches, skits, and parodies. He attacked institutions and conventions of all kinds, from radio executives to weather reporters. There were no sacred cows on Morgan's show. For a time he signed off with crazy weather reports ("Snow tomorrow, followed by small boys with sleds and dignified old men getting conked on the beans by little boys with sleds following snow," or "Muggy tomorrow, followed by Tuegy, Wedgy, Thurgy and Frigy"). It took an official protest by the U.S. Navy to stop his weather put-ons. Of his early sponsors, Alder Elevator Shoes—the company with its "Now you can be taller than she is" slogan—was most vulnerable to Morgan's barbs. Company president Jesse Alder became known to Morgan's listeners as "Old Man Adler." Once Morgan followed a spot claiming that Adlers could add two inches to a man's height with speculation on what would happen to a man's pants in such a miracle. Other early advertising victims were Shell Oil and Ironized Yeast.

Three radio comedians built their reputations on heckling the Establishment. Fred Allen and Arthur Godfrey used needles on their victims, but Henry Morgan used a club. Sometimes the club had a rusty spike in its end. Morgan drove it in with zest. He ripped and tore his way through the early 1940's, clobbering his sponsors with such venomous diatribes that some of them dropped him in outrage. This was all delightful to the millions of people who joined Morgan in hating sponsors and suspecting any commercial delivered in drooling superlatives. And thus, with an acid tongue and a go-to-hell attitude, Morgan became the darling of the era's rebels, the president of a small hard core that considered the barbs of Allen and Godfrey soft. Godfrey kidded his sponsors by inference and innuendo; Morgan blasted them with indictment. The attacks were spontaneous, ranging from cute Godfreyisms on the weak side to jesting charges of fraud on the strong side. In one early show, he ribbed Life Savers for cheating the public by drilling holes in its candy; he offered to peddle the holes as "Morgan's Mint Middles." Morgan's fans thought this outrageously funny. Life Savers people just thought it outrageous. The following morning the candy company canceled its sponsorship.

It was an old story to Morgan. He had been in hot water with sponsors and station executives more than once in his career. Fired from at least one local station for his on-the-air jesting, Morgan built a small but fanatical following shortly after his *Here's Morgan* appeared on WOR. His cult included most of radio's "inner circle"—the comedians, writers, and hosts who had longed for years to do what Morgan did every night. Among his ardent fans was Norman Corwin, who was so impressed by Morgan's style that he signed the comic for a prestigious *Twenty-Six by Corwin* appearance in 1941.

Early in his realtionship with WOR, his bosses learned not to tamper. When they scolded Morgan for losing an account, he related this backstage intrigue in detail for his listeners, then auctioned off the station to the highest bidder. Often he griped about the carefully prepared scripts his sponsors had left him, tore them up loudly on the air, and launched into his own "commercial." It was a sponsor's nightmare. And sometimes, when his jokes didn't quite come off, Morgan reminded his listeners that they could always turn the dial if they thought they'd get a better show from Lowell Thomas.

Morgan's shows were largely ad-libbed; he went on alone, with no rehearsal. The programs depended entirely on his wit and spontaneity. Morgan entered the service in 1943, and when he returned in 1945 he was hired by WJZ, and was back on the New York air complete with previously banned weather reports. Then, on September 3, 1946, ABC brought Morgan coast to coast, in what was for him an elaborate production, airing his *Henry Morgan Show* Wednesday nights in 1946. It was a slick package with actors, announcing by Charles Irving, music by Bernie Green, and his old "Good evening, anybody, here's Morgan" opening, to the fluted tune

"For He's a Jolly Good Fellow." Morgan still did most of his own writing, but somehow the flair was gone; his comedy had lost some of its bite and didn't carry well in 30-minute weekly doses. But after three shows on a sustaining basis, the Eversharp Company decided to bite the bullet and sponsor *The Henry Morgan Show* for Shick ("push-pull, click-click") razors and blades. Morgan had a field day with their spots.

Shick dropped the show December 3, 1947, citing flab in Morgan's material, low ratings, and declining sales as the reason. In typical form, Morgan had his own ("It's not my show; it's their razor") explanation for his audience. He was subsequently picked up by Rayve Cream Shampoo, which he mercilessly drubbed even in a guest appearance on *The Fred Allen Show*. Morgan's final series was on NBC in 1949–50, a Sunday-night show sponsored by Bristol-Myers. It was produced by Kenneth MacGregor, announced by Ben Grauer, and co-starred Arnold Stang and Kenny Delmar.

Herb Shriner Time

Herb Shriner Time was built around the slow Hoosier delivery and simple country style that had made Will Rogers such a hit two decades before. Shriner broke into radio around 1935 on a Fort Wayne, Indiana, barn-dance program, *Hoosier Hop*. His act was also featured on the *Camel Caravan*, *The Chesterfield Supper Club*, and the Phillip Morris program, *Johnny Presents*. But Herb Shriner was not Rogers, and he never caught on in a big way. The show was enough to propel him into a late afternoon CBS variety slot, though; this ran in 1948–49 for Miles Laboratories. In his daily 15-minute stint, Shriner would chatter a bit about back-home Indiana, bring on a guest, and introduce an orchestra number by Raymond Scott and his quintet. That was about it.

Hercule Poirot

Hercule Poirot, the story of Agatha Christie's ingenious (but insufferably immodest) French detective, premièred on Mutual February 22, 1945, and enjoyed a short run as a 30-minute Thursday night series. It starred Harold Huber as the detective, was directed by Carl Eastman, and included a shortwave sendoff by Miss Christie from London. *Poirot* was a fairly decent show. It followed the detective from London to New York, where he set up practice on this side of the Atlantic. Earlier, the Mercury Players had dramatized the most famous of all

Poirot cases,."The Murder of Roger Ackroyd," on the CBS *Campbell Playhouse*, November 12, 1939.

Here's to Romance

Here's to Romance was a pop variety show that began on CBS in 1943 as a vehicle for Buddy Clark, and later Dick Haymes; it shifted gears somewhat during the 1944 season to include even light dramatic offerings. By 1944, the cast included Martha Tilton, Larry Douglas, and the Ray Bloch orchestra, with Jim Ameche as announcer. Special guests staged brief dramatic skits and Robert Ripley even appeared with "Believe-It-Or-Not" incidents from his files. Like Haymes himself, this show lacked staying power, and had disappeared by 1946.

Heritage

Heritage premièred on ABC December 11, 1952, as the "dramatic adventures from the chronicles of ten centuries of Western civilization" and ran for one season. It was a semi-documentary series, "produced in collaboration with leading scholars and educators," and was based on *Life Magazine's* "Picture History of Western Man." Some typical "Heritage" shows were Chaucer's "Canterbury Tales," "The Adventures of Marco Polo," "Tales of the Decameron," "The Notebooks of Science," "Benjamin Franklin," "The Languages of Man," and "School Days: How the Little Red Schoolhouse Molded the Character of our Nation." The series was produced and directed by Sherman H. Dryer with music by Ralph Norman and narration by Charles Irving.

The Hermit's Cave

The Hermit's Cave sent chills up spines during the war years. Today *The Hermit's Cave* comes off as an interesting but corny, relic of the past. But the opening was campy and fun. Skilled use of sound effects by Dwight Hauser set up the show nicely. There was wind. There was howling. There was a feeling of doom, and of gloom too. And finally there was the Old Hermit, standing at the mouth of his cave, warning the weak of heart not to listen:

> *Ghhhooosssttt stories . . . Weeiiirrrrdd stories . . . And murders too! The Hermit knows of them all! Turrrrnnn out your lights!*

Turn them out!. . . Have you heard the story, "Hanson's Ghost"?
Then listen, while the Hermit tells you the story . . .

The Hermit's Cave mangled its victims in the grand old radio tradition. People were chopped, slashed, bashed, mashed, gashed, sliced, diced, and garroted. Sound man Hauser used as many cabbages and lettuces for skull splittings on this show as most people ate in a month of Sundays. But the real interest in *The Hermit's Cave* lay in its personnel. Youngsters Bill Forman and William Conrad were its producers. The music was by Rex Koury. Stories were written by Lou Huston and Herbert R. Connor. The series was produced at Station KMPC, Los Angeles, and was syndicated in 1940–43. The Hermit? That voice of the rusty nails came from the parched throat of Mel Johnson.

High Adventure

High Adventure was one of the better adventure shows but never quite attained the highest level set by *Escape,* which was running concurrently. *High Adventure* came to Mutual in 1947 for a season. The opening was reminiscent of *Escape,* with a deep-voiced narrator sketching in tonight's show in a few terse sentences. The stories were told by members of a "High Adventure Society"—people who like stories of "hard action, hard men and smooth women." Writer-director was Robert Monroe, announcer was Carl Caruso, and music was by Sylvan Levin.

Hilltop House

Hilltop House, "the story of a woman who must choose between love and the career of raising other women's children," was first heard on CBS November 1, 1937. It starred Bess Johnson *as* Bess Johnson, dedicated caseworker at an orphanage known as Hilltop House. Written by Addy Richton and Lynn Stone, the series was produced by Ed Wolfe for Palmolive, and ran on CBS until a cut in the Palmolive ad budget forced its cancellation March 28, 1941. Three days later, the character was revived in a new CBS serial, *The Story of Bess Johnson.* Therein, Bess left the Hilltop House phase of her life behind and settled into her new routine as superintendent of a boarding school. *The Story of Bess Johnson,* written by William Sweets, ran only about a year. But a new version of *Hilltop House* came to CBS in 1948, sponsored by Miles Laboratories. This one ran until 1955, featuring Jan Miner as "Julie of Hilltop House."

Best remembered is the early show. Though it was of a higher calibre than many afternoon serials, *Hilltop House* contained all the strained melodrama that made listening between noon and 5 P.M. such an experience. Picture this scene, from April 1940: It's been two months since John's plane has disappeared; Bess reads again his final words and a lump forms in her throat. Tears spill over her lovely eyelashes. *Oh, John, John . . .* But wait! Bess doesn't know it, but John is alive! His plane crashed in a primitive area inhabited only by Indians. Will he ever find his way out? Will he ever see Bess again? Let's burden John with a severe case of amnesia—an original development if ever there was one—and *Hilltop House* is off and running.

John was only one of Bess Johnson's many internal conflicts. For Bess couldn't ever marry, as long as she wanted to work in the orphanage. And that's a tough one, especially after years of searching for just the right orphanage.

His Honor, the Barber

His Honor, the Barber, a short-lived but extremely entertaining half-hour, told the story of Judge Barnard Fitz of the District Court of Vincent County. The part was played by Barry Fitzgerald, Oscar winner, who had refused all prior offers of steady radio work.

Barber premièred on NBC October 16, 1945, and ran for a season under sponsorship of Ballantine Ale. It was written, produced, and directed by Carlton E. Morse. The show bore most of the Morse trademarks: diversity of plot, depth of character, and plenty of warm, human emotion. Judge Fitz himself had been the barber of a small (pop. 3,543) community before his election to the bench. His "shirtsleeve philosophy" was deeply rooted in human values, and at times the old Irishman could be painfully sentimental. He followed the spirit of the law, and much preferred dispensing kindness than jail terms.

Clashing with the judge's philosophy was that of Sheriff McGrath, "Vincent County's own little Hitler." The sheriff, played by Bill Green, followed a "lock-'em-up-and-throw-away-the-key" philosophy, and based his dealing with prisoners on a literal reading of the law. Often his views clashed with those of the judge in open court, but there he was fighting on the judge's own battlefield and he emerged the inevitable loser. Judge Fitz never failed to find a legal loophole for people oppressed, a trait that endeared him to his lovely, liberal young niece, Susan (Barbara Fuller). In his off-hours, the judge's time was filled with Susan's loves and problems. His relationships with his niece, various townspeople, strangers, and political opportunists kept the series moving well and contributed a bright spot to NBC's Tuesday-night 1945 lineup.

The character of Judge Fitz was created by Nate Slott. Opie Cates provided the music, and Frank Martin was the announcer.

Hit the Jackpot

Hit the Jackpot was another high-jackpot quiz show that swept into radio in the late 1940's. This one, featuring Bill Cullen and the Al Goodman orchestra, ran on CBS for DeSoto as a Tuesday-nighter in 1948–49. Produced by Mark Goodson and Bill Todman, Hit the Jackpot solicited cards from listeners, who were called at random. For guessing a "mystery phrase," prizes often ran over $25,000. Winners got free trips, furniture, services, and sponsor DeSoto threw in a new car. One lucky winner got a $3,000 gold-plated lawn mower in addition to $23,000 worth of prizes.

Hobby Lobby

Hobby Lobby was first heard on CBS October 6, 1937. For two seasons it was a Wednesday-night show, first on CBS for Hudson cars, then (1938–39) on the Blue network for Fels Naptha Soap.

With good reason, Dave Elman was called "the dean of American hobbyists." He collected bits of everything, including pieces of information on unusual hobbies, and wrapped them up in his own radio show. And a popular show it was, spread over a dozen years on various networks. Once the show became established, Elman was flooded with new data on unusual hobbies; thousands of letters poured into the show each week. Elman combed through them himself, looking for the most interesting and unusual to put on the air. Because the show was only on for 30 minutes, less than six unusual hobbies could be explored in detail per program.

Hobbyists ranged from the beekeeper (whose bees escaped into the studio) to the Philadelphia hypnotist who offered to mesmerize 70 percent of Elman's listeners. Elman's subjects included all the oddities of the human condition; the ingenious hobby was presented alongside the silly and frivolous. A few, as summarized by Radio Life, were a baker of musical cakes, a man who taught giants not to be self-conscious, a "debunker" of historical misinformation, a man who cooked bacon on hot coals inserted into his mouth, a speller/thinker/talker of backwards English, a collector of baby elephant hairs, a secretary who created sculpture from burnt toast, a man who could touch his chin with his nose, a woman who collected facts about Friday the 13th, and a club comprised of female war workers all over age 50. In the fall of 1939, *Hobby Lobby* returned to CBS for a Sunday season for Fels Naptha. In 1941 it moved to Saturday for Colgate and ran there until 1943.

One of Elman's most celebrated stunts came in 1942, when he inserted this ad in New York newspapers:

WANTED—TALKING DOG. MUST HAVE VOCABULARY OF 10 WORDS OR MORE, PREFERABLY NO ACCENT. HOBBY LOBBY, PLAZA 8-2900.

The *Hobby Lobby* phones were swamped with barking, howling pranksters. But from it Elman finally turned up several people whose dogs could fairly accurately mimic the English language. One dog arfed, "I love mama" when bribed with hamburger; another growled "Hooray for Roosevelt!" In a turnaround, Elman also presented a man who claimed the ability to talk to dogs.

Hobby Lobby was a fun-filled, often fascinating half-hour. After five years on the air, Dave Elman could well justify his claim as "the man of 100,000 hobbies." The show was revived for a season on CBS in 1945, Thursday nights for Anchor-Hocking Glass. It returned again as a Saturday-afternoon Mutual-sustained show in 1948–49.

The Hollywood Barn Dance

The Hollywood Barn Dance was the West Coast's answer to the two champion hoedowns on the air, and premièred on CBS regional outlets December 4, 1943. It had neither the tradition nor the charisma of *The National Barn Dance* and *The Grand Ole Opry*, but featured the familiar Country-Western mix—two parts music (heavy on the guitar and accordion, podnuh) to one part comedy and philosophy. Master of ceremonies was Cottonseed Clark, who dabbled in "brushwood philosophy" and verse. Regulars included the old Riders Of The Purple Sage (Foy Willing, Kenny Driver, and Al Sloey), singer and strummer Merle Travis, Charlie Linvalle, Kentucky state champion fiddler; Carolina Cotton, Kirby Grant, and the country comic Johnny Bond. Musical director was Foy Willing of the Riders. Because it was situated in the nation's glamor capital, *The Hollywood Barn Dance* often brought in such Western guest stars as Roy Rogers. By 1947,

Merle Travis was emcee. Regulars included cowboy star Ken Curtis, Maureen O'Conner, and Andy Parker and the Plainsmen.

Hollywood Calling

Hollywood Calling was a star-studded, super-expensive giveaway with a $31,000 jackpot that listeners could win in their very own homes. It was created in an effort to regain the listeners who had been wooed away by CBS starting in the fall of 1948.

For the entire life of network broadcasting, NBC had led the way. It had been especially strong in the great comedy shows, and traditionally threw its strongest bastion together on Sunday nights. But CBS ended all that in 1948, when it lured away Jack Benny, the *Amos and Andy* show, and four other top-flight NBC programs. The NBC brass, still reeling from the shock, went into a corporate huddle and came up with *Hollywood Calling* as an answer. It was booked into Jack Benny's slot during summer vacations in the hope that when Benny moved over to CBS, the giveaway would do to him what *Stop the Music* had done to Fred Allen.

And to produce the show, what better man that Louis G. Cowan, architect of the *Stop the Music* plan? Cowan's magic formula went like this: host George Murphy and assorted glamorous film stars would staff the phones, placing their calls to Mr. and Mrs. America wherever they might be listening. Just for answering your phone, you would get a seventeen-jewel watch. For answering a preliminary question on the movies, you won a prize of several hundred dollars' value. Along with that went a chance at the $31,000 "Film of Fortune" jackpot.

NBC, dying to give stuff away, was blatantly trying to buy back its Jack Benny audience. The clues for the preliminary questions were embarrassingly obvious. The new series was first heard July 3, 1949. June Allyson and Walter Pidgeon were tapped for phone duty; they spoke in person to contestants over the air. It was elaborate ad nauseum. *Time* reported that the opener used twenty-one microphones, twelve singers, six arrangers, ten telephone operators, six researchers, fifteen actors, six writers, and a thirty-five piece orchestra.

It was also dull ad nauseum. *Newsweek* noted that the show "failed to excite the approval of a single major radio critic" in its première. And it never got much better. In the fall, when Jack Benny came back on CBS, he clobbered them.

Hollywood Hotel

Hollywood Hotel was the first major network show to come out of the West. It premièred on CBS October 5, 1934, and ran until 1938. It was Louella Parsons' baby.

Miss Parsons, widely read gossip columnist, promoted the concept and became the driving force behind the success of *Hollywood Hotel*. When the show went on the air in 1934, not one national program of importance was originating from the West Coast. Even the staunch *Lux Radio Theatre* was doing straight drama from New York.

The main reason was a telephone company policy that cost networks some $1,000 to reverse radio circuits. New York and Chicago were the audio centers, and Hollywood—sitting out the early radio boom with its priceless aggregation of film talent under wraps —hadn't yet arrived.

It arrived with the opening of *Hollywood Hotel*. Miss Parsons' formula for the show was a two-thirds/one-third mix of drama and variety. She offset the high telephone rate by persuading the top stars of the era to appear free. That was easy enough for Louella; her power and influence as a coast-to-coast columnist were deeply felt in Hollywood, and few stars other than Ginger Rogers wanted to risk crossing swords with her over a refusal to appear. So *Hollywood Hotel* became a mutual back-scratching vehicle, publicizing the stars' movies, promoting their names, and keeping Miss Parsons at the top of Radio Row.

Dick Powell was signed as master of ceremonies; George MacGarrett was director. The format was that of a glamorous Hollywood hotel, with a switchboard opening not unlike that of another popular show of the era, *Grand Hotel*. Duane Thompson, whose feminine voice belied her masculine name, was the switchboard operator; Raymond Paige swung the baton for the "Blue Moon" theme. The show featured guest soloists and a 20-minute movie sketch selected by Miss Parsons. Most of the movies did well after being heard on *Hollywood Hotel*, and in 1938 the radio show itself became a movie, complete with Louella Parsons and the format of the air.

It all ended in 1938 when the Radio Guild launched a campaign against radio "freebies." Miss Parsons' well of free talent dried up overnight, and so did *Hollywood Hotel*. She dropped out of radio for a time to concentrate solely on her writing. But *Hollywood Hotel* was revamped without her; William Powell was brought in as star and host, and production was under the direction of Brewster Morgan. The suave Powell continued the old focus on popular movies, playing in—among others—*Of Human Bondage* with Margaret Sullavan and *Death Takes a Holiday* with Gale Page. Powell even took on part of Ken Niles' announcing burden, promoting movies and longtime sponsor Campbell Soups with equal flair. The stars—now well-paid—kept coming. Luise Rainer, Carole Lombard, and Miriam Hopkins were a few who worked with Powell on *Hollywood Hotel*.

By then there were so many West Coast shows promoting glittering names that *Hollywood Hotel* wasn't too unusual. By 1939 it had folded for good. But California old-timers never forgot that it was the first, and that Miss Parsons—despite her reputation as a sometimes hated gossip columnist—had really brought radio to Hollywood. The dam broke for good in the fall of 1935, when the phone company removed the heavy tariff on shows originating in the West. Within a year, a revamped *Lux Radio Theatre* was in California, doing flashier, more powerful movie adaptations than *Hollywood Hotel* offered. Bing Crosby brought *The Kraft Music Hall* West and Al Jolson opened there in "Shell Chateau." Advertising agencies with heavy radio budgets opened overnight on downtown Hollywood streets, and the networks began pouring money into their West Coast facilities.

By 1937, the Coast had a firm grip on radio's future. A few years later, Chicago was all but washed up, and even New York was playing second-string.

Hollywood Mystery Time

Hollywood Mystery Time was heard Sunday nights on ABC in 1945. It starred Carleton Young as Jim Laughton, an independent producer of movies who found the time to do a little amateur gumshoeing on the side. Working at his side in both celluloid and corpse departments was his pretty secretary, Gloria Dean, played by Gloria Blondell. The show was a poor man's *Mr. and Mrs. North*. In a summertime role switch, Young and Miss Blondell were replaced by Dennis O'Keefe and Constance Moore, another poor man's *Mr. and Mrs. North*.

Hollywood Players

Hollywood Players was an impressive but brief show, premièring on CBS December 25, 1946, and running one season for Cresta Blanca Wines. It replaced the equally impressive *Academy Award* and was comprised of "a company of Hollywood's greatest stars"—Claudette Colbert, Joseph Cotten, Bette Davis, Joan Fontaine, Paulette Goddard, John Garfield, Gene Kelly, and Gregory Peck—who appeared on a rotating basis in original dramas. Sometimes, as in the Christmas opener, the stars played supporting roles to a rising newcomer. On that day, Peck, Cotten, Kelly, and Garfield appeared in support of Janet Leigh, who was making her first radio appearance.

Hollywood Première

Hollywood Première was Louella Parsons' attempt to restore the old Hollywood Hotel formula by luring big names for gratis appearances in return for lavish plugs for their latest film epics. It was first heard on CBS March 28, 1941, and ran until November 28 of that year. The format was like a reduced copy of The Lux Radio Theatre, with a full movie dramatized for about 20 minutes, followed by a "question time" in which Miss Parsons interviewed the guests and asked them questions submitted by listeners. The show, as expected after the Hollywood Hotel fuss, came under fire from the American Federation of Radio Artists for abusing free talent. It lasted less than a year anyway. Sponsor was Lifebuoy Soap; producer was Charles Vanda. Felix Mills' orchestra provided the music, and Harlow Wilcox was announcer.

Hollywood Star Playhouse

Hollywood Star Playhouse was yet another anthology using the Hollywood-superstar formula. Under direction of Jack Johnstone, it came to CBS for Bromo Seltzer on Monday nights on April 24, 1950, with James Stewart as star; moved for the 1951–52 season to Thursday night ABC, and finally came in 1952–53 to NBC on Sundays. It featured original dramas, "tales of suspense, thrills and mystery, written by Hollywood's finest writers and featuring Hollywood's greatest stars." The Hollywood Star Playhouse made an average showing for series of this type, bringing such stars as Deborah Kerr, Vincent Price, and Victor Mature before the microphones. Marilyn Monroe made her radio debut on Hollywood Star Playhouse in 1952. One 1951 ABC episode, "Hour of Truth," with Vincent Price, was unquestionably great radio, but the series itself never made much of a splash. Herbert Rawlinson was host when The Hollywood Star Playhouse opened, and the music was by Jeff Alexander. Jack Johnstone moved with the show to ABC, but Rawlinson was replaced by Orville Anderson, and music was by Basil Adlam.

Hollywood Star Preview

Hollywood Star Preview came to radio in late 1945, and on September 28, 1947, broke into NBC's coast-to-coast Sunday night lineup. In 1948, it became The Hollywood Star Theatre, moving to Saturdays for Anacin, where it ran until 1950. Each week an established member of Hollywood filmdom introduced a newcomer, who played the lead in a 20-odd-minute drama written especially for him or her. After the drama, the newcomer and the old pro were reunited onstage for a bit of chatter, telling how they had met, how the star had first been impressed by the newcomer's talents, and getting in a plug for their latest films. Nat Wolff directed, and musical scores were by Bernard Katz. Generally it was middle-of-the-road drama or light love. Among the offerings: Ray Milland introducing Sally Rawlinson, Henry Fonda introducing Joan Lorring, Ronald Colman introducing Shelley Winters, Adolphe Menjou introducing Don Taylor, Sydney Greenstreet introducing Richard Basehart, Jack Carson introducing Patricia Neal, Rex Harrison introducing Wanda Hendrix, and Douglas Fairbanks, Jr. introducing Helena Carter. Ken Peters announced.

Hollywood Startime

Hollywood Startime was a Blue Network luncheon show that ran Monday through Friday in 1944, featuring interviews with stars of radio and movies as they ate lunch in the RKO commissary. It bore scant resemblance to the Hollywood Startime that was launched by CBS on January 6, 1946. This one was a Sunday-afternoon movie extravaganza for Frigidaire. It made an immediate bid for "prestige drama" status, bringing to the air the now-familiar pattern of movie stars in movie stories, and snapping at the heels of The Lux Radio Theatre and The Screen Guild Players, leaders of the movie pack.

Its production was the equal of Screen Guild and a notch or so behind Lux. Unlike the big two, its run was short. Hollywood Startime was launched into a postwar society recovering from its love affair with film glamor. By then there were so many movie stars on the air that the glitter had faded. The program never got close to Lux or Screen Guild in the ratings department; it faded and died two years after its highly touted première.

It offered some memorable shows, however: The Song of Ber-

nadette with Vincent Price, Lee J. Cobb, and Vanessa Brown; *Riders of the Purple Sage* with George Montgomery and Lynn Bari; *The Lodger* with Vincent Price; and *Talk of the Town* with Cary Grant, Herbert Marshall, and Marguerite Chapman. Music was conceived and conducted by noted composer Alfred Newman, scripts were written by Milton Geiger, and the show, in its first season, was directed by Robert L. Redd.

After its first-year run on Sunday afternoon, *Hollywood Startime* moved into a prime-time Saturday-night slot in the fall of 1946. Herbert Marshall was signed as permanent star-host. Jack Johnstone became director and Wendell Niles continued as announcer. Sponsor was Frigidaire, which reminded listeners every week that "you're twice as sure with two great names—Frigidaire and General Motors."

Honest Harold

Honest Harold, a CBS situation comedy premièring September 20, 1950, and running one season was created by Harold Peary after he abandoned his long-running title role in *The Great Gildersleeve* in June 1950. The show went absolutely nowhere, while *Gildersleeve* continued to thrive under new Gildy Willard Waterman. The show's failure might have been due to a combination of reasons: radio itself was dying then, and few shows created after 1949 made lasting impressions; Waterman did a superb job with the Gildersleeve character, and Peary tried with *Honest Harold* to do Gildy all over again. Surprisingly, this show was the equal of *Gildersleeve* in many respects; the writing was funny, the characters were well-drawn, and direction was by one of the great talents of the era, Norman Macdonnell. Peary played "Honest" Harold Hemp, "popular radio entertainer of Melrose Springs." He lived with his mother and nephew Marvin, and did a homemaker's program on the air. Regular friends included Pete the Marshal, played by Parley Baer; Old Doc Yak-Yak, a strange cross between the crustiness of *Gildersleeve*'s Judge Hooker and the nasal whine of Mr. Peavey; and Gloria, his best girl. Joseph Kearns played Doc, Mary Jane Croft played Evelina, one of Hal's girlfriends; Jane Morgan and Katherine Card played Mother, and Bob Lemond announced. Gloria Holliday, who had played Gildersleeve's scatterbrained secretary Bessie and had later become Peary's wife, played Gloria the switchboard operator at the radio station. The show opened with Peary doing his famous "dirty laugh" from *Gildersleeve*; it closed with his background talk over the credits, much as he had done as Gildy. Peary sang frequently, another throwback to his *Gildersleeve* days. Music was by Jack Meakin. Gene Stone, Jack

Robinson and Bill Danch wrote. Peary gradually slipped out of the network forefront, signing for a local disc jockey show in Los Angeles in 1953.

Honolulu Bound

Honolulu Bound was a comedy-variety show, first heard January 14, 1939, on CBS for Hawaiian Pineapple. It featured gagster Phil Baker, the Andrews Sisters, Harry McNaughton, and Mary Kelly in an islander format. Harry Von Zell was announcer; musical director was Eddie DeLange. The show didn't last, and the following season the pineapple people took on *The Al Pearce Show*. In the final analysis, this was simply an extension of the old *Phil Baker Show*, with McNaughton featured as Bottle the butler, and Baker entertaining between comedy sketches on the accordion.

Hoofbeats

Hoofbeats, a juvenile Western syndicated in 1937, was the air adventures of film star Buck Jones. Packaged and sold for Grape Nuts Flakes, it featured Buck in a rip-roarin' two-fisted program. Although the serial ran for only thirty-nine episodes, *Hoofbeats* was so characteristic of 1930's production that today it remains a classic of juvenile radio. The adventures of Buck and his horse Silver were narrated by a Western hand known only as the Old Wrangler, who reminded his "little pards" to be sure and save them Grape Nuts boxtops. It was mighty fine chuck, and the best way around to corner some mighty fine prizes.

Hop Harrigan

Hop Harrigan was one of the best-known juvenile heroes of the war. Most of Hop's adventures were of warfare and, after all, it was a big war. Captain Midnight, Tom Mix—even Superman—couldn't be on all fronts at once.

And so, on August 31, 1942, *Hop Harrigan*, a refugee from All-American Comics, pushed its way into the crowded Blue Network airspace between 5 and 6 P.M. Hop, played by Chester Stratton, was a daredevil of the air who would have done himself proud in Captain Midnight's Secret Squadron. The *Midnight* influence was more than just coincidental. Writer Albert Aley was sometimes assisted in the scripting by *Midnight* scribes Bob Burtt and Wilfred Moore.

The opening was typical kids' radio—breathless Glenn Riggs shouting, "Presenting Hop Harrigan, America's ace of the airways!" above the drone of Hop's plane, then Hop himself asking for clearance to land:

CX-4, calling control tower: CX-4 calling control tower . . .
Control tower back to CX-4—wind southeast, ceiling twelve hun-dred. All clear . . .
OKAYYY, this is HOP HARRRRIGANNN, COMINGGG INNN!

The serial followed Hop and his pal, mechanic Tank Tinker, on dangerous missions behind enemy lines. Tank (Kenny Lynch) was a bit slow in the brainpower department, but a good guy to have along in a fight. Even after the war, and a shift in 1946 into a final two-year Mutual run, there were more than enough saboteurs, hijackers, and all-American badguys on hand to keep *Hop Harrigan* at the forefront of juvenile adventures. But Hop was essentially a wartime hero. Then the world was full of madmen, and kids needed a superhero to tell them each night that everything was really okay. Hop did that, and Glenn Riggs did the rest. Riggs kept after the home front throughout the war, reminding people to save and turn in waste fats, and to bring paper, tin, and rubber to salvage depots. There were numerous re-minders that the Red Cross needed blood—"the blood given by your family and friends may be responsible for bringing back alive your brother, father, cousin, or neighbor. So keep on punching, gang. Don't even for one minute relax in your efforts to help speed victory . . ."

Because the series was sustained for so much of its six-year run (General Foods took it from 1944 to 1946), there was little else for Glenn Riggs to do but read public service announcements where commercials usually were. The announcements had an aviation slant, and became a memorable part of the show. Riggs told kids about the exploits of men and their flying ships in wartime adventures in Europe and the Pacific. He usually ended with the cry, "Re-member—America needs fliers!"

Riggs' voice blended into the clatter of Hop's engine, and we were off for another night:

CX-4 to control tower—CX-4 to control tower . . . standing by . . .
Control tower to CX-4 . . . all clear!
OKAYYYY, THIS IS HOP HARRRRRIGANNN, TAKING OFF!
SEE YA' TOMORROW, SAME TIME, SAME STATION!

Hopalong Cassidy

Hopalong Cassidy came to Mutual on January 1, 1950, after early-day TV screenings of the 1930's films had made the character a national sensation. The character was created by Clarence Mulford in a series of pulp Western stories. As seen by Mulford, Hopalong Cassidy was a belching, snorting, drinking, chewing relic of the Old West. In 1934, Harry Sherman got film rights to Mulford's stories; he hired William Boyd, a silent screen veteran whose star had declined, to play a badman role. But Boyd identified more with the hero and before the cameras began rolling, Sherman switched the parts. The casting of Boyd was to greatly affect Mulford's character. Hoppy became a knight of the range, a straight-shootin' man of morals who helped ladies across the street but never stooped to kissing the heroine. Under Boyd, Hoppy would never smoke, always believed in fair play, and forever refused to touch liquor.

It was a direct contrast with Boyd's own life. Born in Ohio in 1898, he gravitated toward pioneering Hollywood with disarming good looks and a dream of crashing into films. The dream came true the year after his arrival, when he was hired by Cecil B. DeMille and put to work in a succession of early epics. By the mid-1920's, William Boyd was a big-name star, enjoying all the fruits that went with it. Wine, women, and money were his. He drank, gambled, bought expensive playthings, owned estates, married five times. Boyd lived the lusty life in a house of glass, a fantasy world that shattered and crumbled with the coming of the Depression and talking pictures in 1929.

With his voice, talkies should have been his meat, but Boyd's career was ruined when another actor named William Boyd was arrested for possession of gambling equipment and whiskey. Newspapers ran mugshots of the Hollywood Boyd even as the Broadway Boyd was being booked and charged. Studios canceled his contracts, and it mattered little when the charges were later proved false. The Hollywood studios were convinced that his box office would suffer drastically. Boyd went into a tailspin, and it took Hopalong Cassidy—four years later—to ride out of the West and save him.

Boyd became Cassidy in a literal sense. His personal habits changed, and he lived with his fifth wife from their marriage in 1937 until his death on September 12, 1972. He gave up drinking and carousing and became staunchly devoted to the Cassidy image.

The Hoppy films were respectable B-Westerns. Boyd and Sherman made more than fifty of them through the 1930's and into the early 1940's. Then Sherman, feeling the pinch of rising costs, tried to recoup his losses by cutting back on quality. Boyd balked, and the men split. Boyd continued making Hoppy films on his own, turning out twelve of them between 1943 and 1946. And gradually, after his split with Sherman, Boyd began acquiring all rights to the Hopalong Cassidy character. With TV just around the corner, Boyd had a hunch that his old movies might be in demand. Boyd's acquisition of Hopalong Cassidy was complete in 1948. It cost more than $300,000, sent him in hock to his ears, and changed his standard of living from upper-class to middle-class. But he got the character sewed up just as TV broke upon the scene in 1949; *Hopalong Cassidy* became one of the true sensations of the early tube. The TV films led to a comic strip, then the radio show, which opened to "the ring of the silver spurs." *Hopalong Cassidy* was a distinctive cowboy detective show, for listeners seldom knew the identity of the evil ones until Hoppy tripped them up and brought them to justice. Hoppy was foreman of the Bar-20 Ranch, but spent far more time chasing owlhoots than punching cows.

Boyd had one of radio's perfect voices. His voice could do anything—comfort a bereaved widow one moment, scare the boots off her husband's killers the next. It was strong, virile, and straight to the point. And that Hoppy belly-laugh became famous. It was one of his trademarks, as indispensable as his all-black outfit and his horse Topper.

Hopalong's companion in adventure was grizzled old California Carlson ("the same California you've laughed at a million times"), played by Andy Clyde. First heard Sundays for General Mills, *Cassidy* moved to Saturday CBS in 1950–52. The show was produced and released to independent stations by Walter White Jr.'s Commodore Productions. Soon *Time* reported that the demand for Hoppy shirts and pants was so great that it had created a national shortage of black dye. His endorsement of any product meant spectacular sales instantly, and millions for Boyd. For a little while, the Hopalong Cassidy craze was *it*, as frantic as anything seen in America until Davy Crockett.

The Horace Heidt Show

The Horace Heidt Show's creator, a well-known orchestra leader of the 1930's and 1940's, had more gimmicks than a man needed to make out in radio. He could always be counted on to wrap a new show in a new format, and his name was usually found on some network between 1932 and 1953. Horace Heidt and his Musical Knights first came to radio in 1932, with a show called *Ship of Joy,* sponsored by Shell Oil. The same year they did *Answers by the Dancers,* one of the early dance-interview shows of the air. His *Anniversary Night with Horace Heidt* ran on NBC in 1935, giving married couples a chance at quizzing for prizes. From 1936 through 1938 Heidt was sponsored by Autolite; the first year Monday night on CBS, then Tuesday night on NBC Blue. One of his most popular shows was *Pot o' Gold* in 1938. Heidt's *Tums Treasure Chest* was heard on NBC Tuesday nights from 1940 through 1943. In 1944, Heidt was featured in a Monday night Blue Network show for Hires Root Beer, a program designed to "give a break to boys back from the war." Here, Heidt introduced two guests—recently discharged veterans—and discussed their war records on the air. He asked employers in areas of the veteran's interest to contact their local Blue Network affiliates with offers of work. A teletype was set up on stage to tick off the job offers as they came in.

Heidt's best-remembered show was his *Youth Opportunity Program.* First heard on NBC December 7, 1947, the show ran two seasons on NBC for Philip Morris, then was picked up in 1949, still for Philip Morris, by CBS. Initially a Sunday series, *Horace Heidt's Youth Opportunity Program* moved to Thursday nights for Lucky Strike in 1952. It ended there in 1953. *Opportunity* was really just another talent show, but Heidt captured nationwide interest by taking it on the road. His troupe went from town to town, auditioning local accordionists, piano players, and abusers of the harmonica. Each week, the best of the auditions would be invited to compete in Heidt's on-the-air talent contest; the winners were invited back for more competition until a national champion was crowned. Heidt's first national winner, accordionist Dick Contino, picked up a $5,000 check and rode a brief crest of popularity into his own show. By the end of its first year, Heidt's *Youth Opportunity Program* had edged into the Top 20.

The Hour of Charm

The Hour of Charm featured Phil Spitalny's all-girl orchestra; it came to CBS on January 3, 1935, for Linit Bath Oil on Thursdays.

The idea was a natural; in fact, Phil Spitalny himself would use that same phrase many times in the years to come. Like so many "natural" ideas, this one struck him in a flash, one evening at a concert in 1932. A brilliant girl violinst had just performed and triggered Spitalny's imagination. If an entire orchestra of similarly talented women could be formed, it would just be a natural for radio.

At that time, Russian-born Spitalny was leading an all-male orchestra, which he promptly dissolved to devote his time to the great search. His friends thought he was losing his mind; even his family questioned his judgment. Spitalny had come from a family deeply rooted in music. His childhood in Odessa, Russia had been filled with clarinet, piano, and violin lessons. When he was 15 years old, his mother came to the United States, bringing Phil and his brother Leopold with her. They settled in Cleveland, where both young Spitalnys continued their musical training and played in local bands. Now, after two years as director of a fifty-piece Boston symphony orchestra, after a successful world tour and growing fame as an up-and-coming bandleader in radio, theatres, and records, Spitalny had decided to chuck it and chase a dream.

He began his search for female talent in the large cities, auditioning girls first in New York, then in Chicago, Pittsburgh, Detroit, and Cleveland. But women were expected to pursue homemaking careers; few had the training needed by a top orchestra. In the early months, Spitalny found not one girl with the kind of ability he wanted. Finally at New York's Juilliard School of Music he met Evelyn Kaye Klein, who became his first violinist and concertmistress. They continued the search together, now screening and auditioning in smaller communities as well as big towns. The musicians were signed slowly—a harpist here, a clarinetist there. They listened to more than 1,000 trumpet players, saxophonists, and violinists. At the end of the year, Spitalny had spent more than $20,000 on the search. But he had his first twenty-two-piece all-girl orchestra.

After a three-month rehearsal, the band was booked into the Loew Theatre circuit. From the beginning, Spitalny encountered stiff resistance; people expected the group to be second-rate; prospective radio sponsors wouldn't even listen to auditions. So Spitalny began auditioning by remote, billing the group simply as Phil Spitalny and his Orchestra. *After* a sponsor had signed, Spitalny broke the news.

A female band was a novelty then; it became an instant success, picking up General Electric as longtime sponsor on the Blue Network by the fall of 1936. Its first announcer was Ken Roberts. Rosaline Greene, mistress of ceremonies touted Linit and gave background on the songs. Arlene Francis also served as femcee. Evelyn was billed as "Evelyn and Her Magic Violin." Her 18th century Bergonzi was one of the great instruments of the air. Evelyn, Vivien, and Maxine (the women used only first names on the air) became the three principals; as concertmistress, Evelyn was placed in charge of the orchestra's backstage relationships. Spitalny stepped aside and let the women govern themselves, making decisions only on up-front professional matters such as musical selection, manner of dress, and hairstyles. All members of the orchestra dressed alike, with the exception of the three principals; all were required to wear their hair in "long, soft bobs." Spitalny got into personal problems only when Evelyn couldn't iron them out herself. That was rare. Throughout his career, Spitalny maintained that women were easier to work with than men, and that thirty-five women were easier to handle than one He staunchly defended their abilities, and once offered to bet band-leader Abe Lyman $1,000 that his girls could out-perform Lyman's all-male band. Spitalny said his group had more professional pride, didn't have problems with drink, and when war broke, he was the only orchestra leader in America who didn't have to worry about the draft.

The Hour of Charm was heard Mondays in its 1935–36 season, Sundays in 1936–37, Mondays in 1937–38, and Sundays 1940–46, all on NBC.

The orchestra members owned stock in the orchestra; they formed their own backstage organization, which passed judgment on all offstage matters, personal and professional. A five-member commit-tee was formed to watch over rules, lifestyles, and even dating habits of the band members. "Associations in the all-girl orchestra are much like sorority life," wrote Evelyn in a 1942 Radio Life. "We room together, share our recreations, and even our sorrows. As for temper-ament, Mr. Spitalny won't tolerate it, so all of us are very even dispositioned.

"Whenever a girl wants to go out, she goes to the committee and says, 'I want a date with Mr. So-and-So.' They ask her who the man is, what he does, and for references. If he passes muster, she gets her date. But if the committee feels that it would hurt the orchestra for a member to be seen with the man, the engagement doesn't mate-rialize."

The orchestra specialized in familiar music, played in a style that Spitalny described as a cross between symphonic and popular. All of the girls sang in chorus, some in solo, and all played more than one instrument. Musical ability was Spitalny's first consideration in hiring, but he also strongly considered voice and good looks. Girls couldn't marry without giving six months' notice. It remained a Sunday show after moving to CBS in 1946, running there until 1948, when Spitalny disbanded the orchestra.

Spitalny himself was unmarried until June 1946, when he and Evelyn were wed. They moved to Miami, where Spitalny died in 1970.

The Hour of Mystery

The Hour of Mystery was a summer show, replacing Theatre Guild on the Air from June 9 to September 1, 1946, on ABC. It was sponsored by United States Steel and featured adaptations of well-known mystery stories by well-known Hollywood stars. The opener was "Journey Into Fear," with Laurence Olivier. Others included "Turn on the Heat," June 23, with Frank Sinatra; "The Burning Court," July 14, with John Beal; "Murder, My Sweet," July 28, with William Holden; and "Phantom Lady," August 18, with Franchot Tone. The final show was "The 39 Steps," with David Niven.

House of Glass

House of Glass was Gertrude Berg's attempt at a new serial after the initial cancellation of *The Goldbergs* in 1934. A Wednesday-night feature, it was first heard on NBC April 17, 1935, and ran for only a few months. It told the story of Barney Glass (Joseph Buloff) and his wife Bessie (Mrs. Berg), who ran a small hotel in the Catskills. The show was drawn from the childhood experiences of Mrs. Berg, whose parents had once run a Catskill hotel; it was sponsored by Palmolive.

The House of Mystery

The House of Mystery began as a sustained 15-minute serial on Mutual on January 15, 1945; on September 13, 1945, it changed to a 30-minute Saturday show for General Foods. The show was almost identical under serial and weekly versions. An old-fashioned story-telling session, it opened to creepy organ music and a welcome ("Thiss is the House . . . of Myssstery!") by Roger Elliott, the "mystery man." Elliott, played by John Griggs, was a ghost-chaser, a scientist of the supernatural whose experiences were supposed to prove that "ghosts and phantoms exist only in the imagination," but he took his listeners through some scary territory. He related his yarns to a circle of "ooooo-ing" and "aaaaah-ing" kids, who asked him questions later. The kids were led by Ruth and Johnny (who sounded a lot like the "Johnny" of Philip Morris fame). In the serial version, Elliott read his stories straight from books of great ghost lore, one chapter each day; in the 30-minute version he offered fully dramatized cases from his "own files," complete in each show. This was a fine program for kids, full of mysterious lights, creepy mansions, and stealthy footsteps. After a season on Saturdays, it moved to Sunday—still under General Foods sponsorship—where it ran until 1949.

House Party

House Party came to CBS on January 15, 1945, and became one of radio's longest-running daytime fixtures. Like Art Linkletter's other long-running show, *People Are Funny,* this program grew out of the fertile mind of producer John Guedel.

Linkletter and Guedel had come from diverse and interesting backgrounds. Guedel had a false start as a writer; he gave that up after collecting a ream of rejection slips. He had worked on some of the *Laurel and Hardy* and *Little Rascals* short comedies and gradually eased into radio. Linkletter, Canadian-born son of an Irish family named Kelley, had been adopted as an infant because his natural parents didn't want him. The adoptive parents, named Linkletter, were a poor, religious family. The father, Fulton, was a traveling evangelist, and the boy took their name and kept it through his professional life.

Linkletter broke into radio in 1933 with a staff announcing job at KGB, San Diego. For a time he worked with fairs, broadcasting exposition events for radio audiences; then he freelanced out of San Francisco. During those years of the late 1930's, he appeared in an estimated 9,000 broadcasts doing remotes, hosting jobs, and sportscasts. He became known as possessor of one of the quickest minds and tongues in the business. By the time he came to *People Are Funny* in 1943, Linkletter was as smooth a pro as radio had seen.

Legend has it that Guedel convinced a desperate radio executive—who had been looking fruitlessly for a new five-a-week daytime idea—that he and Linkletter had just the right formula for the sagging slot. He was given an appointment for the following morning and, still without any ideas of specific show formats, told Linkletter what he had done. The two men stayed up all night and worked up the show. In the morning they sold it, booked it, and *House Party* was off and running. First for General Electric, later for Pillsbury and Lever Brothers, *House Party* was heard on the same network for more than twenty years in a Monday-through-Friday 30-minute format.

It was a highly spontaneous show, heavily dependent on Art Linkletter's considerable skill with the ad-lib. *House Party* was much more relaxed than *People Are Funny,* but both shows depended heavily on listener and audience participation. *House Party* dabbled in a bit of everything, from cooking and beauty hints to searches for missing heirs (over the years the show found more than $1 million worth of missing heirs). One of Linkletter's favorite contests was "What's In The House?" a guessing game with progressive clues for grand prizes. In the early years under General Electric, the prizes were household appliances—roasters, toasters, irons, and occasionally refrigerators. Brides and grandmothers were Linkletter's favorite targets.

But far and away the real stars of *House Party* were children, the five or six Los Angeles grammar school kids brought each day by special limousine to the CBS studios. During his twenty-three years with *House Party* on radio, Linkletter interviewed some 23,000 children, each hand-picked by school principals and teachers for intelligence and outgoing personality. Linkletter had many stock questions for the kids—questions about their parents' personal lives that were proven laugh-getters. The simple question, "What does your Mommy do?" drew such answers as "She doesn't do anything," or "Nothing—she's too busy having babies," or "She does a little housework, then she sits around all day reading the racing form." In one moment of priceless pathos, a little boy answered Linkletter's "if you had one wish" question by wishing for his "daddy back from heaven."

Guedel and his father Walter thought up ideas for *House Party*, but Linkletter never rehearsed or used scripts. Still, he was never at a loss for words; sometimes horribly corny puns brought good-natured groans from his audience. But the housewives (comprising three-quarters of his listeners) kept coming back. The cheery "Come on in, it's Art Linkletter's *House Party*" of announcer Jack Slattery became an afternoon standby. The program was last heard on October 13, 1967. Even when dropped from radio, *House Party* continued its strong showing on television.

Husbands and Wives

Husbands and Wives, a spirited program of marital combat, grew out of a light daytime home economics show done on WOR in 1935 by Allie Lowe Miles. Her friend Sedley Brown observed the show one day and decided that if the tempo could be perked up a bit the personal marital chatter of the guests might be interesting for nighttime radio. Thus in the middle of the 1935–36 season, *Husbands and Wives* came to Mutual. By midyear it had moved to the Blue for Pond's Cream. The format featured both Brown and Mrs. Miles. Each week, half a dozen husbands and half a dozen wives—each with a personal beef about marriage—were ushered before the microphones. Brown coached the men, Mrs. Miles the women. Then the tales of woe flowed forth. It was described by *Radio Mirror* as a "three-ring circus of domestic scraps." By 1938, it had disappeared.

I Am an American

I Am an American featured interviews with naturalized citizens who extolled the virtues of their new land and told why they had become Americans. It was a Sunday noontime feature on the Blue Network, running for two seasons, 1940–42. Most of the subjects had attained some degree of fame. Such actors as Elissa Landi, Vera Zorina, and Alla Nazimova were featured.

I Fly Anything

I Fly Anything, an adventure series with Dick Haymes as a free-wheeling cargo pilot named Dockery Crane, came to ABC November 29, 1950, and ran for one season. Crane, so the story went, would "fly anything," anywhere, for a price and a promise of advanture. Supporting cast included a sidekick, Buzz, played by George Fenneman, and a girl named June (Georgia Ellis) to watch the store. It was directed by Dwight Hauser, with music by Basil Adlam, and written by Arnold Perl and Abe Ginniss. *Anything* was predictably corny—a mixture of *Hop Harrigan* and *Boston Blackie,* with some *Fibber McGee* sprinkled through the opening: "I got a tradewind tan, a tall tale about a tribal treasure, a tropical tramp and a torrid Tahitian tomato. You know me—I fly anything!"

I Love a Mystery

I Love a Mystery was first heard on NBC's Pacific Coast outlets January 16, 1939. Lovers of wild adventure in a fast-moving serial found their ultimate radio show here. Carlton E. Morse wrote it. Listeners loved it. Today many people who collect recordings of old radio shows consider it the greatest adventure series ever done.

Jack, Doc, and Reggie were the continuing heroes who led such dangerous lives, from the ghost towns of wind-swept Nevada to the jungles of vampire-infested Nicaragua. Jack Packard, the team leader, was a deadpan hero who exuded quiet strength and courage. Jack, a former medical student, shrugged off superstition and unnatural manifestations. Even while up to his ears in werewolves, he believed that everything had its logical answer, and set out in a straight line to prove that to his comrades' satisfaction. He was the master detective strategist, who always kept his cool in emergencies, no matter what the odds. And—after the hint of a disastrous long-ago romantic fling—he never gave the ladies as much as a tumble.

Doc Long was a likable Texan, a red-headed picker of locks who loved women and constantly craved a fight. Doc was a poker player par excellence, whose long Panhandle drawl, "Honest to my grand-maw," was an effective mask for sharp instincts and keen senses. And Reggie Yorke was the Britisher, prim and proper, but really heavy in any kind of rough and tumble.

The three heroes were easily identifiable to average America. They got down where the going was tough and slugged their way through it. No Lone Ranger tactics for Jack, Doc, and Reggie: they respected the law, but had been known to hide evidence and would seldom be arrested without a fight. Morse gave them failings as well as strengths, and the failings made them human as the strengths made them heroes.

Together they traveled the world, often on official business for their A-1 Detective Agency, just as often as a lark, as three guys looking for excitement. But excitement had a way of finding them even before they formed their loose partnership. They met during the China-Japanese war, when all three were fighting for China. After the war, they formed the detective agency in downtown Hollywood. But usually their cases took them far out of town, to distant and barren lands where native superstition ran rampant.

The opening theme—a frantic train whistle and a haunting organ recital of "Valse Triste"—suggested death. The chime of a clock brought us again to the hour where we last left our three heroes.

Death ran wild through the show. People were murdered in ghoul-
ish, imaginative, and apparently mystifying ways—knifings, shootings, hangings, and slashings. Some characters had their throats torn
out, presumably by werewolves. The embellishments made *I Love a
Mystery* a radio classic. In "The Thing that Cries in the Night," Morse
gave us slashings galore, always coming when a baby cried, in a house
that hadn't sheltered a baby for two decades. His "Temple of Vam-
pires" broadcast was so vivid that the Nicaraguan government lodged
a protest. In another creepy mansion, murders occurred as a strange
organ rendition of Brahms' "Lullaby" echoed through the halls. Like
the baby, neither the organ nor the organist could be found anywhere.

In its original form, *I Love a Mystery* ran five seasons and was
produced in Hollywood. Nine months after the Pacific Coast opening,
the show premièred on a nationwide NBC hookup, broadcasting five
times a week for Fleischmann's Yeast. During its 15-minute days,
Morse batted out one ILAM script a day, working three weeks ahead
in his cubbyhole office near Hollywood's Radio City. Seven days a
week, Morse rose early and hurried to his office, turning out the script
during the five weekdays and writing the 30-minute *One Man's
Family* installments on weekends. He worked with a globe at his right
hand, never knowing where he might send the three soldiers of
fortune next. And, unlike most mystery writers who worked out the
solution in advance, Morse winged it—often he had no idea who the
killer was until near the end, but he plotted carefully and left enough
motivations for everybody.

His pattern of wrapping up each story in about three weeks was
very successful, and it is surprising that more radio writers didn't use
it. Most of radio's serials went on ad infinitum, but Morse usually
concluded his ILAM stories in about fifteen or twenty chapters. Then
it was off to another part of the world, with contrasting atmosphere. It
all took only a few hours a day; by 9:30, Morse was usually finished.
He spent the rest of the day getting production details worked out,
and in the afternoon he and assistant producer Buddy Twiss supervised rehearsal and the East Coast broadcast.

Morse brought in most of the cast from his successful drama, *One
Man's Family*, also sponsored by Fleischmann and a weekly NBC
feature since 1932. Michael Raffetto and Barton Yarborough (Paul and
Cliff on *One Man's Family*) played Jack and Doc. Walter Paterson
(Claudia's *Family* husband Nicky) played Reggie. In 1940, the show
was moved to NBC's Blue Network, still for Fleischmann's, but now a
30-minute Monday-night continuation.

When it underwent this major format change and with the death
of Walter Paterson, Reggie was dropped for a time and a larger role
was written for Jerry Booker, the agency's curvy secretary. Jerry was

played by Gloria Blondell, who looked so much like her famous sister that she was constantly fighting billing as "Joan Blondell's sister." Jerry accompanied Jack and Doc on such adventures as "The Pirate Loot of the Island of Skulls," a superb show of the "temple of jaguars," of darkness and secret tunnels and the high priest Holy Joe. In a shattering climax, Doc Long and Holy Joe met on a rope bridge 150 feet above the temple floor and fought to the death.

I Love a Mystery ran in that 30-minute format until 1942, when wartime restrictions of Fleischmann's products forced it off the air. After only a few months of silence, the serial was revived, turning up March 22, 1943, in the old daily 15-minute form on CBS for Procter & Gamble. That version ended in 1944.

In 1943, near the end of the Hollywood run, Raffetto and Yarborough left the series for a fling at producing, and the part of Jack was played briefly by Jay Novello. Then I Love a Mystery left the air for five years. A new version was produced out of New York, beginning in the fall of 1949, in daily format on Mutual; it used the original scripts. Russell Thorson played Jack, Jim Boles was Doc, and Tony Randall played Reggie Yorke. Mercedes McCambridge, who had made appearances on ILAM as early as 1943, played many female roles on the new version as well. Though many connoisseurs considered the New York series a cheap imitation of the original run, the shows ran true to Morse's early scripts and still made compelling listening. Ironically, this version had the steadiest run without changes, lasting more than two years as a daily 15-minute serial. I Love a Mystery left the air in 1952, leaving a legion of fans and an almost legendary reputation.

Sparked by rediscovery of entire, excellent-sounding ILAM stories, a small but fanatical cult has grown around the show, sweeping in new listeners who never experienced it on the air. Now the flick of a tape recorder switch brings them such Jack, Doc, and Reggie classics as "The Thing that Cries in the Night," or "Bury Your Dead, Arizona." Old-timers hope wistfully that, somewhere, someone will turn up the greatest of all ILAM stories, "The Stairway to the Sun."

I Love Adventure

I Love Adventure was a 1948 summer series that continued the adventures of Jack, Doc, and Reggie of I Love a Mystery. Author-director Carlton E. Morse brought his superheroes to ABC in a 30-minute weekly show that ran from April 25 through July 18, 1948. The New York run of I Love a Mystery was still more than a year away, and this series—produced in Hollywood—brought back the originals: Michael Raffetto as Jack Packard and Barton Yarborough as Doc Long.

Walter Paterson had died, so Tom Collins, the *Chandu* of the West Coast, was tapped as Reggie Yorke.

Morse never was at his best working within the limitations of the 30-minute, complete-in-each-episode format, and *I Love Adventure* just wasn't the same blood-curdling fare that ILAM fans had come to expect. But it did contain some interesting background. In the first episode, listeners were reintroduced to Jack Packard, learning that the three comrades had split up during the war, having disbanded the A-1 Detective Agency and taken up arms for the cause. Jack went into American intelligence; Doc became a fighter pilot after a stint with the Flying Tigers in China, and Reggie joined the Royal Air Force. The three lost touch, until a strange message from the "Twenty-One Old Men of Grammercy Park" brought them together again. The "Old Men" had formed a London-based organization dedicated to fighting the international enemies of peace. Jack and Reggie became field men for the group; they worked alone for eight weeks, then Reggie was dropped abruptly and Doc was thrust without explanation into the show. The music, "Valse Triste," was the same as the theme for *I Love a Mystery*. It was played on the organ by Rex Koury. Announcer was Dresser Dahlstead.

I Love Lucy

I Love Lucy isn't remembered primarily as a radio show, but it did come briefly to CBS around 1952, sponsored by Philip Morris Cigarettes and starring all the principals of the TV show: Lucille Ball and Desi Arnaz as Lucy and Ricky Ricardo, Vivian Vance as Ethel Mertz, and William Frawley as her husband Fred. As in the TV series, Ricky was a struggling bandleader, Lucy his wacky wife. They lived in the upstairs apartment of a tenement owned by Fred and Ethel. Ricky was a hot-blooded Cuban whose broken English was frequently laced with Spanish diatribe. Lucy was given to wild schemes and outbursts of mournful bawling when they went awry. It was an exact copy of the TV show, with the Mertzes fighting with each other, the Ricardos fighting with each other, and the Ricardos fighting with the Mertzes.

I Was a Communist for the FBI

I Was a Communist for the FBI, a syndicated 1952 series growing out of the red scare of the late 1940's and early 1950's, starred Dana Andrews as undercover agent, Matt Cvetic, who infiltrated the top levels of the Communist Party and reported back to the FBI. Cvetic, a real-life double agent, had written his story in books and national magazine articles of the mid-1940's, and Dana Andrews gave a convincing performance in the audio version. The stories were packed with tension, producing plots within plots as Cvetic's relationships within the party changed. The Commies were stereotyped, much as Hitler's Nazis had been a few years before. They were all cold, humorless people whose every waking thought was to enslave the world. That man behind the newspaper—was he a party spy? How about the little old lady walking the dog? Cvetic could never be sure. Party spies were everywhere, and he by his membership was an outcast from his family and all that mattered in his "real" life. The show was good radio entertainment, drumming in its anti-Red propaganda right down to Cvetic's inevitable parting shot: "I was a Communist for the FBI—I walk alone!"

I Was There

I Was There, a dramatic first-person account of true human adventures, was first heard around 1935, and could still be heard on CBS West in 1943. It dramatized three separate incidents in each half-hour broadcast, bringing to its listeners such varied fare as Rene Belbenoit's escape from Devil's Island and the story of the lone survivor of Custer's last stand. Early in the run, the incidents were researched and written by Tommy Tomlinson. Later LaVerne Burton, Ernest Martin, and John Dunkel shared those duties. Many of the shows between 1942 and 1944 revolved around wartime adventures. Narrator then was Chet Huntley. Music was by Lud Gluskin, and the producer was Robert Hafter.

Indictment

Indictment, another respectable late entry in the annals of radio, emerged on CBS January 29, 1956, and ran for three years. It featured murder investigations by the New York assistant district attorney, following cases from inception through tedious checking to an indictment against the accused. Indictment was based on the cases of Eleazar Lipsky, former assistant DA, whose fictional counterpart Edward McCormick fought crime with sidekick Tom Russo. The show was written by Allan Sloane, and directed by Paul Roberts.

Information Please

Information Please, the great quiz of the intellectual, was first heard on the Blue Network May 17, 1938, as a Tuesday-night sustaining show. The idea behind *Information Please*, though unique when the audition record was delivered to NBC in April 1938, was almost incidental to the show's long-running success. What really made this program fly was the mix of personalities who fit the idea so perfectly.

The idea was created by Dan Golenpaul, a promoter who had been around radio for several years when a reversal of the standard quiz format struck him as a viable idea. In most quizzes, contestants were lured from the studio or listening audiences, put on the spot, questioned, and rewarded for correct answers. What about assembling a panel of "experts," letting the audience ask the questions and rewarding the questioners when the "experts" failed?

Golenpaul got little encouragement from radio people, who generally thought such a show would be too highbrow for the masses. He pushed ahead with the idea anyway, and began looking for the people to make it go. As the first member of his panel, Golenpaul got Franklin Pierce Adams, writer and columnist for the *New York Post, Herald Tribune*, and other newspapers. Then Clifton Fadiman was persuaded to come aboard as moderator. Fadiman, longtime editor and critic, had once done a series of radio book reviews, and was book editor of *The New Yorker*.

Somewhat reluctantly, NBC bought the series for $400 a week, and *Information Please* was booked into the spring 1938 schedule. Appearing with Adams were five guest panelists, who split the $400 with Fadiman and Golenpaul. The grand sum of $2 was paid for each question used, and $5 was paid to those who "stumped the experts." It was a lean opening, but *Information Please* began to draw mail almost immediately. Within a few weeks, John Kieran was added to the regular panel, and the show was off and running. By October it had a sponsor, Canada Dry. The fortunes of *Information Please* grew with its fame. By the time the show was six months old, the $400 a week had grown to $2,500, and Golenpaul and company were splitting decent paychecks.

Kieran, sports columnist for the *New York Times*, became Mr. Know-It-All, the hardest panelist of all to stump. His contribution to *Information Please* was inestimable. His wide range of knowledge extended from sports (his specialty) to Shakespeare. By the fall of 1938, a third regular panelist was added in the person of Oscar

Levant. Remaining chairs were filled by notables from every walk of life, each of whom had an area of expertise to be tested by alert listeners.

On the surface, the show was highbrow, but its earthy humor and the trickiness of the questions appealed to the masses as well. The 1938 question, "What sextet recently sang its way to fame?" takes on added difficulty when you remember that Dopey of the Seven Dwarfs was mute. About a dozen questions were used in each show, leaving the panelists time for some impromptu ad-libbing. Often the ad-libs were horrible puns. When John Gunther answered a question about the Shah of Iran, Fadiman asked, "Are you shah?" And Gunther answered, "Sultanly."

Prizes to listeners grew proportionately. The *Encyclopaedia Britannica* was added as a prize in October 1939. In 1940, the program moved to Friday nights for Lucky Strike.

Adams was the expert-in-residence in matters literary: Levant (who was dropped from the show in 1943 after a clash with Golenpaul) was the specialist in music. With their guests, the experts knocked down about 75 percent of all questions submitted to them, but their blunders could be devastating. Authors were quizzed about their own works, and often missed the answers. Louis Bromfield missed questions concerning two of his creations; Elliott Roosevelt bombed on quotations that had appeared in his mother's column the week before; Rex Stout missed a recipe he had created for his fat detective, Nero Wolfe, in the novel *Too Many Cooks*. And Kieran's fans were delighted when "Mr. Know-It-All" knew almost all the answers except the date of his wife's birthday.

Golenpaul had little difficulty selling *Information Please* during the show's heyday. Some 30,000 questions flooded in each week, creating jobs for twelve full-time readers. The questions were sorted, filed, and passed on to an "editorial board" (Golenpaul, his wife Ann, and others). They were filed by subject, so that any guest with offbeat areas of expertise would have a ready-made file awaiting him. Such personalities as Gracie Allen, John Gunther, Fred Allen, Deems Taylor, Lillian Gish, Boris Karloff, Christopher Morley, Bernard Jaffe, Cornelia Otis Skinner, Alfred Hitchcock, Mayor Fiorello La Guardia, Moss Hart, Beatrice Lillie, and Wendell Willkie appeared on the show. Harpo Marx whistled and mimicked his way through a disastrous session. Orson Wells answered every question and then corrected Fadiman three times in his first appearance. Milton Cross and later Ben Grauer were announcers.

Through it all, Golenpaul remained aloof and difficult to deal with. He insisted on complete control over every aspect of the show, eventually even the commercials. When Luckies began chanting its

Jane Ace played an endearing scatterbrain beside her husband, Goodman Ace on *The Easy Aces.* This 1933 shot shows her selecting a Laughing Buddha as a bridge partner at Chicago's Century of Progress Exposition

Jane and Goodman Ace in 1939, posed among some of the original scripts—equivalent to a five-foot shelf—Goodman had written for their show since 1930

(NBC Photo)

Allen teamed with his wife, Portland Hoffa, for his long-running and well-remembered show
(International News Photo)

Left: Fred Allen got his start as a vaude-ville ventriloquist before breaking into radio (Orpheum Studio)

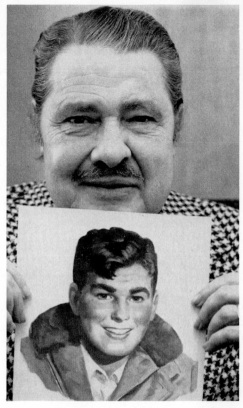

A 1975 photo of Jim Ameche, with an artist's conception of Jack Armstrong, the All-American Boy, played by Ameche from 1933 to 1939 (Wide World Photo)

Amos and Andy were created by Freeman Gosden and Charles Correll. Since both were white, they had to don blackface make-up for *Check and Double Check,* the 1930 Amos and Andy movie released by Radio Pictures (Radio Pictures Photo)

Gosden and Correll before the WMAQ Chicago microphone in their 1928 debut as "Sam and Henry." A year later, they changed their characters' names to Amos and Andy, moved to NBC, and became a national sensation (WABC Photo)

Eve Arden was CBS's schoolmarm of the air in *Our Miss Brooks,* the role that catapulted her out of B-picture obscurity
(CBS Photo)

Gosden and Correll polishing a script in their Beverly Hills office, 1948. Correll had typed the final dialect scripts for over 10 years—so long that he claimed he could no longer spell properly
(Wide World Photo)

Lionel Barrymore played a number of guest roles on various shows, but was renowned for his portrayal of Ebenezer Scrooge in the annual broadcasts of Dickens' "A Christmas Carol"

Major Edward E. Bowes of the long-running *Major Bowes' Amateur Hour,* shown in 1936 with Robert Lipson, a CBS page who made an appearance on the show
(CBS Photo)

William Boyd, whose life became thoroughly intermingled with his movie, radio, and TV role, Hopalong Cassidy, talking with Cecil B. DeMille in 1952

Fanny Brice, whose *Baby Snooks* made
her a radio personality long after her
vaudeville career with Florenz Ziegfeld

In 1964, NBC rebroadcast the highlights o[f] *The Chase & Sanborn Hour* hosted in th[e] 30's and 40's by Edgar Bergen, with hel[p] from Charlie McCarthy. Other guest regu[lars] included (clockwise from top:) Rud[y] Vallee, Eddie Cantor, Don Ameche, W. C[.] Fields, and Dorothy Lamour (NBC Phot[o]

Ray Collins, who won attention as Jim
Gettys in *Citizen Kane*, was a regular
member of Orson Welles' Mercury Theatre
(RKO Radio Pictures)

The Happiness Boys, radio veterans Billy
Jones and Ernie Hare, in formal dress in
1936 (WABC Photo)

Bing Crosby, as he appeared before a microphone in the Paramount Picture *The Big Broadcast of 1932,* in which he was teamed with Stuart Erwin, Leila Hyams, and fourteen other radio stars of the day
(Paramount Pictures)

Cecil B. DeMille, in 1936 in his capacity as host of *The Lux Radio Theatre*
(CBS Photo)

The Fat Man was played by J. Scott Smart the weighty counterpart to the equally successful *Thin Man* detective show

Fibber McGee and Molly were really Jim
and Marian Jordan, who began in vaudeville and played the roles until the show's
demise in the mid 50's

Jean Hersholt, who played *Dr. Christian.* The award Hersholt is holding carried a $2,000 prize for the best script submitted by the listening audience between February 1 and May 1, 1942

hil Harris, who got his start with Jack enny and moved to his own program ith wife Alice Faye

d Gardner was the casual bartender of *uffy's Tavern*

Information Please featuring Clifton Fadiman as moderator, shown here with panelists John Kieran and Franklin P. Adams

Al Jolson in 1948, after a long and successful career in different-format shows for various networks and sponsors
(Herb Ball: NBC Photo)

The 1952 TV version of *Juvenile Jury*, with host Jack Barry and *Jury* members Ronn Molluzzo, Mai-Lan Rogoff, Laura Mangel Charles Hankinson, and Dickie Orlan (NBC-TV Phot

Following page:
The Lone Ranger, was played by Brace
Beemer in the 1940's and 1950's. Later he
raised horses at his home in Michigan and
had been making auto commercials prior
to his death in 1965 (Wide World Photo)

famous "Lucky Strike green has gone to war" in 1942, Golenpaul objected. His claim that the commercial was tasteless brought him under the gun of George Washington Hill, president of American Tobacco. A row ensued and Golenpaul told Hill, in effect, to peddle his smokes on another show. Luckies released Golenpaul from his contract as of February 5, 1943, and a new sponsor—Heinz Foods —was waiting in the wings. By 1943 the show had moved to Monday nights, and listeners who "stumped the experts" could win $57 in war bonds and stamps, in addition to Britannica's twenty-four-volume encyclopaedia and twelve-volume junior set.

In 1945, sponsorship shifted to Mobil Gas, which paid $11,000 a week for the show; in 1946 Parker Pens took over. The 1946 change also marked the first change of network, to CBS on Wednesday nights. It was all unrehearsed, and made an interesting half-hour. Information Please drew some 12 million listeners a week to the sound of the rooster and the tantalizing invitation to "Wake up, America! It's time to stump the experts!" Information Please finished its run in 1947–48 as a Friday-night sustained show on Mutual.

Inner Sanctum Mysteries

Inner Sanctum Mysteries, the famous horror show of the creaking door, was first heard on the Blue Network January 7, 1941, for Carter's Pills. Himan Brown, young producer-director of network radio, got the idea for the greatest opening of the air in one quick flash. In a broadcasting studio where he was working, the door to the basement groaned and squeaked whenever anyone opened it. Turning to an assistant, Brown said, "I'm gonna make that door a star." It was a classic moment, for today—some three and a half decades later—the campy horror of the creaking door may well rank as the single best-remembered sound in radio history, even though the shows are stilted and sometimes badly dated.

Fear hit the senses first, to the sound of organ music, rumbling and deep—so deep that the organ seemed to be under water. Three bars, no more—then, Raymond, our host, turned the doorknob. The door swung open soooo slowly, the creaking broken and uneven on rusted hinges. "Good evening, friends. This is your host, inviting you through the gory portals of the squeaking door. . . ." Then maybe a typically gruesome little joke about losing your heaaaad, or hanging around after the show to beat the high cost of dying. "Heh-heh-heh-hahahahahahaa! And now, if your scalpels are sharpened and ready, we'll proceed with the business of the evening." The humor was a morbid brand that was funny only in a crowd. In a dark room, alone on those wartime nights, with the breeze gently riffling the drapes like the fingers of a wandering spirit, *Inner Sanctum Mysteries* was anything but funny.

The stories were wildly improbable, usually turning on the maddest happenstances. Only on *Inner Sanctum* would a man be haunted for forty years by the wailing of his dead wife, then learn that the wailing actually came from the wind rushing through the hole in the wall where he had sealed her body. Only on *Inner Sanctum* would a man be sentenced to life imprisonment after stealing a scientific formula that has made him immortal.

Tested literary devices were used shamelessly to fool listeners. Most frequent was the trick of telling the story from the viewpoint of the killer. Sometimes the writers let us know he was the killer. Just as often they didn't, when the murderer-narrator hid his true personality behind a cloak of madness and deceit. The writers gleefully pounced on this opportunity for ghostly manifestation. The killer saw things that weren't there. A sudden pang of conscience might conjure up the ghost of an old victim. Circumstances almost meaningless in themselves took on terrifying significance when the beholder was insane.

The stories plodded on toward the inevitable scream of climax. Then Raymond was back, drooling over the cadavers. "Everybody dead but the cat, and we only overlooked him because we couldn't find him . . . Heh-heh-heh . . . Hahahahahahahahahahahahahahahahahaaaaaaaaa . . . And now it's time to close that squeaking door . . . Good niii-iiight . . . Pleasant dreeeaaaammmss . . ." The agonized squeak reversed itself, and the door slammed shut for another week.

After eleven shows in its Tuesday-night format, *Inner Sanctum* moved to Sundays and ran in that time slot until 1942. It moved to CBS on September 4, 1943 and became a mainstay there, first on Saturday nights for Colgate (1943–44), then on Tuesday nights (1944–45), later on Tuesday nights for Lipton Tea and Soup (1945–46), on Monday nights for Bromo Seltzer (1946–50), then moving to ABC Mondays for Mars Candy (1950–51). A final summer series was heard in 1952.

Himan Brown directed the show throughout the run. Raymond was Raymond Edward Johnson, a former jack of all trades who had broken into radio with NBC of Chicago. Great horror men of the screen appeared on *Inner Sanctum Mysteries*, especially in the first year, when Boris Karloff was almost a regular. Among the other notables were Paul Lukas, Peter Lorre, Claude Rains, and Raymond Massey.

The macabre Raymond stayed with the show until the summer of 1945. After a brief transition, the host's role was assumed by Paul McGrath, whose jokes were funnier. But his voice didn't carry quite the edge of menace that Raymond's had.

Announcer early in the run was Ed Herlihy. During the Lipton run, the announcing was carried by the host, who engaged a hostess named Mary in some ghoulishly clever conversation about Lipton Tea and Soup. Later announcers included Dwight Weist and, for Mars Candy, Allen C. Anthony of *Dr. I.Q.* fame.

The final full season was sponsored by Mars Candy, but the show was sustained when it left the air on October 5, 1952, after a summer run on CBS.

Invitation to Learning

Invitation to Learning was a long-running CBS educational show, first heard May 26, 1940, and still going strong fifteen years later. It was a weekly round-table discussion of great books, based on a class at St. John's College, Annapolis, Maryland. The class was developed for radio at the suggestion of college president Stringfellow Barr, who also served on the CBS Adult Education Board. The books ranged in scope from *Moby-Dick* to *Oedipus Rex*, and the participants included Lyman Bryson, Huntington Cairns, and Allen Tate. The first show was a free-wheeling discussion of the United States Constitution.

Irene Rich Dramas

Irene Rich Dramas brought the screen star to radio after a career in movies had begun to wane. She had abandoned a real estate business in 1918, trying her hand in the world of the cinema, and had become one of the bright stars of the silent screen. She played opposite Will Rogers, Wallace Beery, Dustin Farnum, all the top names of her time. With the coming of the talkies her film career dropped off so she turned to—of all things—radio. Her *Irene Rich Dramas* went on NBC Blue for Welch's Grape Juice in 1933. Welch proved to be one of the most loyal of sponsors, carrying the show for more than a decade. In rather an unusual format, it was heard once a week, 15 minutes per episode, with Gale Gordon playing Miss Rich's leading man for some nine years. The serial moved to CBS in the early 1940's, and expired in 1944. Two of the most popular offerings were *Dear John* and *Glorious One*. In *Glorious One*, a 1939 continuation written by Pauline Hopkins, Miss Rich played Judith Bradley, who had been confined to a sanatorium for five years. Now completely cured, she has returned home to find that an old friend has tried to steal her husband Jake (John Lake) and has captured the affections of her eight-year-old son,

Don (Larry Nunn), and 16-year-old daughter, Susan (Florence Baker). The story then was one of a woman's struggle to reestablish herself in her own home.

It Happened in 1955

It Happened in 1955 was an imaginative 15-minute show from Mutual, broadcast in 1945 by member firms of the New York Stock Exchange and the U.S. Treasury Department. It told of life in the future, in brief dramatized stories illustrating man's marvelous achievements-to-come. The series' "guide to the future" was Del Sharbutt. Typical was the show of May 8, 1945: a man seeking a better job must know French fluently to be considered. He has four weeks to learn. Impossible, you say? Not in 1955, the marvelous world of the future.

It Pays to Be Ignorant

It Pays to Be Ignorant, radio's lame-brained answer to the intellectual quiz, was first heard on WOR-Mutual June 25, 1942. In the field of caveman humor, this program was a classic feast of the absurd. Was it a quiz show? Questions were asked, all right, but they were never answered. In fact, the three nitwits who made up the panel spent an amazing amount of time just trying to figure out what the questions were. They were real toughies, like: What beverage do we get from tea leaves? From what kind of mines do we get gold ore? Who came first, Henry VIII or Henry I? *It Pays to Be Ignorant*, then, was radio satire, pure and simple, of such intellectual quizzes as *Information Please* and *The Quiz Kids*, where genius "experts" gave Mr. and Mrs. America a national inferiority complex.

The show was created by Bob Howell, who in 1941 was on the staff of WELI, New Haven, Connecticut. Howell had long thought that a show punching holes in the superiority complexes of the *Information Please* and *Quiz Kid* experts would be a smash. But until he met Ruth Howard, he hadn't done much with the idea.

Miss Howard, who wanted to work in radio, had come to WELI to propose another idea. Howell liked both the idea and the lady. When they were married, Ruth got out Bob's *Ignorant* script and showed it to her father, Tom Howard, an old-time vaudevillian whose career went back to Philadelphia's Dreamland Theatre just after the turn of the century. Ruth thought her father would be perfect as the addled host of the show, and who was Tom Howard to argue with that?

They called it *Crazy Quiz*, and submitted it to a promoter. She sold it, billing Howard as star. As Ruth later told *Radio Life*, Howard got a son-in-law and Howell got a profitable wedding gift at the same time.

The first and most important job in putting on such a show was to assemble just the right blend of maniacs for the panel. The first member was easy. George Shelton was a hoofer whose career in vaudeville had been as long as Howard's. And, because they had teamed as Howard and Shelton on the vaudeville planks for years, the two men knew each other well. Next came Harry McNaughton, a Britisher who had gained his greatest fame playing Phil Baker's butler 'Bottle' on Baker's show. McNaughton had appeared in more than thirty Broadway revues.

Finally, there was Lulu McConnell, the dame of the sawblade voice. She too had spent a lifetime in show business, starring in musicals as an adolescent. George Shelton, Harry McNaughton, and Lulu McConnell made even Mike Clancy of *Mr. Keen* and Gil Whitney of *The Romance of Helen Trent* look smart!

For the three panelists, the format changed little over the seven-year run. Howard, whose sandpaper voice almost rivaled Miss McConnell's, opened with a caustic introduction. He introduced McNaughton as "the celebrated author" of a new book each week—a book like *The High Price of Meat*," or *Goodbye, Mr. Chops*. Inevitably, when his name was called, McNaughton said, "I have a poem, Mr. Howard." The poem, following the insane theme, usually went along these lines:

I eat my peas with honey,
I've done it all my life;
It makes the peas taste funny,
But it keeps them on my knife.

Howard described Miss McConnell for the radio audience in hideous terms. She was "the woman whose face looks as if she had been on a sightseeing tour through a meat grinder." Insults between Lulu and Howard were thick and heavy, especially when a male guest from the audience drew a question from the "dunce cap," and Lulu made one of her inevitable, "Hey, honey, are you married?" remarks.

Finally, Howard got to "the man whose father was an electrician and he was his first shock," George Shelton. Then came the questions, and radio would never be the same. Who was buried in Grant's tomb? Of what material is a silk dress made? What do the letters "U.S." stand for on United States mail boxes?

The three made a shambles of the show, interrupting each other with irrelevancies, insults, jokes, and plays on words. By the time they finished with a question, they had gone off on a dozen tangents and come full-circle back to the subject—only by then nobody remembered what the subject was. As Howard would say, "If you're waiting for the program to improve, you don't know us."

It ran as a Monday-night sustaining show until 1944, when it was picked up by CBS for Philip Morris, becoming a real family affair for the Howards. Ruth and Bob wrote it, each retiring to separate rooms with handfuls of questions submitted by listeners. Each turned out a full script, and the two versions were blended by Tom Howard into one show. Howard's son, Tom Jr., arranged the music for the Mutual run. Later, in its CBS salad days, It Pays to Be Ignorant was given a full orchestra and vocalist. After four years on Friday-night CBS, the show was last heard (1948–49) on Sundays.

It's a Crime, Mr. Collins

It's a Crime, Mr. Collins was a syndicated series, finally turning up on the Mutual network for one season in 1956. It followed the adventures of Greg Collins, "infamous private eye" of San Francisco, through the eyes of his beautiful wife. Yes, Gail Collins told the stories, barely concealing her jealous nature whenever Greg got involved with curvy clients. Naturally, that was all the time.

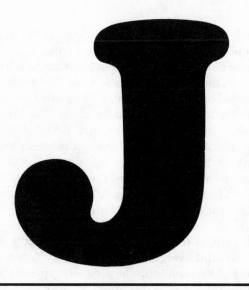

Jack Armstrong, the All-American Boy

Jack Armstrong, the All-American Boy, one of the greatest, longest-running juvenile adventures of all radio, was first heard on CBS from StationWBBM, Chicago, on July 31, 1933. Created by former journalist Robert Hardy Andrews, Jack Armstrong was cast in the Frank Merriwell mold—a super-athlete whose last-of-the-ninth efforts saved games for Hudson High School and glorified team athletics. The series began at Hudson High, where Jack was the prime color-bearer and his cousins were also enrolled as students. Jack's athletic powess gave rise to the famed school song, which became the series theme and is still fondly remembered:

> Wave the flag for Hudson High, boys,
> Show them how we stand;
> Ever shall our team be champions
> Known through-out the land!

But by the time the song was in use, Hudson High was only a memory in Jack's life. Before the series was a year old, Jack had shucked the Merriwell image and had begun to branch out, seeking thrills and adventure in exotic places. With his Uncle Jim Fairfield and his cousins, Betty and Billy Fairfield, Jack Armstrong traveled the primitive paths of the world, challenging the mountain country of Tibet and the waterspouts of the Pacific, hacking through the jungles of the Philippines and chopping footholds in the glaciers of the

311

Andes. Jack, Billy, and Betty were ready to go at the slightest suggestion from Uncle Jim Fairfield, who became their guide in adventure and the ultimate authority figure when big decisions had to be made. Whether it was chasing wildebeests along the veldt in *The Silver Albatross* (Uncle Jim's hydroplane), sailing after Dr. Shupato in the schooner *Spindrift*, or floating lazily above the landscape in the dirigible *Golden Secret*, Jack, Billy, and Betty could be sure that adventure was just ahead, and that their adolescent audience would go breathlessly with them.

As early as the winter of 1933–34, Jack and his friends tracked a ship of pirates to the frozen country for a fierce confrontation on the ice floes. By the mid-1930s, globe-trotting had become a way of life, and Hudson High had to muddle through without its hero. Jack Armstrong had bigger things to do. Jack, Billy, Betty, and Uncle Jim went everywhere, did everything, fought every criminal imaginable as color-bearers of their nation. They were trapped in the Cave of the Mummies, fought the master criminal Dr. Shupato, and trekked into Africa in search of the legendary elephant's graveyard but rarely did they get as much as a scratch for their troubles.

Always they went with the understanding that they would take their schoolbooks and keep up with their studies. But if Jack Armstrong ever cracked a schoolbook in his romps around the world, his fans surely didn't know it. Jack's negligence of school even became a sore point with mothers. Many wrote in with complaints that "that boy isn't ever in school." And while they were complaining, their children were demolishing stocks of Wheaties in stores everywhere, seeking out boxtops for which, along with one dime, a kid could get a Jack Armstrong ring, medallion, pedometer, or bombsight.

Sponsored through most of its run by Wheaties, "breakfast of champions," *Jack Armstrong* was a nightly CBS fixture from 1933 until 1936. It ran on NBC until 1941, on Mutual in 1941–42, and on the Blue Network (ABC) from 1942–50. Armstrong premiums were hot items, since most of them had a direct tie to the story line. The pedometer was "just like the one Jack Armstrong used" to plot the location of a hidden cache of rifles in the Philippines. For another boxtop and another dime, you could have a luminous bracelet, "just like the one Betty wears." The sponsor's inclusion of the premiums in the stories was painfully obvious, but no matter—the kids bought them.

Jack Armstrong was the ruler of the late-afternoon cereal set. Beginning in the depths of the Depression, Jack held his own for more than seventeen years. His daily adventures often continued along the same story lines for months without resolution. Villains would be recycled into the next adventure, the locale would change, and new bad guys would blend in to help the old. But the eternal struggle would continue. Skillful use of constant mini-crises gave the serial an illusion of bustle, while actually the pace was infinitesimally slow. Sometimes the comrades would go off for weeks on some colorful, dangerous side-journey, only to emerge no closer to the real goal than before. Then, just when it seemed that the writers were truly getting bogged down, obstacles were swept away like magic.

The characters were clearly drawn, the voices easy to define. Uncle Jim was clearly the adult voice; Jack was only slightly less manly, while Billy was given to such juvenile exclamations as "Gosh-all-hemlock!" or "Gosh-all-fishhooks, Jack!" And the writers insisted on idiotic name identification with virtually every spoken sentence. Betty served as the token female. She almost always waited in agony while whatever happened happened.

Jim Ameche was the first Jack, and for a brief time his brother Don played Captain Hughes. By the mid-1930's, Don Ameche had departed Chicago for Hollywood stardom, but Jim stayed with *Jack Armstrong* through the Depression years, finally giving it up in 1938. The part was played briefly by St. John Terrell and Stanley Harris between 1938 and 1939, when Charles Flynn took over. Flynn, then 18, was the son of Bess Flynn, writer of the afternoon serial, *Bachelor's Children.* He was to play the part to its end in 1950 (with one brief break in 1943, when Rye Billsbury took over) and continued playing the role after it became *Armstrong of the SBI* in September 1950. As for the rest of the cast, Jim Goss went all the way as Uncle Jim. Billy was played by a variety of actors (notably John Gannon who played the role from 1933 until 1946 and later became a judge of the Cook County Circuit Court, Chicago). Latter-day TV star Dick York played Billy briefly and carried the part into its SBI days. For much of the run, Betty was played by Scheindel Kalish and Sarajane Wells. Many announcers followed David Owen, the first, but the most memorable was Franklin MacCormack of the late 1930's and early 1940's, who talked about premiums and boxtops with zest. Robert Hardy Andrews wrote the early shows; the writing passed to, among others, Talbot Mundy, Colonel Paschal Strong, Irving J. Crump (editor of *Boys' Life*), and James Jewell of *Lone Ranger* fame. The theme and its equally famous tagline, "Have you triiiieeeed Wheaties?" were sung by a group called The Norsemen.

The entire series, during the early war years, was carefully scrutinized by Dr. Martin L. Reymert, well-known child psychologist and director of a laboratory for childhood research at Mooseheart, Illinois. Reymert served as special consultant, checking each script for plot feasibility and wholesomeness. He even had control over some of the sponsor's premium giveaways and strictly prohibited scenes that contained murder or torture. *Jack Armstrong* had a standard to maintain.

More than a million fans joined Jack's "Write-a-Fighter Corps" during World War II. As members, their primary pledge was to send at least one letter a month to a fighting serviceman. But they also collected scraps of paper, rubber, and tin, sold war bonds, and planted victory gardens, and tuned in each night for another adventure and more wartime instructions.

On August 22, 1947, the quarter-hour daily serial ended forever, and *Jack Armstrong* became a 30-minute show broadcast twice a week. In 1950, that version too ended. By 1950, Flynn was pushing 30, but Jack Armstrong was still an adolescent. His perennial adolescence ended there, as the ill-fated *SBI* series loomed on the horizon.

That had been slowly coming since 1945, when Jack, Billy, Betty, and Uncle Jim clashed with the Silencer, a gangland figure shrouded in mystery. The Silencer was embroiled in a bitter gangland war with another mystery criminal, known only as the Black Avenger. When it was over and the Silencer was unmasked, he was found to be one Victor Hardy, a master scientist and inventor who had led a respectable life before amnesia led him down a ten-year path of crime. After a sensational trial, Hardy's memory was restored, leaving him totally dedicated to the path of honor and right. "Because he understands the criminal mind," the announcer told us, "he has dedicated the remainder of his life to the readjustment of criminals and the prevention and correction of crime. In this way, he intends to repay society for those ten years during which he lived outside the law."

It was the beginning of the end for Uncle Jim. He was phased out completely, and Vic Hardy assumed the role of adult authoritarian. Hardy later became head of the Scientific Bureau of Investigation, and drafted Jack, Billy, and Betty into the new series. In the fall of 1950, *Armstrong of the SBI* opened on ABC, again for Wheaties. In this 30-minute twice-a-week show, Jack Armstrong and his friends had grown up overnight, becoming investigators for the SBI. But Armstrong couldn't cut it as an All-American adult, and vanished from the air June 28, 1951.

The Jack Benny Program

The Jack Benny Program though it spanned twenty-three years with great success all the way, was created in pieces. Over the years came the gradual refinements of character and situation, each contributing a small part to a classic in the making. Once character was established and traits were accepted, they were offered as old friends. Thousands of people hated it, but they were vastly outnumbered by the millions who loved it.

The Jack Benny Program was good because it was funny and familiar. The foundation of Benny's house was himself. He built himself up as stingy and vain, and took on all the traits that people find offensive in their fellows. In Benny they came out strangely likeable and in time became an irreplaceable part of Americana.

He worried about his receding hairline; he took inordinate pride in his blue eyes; he fretted about advancing age, and never admitted to being older than 39. The Benny that listeners knew was sensitive about his violin and his ability to play it. He built a vault with multiple locks, to hold the money he'd hoarded over the years, then became paranoid about protecting the vault. So he hired an old guard, who had been living in the vault for so many years that he'd lost all contact with the outside world. If that wasn't enough, Benny had a polar bear named Carmichael, who inhabited the outer basement and once ate a gas man. Benny was such a miser that even the name of his car—Maxwell—was a character-builder. Building on it further, Jack put gas in the car one precious gallon at a time.

Therewith, a surefire formula for radio success. It served Jack Benny for more than 20 years, most of which found him firmly established as America's top-rated comic or snapping at the heels of the leader.

Benny had so many well-remembered gimmicks that listing them becomes a challenge in itself. Most were tried and true, good for a laugh every time. Some, like his train station scenes, were funnier every time they were used. When Mel Blanc barked out, "Train now loading on track three—all aboard for Anaheim, Azusa and Cuc——amonga," the audience howled. And the longer the pause between "Cuc" and "amonga," the bigger the laugh.

Timing was Benny's greatest gift. He was a man of no great wit, a comedian whose reliance on his writers was almost legendary. Fred Allen, his old friendly enemy, once said that Benny couldn't ad-lib a belch after a Hungarian dinner. But he did understand something that was basic to the nature of comedy. He knew what was funny even if he couldn't write it himself; once he had the jokes in hand, Jack Benny knew more about delivery and timing than any other man in the business.

On his level, it became more a question of instinct than learning. Benny's instinct began in Chicago, where he was born Benjamin Kubelsky on Valentine's Day, February 14, 1894. His father, Meyer Kubelsky, was a Jewish immigrant from Poland, who became a back-packing Chicago peddler and later owned a haberdashery store in nearby Waukegan. Benny spent his early life in Waukegan, a fact that eventually made the town famous. In his childhood he was given a $50 violin by his father; at eight, he performed at Waukegan's old Barrison Theatre. A few years later, he was hired by the theatre, doubling as usher and violinist.

Benny always had greasepaint in his blood, but even in young manhood there was no hint that he would someday be one of America's most famous comedians. Had there been no vaudeville, he would muse a lifetime later, he might well have ended up as a violinist in some symphony orchestra. But vaudeville there was, and Benny left school in his sophomore year to try it. He teamed up with theatre pianist Cora Salisbury, touring with small shows in Illinois and Wisconsin under the billing, "From Grand Opera to Ragtime." Two years later, when Miss Salisbury retired, Benny hooked up with pianist Lyman Woods and continued the act along the Orpheum vaudeville circuit.

For six years, he fiddled and never spoke a word or cracked a joke professionally. Then the United States was drawn into World War I, and Benny enlisted in the Navy. At the Great Lakes Naval Training Station, he was tapped to play a benefit for Navy relief. His violin solo bombed, so he tucked the fiddle under his arm and started to talk. He cracked a joke. The people laughed. Forever after the violin was a mere prop for his comedy routine.

After the war, Benny returned to vaudeville. This time he played alone, doing a monologue and playing comic violin. He changed his name from Benny Kubelsky to Ben K. Benny, but in 1921, when his name began going up in lights, he changed it again to avoid confusion with maestro Ben Bernie. Now Jack Benny, he had arrived in big-time vaudeville. He played the Palace in New York and toured in California. In 1926, while playing a West Coast engagement, Benny met Sadie Marks, a hosiery clerk for the Los Angeles May Company. They were married in Waukegan in January 1927, and she began to appear with him on stage. In time, as Mary Livingstone, her name would become almost as well known as his, and their meeting in the May Company would become a stock joke on "The Jack Benny Program."

By 1932, Benny was a top stage headliner. He was playing on Broadway, in Earl Carroll's "Vanities," when columnist Ed Sullivan asked him to appear on a CBS interview show. Benny's routine, heard on the Sullivan show March 29, 1932, began like this: "Ladies and gentlemen, this is Jack Benny talking. There will be a slight pause while you say, 'Who cares?' I am here tonight as a scenario writer. There is quite a lot of money in writing scenarios for the pictures. Well, there would be if I could sell one. That seems to be my only trouble right now, but I am going back to pictures in about ten weeks.

I'm going to be in a new picture with Greta Garbo. They sent me the story last week. When the picture opens, I'm found dead in the bathroom. It's sort of a mystery picture. I'm found dead in the bathtub on Wednesday night . . . "

He was writing his own material then, but even in those early times the emphasis was on inflection and timing. The Sullivan appearance led directly to more feelers into the new medium. Benny listened to *Amos and Andy* and the variety show *Gene and Glenn*. He saw radio as the "coming thing," so he quit Carroll's show to take an offer from Canada Dry for an NBC series. Costarred with Ethel Shutta and her bandleader husband George Olsen and backed by the music of Olsen's orchestra, in a radio format of gags and songs, Benny walked away from his $1,400-a-week stage job and tried a new medium.

His show, premièring on NBC Blue May 2, 1932, was a solid hit. He was later shifted into a Thursday night CBS slot, and in 1933 his show was picked up by Chevrolet for a 10 P.M. Sunday-night NBC run. In 1934, sponsorship went to Jell-O, and the show was set for Sundays at 7 P.M.—the time slot it would keep for the rest of its long run. Benny's first writer was Harry Conn, who did virtually all the routines until 1936. Then Ed Berloin and Bill Morrow came aboard. Al Boasberg joined the growing staff and Harry Conn left for other pastures. Frank Parker was the first male singer, and Benny went through one orchestra a year, from Olsen to Ted Weems to Frank Black to Don Bestor, until Phil Harris began giving him what he wanted in 1936. What he wanted was bouncy, pop music, and not too much of it. He wanted just enough melody to break up the comedy routines, and a bandleader who had the comic ability to blend in and become part of the cast. Harris did that. His greeting, "Hi-ya, Jackson," became one of the series' trademarks. Harris drubbed Benny mercilessly about being vain and cheap. His own character—that of a self-centered, dapper-Dan playboy with curly hair and flashy clothes—was developed to such perfection that, in the late 1940's, it became the focal point of Harris's own show. But even after "The Phil Harris-Alice Faye Show" began on NBC, Harris remained with Benny, helping Mary deflate Jack's puffed-up ego. He lasted until the early 1950's, when Bob Crosby took over the baton chores.

Mary Livingstone was created within the first two years, when a script had a young female Benny fan "crashing" the show to read poetry on the air. The character became Mary Livingstone of Plainfield, New Jersey. After auditioning actresses for the part, Benny gave it to his wife. It was one of his best decisions, for Sadie Marks adapted so well to the brash, peppery role of Mary that her real identity was soon forgotten. Her letters from her mother in Plainfield became a regular routine. Her brother, Hilliard Marks, was Benny's longtime producer-director; Irving Fein was his associate producer and business manager.

People stayed with Benny for years. Eddie Anderson, the gravel-voiced black comic who became known to the world as Rochester, was originally signed for a one-shot appearance as a Pullman porter for the Easter Sunday show of 1937. But Anderson became so popular that Benny brought him back, and finally had him written into the script permanently as valet and chauffeur. Anderson, a San Francisco stage man before he joined Benny, remained with the cast through the radio run and into television.

Don Wilson, after stints as a salesman, singer, and sportscaster, had become Benny's announcer by 1934. He touted the "six delicious flavors" of Jello-O with the booming authority of one who had eaten his share. Wilson was a Denver man, starting on radio in his hometown as part of a singing trio in 1924. A bulky six-foot-two, 220-pound frame went with the booming voice. It was well below the weight of "The Fat Man," but large enough for Benny to make Wilson's waistline one of his great running jokes. At Benny's direction, Wilson began incorporating the middle commercials into the story lines; *The Jack Benny Program* was one of the first shows of the air to use this technique. Some of the later Lucky Strike commercials, with Jack frantically trying to get in a word over the "rat-a-tata-ta-tata-ta-tat" of the Sportsmen Quartet (Marty Sperzel, Max Smith, Gurney Bell, and Bill Days, and earlier John Rarig) were particularly hilarious.

Frank Parker set the pattern for all of Benny's singers. All but Larry Stevens were tenors, and Stevens's light baritone was the tenor's blood brother. All were solid comedians in their own right. Kenny Baker was signed in 1935, establishing the patter of scatter-brained logic that Dennis Day perfected a few years later. Dennis was discovered by Mary Livingstone and was given the job when he answered Benny's summons at the crowded audition with, "Yes, please?" It broke up the house, and became his standard phrase on *The Jack Benny Program*. It was also a perfect key to the kid with the twisted brain he portrayed for Benny. Dennis joined the cast in September 1939. His radio mother, whose hatred for Jack Benny was renowned, was played by Verna Felton. Like other cast members, Day stayed with Benny to the end, his tenure broken only in 1944–45, when Larry Stevens filled his shoes while he was away in the service.

Sponsorship passed from Jello-O to Grape Nuts Flakes in 1942. In 1944, Benny began his long association with Lucky Strike.

By the mid 1940's, the cast and writing crews were solid. Sam Perrin was head writer, assisted by Milt Josefsberg, John Tackaberry, and George Balzer. Each Sunday immediately after the show, they met with Benny in the star's dressing room to discuss the thrust of next week's script. The show was divided into two segments, an opening banter among cast members and a dramatic spoof in the last half. The writers split up the chores, two doing the opening, two working on the drama, and trading off every other week to keep fresh. By Friday the script was in rough draft form, and Benny passed a copy along to Hilliard Marks, who began to acquire the bit players needed for the broadcast. Saturday was rehearsal day; then Benny and the writers did more trimming and revising. Two careful rehearsals followed on Sunday, and the show emerged promptly at 7 P.M. to the theme "Love in Bloom," as one of the best-oiled pieces of precision work on the air.

Contrary to popular belief, Benny's time slot wasn't the air's best. It fell just before prime time, when people were still busy with early evening chores, and it had no built-in carryover audience from a blockbuster program before it. So The Jack Benny Program was the blockbuster, carving out phenomenal ratings that carried through the entire Sunday night schedule. He was the first comedian to give major roles to his supporting cast, the first to reverse the roles, at times becoming the straight man while Phil, Dennis, Rochester, Mary, or even Don got the big laughs. He promoted his stinginess to ridiculous proportions, then reversed that in real life by overtipping in restaurants, giving his cast and writers generous contracts, and raising millions for charity with benefit performances. Benny was a master of the running gag; he knew exactly when to stop a gag, and how it should be stopped. Some gags, like his feud with Fred Allen, were good forever. Others, like his 1945 "I Can't Stand Jack Benny because . . ." contest (which drew 300,000 entries during the month of December, for Victory Bond prizes totalling $10,000) were over in weeks. Only on Benny's show did such phrases as "Now cut that out!" become vital tools of characterization. The people roared at his delayed response, at his "Well!" and "Yipe" and "Wait a minute! Wait a minute! WAIT A MINUTE!!!" Benny could say more with a simple "Hmmmm" than many comedians could say in a page of script.

The show had literally dozens of aspects. There was Andy Devine, who first appeared in August 1937 with the greeting, "Hi-ya, Buck!" and competed intermittently with Rochester for the all-time gravel-voice award. There was Mel Blanc, whose hilarious impersonations of Professor LeBlanc the violin teacher, the sputtering Maxwell, and Carmichael the bear led to his own show. There was Sheldon Leonard, the perennial tipster, who was always lurking in the shadows, waiting to snare Benny with his "Psst! Hey, bud, . . . c'mere!" In the early 1940's, the cast did an annual New

Years show, with Benny playing the old year, Mary playing "Columbia," and various people (one year it was Fred Allen) appearing as
"Uncle Sam." A favorite gathering place of the cast was the corner
drugstore, where the waitress was so sarcastically Brooklyn and
Dennis ordered such oddities as a "cucumber split." Around 1946,
Benny began his annual Christmas shopping shows, with Mel Blanc
as the department store clerk driven to psychoanalysis by Benny's
constant exchanging of presents. He began firing the Sportsmen as
early as 1947, and was still at it in 1954. And on the show of December
9, 1945, Benny introduced Ronald and Benita Colman (who actually
lived eight blocks away) as his next-door neighbors; they appeared
frequently in riotous skits as charter members of the "I Can't Stand
Jack Benny" club. Frank Nelson was superb in his roles of screwball
floorwalkers, doctors, and professional men, marking his entrance
with an inevitable squeal that came out "Yeeeeeeeeessss??!" Finally
there was "Mr. Kitzel," a middle-aged, word-twisting Jewish neighbor, played by Artie Auerbach.

Mary left show business in the early 1950's, giving up her role to
unnamed actresses, but Benny continued his active life to the end.

In 1949, CBS scored the greatest coup in broadcasting, luring
Benny away from NBC with a deal involving $2 million and huge tax
breaks to the comedian. On CBS, Benny continued in his 7 P.M.
Sunday format until May 22, 1955, his last live broadcast on radio.
Reruns of his show continued until 1958. Although his TV show was
dropped in 1964, he continued doing benefits and live performances
and yearly TV specials that drew top ratings. In October 1974, he was
scheduled for a concert in Dallas, but had to cancel because of numb-
ness in his arms. Two months later, on December 26, 1974, Benny
died of cancer.

The Jack Carson Show

The Jack Carson Show, a light comedy-variety program, was first
heard on CBS for Campbell Soups June 2, 1943. Carson continued his
Wednesday-night program until 1947, when the show was discontinued and he took over for Jack Haley as master of ceremonies at The
Sealtest Village Store. The Jack Carson Show grew out of an earlier
Carson-hosted program, The Signal Carnival, in which Carson was
featured as himself. Carnival was running on NBC in 1941, with
Carson flanked by Barbara Jo Allen as Vera Vague, Hal Peary as Mr.
Smugooznok, longtime Carson pal Dave Willock as his nephew Tug-
well, songstress Kay St. Germain (who became Mrs. Carson), and
announcer Johnny Frazer. Paul Conlan produced and wrote. Music

was by Gordon Jenkins. By the time *The Jack Carson Show* came to CBS, Arthur Treacher had come aboard as a regular, and Eddie Marr was the hustling salesman who tried to sell Carson everything. Music was by Freddy Martin's orchestra, and by Dale Evans, who in 1944 was signed as Carson's regular songstress. Despite the well-knowns, *The Jack Carson Show* remains rather an obscure piece of radio. Carson was destined for much wider exposure a few years later as the proprietor of the *Village Store* before returning to his own slot in 1948 with a new cast, including Marion Hutton and Frank De Vol's orchestra. Dave Willock remained as Tugwell until the end.

The Jack Haley Show

The Jack Haley Show featured a comedian who, like Carson, made his mark as proprietor of *The Village Store*. Haley was running the "Store" while Carson was still entrenched in his own show, but there was an earlier *Jack Haley Show* beginning on NBC October 8, 1937, for Log Cabin Syrup, and running on CBS in 1938–39 for Wonder Bread. Haley's show was a similar mix of comedy and musical variety, featuring Virginia Verrill, Warren Hull as emcee, and the Ted Fiorito orchestra. Haley had been a comic on the *Maxwell House Show Boat* when tapped by Log Cabin for his own series.

The Jack Kirkwood Show

The Jack Kirkwood Show began on NBC as a six-a-week morning show, *Mirth and Madness*, in 1943. By mid-1944, it had moved to CBS as *The Jack Kirkwood Show*, running nightly for Procter & Gamble until 1946. Kirkwood, who wrote his own material, was backed by Irving Miller's Orchestra, and was introduced to the theme, "Hi, neighbor, Hi, neighbor; Time to smile and say hi!"

The show consisted of old vaudeville jokes and heavy satire in a strange mix. It usually opened to standup banter between Kirkwood, his wife Lillian Leigh, and announcer Jimmy Wallington, then progressed through a musical number or two, and ended with a little skit by the Little Madhouse Theatre. The Madhouse skits ranged from contemporary to Westerns like "No Matter How Hungry a Horse May Be, He Shouldn't Bite His Fodder." In the Westerns, Kirkwood inevitably was shot and spent the last several minutes dying, muttering, "He got me, I'm goin', I'm dyin', Lil." Included in the cast was vocalist Don Reid and later Jeannie McKean. Gene Lavalle provided more alleged comedy, occasionally hailing Kirkwood, à la Phil Harris, as

"Hi-ya, Jackson!" Around 1948 the Kirkwoods did a series, *At Home With the Kirkwoods,* spoofing husband-wife shows to the extent of knock-down breakfast brawls. Their variety show, *The Kirkwood Corner Store* resurrected some of that format in 1949 on ABC. The Kirkwood show was also heard on Mutual from 1950 to 1953, featuring Wally Brown and Steve "Sam Spade" Dunne.

Jack Oakie's College

Jack Oakie's College was a musical variety show featuring Oakie as the "pres" of a mythical university bearing his name. It was first heard December 29, 1936, as a 60-minute Tuesday-night CBS show for Camel Cigarettes, and running until March 22, 1938. Its college format was totally superfluous, being merely a backdrop for Oakie's guests and skits. Guests included Stu Erwin, Joe Penner, and "MGM's 13-year-old singing sensation, Judy Garland." The Benny Goodman orchestra provided the music during 1937, but all that talent wasn't enough to save it from its own dreariness. The program was a fine example of 1930's radio, still deeply rooted in the bland jokes of the vaudeville stage. The college angle was played to the hilt, with an opening right out of the nearest sorority house:

> Ah-zah zoo zazz
> Zah zoo zazz
> Zah zoo zazz-and-ah
> Razz-a-mah tazz!

The Jack Paar Show

The Jack Paar Show began on June 1, 1947, as a summer substitute for Jack Benny. Paar had also served as Don McNeill's replacement on *The Breakfast Club.* NBC gave Paar a good sendoff, in a situation comedy format strongly reminiscent of Benny's, with a fine supporting cast and a solid writing team. Paar was in and out of radio in several brief summer formats containing various old pros of the air. In 1947 he was supported by Larry Marks, Artie Stander, Larry Gelbart and Sid Dorfman. Hy Averback announced and Bob Nye produced. Later, Jane Morgan, the eccentric landlady of *Our Miss Brooks* played Paar's landlady, Mrs. Morgan. Hans Conried was Oliver T. Hampton, an aging actor, and Frank Nelson was Paar's wisecracking announcer. The writers were Jay Sommers and Hal Goodman, and vocals were by

Carol Richards and Jud Conlon's Rhythmaires. In short, it was a high-class, first-rate production that went absolutely nowhere.

The Jack Pearl Show

The Jack Pearl Show, though it faded early, was one of the major comedy-variety shows of the early Depression. Pearl, who shared a lower East Side heritage with Al Jolson, Eddie Cantor, and a host of top-flight comics, had worked his way up through the revues, vaudeville and burlesque, arriving as a semi-permanent guest on the 1932 *Ziegfeld Follies of the Air*. His comedy was built around dialect; the dialect centered on one Baron von Munchausen, a literal steal from history. The real Baron Munchausen was an eighteenth-century officer in the German cavalry who in his later years took up writing and recorded some of the wildest adventures (supposedly developed from his experiences in Russia) ever set to paper. So it was with Pearl's Baron. As Munchausen, Pearl became the first truly great dialectician of the air. As straight man he had Cliff Hall, who became widely known as "Sharlie." Hall fed the lines; Pearl, in character, responded. "Und dere in frundt off me wuz a green elephant," Pearl would say. Hall would reply, "Now wait a minute, Baron; do you mean to tell me you actually saw a green elephant?" Doubt brought an inevitable explosion from the Baron, followed by the nation's best-known catch phrase: "Vas you dere, Sharlie?" From *Follies*, it was one jump into Pearl's own show, a 60-minute Thursday-night NBC series for Lucky Strike. The Lucky Strike program had begun the year before with Walter Winchell and Walter O'Keefe as stars. By September 8, 1932, Pearl had replaced Winchell as O'Keefe's partner. By 1933 Pearl had moved into a 30-minute Wednesday format for Royal Gelatin; in 1936 he moved to the Blue for a Monday-night Raleigh show, after a short absence. Pearl's show started strong; it was a top-10 blockbuster in 1933, but lost steam quickly. By 1935 he had decided to give up Baron Munchausen and concentrate on situation comedy involving a German tavernkeeper, Peter Pfeiffer. He gave up the tall tales that had characterized his early work, and the *New York Times* reviewer found him "at once a philosopher and less a comedian." Cliff Hall stayed with him through the years. His writers included Billy Wells and Eugene Conrad. The 1936 show featured the music of Tommy Dorsey and the singing of tenor Morton Bowe. Pearl tried several comebacks, one in 1942 and another as late as 1948, when the Treasury Department sponsored him for a summer on NBC.

The Jack Smith Show

The Jack Smith Show was a popular CBS program of light music. Smith started in show business as a student of Hollywood High School in 1931. There he formed a student trio and auditioned for the job just vacated at the Coconut Grove by Bing Crosby, Al Rinker, and Harry Barris. It was a big ambition, but they got the job and held it for almost a year while going to school during the daytime. After graduation, Smith sang on The Kate Smith Show, The Prudential Family Hour, and later became a regular on Kenny Baker's Glamor Manor. His own show was first heard on CBS in 1943. His long-running nightly show for Procter & Gamble, produced by Bill Brennan and arranged by Earle Sheldon, ran from 1945 until 1951 on CBS; it highlighted Smith with popular tunes of the day and great hits of Broadway. Later the music was by Frank De Vol's orchestra, and Smith was joined by Margaret Whiting and Dinah Shore.

Jane Arden

Jane Arden had a short life on the air, running on the Blue Network from June 19, 1938, to June 23, 1939. Sponsored by Ward Baking, this show was about a "fearless girl reporter, the most beautiful woman in the newspaper world—Jane Arden, star reporter for the Bulletin, important newspaper of a big American city." Based on the comic strip by Monte Barrett, it was a five-a-week serial, employing most of the qualities of soap opera and juvenile adventure. Jane, her city editor Eddie Dunn, and a cub reporter named Delaney who wanted more than anything in the world to be a male Jane Arden, were among the principals. Jane was played by Ruth Yorke.

In the end, serials like this seldom made it. Kids didn't like them because of their soap elements; women didn't listen because the adult qualities weren't strong enough. The notable exception was Front Page Farrell, but Jane Arden wasn't a Farrell. It wasn't around long enough.

Jason and the Golden Fleece

Jason and the Golden Fleece was an NBC adventure series of 1952–53 that starred Macdonald Carey as Jason, owner of a café-bar in the French Quarter section of New Orleans. Jason also owned the boat known as the *Golden Fleece*, which frequently was chartered by people on the lam, adventurers, and emotional dropouts. The strange characters who hired Jason's boat made up the bulk of the stories, creating no end of problems for Jason and his bartender-sidekick Louis Dumont. William Conrad played Louis. Music was by Frank Worth; scripting by Herb Ellis and Cleve Herman.

Jeff Regan, Investigator

Jeff Regan, Investigator, began as a CBS summer series in 1948, and is notable mainly as a Jack Webb vehicle. Webb had a couple of seasons of hardboiled drama behind him as *Pat Novak* and *Johnny Madero*, and here he played the same kind of tough private gumshoe: "My name's Jeff Regan. I get ten a day and expenses from a detective bureau run by a guy named Lyon—Anthony J. Lyon. They call me 'The Lion's Eye.' " A bit corny, but there you have it. As Regan, Webb constantly referred to his boss (Wilms Herbert) as "the Lion." The show was written by E. Jack Neuman. Sterling Tracy produced, and organ music was by Dick Aurandt. Webb played the role into 1949, when he left for *Dragnet* and much bigger things. *Jeff Regan* continued into 1950 with Frank Graham in the title role and Frank Nelson as the Lion. William Froug and William Fifield were the writers in the Graham period. With the departure of both Webb and Neuman, the Regan character underwent a drastic change. The chip on the shoulder disappeared, and Regan became a staunch champion of the underdog.

The Jimmy Durante Show

The Jimmy Durante Show evolved out of years of hard work and experience. Although he had been a top show business headliner as early as 1923, Jimmy Durante did not have a regular, continuing radio show until the spring of 1943. Durante had appeared in an NBC summer show Sunday nights in 1934, then he starred in the brief series *Jumbo* for NBC in 1935. *Jumbo* was a lavish production by Billy Rose; Durante played a press agent for two feuding circus owners. But the main thrust of his career during radio's early years was in film and stage work.

Durante was born February 10, 1893, and spent much of his youth lathering faces in his father's New York barbershop. Somewhere between the sixth and seventh grades, he quit school and began selling newspapers. He learned to play piano, and at 17 began his career in a series of Coney Island beer gardens, plinking out tunes for $25 a week. In Terry Walsh's Club, he played while Eddie Cantor —then an unknown waiter—sang. Durante made the full club circuit in the years before the Great War, and by 1916 he had put together a small Dixieland combo for Harlem's Club Alamo. There he met Eddie Jackson, another singer, who was to become his longtime partner. In 1923, he and Jackson opened the Club Durant, and soon they acquired a third partner, a hoofer named Lou Clayton.

Until it was closed by prohibition agents, the Club Durant thrived. It was known as one of the jumpingest joints of old New York, and the team of Clayton, Jackson, and Durante was its prime attraction. With the Durant's closing, the trio went on to even bigger things, finally landing on Broadway in 1928 and on film in the 1929 Ben Hecht–Charles MacArthur epic *Roadhouse Nights*. The formal partnership broke up with the Depression, but Clayton and Jackson remained with Durante for years, following him out to the West Coast and serving as his business managers. There, Jimmy appeared in a score of second-rate films that eventually sent him into a decline.

After a smashing career on stage during and after Prohibition, his star had cooled and might well have burned itself out in the early years of World War II. But radio gave Durante new life as an entertainer. Just after the death in 1943 of his wife, the former Jeanne Olson, Durante accepted a booking on an hour-long variety show, *The Camel Comedy Caravan*. It was to be one of the major turning points in his career.

Durante had never met Garry Moore before that night, but both were billed in different parts of the Camel show. One man, producer Phil Cohan, was struck by the distinctive, contrasting styles in their performances. Cohan couldn't help wondering how they would do as a team.

On the surface, the contrasts were startling. Moore was the young crewcut with the well-oiled tongue. Son of a prominent Baltimore attorney, he had been in radio throughout his professional life. Durante, long-time abuser of the king's English, was the son of an East Side barber; his roots ran to vaudeville and burlesque. As intriguing as their personality differences was the disparity in their ages. Durante was 22 years old when Moore was born, and the subsequent years had seen great changes throughout show business. The men had different ideas, different tastes, and different ways of putting their comedy across. Cohan asked if they would be willing to try a team package, perhaps for a fall shot. They would.

Then, as it sometimes does, fate intervened. Lou Costello had a heart attack, and Bud Abbott refused to carry on their Thursday-night NBC show alone. Cohan pitched his Durante-Moore package to fill the sudden hole, and was told to get it together.

The first show was rushed into production within two weeks, and premiered March 25, 1943. It was a frantic, harried job, and reviewers didn't mind saying so. But in the following weeks, the Durante-Moore team matured and began to carve out an audience of its own.

With his new radio show, Durante established several trademarks immediately. His "Ink-a-dink" style was suddenly known to millions who had never seen him in person. Weekly he belted out the first few lines of his theme, "Ya gotta start off each day wit' a song, yeahhh, even if t'ings go wrong . . ." The age gap between Durante and Moore was emphasized so well (with Durante calling Garry "Junior" and forever saying, "Dat's my boy dat said dat!") that many listeners thought Moore was his son. His nose was played up verbally; his reputation as the "Schnozz" (a term coined by Clayton years before) grew and became radio legend. Durante also talked of his mythical character Umbriago, telling tall tales of their exploits together. And usually he left the audience with his traditional farewell of unknown origin: "Good-night, Mrs. Calabash, wherever you are."

They finished the *Abbott and Costello* commitment and were signed for Camel on CBS. Their show became the new *Camel Caravan*, at least the umpteenth show to go by that name, and it pushed Durante along a comeback trail that culminated in a smash booking at the Copacabana late in 1943. The Durante and Moore team returned in October on CBS, running two years on Friday nights for Camel and for another two years (still on Friday) for Rexall.

The Durante-Moore format followed the same lines as other comedy shows of the time. Moore, as master of ceremonies, told a few flip jokes, then brought on Durante for some dual banter. Somewhere in there, "her nibs, Miss Georgia Gibbs" would be brought out for a song. Then the boys would do a comedy sketch, often based on some occupational enterprise, such as running a circus, becoming scientists, or working on an oil pipeline. Music initially was by Xavier Cougat, who had provided the melodies for the old *Camel Caravan* in its 60-minute variety days. Roy Bargy's orchestra took over in the fall of 1943, and followed Durante—as did announcer Howard Petrie—through most of his radio career.

Moore wrote most of his own material, but Durante ad-libbed his way profusely through the half-hour. Scripts were prepared by a team of gag writers who threw in as many multisyllabled brain-twisters as they could muster. Then some magic in Durante's brain took over, scrambling the words in a way that sounded logical and hilarious. As the magazine *Tune In* noted in 1944, Durante mangled "da big woids just ta hear 'em scream."

In 1947, Moore decided to strike out on his own, so the three-way ownership with Durante and Cohan was dissolved. Beginning with the broadcast of October 1, Durante carried on alone for Rexall on

Wednesday-night NBC. He continued solo for three more years, with Cohan as his producer-director. Without Moore, his show changed shape somewhat. Now he assembled more guest stars; as semi-regulars he brought in Peggy Lee, "butler" Arthur Treacher, and "the Lothario of the lumbago set," Victor Moore.

He was billed as "Rexall's prescription for a pleasant evening," opening each show with his now-famous "Ink-a-dink-a-dink" theme. But he never sang much. Either someone interrupted after the first few bars or Durante himself bellowed, "Stop da music! Stop da music! There's somethin' wrong wit da orchestrial harmonics!" As regular stooges he had Hotbreath Houlihan, a sexy-voiced dame whose "C'mere, big boy" lines were delivered à la Mae West by Florence Halop, and Candy Candido, the moustached comedian whose miracle voice could go mighty high or mighty low. Even sports were featured on the new Durante shows—the last minutes of the 1947 fall shows were given over to football commentaries by Tommy Harmon, all-American grid star, who described the game of the week and offered his pick of the winner.

It was all just window dressing. His show moved to Fridays in 1948 and again Camel picked up the tab. Durante left radio for TV in 1950. In the final analysis, Durante's charm and magnetism carried the show from the early Moore years until its end. Whether he was belting out "I Know Darn Well I Can Do Wit'out Broadway, But Can Broadway Do Wit'out Me?" or venting his exasperation with "Ev'rybody wants ta get into da act!" Durante was a man of the people, a great commoner whose biggest selling point was himself.

Jimmy Fidler

Jimmy Fidler, during his two decades as a network Hollywood gossip reporter, was one of the most controversial men in radio. His first broadcast was in 1932. By 1934 he had his own show, a Wednesday-night 15-minute report, carried on the Blue Network for Tangee lipstick. Fidler became so controversial that his network career looks like a checkerboard. In 1936 he went to NBC Tuesday nights for Drene Shampoo; in 1938 he had Drene shows running on CBS (Tuesday) and NBC (Friday). By 1939 only the CBS show remained. Fidler's disputes with studios and film people forced him from the air briefly, but he returned in 1941 with short-lived shows on CBS and Mutual for Tayton cosmetics. In 1942, he began his long Blue-ABC Sunday-night run for Arrid deodorant. That lasted until 1948, when Mutual picked him up. Fidler's final network run was on ABC in 1949–50, still on Sundays, still for Arrid.

He had been on the Hollywood scene since 1919, coming as an aspiring actor with an eye on a film career. That didn't work out, and in the 1920's Fidler edited movie magazines and worked in public relations for film people. He gave up the print media when his broadcasting career began to perk up in the early 1930's. Despite the reputations of Louella Parsons, Hedda Hopper, and others, Fidler was considered radio's top menace to movies and movie people. He condemned movies he considered stinkers, and condemned people who fit into the same category. His trademarks included a film rating service (four bells for a top-notcher; one bell for a stinkeroo); scathing "open letters" to the stars; his "notes from the little black book"; and a celebrated sign-off: "Good night to you, and I *do* mean *you!*"

By the end of the 1930's, many studios had blacklisted Fidler, refusing him access to their lots. In 1941, he signed with CBS for a Pacific Coast series, but terminated the agreement less than two months later when the network—according to Fidler—tried to censor his scripts and insisted that he give "four bells" to "big" movies. He was picked up by Mutual, and then by the Blue Network, which he promptly got into hot water with his 1942 report that Gene Tierney, beauteous 20th Century Fox star, was smoking cigars in a frantic effort to "acclimatize" herself to her husband's smelly stogies. The outraged studio replied by banning its stars from all NBC radio shows —Red and Blue—but the network, to its credit, stood behind Fidler. Long after his network days ended, Fidler continued doing Hollywood gossip, sending out shows by syndication even into the 1970's.

Joanie's Tea Room

Joanie's Tea Room starred Joan Davis, who first came to radio prominence with an appearance, in August 1941, on NBC's *Rudy Vallee Show*. After rave reviews, she became a Vallee regular in 1942, playing a man-crazy, scatterbrained dame whose chief aim in life was to snare Vallee. When Vallee left the show on July 8, 1943, Miss Davis took over as star, and the show became the *Sealtest Village Store*. The producers, a bit uncomfortable with a female star following Vallee, lost no time booking Jack Haley as her co-star. The two played *The Village Store* until 1945, when Joan quit to join CBS with her own show, *Joanie's Tea Room*.

That program did little more than move her out of the store; basically, she played the same character, with announcer Harry Von Zell as chief foil. The show was heard Monday nights on CBS for Lever Brothers until 1947, but Miss Davis remained with CBS until

1950. The 1946 cast featured Wally Brown, Verna Felton, and Sharon Douglas. Her show was moved to Saturdays in 1947, and to Friday nights for Roi-Tan Cigars in 1949–50. Her last program, titled *Leave It to Joan*, premiered July 4, 1949. Then she abandoned radio for a TV series, *I Married Joan*, with Jim Backus. Before her radio career, Miss Davis had been a veteran of vaudeville and films. With husband Si Wills, she toured until 1936. Her daughter Beverly, then 12, was featured occasionally as Joan's sister in her *Joanie's Tea Room* shows, and her husband was one of her writers. But the height of her popularity was in 1944, when her Sealtest show edged into a formidable spot among radio's top five shows.

Joe Palooka

Joe Palooka, a twice-a-week thriller-comedy, premièred on CBS April 12, 1932. Based on the Ham Fisher comic strip, it told of the "amiable, dim-witted champion of the ring, the store clerk who fights his way to the heavyweight championship of the world." Ted Bergman, who would later become better known as Alan Reed, was starred as Joe, employing his skill with dialect. Frank Readick, one of the earliest stars on *The Shadow*, was pal Knobby. The original series was sponsored by Heinz Rice Flakes, and was heard each Tuesday and Thursday.

The Joe Penner Show

The Joe Penner Show came to CBS on October 8, 1933, after Penner had scored spectacularly on *The Rudy Vallee Show*. Penner's program, also known as *The Baker's Broadcast*, was carried by Vallee's sponsor, Fleischmann's Yeast; it featured a zany comedy of one-liners, music by Ozzie Nelson's Orchestra, and songs by Ozzie's new discovery, Harriet Hilliard.

Penner, who appeared in a derby hat and constantly smoked a cigar, had struggled along as a second-rate comic for more than a decade before Vallee's show swept him to overnight stardom. Born Josef Pinter in a small village outside Budapest in 1904, Penner had been left with grandparents in the old country while his parents came to America seeking a new life. Around 1910, he joined them here. He went through a variety of odd jobs, from apprentice lens-grinder to magazine salesman, before deciding around 1920 to become a comedian. He broke into show business as an aide to Rex, the Mind-Reader and Magician, but the job didn't last; Penner was fired when he accidentally dropped the robe from a floating woman and revealed the wire apparatus holding her up. He got his chance at comedy in 1923, when a comedian in a traveling show he was working threw a tantrum and refused to go on. Penner moved slowly up the vaudeville-burlesque ladder after that, landing in New York in 1930 with the *Vanderbilt Revue*. But he seemed destined for eternal obscurity until he hit upon a phrase in a 1931 Birmingham, Alabama, revue that made his fortune. Part of Penner's act was to constantly interrupt people with such absurd phrases as "Wanna buy an ashcan?" or "Wanna buy a rhinoceros?" On this particular evening, he chirped, "Wanna buy a duck?" and the audience, for some reason best analyzed by psychologists, howled. Penner soon learned that it wasn't a fluke; audiences everywhere appreciated the phrase, delivered precisely in the Penner style. It caught the attention of J. Walter Thompson, the agency handling the Vallee show, and Penner was on his way.

It has been estimated that each word of the "Wanna buy a duck" phrase was worth $250,000 to Penner's fortunes. His weekly income rocketed from $500 to $7,500 with the 1933 première of his own show. Penner began to pose in publicity stills with a duck in a basket. He named the duck "Goo-Goo," and Mel Blanc gave it voice on the air. Soon he developed new phrases that exaggerated words and played on sarcasm: "You NAH-H-STY man!" "Don't ever DOOOO that!" "WOOEE is me!" In June 1934, he was voted radio's outstanding comedian. But Penner was dissatisfied with *The Baker's Broadcast*. He quickly tired of reading the canned scripts churned out by a stable of writers, and he approached the agency for a change in format. The show was then nestled comfortably in the middle of radio's top 10, and the agency took a hard-line "why argue with success?" approach.

Penner quit the show cold, and stayed out of radio for a year. He returned in the fall of 1936, with a CBS Sunday show for Cocomalt. This one was built around situation comedy featuring the Park Avenue Penners, an aristocratic family of which Joe was "the black sheep." Joy Hodges and Gene Austin provided the vocals. Ozzie and Harriet Nelson had stayed with *The Baker's Broadcast* under new host Robert Ripley, so Penner got Jimmy Grier's orchestra for musical backup. Harry Conn, Jack Benny's first writer, handled Penner's scripts; Bill Goodwin announced. But the new show never quite attained the popularity of the old. It started strong but faded slowly through the 1930's, ending in 1940 as a washed-out Blue Network affair for Ward Baking. Penner went back on stage. On January 10, 1941, while in Philadelphia for a production of *Yokel Boy* he was stricken with a heart attack and died at the age of 36.

John Charles Thomas

John Charles Thomas, "America's beloved baritone" and longtime star of the Metropolitan Opera, came to NBC January 10, 1943, with a Sunday-afternoon show of popular music and Americana. Thomas, whose theme was "Home on the Range," sang such songs as "Erie Canal" and "All the Things You Are" for Westinghouse. He was backed by the music of Mark Warnow and the Lyn Murray Chorus, later by the Victor Young Orchestra and the Ken Darby Chorus. Intermingled with the songs were stories by John Nesbitt from his "Passing Parade." The show ran in its 2:30 P.M. EST Sunday 30-minute format until 1946.

John Steele, Adventurer

John Steele, Adventurer, was first heard on Mutual April 26, 1949, and was carried as a sustained show through 1956. It featured Don Douglas as Steele, who told tales of adventure and intrigue, and was another solid show that just came along too late. Steele's stories were often set in exotic back country, in the jungles of the Amazon, or on a remote island where the only building was a lonely lighthouse. *John Steele* was written and produced by Robert Monroe. Musical score was by Sylvan Levin.

Johnny Madero, Pier 23

Johnny Madero, Pier 23 ran Thursday nights on Mutual between April 24 and September 4, 1947. It is notable as Jack Webb's first significant appearance with his now-famous staccato style, and has direct ties to Webb's other hardboiled role, *Pat Novak, For Hire.*

Madero and Novak were both a light-year away from the Webb characterization that would emerge as Joe Friday on *Dragnet* two years later. *Johnny Madero* was a refugee from the street wars, virtually a copy of *Novak,* which had begun on a limited West Coast network in 1946. *Novak* originated in San Francisco, and within months of its première had built up a strong local audience, all connoisseurs of Webb's smartmouthed delivery. But by 1947, *Novak* writer Dick Breen and star Webb had left San Francisco for the greener pastures of Hollywood, and Webb was replaced as Novak by Ben Morris. Morris never really did the part justice, and faced a terrible disadvantage after the months of Webb. The inevitable happened; Webb's fans began to clamor for a return to the originals, and it wasn't long before Breen and Webb teamed up in Hollywood for *Johnny Madero*.

To call *Madero* similar to *Novak* is like casually describing the similarities of Siamese twins. Like Novak, Madero rented boats in San Francisco, and did "anything else you can blame on your environment." That often meant tailing someone, usually a dame; it led through a tangled mass of clients, bad guys, waterfront double-talk, and inevitably, to murder.

Johnny Madero took it in stride. We saw the world through his eyes, with a vivid opening set to the deceptively gentle sounds of water lapping against the pier. Webb's monologue was typical: "You know, the only time San Francisco really gets hot is when a tourist calls it Frisco, and then it gets warm enough to give a sleigh dog a Southern accent. Down around the waterfront, they don't care so much, and for a buck you can insult anybody but Joe DiMaggio. The piers stretch out like a big yawn, from south of the ferry building clear to the China docks. And pushed over on one side so you won't notice, about the same spot you'll find dust in a bride's parlor, you find Pier 23. From there it's a short skip to Johnny Madero's boat shop—my place. The sign outside looks honest, but down here the only sign people pay any attention to is rigor mortis . . ."

The regular characters on *Madero* were few; the series turned more on Webb's hardboiled quips than on any significant innovation of plot. Madero led with his tongue, wisecracking his way through even the grimmest scenes. He worked alone, taking time out for just a quick consultation with Father Leahy, the waterfront priest. Father Leahy was a bit unscrupulous for a man of the cloth, but he could always be counted on in a pinch. Like Jocko Madigan of *Pat Novak*, Father Leahy served chiefly as the hero's legman. Somehow he had developed some excellent underworld contacts, and through his grapevine he kept a sensitive finger on the pulse of the waterfront. Between them, Madero and Leahy managed to keep one step ahead of the menacing cop Warchek, well-played by William Conrad.

In something of a departure from his comic roles, Gale Gordon took the part of Father Leahy. Dick Breen created the character, and the snappy dialogue was put together by Herb Margolis and Lou Markheim; the show was directed by Nat Wolff. Music was by Harry Zimmerman; announcer was Tony La Frano.

Although it was on the air only during the summer of 1947, *Johnny Madero* led ultimately to a reinstatement of *Pat Novak* in 1948—again starring Webb and this time on a coast-to-coast ABC hookup.

Johnny Presents

Johnny Presents was an NBC Tuesday-night variety show that ran from 1939 through 1946 under several formats. In its early 30-minute format, it featured music by the Ray Bloch orchestra, vocals by the Swing Fourteen and the Marsh Sisters (Beverly and Audrey), and a mini-drama. One of the regular dramatic features, beginning in 1941, was "Nancy Bacon Reporting," a newspaper skit starring Una Merkel. By 1943, it had become "Johnny Presents Ginny Simms," in which beauteous Ginny interviewed servicemen, arranged family reunions, gave away gifts, and sang songs. Myron Dutton produced and wrote this show, which ran until 1945. Cal Kuhl produced in 1945, and music was by Cookie Fairchild. Then Miss Simms departed for another sponsor (Borden Milk for CBS Friday nights where she was heard until 1947), and Johnny Presents reverted to its variety format. it still featured Ray Bloch and was still heard on NBC Tuesdays at 8 P.M., but now the vocal star was Barry Wood. That version ran one season. As for Johnny, he continued to "Calll forrr Philllippp Morrraaaiiss" on other PM-sponsored shows.

John's Other Wife

John's Other Wife was a soap opera far outstripped by its catchy, widely mimicked title. First heard on NBC September 14, 1936, it told the story of John Perry, his wife Elizabeth, their kids, and their "beloved Granny Manners." The show was developed by Frank and Anne Hummert; it wallowed in melodrama throughout its six-year run. John's Other Wife never had the audience that some of the Hummerts' greater lights commanded, and it spent its final year—1942—as a Blue Network filler. The show was gleefully parodied by Fred Allen and other comedians, who developed the "other wife" theme (John's other wife was actually only his secretary) in numerous comedy skits. Matt Crowley, Luis Van Rooten, and William Post, Jr. were among the actors who played department store owner John; Elizabeth was played by Adele Ronson and later by Erin O'Brien-Moore.

The Johnson Family

The Johnson Family was truly a one-man show, with Jimmy Scribner—a white man—playing an entire hamlet of Southern blacks. His location was the mythical village of "Chicazola, way down

South." The show was first heard in 1934 at Station WTAR, in Scribner's home town, Norfolk, Virginia. Soon he took it to WBAL in Baltimore and WLW in Cincinnati; in 1936, *The Johnson Family* was booked on the Mutual network. Scribner continued doing his shows from Cincinnati until 1945, gradually refining his characters and adding new voices until he was playing twenty-two separate parts.

Scribner went into radio from a boring job at a Ford Motor Company assembly line. Even in the early days, he was handling eight or more roles. He was Papa and Mama Johnson, their daughter Lucy, Lucy's boyfriend Peewee, Peewee's stuttering friend Stumpy, Grandpa, Lawyer Philpotts, Deacon Crumpet, and others. The characters were all based on people Scribner had known in his youth. Scribner did everything for this show but play the organ. He wrote it, usually doing the scripts on a day-to-day basis and frequently ad-libbing as he went; he handled the sound effects and even played the banjo when the need arose. His show became especially popular in the South, and Scribner received many letters from fans marveling at his ability to switch vocal characteristics so quickly without getting mixed up. He told *Newsweek* in 1937 that arguments between the characters gave him the most trouble. His show was on intermittently on Mutual in the 1940's, and ran until 1950.

Joyce Jordan

Joyce Jordan had more substance than most soap operas, being the "moving and dramatic story of a woman doctor—of her struggle to be a woman and a doctor at the same time." *Joyce Jordan, Girl Interne* began on CBS May 30, 1938, and was inspired by a real-life quarrel between a young girl interne and her beau. The quarrel happened on a city bus. The girl wanted a career; the boy wanted to get married. The girl thought that women could mix marriage with career; the boy thought that woman's place was in the home. Sitting behind them on that long-ago bus ride were Himan Brown, young radio producer, and Julian Funt, script-writer. Both men immediately recognized the germ of an idea. *Flash! A serial about the love problems of a girl interne!*

Scheindel Kalish, who had changed her name to Ann Shepherd since playing little Betty Fairfield on *Jack Armstrong, the All-American Boy,* was chosen as Joyce. Myron McCormick played her husband Paul, a not-quite-so-understanding newsman. The early shows developed this basic conflict between home and calling to the hilt, and soon it became apparent that Paul would have to go. By the mid-1940's, Joyce was single again. She was also established, having passed her medical exams during the 1942–43 season. With her new "doctor" title came a new title for the serial; *Joyce Jordan, M.D.* Joyce practiced in the little town of Preston, and became a brilliant surgeon at Hotchkiss Memorial Hospital. Betty Winkler and Elspeth Eric played Joyce in the later years. Writer Julian Funt, who had edited medical journals before coming into radio, gave the show plenty of hospital flavor. *Joyce Jordan* held the CBS fort for General Foods until 1945, then moved to NBC for Dreft where it ran until October 8, 1948. It evolved into *The Brighter Day.* Joyce, meanwhile, enjoyed a brief ABC revival in 1951–52.

Judy and Jane

Judy and Jane was one of radio's earliest soap operas, a Hummert effort first heard on Midwest stations of NBC Blue October 10, 1932. It told the story of beautiful housewife Jane Lee and her wisecracking friend Judy, and was distributed to stations by transcription. Judy was played for a time by Joan Kay and for more than twelve years by Margie Calvert; Jane's part was taken by Donna Reade, Margaret Evans, Ireene Wicker, and Betty Ruth Smith. Sponsor was Folger's Coffee, the announcer was Jack Brinkley. On its regional network, *Judy and Jane* was still going strong in 1943.

The Judy Canova Show

The Judy Canova Show featured the reigning "queen of the hillbillies." Beginning July 6, 1943, as a Tuesday night CBS comedy for Colgate, Judy Canova moved to NBC in 1944 and ran until 1953, mostly as a Saturaday-night Colgate warmup for *Grand Ole Opry.*

In this case, the warmup had higher ratings than the main event. *The Judy Canova Show* struck closer to what middle America called home. Judy played a bumpkin from the sticks whose shotgun, wolf traps, and calico created a major pigtail fad on college campuses everywhere in the fall of 1943.

Her real name was Julia Etta; she came from Jacksonville, and crashed the hillbilly gates in 1933 when she applied for a hoedown job at a rustic New York club. The image stuck, despite some attempts later to cast it off. In New York, Judy was spotted by the old star-maker Rudy Vallee, and her career as a dyed-in-the-wool country gal was launched.

She came to radio after a fling in movies and one Broadway musical, and some fine talent was lined up in support. Hans Conried, as Judy's house guest, Mr. Hemingway, played the grouchy character he did best. Verna Felton was her friend Miz Pierce, and Ruby Dandridge was Geranium the cook and maid. Sheldon Leonard played Joe Crunchmiller, Judy's Booklynese boyfriend. But the best supporting role went to Mel Blanc. As Pedro, the goofy Mexican handyman, Blanc became one of the best-known members of the cast. His weekly line, "Pardon me for talking in your face, señorita; thirty days hacienda, April, June and sombrero—I theenk" was a national joke. Pedro's lines were always thrust suddenly into the scenario, as in this brief excerpt:

> JUDY: Sure am lookin' forward to gettin' into television. Ooooo, just think—in time, I'd meet all kindsa handsome leadin' men . . . Clark Gable, Ty-roney Power, Robert Taylor . . .
> MIZ PIERCE: Ah, poof, Judy! What have they got after you take away their charm and smiles and manners?
> JUDY: I don't know, but you can deliver me a carload of anything that's left over. Oooo boy, I can jest see myself in a love scene with one of them virilly stars. He holds me tenderly in his masculiny arms, looks in mah shinin' peepers, an' he says . . .
> PEDRO: Pardon me for talking een your face, señorita!

Joe Rines produced the show; music was by Charles "Bud" Dant; Howard Petrie announced. The show was largely situation comedy, loosely wrapped around songs by Judy, The Chaperones, and the Sportsmen Quartet. Judy's songs—usually two per show—were done in and out of character. Often she sang "musical stories" in hillbilly voice, then did a serious number in her natural voice. The fact that she trained in grand opera did little to help her break out of the hillbilly mold, and today she is remembered primarily for the pigtailed images she created during her decade of *The Judy Canova Show*.

Junior Miss

Junior Miss was Judy Graves, the character created by Sally Benson in the pages of *The New Yorker* magazine. Judy survived jumps from the printed page to stage and screen, but had a difficult time getting established on radio. The first *Junior Miss* premièred on CBS March 4, 1942, starring Shirley Temple. It failed because of its high cost ($12,000 a week). A second effort in 1946 failed because of poor characterization in the scripts. Finally, in 1948, *Junior Miss* came to CBS as a Saturday-morning show of some charm and staying power—enough to hang in there for five seasons, anyway. Sponsored by Lever Brothers, it featured Barbara Whiting, Margaret's

16-year-old sister, as Judy. Beverly Wills, Joan Davis's daughter, played Judy's pal Fuffy Adams, who lived downstairs. Peggy Knudsen was Judy's sister Lois. Gale Gordon played father Harry Graves and Sarah Selby was mom. Writers were Henry Garson and Bob Soderberg; Fran Van Hartesveldt produced. The stories were cut from the *Corliss Archer* cloth, exploring the trials and tribulations of being a teenager. The cast for this last version of *Junior Miss* remained intact through the five-year run. The show ran five times a week in 1952–53 and was last heard on Thursdays in 1954.

Just Plain Bill

Just Plain Bill was one of the greatest successes of Frank and Anne Hummert. *Bill* was among the first dozen soaps of the air, broadcasting his initial show for CBS and Kolynos on September 19, 1932. Nobody knew it then, but *Just Plain Bill* would become one of the best-loved, longest-running shows in radio history.

The serial exploited one of the Hummerts' favorite themes, life in a small town. It told of Bill Davidson, a barber in the mythical village of Hartville, and was "the story of a man who might be living right next door to you; the real-life story of people just like people we all know."

Yes, Bill Davidson was another of soapland's homespun philosophers. But it was Bill who established the pattern for the others. *Just Plain Bill* was on the air when *David Harum* was little more than a gleam in Bab-O's sink. Bill Davidson was the male Ma Perkins, and predated that staunch old mother of the air by almost a year. He lathered faces, gave advice, and provided a sympathetic sounding board for the troubles of Hartville and the world.

Bill was a widower, and trouble seemed to come most regularly to the immediate members of his family. Much of the action centered on his daughter Nancy, her husband Kerry Donovan, and their son Wiki. Kerry Donovan, a jealous, moody highbrow who sometimes dabbled in politics, was often the target of blind hate and vicious backbiting—hard feelings against him often manifested in campaigns against Bill or the family. Despite the soft theme of the show and the gentle nature of his philosophy, Bill Davidson—like most heroes of afternoon drama—had his share of murders to solve.

Through it all, he remained such a man of integrity, such a God-fearing proponent of the Golden Rule who generally found good even in the town's worst blackhearts, that Bill was asked for help and advice by thousands of his listeners. Mail poured in, describing all manner of personal problems and strife and hoping for a quick solution from Bill's sensitive pen. The voice behind all that philosophy belonged to Arthur Hughes, a Broadway veteran who stepped into Bill's shoes for that first broadcast and went all the way, until TV and the demand by affiliates for more local time finally squeezed the show out of radio more than twenty years later.

Bill's daughter Nancy was initiated and played for most of the run by Ruth Russell; James Meighan was Kerry Donovan. Scores of characters were developed over the run, and dozens of actors were brought in to play them. Robert Hardy Andrews, who created *Jack Armstrong, the All-American Boy*, was the show's first writer; Martha Atwell and Art Hanna were longtime directors. Ed Herlihy, André Baruch, and Fielden Farrington are the best-remembered announcers.

Just Plain Bill was a 15-minute giant of the air, surrounded by themes most unusual to daytime drama. Instead of the traditional organ, *Bill* was introduced to the strumming of Hal Brown's guitar, picking out the countrified tones of "My Darling Nellie Gray." A different theme was used for the closing; Brown put down the guitar and picked up the harmonica, ripping off a rousing rendition of "Polly Wolly Doodle." In its later years, "Nellie Gray" was used as an internal bridge and "Polly" became the opening and closing themes. Brown's guitar was used for the internal music, an unusual technique for soap opera. With one change of network—to NBC in 1936—Bill carried on for more than twenty-two years, until October 1955.

Juvenile Jury

Juvenile Jury wasn't *Quiz Kids*. This show simply assembled a panel of five normal but articulate kids aged 5 to 12 and let them air their views on the problems of other kids in their age group. The answers they gave were so delightful, original, and—in many cases—hilarious that *Juvenile Jury* became one of the stellar attractions of Sunday radio. Art Linkletter had been interviewing kids on *House Party* with the same results, but until *Juvenile Jury* came along, no major 30-minute weekly show had been built solely around the concept of juvenile questions and answers.

The idea originated with Jack Barry, who became the show's master of ceremonies. The first *Juvenile Jury* was heard in New York on Station WOR, May 11, 1946. After a five-week trial, the show went on the national Mutual hookup June 15. It started as a Saturday show, but soon moved to Sunday for Gaines Dogfood. There it was heard for five years, finally leaving Mutual in 1951. NBC picked it up for a final season the following year, and *Juvenile Jury* was last heard in 1953.

The kids handled such questions as "When should a girl start wearing lipstick?" and "How much allowance should an 11-year-old boy get?" Maryann Maskey, a 7-year-old juror, answered the question, "Should the father or the mother do the spanking?" in such an original manner that her comment made the pages of *Time*. "The mother should do it," she said. "She's home most of the time and knows the child really tried to do good—an', an', besides, she can spank more lighter than the father."

The show was unrehearsed and employed no writers. Each week Barry and his co-owner, producer Dan Ehrenreich, selected the questions from more than 5,000 sent in by children, teachers, and parents. Onstage, Barry delivered the questions in a forthright manner, without suggestion or obvious prompting. His delivery paid off in spontaneity and flow. The kids fenced over sticky problems of school dress and study habits, and even over kissing. Sometimes young guests were brought in to deliver their cases in person. They found that the "Jury" wasn't an automatic rubber-stamp for the side of the juvenile; the kids displayed a strong sense of fairness, and frequently stuck up for the parent.

Barry thought of the show while doing a juvenile amateur program in New Jersey. When he moved over to WOR, he saw a chance to put an audition record together when five children were brought in for an *Uncle Don* broadcast. When Uncle Don signed off, Barry regrouped the kids in a sound studio and fired some impromptu questions their way. The answers he got convinced him finally that *Juvenile Jury* was a solid radio idea.

Using most of the children from that *Uncle Don* show, Barry got *Juvenile Jury* booked on Mutual. The Early "Jurors" included Maryann Maskey, Buddy Robinson, Ginger Henkel, Glenn Mark Arthurs, Art Stone, Marilyn Kandler, and Francey Aransohn. Gradually they were replaced, as the continuing need for new blood became apparent. Talent hunts were launched in the schools, and children were auditioned by referrals. Among the later "Jurors" were Elizabeth Watson, Peggy Bruder, Dickie Orlan, Patsy Walker, and 5-year-old Robin Morgan, who had her own radio show of chatter and records before she learned to read.

Kate Hopkins, Angel of Mercy

Kate Hopkins, Angel of Mercy was a CBS soap opera of short duration, first heard October 7, 1940, for Maxwell House Coffee. It featured Margaret MacDonald as nurse Kate Hopkins, and was chiefly notable as a writing vehicle for Gertrude Berg, whose energy then was going into her famous serial, *The Goldbergs*. Despite Mrs. Berg's talent for the serial drama, *Kate Hopkins* never quite made it, and had vanished by 1943.

The Kate Smith Show

The Kate Smith Show was first heard on NBC, in a late-night (after 11:30) 1930 format that failed to click. But the following year Kate went to CBS, beginning an association that would last for almost two decades, producing one of the top-rated shows of its time.

Kate Smith was a simple gal from Greenville, Virginia. She was born May 1, 1909, and was bitten early by the acting bug. Her parents bucked her plans to crash show business, but Kate had something that was bigger than all their objections. She had an honest-to-gosh contralto voice that could rattle the timbers of an auditorium.

She went to New York in 1926, after being "discovered" by showman Eddie Dowling in a Washington vaudeville house. Kate was signed for *Honeymoon Lane*, a show that opened September 20, 1926. She played a character called Tiny Little—singing, clowning, and dancing the Charleston. After a turn on the road with *Hit the Deck*, she landed on Broadway in *Flying High* with Bert Lahr.

By then she had carved out a certain notoriety of her own, but her career was quickly dead-ending into a wall of fat jokes. Bert Lahr ridiculed her weight shamelessly, getting his laughs at Kate's expense, and journalistic morons pounced gleefully on the Fat Kate Smith bandwagon. They tagged her a "find of huge proportions," and the cutesy patter of their typewriters drove the overweight songbird to tears and almost out of the business.

That was during the 1929–30 season; radio was still an infant, and Ted Collins just a name that sounded something like a cocktail. People who thought of Ted Collins as just another announcer hadn't done much probing into the life of Kathryn Elizabeth Smith. Even a superficial look reveals that Ted Collins was truly the man behind the woman, that he molded and guided and influenced Kate Smith's career from beginning to end. Kate herself was always first to admit it.

Collins was then recording manager for the Columbia Phonograph Company. One of his primary jobs was to seek out and develop new recording talent, so he frequently caught the musicals of Broadway and Washington. One night in 1930, he dropped in on *Flying High*, and was impressed by the voice of Lahr's 21-year-old punching bag. After the show, he dropped around to her dressing room and proposed that she try the recording business.

Miss Smith, who by then was on the verge of tears over the fat gags, thought that was a splendid idea. A verbal agreement was reached between them. Kate would sing, Ted would fight the lions, and they would split in even partnership whatever they earned. For years they operated that way, with only a verbal understanding, even after their Kated Corporation became a million-dollar business.

Collins got Miss Smith booked into NBC, but her near-midnight slot was little more than a throwaway. On May 1, 1931, she began her long association with CBS in an early-evening 15-minute four-a-week program of songs. Her first sponsor was LaPalina Cigars. But this too was a time slot nobody wanted; Miss Smith was scheduled directly opposite *Amos and Andy*, which was then riding the crest of a national craze. Under the circumstances, Kate made a fine showing, pulling enough mail to get her own sponsor. For the next sixteen years (with tongue in cheek, considering the early newspaper critics), she was a radio giant.

Collins, in the truest sense, became her guiding light. She deferred to his judgment completely, doing whatever he said however he said it. Simplicity became her password; Collins brought out her true character, that of a warmhearted gal from Virginia who talked to people as if they were all "just folks." She became "the songbird of the south," opening with just her theme—"When the Moon Comes Over the Mountain"—and her friendly greeting, "Hello, everybody, this is Kate Smith." Her "Thanks for listenin' " became one of radio's great taglines. Jack Miller was perennial bandleader, and her announcer was André Baruch.

The Hudson Motor Car Company took on the songbird in 1934, in a 30-minute Monday-night amateur hour setting. Miss Smith returned to the 15-minute three-a-week format in 1935, broadcasting for A&P. In 1936, her 60-minute variety show was carried by A&P on Thursday nights, and in 1937 she signed a long-term pact with General Foods, which carried her through 1947 and the end of her CBS years. Her programs for General Foods included Thursday nights with Glenn Miller's orchestra for Calumet Baking Soda (1937–38), Thursday nights, again with Miller, for Swansdown (1938–39), Friday nights for Grape Nuts Flakes (1939–42), and Friday nights (1942–44), Sundays (1944–45), Fridays (1945–46), and Sundays (1946–47) for Sanka Coffee. Her 235-pound frame cast as big a shadow as Dashiell Hammett's *Fat Man,* but under Collins' guidance it became something respectable. Miss Smith was a radio personality to be reckoned with. "I'm big and I'm fat, but I have a voice, and when I sing—boy, I sing all over," she once told Newsweek. In the late 1930's, at the height of her career, she and Jack Benny had the only noncancellable contracts in radio. Legally, only war could force Kate Smith off the air.

One of her greatest coups was getting exclusive rights to Irving Berlin's classic "God Bless America," which she introduced on her show in the fall of 1938. Week after week she alone sang the song, bringing it such popularity that there was serious talk of making it the national anthem. That same year Collins signed her for a three-a-week (later daily) noontime feature, *Kate Smith Speaks,* which became a long-running vehicle of folksy chatter, news, and philosophy. This show was broadcast directly from her Park Avenue apartment. Collins read news dispatches phoned in just before airtime from United Press headquarters; Miss Smith rambled about the good things in life, and they chatted pleasantly about miscellaneous generalities of life. The noon show became one of the top-rated offerings of its kind, drawing a daily audience of about 10 million. She was consistently ranked among America's most outstanding women and was often termed (after a 1939 *Time* reference that stuck) "the first lady of radio."

Kate Smith was known as one of the great patriots of the war years, and became one of the top benefit performers of the air. She raised millions for orphanages and war bonds, and pushed the American way at every opportunity.

By the mid-1940's, she had won a trunkful of awards, citations, and keys to cities. Her show was trimmed to 30 minutes in 1945. Miss Smith signed with ABC in 1949, for one season in a 60-minute variety show, *Kate Smith Calls*. She returned to the air with a five-a-week 1957–58 show on Mutual. Her daytime show, *Kate Smith Speaks*, was first heard April 4, 1938, and ran until 1947 on CBS for General Foods. It was heard on Mutual thereafter, broadcasting its finale in 1951.

Collins died in 1964. But Kate Smith is still much in evidence in the 1970's, seen often as special guest on major TV variety shows.

Kay Kyser's Kolloge of Musical Knowledge

Kay Kyser's Kollege of Musical Knowledge had its roots in an earlier Mutual show. First heard early in 1938 as *Kay Kyser's Kampus Klass*, it contained the basic elements that would go into the more famous *Kollege*.

Chief element was Kyser himself. His warm southern drawl and standard greeting "Evenin', folks, how y'all?" wasn't a put-on. Born James King Kern Kyser in North Carolina on June 18, 1906. Kyser modified the name, and by his college years he was simply called "Kay." His first band, formed in 1926 at the University of North Carolina, played mostly college functions. But by 1933 Kyser had hit the big circuit, with appearances at Chicago's famous Blackhawk Hotel. His early trademarks included singing song titles and announcing numbers with four bars from the melody.

He first played on the air in San Francisco in a 1933 broadcast from the Bal Tabarin Cafe, but his radio work attracted little public acclaim until the *Kollege of Musical Knowledge* premièred in 1938.

Kyser's Kollege of Musical Knowledge was a real novelty when it first hit the air. The great era of giveaway shows hadn't yet begun, and Kyser developed within his 60 minutes an unusual blend of comedy, music, and contest, with up to $400 cash for contestants who could answer the "kollege brainbuster question." Kyser pushed aside his baton for the cap and gown of the quizmaster on this variety hour of questions and answers. And the cap and gown, in this case, was more than just a figure of speech. Kyser developed the *Kollege* theme completely, actually wearing "the old perfessor's" getup for the benefit of his studio audience. His band members came similarly in character, with beanies and lettered sweaters of campus days. But the real "class" of Kyser's show was his audience. If a contestant got stumped by a question, Kyser's cry, "Students!" brought an immediate answer from the crowd.

Within a year of his radio debut, Kyser and his band were featured in a movie, *That's Right, You're Wrong,* a title taken from one of his famous *Kollege* trademarks. Often in the quiz, Kyser would inform guests that they must answer his true-false questions backwards, giving a "false" answer to a true question. When they did, he shouted, "That's wrong, you're right!" When they failed, it was, "That's right, you're wrong!" Another well-remembered phrase was Kyser's use of "roger" for "right" or "correct." "Is it a roger or a wronger?" he would ask.

By late 1938, Kyser had moved to NBC, picked up Lucky Strike as sponsor and the name was changed. *Kollege* ran on NBC for Luckies for five years, broadcasting Wednesday nights in a 60-minute musical quiz format. His longstanding theme was "Thinking of You."

Many members of Kyser's original band continued with him through the years, becoming well-known personalities in their own right. Vocalists included Ginny Simms, Harry Babbitt, Sully Mason, Mike Douglas of later TV fame, and the King Sisters—Luise, Donna, Alyce, and Yvonne. During the war, Georgia Carroll, a young movie starlet, joined Kyser as a singer, and they were married on June 7, 1944.

Probably the most popular member of the group was Merwyn A. Bogue, who developed a comic haircut with bangs and became known as "Ish Kabibble." As Ish, he did novelty songs; he stayed with Kyser from the beginning of his career to his retirement in the early 1950's. Ed Cashman was early director; Frank O'Connor produced; writers included Henry Garson and Martin Work; Ken Niles announced. Later announcers were Bud Heistand, Verne Smith and Bill Forman, who doubled as the "versatile dean of public speaking." "Dean" Forman was billed as "39 throats behind a single collar button," and was highly touted for his ability with accents. One of the guessing games on the wartime *Kollege* involved contestants trying to peg Forman's dialects.

Kyser and his *Kollege* troup were among the nation's top entertainers for the armed forces. It was estimated that his band played more than 500 shows from camps, bases, and hospitals during the war years. In 1944, sponsorship went to Colgate; in 1946, the show was trimmed to 30 minutes. It moved to Saturday nights in 1947, and left the air late that year. It was picked up by ABC as a 30-minute daily show for Pillsbury, and was last heard in 1949.

Keep 'Em Rolling

Keep 'Em Rolling was a Sunday-night Mutual show, premièring November 9, 1941, and sponsored by the Office of Emergency Management in the interests of national defense. It promoted the theme of a strong America, built into a 30-minute variety format. Like the popular Treasury Department shows, *Keep 'Em Rolling* had its pick of top Hollywood and Broadway talent on a gratis basis. For its opener, the producers chose Maurice Evans to dramatize Maxwell Anderson's *Valley Forge*; government officials were interviewed on the world crisis, and Clifton Fadiman was brought in as moderator. Ethel Merman belted out the *Keep 'Em Rolling* theme, "The Flame of Freedom Is Burning," written especially for the show by Richard Rodgers and Lorenz Hart. Music was by Morton Gould and the series was produced by Arthur Kurlan.

Keepsakes

Keepsakes was a Sunday-night Blue Network program of concert music starring opera star Dorothy Kirsten and sponsored by Carter Products. It was on the air from September 1943 through September 1944.

Kitty Keene, Incorporated

Kitty Keene, Incorporated, was the name of a fictitious detective agency, first opening for business on NBC Red September 13, 1937. Kitty was another soapy heroine from the tragedy mill of Frank and Anne Hummert, but she rushed in where most soapers feared to tread. She was an honest-to-bubbles female detective, complete with a mysterious past and a beautiful face. In the grand tradition of Helen Trent, Kitty Keene retained her "woman of mystery" image, seldom discussing her past life even with her daughter Jill. She had once been a *Follies* showgirl, and that is all even we-the-listeners knew. Kitty's fight for happiness was wrapped up in the problems of Jill and her husband Bob. The show was packed with melodrama, and stands today as high camp. *Music! Violins!* The most heart-rending version of "None But the Lonely Heart" imaginable, and *Kitty Keene* is on the air.

The show originated from the WBBM Air Theatre in Chicago, with Beverly Younger, Gail Henshaw, and Fran Carlon all serving stints as Kitty. Janet Logan was Jill and a young Bob Bailey was Bob. Lenton Huntley wrote the epic, and the sponsor was Procter & Gamble, for Dreft. In retrospect, *Kitty Keene* is fascinating early soap. But again, it illustrated the folly of combining soapsuds with detective elements. The show disappeared during the 1941 season, about four years after its première.

Knickerbocker Playhouse

Knickerbocker Playhouse was a blatant First Nighter copy. Instead of riding up to the theatre in a cab, we went in through the back door and watched the play from backstage. But most of the other First Nighter elements were there. We had a host with a deep First Nighter voice, appropriately named Mr. Knickerbocker. He chatted amiably with announcer Gene Baker, giving us a verbal bill of fare. Instead of an usher, we had a stagehand bustling about, reminding us that the play was about to begin. We had a buzzer and the announcement, "Curtain going up!" at the opening of each play. And as if that wasn't enough, the lighthearted plays themselves bore striking resemblance to those usually done on The First Nighter Program. They were original works, usually light comedies. But they were decent radio, and for that we can forgive Mr. Knickerbocker all his transgressions into First Nighter territory. After a 1939 Sunday night CBS summer run, the show was booked into NBC Red September 21, 1940, and ran for about 15 months in its basic Saturday-night format for Drene Shampoo. Then, on January 24, 1942, Abie's Irish Rose became a continuing drama in the Knickerbocker Playhouse, and the old anthology format disappeared. Abie's Irish Rose eventually became a show in its own right, and the Knickerbocker Playhouse just trickled away.

The Kraft Music Hall

The Kraft Music Hall was a major NBC variety show, beginning June 26, 1933, as a revue for Paul Whiteman and his orchestra. It featured Jack Fulton, tenor, Roy Bargy, Ramona and, as master of ceremonies, the intellectually wisecracking music critic, Deems Taylor. Al Jolson took the mike late in 1933, and left the following year, soon to be starred in Shell Chateau. Bing Crosby came aboard in 1935, and remained at the helm until 1946. The Kraft Music Hall was trimmed from 60 to 30 minutes in 1942. During the year of transition after Crosby's departure for Philco, the emcee job was handled by Eddie Foy and others. Jolson returned to his old job in the fall of 1947. Nelson Eddy and Dorothy Kirsten held down the summer Music Hall for two years. The regular show lasted until 1949 under Jolson. See Bing Crosby and Shell Chateau.

Ladies Be Seated

Ladies Be Seated evolved from a show first heard on the Blue Network in 1930 called *Sisters of the Skillet*. *Sisters* featured Ed East and Ralph Dumke in a parody of a household hints show. In 1943, East and his wife Polly reorganized the format for the Blue Network, and presented a five-a-week 30-minute afternoon show called *Ed East and Polly*. It revolved around heavy audience participation and gags, in much the same vein as Art Linkletter's *House Party*. In 1944, the name was changed to *Ladies Be Seated*; Quaker Oats came aboard as sponsor in 1945, and the show continued until 1950, the final year for Philip Morris. By 1946, Johnny Olson had replaced East as emcee; Tom Moore handled the show in its final year. Producer Philip Patton thought up many of the gags, which ranged from blindfold husband-wife pranks to spaghetti-eating contests. In addition, there was a musical quiz, in which people won valuable prizes for filling in the missing words to songs. In its last days, *Ladies Be Seated* was giving away about $6,000 worth of merchandise a week.

The Land of the Lost

The Land of the Lost, first heard on ABC October 9, 1943, followed the adventures of young Isabel Manning Hewson and her brother Billy, "in that wonderful kingdom at the bottom of the sea, where all things lost find their way, and where the world is bathed in a shimmering green light."

The stories were written and narrated by Miss Hewson in her all-grown-up voice. In each episode, she told about her childhood adventures with Red Lantern, the talking fish who glowed under water, lighting the way for Isabel and Billy past the curtain of magic seaweed to "The Land of the Lost."

The magic seaweed enabled them to breathe underwater, and there they had marvelous adventures that only a preschooler could understand. *The Land of the Lost* was an enchanted kingdom of white sands and pearly palaces, ruled by an invisible monarch named King Find-All. Here came everything lost upon earth—hats, rings, umbrellas, toys—to form the kingdom's streets and avenues and begin their lives anew. There were the Street of Lost Shoes, the Hall of Lost Lamps, the Treasury of Lost Coins, and Lead, Pencil-vania, where all lost pencils go.

Here too were strange and mysterious sea creatures—Mike Pike with his "fin-feriority complex"; Kid Squid the boxing octopus, and Ralph Royster the singing oyster. There was a Lost Game Preserve, where all the lost games of the world (Parcheesi, backgammon, etc.) are kept on file. And in all of radio, Isabel and brother Billy were the only humans who knew of the kingdom and how to get there.

Betty Jane Tyler and Ray Ives played Isabel and Billy as kids; Junius Matthews and William Keene played Red Lantern, "the wisest fish in the ocean." Cyril Armbrister directed, with vocal arrangements (singing mermaids and such) by Peggy Marshall. Lyrics were by Barbara Miller, and Michael Fitzmaurice was announcer.

The series began on ABC Saturday mornings, shifted to Mutual in 1945, and had returned to ABC by 1947, finishing its run there in 1948. During the last year, the sponsor was Bosco chocolate-flavored syrup.

One of its best-remembered features was "Lucky Seven Time." Seven lucky kids who had written in describing lost treasures were given as near a likeness as the producers could find, the awards based on most interesting letters. Miss Hewson referred affectionately to her young listeners as "pollywogs," and reminded them frequently of the show's motto: "Never say lost."

Lassie

Lassie, the amazing collie owned and trained by Rudd Weatherwax, came to ABC June 8, 1947, in a 15-minute weekly show for Red Heart Dog Food. The series followed the successful MGM film, *Lassie Come Home*, and promoted Lassie as the wonder dog of many adventures. Weatherwax narrated the show, tossing Lassie cues for various barks, whines, growls, and whimpers suggested by the scripts. The dog usually handled her lines like an old trouper, but in occasional periods of stubbornness two animal imitators were on hand as fill-ins. They also doubled as the "other dogs" in the scripts. Weatherwax fell into the Lassie bonanza when a Hollywood man brought the dog to him for training. Rather than pay the training bill, the owner decided to give the dog away. For a time, Weatherwax let Lassie run free, then decided to take her in for a tryout when he heard that MGM was casting the film. At first she was rejected, but when the studio couldn't find just the right Lassie, Weatherwax tried again. This time, he had shined Lassie's coat and spent a lot of time putting her through basic movie training. She got the part and ultimately the radio show. Hobart Donovan wrote the radio scripts, Frank Ferrin produced, and Harry Stewart directed. *Lassie* was heard for one year as an ABC Sunday show. It moved to NBC Saturdays in 1948, still for Red Heart, and ran until 1950.

Leave It to the Girls

Leave It to the Girls came to Mutual on October 6, 1945, a creation of Martha Rountree, whose credits later included the prestige newsmaking show *Meet the Press*. At first Miss Rountree saw the show as a serious panel discussion among four career girls of problems submitted by the listening audience. As it developed, however, the show became far more comical than serious. Paula Stone was moderator, and producer Rountree tried for a panel comprised of one serious type, one calculating, one mature, and one punster à la Gracie Allen. The panel fielded such listeners' problems as: How does a man who has told his girlfriend he is a rich playboy tell her, now that they are engaged, about his real position, simple salesman? How does a mother handle her daughter's ambition to become an actress? Usually there was one slick-talking male on hand to "defend the men of America." George Jessel and Henry Morgan were among the "defenders"; they were equipped with a whistle that brought the focus to the male viewpoint. Among the panelists: Dorothy Kilgallen, Robin Chandler, Eloise McElhone, Ilka Chase, Lucille Ball, Sylvia Sidney, Constance Bennett, and Edith Gwynn. The show was heard as a Mutual sustainer Saturday nights from 1945 through 1947, and on Fridays until 1949.

Leonidas Witherall

Leonidas Witherall was a summertime detective series premièring on Mutual June 4, 1944, and also heard in 1945. It was based on a character created by Alice Tilton, and featured Walter Hampden as Leonidas and Agnes Moorehead as Mrs. Mollett, his housekeeper. An interesting character, Leonidas led a triple life. First, he was owner and teacher at Meredith, "an exemplary school for boys in a present New England town." On the sly, he was creator and writer of *Lieutenant Hazeltine,* a radio detective who was "master of every situation." Finally, Leonidas was himself an amateur sleuth, forever stumbling into cases of intrigue and murder. And always in his real-life cases, he found himself in intense competition with his fictional hero, Lieutenant Hazeltine. How, everyone naturally wondered, would Hazeltine handle this? The series was produced by Roger Bower.

Oh, yes—there's one more thing about Leonidas. His beard made him a dead ringer for William Shakespeare. People were always asking Leonidas if they'd met him in the public library. Some went as far as to call him Bill Shakespeare. Others call him just plain—uh—Bill.

Les Miserables

Les Miserables was presented in a special seven-part production on Mutual in the summer of 1937. This program boldly heralded the arrival of radio's greatest repertory. Appearing with Orson Welles across the seven-week run of Victor Hugo's masterpiece were Martin Gabel, Ray Collins, Alice Frost, Agnes Moorehead, Everett Sloane, Bill Johnstone, Peggy Allenby, Estelle Levy, Hiram Sherman, Betty Garde, Adelaide Klein, and Frank Readick. A year later, many of these players would follow Welles to CBS for the opening of *The Mercury Theatre on the Air.*

But *Mercury* was still a year away when Mutual took on Welles and his group, gave them a free hand and opened an unusual run of successive Friday-night slots. Welles played Jean Valjean, poor thief persecuted beyond all reason by the ruthless Inspector Javert. Valjean's trouble began with the theft of a bread loaf, multiplied with his repeated attempts to escape from prison, and culminated years later on his deathbed.

Gabel played Javert. Cosette, the orphaned girl who became Valjean's only source of joy, was played by Estelle Levy. The show began July 23, 1937, and ran until September 3.

Let George Do It

Let George Do It was a West Coast mystery-detective show first heard on Mutual-Don Lee in 1946. Bob Bailey, who would go on to better things in *Yours Truly, Johnny Dollar,* played private eye George Valentine. George got his cases with a newspaper ad à la *Box 13:* "Personal notice—danger's my stock-in-trade. If the job's too tough for you to handle, you've got a job for me, George Valentine. Write full details."

In the early shows, George's brawn was underplayed and his skill at solving scientifically all manner of murder and mayhem was brought to the fore. He was assisted by a rather dumb office boy named Sonny (Eddie Firestone, Jr.) and a secretary–girl Friday named Claire Brooks ("Brooksie" to George) played by Frances Robinson. Joe Kearns was Caleb the elevator man. Owen Vinson produced and Polly Hopkins wrote the scripts. A later, syndicated version featured Virginia Gregg as Brooksie, in a typical "snare the boss" man-chasing role. Don Clark directed this one; scripts were by David Victor and Jackson Gillis. Eddie Dunstedter pounded the organ. In all, it was quite respectable for a canned show, but George was just another detective with a gutsy style and a nose for trouble.

Let's Pretend

Let's Pretend was known as "radio's outstanding children's theatre." For more than twenty-three years, through two distinct formats, it delighted the very young with tales of witches and goblins, princes and princesses, leprechauns and talking animals.

Let's Pretend in its best-known format, began on CBS in 1939. It grew out of an earlier show, *The Adventures of Helen and Mary,* which was first heard on the same network September 27, 1929. As *The Adventures of Helen and Mary,* the show was already going strong when CBS hired young Nila Mack away from her hometown radio station and put her to work in children's radio.

Miss Mack had been an actress on Broadway and in vaudeville before coming to radio. For more than six years she played with Alla Nazimova's troupe, then left the stage to join the CBS staff around 1928. She left the network to return home, but returned in 1930 as director of *Helen and Mary.* She wrote the scripts, adapting her stories from the Arabian Nights, from Hans Christian Andersen, from the Brothers Grimm and Andrew Lang. She directed the productions and held auditions for budding child stars. Under her direction, *Let's Pretend* became the finest show of its kind, winner of almost fifty national awards.

In its heyday, after Cream of Wheat came aboard as sponsor, the show opened to the bouncy rhythm of maestro Maurice Brown's music, the cheering of kids in the studio, and the *Let's Pretend* theme. Together the cast sang:

Cream of Wheat is so good to eat
Yes we have it every day;
We sing this song, it will make us strong
And it makes us shout "Hooray!"
It's good for growing babies
And grown-ups too to eat;
For all the family's breakfast
You can't beat Cream of Wheat!

Host for the half-hour was "Uncle" Bill Adams, who opened each session with "Hel-loooooo, Pretenders!" The studio audience roared back, "Hel-looooo, Uncle Bill!" Then Bill would say, "How do we travel to Let's Pretend?" and one of the kids chimed in with something like, "Why don't we go on a railroad train?" It might also be a stratocruiser or a flock of geese; whatever, it became a signal for the sound man to get busy and fill the studio with train, plane, or goose noises. "All aboard! All aboard for Let's Pretend, Rumpelstiltskin, and points east!" And the train huffed its way out of Pretender Station for another 30 minutes of fantasy.

Let's Pretend was a foundation of Saturday-morning radio. A 1943 *Newsweek* reviewer found the show "filled with kings and queens and princes who ride talking horses through enchanted forests. It has beauteous maidens who must be rescued from witches, dragons, gnomes, dwarfs and other mythical fauna. Its characters travel in golden coaches, wear purple robes, pass through emerald halls to jade rooms, and drink from golden goblets."

Miss Mack dramatized such favorites as *Cinderella, The Sleeping Beauty,* and *Rumpelstiltskin.* For each holiday she wrote an original drama. One of them—*The House of the World*—was repeated each year at Christmas. Miss Mack believed that child actors could best convey the sense of awe and magic that she wanted for her show, and she enjoyed working with young people anyway. Many of the children who saw early duty on *Let's Pretend* became stars in adult life. Roslyn Siber went on to play Rosalie in *The Goldbergs.* Nancy Kelly became a star of screen and radio. Billy Halop was one of Hollywood's Dead-End Kids. Billy and Bobby Mauch went to Hollywood for the filming of *The Prince and the Pauper* in 1937, and Billy played in a series of films based on Booth Tarkington's *Penrod.* Jimmy Lydon was Henry Aldrich on the screen. Pat Reardon went to Broadway for *Junior Miss.* Other well-knowns who played in *Let's Pretend* were Skip Homeier, Walter Tetley, and Marilyn Erskine.

But the show also developed original talent, people who remained "Pretenders" to the end. Sybil Trent was discovered by Miss Mack in a New York "community sing," and served on the show into young womanhood. She was a "Pretender" in the early days of 1941, and was still aboard when the show went off in 1954. Jack Grimes, Miriam Wolfe, Michael O'Day, Gwen Davies, and Arthur Anderson were others who spanned the years. "Pretenders" of the early and middle 1940's included Hope Miller, Albert Aley, Edward Ryan, Patsy O'Shea, Lorna Lynn, Patricia Ryan, Jack Ayres, Alec Englander, Mary Ellen Glass, Barbara Adams, Larry Robinson, and Robert Lee. Studio technician in those years was Fred Hendrickson; announcers included George Bryan and Jackson Wheeler.

In 1943, CBS finally permitted a sponsor, Cream of Wheat, to carry the show. Cream of Wheat dropped it in 1952, and *Let's Pretend* was again sustained by the network.

By the 1950's, a mixed cast of steadies and newcomers dominated the show. Adult roles were now played by children who had grown up on the show. Evelyn Juster, Lillian Collins, Daisy Alden, Roger Sullivan, Rita Lloyd, Donald Madden, Lynn Thatcher, Stanley Martin, Diana Hale, Bill Lipton, Jack Jordan, Vivian Block, Robert Moran, Kingsley Colton, and Michael Dreyfus were carrying many of the parts.

Nila Mack died on January 20, 1953, and the writing was assumed by Johanna Johnston. Announcer was Warren Sweeney. Uncle Bill stayed to the end. In the last two years, the Nila Mack Award was given to the player who gave the year's best performance. It became a coveted honor, and a great tribute to the woman whose pen slew a thousand dragons. The last show was heard on October 23, 1954.

Let's Talk Hollywood

Let's Talk Hollywood was the *Information Please* of the film world, with a panel of Hollywood experts assembled to field movie questions from listeners. Listeners got a free subscription to *Photoplay* magazine if their question was used on the show. If they "stumped the experts," they won a "gold pass" good for free admission all year at their favorite theatres. The show was first heard July 4, 1948, on NBC and ran through the summer as a replacement for *The Jack Benny Program*. George Murphy was master of ceremonies. Regulars included Eddie Bracken, Edith Gwynn, and Erskine Johnson. Benny's sponsor, American Tobacco, carried *Let's Talk Hollywood* through its summertime run.

Life Begins at 80

Life Begins at 80 was a Jack Barry creation, patterned after his highly successful *Juvenile Jury*. In *Jury*, Barry assembled a panel of children to discuss the problems of their peers. In *Life Begins at 80*, the panelists, all octogenarians or older, spoke uninhibitedly about the troubles of the world. It was first heard on Mutual as a summer replacement July 4, 1948, outgrew its temporary status, and ran until September 24, 1949. It was also heard on ABC in the early 1950's.

Regular panelists included Fred Stein, 81; Eugenia Woillard, 83; Joseph Rosenthal, 84; and Georgiana P. Carhart, 83. Stein and Mrs. Woillard could always be counted on to disagree; Rosenthal was a deep thinker and Mrs. Carhart was a blatant flirt. Barry created the show in the wake of the *Juvenile Jury* success, thinking rightly that oldsters would be as free of tongue as youngsters. They were even more so; occasionally their comments were so candid that they bordered on risqué and, once started, they weren't as easy to hush. Barry couldn't take a chance on running this show live, as he did with *Juvenile Jury*, so he taped it and later edited out the indelicate parts. Despite the obvious humor of the show, it never attained the popularity of *Juvenile Jury* and lasted only a year. Barry used guests and rotating systems for the panel's fifth chair. Other regular panel members were Rose Baran, 89; Mrs. Ella Pomeroy, an ordained minister who admitted to "81-plus"; Pop Gordon, 92; and Captain Edwin Lane, 81, a former man of the sea with a long white beard. Producer, as on *Jury*, was Dan Ehrenreich. Barry often closed the show with a short piece of philosophy from writer Julia Ward Howe, who wrote of old age, at 90, that "all the sugar is at the bottom of the cup."

Life Can Be Beautiful

Life Can Be Beautiful had a plot that couldn't fail. Carol Conrad was young, afraid, and alone; a product of the big-town slums and not yet out of her teens. Seeking shelter, she found it with one of the grand old philosophers of daytime radio. For on that day—September 5, 1938—Carol found Papa David Solomon, owner of the Slightly Read Bookshop, and began her new life as his ward.

With the new life came a new name. Carol became the fiery, impetuous "Chichi," girl of the streets. Seeking a hiding place from Gyp Mendoza, the neighborhood bully, she was taken in by kindly old Papa David, who let her sleep on a pallet in the back room of his store. The pallet became a bed; the back room became Chichi's room, and for the next fifteen years she and Papa David shared their lives, troubles, and adventures.

That was the beginning of *Life Can Be Beautiful*, "an inspiring message of faith drawn from life, written by Carl Bixby and Don Becker and brought to you by Spic And Span." As she grew up, Chichi became a daughter to the old man. Her life, and the men in it, became the great concern of Papa David's last years.

That was why Papa David must have been particularly gratified when Chichi decided to marry Stephen Hamilton. Stephen was like a son to Papa David. A hopeless cripple, he too had been taken in by the kindly old book dealer. Papa David had given Stephen a job in the Slightly Read Bookstore when no one else would hire him. Chichi was impressed by Stephen's intellect, amazed that she could be loved by a man so much greater than she. A long-running romance was triggered; Stephen was partly cured of his paralysis through an amazing operation, then lost his legs in a later accident. Some listeners began clamoring for marriage. Bixby and Becker yielded to the outcry. Chichi and Stephen were married.

Almost immediately, the writers realized their mistake. Stephen was like a millstone around her neck. So after involving him with another woman and getting him entangled in a jewel heist, they killed him off with a heart attack. Stephen, one of the great sympathy characters of daytime radio, turned blackheart at the end. Even Chichi's baby died, the result of pneumonia caught when Stephen foolishly took him out unprotected in the rain.

Chichi, free again, became one of the most eligible singles of the matinée airwaves. The one consistent man in her life, her "chum from the streets" Toby Nelson, loved her passionately but without hope. Toby was just her pal (she was always "Cheech" to him), a shoulder to cry on when things got too tough. He was around for most of the run, disappearing to Korea a couple of years before the serial was dropped in 1954.

Life Can Be Beautiful was one of the best-loved of radio's soaps. To the actors who worked on it, the show became known by its first letters, LCBB, which translated over the years into the pet name "Elsie Beebe." Ralph Locke went all the way as Papa David, and died soon after the show left the air. Alice Reinheart played Chichi for the first eight years, and then the part was taken by Teri Keane, who finished it. Toby was Carl Eastman. Stephen Hamilton was first played by John Holbrook, later by Earl Larrimore.

Becker and Bixby shared the writing duties, each taking over for several weeks at a time and working out their plots by telephone. They began each show with some piece of heavy philosophy: for example, "John Ruskin wrote this: 'Whenever money is the principal object of life, it is both got ill and spent ill, and does harm both in getting and spending. When getting and spending happiness is our aim, life can be beautiful.' " And "Longfellow expressed the opinion that the Sabbath is the golden clasp that binds together the volume of the week . . . By the way, how long has it been since you've been to

church, where you'll find new assurances that life can be
beautiful. . . ?"
Despite the tearstained plots, Becker and Bixby thought of their
serial as a beam of hope in a dark world. It proved—they told *Time* in
1953—that, "however dark the world, this too will pass."

The Life of Riley

The Life of Riley was first heard on NBC in the summer of 1943. By
January 16, 1944, it had become a Sunday Blue Network show for the
American Meat Institute.

Chester A. Riley, radio's riveter and resident hardhat, might have
been the Archie Bunker of the 1940's. Riley didn't have Bunker's open
bigotry, but his expression of disgust, "What a revoltin' development
this is," became one of America's favorite sayings. William Bendix
was just about perfect as Riley. Rather a latecomer to the profession,
Bendix didn't act at all until he was 30, when the grocery store he was
running was closed by the Depression. For three years he worked with
the New Jersey Federal Theatre Project. Stock and Broadway followed, with Bendix scoring a stage triumph in William Saroyan's
1939 Theatre Guild play, *The Time of Your Life.* He began making
films in the early 1940's, and through the decade became known as
one of the screen's top character actors, turning in solid performances
in such films as *Lifeboat* and *Guadalcanal Diary.* Riley was probably
his best character—certainly his best-remembered part.

Riley was developed as the typical hard-working Joe, a guy who
did his job when he could find one, paid his bills when he had the
dough, raised good, lively kids, went to church as often as his wife
could drag him, probably bowled Wednesday nights and drank beer
before dinner. Riley was easily exasperated, but not easily defeated.
And he was most difficult to defeat when fighting for a flimsy cause.
Riley's character really came through best on thin ice. A leaking roof,
problems at the plant, or the manifestations of his kids' growing pains
were enough to send Chester A. Riley into pandemonium. Before he
was finished, what had been a minor problem was a Grade-A disaster.
Through it all, wife Peg tried to remain level-headed and understanding, but even she sometimes lost her cool before the 30 minutes were
up. The kids, Junior and Babs, watched their father's antics with
mixed awe—half fascination and half apprehension. They knew they
might be next on Chester A. Riley's list of targets.

Supporting players got a healthy share of the laughs. Gillis,
Riley's co-worker and pal, was also the fly in Riley's ointment. He
played a part quite like Ozzie Nelson's Thorny, only with more

sarcastic cynicism. Uncle Baxter became Riley's permanent house-guest, avoiding paying rent by reminding Riley constantly of the pint of blood he had given him in the past. Digby O'Dell, "the friendly undertaker," had a part similar to that of Peavey, the druggist of *The Great Gildersleeve*. Digger, as Riley called him, had one walk-on during the show in which Riley unleashed his problems and braced himself for a series of undertaker jokes. Digger's character was developed to the extreme; it became one of the funniest elements of the show. Well-played by John Brown—and far removed from his roles of Thorny on *Ozzie and Harriet*, Al on *My Friend Irma*, and Broadway on *The Damon Runyon Theatre*—Digger had a cold, clammy voice and was ghoulishly fascinated by death. He ended his brief appearance on each show with the stock farewell: "Cheerio; I'd better be shoveling off." Brown also played neighbor Gillis. Paula Winslowe played Peg for most of the run, and the kids were handled by, among others, Conrad Binyon and Sharon Douglas. Barbara Eiler replaced Sharon Douglas in January 1947; by 1945 Scotty Beckett was Junior, and later the part was played by Tommy Cook and Bobby Ellis. Hans Conried was the snide Uncle Baxter. Irving Brecher produced and Don Bernard was the show's first director. Writers included Alan Lipscott and Reuben Ship.

In 1945 *Riley* moved to Saturday-night NBC for Prell; it moved to Fridays in 1948, and changed sponsors—to Pabst Blue Ribbon—in 1949. Then it ran until 1951 as a Friday-night NBC show. Like *Ozzie and Harriet*, *The Life of Riley* was virtually unscathed by the arrival of television. It made the transition easily, with Bendix carrying on as ever, after the initial shows had featured Jackie Gleason as Riley. Bendix died in 1964.

Life with Luigi

Life with Luigi utilized one of the most difficult of all the audio arts—dialect humor. Being funny is much harder than being frightening, and being funny in a strange tongue magnifies the difficulty beyond the scope of all but a few talented actors. One such actor was J. Carrol Naish; another was Alan Reed, and a third was Hans Conried.

Bring the three together and you have *Life with Luigi*, a situation comedy about Italian immigrants, created by a Jew from New York and starring an Irishman in the title role. *Luigi* came to CBS September 21, 1948 as a 30-minute comedy. For a year it was sustained, then was picked up by Wrigley's Spearmint Chewing Gum, which carried it mostly as a Tuesday-night feature until 1953, when it left the air.

Life with Luigi ranks just behind *Amos and Andy, Lum and Abner,* and *The Goldbergs* in its warm, exaggerated portrayal of life for the minorities in America. Each week Luigi told of his adventures in a letter to his Mama Basko in Italy: "Dear-a-Mama-Mia! It's-a now summertime in-a-Chicago, and everybody's-a-feelin' very very hot-a!" That was a perfect lead-in for a show about the beach, and Luigi tried almost desperately during the half-hour to make his Mama-Mia understand how much he was learning about American life.

He had come from Italy in September 1948, sponsored by his countryman Pasquale, who owned a spaghetti palace in the Little Italy section of Chicago. Luigi's overpowering hope was that someday he would become an American citizen; to achieve that end, he began studying citizenship and government at night school. There, supervised by a buxom teacher named Miss Spalding, Luigi and other immigrants from other lands began to learn about George Washington and the United States Constitution. He met classmates Olsen, Horowitz, and also Schultz, a crusty German whose rheumatism was always killing him. Often the class played a strong part in the development of Luigi's stories.

But most of the action was set outside the classroom. Soon after his arrival in Chicago, Luigi rented a building adjoining Pasquale's Spaghetti Palace and opened an antique store. It didn't take him long to realize why Pasquale had brought him to America. Pasquale wanted to marry off his fat daughter Rosa, and he had Luigi tabbed as prospective son-in-law. Luigi was simply awed by Rosa's 300-pound frame, squeaky voice, and horrid laugh that belched out whenever Pasquale called her name. Pasquale's introduction of Rosa became one of the great running gags of the show.

Luigi and Pasquale were superbly played by J. Carrol Naish and Alan Reed. Reed, whose real name was Teddy Bergman, perfected Pasquale as a good-natured villain ranking with the Kingfish of *Amos and Andy.* Pasquale plotted against every enterprise that did not advance the cause of his daughter's marriage. He was a ruthless saboteur of Luigi's love life, masking his venom with the cheery greeting, "Luigi-mah-friend! 'Ello, Luigi, 'ello, 'ello!" And when Luigi's dreams were shattered—as Pasquale knew they would be —Rosa was always on hand to help pick up the pieces of Luigi's broken heart. "Just-a-so happen I'm-a-bring-a my little baby with-a-me. I'm-a-gonna call-er over. Oh Roooosa! Roosssa! *ROSA!!*"

The show was created by Cy Howard, who gave up a dead-end selling job to become one of radio's latter-day success stories. Howard already had *My Friend Irma* on the air when *Life with Luigi* came to CBS. Soon both were highly popular. *Luigi* was scheduled in direct competition with Bob Hope. But within the year, the new show was giving Hope run for the rating. Had *Life with Luigi* started earlier, it might have had one of radio's longest runs.

The shows were written by Mac Benoff and Lou Derman, directed by Benoff. Hans Conried played Schultz, Jody Gilbert was Rosa, Mary Shipp was Miss Spalding, Joe Forte was Horowitz and Ken Peters was Olsen. Luigi's young friend Jimmy was played by Gil Stratton, Jr., and occasionally by Alan Reed, Jr. Music was by Lyn Murray and later Lud Gluskin. The musical theme was a mixture of "Chicago" and "Oh, Marie," with the latter played softly on the accordion over closing credits and Luigi's "So long, Mama-Mia. Your lovin'-a-son-a, Luigi Basko, the li'l immigrant!"

The Light of the World

The Light of the World was an unusual soap opera, sponsored by General Mills in 15-minute serial form, but using the Bible as the core of all stories. The language was modernized and the stories flowed with the usual array of crises and heartbreaks, but each story came in substance from the Old Testament. Radio writers predicted an early demise for the series when it first came to NBC on March 18, 1940. The public, they said, would never stand having its Bible treated like a refugee from the soap vat.

As usual, they were wrong. *The Light of the World* thrived, and its audience grew steadily through the early 1940's. The scripts, written by sisters Katharine and Adele Seymour, tried to draw out the ancient characters and present their personalities in modern terms. Their efforts drew heavy fan mail and brought a heavy responsibility to be true to the original writings while keeping in the serial mold. A nonsectarian advisory board was established to review the scripts, and for each role, scores of actors were auditioned by producer-director Basil Loughrane. Bret Morrison, whose distinctive voice was also heard as *The Shadow*, narrated; Jim Fleming, Stuart Metz, and Ted Campbell were announcers, and Clark Whipple provided music on the organ. Sound effects were almost nonexistent, except for the occasional swish of robes or the rustle of opening parchment. The show was dropped by General Mills during a flour shortage in March 1946. But church groups across the land—many of which had used the program for Bible study—began clamoring for its return. It was returned to the lineup December 2, 1946, with an eleven-part adaptation of the Adam and Eve story. It starred Philip Clarke as Adam, Eleanor Phelps as Eve, and Mandel Kramer and Chester Stratton as sons Cain and Abel. Typical of soaps, it played heavily on Cain's unpredictable nature. *The Light of the World* lasted until 1950.

Lights Out

Lights Out, radio's ultimate horror show, was first heard locally, on Chicago station WENR, as a late-night 1934 15-minute feature. The show was created by Wyllis Cooper, then a staffer at NBC's Chicago studios. On April 17, 1935, it opened Wednesdays on NBC Red.

Cooper tried to make *Lights Out* reach new highs in intensity, and he succeeded admirably. Tucked away in an after-midnight slot in its early days, the show offered imaginative plays so filled with sinister, throat-clutching sound effects that it created a sensation. Like the plays, the openings made the best possible use of frightening imagery. Churchbells and a gong were the standard trademarks. An announcer broke the stillness with, "LIGHTS OUT, EV-RYBODY!" and the bell began its slow tolling of twelve chimes. Near the end, the wind came up. "This is the witching hour . . . It is the hour when dogs howl, and evil is let loose on the sleeping world . . . Want to hear about it? . . . Then turn out your lights!"

Upon Cooper's departure for the West Coast in 1936, NBC brought in Arch Oboler, a young playwright who had done some work for Rudy Vallee and for *Grand Hotel. Lights Out* really became Oboler's show. It was he who took it through the best years just before the war—these were the years when Oboler first began to experiment with some of the audio techniques that later made him famous.

So strong were the plays that some listeners still remember the basic plot lines. Highest on the list of memory teasers are "Cat Wife," a Karloff offering about a man whose wife turns into a human-sized cat, and "Chicken Heart," the tiny organ that grew and grew and grew, until—with a dull thump-THUMP, thump-THUMP, thump-THUMP—it consumed the world. *Lights Out* fan clubs sprang up. In 1937, when NBC tried to drop the show, hundreds of protests forced the scary program back into its late-night time slot, deliberately chosen so that the young might not be exposed to such mayhem.

Under Cooper and later under Oboler, the most grisly sound effects imaginable were employed. When people were electrocuted, sound men held frying bacon up the the mike and made sparks fly with a telegraph key attached to a dry cell battery. Bones were broken by smashing spareribs with a pipe wrench. Maple syrup dripping on a plate sounded just like drops of blood, and heads were lopped off with the precision swing of a sound man's blade chopping through a head of cabbage.

When Oboler created his famed tale of a man turned inside out by a demonic fog, the sound was created by soaking a rubber glove in water and turning it inside out while a berry basket was crushed. When a script called for the sound of a body splattering against pavement, a soaked rag was hurled against a cement slab. A sharp knife through a piece of pork gave a realistic impression of ripping flesh. And in what *Radio Guide* once described as "the most monstrous of all sounds," cooked spaghetti was squished and squashed to connote human flesh being eaten.

Under Oboler, *Lights Out* really came into its own as an instrument of the macabre. From his first show in May 1936, Oboler approached each new script as a challenge. After two years of constantly trying to top himself, Oboler quit and began his famous *Plays* series. But while he was there, both he and *Lights Out* became nationally renowned. The show was the true testing ground of his developing style. Many Hollywood stars, including Boris Karloff (then at the height of his fame as a film monster) made the trip to Chicago just to appear in Oboler's grim little 15-minute theatre.

Lights Out continued for a year after Oboler's departure, the scripting and directing done by NBC Chicago staffers. The show ran until August 16, 1939. In 1942, Oboler found his bank account sadly depleted after two years of doing government propaganda shows for nothing. So on October 6, 1942, he resurrected *Lights Out* from New York as a 30-minute Tuesday-night CBS entry for Ironized Yeast, later moving it to Hollywood and using many of his original scripts from the Chicago days. The new show had a lighter gong, creating the illusion of a chiming clock. With each chime, the announcer spoke one word—"It . . . is . . . later . . . than . . . you . . . think!" In this new format, Oboler worked with a floating cast of semi-regulars, including Irene Tedrow, Lou Merrill, Gloria Blondell, Wally Maher, Ted Maxwell, Earle Ross, Tom Lewis, and Templeton Fox. That one ran until September 28, 1943. *Lights Out* just trickled away after that. There were several subsequent attempts to revive it; two brief runs were heard on NBC during the summers of 1945 and 1946.

By the mid-1940's, the great contribution of Wyllis Cooper, who had been the prime mover behind the early *Lights Out*, was all but forgotten. A final series came to Mutual July 16, 1947. This last try—written by originator Cooper and Paul Pierce and starring Boris Karloff—lasted only a month. Then it was gone. *Lights Out* went into television in 1949, running until 1952. But the TV version never really achieved the popularity of the radio show, for those lurkers of the crypt whose inner ears still go thump-THUMP to the faint, faraway echo of a chicken heart.

Lincoln Highway

Lincoln Highway, first heard on NBC March 23, 1940, was a Saturday-morning show of big-time quality, featuring top stars of Broadway and Hollywood who usually were only available for prime-time evening shows. Its stories took place along the Lincoln Highway, a 3,000-mile strip of pavement stretching between Philadelphia and Portland, Oregon. *Lincoln Highway* was an anthology of life written by Jack Hasty, Brian Byrne, and Ed Sherry. Among the stars were Ethel Barrymore, Joe E. Brown, Harry Carey, Claude Rains, Victor Moore, Gladys George, Henry Hull, Luther Adler, Burgess Meredith, Joan Bennett, Betty Field, and Luise Rainer. Sponsored by Shinola Polish, it was billed as "radio's big, dramatic show in the morning." It ran for two seasons, gathering an audience of more than 8 million before its demise in 1942.

Linda's First Love

Linda's First Love, an obscure, corny, violin-filled serial for women, was syndicated in the early 1940's. It told the "true-to-life story of a girl in love with the world about us, and in love with wealthy young Kenneth Woodruff. She is a shop girl; he a young society man. The romance is frowned upon by Linda's friends and family, and Linda faces the world with her dream of happiness—alone." Should Linda go on fighting for Kenneth, despite the opposition of his dictatorial mother? Or should she return to faithful, steady Danny Grogan? Listeners were solicited for answers to that question, and the five best letters each week won for their writers seventeen-jewel Gruen watches. Arline Blackburn played Linda in this washboard weeper.

The Lineup

The Lineup took its listeners "behind the scenes of a police headquarters in a great American city, where under the cold, glaring lights pass the innocent, the vagrant, the thief, the murderer." Bill Johnstone, one of the early stars of *The Shadow*, took the role of Lieutenant Ben Guthrie, with Wally Maher as his sidekick, Sergeant Matt Grebb. The dramas were built around a police lineup gimmick, with Maher instructing suspects in a flat, bored monotone. The scripts were fast and realistic, with Johnstone's easy-going character played for dramatic effect against Maher's hot-headed gruffness. Raymond Burr, Jeanette Nolan, Sheldon Leonard, and Howard McNear were among the supporting players on *The Lineup*. Writers were Blake Edwards and, later, Morton Fine and David Friedkin; Jaime Del Valle was producer-director, getting his story ideas from newspapers and from slumming with cops on the beat. Elliott Lewis also served as producer. Music was by Eddie Dunstedter. The CBS series was first heard on July 6, 1950, and ran for three years—on Thursday, then Tuesday, and finally Wednesday.

Little Orphan Annie

Little Orphan Annie made its first appearance on April 6, 1931, as a six-a-week juvenile adventure serial on the Blue Network. In those days of box microphones and primitive hookups, *Annie* was the first of its kind, the genesis of the children's serial format, carving out a strong following among grade-school children and setting the pattern that would carry through radio in the coming decades.

The radio show was a reasonably faithful adaptation of the comic strip by Harold Gray. In the early days, the *Orphan Annie* theme was one of the best-known ditties of the air. It began

Who's that little chatter-box?
The one with pret-ty auburn-locks?
Who-oo can it be?
It's Little Orphan An-nie!

and was punctuated with " 'Arf,' says San-dy" interruptions at regular intervals. Later the words were dropped, when the show became *Adventure Time with Orphan Annie*. It opened à la *Captain Midnight*, with the drone of an airplane, the sound of a train whistle, and the hoot-hoot of a steamer. The *Annie* theme was played by organ, minus the words, and announcer Pierre André leaped straight into the Ovaltine vat.

The pattern was heavily descriptive action, carried mainly by dialogue and peopled by child heroes under 10. Annie, taken in as a child by a rural couple (Mr. and Mrs. Silo), went adventuring with her pal Joe Corntassel in the make-believe world of Tomkins Corners. Shot through the radio series were all the other memorable Gray characters: Daddy Oliver Warbucks, Punjab the Giant, and Captain Sparks. Later, her adventuring branched out from Tomkins Corners to include more exotic locales. She chased gangsters, criminals, and pirates with the best of them and remained a serial mainstay for more than a decade.

Shirley Bell played Annie from Chicago. The part was also played by Janice Gilbert. Allan Baruck and Mel Tormé served stints as Joe Corntassel. A separate production headed by Floy Hughes originated in San Francisco in the first two years, but was dropped in 1933, when the coast-to-coast Blue Network lines were completed.

Annie was one of the great premium-givers of all radio, dispensing decoders and shake-up mugs, all for a dime and/or the aluminum strip seal from the inside of an Ovaltine can. Ovaltine, which gave away the mugs as ideal promotions for the product ("It's a two-in-one gift; when you put the top on, it makes a keen shaker for mixing your ice-cold chocolate-flavored Ovaltine shakeup; and then, when you take the bright red top off, *presto!* The shaker turns into a swell, big drinking mug!") carried *Little Orphan Annie* through the 1930's, then abandoned the little heroine around 1940 to take up with *Captain Midnight*. After that, *Little Orphan Annie* gradually lost ground, and had disapperaed from the air by 1943.

The Little Show

The Little Show was the result of a strange collaboration between performer Robert Q. Lewis and writer Goodman Ace. It ran on CBS in 1947 and despite the obvious talent involved, never went anywhere. Lewis and Ace developed *The Little Show* in the mold cast by Henry Morgan, with outrageous digs at soap operas and other radio traditions. Perhaps there was room for just one Morgan in radio. Or perhaps, as Ace suggested, the network botched it by taking his original idea—a tight 15-minute show built around Lewis' quips —and making it a slick 30-minute package with orchestra and live audience. Anyway, the show was exactly what its name implied.

Lone Journey

Lone Journey was an on-again, off-again soap opera, first heard on NBC May 27, 1940, for Dreft. It ran three years before being replaced by *The Dreft Star Playhouse* in June 1943. *Lone Journey* was revived for a brief CBS run in 1946, under sponsorship of Carnation Evaporated Milk, and was revived again—the time on ABC for Lever Brothers—in 1951. The show was written by Sandra Michael in collaboration with her brother Peter. Miss Michael, one of daytime radio's most distinguished writers, had won a coveted Peabody Award in 1942 for another serial, *Against the Storm*. *Lone Journey* was based on people she knew in Montana and was drawn from real events. It told the story of Nita and Wolfe Bennett, ranchers in Montana whose Spear-T Ranch was set near the real mining town of Lewiston. Les Damon was Wolfe, and the part later was played by Staats Cotsworth. Eloise Kummer, Betty Winkler, and Claudia Morgan took stints as Nita. The show disappeared for good in 1952.

The Lone Ranger

The Lone Ranger was first heard January 30, 1933, on Detroit station WXYZ. The show was truly a product of Depression America. Soon after the stock market crashed, George W. Trendle and John H. King decided to go into radio. Trendle was a lawyer turned theatre executive, King a theatre palace pioneer who was said to have built one of the first movie houses in the nation. In partnership, they bought Detroit's station WXYZ, then a CBS outlet. Trendle made some immediate changes. He looked for more creative programming at the local level, and began to put together a company of acting talent for WXYZ productions. CBS wouldn't permit any tampering with its prime-time schedule, so Trendle severed his connections with the network and prepared to go on alone. Independence was particularly precarious in those days, and Trendle's decision to cast off his affiliation was a gutsy one.

The station was soon dropping hundreds of dollars a week, but Trendle had an idea. He would develop a new show, a Western of unprecedented wholesomeness, with a bigger-than-life hero distinguishable from all others. He set down some basics and submitted them to his staff for reaction, took their suggestions under advisement, and emerged with a rough outline of his hero. The outline led ultimately to this general background:

In Bryant's Gap the canyon narrows and the cliffs rise high on either side, and the wind whistles through the rocks that have cracked away and fallen. Just inside the gap is a small, grassy hill, an enigma in the bleak surroundings of rock and wind-blown sand. Beyond the hill, at the base of the cliff, a deep cave cuts into the rock. Nearer, just coming into view now, five crude wooden crosses mark the top of the hill. They have been here a long time.

Many years ago, six Texas Rangers chased the ruthless Butch Cavendish gang through the badlands for a final showdown at Bryant's Gap. The party was headed by Captain Dan Reid, and among those in his command was his younger brother John. The Reid brothers had been partners in a rich silver mine strike before duty called; they planned to return to the mine when their service with the Rangers was through.

But they rode into an ambush. The Cavendish gang fired down upon them with high-powered rifles from both rims of the canyon. Trapped on the smooth floor, Captain Reid asked one final promise of his younger brother: "My wife and son Danny are coming out here soon. If you get through this, work our silver mine and see that they get my share."

John Reid knew that the odds were against him. His brother fell, then John too was hit. From the rim, the Cavendish gang watched the massacre for a long time. Nobody moved.

Satisfied, Butch Cavendish rode away with his men. The floor of Bryant's Gap was still again.

That night an Indian examined the bodies by moonlight. One man lived. The Indian carried young John Reid to the cave, where he bathed and dressed the wounds. Then he buried the five Texas Rangers and, realizing that the outlaws might return, he made a sixth grave and left it empty. Only when the fiendish Butch Cavendish was brought to justice could the sixth mound be dismantled and the earth smoothed over.

For four days the Indian cared for the lone surviving Ranger. At last John Reid's eyes fluttered open. At once Reid recognized the Indian as a childhood friend whose life he had once saved.

"Your name is Tonto," he said.

"You remember," the Indian replied with satisfaction.

"Years ago you called me kemo sabe," Reid said.

"That right, and you still kemo sabe. It mean 'faithful friend.' "

Reid asked about the fate of his companions.

"You only Ranger left," Tonto said. "You Lone Ranger."

And so, in the cave below Bryant's Gap, John Reid became the Lone Ranger. There he donned the mask that would become his trademark. He buried his old identity along with his five comrades, and he and Tonto made a pact: "As long as you live, as long as I live, I will ride with you!"

To transfer the character from idea to script, Trendle hired Fran Striker, a young, hungry writer from Buffalo who had worked with the station on another project. Striker had talked with his pioneering uncle, who had once worked in a Denver saloon, and he had some ideas of his own. It was Striker who fleshed out Tonto, who filled the Ranger's guns with silver, and who added the cry, "Hi-Yo, Silver!"

The silver mine became the Ranger's chief source of income and the source of the silver bullets that filled his sixgun. He found a wild white stallion, named him Silver, and made silver shoes for the horse's feet. He hired an honest old man "of modest needs" to work the mine. Then he set out to find his lost nephew, Dan Reid, and to bring the men of the Cavendish gang to justice.

Such was the fictional heritage of The Lone Ranger, one of the most famous champions of all radio.

Through the month of December 1932, Striker and Trendle worked on the character, refining the image until—to Trendle—it was just about perfect. Trendle vetoed Striker's suggestion that the Ranger be humanized with a sense of humor. Nor did Trendle agree with others in his staff that the Lone Ranger should talk in Western slang. Trendle wanted a masked man with grim dedication to his single purpose, a man who never clipped a 'g' or failed to use good grammar. The Lone Ranger had a code, and he never broke it. And it was Trendle's belief that kids would buy it.

And they did. When the show was less than four months old, it drew more than 24,000 replies to its first premium offer. About 70,000 children turned out to see the masked man in person at a school function, creating pandemonium for traffic police and causing the producers to keep the Lone Ranger under wraps thereafter. The show's fame and range grew rapidly.

For most of its first year, it was sustained by the station, and offered its first show for Silvercup Bread November 27, 1933. Gradually the program's fame spread beyond the confines of its small Michigan audience, going to WGN Chicago, then to WOR, New York. These three stations formed the backbone of the Mutual Network in 1934, with WOR as its hub and The Lone Ranger as its biggest early-evening attraction. With the formation of the Mutual Network, The Lone Ranger was heard throughout the East and Midwest.

For the next twenty-two years, the masked man and his Indian companion filled the air with Western thrills. "A fiery horse with the speed of light, a cloud of dust and a hearty Hi-Yo Silver! The Lone Ranger rides again!"

From the beginning of its run, The Lone Ranger was a Western of new and original flavor. It was the first juvenile adventure set to classical music. Even today, many people think Rossini's classic "William Tell Overture" originated on The Lone Ranger. The masked man became the most respected champion of the fictional West, as much a part of Americana as Lewis and Clark. He was a tough, hard man with a will of iron and an unswerving sense of justice. He had few weaknesses, and meted out law and order with the objectivity of a computer. And even though he never smoked or drank, never shot to kill, and subscribed to the highest ideals of American life, the Lone Ranger maintained his credibility to the end.

In more than two decades of broadcasting, only one man comes to mind as having died at the Lone Ranger's hand, his deadly enemy,

Butch Cavendish. Even then, it was clear-cut self defense. After breaking out of federal prison, Cavendish tracked the masked man and his young nephew back to Bryant's Gap, and they fought a battle to the death on the cliffs high above the massacre site.

Trendle had as much trouble with the Lone Ranger's voice as he had with the image. A man remembered by Trendle only as Jack Deeds was the first to play the part, but he was replaced within the month by George Seaton, who would become a film director. He too proved unsuitable and in May 1933 an unheralded WXYZ staffer named Earle Graser got the role. In Trendle's opinion, Graser's voice carried just the right blend of intelligence and authority; in time it would become as well-known as the president's voice. Graser, who had joined WXYZ in 1931, was to play the Lone Ranger for the rest of his life. For more than eight years, this law school graduate with three college degrees was the masked rider of the plains, for whom "danger lay at the end of every trail." Ever in character, Graser championed the cause of right and vigorously promoted automobile safety. National safety clubs were formed in his name.

Regional networks were added, and in January 1937, the Don Lee Network introduced the show to children of the West Coast. Silvercup Bread continued as sponsor until early 1939, when Bond Bread began paying the bills. General Foods became the sponsor in 1941.

Then, early on the morning of April 8, 1941, the unthinkable happened. Just outside the little town of Farmington, Illinois, Graser was killed in an automobile accident. His death created a crisis. For a time, the Lone Ranger was written out of the show, leaving Tonto to carry on alone. When the Ranger did come back, it was with the slightly huskier tones of Brace Beemer, who had announced the show under Graser. Beemer, a farmer's son, had won a Purple Heart for service in World War I. He picked up where Graser had left off, with no lapse in quality and no blatantly disturbing change of characteristics. The Lone Ranger went on as before, and Beemer played the part from 1941 through 1955. He died in 1965.

In May 1942, the Blue Network outbid Mutual for the show, and by 1945 it was estimated that the Lone Ranger and Tonto had put away nearly 2,000 crooks. The voice of Fred Foy, best-known of the Lone Ranger announcers, rang out with authority:

> With his faithful Indian companion Tonto, the daring and re-sourceful masked rider of the plains led the fight for law and order, in the early western United States. Nowhere in the pages of history can one find a greater champion of justice. Return with us now to those thrilling days of yesteryear . . . From out of the past come the thundering hoofbeats of the great horse Silver! The Lone Ranger rides again!

Virtually the entire dramatic staff at WXYZ worked on *The Lone Ranger,* giving the show a rotating cast of up to fifty. Yet many distinctive voices turned up again and again. John Todd went virtually all the way as Tonto. Paul Hughes played dozens of roles, from badmen to pompous army colonels to the Lone Ranger's friend, Thunder Martin. With his unusual way of slurring words, Hughes had the third most recognizable voice on the show.

Trivia buffs will remember that Tonto's horse was named Scout; Dan Reid's horse was Victor. Directors and producers of the show included James Jewell, Charles Livingstone, and Fred Flowerday. Striker became chief writer, turning out 60,000 words a week in radio scripts, *Lone Ranger* comics, and novels and overseeing scripting of Trendle's other great juveniles, *The Green Hornet* and *Sergeant Preston of the Yukon.* Striker was a singular talent. Listeners were comfortable with his style. Striker made sure they knew about the masked man's disguises too. The fans never needed the admiring words of the sheriff to know that, "shucks, that warn't no prospector, boys. He's the Lone Ranger!"

The Lone Ranger continued as a three-a-week Blue-ABC show until May 27, 1955.

The Lone Wolf

The Lone Wolf was a sustaining Mutual detective show, based on the stories by Louis Joseph Vance and running Tuesday nights during the 1948–49 season. "Lone Wolf" was the pet name for Michael Lanyard, just another radio gumshoe. He got the name because he worked alone and was single. When he wasn't up to his neck in cadavers, Lanyard could usually be found sipping highballs at the Silver Seashell Bar and Grill, his favorite haunt. It was more than a little reminiscent of another detective series, *The Falcon.* When the show started in 1948, Gerald Mohr played Lanyard and Jay Novello was his butler. By 1949 Walter Coy starred as Lanyard, and Rex Koury provided music on the organ.

Lonely Women

Lonely Women, strictly a wartime soap opera with a wartime theme, told of women separated from their men by war. Written and conceived by Irna Phillips, the action revolved around Marilyn Larimore, a Fifth Avenue model, and Judith Clark, a lovesick secretary, played by Betty Lou Gerson and Barbara Luddy. Other prominent "lonely women" were Marilyn's sister Bertha Schultz (Patricia Dunlap), Jean

Evans, a confused young girl (Eileen Palmer), Nora the housekeeper (Nannette Sargent), and Peggy the elevator operator (Harriette Widmer). Mrs. Schultz was played by radio's "mother of the air," Virginia Payne. *Lonely Women* began as strictly an all-girl affair, but gradually broadened its scope to include men. It was sponsored by General Mills on NBC, and ran one season beginning June 29, 1942.

Lonesome Gal

Lonesome Gal was first heard at Station WING, Dayton, Ohio on October 13, 1947. For two years it remained strictly a local disc jockey show, with sultry, sexy Jean King wooing the guys in her most haunting style and best come-hither voice. Miss King, identified only as "Lonesome Gal," spoke in as intimate a manner as radio would allow, as though she and her one male listener were alone over candlelight and wine. She called him "muffin" and "baby" and, judging from the frantic phone response from lonely men across town, must have hit a universal emotion.

In December 1949 she decided to syndicate the show; within six months she had more than fifty stations and an income of six figures. Her show was unusual syndication fare, because each broadcast was completely localized, including local commercials which she wrote and read herself. Miss King accomplished the localization by maintaining active correspondence with Chamber of Commerce officials in cities where the show was running; thus, she was able to describe town parks, monuments, and streets as though she had actually been there. But it meant a hectic grind, writing and recording almost 300 separate shows a week. Miss King, a refugee from the *Tarzan* films, had played briefly in *I Love a Mystery* in 1943, but had dropped out of radio to try movies. She had no money and no job when she hit Dayton, and happened to land at WING at just the right moment. Soon she was purring "Hiiiieee, baaayyybeee," driving men nuts, and wearing a mask for all public appearances.

Lora Lawton

Lora Lawton, yet another in the almost endless line of Hummert soaps, told the story of "what it means to be the wife of one of the richest, most attractive men in all America—the story of the conflict between love and riches in a world so many dream of, but where so few dreams come true." It hadn't always been so. When she arrived on the NBC scene on May 31, 1943, Lora Lawton was merely a housekeeper for Peter Carver, head of the Washington-based Carver Ship-building Company. But Lora and Peter eventually married, and *Lora Lawton* slipped into the familiar Hummert themes of jealousy, marital strife, and half-crazy suitors. In one late 1947 sequence, Peter was whisked away to a lonely farmhouse on the coast of France by Ilsa Bourg, "a strange girl with whom he has become so involved."

Lora Lawton set the pace for premium giveaways on daytime radio. In the same 1947 sequence, listeners were offered a set of brightly colored Christmas cards, "just like the ones that brought Lora and Peter together again." Longtime sponsor of *Lora Lawton* was Bab-O. The show was gone by 1950. Joan Tompkins initiated the role; by 1946 it had passed to Jan Miner. Peter Carver was played by Ned Wever and James Meighan. Other prominent cast members were Ethel Wilson as May Case, Peter's secretary and Lora's trusted confidante; William Hare as Angus MacDonald, Peter's brother-in-law; and Lawson Zerbe as Lora's brother-in-law Rex. Marilyn Erskine played Gail Carver, Peter's spoiled young sister who married Angus MacDonald. James Van Dyk played Clyde Houston, editor of the magazine where Lora worked; Elaine Kent was Clyde's wife Iris, and Ann Shepherd was heard as 1947 troublemaker Hillary Strange. The show's theme was first sung, later played on the organ: "Just a little love, / A little kissssss, . . ."

Lorenzo Jones

Lorenzo Jones was Frank and Anne Hummert's new approach to afternoon soap opera serials. Soaps had always been filled with misery and unhappiness—how about a show built around comedy? They first tried it on the air April 26, 1937, in a late-afternoon 15-minute slot on NBC. The audience kept buying it for eighteen years.

While it lasted, *Lorenzo Jones* was part of a "just-before-Jack Armstrong" tradition, an hour that also included *Backstage Wife* and *Stella Dallas*. It was NBC's last gasp of tear-soaked melodrama before the kiddies' hour, and the Hummerts saw no reason to go out with a frown. And so, to the bouncy rhythm of "Funiculi, Funicula," came Lorenzo Jones, a mechanic at Jim Barker's garage whose two great loves in life were his wife Belle and tinkering around with inventions (not always in that order).

Lorenzo left us with the hope that we had been able to "smile a while" at his capers. The capers usually concerned some hare-brained scheme or impractical concoction, such as the sulphur water cure-all that got him arrested for selling medicine without a license. Lorenzo's inventions often turned out that way. Once in the late

1940's he devised a triple-spouted teapot, with spouts for strong, medium, and weak. The ever-patient, devoted Belle suffered through them in silence. To overcome the lack of melodrama, the Hummerts added strong doses of listener identification:

> We all know couples like lovable, impractical Lorenzo Jones and his devoted wife, Belle. Lorenzo's inventions have made him a character to the town, but not to Belle, who loves him. Their struggle for security is anybody's story, but somehow with Lorenzo it has more smiles than tears.

Lorenzo Jones continued as the afternoon bright spot for almost fifteen years. Then suddenly the show turned away from smiles and began to employ some of the Hummerts' favorite tricks. Lorenzo got mixed up with thieves and criminals. He became yet another victim of total amnesia. The amnesia factor continued for months, then years. Finally, just in time to bid his fans farewell, Lorenzo was whisked back to reality and loving Belle's arms. Rather a strange climax to a show that had built its reputation around a "smile a while" theme.

Karl Swenson, who dropped a budding medical career to go into radio in 1937, went all the way as Lorenzo. Belle was played by Betty Garde and Lucille Wall. Frank Behrens played Jim Barker and Joseph Julian was Lorenzo's friend Sandy Matson. Grady Keddy and others played Barker's wife Irma. Sterling Drugs carried the show for Phillips Milk of Magnesia and Bayer Aspirin until 1949, when Procter & Gamble took over. Like most of its contemporaries, *Lorenzo Jones* was snuffed out by TV lights in 1955.

Louella Parsons

Louella Parsons tried her first Hollywood talk show locally in 1928 for Sunkist oranges. It was an interview format, notable mainly for its failure. Miss Parsons, Hearst columnist from the film city, also served as hostess for the dramatic shows *Hollywood Hotel* and *Hollywood Première*. Her best-remembered gossip program was her Sunday-night show for Jergens Lotion, which ran on ABC from 1945 through 1951. She was given the 9:15 P.M. slot after successfully substituting for Walter Winchell, ace Jergens news gossip, who had the quarter-hour beginning at 9 o'clock. That gave Jergens a full half-hour corner on the gossip market, with Winchell reporting out of New York and Miss Parsons following immediately from Hollywood. While preparing for her own show, Miss Parsons always kept a wide-open ear cocked to Winchell, cringing whenever he beat her on an item of West Coast origin.

Luke Slaughter of Tombstone

Luke Slaughter of Tombstone was ushered into CBS February 23, 1958, in an era that saw a rash of new Westerns (Frontier Gentleman, Fort Laramie, Have Gun, Will Travel) and little else. This one starred Sam Buffington as Luke Slaughter, Civil War cavalryman turned Arizona cattleman. "Across the territory, from Yuma to Fort Defiance, his name was respected or feared, depending on which side of the law you were on . . . Man of vision . . . Man of legend . . . Luke Slaughter of Tombstone!" It opened à la Have Gun, with Buffington/Slaughter delivering his ultimatum:

> Slaughter's my name, Luke Slaughter. Cattle's my business. It's a tough business; it's big business. And there's no man west of the Rio Grande big enough to take it from me.

The series was directed by William N. Robson, with writing by Fran Van Hartesveldt and a musical score by Wilbur Hatch.

Lum and Abner

Lum and Abner was a leisurely quarter-hour stroll through the sticks. The old "Jot 'Em Down Store" first opened for business in April 1931, on Station KTHS, Hot Springs, Arkansas. Lum was Lum Edwards and Abner was Abner Peabody—in real life Chester Lauck and Norris Goff, but fans rarely if ever heard those names. What they did hear was dialect humor in the Amos and Andy tradition—an effective mix of comedy and soap opera—but supplanting the burnt cork of blackface with the whiskers and tattered clothes of the hillbilly.

Lauck was a small-town finance clerk and Goff was a grocery man in the same town when a benefit performance for a local Lion's Club turned their lives around. Both were born-and-bred natives of Arkansas. Lauck was born February 9, 1902, at Alleene; Goff May 30, 1906, in Cove—just a few miles away. As kids they both moved "up the road" to Mena, Arkansas, with their families and there they met in grade school. Goff developed a reputation of being able to handle himself with older boys; early in life he got tagged with the nickname "Tuffy," and he and Lauck became good friends. During the summers, they worked in town—Goff in his father's grocery store, Lauck in his dad's lumber yard. After work they would get together for some home-folks mimicry, experimenting with voice patterns and homespun characterizations. There, in those lazy 1920's summertime days, the nucleus of *Lum and Abner* began to form.

Both men still had some living to do first. Contrary to their radio images, both were college educated. They entered the University of Arkansas, but Goff switched to Oklahoma and Lauck went away to Chicago. After graduation they returned to Mena, marrying childhood girlfriends and settling into steady jobs. It might have ended there, except for the 1930 benefit that led to a radio audition that led to *Lum and Abner.*

The boys thought they were great blackface comics. Their first plan was to take their blackface act to the audition. But when they got to the station they found the wings full of Amos and Andy imitators. They shifted their focus on the spot, dragged out their "fellers from the hills," and logged their skit as "Lum and Abner." Lauck became Lum; a strange name. He had never known anybody named Lum. Goff was Abner, a solid hillbilly name lifted from a real man in the nearby village of Waters. The Jot 'Em Down Store, which Lum and Abner owned in partnership, was inspired by the general store owned by Goff's dad. And with those crude elements, *Lum and Abner* was on the air. By July 1931 *Lum and Abner* had moved to Chicago as a summer replacement for the NBC variety show *Gene and Glenn*; the earliest sponsor was Quaker Oats. By 1935, the five-a-week show was on the Blue Network for Horlick's Malted Milk. The show would be on the air, on various networks, for various sponsors, for the next twenty-two years.

As the show developed, the characters took shape and came alive. Abner was the whining gambler who loved checkers and horse trading; Lum was more careful about money and legal wheeling-dealing. Both were vulnerable to con men. New characters, all played by Lauck and Goff, were added as the show progressed. Goff became Squire Skimp, local loan shark and con man extraordinaire. Goff also played Dick Huddleston, postmaster and owner of a rival store in Pine Ridge, mythical community where the Jot 'Em Down Store was located. Lauck was Cedric Weehunt, the village idiot, and Grandpappy Spears, whose greatest pastime was beating Abner at checkers. Most of the action took place in the store, in the back-and-forth dialogue between two or more of these rustic characters. Eventually more characters of great contrast, such as the weak-kneed Mousy Gray (Goff) and the town tough Snake Hogan (Lauck), were added. But the series was several years old before a woman's voice—even a mimic—was heard in Pine Ridge. By the mid-1930's, several female characters had been introduced, but their parts were all done offstage. Abner talked often of his wife, Lys-beth; there was much discussion about Sister Simpson and Lum's heartthrob, Evalena. Later, real women were added to the cast; Zasu Pitts joined Andy Devine, Clarence Hartzell, and Cliff Arquette and became a semi-regular in the 30-minute days. But in the beginning, with Lauck and Goff carrying the entire show, there was just no place for a feminine voice.

The partners did it all in the early days. They did their own writing, and often ad-libbed their way through half the show. As *Lum and Abner* prospered, writers and elaborate sound effects and the music of Opie Cates' orchestra were added. Hartzell played Ben Withers, a hilarious character cut from the cloth of his great Uncle Fletcher performance on *Vic and Sade*.

Though it was seldom described, the Jot 'Em Down Store took on vivid characteristics. One of the memorable sound effects—possibly because there were so few—was the squeaking screen door whenever anyone entered. Here hung all manner of country necessities, from buggy whips and harnesses to washtubs and garden tools. It seemed real because it *was* real. A few miles from Mena, in the small village of Waters, there really were stores like that. There really was a Dick Huddleston, who knew Lauck and Goff well. Even Waters had its day in the *Lum and Abner* limelight. In April 1936, in celebration of the show's fifth year on the air, Waters went through an act of Congress and got its name changed. Pine Ridge had arrived.

The show switched to CBS for Postum in 1938, running three times a week until 1940, when the stars dropped out of radio for a year to make movies. In 1941, *Lum and Abner* returned as a four-a-week Blue feature for Alka Seltzer, running in that format on ABC until 1947. In the fall of 1948, it opened on CBS for Frigidaire as a half-hour Sunday situation comedy. Until the 1948 30-minute version, a conscious effort was devoted to simplicity. There were few sound effects and little music. The show's theme, "Evalena," was composed and played on the organ by Sybil Chism Bock, wife of a network publicist, who had also served for a time as organist on *One Man's Family*. The episode of the day was usually a one-act dialogue, punctuated heavily by Lum's grumbling and Abner's catch phrase, "I-doggies, Lum . . ."

The show moved to Wednesday in 1949, and the Ford Motor

Company became the sponsor. A final run of 15-minute shows began on ABC in the early 1950's. *Lum and Abner* broadcast its final show May 15, 1953.

The Lux Radio Theatre

The Lux Radio Theatre was first heard on NBC October 14, 1934, dramatizing a mixture of movie and Broadway plays from New York. It was originally a Sunday-afternoon show, but moved into its long-running Monday-at-9 P.M. slot when it jumped to CBS on July 29, 1935.

Less than a year after its arrival on the air, *The Lux Radio Theatre* began to sag. Directed by Tony Stanford from New York, the show faced a severe shortage of adaptable Broadway material; ratings had dropped more than four points. Unless something changed, the show was doomed.

Given the job of making something change was Danny Danker, an executive with J. Walter Thompson, the ad agency handling the Lux account. Danker saw, even in those dark Depression days, that the trend of radio drama was toward Hollywood, where a radio show had almost unlimited access to the most famous names in entertainment. Louella Parsons had already broken the ice with *Hollywood Hotel*, the first big West Coast glamor show, and some of the variety programs even then were setting down roots in the film city. Danker reasoned that a super-extravagant production featuring top stars in movie scripts would be exactly the right prescription for the ailing show. That was his recommendation; *The Lux Radio Theatre* moved from New York to Hollywood on June 1, 1936.

Continuing the thinking along extravagant lines, the agency hired Cecil B. DeMille as producer-host. There were no illusions that DeMille would be cheap; Lever Brothers knew he would cost them money—DeMille's ideas of "bigness" had always carried hefty price tags. This was the same film director who had parlayed a "damn the cost" attitude into Hollywood immortality, turning out Biblical epics like *The Ten Commandments* and *King of Kings*, covering studio lots with elaborate, costly sets, and going through as many as 10,000 extras a day to achieve a single effect. His salary alone for the Monday-night performances was $1,500 (later raised to more than $2,000) a week. And even though DeMille was producer in name only, the deeper illusions of Hollywood glamor had a hefty price tag. A flat fee of $5,000 was soon established (Clark Gable got $1 over top scale, just to be able to say he was the highest-priced star) for big-name Lux talent. A run-of-the-mill production used two such names, and special shows contained three or four. Frequently the tab for a single program ran well over $20,000.

Broadcast from the Music Box Theatre on Hollywood Boulevard, *The Lux Radio Theatre* served notice with its first West Coast production that the new era had arrived. *The Legionnaire and the Lady* starred Clark Gable and Marlene Dietrich. It was followed on June 8 by *The Thin Man* with William Powell and Myrna Loy, and on June 15 by Al Jolson and Ruby Keeler in *Burlesque*. Other highlights of the first year included *The Voice of Bugle Ann* with Lionel Barrymore and Anne Shirley; *Chained* with Joan Crawford and Franchot Tone; *Main Street* with Barbara Stanwyck and Fred MacMurray; *The Jazz Singer* with Al Jolson; *Saturday's Children* with Robert Taylor and Olivia de Havilland; *Men in White* with Spencer Tracy, Virginia Bruce, and Frances Farmer; *Mr. Deeds Goes to Town* with Gary Cooper; *A Farewell To Arms* with Clark Gable and Josephine Hutchinson; and *The Plainsman* with Fredric March and Jean Arthur. It became a Monday night powerhouse, consistently among radio's top 10 shows throughout the 1930's and 1940's.

Danker understood that you get what you pay for, and thought the stars' on-the-air endorsement of Lux soap would be worth the price. Danker died in 1944, but lived long enough to see his theory work on both fronts. Housewives flocked to stores to buy Lux, and *The Lux Radio Theatre* became one of radio's all-time great attractions.

There were a few close calls, but year after year the program went off on schedule. *The Plainsman* almost didn't make it—stars Gary Cooper and Jean Arthur came down with an eleventh-hour flu bug. Fredric March, brought in as a replacement for Cooper, stayed up all night before the show, taking a cram course in a Western dialect he had never before used. With Robert Taylor's first appearance, a flock of adoring women crashed the theatre through an open fire escape door, shutting out many who had tickets. Lux was like that. Every Monday was like a new opening night, with new stars, the glitter of marquee lights, and a flock of persistent autograph hounds who even tried to break into rehearsals.

Danker had wanted an extravaganza, and he got it. In the DeMille years, more than fifty people were required for each show. Sometimes the stage couldn't hold them all. Louis Silvers' orchestra alone numbered twenty-five. Sound men, technicians, and a solid supporting cast of radio's best professionals (underpaid even while stars' salaries soared) rounded out the spectacle. The show began to fit together on Thursday afternoons, when the cast assembled for initial readings. Another rehearsal followed at noon Friday, and a third was on Saturday. Two dress rehearsals came Monday—the first a 10 A.M. run-through; the final about 90 minutes before air time. By 9 o'clock everything was ready. The stars took their places at the CBS microphones, announcer Melville Ruick chanted "Lux presents *Hollywood!*" and Silvers' melodians launched into the traditional Lux theme.

Just the thought of broadcasting to 30 million people terrified even the biggest name stars. Grace Moore, Ronald Colman, Cary Grant, Gary Cooper, Barbara Stanwyck, and William Powell all confessed to cases of mike fright. Joan Crawford was openly frightened at her first *Lux* performance. Paul Muni was so rattled by the prospect that to work out the tension he once played a violin right up to air time. To the supporting cast, it was an old story; most of them were old hands before the microphone. Regular *Lux* supporting players were Lou Merrill, Margaret Brayton, Florence Lake, Eddie Marr, and Lurene Tuttle, the wife of announcer Mel Ruick.

The plays, adapted by a stable of writers that included Sanford Barnett and Carroll Carroll, were done in three acts of about 15 minutes each. The show's exclusive sound man was Charles Forsyth. In the early days, DeMille told behind-the-scenes stories of Hollywood, interviewing stunt men and other unsung heroes between the second and third acts. Then the stars came back for a curtain call, which consisted of small talk with DeMille about current pictures and past experiences. The ladies gave *Lux* its due, and it was over till the next week—$20,000 worth of glitter and fame.

DeMille became an institution on the show. He conveyed an almost frantic "show must go on" image, refusing to let even minor illness stop him from appearing. For the January 9, 1939 broadcast of *Mayerling*, he was brought to the studio by ambulance, having been restricted to bed by doctors following an operation, and spoke his lines from a cot. On other occasions, he came straight from his movie set, arriving in riding breeches and boots.

It was all an effective charade, for DeMille never did direct *The Lux Radio Theatre* in the real sense. He simply hosted it as an easy way to pick up $2,000, and probably would have stayed to the end except for a bitter spat with the American Federation of Radio Artists (AFRA), which ultimately forced him off the air.

AFRA had assessed its members $1 in a campaign to strengthen union control in radio. DeMille was violently opposed to more union influence, and he refused to pay it. A lengthy court battle ensued, pushed by DeMille to the United States Supreme Court. DeMille lost, and with the beginning of the 1945 season faced the inevitability of paying up or getting out. He got out. On January 29, 1945, Lionel Barrymore replaced him as host, serving two weeks as "guest producer." Other "guests," such as Walter Huston, Irving Pichel, William Keighley, Mark Hellinger, and Brian Aherne, carried the show through the year. On November 5, 1945, William Keighley was announced as permanent host.

Keighley, who had been directing films in the early 1930's, had the same solid radio image that DeMille projected. He came to Lux from the Army Air Corps, where he had served during the war as head of motion picture services. Keighley remained with the show for six years.

Frank Woodruff, listed as assistant director under DeMille, became director, in another piece of audio trickery. He actually had been director all along, a job that later passed to Fred MacKaye. John Milton Kennedy was announcer through the mid-1940's, and Ken Carpenter announced in the 1950's.

The show was dropped by CBS after the broadcast of June 28, 1954, and was revived by NBC September 14 as a Tuesday-night show. Irving Cummings became permanent host around 1952, surviving the network jump in the fall of 1954, to ring down the final Lux Radio Theatre curtain on June 7, 1955.

Ma Perkins

Ma Perkins brought to listeners the world over Oxydol's "mother of the air." This program was first heard as a local feature on WLW, Cincinnati, August 14, 1933. After a three-month trial, sponsor Procter & Gamble brought the serial to Chicago in a coast-to-coast NBC slot. It started on NBC December 4, 1933, and was also sold to CBS in 1942. *Ma Perkins* had rare double network status for six years, doing a 1:15 P.M. stint for CBS and the NBC show two hours later. At the height of its fame, the serial was also heard in Canada, Hawaii, and throughout Europe via Radio Luxembourg.

Among the great homespun philosophers of old-time radio, none is remembered with more affection and pathos than Ma Perkins. Flowing into kitchens each afternoon to a slight variation of "My Old Kentucky Home," *Ma Perkins* was one of radio's most important daytime serials, spanning almost the entire life of network broadcasting. This Frank and Anne Hummert creation was a softer show than others more closely identified with the Hummerts. Certainly less melodramatic than *The Romance of Helen Trent*, it followed the life of a widow who managed a lumber yard in Rushville Center, U.S.A. Ma was a tough old bird with a heart of gold, described by *Time* just before her twenty-fifth anniversary as "a shrewd combination of Dr. Christian, David Harum and Tugboat Annie." She was another of radio's great commoners, a woman's answer to *Just Plain Bill,* and even more durable than that perennial Hummert favorite. Ma's busy life was never too crowded for another problem. She lived by the

Golden Rule, but wasn't above diving into a verbal slugfest when she
saw a wrong to be righted. In her years on the air, Ma became Rushville Center's conscience, its best-loved sounding board, its guide.

All this in addition to raising three children and managing a
business. Ma's kids were John, Evey, and Fay. John was killed in
World War II, and was buried "somewhere in Germany, in an unmarked grave." Evey, rather a gossipy snip at times, married Willie
Fitz, who became manager of Ma's lumber yard, and they had a son
named Junior. Fay, Ma's pet, married Paul Henderson while she was
"still a girl." He died, leaving her to raise their daughter Paulette
alone.

Rounding out the cast of regulars was Shuffle Shober, Ma's partner. Shuffle possessed many of Ma's personal qualities: tough honesty combined with an instinctive understanding of the human spirit.
Though he wasn't as articulate as Ma, Shuffle often saw through
deceit much faster. Ma subscribed to the principle that all people
deserved trust until they proved otherwise. With Shuffle, it was often
the other way around.

Many's the night they sat together on Ma's Rushville Center
porch, philosophizing about their loved ones and the world around
them. On those warm wartime evenings they would often talk
until—one by one—the lights on the block went out and the night
sounds rose up around them. Then, with the problems still unsolved
but somehow easier to bear, Shuffle would shuffle off, leaving Ma
with a feeling of contentment and thankfulness for the blessings of
life.

Ma Perkins had its share of dark moments. When son John was
killed, the network was deluged with letters addressed to "Ma" carrying heartfelt messages of sympathy. People were killed, divorced, and
disgraced on *Ma Perkins*. Ma was cheated by unscrupulous cousins,
and once worked overtime to expose a baby black market. Through it
all, she carried herself with dignity, winning high marks for her show
in the Radio Hall of Fame.

In an incredible stint, Virginia Payne went all the way as Ma,
never missing a single performance. Miss Payne, just 23 years old
when the program first went on the air, was 50 when it ended. She was
a daughter of a Cincinnati doctor, breaking into radio at WLW. There,
she played *Honey Adams,* a singing Southern heroine in an early
radio epic (Jane Froman is said to have been Honey's singing voice)
and, during the summer of 1933, she was tapped for *Ma Perkins*.

Unlike her fictional heroine, Virginia Payne was highly educated.
She held two degrees from the University of Cincinnati. Her performance as Ma Perkins was convincing and real from the beginning,
boosting sales of Oxydol and soaring to rating marks that competed

Lonesome Gal, whose sultry disc jockey voice tickled male listeners, finally revealed her identity in 1953. She was Jean King Rousseau, wife of radio producer Bill Rousseau (Wide World Photo)

Lum and Abner—in real life—Chet Lauck and Norris Goff—used their authentic Arkansas background as inspiration for their mythical airtime town of Pine Ridge, and its Jot 'Em Down Store

Peg Lynch with some of the millions of words of scripts she wrote for shows such as *Ethel and Albert*

Meet Corliss Archer starred Janet Waldo as Corliss and Sam Edwards as her boyfriend Dexter Franklin

Agnes Moorehead reading the script of
her famous "Sorry, Wrong Number,"
which appeared as a play on *Suspense*
(CBS Photo)

Carlton E. Morse, the originator and writer
of many shows including *One Man's Family* and *I Love a Mystery*

The Nelsons, *Ozzie and Harriet,* as they appeared in 1937, when they were still providing music for other stars' variety shows

One Man's Family starred Minetta Ellen as matriarch Fanny Martin Barbour and J. Anthony Smythe as her husband Henry

J. Carrol Naish played "the li'l immigrant" Luigi Basko on CBS's *Life with Luigi*
(CBS Photo)

Robert Ripley before the microphone in the early 1930's for his radio version of *Believe-It-Or-Not*

Will Rogers on *The Gulf Show* in the early 1930's

Eleanor Roosevelt's *It's a Woman's World*
aired on Friday nights over WABC in 1935.
Her proceeds were donated to charity

Frank Sinatra (right) got his start in 1937
as one quarter of The Hoboken Four on
Major Bowes Amateur Hour
(Wide World Photo)

Kate Smith in 1931, joined by studio guest
Morton Downey and Bing Crosby
(CBS-WABC Photo

Bill Stern, ace sportscaster, before the NBC mike in 1942 interviewing Leslie Howard on a two-way hookup

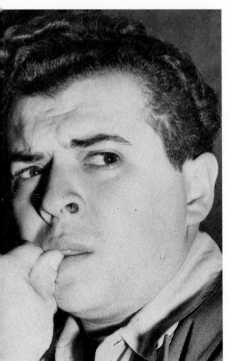

Ezra Stone, a veteran of theatre and movies, played Henry Aldrich on *The Aldrich Family* (Wide World Photo)

Pianist Alec Templeton of *Alec Templeton Time*, in 1950

Lew Valentine of *Dr. I.Q.*

Orson Welles as he appeared in 1938 on *The Mercury Theatre on the Air*

His October 30 broadcast of "The War of the Worlds" caused a national panic. Here Welles sheepishly explains to reporters how it all came about

(International News Photo)

Wendy Warren and the News was a soap opera, beginning with actual news of the day and progressing to the woes of Miss Warren, played by Florence Freeman, here preparing for her first broadcast

(CBS Photo)

In 1950, Douglas Edwards was still leading in with news of the day, and Florence Freeman still leaving the studio for greater adventures after Douglas's "broadcast"

ack Webb, who played Sergeant Joe 'riday in *Dragnet* as well as other private-ye roles like *Pat Novak*

Willard Waterman, who took over *The Great Guildersleeve* role after Harold Peary had originated the character on *Fibber McGee and Molly* (NBC Photo)

Alexander Woollcott, critic, wit, and raconteur, hosting *The Town Crier* in 1935 (CBS Photo)

d Wynn, in costume for his role as "Tex-
:o's Fire Chief," 1933

Robert Young as head of the house in
NBC's *Father Knows Best* (NBC Photo)

with nighttime shows. Whenever she appeared in public, Miss Payne dressed up as Ma Perkins and played the role.

CBS acquired sole possession of the show in 1948, and *Ma Perkins* continued there until its demise on November 25, 1960. And when her show was finally canceled, it was Virginia Payne who summed it all up, touching the highlights in an emotional farewell.

Ma Perkins again. This was our broadcast 7,065. I first came to you on December 4, 1933. Thank you for all being so loyal to us these twenty-seven years.

The part of Willie has been played right from the beginning by Murray Forbes. Shuffle was played for twenty-five years by Charles Egleston, and for the last two years by Edwin Wolfe, who was also longtime director. The Fay you have been hearing these past few years has been Margaret Draper, and the part was played for many years by Rita Ascot. For fifteen years our Evey has been Kay Campbell; Helen Lewis plays Gladys, and Tom Wells has been played by John Larkin and Casey Allen. Our director is Richard Leonard. Our writer for more than twenty years has been Orin Tovrov.

Ma Perkins has always been played by me, Virginia Payne. And if you'll write to me, Ma Perkins, at Orleans, Massachusetts, I'll try to answer you.

Good-bye, and may God bless you.

The Magic Key

The Magic Key was a major variety series of the mid-1930's featuring a fascinating mix of highbrow and lowbrow entertainment. Top symphony musicians and opera stars were billed with such common radio acts as Lum and Abner, Colonel Stoopnagle and Budd, Amos and Andy and Rudy Vallee and his Connecticut Yankees. It premièred September 29, 1935, bringing "through the magic eye of RCA, news and entertainment from several parts of the world." Music was provided by Frank Black and the NBC Symphony Orchestra, with frequent cutaways to such distant points as Montreal, Chicago, and New Orleans, where commentator John B. Kennedy might file a special report on Mardi Gras before flitting away to the high country for a subsequent special on winter sports. *The Magic Key* was a lavish show, bringing together the orchestras of Ray Noble, Guy Lombardo, and Richard Himber in a single act, offering fully dressed scenes from forthcoming films, and concerts by Eugene Ormandy and the Minneapolis Symphony. Among the stars who appeared were Lauritz Melchior, Joan Bennett, Fred MacMurray, Francia White, Gene Raymond, Ruth Etting, Cornelia Otis Skinner, the Pickens Sisters, and Adele Astaire, sister of Fred, then trying to make it as a comedienne. Linton Wells became "roving reporter" around 1937. The 60-minute Sunday show, heard until 1938, closed with its two well-known announcers tossing their tag lines back and forth:

"This is Ben Grauer . . ."
"And Milton Cross . . ."
"Speaking for one member of RCA . . ."
"The National Broadcasting Company."

The Magnificent Montague

The Magnificent Montague was a situation comedy premièring on NBC November 10, 1950, and running one season for a variety of sponsors including Anacin, Chesterfield, and RCA Victor. It followed the exploits of Edwin ("The Magnificent") Montague, former Shakespearian actor who has had to turn to (ugh!) radio to make a living. Edwin, who at the height of his glory twenty-five years ago married his leading lady Lily Boheme, has fallen on hard times. Now he plays Uncle Goodheart on the air, at the same time maintaining his membership in the exclusive Proscenium Club for practitioners of the Bard's work. His overpowering fear is that Proscenium members will learn of his double life as Uncle Goodheart. Edwin and Lily live in a New York apartment with their maid Agnes, a stereotyped smart-mouthed Brooklyn housekeeper.

The series had its moments, but had little staying power. To play Montague, producer-director Nat Hiken lured Monty Woolley to the mike. Woolley was no stranger to radio, having appeared briefly in an equal billing CBS format with Al Jolson in 1943, and in a show with Sammy Kaye for Old Gold Cigarettes in 1943–44. Renowned for his flawless beard, Woolley even looked the part; he was assisted by Anne Seymour as wife Lily and Pert Kelton as Agnes. Jack Ward was at the organ.

Maisie

Maisie was both a network and a syndicated series, first seeing action on July 5, 1945, in a two-year CBS series for Eversharp. Based on the MGM movie series, it starred Ann Sothern as Maisie Revere, the

Brooklyn beauty who saw the world as a Jane-of-all-trades but usually ended up dead broke in some out-of-the-way dive. The series was directed by Tony Stanford. On November 24, 1949, WMGM, New York, began syndicating a *Maisie* series, written by Arthur Phillips and announced by Jack McCoy. Harry Zimmerman composed the music, and Miss Sothern was supported by people from radio's top ranks—Hans Conried, Sheldon Leonard, Ben Wright, Lurene Tuttle, Marvin Miller, Joan Banks, Elvia Allman, Bea Benaderet, Peter Leeds, Patrick McGeehan, and Frank Nelson. The show was marked by Maisie's rather dense Brooklyn chatter and her penchant for getting into other people's problems. The opening was sheer 1940's: the click-click of Maisie's heels, followed by the long, slow whistle of a wolf. A fresh voice: "Hi-Ya, babe! Say, how about a lit——" A sharp slap, a pained "Ouch!" and Sothern with the put-down—"Does that answer your question, buddy?"

Major Bowes' Original Amateur Hour

Major Bowes' Original Amateur Hour was first heard on WHN, New York, in 1934. Bowes was born on June 14, 1874, in San Francisco. He served as a major in intelligence during World War I, and was a keen man with an acute business sense. In partnership, he built the Capitol Theatre in New York, where the pioneering radio show *Roxy and his Gang* began broadcasting around 1923. When Roxy left the Capitol three years later, Major Bowes began a forerunner of the *Amateur Hour*, a 60-minute session of music, poetry, and talk called *Major Bowes' Capitol Family*. He was heavily involved in live theatre and in film distribution until 1935, when he dropped out of his other enterprises to devote full time to his amateur show.

"Around and around she goes, and where she stops nobody knows." That was the major's "weekly wheel of fortune" spinning, a phrase he used in opening the show and one that became its most famous trademark. On March 24, 1935, the show went coast to coast on NBC for Chase & Sanborn. It moved to CBS for Chrysler on September 17, 1936, remaining a Thursday fixture for nine years.

The rise of Major Edward Bowes in the summer of 1935 led directly to a new national fad. The fad became a mania and, for many, a passionate way of life for a time. *The Original Amateur Hour* offered hope to the unsung genius waiting for the Big Break. Amateur fever it was, and by autumn of its first year America was on fire with it. Bowes' program had leaped from nowhere into first place on the rating charts. And for anyone with bus fare and a harmonica, it was the one chance left at the big brass ring.

People came from all parts of the nation to have a crack at Major Bowes and his amateur show. Many sold their homes, put their instruments on their backs and headed East. Poor blacks came out of the South; cowboys from the West. Most had sung or played in whistle stops back home, perhaps with three-piece combos held together by long strings of one-night stands.

By the middle of its second year, The Original Amateur Hour was receiving 10,000 applications in a single week, hearing between 500 and 700 in audition, selecting 20, and sending the rest back into the streets. Alone in the big city, with no friends and few skills, many ended up on the city's already bulging relief rolls.

In one month of 1935 alone, Newsweek estimated that 1,200 amateurs had applied for emergency food and shelter. Bowes, anticipating a share of blame for the city's welfare problems, had established a rule that only residents of New York or its burroughs were eligible to participate on the show. But this did little to stem the incoming tide. Once a person was committed to the dream of fame and fortune, establishing New York residence was easy. And so they came, players of jugs and washboards, tap dancers, foot shufflers, piano players, mimics, tellers of old jokes, duos and trios and quartets and more. There were harpists and yodelers and chime-ringers and harmonica players. The harmonica may have its virtues, but we seldom heard them on Major Bowes. There were flutists and ukelele pickers, fiddlers who wanted more than anything in the world to be violinists; and there were singers—baritones, tenors, and sopranos —singers of "The Lord's Prayer" and "This Is My Country" and "The Battle Hymn of the Republic."

Within a few years, Bowes' weekly income from the radio show alone had soared to $15,000. In addition, he put together traveling companies of amateurs to play live performances in towns around the nation. Sometimes Bowes had dozens of these companies on the road at once, bringing in another $15,000 a week. Out of this pot he paid his help, but even after the bills were paid, he still had a tidy sum left over. In 1939, Time guessed that the major's weekly net was around $15,000.

The traveling companies were comprised of "winners" and "finalists" from the radio show. Each week the amateurs were subjected to a vote of the people. Listeners voted by phone and by mail, sometimes swamping CBS with 30,000 votes. Once a week a city along the network was selected by Bowes as an "honor city." That edition of The Original Amateur Hour was dedicated to the honor city, and phone banks were set up locally, allowing the residents to vote by phone. Winners were brought back for an encore, and three-time winners became finalists for the year's championship.

Few ever got to that level; fewer yet made it into the world of professional entertainment. Many of the amateurs, when they finally made it as participants, hadn't eaten in days. On the night of the broadcast, Bowes took the twenty-odd who had successfully auditioned that week to a restaurant for dinner. There they could eat anything they wanted, and in whatever quantities. And there Bowes learned about his people in a relaxed atmosphere, gaining personal background on which to build his questions. The amateurs also got $10 for their troubles. But once on the air, Bowes could be ruthless. His gong indicated sudden death for a performer, and the major always kept a bodyguard nearby in case the going got rough.

Looking back, the show produced few real stars and not even too many obscure professionals. A handful graduated to nightclubs; some went into grand opera; most gave up the dream and went back home to settle down to the common life. Of more than 15,000 amateurs who appeared on the show, only one stands out as a find of superstar proportions. That happened in 1937, when Major Bowes introduced a group of kids called the Hoboken Four. Their names were Frank Tamburro, Jimmy Petro, Patty Prince, and Frank Sinatra.

Gradually the amateur fever cooled, but Bowes' program remained a formidable CBS entry throughout the decade. It was 60 minutes long until 1942, when it was cut in half.

Bowes died June 13, 1946, and for a few years the show died too. Then on September 18, 1948, an old Bowes man named Ted Mack resurrected it on ABC, using the old Bowes formula—wheel of fortune, traveling amateur shows and all.

Mack had been with Bowes from the beginning, directing auditions and later directing the show itself. He had headed several of the major's road companies, doubling as clarinetist and master of ceremonies. He was especially suited to revive the show, but by then the fever had gone and radio itself was on the way out. This version, though it had only a shadow of the major's old rating, lasted four years and became one of the early shows of TV. Mack's *Original Amateur Hour* was heard Wednesday nights for 60 minutes in its first season, then was cut to 45 minutes, and moved to Thursday. It was sponsored by Old Gold Cigarettes and ran until 1952.

Major Hoople

Major Hoople, a situation comedy based on Gene Ahern's comic strip, *Our Boarding House*, was first heard on the Blue Network June 22, 1942. It followed the adventures of "Major" Amos Hoople, a windbag who claimed former association with every military fighting outfit ever mustered. Hoople also claimed to be descended from a long line of English barons, one of whom had served in every prominent skirmish of history. With his wife Martha, the Major ran the Hoople Boarding House, boring guests to tears with his bungling and puffed-up accounts of how he captured San Juan Hill and won the Boer War single-handedly. Chief doubter of the Hoople claims to fame was Tiffany Twiggs, the star boarder who had been with the Hooples so long that he was accepted as a member of the family. Arthur Q. Bryan played Hoople, Patsy Moran was Martha, and Conrad Binyon played their little nephew Alvin. Mel Blanc was the sneering, sarcastic Twiggs. When the series began, it was written by Jerry Cady and produced by Arnold Maguire. After it outgrew its replacement status, Phil Leslie took over scripting and Louis Quinn produced.

The Man Behind the Gun

The Man Behind the Gun was a series of gutsy war stories "dedicated to the fighting men of the United States and the United Nations" and presented weekly "for the purpose of telling you how your boys and their comrades-in-arms are waging our war against Axis aggression." It came to CBS October 7, 1942, and was heard into 1944, dramatizing true war incidents. One 1943 show was seen through the eyes of a Royal Air Force pilot, but was intended as a tribute to the entire RAF. Ranald MacDougall wrote the show, which was directed by William N. Robson, narrated by Jackson Beck, and scored by Nathan Van Cleave.

The Man Called X

The Man Called X came to CBS July 10, 1944, as a half-hour of international intrigue. Directed by William N. Robson and scored by Gordon Jenkins, it starred Herbert Marshall as Ken Thurston, "the man called X." Beginning as an FBI show, it was booked into the Monday night Blue-ABC schedule for Lockheed that fall and soon became the globetrotting series best remembered. Thurston, the announcer told us in those early episodes, "is the man who crosses the ocean as readily as you and I cross town; he is the man who travels today as you and I will travel tomorrow; he is the man who fights today's war in his unique fashion, so that tomorrow's peace will make the world a neighborhood for all of us." Marshall, the English actor whose specialty was suave roles, did a bang-up job as secret agent Thurston. His smooth delivery kept *The Man Called X* on a higher plane than such later copies as *Dangerous Assignment*. Thurston worked places like Cairo, Monte Carlo, India, Beirut, and the Riviera. There was usually a beautiful woman, often a lady of mystery and exotic background. Sometime during the 30 minutes, Thurston would bump into his sidekick, Pagan Zeldschmidt, who had a streak of larceny in his soul but somehow managed to stay right with the law. Pagan was played by Leon Belasco. In its year for Lockheed, *The Man Called X* was produced and directed by Jack Johnstone, narrated by John McIntire, and scored by Claude Sweeten (later Felix Mills). On June 12, 1945, the show went to NBC, taking Bob Hope's place for the summer. It returned on NBC in 1946. By 1947, *The Man Called X* had turned up on CBS for Frigidaire. Jack Johnstone went along, Wendell Niles became announcer, and the music was by Johnny Green. Later in the CBS run, Dee Engelbach directed. It ended September 26, 1948. A final *Man Called X*, again starring Marshall, ran on NBC from 1950 through 1952.

The Man from Homicide

The Man from Homicide was a police show premièring on ABC, June 25, 1951. Dan Duryea was starred as Lieutenant Lou Dana, tough cop par excellence. Dana wasn't above using borderline third degree tactics on punks and wiseacres, and when he couldn't extract information by the book, he went to work with his fists. Dana justified it with his catch-phrase: *"I don't like killers!"* He always got his man, in some cases, his woman. The series featured Bill Bouchey as Inspector Sherman, and Lawrence Dobkin as Dave the sergeant. It was directed by Dwight Hauser and scored by Basil Adlam. Orville Anderson announced.

A Man Named Jordan

A Man Named Jordan was an adventure serial, first heard on CBS January 8, 1945, and running for about two years in daily 15-minute form. It told of Rocky Jordan, proprietor of the Cafe Tambourine, a small restaurant "in a narrow street off Istanbul's Grand Bazaar" where the smoke of Oriental tobacco mingled with the babble of many tongues to create a great atmosphere for a radio show. Rocky's sidekicks at the Tambourine included a native man Friday named Ali, girlfriend Toni Sherwood, and pal Duke O'Brien. Unlike many heroes of action serials, Rocky was rough-cut and formidable. He might have fit well into *I Love a Mystery*. His ethics were built on practicalities, not sentiment. Rocky did what he had to do to survive "in all those places of the world where intrigue and danger go hand-in-hand, where death and disaster are the rewards of weakness." Strongly motivated by profit, his search for fortune was conducted under risky circumstances. Jack Moyles, a Roosevelt-Churchill imitator who had played roles in *Night Editor* and *The Whistler*, was Rocky from the beginning. Dorothy Lovett, Jay Novello, and Paul Frees had supporting roles. The show was written and directed by Ray Buffum. In 1949, the character was resurrected for a half-hour series, *Rocky Jordan*.

Mandrake the Magician

Mandrake the Magician, based on the King Features comic strip by Lee Falk, was syndicated in 1940, running in 15-minute serial form on WOR between November 11, 1940, and February 6, 1942. As in the strip, Mandrake lived with his servant Lothar, a giant who could "rip a crocodile's jaws apart or break the back of an anthropoid ape." They lived in a "house of mystery and many secrets." Mandrake, Lothar, and the beautiful Princess Narda battled evil elements, serving up generous portions of mysticism along the way. Raymond Edward Johnson, who would later gain fame as the host of *Inner Sanctum Mysteries*, played Mandrake. His voice was ideal as the man of a thousand secrets, whose chant "invovo legem magicarum" invoked the laws of magic and set into play the bag of tricks.

The Manhattan Merry-Go-Round

The Manhattan Merry-Go-Round began as a mix of comedy and music, but eventually became the Hummert version of *Your Hit Parade*. Yes, the producer of this long-running music show was the same Frank Hummert who, with his wife Anne, turned out *Just Plain Bill*, *Backstage Wife*, and soap operas ad infinitum. *Manhattan Merry-Go-Round* was Frank's show; he ran this while Anne supervised the soaps, taking his melodies from sales of sheet music and record sales tabulations in the best *Your Hit Parade* tradition. It was first heard for Dr. Lyon's Tooth Powder on the Blue Network around 1933, and held its 30-minute, NBC Sunday-at-nine time slot for more than 15 years, finally bowing out in 1949.

In its own way, *Manhattan Merry-Go-Round* was as distinctive as *Your Hit Parade*. It was built around the concept of a wining-dining whirl of New York night clubs, where the top tunes of the week were "sung so clearly you can understand every word and sing them yourself." In its early years, *The Manhattan Merry-Go-Round* featured such famous guests as Jimmy Durante and Beatrice Lillie, but later the show acquired a steady cast which, in a fantasy format, crashed New York's most famous clubs every week. The Merry-Go-Round plugged such real nightspots as The Diamond Horseshoe and The Stork Club, and in 1945 Newsweek reported that mention on the show was worth a small fortune to the clubs in out-of-town trade. Actually, the cast never got out of the Hummert studio, but the listeners got the sensation of the whirlwind tour—so much so that they sometimes asked to see the cast members when they came to New York to visit the real clubs. Rachel Carlay was the featured singer of the prewar period. Later, Thomas L. Thomas headed a cast that included Marian McManus, Dick O'Connor, Dennis Ryan, Barry Roberts, Victor Arden's band and "The Boys and Girls of Manhattan." Ford Bond, longtime announcer, opened the show, and the chorus, "Jump On the Manhattan Merry-Go-Round" became one of the great nostalgic bellringers of old-time radio.

"Jump on the Manhattan Merry-Go-Round,
We're touring alluring old New York town.
Broadway to Harlem a musical show,
The orchids that you rest at your radio.
We're serving music, songs, and laughter,
Your happy heart will follow after.
And we'd like to have you all with us,
On the Manhattan Merry-Go-Round."

Manhattan Mother

Manhattan Mother, a soaper about New York, was produced in Chicago and ran for a year on CBS for Chipso Soap. It followed the life of Patricia Locke, estranged from her husband Lawrence and alone in the big city with her little daughter to raise. In her long hours of loneliness, Pat turned to old friend Sam Newell, whose unrequited love for her is complicated by wife Sonja, "the ravishing Russian." Margaret Hillas and Kay Brinker played Pat, and the serial ran from March 6, 1939, through April 5, 1940.

The March of Time

The March of Time, probably the best-known news documentary on the air, was first heard on CBS March 6, 1931. It was a Friday-night fixture, sponsored and produced by Time Magazine. This program was an attention-grabber, the only radio show that sounded just like a Movietone newsreel, complete with interviews and "news of the day" music.

The March of Time was built around the words of a rapid-fire, super-intense narrator known as "the voice of time," who bridged the scenes of that day's events with terse comment. Harry Von Zell and Ted Husing were the earliest "voices," but the longest-lasting, best-known was Westbrook Van Voorhis, who took part in the show from its first year, giving staccato readings that worked perfectly with Howard Barlow's bouncy newsreel music. "As it must to all men, death came today . . ." Van Voorhis inevitably said in announcing the passing of a world leader. His "Time—marches on!" usually ended the show, serving also as a dramatic period to the last scene. The sound track of The March of Time almost demanded pictures, so a skilled crew of actors and sound men were employed.

Listeners "saw" the rise of Hitler, the indictment and trial of Bruno Richard Hauptmann in the kidnap-murder of the Lindbergh baby, the abdication of King Edward VIII. They "saw" the national controversy over Roosevelt's New Deal policies; they "watched" Italy turn aggressor and consume Ethiopia, and they had a ringside seat for the Spanish Civil War. Many listeners, convinced that the dramatizations contained the actual voices of newsmakers from the scene, wondered aloud how it was done.

It was done with some clever mimicry. At first, because of poor international hookups in the early days of network radio, The March of Time dramatized everything it used on the air. Under the direction of Donald Stauffer, actors fluent in dialect and the voice patterns of the famous were brought before the March of Time microphones again and again, until they became almost regulars. Jack Smart, one of the earliest March of Time actors, sometimes played as many as half a dozen parts in a single show—roles ranging in scope from English sophisticates to American drunks, from Prussian generals to Chinese commoners.

In 1943, Radio Life highlighted a decade of March of Time broadcasts, noting that the review captured the entire movement of recent history. The first story done on March, the magazine noted, was the renomination of "Big Bill" Thompson as mayor of Chicago. Hitler appeared only twice that year. Most of the action was focused on domestic issues, with Americans mainly concerned about presidential politics and the Depression. Herbert Hoover, Mahatma Gandhi, King Alfonso of Spain, Huey Long, and Al Capone (in that order) were the people most often impersonated on this program.

Hoover remained the dominant figure in 1932, with Franklin D.

Roosevelt getting top honors between 1933 and 1937. Americans were still most concerned with problems at home, and The March of Time did more New Deal stories during that period than any other kind. Toward the end of the 1930's, people began to look outward at Japan's invasion of Manchukuo, at the rise of Hitler, at Italy's invasion of Ethiopia, and at the Spanish Civil War.

Dwight Weist became one of the busiest March of Time actors of the run. He played Hitler through the 1930's, and his additional characterizations of labor leader John L. Lewis, Mayor Fiorello La Guardia, and the "man in the street" gave him a reputation around the trade as "the man of a thousand voices." Listeners heard Frank Readick, "The Shadow" of 1931, become New York Mayor Jimmy Walker of 1932.

For the bulk of its run, the program was sponsored and produced by the magazine. Only briefly, in the 1933–36 period, did outside sponsors get a piece of the action. From 1933 through 1935, Remington-Rand was the sponsor; in 1935 it went into a 15-minute nightly format, which lasted a year. Wrigley's Gum had it during the 15-minute days of 1936. But Time always let it be known that its editors—not the sponsors—had the final say on the news of the day. "The makers of Wrigley's Spearmint Gum have no more control over The March of Time than they have over the editorial policies of the newspapers or magazines in which they advertise," the announcer said, opening a 1936 edition. "Right up to the minute this program goes on the air, the news of the day is flashing into the studios in New York, where the program originates. Wrigley's is content to sit back, as you are doing now, to see what the editors of Time have in store for us."

And now, The March of Time!

Bugles up; Van Voorhis in with a drum roll. Newsreel music, and another day of history evaporates into ether.

In dramatizing an execution in 1936, Van Voorhis' crisp "Time—Marches On!" coming a second after the gunshots was just about dramatically perfect.

Some people thought it was too much, though, and The March of Time drew its share of criticism for being melodramatic and pretentious. But few who heard it could deny its magnetic listener appeal. As it matured and radio hookups improved, the show gave an illusion of being right on top of the news. Time had correspondents in every corner of the globe. More than 300 reporters were on call to jump at the command of the radio editors. Sometimes late-breaking news forced writers to rework huge sections of script at the last minute in the great tradition of newsgathering.

The March of Time returned to the half-hour format in 1936, and was heard Thursday nights. In 1937, it moved to NBC, where it alternated between Blue and Red Networks on Friday and Thursday nights. With the change of networks, Donald Voorhees became director of music, but the show retained its urgent newsreel flavor. Keene Crockett was for a time director of sound effects. He utilized more than 7,000 in-house sounds from NBC's vast recorded sound library, and exercised great care in researching the sound patterns. Such questions as how long a bomb takes to fall 5,000 feet, or whether Big Ben chimes in a low E or G were standard sound problems.

In 1938, Hitler became the top-mimicked figure on the show. A few years later Roosevelt slipped to third behind Japan's Saburo Kurusu and Russia's Joseph Stalin. Rubber and steel and shortages became top stories at home. People wanted to know how other people were coping; when Jack Benny donated his Maxwell to the scrap drive, The March of Time was there to record it.

Everett Sloane joined the program in 1943. Others who worked on the series were Orson Welles, Agnes Moorehead, Martin Gabel, Kenny Delmar, and the husband-wife team of John McIntire and Jeanette Nolan. Directors after Stauffer included Homer Fickett, who would later become associated with the great historical show Cavalcade of America. William Spier, who would build a reputation as radio's "master of the macabre" through his work in such thrillers as Suspense, was director in 1932.

The new era in communications brought a decided shift of emphasis in March of Time programming. In the 1940's, dramatizations were phased out as much as possible, and news actualities were used much more frequently. Time reporters around the world were expected to broadcast interviews and action from the scene. When dramatizations were necessary, the reporters gave the newsroom vivid personality profiles on the people being impersonated. The profiles included everything from voice inflection to the tiniest gestures.

Amid the clatter of teletype machines, The March of Time was slapped together from Berlin, Singapore, and China. Newsmen contributing included Harry Zinder from Cairo, Robert Sherrod and George Strock from Australia, William Fisher and Theodore White from New Delhi, and Walter Graebner from Moscow. The tempo increased with the war; giants on all fronts—from shipbuilding tycoon Henry J. Kaiser to moviemaker Darryl Zanuck—were hauled before the March of Time microphones. The program was last heard on ABC in 1945.

Mark Trail

Mark Trail appeared on Mutual January 30, 1950, as a three-a-week 30-minute adventure show for Kellogg's Corn Flakes and Pep. The show followed a loosely connected story line, and was fairly faithful to the Ed Dodd comic strip. Mark Trail was a man of the woods, an outdoorsman whose greatest enemies were the spoilers. His adventures in the wilds often involved crooks, bullies, and badmen, but Trail—with the help of his friends Scotty and Cherry—always cut them down to size. In 1951, the series moved to ABC, where it became a five-a-week, 15-minute serial in 1952. Mark faded away into the wilderness later that year.

Matt Crowley initiated the title role, Ben Cooper played Scotty. Staats Cotsworth took over as Trail when the show was serialized. Drex Hines directed; Jackson Beck was announcer. His opening became the show's best-remembered feature:

> Battling the raging elements!
> Fighting the savage wilderness!
> Striking at the enemies of man and nature!
> One man's name resounds from snow-capped mountains
>   down across the sun-baked plains . . .
> MAAARRRKKK TRAIL!
> Guardian of the forests!
> Protector of wildlife!
> Champion of man and nature!
> MAAARRRKKK TRAIL!

The Martin and Lewis Show

The Martin and Lewis Show came to NBC April 3, 1949, in the network's frantic scramble to find new talent for the Sunday-night void created by the CBS talent raids. At that time, Dean Martin (singer) and Jerry Lewis (maniac) were at the beginning of their rise to superstardom. They were virtually unknown to a radio audience accustomed to hearing Jack Benny and *Amos and Andy* on Sundays. Martin and Lewis had met while working together in an Atlantic City nightclub. Their rise was billed as "overnight" on the new radio show, but actually it took two years of nightclub bookings to accomplish. The radio show did little to advance their reputations, and followed the familiar Martin-Lewis movie pattern. Dean was the singing straight man and Jerry was squeaky-voiced idiot who heckled everybody in sight. At first the network sustained the show, giving the boys a good, well-funded sendoff. Lucille Ball and Bob Hope were among the guests. Later, as the Martin-Lewis movies for Hal Wallis began to attract a following, the radio show picked up some momentum, but never quite enough. It expired in 1952. Sponsors included Anacin and Chesterfield. The program was produced and directed by Robert L. Redd and later Dick Mack, written by Ed Simmons and Norman Lear, with music under the direction of Dick Stabile.

Martin Kane, Private Detective

Martin Kane, Private Detective came to Mutual on August 7, 1949, as a Sunday-afternoon program for U.S. Tobacco. It starred William Gargan as Kane, the gumshoe of the calculating mind and the penchant for danger. Despite Kane's basically quiet nature, Radio Life reported in 1950 that he had been "drugged, beaten, locked in a chamber with poison gas seeping in, thrown in the river, stabbed, shot, tied up in a burning building and locked unarmed in a room with a homicidal maniac bearing a meat cleaver." In short, this was an action show of the first magnitude. Kane made an almost effortless transition into early TV in 1950. Soon thereafter Gargan decided to give up the role for a fling at producing. He hand-picked Lloyd Nolan as his replacement, and the radio show ran until 1952. Gargan, meanwhile, would return in 1951 in a new NBC Wednesday night radio private-eye role, Barrie Craig: Confidential Investigator, which was heard until 1955.

Mary Margaret McBride

Mary Margaret McBride arrived in radio via Station WOR in 1934, and for the next two decades Mary Margaret was one of the hottest sales personalities of the air—the woman's answer to Arthur Godfrey.

She began as a reporter for the old Cleveland Press, graduated to writing magazine articles and, by the late 1920's, was considered one of the outstanding freelance writers in the country. The Depression dried up many of her markets, so she turned to radio. In 1934 she began broadcasting for WOR as "Martha Deane," grandmother, in a talk show that called for her to discuss each day the doings of her brood. In reality, she had no grandchildren (she never even married), and one day she tired of the charade. She told WOR that from then on she was going to level with her listeners and talk about what she found interesting. She happened to be on the air when she told them, so the decision was irrevocable. She continued to be Martha Deane, but without the grandchildren and the fancy window dressing.

By 1937, she had attracted attention at CBS, which hired her for a 15-minute talk show under her own name. She continued with the *Martha Deane* WOR broadcasts until 1940, when she quit to devote all her time to the network. In 1941, NBC gave her a shot at a 45-minute show; she leaped at it, running for a decade in a 1 P.M. EST time slot.

Her greatest fame came during the 1940's. Her format was built around celebrity interviews (which took up the first 30 minutes) and household chatter and plugs for a dozen sponsors (which took up the last 15 minutes). Often she ran plugs together, talking of two or more products in a single sentence. Her guests attributed her success to her ability to make them feel at home. She listened attentively and with appreciation of what they were saying, drawing them out on personal anecdotes that, perhaps, they hadn't even intended to tell.

Her theme during those years was "Beautiful Lady." Her business manager, who first pushed her into radio, was her old friend Stella Karn. Longtime announcer was Vincent Connolly, who was often chided on the air by Mary Margaret for his apparent reluctance to get married. His introduction was a classic of simplicity: "It's one o'clock and here's Mary Margaret McBride."

Probably without knowing it, she tapped into the source of Godfrey's great strength—a pleasant mix of folksy chatter and interview, combined with honesty and candor. Like Godfrey, she believed in the products she advertised. Early in her career, she established the practice of promoting nothing that she hadn't tried herself; later she strengthened the policy by insisting on laboratory proof of advertising claims. Sponsors who balked could go their own way. Mary Margaret McBride had a giant audience in New York alone, and there were always between twenty and thirty sponsors waiting in the wings.

Sponsors have a way of swarming around anyone who can sell their wares, and Mary Margaret McBride could. Sales of McBride-mentioned items leaped overnight, sometimes as much as tenfold. Listeners buried her under 5,000 letters a day. Once she gave 3½ million letters to the wartime paper drive. Her fans sent gifts on her birthday—lucky rabbits' feet, scarves, kitchen utensils, and pounds and pounds of candy to add to her already ample figure. Sponsors didn't fool around with someone who could draw response like that. They just bought into her show and crossed their fingers.

In 1950, she moved to ABC for a 30-minute daily program. She died in April 1976.

Masquerade

Masquerade was a brief Irna Phillips serial, heard on NBC from January 14, 1946, until August 29, 1947. It was part of the "General Mills Hour," in which characters from four Phillips dramas spilled over into each other. The action of *Masquerade* was set in the small town of Fairfield, Iowa, which was also described as the home town of a leading character of *The Woman in White*. Of four serials in the "Hour," *Masquerade* was the most forgettable and the first to fall. The show originated in Chicago, then underwent a large-scale change of cast when Miss Phillips moved her shows to the West Coast in the summer of 1946. Les Mitchel directed in Hollywood; Dick Aurandt played the organ and Carl Wester produced. Players included, from Chicago, Art Seltzer, Beryl Vaughn, Jack Petruzzi, Jack Swingford, Mary Marren Rees, Geraldine Kay, Sondra Gair, and Ned LeFevre. Miss Gair and LeFevre followed the show to California, where they were joined by Herbert Rawlinson, Grif Barnett, Nancy Gates, Janet Scott, and Francis X. Bushman.

Mayor of the Town

Mayor of the Town was set in Springdale, the mythical town for this warmhearted series of human interest dramas. The town, 75 miles from Capitol City and 20 miles from the war plant boomtown Crescent City, was off the well-worn path. The series, running on various networks between September 6, 1942, and 1949, gave a realistic portrait of rural living.

It told the story of the mayor, his housekeeper, his young ward, and their neighbors. Ever in character, Lionel Barrymore played the mayor, who cared more about his constituents' problems than about political persuasion. Barrymore grumbled and grunted through his role in "grand old man" fashion and even found time—once each year—to turn Springdale into a special theatre for his traditional offering of Dickens' *A Christmas Carol*.

Agnes Moorehead played Marilly, the mayor's whining house-keeper, whose warpath antics often sent one and all scurrying for the back fence gate. Conrad Binyon was Butch, the mayor's ward, who could usually be found hanging on the gate waiting for the mayor at the end of a long day of administrative bickering.

Butch had come to live with the mayor when his mother died and his father went to fight with the Seabees. On summertime nights,

Butch played under streetlamps and chased fireflies with his friends, Bitsy Morgan, Peewee Taylor, and Sharlee Bronson. Sharlee, played by Gloria McMillan, became Butch's best girl. Holly-Ann, the mayor's granddaughter, was played by Priscilla Lyon.

Naturally, Barrymore was the star. He brought the show its special warmth and made it tick. Descended from radio's most prominent acting family, Barrymore had a fondness for radio that was evident in this role. He insisted on meticulous attention to detail, even though others were in charge of production. Barrymore had a way of knowing what lines were wrong and why; his town became as well-known to listeners as any in fiction. Regulars didn't need a map to know where Elmwood School was. Hill Street, Spring Street, River Street, Mulberry, and Market were all familiar names. Springdale had its "wrong side of the tracks," too, where pool halls, bars, and dives clustered around the seedy Avon Hotel.

Mayor of the Town first came to NBC September 6, 1942. After a month it moved to CBS where it ran Wednesdays for Lever Brothers (1942–43), then on Saturdays for Noxzema (1944–47). It moved to ABC, still for Noxzema, in 1947–48, and was last heard on Mutual Sunday nights in 1948–49. Producer was first Murray Bolen, then Knowles Entrikin. Music was by Gordon Jenkins and later Bernard Katz. Howard Breslin and Charles Tazewell shared the writing in the middle years, each turning out a script every other week.

Meet Corliss Archer

Meet Corliss Archer was based on F. Hugh Herbert's stage play, *Kiss and Tell*. It first came to CBS in 1943, and in 1944 became a late afternoon Sunday show for Anchor Hocking Glass, Herbert's inspiration for *Meet Corliss Archer* had been the growing pains of his own two daughters, Diana and Pamela, and both real-life daughters wanted the part of Corliss. Herbert turned thumbs down on that with the excuse that he didn't want either of them becoming professionals at 13. It got him out of a tight spot, and initially the role went to Priscilla Lyon, with Janet Waldo carrying the part most of the run.

Among the great radio comedies involving adolescents, *Meet Corliss Archer* ranked consistently near the top. As the CBS version of NBC's *A Date with Judy*, Corliss herself emerged as Judy Foster's blood sister. The girls were virtually identical; in fact, Janet Waldo and Louise Erickson (Corliss and Judy) each had several parts in the other's shows. But Corliss' real strength lay with the men in her life. They were her father, Harry Archer, and her boyfriend, Dexter Franklin. Dexter's character developed through the 1940's, and ultimately became one of the strongest seen in adolescent situation comedy. It began with his laugh, a deep nasal bellow that became a series trademark. It deepened with his poor-boy's way of looking at life. Dexter was a man of such simple needs that all the problems of his world could be solved with a buck. His character was capped by his uncanny ability to botch everything he touched. Archie Andrews, Henry Aldrich, and Judy's boyfriend Oogie Pringle all had that ability. What they lacked were the deeper touches of character that made us care and suffer along with them. Irving Lee was cast as Dexter, Frank Martin played Mr. Archer, and Mrs. Archer (Janet) was played from the start by Irene Tedrow. By the fall of the first year, Bill Christy had taken the Dexter role, and Corliss was played by Janet Waldo. Miss Waldo, spotted by movie talent scouts while still a student at the University of Washington, had been brought to Hollywood for a film part. Bored with the inaction of the studio after her first movie, she turned to radio with performances on *The Lux Radio Theatre*, *Those We Love*, and *Cavalcade of America*. For a time she played Cliff's wife Irene on *One Man's Family*. Then came *Meet Corliss Archer* and the breathless adolescent she would play to "golly-gee" perfection for the next decade.

The show really began to mature with the arrival of Sam Edwards as Dexter. He was Corliss' lifelong sweetheart, and his elephant-roar, "CORR-LAISS!" across the hedge at eight o'clock in the morning was one of the running gags of the show. Usually he became the victim, the pawn in Harry Archer's unending war against the female sex. Corliss' father, a gruff lawyer, was the typical father image of his time—cynical, dry, and full of schemes, but with a heart of gold that always managed to shine through.

When Fred Shields took the role of Harry Archer, the scenario was complete. *Corliss* moved to Thursdays in 1944 and to Sundays in 1947, where it ran one season for Campbell Soups. In 1949, the program was picked up by Electricity Co-Ops, which sponsored it through 1953 on Sunday (1949–51), on Saturday (1951–52), and on Friday (1952–53). In 1952, it moved from CBS to ABC. It was revived on CBS for a final run in 1954–55. In the final year, Corliss and Dexter were played by Lugene Sanders and David Hughes, and the show melted away to an echo of its old vitality.

Meet Me at Parky's

Meet Me at Parky's was a mid-1940's situation comedy, featuring Harry Einstein as Parkyakarkus, owner of a Greek restaurant. Einstein created the character as a boy, mimicking the Greek workers at his father's importing warehouse. He began entertaining at school functions, and finally made it into radio when he gave up the adult world of advertising copywriting. His "Parkyakarkus" debut was on Boston radio in 1932. That same year he hit the big-time with *The Eddie Cantor Show*, where he remained as a regular. Einstein took "Parky" to *The Al Jolson Lifebuoy Show* in 1938, then dropped out of radio in 1941. So *Meet Me at Parky's*, when it opened on NBC June 17, 1945, was something of a comeback. The series featured Einstein's self-written slapstick, the songs of Betty Jane Rhodes and David Street, and the music of Opie Cates. The show ran for two years as an NBC Sunday-night show for Old Gold, then moved in 1947 to Mutual for a final season as a Sunday sustainer.

Meet Millie

Meet Millie, a light situation comedy revolving around secretary Millie Bronson, her Brooklyn Mama, and her addled boyfriend Alfred, came to CBS July 2, 1951, a Monday night sustainer with Audrey Totter in the title role. It moved to Saturdays before the year was out and was heard Thursdays from 1952 through 1954 for a variety of sponsors. In late 1952, when CBS took on the series for its TV schedule, Miss Totter's studio refused to let her play the video version. Elena Verdugo was tapped for that. Verdugo subsequently got the radio job when Totter resigned.

Meet the Meeks

Meet the Meeks was a moderately horrible Saturday-morning situation comedy, heard on NBC to the detriment of Swift Meats from 1947 until 1949. It followed the Mortimer Meeks who lived in "the little green house with the white shutters" on Elm Street in Civic Center. The alleged plots revolved around the attempts of Mortimer and the family (daughter Peggy and Uncle Louie) to cope with wife Agatha's frequent tirades. When Agatha decided to go on a health kick, the whole family had to suffer through spinach juice, cold showers, and open windows ad nauseum. Forrest Lewis, utilizing his best henpecked Mr. Peavey voice, played Mortimer. Fran Allison and Cliff Soubier played supporting roles.

Meet the Missus

Meet the Missus was a typical audience participation show heard on CBS West Coast stations around 1944–50. Jack Bailey was master of ceremonies when the show opened, a job that later fell to Jay Stewart, Harry Mitchell, and Ed East. Director was Harry Koplan, who later became emcee. The show drew ladies from the audience in the House Party tradition, poking good-natured fun at them and giving them gifts for their troubles. The program was broadcast from Earl Carroll's Hollywood theatre-restaurant, giving the emcee a chance to wander among the tables searching for victims. Standard features were the "question of the day" (in what year was chewing gum invented?—1869) for a "grand prize," and the "walk down lovers' lane." In the latter, couples married the longest and most recently were brought up on stage to "represent all lovers everywhere," and engage in some banter. The oldsters usually gave the youngsters some advice, as when one man told the young groom to "establish an alibi early."

Meet the Press

Meet the Press was created by Martha Rountree, who had been a struggling New York freelance writer when she cracked into network radio with a new kind of public affairs show. With its first broadcast on Mutual in 1945, Meet the Press was promoted as a joint venture between the network and the American Mercury, "the distinguished magazine of opinion." Mercury editor, Lawrence Spivak, became a permanent member of the panel, and Miss Rountree served as the show's producer. She was responsible for selecting and persuading the top headline-makers in the country to come before the microphones and "meet the press."

It was no small job for a 30-year-old fiction writer. But Miss Rountree, who had once been on the writing end of the news herself, succeeded in getting such controversial figures as John L. Lewis, Walter Reuther, Mayor Fiorello La Guardia, and GOP chairman Herbert Brownell, Jr. to face the journalists. The show became an instant success as a newsmaker in its own right, and soon was receiving regular coverage by both major news wire services.

Bill Slater served as early moderator for the top journalists of the era, such inquisitors as Tex McCrary and Dorothy Thompson. The newsmakers, subjected to on-the-spot grillings, often reacted with sarcasm and anger. John L. Lewis rattled his union sabre on one show, made coast-to-coast headlines by threatening a national coal strike. When McCrary asked La Guardia if he had ever used his position as mayor to try to get reporters fired, La Guardia snapped, "That's a damn lie."

Pretty strong for 1945, but that's what made *Meet the Press* go. Thirty years later, it's still going, as a Sunday NBC TV show.

The Mel Blanc Show

The Mel Blanc Show came to CBS after Mel Blanc was already a well-known name. With his "57 varieties" of dialect, voice characterization, and vocal sound effects, Blanc was one of the busiest men in Hollywood. He had started collecting his dialects and characterizations as a child in Portland, Oregon. His first mastered dialect, a thick Yiddish, was filched from an old Jewish couple who ran a grocery store in his neighborhood. Gradually he worked into Portland's Chinatown, adding tongues of the Orient to his downtown Jewish. By the time he was in high school, Blanc was an entertainer of semi-professional competence, doing occasional skits and numbers on local radio with his brother Henry. He became director of the Orpheum Theatre in Portland when he was 22, and in 1933 took to the air locally with his one-man show.

Encouraged by wife Estelle, he moved to Hollywood in 1935 and began casting around the network waters. His first bite came from KFWB; it led to an appearance on *The Joe Penner Show*. Blanc ultimately became Penner's infamous duck, and his reputation as a master of dialect, comic animal imitator, and one-man sound effects system began to grow.

Sometimes he worked on a score of radio shows in a week. He played Tiffany Twiggs, star boarder on *Major Hoople*; he was the Happy Postman with Burns and Allen; he had continuing roles as Botsford Twink on *The Abbott and Costello Show* and as Uncle Petie and Rover the dog on *Tommy Riggs and Betty Lou*. Blanc was August Moon on *Point Sublime*. He played many parts on *The Jack Benny Program*, from Jack's huffing, chugging Maxwell to Carmichael the polar bear; from Professor LeBlanc the violin teacher to the train barker who reeled off "Anaheim, Azusa and Cuc——amonga!" Mel was Pedro, the Mexican handyman of "pardon me for talking in your face, señorita" fame on *The Judy Canova Show*. He was Floyd the barber (a part also played by Arthur Q. Bryan) on *The Great Gildersleeve*. And as if that wasn't enough for one man, he was also the voices of Bugs Bunny, Porky Pig, Daffy Duck, Tweety Pie, and company in Warner Brothers' Looney Tunes.

CBS got the message in 1946. On September 3, Blanc's show premièred for Colgate-Palmolive as a Tuesday-night 30-minute situation comedy. In it, Blanc played two major roles. As Mel Blanc, he used his natural voice, playing an addled young man who ran the Fix-It Shop. In his stuttering Porky Pig voice he played Zookie, Mel's helper in the shop. Zookie opened the show with a "Hello every b-buh-bbb-uh-b-uh-bbb-uh—HI!" Mel's image was that of a scatterbrain who should have been anything but a fixer of broken objects. Somehow things always went out of Mel's shop in worse shape than they had come in, much to the disgust of Mr. Colby, owner of the neighborhood supermarket and grouchy father of Mel's girlfriend Betty.

Unfortunately Blanc's own show, on the air for just a year, never fully displayed his great ability as well as his better supporting roles. *The Mel Blanc Show* revolved around his efforts to impress Betty and her father with his initiative—these always ended in disaster for Mel, but gave him the chance to explore the full range of his talented throat. In one show, for example, Blanc ruined Mr. Colby's new radio, then tried to conceal his bungling by hiding behind the set and creating all the programs as Colby turned the dial. In another show, Mel exchanged Betty's Christmas present so often that he had to resort to a wide variety of disguises and voices to befuddle the exchange woman.

In the scripts, Mel belonged to a lodge known as the Loyal Order Of Benevolent Zebras. Their password, "Ugga-ugga-boo, ugga-boo-boo-ugga," was one of the show's catch phrases. CBS-Colgate sent Blanc off in good company, with Mary Jane Croft as Betty, Joseph Kearns as Mr. Colby, Hans Conried as Mr. Cushing the Lodge president, and Alan Reed as Mr. Potchnik the piano teacher. Others who played occasional roles were Bea Benaderet, Leora Thatcher, and Earle Ross.

The show was produced and directed by Joe Rines, with music by the Victor Miller orchestra. Writers were David Victor and Herb Little, Jr., and later Mac Benoff. Announcer was Bud Easton.

Melody Puzzles

Melody Puzzles was an obscure music-quiz show running on the Blue Network for Lucky Strike in 1938. Skits were performed and contestants guessed song titles from clues hidden in the skits. Then the songs were sung by Buddy Clark and/or Freda Gibbson (Georgia Gibbs). Master of ceremonies was Fred Uttal, and the music was by Harry Salter's orchestra.

The Mercury Theatre on the Air

The Mercury Theatre on the Air came to CBS on July 11, 1938, after a smash season on stage. Despite low ratings, it would make Orson Welles' name a household word before its first year was up. Welles, born in Kenosha, Wisconsin, May 6, 1915, was the son of a pianist-inventor, and his love of performing developed early. By his tenth year he had played Peter Rabbit for a Chicago department store and had been paid $25 a day for it. He was a professional. Two years later, he staged a school production of *Julius Caesar*; in typical form, he played three major roles himself. Welles went to Ireland in 1931, ended up broke in Dublin, and talked himself into a solid role in the Gate Theatre production of *Jew Suss*. It wasn't that easy back home. After a series of frustrations and a vacation in Morocco, Welles decided to play the contact game. He parlayed a meeting with Thornton Wilder into a meeting with Alexander Woollcott, and that into a tour with Katharine Cornell. The tour culminated in New York, with the 1934 production of *Romeo and Juliet*.

Backstage, Welles was introduced to John Houseman, a young man who had abandoned the grain business for the insecure, exciting world of theatre. Houseman was then producing an Archibald Mac-Leish play *Panic*, and had been so impressed by Welles in *Romeo and Juliet* that he wanted him for the lead. That was the first step toward the Mercury Theatre.

With Houseman, Welles took over a WPA Negro unit in 1936 and prepared to stage *Macbeth* as a Haitian melodrama. The Shakespeare classic, done with an all-black cast, led to other WPA shows, including *Dr. Faustus* and Marc Blitzstein's *The Cradle Will Rock*. The Federal Theatre, under the gun for staging too many plays with labor themes, decreed that *Cradle* would not open. But the two borrowed a theatre, defied a rule banning them from the stage and offered the performance in the aisles.

In 1937, when *Mercury's* first stage production was still four months away, the group that would become the Mercury Players offered an ambitious production of *Les Miserables* on Mutual. Later that year, Welles and Houseman leased New York's old Comedy Theatre, renamed it Mercury, and began putting together their modern version of *Julius Caesar*, which opened on November 11, 1937.

Welles, appearing as Brutus in a blue serge suit, brought the fascism of modern Italy under artistic scrutiny in Shakespeare's 300-year-old play, and set the Welles legend in motion.

Getting the play opened was a financial struggle, but after opening night the money woes melted away. *Julius Caesar* was a smash, critically and financially, and the Mercury Theatre was on its way. A small core of talent formed around Welles. Joseph Cotten, Agnes Moorehead, Martin Gabel, and George Coulouris were early Mercury players. Welles handled the directing and producing; Houseman held up the business end.

Their antics that first year were spectacular. They did George Bernard Shaw's *Heartbreak House*—all three hours of it—Thomas Dekker's *Shoemaker's Holiday*, and *Danton's Death* by Georg Büchner. The critics were ecstatic; they bestowed upon 22-year-old Orson Welles the titles of "genius" and "wonder boy." With that kind of press, it didn't take CBS long to offer Welles an even greater stage, "the Broadways of the entire United States." And when the CBS offer came, in the summer of 1938, the two men prepared for the additional burden of radio, and a schedule that Houseman would describe years later as "health-wrecking." The show was originally slated for nine Monday-night 60-minute dramatizations of classics from literature.

Welles, at 22, was already a radio veteran when *The Mercury Theatre on the Air* was formed. By 1935, he had become almost a regular on *The March of Time*, and since March 1937 was heard weekly as Lamont Cranston in *The Shadow* for Goodrich Tires. By 1937 Welles was averaging $1,000 a week from his radio roles. But *The Mercury Theatre on the Air* would be no mere reading of lines. It was Welles' baby, all done in his "first-person singular," from the start. He would be the star, narrator, writer, producer, and director —in addition to his continuing stage career at the Mercury.

The best talents from radio were assembled for the new show. Karl Swenson, Alice Frost, Kenny Delmar, and Frank Readick joined Miss Moorehead, Gabel, Coulouris, and Ray Collins in early Mercury dramas. Howard Koch was hired as writer of first drafts, which Welles would painstakingly pick apart later. Keeping with the show's prestige image, Tchaikovsky's "Piano Concerto no. 1 in B-Flat Minor" was adapted as its theme. Bernard Herrmann, CBS resident melodian, was assigned the score, and Dan Seymour was announcer. Houseman became the show's editor, and Paul Stewart was associate producer. Davidson Taylor was sent in to supervise for CBS.

It was a concentrated shot of talent for a 60-minute dramatic series. *The Mercury Theatre on the Air* opened July 11 with Bram Stoker's *Dracula*. Welles played two roles, Dr. Seward and Count Dracula; Gabel was Dr. Van Helsing, Coulouris was Jonathan Harker,

Collins the Russian captain, Swenson the mate, Miss Moorehead Mena Harker. In the weeks that followed, Welles offered *Treasure Island, A Tale of Two Cities, The 39 Steps, Three Short Stories, Abraham Lincoln, Affairs of Anatole, The Count of Monte Cristo, The Man Who Was Thursday, Julius Caesar, Jane Eyre, Sherlock Holmes, Oliver Twist, Hell On Ice, Seventeen,* and *Around the World in 80 Days.*

With the new fall season, *The Mercury Theatre* became a regular, moving on September 11 into an unenviable Sunday-night time slot opposite Edgar Bergen's *Chase & Sanborn Hour.* Bergen then had America's top-rated show, pulling in a Crossley-estimated 34.7 percent of the total audience. After seven broadcasts in its new Sunday slot, *The Mercury Theatre* was rated at 3.6 percent. But on Hallowe'en eve, Welles and his group staged the ultimate in radio thrillers, a science fiction fantasy that sent people running into the streets in terror. That night a series of disjointed events went into motion that would make *The War of the Worlds* the most famous single radio show ever broadcast.

First came basic dissatisfaction of the Mercury staff with the story. H. G. Wells' fantasy about invaders from Mars who landed in England with their terrible mechanical fighting machines seemed highly futuristic when it was published in 1898. Forty years later, the *Mercury* staff fretted over its credibility. Writer Howard Koch phoned Houseman the Tuesday before the broadcast, distraught over the assignment. There was no way this ancient epic could be adapted effectively for modern radio.

Houseman considered changing plays. *Lorna Doone* was available, but coming on the heels of several traditional classics, it seemed a dull alternative. Houseman phoned Welles, who was deep in rehearsal for the *Mercury* play, *Danton's Death.* Welles wouldn't come to the phone, so Houseman told Koch to go ahead with the script, and he—Houseman—would come over and help.

By the time Houseman had arrived, Koch had gotten his Martians down to earth and was spreading poisonous black smoke across the marshlands of New Jersey. The two men hammered at the script for almost 36 hours, finally wrapping it up on Wednesday night, four days before the broadcast.

On Thursday morning, the cast was assembled for the first rough rehearsal. The rehearsal was recorded and played back that night in Welles' office. Everyone was despondent. As written and rehearsed, *The War of the Worlds* just didn't make it. Somehow it had to be modernized, its newscast simulations heightened and intensified. Real names and details had to be added, to give the illusion of up-to-the-minute reality. Already the London setting of the novel had

become Grover's Mill, New Jersey. Now narrative became news bulletin as the staff worked over the script through the night. Horrid
present-tense reports of thousands killed, of poison gas spreading
westward, of route instructions for getting out of town, were written
in. More bulletins were added, of fires and of people crushed in the
mad stampede away from the scene. "Seven thousand armed men,
pitted against the single fighting machine of the invaders from
Mars—120 known survivors . . ."

Friday afternoon, the revised script was passed by the CBS censors, with few alterations. The Hotel Biltmore was changed to the Park
Plaza; President Roosevelt was changed to the nameless "secretary of
the interior;" a few other actual names were deleted. Welles still
hadn't come to the studio by Saturday, so the afternoon rehearsal was
done without him. Frank Readick, who played newsman-in-the-field
Carl Phillips, had dug out the transcriptions of Herb Morrison's on-
the-scene report of the Hindenburg crash at Lakehurst, New Jersey.
Morrison's emotional broadcast, filled with weeping as scores of
people died before him, became Readick's model in describing the
horrors of the Martian heat ray.

For all purposes, The War of the Worlds was ready to air. Then
Welles began to add his magic touches. Early news bulletins were
dragged out and lengthened, over the objections of staff. The first
orchestra number—"La Cumparsita" by the fictional Ramon Raquello
and his Orchestra—was beefed up; a later number by "Bobby Milette"
was also lengthened. Welles' theory was simple: "The War of the
Worlds" would work by contrast. The slow passage of time early in
the show would contribute to the illusion of reality; then the tempo
would pick up dramatically, with the opening of the Martian cylinder, and would rush to climax with express-train speed.

They were exactly 12 minutes into the broadcast when things
began happening. Precisely at that minute, Edgar Bergen brought out
a singer on NBC, and an estimated 3 to 6 million listeners went
dial-twisting. Most of them froze when they heard shrill news bulletins about something happening on Mars. Hitler's antics had the
nation jumpy anyway; when reports of a warlike confrontation in
eastern New Jersey began shaping up, few listeners changed the
station.

As a result, they missed the full opening signature, which made
clear that the Columbia Broadcasting System and its affiliated stations were presenting Orson Welles and The Mercury Theatre on the
Air in The War of the Worlds, by H. G. Wells. What they did hear was
"Carl Phillips," giving an on-the-scene report of a cylinder of unknown origin hitting earth "with almost earthquake force" near
Grover's Mill, New Jersey.

Ladies and gentlemen, this is the most terrifying thing I have ever witnessed—wait a minute! Someone's crawling out of the hollow top—someone or . . . something. I can see peering out of that black hole two luminous discs. Maybe eyes, might be a face . . . Good heavens, something's wriggling out of the shadow like a gray snake. Now it's another one . . . They look like tentacles . . . I can see the thing's body now—it's large as a bear. It glistens like wet leather. But that face, it's . . . it's . . . ladies and gentlemen, it's indescribable; I can hardly force myself to keep looking at it, it's so awful. The eyes are black and gleam like a serpent; the mouth is . . . kind of V-shaped, with saliva dripping from its rimless lips that seem to quiver and pulsate. The monster or whatever it is can hardly move; it seems weighted down possibly by gravity or something. . . .

Things happened fast from there. The monster rigged its fighting machine, with Phillips giving a running account, and the war of the worlds began. The heat ray turned soldiers to screaming flames; fires spread everywhere, and suddenly Phillips was cut off the air. A piano interlude, another Welles innovation, heightened the horror with its soft touches. Then the bulletins began pouring in.

Red Cross emergency workers dispatched to the scene . . . bridges hopelessly clogged with frantic human traffic. . . .

Finally came the announcement that capped it:

Ladies and gentlemen, as incredible as it may seem, both the observations of science and the evidence of our eyes lead to the inescapable assumption that those strange beings who landed in the Jersey farmlands tonight are the vanguard of an invading army from the planet Mars . . . The monster is now in control of the middle section of New Jersey and has effectively cut the state through its center. Communication lines are down from Pennsylvania to the Atlantic Ocean. Railroad service from New York to Philadelphia discontinued, except routing some of the trains through Allentown and Phoenixville. Highways to the north, south, and west are clogged with frantic human traffic. Police and Army reserves are unable to control the mad flight. By morning the fugitives will have swollen Philadelphia, Camden and Trenton, to twice their normal populations. Martial law prevails throughout New Jersey and eastern Pennsylvania. . . .

Bulletins too numerous to read are piling up in the studio here. The central portion of New Jersey is blacked out from radio communication due to the effect of the heat ray upon power lines and electrical equipment. . . .

The panic began in New Jersey and spread north and west. Men staggered into bars, babbling about the end of the world, and bartenders tuned in just in time to hear Kenny Delmar's icy message as "the Secretary of the Interior." Honoring the censors' ultimatum not to use the President's name, Delmar nevertheless put on his best Roosevelt voice. Word spread that Roosevelt was on the air, giving the public emergency instructions. Martian cylinders were falling all over the country now—in Newark, people wrapped their faces in wet towels and took to the streets in flight. A hospital there treated more than twenty people for shock. At a college campus in North Carolina, students fought over the few available telephones. The editor of the *Memphis Press–Scimitar* called his staff back to work for an extra edition on "the bombing of Chicago." A woman in Pittsburgh was saved by her husband in an attempt to swallow poison. A power shortage in a small Midwestern town at the height of the show sent people screaming into the streets. In Boston, families gathered on rooftops and imagined that they could see the glow of red against the night sky as New York burned.

The panic spread into the South—there were wild rumors that New York had been hit by a planetoid, with casualties running into millions. People gathered in churches from Richmond to Birmingham, praying to their Maker, and from towns near the Rockies people scattered into the hills, losing themselves so thoroughly that sheriffs' posses ultimately had to track them down.

And inside Studio One at CBS, Welles and his company went blissfully on, doing their thing in complete ignorance of the wholesale havoc they were creating across the country. At the end of Kenny Delmar's "Secretary of the Interior" speech, CBS supervisor Davidson Taylor was called to the phone. It was the CBS front office, with frightening reports of affiliate reactions to the show. Taylor was ordered to break into the drama with an announcement that *The War of the Worlds* was only fiction. By the time he got back to the control booth, the 40-minute break was imminent anyway. Ray Collins, as the last surviving news announcer, was describing the poisonous black smoke spreading across New York. In another moment, Collins too had died a choking on-the-air death, and an announcer said, "You are listening to a CBS presentation of Orson Welles and *The Mercury Theatre on the Air*, in an original dramatization of *The War of the Worlds*, by H. G. Wells."

There followed 20 minutes of straight drama, with Welles in his role of Professor Richard Pearson describing the aftermath of the war. In the punchline, the Martians were killed off by earth bacteria, and all was right with the world.

By then, Welles had an inkling that all wasn't right with his world. Outside the studio, police with billy clubs were swarming through the halls. Welles closed the show with assurance that *The War of the Worlds* had "no further significance than as the holiday offering it was intended to be—the *Mercury Theatre's* own radio version of dressing up in a sheet and jumping out of a bush and saying boo."

Then, certain that his career was finished, Welles went out to face the interrogations of the police and press. The next few hours were later described by Houseman as a nightmare, with reporters grilling them on reports of deaths and suicides nationwide. They learned soon enough that no one had died. And far from being destroyed, Welles' career was made by *The War of the Worlds*. His name was no longer familiar only to elitist theatre groups. Literally overnight, the Welles legend was crowned and cemented into the folklore of America. The publicity brought them a sponsor—Campbell Soups at a fat $7,500—and the name of the show was changed to *The Campbell Playhouse* with the beginning of the second season September 10, 1939. The series ended in 1940. Welles brought an unusual *Mercury* format to CBS September 15, 1941, broadcasting in 30 minutes for Lady Esther under the name *Orson Welles Theatre*. It ran until 1943, the last year as a sustainer. In 1946, the Mercury Players were heard in a summer season for Pabst Blue Ribbon, broadcasting half-hour classics from June 7 through September 13.

Two strange footnotes later brought the memory of the Martian scare into focus again. In 1939, a similar script was broadcast in Charleston, South Carolina. It was called "Palmetto Fantasy," and concerned a deadly anti-aircraft ray that went out of control and plunged into the Santee reservoir. Hundreds of people supposedly had been killed. Station WCSC in Charleston was deluged with frantic phone calls; so were police stations and newspaper offices. And in another incident, a South American station carried Welles' *War of the Worlds* with the same widespread panic. But this time, when the people learned of the hoax, they set fire to the station and killed several announcers.

Michael Shayne

Michael Shayne, the "reckless red-headed Irishman" created in detective novels by Brett Halliday, was first heard on the West Coast Don Lee Network on October 16, 1944. After two years as a regional show, *Michael Shayne* moved to Mutual in the fall of 1946 as a 30-minute thriller. In its earliest form, Shayne was played by Wally Maher, his girlfriend-secretary-sidekick Phyllis Knight was Louise Arthur, the Inspector was played by Joe Forte, and the series was produced by Bob Nye. By the time it went coast to coast, Cathy Lewis had taken the role of Phyllis, Dave Taylor was producer, and the scripts were by Richard de Graffe. The show followed Shayne, a private eye, through cases of rough-and-tumble murder, with a sprinkle of Phyllis's feminine intuition thrown in and a dash of her unabashed longing for a more permanent relationship with the hero added as a final touch. Maher, long known for his air portrayals of gangsters and heavies, came to the show fresh from being eaten alive by crocodiles on *I Love a Mystery*. Others in the network cast were Charlie Lung, Harry Lang, GeGe Pearson and Anne Stone. A version was syndicated by Don W. Sharp Productions. The syndications, directed by Bill Rousseau, starred Jeff Chandler as Shayne. His was a considerably more hard-boiled portrayal than Maher's. Still another version ran on ABC in 1952, starring Robert Sterling.

Midstream

Midstream, "where the currents of life are swiftest, where the problems of life are greatest, where the temptations of life are strongest. This is the story of Charles and Julia Meredith, who have reached the halfway mark between the distant shores of birth and death." If that opening sounds somewhat sudsy, it's with good reason. *Midstream* was one of the gushiest soaps to grace the 1939 NBC season. Actually getting its push in a 1938 debut on Cincinnati's WLW, this program came to the network May 1, 1939, churned and foamed until 1940, when it was quietly put to rest. Hugh Studebaker was Charles; Betty Lou Gerson played Julia. This obscure soap was penned by Pauline Hopkins and sponsored by Teel Soap.

The Million-Dollar Band

The Million-Dollar Band came to NBC May 29, 1943, as a 30-minute series of music for Palmolive Soap. It spotlighted the top musicians of the nation, many of whom had played with Benny Goodman, Glenn Miller, and other name bands, and the singing of Barry Wood, late of *Your Hit Parade*. One guest bandleader would appear each week to wave the stick over the *Million-Dollar Band*. The first show featured Charlie Spivak. The most unusual policy of this show was its weekly giveaway of diamond rings. Each program awarded five rings from Tiffany's to listeners who wrote the most interesting letters, specifying why certain pieces of music were sentimentally important to them and what touching memories the songs stirred up. The show carved out a respectable rating in its Saturday-night summer slot to break into the regular NBC fall lineup. It took on comedienne Patsy Kelly and became *The Palmolive Party* April 1, 1944, expiring soon after.

Millions for Defense

Millions for Defense was one of the first big Treasury Department bond shows of the war. Its debut, July 2, 1941, predated Pearl Harbor by five months, serving notice that hard times and a general tightening of belts was just ahead. The show took the place of Fred Allen's *Texaco Star Theatre* during the summer on CBS, and Allen himself served as the first week's master of ceremonies. It was a 60-minute variety hour and, typical of these wartime bond shows, had its pick of top Hollywood talent on a gratis basis. Bob Hope, Bing Crosby, and Dorothy Lamour appeared on the show of July 9; subsequent guests included Bette Davis, Lily Pons, Bud Abbott and Lou Costello, Tyrone Power, and Claudette Colbert. It became very popular during the waning months of the summer owing to its lavish format, and when Allen's show returned in the fall, *Millions for Defense* was picked up for a time on NBC. Then came Pearl Harbor, and Treasury shows were everywhere. Charles Vanda produced this one.

The Milton Berle Show

The Milton Berle Show was the most notable failure of the airwaves. Berle tried radio no less than six times between 1939 and 1949, when he finally gave up and went into television, where he could use his goofy teeth and elaborate mugging in costume to its greatest effect. But Berle's radio shows were all marked by similar traits—low ratings and brief runs. None lasted more than a year, adding solid evidence to the old theory that there are visual comics and comics of the ear.

He was born Milton Berlinger in New York in 1908, and graduated from street entertaining to acting as a child in silent films. Eventually he became a Broadway headliner, a field that led inevitably to radio.

His first radio appearance was in 1934. He appeared as a regular on the 1936 CBS show *Community Sing* for Gillette, then landed his own show—a Saturday night version of *Stop Me if You've Heard This One*—on NBC for Quaker Oats in 1939. It died soon, but Berle came back in 1941, with a Friday night sustainer on the Blue Network.

His radio shows contained the same brand of slapstick that ultimately carried him to fame. He swapped insults with announcers and supporting cast, embellished clichés, and was shameless in his theft of other people's jokes. If it was funny, Berle used it, and it mattered not a whole lot that someone else might have used it first. So blatant was Berle at stealing material that he became known in the trade as the "thief of badgags." Fred Allen called him a "parrot with skin on." Bob Hope told a *Time* reporter that "when you see Berle, you're seeing the best things of anybody who has ever been on Broadway. I want to get into television before he uses up all my material."

Berle's comedy depended on pained grimaces and a "What's up, doc?" delivery. In 1944, he brought his most unusual show to the Blue Network for Eversharp Pens titled *Let Yourself Go;* this one later ran on CBS and was ideally suited to Berle's personality, being a half-hour of stunts designed to dissolve social inhibitions. Contestants, selected from show business and from the studio audience, were invited onstage to tell Berle and announcer Ken Roberts of their long-suppressed yens. Then they shed their dignity (and nobody was better at that than Berle) and "let themselves go." The contestants got $25 and were judged for a $100 grand prize, awarded each week to the one who did this best. Some wanted to break eggs in Berle's face; some wanted to be firemen or throw snowballs. Whatever the urge, Berle did his best to accommodate, acting the eternal stooge to the roars of the studio audience and the silence of those gathered around the radio sets, who could only try to imagine what all the people were laughing at.

The funniest Berle offering was his 1947 *Milton Berle Show* for Philip Morris. For whatever reason, this too went down the drain. By 1948, Texaco had replaced Philip Morris, and it was with Texaco that Berle sailed into NBC-TV in 1949, becoming nationally famous as "Mr. Television."

The 1947 series featured Pert Kelton, Mary Shipp, Jack Albertson, Arthur Q. Bryan, Arnold Stang, and Ed Begley. As with *Let Yourself Go,* music was by Ray Bloch. Announcer Frank Gallop added greatly to the program, needling Berle unmercifully with his deep, dry scorn.

Mischa the Magnificent

Mischa the Magnificent was a summertime CBS comedy, premiering July 5, 1942, and running through the summer. Mischa Auer, the Russian actor who had been in films since the late 1920's, was cast as himself—a man writing the memoirs of his golden youth. Each episode, scored to the theme, "The Volga Boat Man," explored some deeper aspect of his past, from Mischa the lover to Mischa the famed opera singer. His standard greeting to anyone on the show was, "Greetings, my little cabbage." *Mischa the Magnificent* was produced by Paul Pierce and written by Carl Hertzinger.

Mr. and Mrs. Blandings

Mr. and Mrs. Blandings was a particularly weak comedy effort, especially considering the talent involved. Based on the movie *Mr. Blandings Builds His Dream House* (in turn based on Eric Hodgins' best-selling novel), the show brought to the NBC mikes the star of the film, Cary Grant and his real-life wife, Betsy Drake. The Grants played Jim and Muriel Blandings, young city people who took up residence in the country, coming fully equipped with Jim's occasional forgetfulness and Muriel's occasional jealousy. Their marital bliss was broken by frequent misunderstandings, some so farfetched that the show was blasted from all sides by media critics. Grant, particularly stung by the critical brickbats, blamed weak writing, and rejected several scripts until his wife produced one he considered suitable. *Mr. and Mrs. Blandings* opened as an NBC Sunday-night feature on January 21, 1951, and closed less than a year later. The sponsor was Trans World Airlines. Gale Gordon and Sheldon Leonard provided solid help in supporting roles, but it wasn't enough to save the series from its own inertia. Nat Wolf was producer-writer when it opened, and the director was Warren Lewis.

Mr. and Mrs. North

Mr. and Mrs. North began as a CBS comedy in 1941. When he wrote the first *Mr. and Mrs. North* stories, Richard Lockridge made Pam and Jerry a lighthearted, comfy couple whose amusing domestic adventures were gobbled up by *The New Yorker*. It wasn't until 1940, when Lockridge teamed up with his wife Frances, that the Norths met murder and snowballed their way to the most successful amateur husband-wife crimefighting team of the time. *The Norths Meet Murder* had been published and the characters had made the transition to stage and film before radio got its teeth into *Mr. and Mrs. North*. But in the initial show, the murder element was completely ignored. Pam and Jerry reverted to situation comedy in performances by Peggy Conklin (who also played Pam in the play) and Carl Eastman. It was just a light situation romance, produced and written by Howard Harris and Martin Gosch. Donald Voorhees provided the music, and this version soon blew away.

In its widely remembered mystery form, the show opened on NBC December 30, 1942. Within a year of its debut on NBC, the new *Mr. and Mrs. North* was one of the most popular thrillers of the air. Generally finishing just behind *Mr. District Attorney* in the crime popularity charts, Pam and Jerry North became the souls of normality. They solved only common murders—the shootings, the stabbings, the crimes of passion—leaving the more exotic cases to official gangbusters. Neither was trained in the art of deduction. Jerry was just a "normal" book publisher who happened, once a week, to stumble over a corpse. Pam was his "normal" housewife who loved cats, talked in riddles and usually managed through clever detection and women's intuition to figure out the killer's identity just ahead of the men.

The other man in the cast was Lieutenant Bill Weigand, who saw so much of the Norths that he eventually became their friend. Weigand got used to the idea after a while: wherever the Norths would go, murder always followed. If they went on a train trip, a corpse would be stuffed in an upper berth. Look in the bathroom, body in the bathtub. Just one of the many nuisances that a busy publisher had to cope with. Ultimately, it was the secret of the Norths' success. The idea of "normal" people encountering murder was sheer escapism, and soon the show had 20 million fans. Everything but their apartment was geared to the "common" listener.

The Norths lived at 24 St. Anne's Place, a mythical apartment in New York's Greenwich Village. Their acquaintances in the neighborhood bordered on the bizarre: floaters through the underworld, neighborhood sellers of tips, and a talkative cabbie named Mahatma McGloin were among their contacts. Early in the series, they were also burdened by a 14-year-old niece who managed to happen upon a few bodies without any help from Pam or Jerry.

For five years the show ran as an NBC Wednesday-nighter, first for Woodbury Soap (1942–45) and then for Jergens Lotion (1945–47). *Mr. and Mrs. North* moved to CBS for Colgate-Palmolive in 1947 and was heard on Tuesday nights until 1954. Then the show moved to Monday, sustained by CBS. Late in the run, it became a five-a-week 15-minute serial. Pam and Jerry were played by Alice Frost and Joseph Curtin. In its closing days the roles were taken by Barbara Britton and Richard Denning, who played the Norths into TV. Frank Lovejoy played Weigand, a role also done by Staats Cotsworth and Francis DeSales. Betty Jane Tyler was niece Susan, Mandel Kramer was cabbie McGloin, and Walter Kinsella played the forever exasperated Sergeant Mullins. The show was produced first by S. James Andrews, later by John W. Loveton. Heavy use was made of "mood music," which was written and conducted by Charles Paul.

Mr. Chameleon

Mr. Chameleon was the "famous and dreaded detective" who often used a disguise to track down a killer. Thus the subtitle, The Man of Many Faces.

The disguise was at all times recognizable by the audience and so were the hero's obvious soap opera tactics. But then, Mr. Chameleon was a creation of Frank and Anne Hummert. Chameleon—as drawn by the Hummerts, was "famous and celebrated," operating out of Central Police Headquarters in his relentless pursuit of criminals. A case was "famous" the moment it was assigned to Chameleon, even if the body was still warm and the killer was still on the premises.

Like his blood brother Mr. Keen, Mr. Chameleon really needed no help in his crime fighting. But the Hummerts gave him Detective Dave Arnold anyway. It was a trick dating back to Sherlock Holmes and Watson, perhaps beyond—that of giving the brilliant hero a none-too-bright sidekick to ask the dumb questions and make sure the Great One had plugged all the holes. Often with Mr. Chameleon that wasn't necessary; the listeners were sometimes two jumps ahead of Chameleon himself. But we got Detective Arnold anyway.

About three-quarters of the way through each play, Chameleon usually disappeared, returning in disguise. Often the disguises were superfluous and useless, designed chiefly to throw the killer off guard by making him think that the "famous and dreaded detective" was no longer at the scene. In one episode the disguise was so bad that even the killer saw through it immediately. But the "man of many faces" had a name to uphold, and the disguises kept coming.

Mr. Chameleon came to CBS for Bayer Aspirin July 14, 1948. Like most Hummert shows, it immediately grabbed a sizable chunk of the Wednesday-night audience. Karl Swenson played Chameleon; Frank Butler was Dave Arnold. The show ran until 1951 for Bayer, then moved into the CBS Sunday lineup where it was heard for one more year as a sustaining show.

No matter what one thinks of the Hummerts, they sure knew their American public.

Mr. District Attorney

Mr. District Attorney was first heard on NBC April 3, 1939, in a nightly 15-minute serial format. Thomas E. Dewey, New York's racket-busting district attorney of the late 1930's, was the inspiration and model for this crime show. Dewey's front-page war against corruption and racketeers swept him to the governorship of his state, and culminated in two strong runs for the presidency.

Ed Byron had been knocking around in radio for several years, at one time pumping out scripts for WLW, Cincinnati, for as little as $1 each. In 1939 Byron, ready for some professional growth, was convinced that his future lay in independent production of radio shows, so he formed Byron Productions and went fishing for that elusive Something Different.

Dewey was exactly the kind of hero Byron had in mind: a tough, crusading D.A. who wouldn't hesitate to go after the "big boys" of organized crime. Almost single-handedly Dewey had changed the image of the district attorney from the incompetent inquisitor portrayed by Hollywood to the white-collar sleuth of news flashes and banner headlines. That was "Mr. District Attorney," the man Ed Byron prepared to bring to the air in the spring of 1939.

Phillips H. Lord, veteran producer of crime shows, had coined the title. When the show opened as a nightly serial, Dwight Weist played the unnamed D.A., who had just been elected after a bruising campaign against the racketeers and corrupters. Throughout the network run, the D.A. remained nameless. To his sidekick Harrington and his secretary Miss Miller, he was known as "Chief" or "Boss." To the people he became simply "Mr. District Attorney," a staunch authority figure cut from the frills of Lone Ranger cloth. On June 27, 1939, the show shifted to 30 minutes weekly, running through the summer as Pepsodent's replacement for vacationing Bob Hope. When Hope returned, Pepsodent also kept Mr. District Attorney, moving the show into the Blue Network's Sunday-night schedule. It didn't take long for the half-hour version to begin sweeping the ratings charts, vaulting into the top 10 and staying there for several years.

During the summers when the big-name comedians were on break, Mr. District Attorney led all shows in ratings. In 1940, the D.A. moved to NBC Wednesdays for its long Bristol-Myers run. It came each Wednesday, shrilly pushing Vitalis, Bufferin, Ipana, and Sal Hepatica. The opening was a zinger, still fondly remembered by people who followed it through the years.

> MISTER DISTRICT ATTORNEY!
> CHAMPION OF THE PEOPLE!
> GUARDIAN OF OUR FUNDAMENTAL RIGHTS TO LIFE,
> LIBERTY AND THE PURSUIT OF HAPPINESS!

Then a rousing fanfare by Peter Van Steeden's orchestra, and the echoed oath of the D.A.: ". . . and it shall be my duty as district attorney not only to prosecute to the limit of the law all persons accused of crimes perpetrated within this county, but to defend with equal vigor the rights and privileges of all its citizens."

Byron took that oath seriously. His D.A. was a man of great compassion as well as a vigorous prosecutor of criminals. Byron himself, a former law student who had assembled 5,000 books on crimes and criminal justice, made weekly excursions with his writer, Robert Shaw, to some of the city's best dives. There he rubbed elbows with thieves and punks in his unending search for material. Byron and Shaw visited bars where cops and reporters mingled after work. By his 40th birthday, Byron was near expert on the con game. *Newsweek* found his talk pithy and crude, "as if he mixed with no one but gangsters."

But the result was a show of startling realism for its time. *Mr. District Attorney* had the air and pace of the front pages. So alert was Byron to crime trends (con games in the spring, juvenile delinquency and husband-wife murders in the fall; burglaries in the winter) that he often scooped the press. In 1942, his June 17 script about Nazi submarines dropping off spies along the Atlantic Coast brought him a visit from FBI agents. The G-Men had just picked up a group of Nazis in almost the same manner described on *Mr. District Attorney*. They were about to blow their own horns in a press release when Byron took the wind out of their sails. In another case, when *Mr. District Attorney* raided a phony sanatarium in the early 1940's, the raid was timed to the day with a real raid on a real sanatarium by real cops —though the script had been written weeks before. The program aired a show about an insane veteran shooting people in the streets on the same day that a real vet went berserk and began shooting up Camden, New Jersey. By reading five daily newspapers and keeping abreast of city trends, Byron was able to carve out a reputation for his show as an uncanny forecaster of news events.

The series won many awards for excellence, doing scripts on racial prejudice and social issues as well as crime stories. Its cast and crew remained for most of the run. Vicki Vola went all the way as Miss Miller; Len Doyle played Harrington, the ex-cop turned D.A.'s investigator, for most of the run. Jay Jostyn came aboard as Mr. District Attorney in October 1940 and stayed through the network run. His portrayal won the personal approval of Thomas E. Dewey himself. At the 1940 Republican National Convention, several delegates cast persistent votes for Dewey over the eventual winner Wendell Willkie on the strength of the radio show alone. *Mr. District Attorney* was heard on NBC Wednesdays for B-M products Vitalis and Sal Hepatica until 1951, when Bristol-Myers followed it to ABC for a final season on Fridays. With the closing of the network run, a new series was syndicated by Ziv in the early 1950's. This one starred David Brian as Paul Garrett. At long last, after years of fighting rackets and crooks, the D.A. had earned his right to a name. This version became the basis for a TV series.

Mr. Feathers

Mr. Feathers was a lighthearted situation comedy first heard on Mutual November 9, 1949. It starred Parker Fennelly, the Titus Moody of *The Fred Allen Show*, as a homespun philosopher "not quite like any next-door neighbor you ever had." Mr. Feathers ran a drug store in "the untroubled and quite untypical town of Pike City." As Mr. Feathers, Fennelly had the usual run of village idiots to contend with, and despite his great talent and dry New England wit, the series never quite made it and was gone by 1951. The show was created especially for Fennelly by Gerald Holland. *Mr. Feathers* was produced by Herbert Rice and directed by Rocco Tito, with music by Ben Ludlow.

Mr. Keen, Tracer of Lost Persons

Mr. Keen, Tracer of Lost Persons was first heard on NBC October 12, 1937, as a three-a-week 15-minute serial for Bisodol. Mr. Keen might legitimately be called Mr. Chameleon's "grandfather." His show was about eleven years older, and he would have been at least 60 by the time *Chameleon* hit the air in 1948. Keen and Chameleon were almost exactly alike, both drawn from the joint well of Frank and Anne Hummert, both working on the same kinds of murder cases, both using simple methods of catching killers and both using dumber-than-thou assistants. The *Mr. Keen* show moved to CBS in 1942, remaining a serial until 1943, when it became a weekly half-hour for Kolynos on Thursday nights.

In the beginning, Mr. Keen lived up to his billing, tracing lost persons through their personal jungles in fairly tight stories. But with the half-hour version, tracing became a lost art; Mr. Keen and Mike Clancy became primarily homicide detectives, even though they kept the distinctive "tracer" moniker and the long-remembered theme, "Someday I'll Find You." They seemed to have no official position, yet—as Clancy often said, "We usually work along with the police, ma'am." But they did have arrest powers. They barged into private homes without search warrants, Mr. Keen leading the way with kindly charm and soft persuasion, but always flanked by the boneheaded Clancy in case the going got rough. Whenever Keen's Mike Clancy put his alleged brain to work, a vacuum developed over the Atwater-Kent and remained there for days.

Clancy was incredible. "Saints preserve us, Mr. Keen, do you mean . . .?" he said, week after week. Ever the patient and kindly investigator, Mr. Keen replied sagely, "Yes, Mike," as though explaining the facts of life to his small child. One of the great portraits in the Radio Hall Of Fame is of Mike Clancy—mouth open, scratching his head.

The show ran Thursdays on CBS for the Whitehall Drug Company from 1946 through 1951, Thursdays on NBC for Chesterfield in 1951–52, and Friday nights on CBS for a variety of sponsors from 1952 through 1954. As the show matured, it seemed to follow a reverse trend and disintegrate, eventually settling into a steady grind of half-hour melodrama. That was the format until the early 1950's when *Mr. Keen* again became a 15-minute NBC serial, with nightly episodes and stories that concluded each week, and at times running concurrently with the 30-minute version. By then there was little to distinguish *Mr. Keen* from *The Romance of Helen Trent* or any of the Hummerts' other daytime serials. The dialogue was campy and unreal, employing the age-old Hummert technique of identifying the speaker and the subject fully with every sentence:

MISS CARSON: Before I open this door, Mr. Keen, let me tell you something. No one in this house right now had anything to do with the murder of young Donald Travers, my niece's husband.

MR. KEEN: That remains to be proven, Miss Martha.

MISS CARSON: My niece Jane Travers should never have sent you here.

MR. KEEN: Jane Travers only wanted to help you prove your innocence, Miss Martha.

Bennett Kilpack was the longest-running Mr. Keen; Philip Clarke took over late in the run and finished the series. During the show's salad days, Kilpack's fan mail was of much the same sort received by actresses who played in Hummert soaps: listeners asking for help tracing boyfriends, children, husbands, or wives who had simply vanished. Jim Kelly was Mike Clancy, and Richard Leonard directed. Dialogue was generally attributed to Frank Hummert, but was turned out at his direction by the usual Hummert assembly line.

Mr. President

Mr. President came to ABC June 26, 1947, with stories of "Mr. President, at home in the White House—the elected leader of our people, our fellow citizen and neighbor. These are little-known stories of the men who have lived in the White House—dramatic, exciting events in their lives that you and I so rarely hear." The shows, meticulously researched, were designed to capture the human side of the chief executive. The president was never identified by name during the story; listeners were invited to guess his identity, which was later revealed in a brief epilogue. To play the president, the producers looked for "an actor with the aggressiveness of Teddy Roosevelt, the warmth and humility of Abe Lincoln, and the tenacity of Andrew Jackson." They came up with Edward Arnold, a solid choice. Arnold soon immersed himself in the job, reading all he could find each week on the upcoming presidents, though he never tried to characterize the role. "They're all Edward Arnold," he said once, "otherwise the guessing game would be lost."

Arnold had an intense interest in politics, and once during the series almost ran for Senate on the Republican ticket. He became friends with President Harry Truman, who often chided him on his Republican philosophy and referred to him as "Mr. President." The series was created by Robert G. Jennings, produced and directed by Dick Woollen and written by Jean Holloway who, for a time, got unusual billing up front with Arnold. Other writers included Bernard Dougall and Ira Marion. After a summer stint on Thursdays, Mr. President ran on ABC for three years as a Sunday feature, then moved to Wednesday for another three-year run. Mostly sustained, it finally passed away in 1953.

The Mollé Mystery Theatre

The Mollé Mystery Theatre was the best-known title of a series that premièred on NBC September 7, 1943, and ran under several formats on several networks between 1943 and 1954. Alexander Semmler composed the music; Dan Seymour announced and plugged Mollé in a memorable commercial jingle:

It's smooth . . . so smooth . . .
It's slick . . . so slick . . .

It's a smooth smooth slick slick shave you get
With M-O-L-L-E!

For Mollé, the show was heard on NBC in 1943–44 (Sundays), on Mutual in 1944–45 (Sundays), and on NBC in 1945–47 (Fridays). It featured the "best in mystery and detective fiction," with tales running the gamut from such old masters as Edgar Allen Poe to modernists Raymond Chandler, Joseph Ruscoll, and William Irish. The stories were selected and introduced by Geoffrey Barnes, the on-the-air pseudonym of Bernard Lenrow. Described in NBC publicity releases as "a connoisseur of mysteries," Lenrow had been hooked on the genre in the late 1920's, and had since read 100 mystery novels a year.

In all, *The Mollé Mystery Theatre* was respectable radio, with many old pros of the medium taking the parts. Elspeth Eric, Joseph Julian, Frank Lovejoy, and Richard Widmark were a few who appeared. In 1947, Mollé dropped the show, and it became simply *The Mystery Theatre*, broadcasting on NBC Friday nights for Sterling Drugs. In 1948, it moved to Tuesday-night CBS, where in 1951 it became the melodramatic *Hearthstone of the Death Squad*. *Hearthstone* ran on CBS Thursdays, featuring Alfred Shirley in a Mr. Chameleon-type role under the direction of Frank and Anne Hummert. Meanwhile, the *Mystery Theatre* format, still under Sterling Drug sponsorship, turned up Wednesday nights on ABC, where it featured police cases investigated by "Inspector Mark Sabre." Robert Carroll played the suave Mr. Sabre in a series that lacked the zip of the old Mollé days.

Murder and Mr. Malone

Murder and Mr. Malone starred Frank Lovejoy as John J. Malone, "fiction's most famous criminal lawyer." It was based on the Malone novels and movie scripts by Craig Rice, and was heard on ABC Saturday nights from January 11, 1947, through 1948. Lovejoy played the kind of part he did best—that of a cynical, somewhat humorless man with a keen analytical mind sharpened by years of courtroom fencing. The show was sponsored by Wine Growers, produced by Bernard L. Schubert, and directed by Bill Rousseau. John Duffy scored; Art Gilmore announced.

On September 21, 1949, the show was revived on ABC Wednesday nights as *The Amazing Mr. Malone*. Lovejoy had gone to other things, and the role was played by Gene Raymond.

Murder at Midnight

Murder at Midnight was a series produced by KFI, Los Angeles, and syndicated in 1946. It featured tales of the supernatural and macabre by radio's top writers and performers. Elspeth Eric, Mercedes McCambridge, Berry Kroeger, Betty Caine, Carl Frank, Barry Hopkins and Lawson Zerbe were Murder at Midnight regulars. The stories were wild tales of death and the uncanny—of severed hands coming to life; of death appearing as a man in a black beard. It told of "the witching hour . . . when night is darkest, our fears the strongest, our strength at its lowest ebb. Midnight—when graves gape open and death strikes! Thus comes 'Murder at Midnight.' This show tried to do what Inner Sanctum did so memorably on the networks; the stories were often the equal of Inner Sanctum yarns, but the format wasn't in the same ballpark. Writers included Robert Newman, an old Inner Sanctum alumnus, Joseph Ruscoll of Mollé Mystery Theatre, Max Ehrlich of Suspense, and William Morwood of Bulldog Drummond. Charles Paul contributed the creepy organ music; the director was Anton M. Leader. And that sinister-voiced narrator whose voice dripped "MURRR-DERRR——A-A-ATTT MID-NIGHT!" was none other than Raymond Morgan, a former Long Island minister who had given up the cloth for the excitement of radio.

Murder by Experts

Murder by Experts was a fine Mutual mystery-detective series sustained on Monday nights from September 26, 1949, through 1951. Offered here were tales chosen by the world's leading writers of mystery fiction. Hosts were also top writers—for a time John Dickson Carr and Brett Halliday. The stories were highly charged plots of crime and passion, bearing out the adage that the best is produced by the best. Most of the murders on Murder by Experts were simple crimes without gimmickry, gadgetry, or fancy embellishment, but heavily laden with human emotion. Emerson Buckley provided the music. Serving jointly as producer-directors were Robert A. Arthur and David Kogan, the writing team from Mutual's Mysterious Traveler.

Murder Will Out

Murder Will Out wasn't the newest idea on the air when it premièred on the Blue Network early in 1945. This Tuesday-night mystery quiz followed the same basic formula as Ellery Queen's *Armchair Detective* shows—fully dramatized murder mysteries, followed by guesses from the audience on "who done it." Writer-director Lew Lansworth did have a few new twists. His stories contained no trick clues, but were followed chronologically by police, with clues being considered in the order found. They were based on real cases, and the clues unfolded as they had in real life, putting listeners at the same level as the cops. The cops in these dramas were Inspector Burke, played by Edmond MacDonald, and Detective Nolan, played by Eddie Marr. With their drama finished, announcer Larry Keating brought four people onstage for the guessing game. It was a man-versus-woman affair, with two representatives from each sex and war bonds as the prize. (The ladies usually won.)

The Music Appreciation Hour

The Music Appreciation Hour was one of radio's early music education series. Its creator, Walter Damrosch, came to radio after a long and distinguished career as a leader in concert music. He served as assistant director of the Metropolitan Opera and for many years after the turn of the century was leader of the New York Symphony Orchestra. His first experiment with radio came in 1925 when he conducted the first full symphony concert of the air. In 1927, he joined NBC, where he premièred his long-running *Music Appreciation Hour* on the Blue Network in the winter of 1928. The show's purpose was to bring the deeper meanings of music to the younger generation; from the beginning, *The Music Appreciation Hour* was seen as a tool of education. Heard Friday mornings at 11 A.M., it became part of hundreds of curriculums in its first year. The 60-minute format was divided into segments for grammar-school and high-school students; both segments were so structured as to provide learning experiences for college-level students and adults as well. Damrosch always fully explained a piece, then led the orchestra in the playing. NBC prepared a series of workbooks, which were available to schools at a small cost. *The Music Appreciation Hour* ran until 1942. Damrosch died December 22, 1950.

Musical Bouquet

Musical Bouquet was a Sunday-afternoon ABC entry of 1945. Produced by Mildred Fenton, it featured 30 minutes of popular romantic music and song, narrated by the "word pictures" of host Bret Morrison. Louise Marlow and French-Canadian singer Paul Frenet were the soloists. Music was by the Earl Sheldon Orchestra.

The Musical Steelmakers

The Musical Steelmakers featured amateurs turned semi-professionals in a Sunday-afternoon program. It started on Station WWVA in Wheeling, West Virginia in 1936, featuring the musical talents of Wheeling Steel Corporation employees. The workers served on the program in addition to their regular duties at the plant, putting in a minimum ten hours a week rehearsal. Secretary Regina Colbert became one of the series' leading singers; so did Alma Custer, a receptionist. Other "Steelmakers" included Lois Mae Nolte as emcee, John Wincholl as the show's "Old Timer and Interlocutor," Mary Bower as harpist, Carlo Ross, Bill Griffiths, and the Evans Family. Music was conducted by Lew Davies. The show became so popular locally that in 1938 it was picked up by Mutual, where it ran as a late-afternoon Sunday feature for three years. In 1941, *The Musical Steelmakers* went to the Blue, where it continued for another three years. Wheeling Steel sponsored the network version too, and the show originated from the Capitol Theatre in Wheeling.

My Favorite Husband

My Favorite Husband was Lucille Ball's first regular radio show, premièring on CBS July 5, 1948. Co-starred was Lee Bowman and thereafter Richard Denning; the two played Liz and George Cooper, "two people who live together and like it." George was a banker; their home, "a little white two-story house" located at 321 Bundy Drive in the "bustling little suburb of Sheridan Falls." Miss Ball was the zany housewife she would perfect a few years later on the TV show *I Love Lucy*. Since the Coopers had a maid—Katie—to do all the household dirty work, Liz's chief function lay in the creation of those weekly domestic snarls that made life so interesting for hubby George. And George helped out by being the typical screwy husband, sometimes forgetful, sometimes lovable—the stereotyped radio male. George's partner in crime was his boss, the short-fused banker Rudolph Atterbury. Liz's favorite cohort was the boss' wife Iris, whose greeting, "Ah, Liz-girl, George-boy" is one of the best-remembered lines on the show. Gale Gordon played Atterbury with his usual sarcasm; Bea Benaderet was his wife Iris. Ruth Perrott was Katie in this comedy. The show was produced by Jess Oppenheimer and written by Bob

Carroll, Jr. and Madelyn Pugh. After its initial summer season, it ran three years on CBS for General Foods, on Friday nights from 1948 until 1950, and Saturdays during 1950–51. Lucy was in good form, right down to the famed crying fits.

My Friend Irma

My Friend Irma was first heard on CBS early in 1947. The program bore the unmistakable stamp of Cy Howard, the reformed introvert who a year later gave us *Life with Luigi.* Irma was a law firm stenographer by trade; she lived in a ramshackle apartment run by the crusty Mrs. O'Reilly, and her world—like Luigi's—was peopled by strong, identifiable characters. Her roommate, Jane Stacy, was almost her opposite—completely sane, dependable, logical in every way that Irma was not. Jane narrated the stories, telling of her life with the screwy Irma and mixing the narrative with love and exasperation at the antics of her peabrained roommate. The big element in Jane's life was her love of her millionaire boss. "Wouldn't it be great if I would end up being Mrs. Richard Rhinelander the third?" she asked Irma one night in a moment of weakness. "The third?" replied Irma, "what good will that do if he's got two other wives?"

Marie Wilson broke the mold for dumb blondes everywhere. In October 1947, when *My Friend Irma* was less than six months old, a *Time* reviewer described it as a follower "in the artfully stumbling footsteps of Gracie Allen, Jane Ace, and other attractive dunderheads." In fact, this show would soon be the leader. Jane Ace, chiefly a master scrambler of words, was a dunderhead of a different kind. In the realm of the logically illogical featherbrained blonde, Gracie Allen was Miss Wilson's only peer. And even Gracie couldn't top Irma Peterson.

Only Irma would answer a question about compulsory military service by saying that "a girl shouldn't have to go out with a sailor unless she wants to." A newscast telling of racketeers operating swindle shops on Second Avenue was followed by Irma's entrance and her inevitable announcement that she had found some fantastic bargains shopping—guess where.

When the show first hit the air, Cy Howard did everything from writing to directing. He was hungry then, eager to escape the humdrum life of the salesman. But despite immediate success in the ratings (*Irma* had a healthy Hooper of 20-plus before the first season was out), the show sold to Lever Brothers only after twenty weeks of bartering. Ultimately Howard brought in Parke Levy as writer-director and Stanley Adams as writing assistant. Lud Gluskin's orchestra provided the music, and the "Friendship! Friendship! Just a perfect blendship" theme played on Jane's true affection for her crazy friend Irma.

Jane always had Irma's interests at heart. That was why she frequently tried to discourage the romance between Irma and the street hustler Al. "Al has no job, no money, no clothes, no car, no prospects and no future," she once told Irma. "I know," Irma said, "but I have to stick with him in case things get tough." Al's Brooklyn voice was patiently understanding. "Hi-ya, chicken," he said in weekly greeting, and Irma's troubles began to melt away.

Good for one walk-on per show was Professor Kropotkin, the violinist of the Paradise Burlesque who lived in the flat downstairs. The professor carried on a running battle of insults with Mrs. O'Reilly: his entrance was always marked by a soft knock at the door and his sheepish German voice: "It's only me, Professor Kropotkin."

The parts were played by radio's best-known voices. Cathy Lewis was Jane, John Brown played Al, Hans Conried was Professor Kropotkin, and Gloria Gordon was Mrs. O'Reilly. Leif Erickson played Richard Rhinelander the Third and Alan Reed was Irma's boss, the crotchety lawyer Mr. Clyde.

So popular was the show that it was brought to the screen by Hal Wallis in 1949. Marie Wilson made the transition, but the movie My Friend Irma served primarily as the launching pad for the careers of Dean Martin and Jerry Lewis. Irma ran on Monday nights from 1947 until 1951; it moved to Sundays in 1951, and to Tuesdays in 1952 for Camel Cigarettes. In 1953–54, its final season, My Friend Irma was carried by a variety of sponsors on Tuesday nights.

My Little Margie

My Little Margie is best remembered as a TV show, but an almost identical audio version ran on CBS Sunday nights under the sponsorship of Philip Morris from December 7, 1952, through 1955. Margie was Margie Albright, who lived with her father Verne—a busy executive with Honeywell Industries—in an apartment "high atop New York's Fifth Avenue." The comedy usually revolved around father Verne or boyfriend Freddie. They were natural enemies, though Freddie did his best in his bumbling way to gain Verne's confidence. Margie, a natural female schemer in the best radio tradition, was aided and abetted by her friend and neighbor, an older woman named Mrs. Odetts. As in the TV version, Margie and Verne were played by Gale Storm and Charles Farrell. Verna Felton was Mrs. Odetts, Gil Stratton, Jr. was Freddie, and Will Wright played Verne's often grouchy boss, Mr. Honeywell. The show was based on characters created by Frank Fox, produced, directed, and transcribed by Gordon Hughes with Hal Roach, Jr. and Roland Reed, and written by Lee Carson.

My Son and I

My Son and I was an obscure CBS soap, first heard October 9, 1939, for Swansdown Cake Flour and running just about a year. It followed the trials of Connie Vance, former vaudeville trouper whose husband had passed on to his great reward, leaving her with a young son to raise. The story concerned Connie's fight for security. She had time in her brief year to be kidnapped and held prisoner in a remote Mexican hideout, with son Buddy Watson and old Aunt Minta as her co-captives. Betty Garde played Connie; Kingsley Colton was Buddy and Agnes Young played Aunt Minta. Charles Paul was at the organ.

My True Story

My True Story, broadcast in cooperation with the magazine, came to ABC February 15, 1943, as a five-a-week, 30-minute morning dose of heartbreak, complete in each show. The glaring headline from the 1948 cover of True Story magazine gives a good synopsis of the show's content. Whether it was "Lost and Alone, I Loved My Sister Too Much" or "Anyone Would Have Been Better than the Man My Daughter Married," the radio version was just about as maudlin. Scores of people worked on the series over its fifteen-year ABC run, and even when that expired in 1959, NBC picked it up for another two-year stint. My True Story told the stories people liked to read and hear—of those in trouble, of people motivated by "strange, selfish desires," of others torn by discovery that a loved one had feet of clay after all. The magazine is still peddling that formula.

The Mysterious Traveler

The Mysterious Traveler first rode the rails on Mutual in 1943 as a Sunday-night sustained show. The series ran on Mutual for nine years, bowing out in 1952, never having had a sponsor.

All memorable radio characters had their distinctive entrees. The Whistler came whistling out of the night; Captain Midnight zoomed down in his airplane; the Shadow was just there suddenly, knowing all evil that lurked in the hearts of men. The Mysterious Traveler came on a train. "This is a Mysterious Traveler, inviting you to join me on another journey into the strange and the terrifying. I hope you will enjoy the trip, that it will thrill you a little and chill you a little. So settle back, get a good grip on your nerves and be comfortable—if you can . . ."

Maurice Tarplin brought just the right amount of morbid mischief to the Traveler's voice. Like the Whistler, he never appeared in the stories; he narrated from on high, from an omniscient perch within the soul of his hero. The stories ran from wild "end-of-the-world" science fiction to straight crime. In some ways, The Mysterious Traveler was as close to Escape in story content as it was to The Whistler.

"Behind the Locked Door," the all-time classic Mysterious Traveler show, was requested again and again by listeners. A pair of archaeologists found an old cave buried behind a landslide. Blasting away the rubble, they saw the remains of an ancient wagon train. Gradually Professor Stevens pieced together the story. The pioneers, pursued into the cave's mouth by attacking Indians, were sealed alive. But what if they hadn't all died? What if some thrived underground, reproducing themselves through the ages? What if people still lived in this dark world, five generations removed from civilization? What would they look like?

Slowly the horror of their situation began to creep over them. Their guide was attacked; they found him with his throat torn out. Then their lights flicker and go out; alone, in total darkness, they prepare to meet the monsters of the cave. The story ends with a scream of terror, blending into the clackety-clack of the Traveler's train: "Oh, you have to get off here! I'm sorry! I'm sure we'll meet again. I take this same train every week at this same time . . ."

The Traveler was always pulling endings like that. We never quite saw the monster, but maybe in a way that was better. Anyway, that's how the stories flowed from the typewriters of Robert A. Arthur and David Kogan, who also produced and directed.

As with most unsponsored anthologies, The Mysterious Traveler avoided "star" players and instead drew its talent from the world of the unsung radio professional. Scores of musicians, announcers, and actors—representing many of the medium's best pros—worked on the show over its nine-year run.

Mystery in the Air

Mystery in the Air was a title given to at least two summertime crime-mystery series sponsored by Camel Cigarettes on NBC in the mid-1940's. One *Mystery in the Air* premièred July 5, 1945, and ran as a thirteen-week replacement for *The Abbott and Costello Show.* It featured Stephen Courtleigh as detective Stonewall Scott, with the support of Joan Vitez as Dr. Alison, Ed Jerome as Dr. Dietrich, and Geoffrey Bryant as Tex. This one was written by Robert Newman and directed by Kenneth MacGregor. *A Mystery in the Air* again took the place of *The Abbott and Costello Show* for the summer beginning July 3, 1947. This was a fine radio show, starring Peter Lorre in dramatizations of great crime classics. Lorre delivered supercharged, intense performances as tormented, driven men. The shows included "The Marvelous Barastro," "The Lodger," "The Horla," "Beyond Good And Evil," "The Mask of Medusa," "Queen of Spades," "The Black Cat," and "Crime And Punishment." Harry Morgan, then going by the name Henry Morgan, was announcer. Others supporting Lorre included Agnes Moorehead, Russell Thorson, Barbara Eiler, John Brown, Peggy Webber, Joe Kearns, Luis Van Rooten, Herb Butterfield, Howard Culver, Jane Morgan, and Ben Wright. Michael Roy was commercial announcer, and the show was directed by Cal Kuhl.

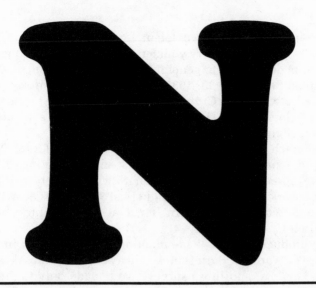

The National Barn Dance

The National Barn Dance was first heard on Chicago Station WLS, in April 1924, and was a Saturday night mainstay for more than 20 years. The clang of cowbells, a fiddlin' rendition of "Hey, Hey, Hey, the hayloft gang is here," and greetings by host Joe Kelly ushered in America's first radio hillbilly show. "Hello, hello, hello, everybody, everywhere; well, well welcome to your ole Alka Seltzer National Barn Dance." For genuine country entertainment, only *Grand Ole Opry* gave this show a run for its money.

Barn Dance came from Chicago, but its people came from everywhere. And over the years they changed their show little. For more than twenty-five years the program followed the same basic pattern set that April in 1924, when WLS was in its first week on the air.

By 1928, the demand for tickets had far outgrown the studio's ability to accommodate. With the move into the 1,200-seat Eighth Street Theatre, *The National Barn Dance* began to dress up for its audience—a real audience now, and a paying one at that. While the Eighth Street Theatre stood half empty other nights of the week, the people packed it on Saturday nights, paying 75 cents each (35 cents for kids) for a four-hour hoedown. Listeners got only a 60-minute slice, later trimmed to 30 minutes, punctuated by commercials for Alka Seltzer, a new product that had come aboard just before the network run began. And they got a verbal description of the window dressing—the straw bales the cast sat on, the haypile in the corner of the stage, the jeans and pigtails. Like its Nashville cousin, *The Na-*

tional Barn Dance featured talent from the sticks, natural talent, players by ear, and country yodelers who had learned songs handed down from generation to generation. *Barn Dance* went on a national hookup on September 30, 1933, in a 60-minute hoedown format on the Blue Network. Like *Grand Ole Opry*, which came to network radio six years later, *Barn Dance* became one of the stalwarts of the Saturday-night schedule.

For much of their respective runs, *The National Barn Dance* and *Grand Ole Opry* were locked into a neck-and-neck ratings battle, with the point spread shifting year to year. Since they were by then on the same network (NBC) the same night (just 30 minutes apart), many of the people who tuned in *Barn Dance* at 9 o'clock probably stayed around for *Grand Ole Opry*.

As producer Walter Wade mentioned to *Newsweek* in the early 1940's, *The National Barn Dance* held a consistent Crossley rating of 10 to 15 points, and those surveys were made only in large urban areas. Wade, who supervised for Alka Seltzer, was a *Barn Dance* charter member. He and co-producers Peter Lund and Jack Frost were on hand for the first network show. Genial master of ceremonies Joe Kelly, another charter member, would later originate *The Quiz Kids*, also for Alka Seltzer. Others on hand for the network opener were Luther Ossiebrink, "Lulu Belle" (Myrtle Cooper), and long-time announcer Jack Holden. Ossiebrink, as Arkie the Arkansas Woodchopper, did the do-si-do honors, calling the square dances while the couples actually whirled on stage. There were no faked dances; the show had its paid audience to consider too.

Lulu Belle was a regular who predated the arrival of the network. Born Myrtle Cooper, she came out of Bonne, North Carolina, at her father's urging, to become the leading *Barn Dance* female ballad singer. Soon after the network piped in, Lulu Belle was teamed with "Skyland Scotty" in singing-yodeling hillbilly numbers. Scotty was Scott Wiseman, another native of North Carolina, born just 40 miles from Myrtle Cooper's home. But they both came to Chicago to meet on *The National Barn Dance*. Their courtship and wedding was one of the show's romantic high points.

The *Barn Dance* developed many personalities who never got into the on-the-air part of the show. The NBC segment, marked by the cowbells and the background babble of constant voices, featured a set of regulars. Most popular were the Hoosier Hot Shots, a quartet of musical funnymen who parlayed a hand-operated klaxton, a set of bulb horns, and a series of washboards into radio's highest-paid novelty act. The Hot Shots (Paul "Hezzie" Trietsch, his brother Ken, Frank Kettering, and Charles Otto "Gabe" Ward) came aboard in 1933, and remained with the show through most of its run.

For a time, Pat Barrett donned his cotton chin whiskers and became the show's Uncle Ezra, the same part he played on his own Station E-Z-R-A show, then heard three times a week on NBC. In the early 1940's, Pat Buttram became a Barn Dance regular, telling tall tales as "the sage of Winston County, Alabama" in the same croaky-voiced characterization he used on Gene Autry's Melody Ranch. During those years, the Dinning Sisters—Jean, Ginger, and Lou —broke up the corn with some arrangements of swing and popular sweet tunes. Glenn Welty arrived to lead the orchestra. Others included Sally Foster, the blonde ballad singer; baritone Skip Farrell; Lieutenant Commander Eddie Peabody, the Navy's banjoist-in-residence; Joe Parsons, who sang sad numbers with his hat on; Grace Wilson, "the girl with a million friends"; Louise Massey and the Westernaires; Lucille Long, contralto and singer of classics; Henry Burr, tenor; and Ted Morse and his Novelodeons.

In 1941, the show moved into another new home, the Chicago Civic Theatre; on July 4, 1942, its network time was cut to 30 minutes; it continued on NBC for Alka Seltzer until 1946. It was revived on ABC for Phillips Milk of Magnesia in 1948, but attracted only a small part of its former audience, ending in 1950.

NBC Presents: Short Story

NBC Presents: Short Story was an anthology of modern stories written by contemporary masters of the form. It opened February 21, 1951, with an adaptation of Ernest Hemingway's "Thirty Grand." During the year's run, the show offered stories by William Faulkner, Sherwood Anderson, John Steinbeck, Stephen Vincent Benét, Sinclair Lewis, Ray Bradbury, Ring Lardner, Erskine Caldwell, and John Galsworthy. One of the most famous was "The Lottery," by Shirley Jackson. The show was sustained by NBC on Wednesday night, and was last heard March 14, 1952.

The NBC Radio Theatre

The NBC Radio Theatre was a last gasp at quality daytime drama. It ran in 1959, too late by almost everybody's standards, and featured a rotating company of stars in daily hour-long dramas. The company was comprised of Eddie Albert, Lee Bowman, Madeleine Carroll, Gloria DeHaven, and Celeste Holm. The stories were of people "at a climactic moment of their lives." It was a noble effort, burdened from the outset by too many sponsors, too many commercials, and too few listeners. It was produced and directed by Himan Brown who, fifteen years later, would still be valiantly trying to resurrect network radio with *The CBS Radio Mystery Theatre.*

The NBC University Theatre of the Air

The NBC University Theatre of the Air came to radio July 30, 1948, with 60-minute adaptations of modern novels, tied to college-supervised home-study courses. It offered such works as Robert Penn Warren's *All the King's Men* with Wayne Morris and Graham Greene's *Ministry of Fear* with Alan Mowbray. But the producers always invited listeners to use the broadcast as a springboard for a reading of the novel. The University of Louisville and Washington State College initially offered home-study courses in connection with *The NBC University Theatre of the Air,* and other colleges were announced on the show as they were added. Intermission time featured a well-known author or critic talking about the writer whose work was being featured and adding perspective to the play being performed. The show was programmed in semesters, with each featuring British and American authors of a certain era. Radio drama was seldom better than this. Among the shows were *A Farewell to Arms* by Ernest Hemingway, with John Lund and Lurene Tuttle; *An American Tragedy* by Theodore Dreiser, with George Montgomery; *Arrowsmith* by Sinclair Lewis, starring Van Heflin; *Of Human Bondage* by W. Somerset Maugham, with Brian Aherne and Angela Lansbury; *The Grapes of Wrath* by John Steinbeck, starring Jane Darwell from the screen cast; *The Red Badge of Courage* by Stephen Crane, starring John Agar. In 1949, the show won radio's highest award, a Peabody, which cited Hemingway's *Short Happy Life of Francis Macomber* with Preston Foster as one of its best offerings. The series was directed by Andrew C. Love from Hollywood, and the supporting roles were done by radio's outstanding professionals. This program ran for three years, on Sundays from 1948 through 1950 and on Wednesday nights in 1950–51. In 1949, the name was changed to *NBC Theatre.* The producers felt that the word "University" was scaring off listeners and causing low ratings.

Never Too Old

Never Too Old was an interview show conducted by Art Baker on Mutual–Don Lee in 1945. Baker interviewed senior citizens (they had to be at least 70 to get on the show) from all walks of life—veterans of the Spanish-American War; cub reporters of the 1880's; people who were young when the century turned. The interviews were nostalgic and reflective, and Baker was ever the appreciative listener.

Nick Carter, Master Detective

Nick Carter, Master Detective, premièred on Mutual April 11, 1943, featuring "that most famous of all manhunters, the detective whose ability at solving crime is unequalled in the history of detective fiction." With Nick, the claim was partly justified. Beginning as a character in the 1886 pages of Street and Smith's New York Weekly, Nick Carter made a highly successful jump to radio.

Keeping with the old Street and Smith image, the stories were all subtitled ("The Corpse in the Cab," or "Nick Carter and the Murder in the Park").

The early shows opened with the sound of someone frantically knocking at the door to Carter's brownstone office. Bang-bang-bang-bang! No answer. Bang-bang-bang-bang!! No answer. BANG-BANG-BANG-BANG!!! Then the door was jerked open and Patsy's startled voice cried: "What's the matter, what is it?" Another case for Nick Carter, Master Detective!

As a radio character, Nick wasn't quite good enough to pull himself completely clear of the Mr. Keen syndrome. The dialogue contained much of the Keen-Chameleon triteness, though the puzzlers themselves were usually somewhat better. Nick Carter was, in the end, a series of murder mysteries in the classic tradition, with the murderer revealed at the end after Nick had gathered and deciphered a lengthy series of clues. Then, of course, there would be an epilogue, in which Nick would explain what each clue meant and how it had contributed to the killer's doom. The killer usually made one final run for it, screaming "You'll never take me alive, Carter," and as often as not met some gruesome death.

Like Mr. Keen before him and Mr. Chameleon afterward, Nick worked with assistants kept in a state of perpetual fascination at his unprecedented brilliance. Nick's friends were the beautiful, talented gal Friday–secretary Patsy Bowen, and the "demon reporter" Scubby Wilson. Patsy was worth ten of Mr. Keen's Mike Clancy. A serious student of Nick's ways, she once, during his absence, took command of a murder case and solved it all by her lovely self. Scubby was just there. A demon he wasn't. Together they made life miserable for Sergeant Mathison (Matty to us) of the police department. Matty, following in the hard-headed footsteps of Commissioner Weston of The Shadow, griped and moaned at the slightest suggestion that his success in homicide was due to his acquaintance with Carter; Patsy liked to remind him once in a while, just to keep him honest. Heard on Mutual for more than ten years, the show became a great favorite despite its sometimes hokey nature. Lon Clark, opera singer turned radio actor, was nicely suited for the title role. Patsy was played by Helen Choate until mid-1946, when Charlotte Manson took the part. Scubby was John Kane and Sergeant Matty was Ed Latimer. Music was by Lew White, and later by George Wright. The production was written, directed, and produced at WOR, New York, by Jock MacGregor.

Nick Carter, Master Detective ran until 1955, often as a Mutual sustainer. Its sponsors included Lin-X Home Brighteners (1944–45) and Cudahy Meats (1946–51); its longest-running time slot was Sundays from 1944 through 1954.

But the character turned up again in the 1970's as star of a televised Movie of the Week. Like his nineteenth-century contemporary Frank Merriwell, the master detective seems good for periodic revivals every three or four decades.

Nightbeat

Nightbeat brought Frank Lovejoy before the NBC microphones in 1950 for a weekly half-hour of newspaper adventure. Lovejoy played Randy Stone, top reporter for the Chicago Star. His assignment: Nightbeat. That meant roaming Chicago looking for human interest stories, turning over rocks and exposing the worms for the Star cameraman's bulbs. Lovejoy being Lovejoy, many of the stories revolved around crime and criminals, but Nightbeat was a fine series of plain human drama. It premièred February 6, 1950, and ran for about two years, sustained for most of the run, but sponsored during the summer of 1950 by Wheaties. Produced and directed by Warren Lewis, it drew supporting players from radio's best. William Conrad, Lurene Tuttle, Joan Banks, Herb Butterfield, and Peter Leeds were among the Nightbeat players. They created the situations; Lovejoy wrapped them up in a final crisp command: "COPY BOY!"

Nightmare

Nightmare was a rather weak Mutual effort premièring October 1, 1953, and running one season. It starred Peter Lorre as "your exciting guide to terror." Lorre told and starred in tales of the macabre, but the whole thing had rather a canned effect. It was transcribed in Hollywood. The epigraph: "Out of the dark of night, from the shadows of the senses, comes this—the fantasy of fear." Lorre's talent was much better utilized on his earlier NBC show, *Mystery in the Air.*

Niles and Prindle

Niles and Prindle was a Blue Network comedy revolving around two friends who argued about anything, anywhere, anytime. It ran in 1945, and featured the team of Wendell Niles and Don Prindle, really longtime friends.

Ninety-Nine Men and a Girl

Ninety-Nine Men and a Girl was a 1939 CBS variety show. The girl—"The Incomparable Hildegarde"—had come a long, long way from the Hildegarde Loretta Sell of Milwaukee days. Those were Depression days, and Hildegarde a dime-store clerk. She gave it all up for the lively world of vaudeville, and when star-maker Gus Edwards got her under his wing in 1932, "The Incomparable Hildegarde" was on her way. She hit the big-time nightclub circuit in London and Paris, returning to America with one name and a flair for the continental. It didn't take long for the U.S. tire dealers to sign her for *Ninety-Nine Men and a Girl.* The ninety-nine men were the musicians of Raymond Paige's orchestra, which backed up the throaty songstress in her Wednesday-night offerings of such numbers as "Why Do I Love You?"

Nitwit Court

Nitwit Court was the 1944 edition of *The Ransom Sherman Show,* an outrageous parody of John J. Anthony's *Goodwill Hour,* with Sherman as the screwball "judge" who dispensed advice on personal problems. A summer series, it premièred July 4, 1944, on the Blue Network. Sara Berner co-starred as juror Bubbles Lowbridge, with Mel Blanc and Arthur Q. Bryan playing various roles. Sherman was a master at devising these brief, funny formats. It's surprising that so few of them lasted.

Noah Webster Says

Noah Webster Says was the result of Haven MacQuarrie's lifelong interest in words, and the dictionary was the final authority for this quiz, first heard on NBC in 1942. Listeners sent in lists of words, and the contestants had to define them. Each show had time for about eight contestants who were each given a list of five tough words. One dollar was won for the first correctly defined word; another $2 for the second; $3 more for the third; $4 for the fourth; then came the chance to risk $10 or win $50 for the fifth word. Winners were brought back for a "final exam" to divide the money lost by the contestants. The show was virtually a one-man operation—created, written, produced, and directed by Haven MacQuarrie, who also served as moderator. (Contestants aside,) the only other people on the show were the announcer (Doug Gourlay and later John Storm) and Professor Charles Frederick Lindsley of Occidental College. Lindsley served as the "judge"—the final word on Noah Webster's definitions.

MacQuarrie got the idea for this show in 1942, and by spring of that year it had premièred on NBC Pacific Coast stations. In June it was sent coast to coast. MacQuarrie's previous air credits had been in *Do You Want to Be an Actor?* and *The Marriage Club*. His dictionary show spurred formation of Noah Webster Clubs around the nation. In 1944 when "Believe-It-Or-Not" specialist Bob Ripley invaded MacQuarrie's territory by declaring in a newspaper column that only six words in the English language ended with the letters "cion," MacQuarrie promptly found a seventh. His show was sponsored by Wesson Oil and Snowdrift, and was shifted into many different time slots. On July 6, 1943, it became the summer replacement for one of the great maligners of the king's English—Ed Gardner of *Duffy's Tavern*. The show was still running on NBC in 1951.

Nobody's Children

Nobody's Children, first heard on Mutual July 2, 1939, was created and conducted by actor Walter White, Jr., as the result of his interest in the problems of orphaned and homeless children. White and his wife had been told (wrongly) that they might never have children of their own. His subsequent research took him into orphanages and homes for abandoned children, and he began to see a potential radio show developing. The show that ultimately hit the air originated at KHJ, Los Angeles, and discussed cases at the Children's Home Society of L.A. The orphans themselves were brought to the microphones for interviews, then a famous guest star discussed the child's case.

Placements from the home rose dramatically in the first six months the show was on. Barbara Stanwyck, the first guest, postponed her honeymoon with Robert Taylor to do the show. Others who appeared were Otto Kruger, Jack Benny, and Jeanette MacDonald. Fay

Bainter burst into tears after touring the home. It was the first time in history that microphones had invaded the sanctity of a children's home, but White always made certain that the kids were well-insulated. Only fictitious names were used, and the discussions of individuals never began until the subjects were well out of earshot. *Nobody's Children* ran through 1940 and returned for a summer season in 1941.

Of Men and Books

Of Men and Books was a Saturday panel discussion of new and important books featuring writers and others interested in the literary scene. The series ran on CBS from 1940 through 1947, but was also heard as a summer show beginning June 7, 1939. In one early show, T.V. Smith debated himself on the season's newest books. Professor of philosophy at the University of Chicago and a United States Representative from Illinois, Smith first considered the book as a professor, then tore apart his own conclusions as a congressman.

Official Detective

Official Detective came to Mutual in 1946 and ran for more than eleven years. It was just an average cops-and-robbers show, telling of the inner workings of a large city police department. The same thing was done better on *The Lineup* and much better on *Dragnet*. *Official Detective* featured Craig McDonnell as Detective Lieutenant Dan Britt and Tommy Evans as Sergeant Al Bowen. The program was presented in cooperation with *Official Detective* magazine, and was produced and directed by Wynn Wright. It was a 15-minute series heard Sunday afternoons in 1946, but expanded to 30 minutes Tuesday nights when Pharmaco came aboard as sponsor in 1947. It was sustained on Tuesdays from 1948–52 and was carried by various sponsors on Thursdays from 1952–57.

On Stage

On Stage, the Cathy and Elliott Lewis CBS production, came to the airwaves in January 1953 and left in 1954; two brief seasons of sustained drama virtually forgotten today. But when On Stage first arrived, Cathy and Elliott were at the peak of their joint careers. She was playing Jane Stacy in My Friend Irma in both radio and TV and was appearing in numerous Suspense shows. He was directing Suspense and appearing in many of the plays. At the same time, Lewis was directing Broadway Is My Beat, Crime Classics, and The Phil Harris–Alice Faye Show, in which he played a leading comic role. Their intense involvement led to their reputations as "Mr. and Mrs. Radio."

Elliott Lewis had about as active a radio career as anyone in the business. He gravitated toward Los Angeles in the late 1930's, gave up a vague notion of becoming a lawyer, and began playing New York toughs on the air. By 1940 he was an established character actor, but the war threatened to cut his career short. Instead, Master Sergeant Lewis went into Armed Forces radio, handling more than 100 series and shows and emerging from the service an established microphone veteran. In November 1940, he met Cathy, who had come to Hollywood in 1936 to become a singer. She found greater opportunity in dramatic radio, appearing on such chillers as The Whistler, I Love a Mystery, and the pre-Elliott Suspense. They met while both were doing The Woodbury Playhouse and were married April 30, 1943. Cathy didn't even change her name—much; she was Cathy Llewis before her marriage.

On Stage was the natural professional result of the union—an intense 30 minutes of drama running from classic to adventure to borderline sentimental. They appeared in Candide, The Midnight Ride of Paul Revere and The Lady or the Tiger, and did original works of contemporary life by such scripters as Shirley Gordon, E. Jack Neuman, Antony Ellis, and the team of Morton Fine and David Friedkin. The stories were sometimes experimental but always involved a heavy man-woman theme.

Lewis played the male leads and served as producer-director. Among the supporting stars were Peggy Webber, Clayton Post, John McIntire, William Conrad, Howard McNear, Mary Jane Croft, Lou Merrill, GeGe Pearson, John Dehner, Ben Wright, Barney Phillips, Tony Barrett, Byron Kane, Edgar Barrier, and Harry Bartell. The music was composed by Fred Steiner and conducted by Lud Gluskin. The

"Cathy and Elliott Theme" was by Ray Noble. George Walsh was announcer.

One Man's Family

One Man's Family was first heard on a small West Coast NBC network April 29, 1932, and lasted until the final days of network radio. Carlton E. Morse, one of radio's legendary writers, fashioned this long-popular program after John Galsworthy's Forsyte Saga. Born June 4, 1901, in Jennings, Louisiana, Morse had always possessed a yen to write, and moved into journalism with the Sacramento Union during his days at the University of California. For a time he practiced on San Francisco newspapers, then worked briefly for the Seattle Times. Morse went to NBC in 1930, writing many serials and adventure shows now forgotten. His proposal for a serial about an upper-middle-class Sea Cliff family brought stifled yawns to the lips of NBC executives who could see no appeal in it. But in those early days, talent was sparse and time was there to be filled.

By May 13, 1932, the show had been picked up by the full Western states' network. One year later, May 17, 1933, One Man's Family went coast to coast. Originally heard in weekly 30-minute installments on Friday nights, the serial moved to Wednesdays with its introduction on the full network. Its earliest sponsor was Wesson Oil–Snowdrift, then Kentucky Winner tobacco. In March 1935, Standard Brands became the long-running sponsor first with Royal Gelatin, later Tenderleaf Tea. For its first five years, One Man's Family was broadcast from San Francisco, home of the Barbour family, whose adventures it followed; then the show—cast and all—moved to Hollywood. One Man's Family ran on NBC Wednesday nights until 1939; then it moved to Sundays, where it continued for another decade.

Morse created an American dynasty with his famous serial. For twenty-seven years the Barbour clan of Sea Cliff, San Francisco, was America's family of the air. Generations watched themselves grow up and grow old with the Barbours; they watched the Barbours grow, too. Like the Barbours, Morse had come from a large family with deep roots. His father, mother, three brothers, and two sisters held yearly reunions, gathering each Christmas in the same tradition practiced by the Barbours. In 1942, sixty-eight people gathered for the Morse reunion.

But nothing was eternal on One Man's Family; even the solid, steady American family tree over which the creator labored and so often philosophized had its decay and its shortcomings. The result was a feeling of reality that no other radio show could duplicate. *One Man's Family* moved with the slowness of life itself, working on tiny pieces of characterization and subtle, underlying conflict. The people came alive: they grew up, married, grew old, and some died. *One Man's Family* was simply the most addictive show of its time.

Listening to the tapes that go back over a quarter-century confirms that judgment. Taken singly, the chapters of *One Man's Family* are dull and occasionally oversentimental. The problem is that no one can pick up a novel, turn to the middle, and expect to be carried along instantly. Taken in vast units of entire serials, the underlying characterizations go to work, the family becomes as real as the old friends halfway up in the next block. With collectors of radio shows, *One Man's Family* dominates the dinnertimes, the early mornings, the off-hours. The TV stands dark in a corner, and the Barbours live again.

Henry Barbour came to San Francisco as a very young boy with his parents. Transplants from Ohio, the Barbours were confirmed San Franciscans from that first spring day in 1879. Henry made friends with the boys of the neighborhood, notably Glenn Hunter and Fred Thompson, who would become judge and doctor in adulthood. Henry's good-natured, lifelong rivalry with Hunter and Thompson began in 1893 at a party in the Palace Hotel, when the three scrambled for the attentions of a good-looking girl named Fanny Martin. Henry won that courtship; he and Fanny were married on May 10, 1896. They established a home at Sea Cliff, just below the spot where the Golden Gate Bridge would be built many years later. Five children—Paul, Hazel, Claudia, Clifford, and Jack—were born to the Barbours. These children and their children made up the deep interlaced drama of *One Man's Family*.

Henry Barbour, a stock broker, founded the Henry Barbour Stock Brokerage House on Montgomery Street in 1912. For more than three decades the firm prospered under his tight reign, and was finally sold for $450,000—a sum more than adequate to serve the Barbours' needs in retirement. In his later years, the family garden was Henry's great pleasure. He became crusty and old-fashioned in a modern, changing world. Completely dedicated to family life and the American way, he would not tolerate anyone who did not share those ideals. The bigger the family the better, thought Henry Barbour in those long-ago days before population problems. "If we, by example, can in some small way further the desire in America for family tradition and family loyalty, we will have served a worthy purpose," he said in 1940.

Henry became the mouthpiece for many of the author's own ideals, but his sermons and obvious moralizing were tempered by his feet of clay. He carped too much; when he took to a cause he was relentless in his attempts to ramrod it past his reluctant family. He

ONE MAN'S FAMILY

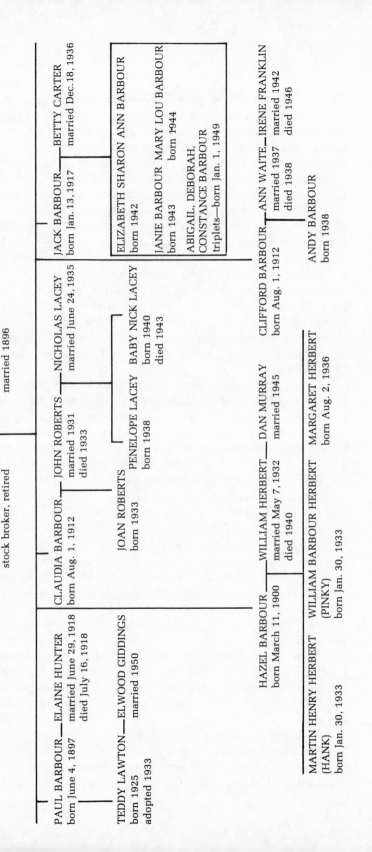

HENRY BARBOUR
born 1875
stock broker, retired

FANNY MARTIN BARBOUR
born 1878
married 1896

PAUL BARBOUR—ELAINE HUNTER
born June 4, 1897 married June 29, 1918
died July 16, 1918

CLAUDIA BARBOUR—JOHN ROBERTS
born Aug. 1, 1912 married 1931
died 1933

JACK BARBOUR—BETTY CARTER
born Jan. 13, 1917 married Dec.18, 1936

NICHOLAS LACEY
married June 24, 1935

TEDDY LAWTON—ELWOOD GIDDINGS
born 1925 married 1950
adopted 1933

JOAN ROBERTS
born 1933

PENELOPE LACEY
born 1938

BABY NICK LACEY
born 1940
died 1943

ELIZABETH SHARON ANN BARBOUR
born 1942

JANIE BARBOUR MARY LOU BARBOUR
born 1943 born 1944

ABIGAIL, DEBORAH,
CONSTANCE BARBOUR
triplets—born Jan. 1, 1949

HAZEL BARBOUR
born March 11, 1900

WILLIAM HERBERT—DAN MURRAY
married May 7, 1932 married 1945
died 1940

CLIFFORD BARBOUR—ANN WAITE—IRENE FRANKLIN
born Aug. 1, 1912 married 1937 married 1942
died 1938 died 1946

MARTIN HENRY HERBERT
(HANK)
born Jan. 30, 1933

WILLIAM BARBOUR HERBERT
(PINKY)
born Jan. 30, 1933

MARGARET HERBERT
born Aug. 2, 1936

ANDY BARBOUR
born 1938

picked and picked and picked until the family was at the brink of explosion. When things went wrong, he sulked and brooded. His suspicion of strangers—especially strangers who wanted to marry into his family—approached upper-middle-class snobbishness. Once the outsiders had won him to a cause, he was their staunchest ally. But Henry resisted change; he fought new ideas and resisted any implication that he was not still the head of the house of Barbour.

Even while his sermons made Henry Barbour the grandfather of all America, his flaws made him believable and human. Despite his bullheaded nature, his overbearing personality, and his sometimes aristocratic airs, he emerged as a warm, lovable human being. His expression, "yes, yes," became the show's trademark, and Henry himself its strongest element. This was due in no small measure to a magnificent 27-year portrayal by J. Anthony Smythe, a native San Franciscan of long stage experience. Smythe, a bachelor, served *One Man's Family* from its first day to its last. Fanny was played nicely for twenty-three years by Minetta Ellen, and for the last three years by Mary Adams.

Minetta Ellen and J. Anthony Smythe had met years before, when both were working the boards in Oakland. There they appeared together in many plays, often as a married couple, but it was as Fanny and Henry that they attracted their greatest audience. As Fanny, Miss Ellen became the peacemaker of the family, forever trying to undo the damage that Henry had created. Her exasperation with his antics knew no limits, yet they remained a devoted couple with no second glances at the past. Sometimes Fanny teased Henry with the suggestion that she had chosen him by a simple process of elimination (Fred Thompson, she said, always smelled like antiseptic, and Glenn Hunter was too much a ladies' man for her liking); Henry shrugged it of with a "yes, yes," and went on down to his garden. Fanny tried, but often peace at the Barbours was not easily accomplished. Events would run their course, and all she could do was watch them in silence.

Paul Barbour, eldest of the five children, was an aviator, writer, and philosopher. Born June 4, 1897, he soon assumed a second-in command status behind his father. Often family members would confide in Paul what they would never tell Henry. The old man, sensing this, sometimes felt that his son had taken his place as head of the family, and brooded over it whenever the breach became too obvious.

Paul was a fighter pilot in World War I. In Europe, he met and married Elaine Hunter, an army nurse. They had less than a month together before Paul was assigned to France. On a mission over France, his plane was shot down and he was wounded. Meanwhile, an epidemic swept through the hospital where Elaine was working, and she died before Paul could return to her.

Paul would carry the physical and psychological scars of those days for the rest of his life. Always afterward he walked with a slight limp, and though he came close several times, he never remarried. He moved into a cozy writer's loft apartment in the family home; the apartment became a sanctuary for anyone who needed his counseling. In 1933, it also became a home for Teddy Lawton, a 9-year-old orphan girl Paul found swinging on a gate. Paul legally adopted Teddy, and she lived in a room just off the attic. She became a strange mixture of joy and pain for him—joy in her growing years; pain in her misdirected feeling for him. It was Teddy who finally drove a wedge between Paul and the lovely widow Beth Holly, his earliest serious romantic attachment. Beth Holly, played by Barbara Jo Allen long before she created her comedic Vera Vague for Bob Hope and other big-time comics, often had Paul to her apartment for Sunday-morning breakfasts, where they would sit over coffee and talk away the troubles of the world. But Beth refused to compete with a child, and gradually the romance melted away. Paul had become the most important male figure in young Teddy's life—so important that he colored her adulthood as well. Always she compared prospective suitors to Paul; always they paled in comparison. She was unable to function in a marriage relationship; her feeling for Paul was largely responsible for the failure of her marriage to the dentist Elwood Giddings (Tyler McVey).

Winifred Wolfe literally grew up playing Teddy. She was 11 when she first took the part, and stayed with it for more than a decade. After her own marriage in 1945 (performed at author Morse's home), the part of Teddy was written out of the scripts for a time. Teddy was an army nurse, assigned to Europe. When she returned, it was as a fully matured but still troubled woman, played by Jeanne Bates. Paul was played for most of the run by Michael Raffetto, the original Jack Packard of Morse's adventure serial, *I Love a Mystery*. Raffetto, an unsung film pioneer and former San Francisco attorney, had broken into radio at NBC in San Francisco, with his own early series, *Arms of the Law*. Through many of the golden years of *One Man's Family*, Raffetto served as assistant writer and director in addition to playing Paul. His voice was ideal as the man of great strength and tenderness, the deep thinker, the wide reader, the lonely man despite all his family ties. Raffetto played Paul until his voice began to fade, and in July 1955 Russell Thorson took the part, playing it until the series ended four years later.

Despite the obstacles they threw into his romantic path, the family wanted Paul to marry and find happiness. Often they tried to nudge him into marriage with Nicolette Moore (Jeanette Nolan), a governess at brother Jack's house. Through it all, Paul and Nicolette remained good friends. His most serious romantic attachment of later years was with Christine Abbott (Mary Jane Croft), a widow and a noted concert pianist. But that romance was foredoomed: Christine's brother Rexford Frome was a psychopath, and Father Barbour was violently opposed to any contact with the Fromes.

For a time, Paul ended each chapter with a short perspective on the day, closing with, "That's how it is with the Barbours today."

Hazel Barbour was born March 11, 1900. A leggy girl, she grew up with a strong sense of responsibility and motherhood. She married William Herbert on May 7, 1932, and bore twin boys exactly nine months later. The boys were named Martin Henry and William Barbour Herbert, but became known by the family names of Hank and Pinky.

A daughter, Margaret, was born in 1936. Hazel's husband died in 1940; after a long courtship she married Dan Murray in 1945. The Murrays made their home in Sea Cliff, "three blocks down and two blocks over" from the family estate. Dan Murray worked hard and made them a good life. Hazel's top problem was with her son Pinky.

Pinky suffered through all the foibles of adolescence. Everyone who didn't see eye to eye with Pinky was "out of touch with the times." He failed miserably at almost everything: flunked out of Stanford, piled up huge debts and tried to shirk his responsibility to repay them. His failures were even more notable when compared with the achievements of his brother Hank, straight-A student and good at everything.

Most of the serial's final days revolved around the troubles and relationships of Hank and Pinky, but by then it was a shadow of its old days. The grandchildren simply never took the place of the children as leading players. In the golden era, Hazel was probably the least troublesome of all the Barbours. She was solid; her judgments were usually sound. The part was played all the way by Bernice Berwin, who had started on radio in college, graduated to NBC in 1928, and had worked with Morse many times before One Man's Family was brought to the air.

Bert Horton played Hazel's first husband, William Herbert. Dan Murray was played by Wally Maher, Bill Bouchey, Russell Thorson, and Ken Peters. Hank was portrayed by Conrad Binyon, Dickie Meyers, and Billy Idelson over the years. And the troublesome Pinky was played by Richard Svihus, Dix Davis, Eddie Firestone, Jr., Tommy Bernard, George Pirrone, and Idelson. Dawn Bender played Margaret.

The Barbours were noted for multiple births, and for the deaths of the natural members' spouses. So it was with Claudia and Clifford, twins born August 1, 1912.

In youth they were inseparable. Claudia was restless and sometimes openly rebellious; Cliff was calmer on the surface but tightly wound inside. "Once they divided up the world between them," Fanny wrote in her 1940 Memory Book. "Cliff took the sky because it was quiet and peaceful. Claudia took the ocean because it was changeable and restless—and I guess that describes Claudia's nature as well as anything could."

Claudia's nature led her into an early marriage with John Roberts, Jr. It ended with his death in 1933, but left her with a young daughter, Joan. In 1935 Claudia met a wealthy Englishman named Nicholas Lacey; they were married the same year. Nicky brought some stability to the restless Claudia's life. Their daughter Penelope was born in 1938; a son, Nicky Jr., in 1940. In the interim, Nicky had bought a 400-acre ranch about 40 miles down the peninsula from San Francisco. They called it the Sky Ranch. Here they raised thoroughbred horses, and the family spent many pleasant weekends and summers. There was a pool and heavy wood, a pasture to the south and a valley to the west. The stable held seventy-five horses.

The Lacey home in San Francisco was just five houses down from the family estate. With Jack sandwiched between and Hazel only a few blocks away, the family maintained its togetherness long after the children were grown and married.

But the war brought tragedy, when Nicky was sent on a mission to Europe. It was decided that Claudia and her two young children would accompany him, while Joan would remain with the family in San Francisco. Claudia and the children left for Washington on August 29, 1943. Soon the family received word that their Scandinavian liner to Europe had been torpedoed by the Germans. All were presumed lost. For more than two years, Claudia, Nicky, and the children were written out of the script and were presumed dead by family and listeners alike.

In fact, they were prisoners in a German concentration camp. Little Nicky didn't survive the ordeal; he died in his mother's arms during the long train ride to the prison. But in 1945 came the first report that Claudia, Nicholas, and Penelope might still be alive, and Paul was off to Europe on a long search, and one of the show's most memorable stories.

The part of Claudia was initiated by Kathleen Wilson who, like Bernice Berwin, had played in previous Morse programs. Miss Wilson played Claudia for more than eleven years, until that ill-fated trip to Europe. When Claudia was returned to her home in October 1945, the role was assumed by Barbara Fuller, who took it to the end in 1959.

Floy Hughes stood in occasionally for Miss Wilson in the early years; Laurette Fillbrandt played Claudia for Miss Fuller during the summer of 1949. John Roberts, Claudia's first husband, was Frank Provo; their daughter Joan was played by Ann Shelley and Mary Lou Harrington. Joan inherited much of her mother's rebellious nature, and was a source of constant worry to Claudia (who saw a little too much of her own fiery youth mirrored there). With Claudia's marriage to Nicky, and the subsequent births of Nicky Jr. and Penelope (Anne Whitfield), Joan went through a long identity crisis. She felt cast out of her mother's life; an outsider within the family. When Claudia and Nicky took the babies to Europe and left Joan with the family, the feeling only intensified. Like her mother, Joan went through a troubled adolescence, eventually settling down in marriage with Ross Farnsworth (Vic Perrin), and producing the first great-grandchild, Paul John Farnsworth. The part of Nicky was first played by Walter Paterson, the original Reggie of Morse's *I Love a Mystery*. When Paterson died in September 1942, Morse sent Nicky away on a mission for British Intelligence. He subsequently returned in portrayals by Tom Collins, Dan O'Herlihy, and Ben Wright.

Clifford's life was even more tragic than that of his twin sister. But it was tragedy of a different kind, and he handled it in a different way. The deep personal losses of his life accumulated and crushed his spirit. By 1949, he was a ghost, a shell.

It began in 1937, with his marriage to Ann Waite. Ann (Helen Musselman) was a piano prodigy whose life was her music. Cliff resented that and they fought. Ann left him, even then carrying his child. The baby boy was born in secrecy. Then Ann tried to run home to her overprotective father and died trying to leave the hospital just after the birth.

The family brought the baby home from the hospital. Cliff, completely devastated, refused to look at the child. For eight years Cliff's son was nameless. Cliff called him "Skip" and then "Skipper"; finally, after much prodding by Mother Barbour, the boy was named Andrew.

In the interim, Cliff had married Irene Franklin, a sweet young thing of soft voice. Their wedding of June 28, 1942, consumed an entire half-hour show, as had the ceremonies of Claudia and Nicky and Hazel and William Herbert. Irene was a frail girl, first played by 16-year-old Naomi Stevens, yet another graduate of *I Love a Mystery*, and later by Janet Waldo. That marriage lasted four years, but it too came to a tragic end. In a 1946 sequence, a murder suspect, Gregory Lusck (who had been hiding out on the Sky Ranch), made a desperate run for freedom. Irene, on her way to the ranch, encountered Lusck's careening car on a winding mountain road and both were killed instantly in the crash.

Cliff, now completely shell-shocked, moved into the family home and stayed there for several years, living off his parents and making no effort to support himself. His moods of quiet meditation were broken by frequent quarrels with his father, who tried in his usual heavy-handed manner to push Clifford into some plan of action. For a time Cliff went through a mental lapse, unable to remember the past eleven years. Gradually he warmed up to his son, and began seeing women again. Young Andrew saw Roberta Evans (one of Cliff's first girlfriends of this period) as a threat, and injected more conflict with his open dislike of her. In 1950, Cliff met Maudie Pemberton, a girl rooming with Teddy during her separation from Elwood Giddings. A spunky girl, Maudie got Cliff back on the road to self-respect. She got him to work, and that made her a champion in Father Barbour's eyes. But like a house of cards, it all came tumbling down when Maudie refused Cliff's offer of marriage. Cliff returned to his moping ways, and Henry wrung his hands in distress.

Young Andy was played variously by Mary Lansing, Henry Blair, Michael Chapin, and David Frankham. Barton Yarborough, a fine radio actor, played Cliff from the beginning of the run until his death on December 27, 1951. Yarborough, who also played Joe Friday's sidekick Ben Romero on Dragnet and the red-headed Texan Doc Long on I Love a Mystery, really did hail from Texas. He ran away from home as a youth, joining a road show, then crashing vaudeville. Yarborough was one of Morse's little company of longtime regulars, and was all but irreplaceable as Cliff. When he died, Cliff was written out of the show. He moved to Scotland, listeners were told, where he married Mary McLeod and made a successful new life for himself. The family kept tabs on his movements by his infrequent letters, which were always shared with the audience. Cliff lived happily ever after—rather a pat finish to a moody, complex, but likable character.

Jack Barbour, born January 13, 1917, was the baby of the family. Of all the Barbours, Jack was most like the average American family man. His life was marked by few deep tragedies; instead, it became an unending battle to stay ahead of bill collectors, put food on the table, and shoes on little feet. And Jack had a lot of little feet to keep in shoes.

His marriage to Sea Cliff's Betty Carter in 1936 brought him, ultimately, six children. All were girls, and three were born at once. Daughters Elizabeth Sharon Ann, Mary Lou, and Jane were played interchangeably by Susan Luckey, Mary Lansing, and Susan Odin, and others took the parts at various stages of growth. The triplets —Abigail, Deborah, and Constance—were played by Leone Ledoux. Jack's wife Betty was Jean Rouverol and later Virginia Gregg. Page Gilman was Jack for the entire series. He was 14 years old when One Man's Family went on the air; he was a middle-aged 41 when it went off. When Gilman went to the Pacific in World War II, Morse sent Jack along with him. But Jack survived, returning to the study of law and eventually becoming a junior partner in the law firm of Henry's old friend, Judge Glenn Hunter.

These were the principal characters of *One Man's Family*. It ran 3,256 chapters wrapped into 134 "books." When Standard Brands dropped the show in 1949, the mere hint that NBC might also drop it brought 75,000 letters of protest from the faithful. It continued for a time as a Sunday-night sustained serial. On June 5, 1950, *One Man's Family* went into a 15-minute nightly format for Miles Laboratories. On July 4, 1955, it was moved into a daily matinee slot.

Although the series officially ended May 8, 1959, some eager affiliates chopped it off two weeks earlier. It just stopped there one April day, and the people who followed the Barbours for 27 years were left hanging. Father Barbour was left brooding over the problems of grandson Pinky. The show should have had a "family gathering" ending—one last grand splash, with all surviving members present and accounted for. There would be a letter from Cliff in Scotland. Father Barbour would read it aloud, pausing fcr editorial comment with every other sentence. Finally Fanny would tire of Henry's mutterings, and would ask Paul to read the letter. Henry would grumble under his breath as always. Then there would be time for family reminiscences. Memories would be long and fluid. Claudia would recall the horrors of her wartime experiences; Henry and Fanny would philosophize and talk about how it all began. Finally there would be a family projection for the future. It would all be shamelessly sentimental, but lifetime listeners deserved no less. What they got was a snuffed-out finish to a 27-year slice of life.

One Out of Seven

One Out of Seven provided early experience for Jack Webb and was a very strong opponent of racial injustice. The show was broadcast on a partial ABC hookup from San Francisco early in 1946, and featured Webb as a narrator and in many character roles. Often his was the only voice heard in the documentary-drama, an assignment that called for a variety of dialects from black to Jew. Webb brought them off in good form. The material used on *One Out of Seven* was taken from the news of the past week, "from authoritative files" and from the dispatches of Associated Press, United Press, and International News Service. "From these past seven days, the editors in our San Francisco newsroom have chosen the one story they have judged worthy of re-telling. This is one out of seven!" The stories were usually tough attacks against bigots and merchants of hate. Webb emphasized that the material was first used by the wire services, and the network "assumes no responsibility for the attitude such statements reflect." But, oh, the arrangement! The show of February 6, 1946, was a prime example—Webb and company took on Mississippi Senator Theodore G. Bilbo, arch foe of minorities. Bilbo's own words were read back to him in the most damning style imaginable, and the narrative was continuously punctuated by Webb's inserts: "Senator Bilbo is an honorable man, and we do not intend to prove otherwise."

Truly a gutsy show for radio of the era, *One Out of Seven* was written by James Edward Moser and directed by Gil Doud.

The O'Neills

The O'Neills was a soap opera giant during the turbulent 1930's. Beginning as a three-a-week nighttime serial, it told the story of a close-knit family in the small town of Royalton.

It was first heard June 11, 1934, on Mutual and went to CBS December 10, 1934. On October 8, 1935, the O'Neills moved into a late-afternoon slot on NBC for Ivory Soap. By the late 1930's, its Hooper rating had approached 10 points, almost a phenomenon for afternoon radio, and the show was carried on both NBC and CBS. The two networks jockeyed w·th *The O'Neills* through the last three years of its run, and it passed quietly from the scene June 18, 1943.

Mother O'Neill, a widow, had been left to her own resources in the raising of her children Danny and Peggy. She was the matriarch in the grand tradition, a 60-ish woman whose stock in trade was wisdom and understanding. Her children grew into fine citizens, though Peggy was a bit impetuous and Danny sank into one long period of depression after the childbirth death of his young wife Sally. Peggy married Monte Kayden, an ambitious entrepreneur whose intentions were often better than his judgment. They had three children. Monte's chief goal in life was to make a fortune, and for a time he pursued that end so ruthlessly that it almost cost him his family.

Two adopted members of the family were Janice and Eddie Collins, taken in by the O'Neills after the death of their father in an accident. Janice came to the family full of growing pains and teenage curiosity, which Mother O'Neill helped ease with love and kindness. Almost members of the family were Morris Levy and Mrs. Trudy Bailey. Morris ran a hardware store in Royalton; he was Mother O'Neill's closest friend and confidante. He was the show's philosopher, the inevitable shirt-sleever who was never too busy to listen, who took up the slack and provided Peggy and Danny a strong male figure after the death of their father.

Morris Levy was loved dearly by Mrs. Bailey, the meddlesome (but lovable) busybody who lived upstairs in the O'Neills' two-family house. With the tenacity of Father Barbour (the meddlesome head of *One Man's Family*), Mrs. Bailey poked her nose into everyone's business. She was forever "fresh out" of something, and in one of the serial's most repeated, most memorable scenes, Mrs. Bailey would call down the dumbwaiter to ask Mother O'Neill if she had any of this or any of that. Her campaign to win Morris Levy's heart finally ended successfully, and they were married in the early 1940's.

The O'Neills was a solid family soap opera, padding along to the theme "Danny Boy" in the footsteps of *Ma Perkins* and *One Man's Family*. Kate McComb played Mother O'Neill; Jimmy Tansey was Danny; Peggy was played over the years by Betty Caine, Violet Dunn, Betty Winkler, and Claire Niesen. Jane West, who played Mrs. Bailey, also wrote the show. Morris Levy was played by Jack Rubin, who directed for a time. Janice Gilbert was adopted daughter Janice; Jimmy Donnelly was Eddie Collins, and Chester Stratton played Peggy's husband, Monte Kayden.

The Open Door

The Open Door was writer Sandra Michael's try at a second quality afternoon serial. Her first was *Against the Storm*, winner of the 1942 Peabody Award. As with that program, Miss Michael's new serial was bucking all the odds when it appeared on CBS June 21, 1943, as a replacement for the just-canceled *O'Neills*. Despite its acknowledged quality, *Against the Storm* hadn't been able to overcome low ratings, and so it was with *The Open Door*. This time, bucked up by husband John Gibbs as producer, Miss Michael fashioned a series of slow-moving, character-building vignettes around Erik Hansen, the dean of the fictitious Vernon University. The "stories" involved the people he came to know and love, their problems, their lives and loves. Dean Hansen was almost a lateral transplant from *Against the Storm*—he had been Pastor Hansen there and had been played by the same actor, Dr. Alfred Dorf. He was a staunch man who cared about people and truly believed in being his brother's keeper. The agency handling the Standard Brands account didn't feel quite that way toward Miss Michael. Pressured to boost the show with melodrama, she resisted and finally quit, forcing its demise June 30, 1944, just a year after it had opened. Miss Michael had known Dorf—in real life a minister —since her childhood in Denmark. He had come to America to establish his church, Our Savior Church in Brooklyn. Dorf was her real-life inspiration for the Hansen character, whose life she saw intermingling with those of outsiders who sought his advice. In the end, radio just wasn't ready for this.

The Open House

The Open House was a CBS Hollywood effort, circa 1944. The idea was to introduce radio stars in an informal, chatty atmosphere and let them talk about themselves. Robert Young, Groucho Marx, Billie Burke, Ruth Hussey, and others were interviewed by hostess Ona Munson and encouraged to tell all about their work, their childhood, about anything that might bring them closer to listeners. The series was created by Beverly Barnes. Her husband, Jay Stewart, announced, Anita Ellis sang a song or two, and the music was by Lud Gluskin.

The Open Road

The Open Road showed what some people would do to get their break in radio. Red Quinlan was just out of high school in Chicago—the year was 1934. He dreamed up a serial based on the adventures of "kids of the road"; for material, he proposed thumbing and riding the rods across the country and back. One sponsor gave him some mild encouragement, and Quinlan was off. Some 6,000 miles later he was back, with enough anecdotes to interest NBC. His show, The Open Road, ran briefly during the summer of 1935. Quinlan painted life on the road as difficult, full of fights with railroad bulls and frantic running to elude police. Someone without money could still go to jail for vagrancy in 1935.

Our Daily Food

Our Daily Food, a show typical of early radio, was a 15-minute discussion of recipes, food possibilities, and menus. Sponsored by A&P food stores, the series told, among other things, how to make hot chocolate, how a grape juice factory functioned, how to start a school lunch program. It ran on NBC Red and Blue from 1930 until 1932.

Our Gal Sunday

Our Gal Sunday was one of the four well-known, much-beloved soap operas that CBS terminated on January 2, 1959, after decades of afternoon misery. The others were *This Is Nora Drake, Backstage Wife,* and *The Road of Life.*

Two of the four were Hummert productions and the most famous—*Our Gal Sunday* had come a long way from the Depression-era mining camps of Silver Creek, Colorado. That's where Sunday, an unwanted waif, was born and brought up by lonely grubstakers. The story of her rise from the camps was told daily for more than twenty years, drifting into kitchens at quarter to one to the mournful theme, "Red River Valley."

And now, *Our Gal Sunday,* the story of an orphan girl named Sunday, from the little town of Silver Creek, Colorado, who in young womanhood married England's richest, most handsome lord, Lord Henry Brinthrope—the story that asks the question, can this girl from a mining town in the West find happiness as the wife of a wealthy and titled Englishman?

The question was first asked on March 29, 1937; it wasn't answered until 1959. The interim was filled with some of the most heart-wrenching melodrama ever sent forth from the Hummerts' soap mill. It had all come down to the final day.

Faithful listeners had been through few moments when even the hint of happiness had come into Sunday's life. Always she managed to snatch agony from the jaws of bliss and continue down the tear-stained afternoon path. She suffered through years of Lord Henry's uncontrollable, unjustified jealousy, then saw her little boy Davy crippled by a hit-and-run driver. She cradled the head of her dying friend, the "brilliant, handsome" lawyer Kevin Bromfield, after he was struck down by a bullet meant for her. And in 1946 she suffered numerous indignities at the hand of Lord Henry's childhood friend, Thelma Mayfield, who came to Black Swan Hall (their spacious Virginia estate) to boldly announce that one day she—Thelma —would be mistress there.

Henry's blue blood jumped vigorously at the sight of a beautiful woman, but there was never any other man for Our Gal Sunday. So fickle was Henry that once, when the question of their adopted child's real parentage came up, Sunday thought for a time that it might be the result of Henry's i-l-l-e-gi-t-i-m-a-t-e wanderings.

But for the most part, *Our Gal Sunday* was free of children; her own kids Davy and Caroline were heard from only when the complications of youth were needed. Her chief problem in life was Lord Henry.

She was put down so often by so many of Lord Henry's stuffy British relatives that the epigraph had an almost ironical ring to it.

Bloodlines be damned: the real question in listeners' minds was whether Lord Henry Brintrope was good enough for Our Gal Sunday. And that was exactly what the Hummerts wanted.

As with many long-running soaps, Sunday assembled a loyal cast of regulars who stayed with it for years. Only two actresses played Sunday. The role was originated by Dorothy Lowell, who stepped aside in 1946 when Vivian Smolen took over. Lord Henry was played to aristocratic perfection by Alistair Duncan and by Karl Swenson, who used the same voice for the Hummerts' nighttime thriller, Mr. Chameleon. Joseph Curtin and Fran Carlon were Peter and Irene Galway, Sunday's close friends who lived in an estate bordering Black Swan Hall. Only five writers served the show, and Our Gal Sunday was written by Jean Carroll for the last fourteen years of its run. The most consistent sponsor over the twenty-two years was Anacin.

Incidentally, Our Gal Sunday did find happiness. She and Lord Henry left Black Swan Hall for a dramatic pilgrimage to his ancestral stamping ground. It had all come down to Ethel Barrymore's famous line, delivered seventy years ago in the Broadway play Sunday, which inspired the serial: "That's all there is, there isn't any more."

Our Miss Brooks

Our Miss Brooks was a show that teachers everywhere took to their hearts from the first broadcast. Here at last was a teacher seen as something other than a sexless tormentor of tenth-grade morons. Connie Brooks, the show's heroine, taught English at Madison High School, in a town of mid-America that somehow had a little piece of everywhere built into its foundations.

Perhaps that was the secret of the program's success. For teachers, Our Miss Brooks was all too human, finding plenty of time during the weekly half-hour comedy format to complain about her lowly salary (how teachers identified with that!) and to chase Philip Boynton, the bashful biology teacher.

The show premièred on CBS July 19, 1948, and was one of the network's most popular comedies for nine years. For six years, Colgate sponsored the program; then Toni Home Permanent began footing the bills. With Ozzie and Harriet, Life with Luigi, and The Phil Harris–Alice Faye Show, Our Miss Brooks was one of the last bright lights of radio situation comedy.

The title role was perfect for Eve Arden, a refugee from the B-movies. She was born Eunice Quedens but left that name in Mill Valley, California. When she set out with a touring theatrical group to see the world she combined the names on cosmetic bottles on a dressing room table—from "Evening In Paris" and "Elizabeth Arden," Eve Arden was born. With her touring company, she played barns and hotel lobbies in the early 1930's and finally landed in the *Ziegfeld Follies* of 1936. Hollywood beckoned the following year, and she embarked on a film career.

Her earliest notable acting credit was in *Oh, Doctor*, a 1937 celluloid cheapie. Following that, Miss Arden played gun molls and wisecracking babes in more than fifty horrible Hollywood capers, among them *The Forgotten Woman* (1939), *Slightly Honorable* (1940), and *She Couldn't Say No* (1941). Those B roles began to taper off only after *Our Miss Brooks* had become a national hit and she could afford the luxury of selecting her own slots. Her comic gifts had long been overlooked by filmdom, so it was in radio that she found her greatest success. She brought to the character a sarcastic wit that became its strongest trademark.

Writer Al Lewis captured the human side of Connie Brooks. Each year Miss Arden received thousands of letters from teachers frustrated with their own circumstances. At least half a dozen high schools offered her jobs teaching English. She turned down the jobs, but sometimes spoke at PTA meetings.

The schools couldn't have afforded her anyway. By then she was making $200,000 a year for being the tart-tongued schoolmarm of the air.

Her supporting cast was distinguished and funny, proving again that a show seldom flies with only one sail. Jeff Chandler, who died in 1961 without quite attaining the superstardom some producers had predicted, was Philip Boynton. It was one of his few tries at comedy, precisely the reverse of his later rough-cut, machismo screen image. Chandler handled the part extremely well, stumbling over words and laughing nervously whenever he was the center of attention. He was the perfect bashful boyfriend, even growing red-faced at the mention, in mixed company, of his frogs' breeding habits.

Probably the funniest character in the show was Osgood Conklin, Madison High's harried principal. Gale Gordon, who had played Mayor La Trivia on *Fibber McGee and Molly*, was at his best in these roles of blustery windbags, and Conklin was probably his best all-around radio role. It provided at least one solid stack-blowing per show.

Rounding out the cast of important regulars were Leonard Smith, Jane Morgan, and Richard Crenna (Dick in those long-ago days of bop and bobby-soxers). Smith played the school idiot, Stretch Snodgrass. Miss Morgan was heard as Mrs. Davis, owner of the apartment building where Miss Brooks lived. Mrs. Davis was always naive and sometimes seemed slightly senile, making remarks in a patter of logical lunacy taken from the Gracie Allen–Marie Wilson cloth.

Crenna was Walter Denton, the show's Henry Aldrich, who often drove Miss Brooks to school in his alleged automobile (remember the leaky top on rainy days?). Walter was another thorn in Conklin's side because he was in love with the principal's daughter Harriet. Harriet was played with Corliss Archer breathlessness by Gloria McMillan. Crenna would later become Luke on the Walter Brennan TV show, *The Real McCoys*, and today can be seen in a variety of serious film roles. But in 1949 he was Walter Denton, Jeff Chandler was just getting a foot in Hollywood's door, and Gale Gordon was one of radio's greatest character actors. Wilbur Hatch provided music.

They came to work on Sunday, arriving at the Hollywood studio at mid-morning for an informal reading of script. Lines and cues were learned, and a more polished rehearsal followed in the early afternoon. At 3:30 Pacific time, the show was broadcast live to the East Coast and taped for later replay in the West.

Radio comedy is often stilted and badly dated, but *Our Miss Brooks* is still funny and warm. So completely did Eve Arden assume the part that even today she is best remembered as the English teacher of Madison High. Her voice is immediately recognizable in any TV guest shot, and sometimes it can be distracting. It's hard to imagine Our Miss Brooks playing, as she has recently done, the part of a heavy.

Our Secret Weapon

Our Secret Weapon came to CBS August 9, 1942, and by 1943 was being heard as a 15-minute Friday-night propaganda show sponsored by Philco. It brought to the microphone Rex Stout, creator of detective Nero Wolfe, in a give-and-take session of Axis lie-debunking. Stout did most of the giving. Each week the current crop of lies being broadcast by the Axis powers on shortwave radio was collected by Jack Gerber and his staff at the CBS shortwave listening station. Stout selected those he wanted to use; Sue White, the series' creator, did the legwork, digging out the truth. Then Stout wrote a tough, punchy script, dousing the lies with the Allied version—in those innocent days called truth. The series was a direct counter to the strategy of German propaganda minister Joseph Goebbels, who flooded the air with claims of German-Italian-Japanese superiority and American bungling. When the Axis claimed that most top American athletes were German, the ancestry of baseball's top hitters was researched. The lies were then read rapid-fire by an announcer, and debunked in equally strong terms by Stout. For frequent dramatizations of ranting

Nazi speech, Paul Luther was brought in as Hitler. Guy Repp played Mussolini and Ted Osborne was Hirohito. The series ran for more than a year.

Our Secret World

Our Secret World was an unusual Mutual wartime series, running its short life in the fall of 1942. It was simply a series of spoken love letters, intimate little snatches of love talk between husbands and wives torn apart by a war in another part of the world.

Out of the Deep

Out of the Deep was the story of deep sea diver and soldier of fortune Gunner Carlisle, owner-shipper of the *Blue Falcon*, a salvage ship that sailed the oceans of the world in search of fortune and adventure. An average adventure series, this came to NBC December 1, 1945, and ran for about a year. It featured Ted Maxwell as the skipper. Maxwell also did the writing; Homer Canfield was producer-director, and Don Stanley announced.

Pacific Story

Pacific Story was a late-night (11:30 P.M.) semi-documentary, running on NBC in 1943–45. Jennings Pierce, the network's West Coast director of public service programming, and Inez Richardson of Stanford University had an idea that after the war, with Europe in ruins, the Pacific would emerge as the center of world political and social action. They thought people should know something about it. The network hired Arnold Marquis, former foreign correspondent, to write and produce the show, then began accumulating reference material for a master file and lining up experts on matters Pacific. As special counsel, NBC brought in Owen Lattimore, former emissary to China for President Roosevelt. Among the guests were Henry Luce of *Time-Life* and author Pearl S. Buck. Gayne Whitman narrated.

The Packard Show

The Packard Show was a concert program, later a variety hour. It was first heard on the Blue Network in 1934 in a 30-minute Tuesday-night format. In 1935 the show moved to CBS, keeping the same time slot, with Lawrence Tibbett as regular soloist. The variety hour premièred September 8, 1936, moving into a 60-minute Tuesday-at-9:30 time slot. Fred Astaire, then at the height of his fame as a dancer, was signed as singing star; Charlie Butterworth was comical co-star, and they were backed by singers Francia White, Trudy Wood, and Jimmy Blair. The production was wrapped up for Packard ("ask the man who owns one") by the music of Johnny Green's orchestra. Trudy Wood, a clear-voiced soprano, was pulled out of the chorus by Astaire for an on-the-air duet in her second week with the show, and went on to become the *Packard Hour* headliner when Astaire and Butterworth broke for summer vacations.

The trouble was, Astaire never came back. The sponsor did a quick shuffle and Lanny Ross, erstwhile *Show Boat* star, was co-featured with Walter O'Keefe when *The Packard Hour* opened for 1937. Butterworth, in his comedy routines, was teamed with Cliff Arquette, and Florence George was tapped as Packard soprano. The new version was decked out in a Mardi Gras format, with Don Wilson announcing and music by the Raymond Paige orchestra. But from the beginning the show had never run smoothly. Astaire even missed the first broadcast, leaving Jack Benny and Ginger Rogers to host the show, and there were consistent rumors of backstage rifts between Astaire and Butterworth. After a few rather disjointed seasons, Packard called it quits. It could have been big-time radio, but never quite made it.

Painted Dreams

Painted Dreams is generally considered radio's first soap opera. Created by Irna Phillips in 1930, it was aired by WGN Chicago, where Miss Phillips had landed after abandoning a teaching career. She appeared in the serial in addition to writing it. When WGN spurned an offer from the network to carry *Painted Dreams* nationwide, Miss Phillips angrily quit her job and went to work for NBC. A suit filed by Miss Phillips to retain the rights to *Painted Dreams* was not successful, but she gained her revenge by bringing thinly disguised versions of the same characters to a new drama. That show, *Today's Children*, was one of the great success stories of the early years, while *Painted Dreams* soon faded into obscurity. After three years on WGN, *Painted Dreams* did go network; it was brought to CBS late in 1933 under writer Bess Flynn. It told the story of the Moynihan family—a mother and daughters. In Miss Phillips' version, she played Mother Moynihan, with Ireene Wicker cast as one of her daughters. In the CBS version, author Flynn took the lead. The Flynn version disappeared in 1934.

The Palmolive Beauty Box Theatre

The Palmolive Beauty Box Theatre was a series of light operettas, first heard on NBC in 1934. John Barclay starred in the early shows, with support from Jane Froman and other leading singers of the era. Gladys

Swarthout was a semi-regular through the first year. But despite its talented cast, *Beauty Box Theatre* was in trouble. Ratings dropped consistently; the show moved to CBS in 1935, and trimmed from 60 to 30 minutes in 1936. Then came one of radio's frequent bombshells.

None ever hit with greater force than NBC's news, early in 1937, that Jessica Dragonette was leaving her *Cities Service Concerts* after seven years on the show. The network didn't say it, but magazine snoops smelled a dispute beneath the surface, and *Radio Mirror* predicted that Miss Dragonette would soon land feet-first on a program "to be sponsored by a famous soap manufacturer, on a network yet to be chosen, but probably CBS."

Even before the ink was dry, Miss Dragonette had agreed to star in the sagging *Palmolive Beauty Box Theatre.* Her entry was so smooth that her legion of fans hardly had time to miss her. But they buried NBC and Cities Service under an avalanche of protests anyway. On the *Palmolive Beauty Box Theatre*, she sang such operas as *The Student Prince, The Merry Widow, The Chocolate Soldier*, and *Rio Rita.* The format also gave her a brief chance to act, which was the central issue behind her split with Cities. Her male leads were prominent stars of the Metropolitan Opera, and the orchestra was under the direction of Al Goodman. The singing was supplemented by the narrative bridgework of announcer Jean Paul King. Despite its prestige format, *The Palmolive Beauty Box Theatre* indulged in premium giveaways just like afternoon kid shows. (One of its gifts was a Dionne quintuplets cutout book, guaranteed to "thrill the children.")

By the time she came to *Beauty Box Theatre*, Miss Dragonette was radio's première performer, a superstar even by today's standards. She virtually grew up in the medium, singing on the first around-the-world broadcast while still a schoolgirl in pigtails. Born poor, she worked her way through school and musical training, and was selected as one of America's first good-will song ambassadors to Latin America. Her disagreement with Cities led her ultimately to radio's exit door; she made fewer and fewer appearances after *The Palmolive Beauty Box Theatre* closed in 1937. In the early 1940's, she was a regular on Pet Milk's *Saturday Night Serenade*, the long-running CBS series of concert and popular music. Finally she disappeared completely, leaving an army of adoring fans and a lingering, almost legendary reputation as the first great voice of the air.

The Passing Parade

The Passing Parade was John Nesbitt's version of *Believe-It-Or-Not.* It was a series of yarns almost too incredible to believe but thoroughly documented by Nesbitt and others. Nesbitt, a student of Shakespeare and an actor early in life, broke into radio announcing for a station in Spokane. The idea for this program came with the death of his father, who left a trunk containing news clippings and papers telling of strange happenings around the world. Nesbitt began to investigate some of these accounts, and the result was *The Passing Parade,* which was picked up by the networks and ultimately found its way to the screen in a series of short subjects which Nesbitt also wrote and produced.

The show didn't attain a solid, continuing status on the networks, but was shifted into various times and formats. *Passing Parade* was heard as early as July 24, 1938, serving as a summer substitute for Phil Baker. On June 29, 1943, it became the summer replacement for *Fibber McGee and Molly.* During that same period, Nesbitt became part of John Charles Thomas' Sunday NBC Westinghouse show. In 1944, he did three shows a week for CBS, in addition to his Sunday Westinghouse stint at NBC. In 1948, he was signed by Mutual for a daily 15-minute afternoon show. Nesbitt told his stories "straight" without sound effects or music—a major difference between his show and Ripley's *Believe-It-Or-Not.* Occasionally, when the situation demanded, Nesbitt would slip into dialect. Usually he told two stories in each program, with an intermission for some band music by such as Victor Young's orchestra. Nesbitt's stories often contained unexplainable elements, heightening their interest. He told adventure tales, stories of daring prison breaks, of the man who lived for four years in a cupboard. A prolific, fast writer, he often waited until the last few minutes to begin preparing his script. But a staff of up to fourteen people helped him with research.

Passport for Adams

Passport for Adams was Norman Corwin's wartime globe-trotting adventure series, first heard on CBS August 17, 1943. It starred Robert Young as Doug Adams, "the country editor who's been sent on a trip around the world to visit the cities and talk to the people of the United Nations." The series, fully dramatized, was nevertheless semi-documentary in nature, explaining the customs and people of our fighting Allies as seen through the eyes of Adams. Accompanying Adams on his jaunt was "Quiz" Quisinberry, a slang-ridden, girl-hungry New York photographer. *Passport for Adams* maintained Corwin's high standard and reflected his intense interest in world affairs. His sixth script, telling of the state of Israel during a visit to Tel Aviv, was later used as a single story in his *Columbia Presents Corwin* series. Music for *Adams* was composed by Lucien Moraweck and conducted by Lud Gluskin. Scripts were also written by Ranald Mac-Dougall.

Pat Novak, For Hire

Pat Novak, For Hire—"That's what the sign outside my office says. Down on the waterfront in San Francisco, you don't get prizes for being subtle. You want to make a living down here, you got to get your hand in the till any way you can. You rob Peter to pay Paul, and then you put it on the cuff.

"So I rent boats and tell a few white lies if the price is right. It's a happy life, if you don't mind looking up at a headstone, because sooner or later you draw trouble a size too big."

Thus spoke Pat Novak, first cousin of *Johnny Madero* and the character who propelled Jack Webb to national prominence as radio's prime toughguy. The only things that separated Novak from Madero were the names and a little distance. *Pat Novak* was first heard in 1946, broadcasting from San Francisco and reaching a limited West Coast ABC network. After playing the part for several months, Webb left for Hollywood; *Novak* was continued by Ben Morris, but his portrayal was dull compared with Webb's. An outcry arose from Webb fans, and the result was *Johnny Madero*, a Mutual summer series of 1947 that reunited Webb and *Novak* writer Richard Breen in almost an exact copy of the *Novak* format.

Johnny Madero disappeared at the end of summer. The Ben Morris versions of *Pat Novak* continued through the 1946 season, broadcasting from KGO, San Francisco. That show featured Jack Lewis as Novak's pal Jocko Madigan and John Galbraith as Inspector Hellman, Novak's enemy with a badge. A steady demand persisted on the West Coast for a return of Webb as Novak, and it finally happened. By February 1949 the series had been picked up by ABC as a coast-to-coast show, and was billed for a time as the network's "most unusual" crime-detective series. The new series picked up where the original left off, Webb filling the air with hilarious clichés and purple dialogue: "The street was as deserted as a warm bottle of beer . . . a car started up down the street and the old man couldn't have made it with a pocketful of aces . . . I caught a glimpse of the license plate in a dull, surprised way, the way you grab a feather out of an angel's wing. . . ." Webb and Novak kept them coming, half a dozen per minute. Their style was what made this series go.

Like most private sleuths, Novak had an assistant—Jocko Madigan, wharf bum, "an ex-doctor and boozer—to him a hangover is the price of being sober—but an honest guy." The stories all went in the same direction. Novak would be hired to do something simple —tail a blonde, deliver a package. Inevitably, it led to murder. Along the way, he got slugged, and awoke with the room full of coppers. The only way to clear himself was to find the real murderer, fast. Jocko would be dragged out of some bar to do the legwork, while Novak waded into the enemy den with his fists and mouth working overtime. Week after week the same plot was used, and Novak was known by Jocko and others as "Patsy"—everybody's patsy.

He was especially Hellman's patsy. Hellman was the brutish police inspector who hated Novak enough to throw the switch on a jaywalking charge. He thought nothing of beating Novak occasionally, just for the hell of it. Novak responded with more smartmouth, and on it went. The series was simply a showcase for Webb's quips. He was the ultimate radio hardboiler, so distinctive that he was even parodied on a rival show. In 1949, the producers of Richard Diamond gave their hero a funny-rude rival, containing many of the Webb-Novak mannerisms and named, not coincidentally, Pat Cosak.

Tudor Owen, a British actor whose career spanned London stage, movies, and television, played Jocko Madigan in the Webb network version. Raymond Burr was perfect as Hellman. The show was produced and directed by William Rousseau, and music was by Basil Adlam. George Fenneman was announcer. It ran through the 1949 season.

Paul Whiteman Presents

Paul Whiteman Presents was a 30-minute NBC replacement for Edgar Bergen in the summer of 1943, bringing together Whiteman's thirty-five-piece orchestra and hostess Dinah Shore in the smash hit of vacation time. The show was a high-budget variety hour, carried by Bergen's sponsor, Chase & Sanborn and featuring songs, jokes, and top guest stars. The high point came on July 4, when Bing Crosby got together with his old partners Harry Barris and Al Rinker to form the first professional reunion of the Rhythm Boys since their beginnings with Whiteman's band in 1930. Among the other guests over the thirteen-week run were Eddie Cantor, George Burns and Gracie Allen, Red Skelton, Ed "Archie" Gardner, and Jimmy Durante. Paul Whiteman Presents premièred June 6 and went off August 29. The format called for one major guest star and a member of the "Whiteman Alumni Association" to appear each week. The "Alumni" were such old Whiteman associates as Ferde Grofé, Johnny Mercer, and Matty Malneck. Bill Goodwin was announcer, and the theme was (what else?) "Rhapsody in Blue."

Paul Winchell and Jerry Mahoney

Paul Winchell and Jerry Mahoney came to Mutual November 29, 1943, in a Monday-night variety show that featured singer Imogene Carpenter and the Russell Bennett Orchestra. Winchell was a ventriloquist, riding the crest of the Charlie McCarthy wave, and publicity shots of his dummy Jerry Mahoney bore a startling likeness to Edgar Bergen's Charlie. Winchell was a better ventriloquist too, as TV later proved. But on radio people didn't care how badly your lips moved, and in 1943 he was trodding old turf. There was just one Charlie.

The Pause That Refreshes on the Air

The Pause That Refreshes on the Air was a title used several times by Coca-Cola. One early *Pause* show, running on NBC in 1934–35, featured Frank Black, "sixty-five musicians and twenty-five vocalists." On December 1, 1940, a new *Pause* opened on CBS. It was a distinctive program of concert music under direction of Russian-American conductor Andŕe Kostelanetz. Kostelanetz had been with CBS since 1933, broadcasting for Chesterfield with such headliners as Lily Pons and Lawrence Tibbett and later for Ethyl Gas as *Tune-Up Time.* Now came Coca-Cola, searching for a Sunday-afternoon format that would best fit its "pause that refreshes" slogan. After listening to several maestros of the swing school, Coke settled on the Kostelanetz forty-five-member orchestra. Violinist Albert Spalding was tapped as the show's narrator, John Charles Thomas was featured singer, and guest soloists were booked from the opera world. The show immediately picked up a respectable audience, and the orchestra was praised by *Newsweek* for the "distinctive shimmering effect" of its sixteen violins. It ran in its 30-minute, Sunday-at-4:30 time slot until 1944, when Coke moved its advertising dollar elsewhere. Kostelanetz turned up again in 1946, doing his thing for Chrysler.

In 1947 Coke reinstated the *Pause that Refreshes* format, complete with the Kostelanetz orchestra. By 1948, Percy Faith was broadcasting under that banner Fridays on CBS, in a format that co-starred singer Jane Froman.

The Penny Singleton Show

The Penny Singleton Show was heard on NBC in the summer of 1950. Miss Singleton, best known as the Blondie of radio and movies, now played Penny Williamson, a widow who lived in Middleton and sold real estate to support her two daughters. The situation comedy was basically a soft and early blow for women's lib, portraying Penny and her daughters as highly competent, self-sufficient females in a sea of male ineptitude. Chief bunglers and fierce competitors for her hand were Horace Wiggins, her partner in the realty firm, and crusty Judge Beshomer Grundell. A top cast of radio professionals appeared in support: Jim Backus played Wiggins; Gale Gordon was Grundell, and Bea Benaderet was Margaret, Penny's nasal cook. Her daughters in the show, Sue and Dorothy ("DG" for short) were named for Penny's real-life daughters, and were played by Sheila James and Marylee Robb. Max Hutto directed.

People Are Funny

People Are Funny evolved from an earlier show, and made its nationwide première on NBC on April 3, 1942.

John Guedel was an unknown who had started his professional life as a ditchdigger with the WPA after his family fortune was depleted in 1929. He subsequently became a traveling salesman, sleeping, when he couldn't afford hotels, in parks and occasionally (for the ultimate in peace and quiet) in graveyards. In the late 1930's he landed in show business as a writer for Hal Roach. His thoughts of becoming a freelance writer were ended by a string of 100 rejection slips, and he was in a doctor's waiting room in 1942 when a chance reading of a radio trade magazine turned his life around.

The article described a current radio show that was being cancelled. Always the promoter, Guedel had just the formula for the vacant slot. In 1938, he had produced a local game show, *Pull Over, Neighbor*, which he had sold with a $30 audition record. The show had later become known as *All Aboard* when sponsorship went to a railroad. Now Guedel reorganized the format, called it *People Are Funny* and dashed off a note to the agency handling the account.

A few days later, he was outlining *People Are Funny* to the agency by phone.

The idea was simple enough: it was to be a stunt show, with prizes of cash and merchandise—but there was a twist. Each stunt would be carefully designed to reveal a humorous facet of character—to prove that "people are funny." The agency liked it; within weeks, the show was whipped together and was put into an NBC Friday-night slot.

The stunts were written by Guedel's father Walter; Art Baker, then one of the most popular emcees on the coast, was brought in as host. He had been with the show in its *Pull Over, Neighbor* days; now, for the first six shows, he was joined by young Art Linkletter, a brash San Francisco announcer whose growing specialty was audience participation. Linkletter and Baker served as co-hosts, rather an unusual setup for an unusual show. Then Linkletter went back to his San Francisco duties and Baker continued the show alone.

For six years it was a Friday-night show, sponsored until 1945 by Wings Cigarettes, and until 1951 by Raleigh.

For seventy-eight weeks Baker ran the program, holding a solid rating throughout. On October 1, 1943, he was abruptly dropped by Guedel, and Linkletter was brought in again from San Francisco. The parting had not been an easy one. Baker, charging that Guedel had broken his five-year contract and brought in Linkletter at a lower salary, promptly sued. But it all came to naught, and *People Are Funny* was suddenly Linkletter's show. He continued at the helm for more than fifteen years, taking it into TV as well. Linkletter became so well established as the genial *People Are Funny* host that even its longtime listeners eventually forgot that the show had once been handled by someone else.

Linkletter pulled thousands of pranks. Once a week, a contestant was selected from the studio audience and sent out to do some outrageous stunt in public. The contestant couldn't reveal to passersby that he was on assignment from *People Are Funny*, and Irvin Atkins (Guedel's man Friday) went along on "outside" stunts to make sure that nobody broke the rules.

Five minutes before the show went off the air, the contestant was returned to the studio to tell how he had fared. In the interim, various pranks would continue inside, using other people from the audience. Linkletter was shameless in his glee as people got doused with water, hit with pies, or endured some similar hilarious trick. Once he sent a man out to make a dress for a manikin on the crowded corner of Sunset and Vine. In another wild stunt, a man and his wife were sent out, camouflaged as trees. Still another man was sent to register at the posh Knickerbocker Hotel with a seal as his weekend "girl friend." Linkletter sent contestants out to "give away money" (many had a surprisingly tough time doing that), and once he gave a contestant $20,000 to "play the stock market for a week." In 1945, he began one of his most celebrated stunts, dropping twelve little boxes sealed in plastic balls into the Pacific Ocean, and announcing a $1,000 prize to the first person who found one. The first ball was found two years later by a native of the Ennylageban Islands.

One of the popular early stunts was called "You Bet Your Life." Here, contestants competed for the sponsor's cigarettes with a chance to win up to forty cartons. It was a prelude to another Guedel program, created five years later, which became famous in its own right as a showcase for Groucho Marx. In 1948, *People Are Funny* moved to Tuesday nights, where it remained through its long run. In 1951, it moved to CBS, still on Tuesdays, for Mars Candy, and in 1954 it returned to NBC for Toni. *People Are Funny* lasted until 1959.

The People's Platform

The People's Platform, a project of the CBS Adult Education Board, was first heard in July 1938 as a 30-minute discussion of current events. Chairing the discussions was Lyman Bryson, a noted educator who had been appointed chairman of the CBS board the previous January. Bryson brought into the studio a hand-picked panel of four people. The guests were served dinner as an icebreaker, and had an opportunity to chat before the show. Most were experts in the field under discussion, or at least had a good working understanding. Bryson remained with *The People's Platform* for seven years, and the show continued until 1952. Initially on Wednesdays, it moved to Sundays by 1939 and Saturdays in 1940, where it stayed until 1946. It then returned to Sunday, where it remained for the rest of the run.

The People's Rally

The People's Rally was a strange Sunday-afternoon mixture that came to Mutual in 1938. Within the 30-minute format, commentator John B. Kennedy and guests debated such searching questions as the effect of the Neutrality Act. Then quizmaster Bob Hawk offered a spirited mini-version of his "Quixie Doodles" audience stumpers. It was rare programming for public interest and quiz to be mixed, but *The People's Rally* faded from the air after one year. While it was there, it was sponsored by Mennen.

Pepper Young's Family

Pepper Young's Family, was a low-key soap opera about life in middle America. An organ, a slow piano, and the haunting theme "Au Matin" set the stage. From their home in the mythical town of Elmwood, the Young family spun a twenty-three-year tale of love, hate, sorrow, and finally madness, enduring on NBC from 1936 through 1959.

The serial was written by Elaine Carrington, who gave up writing for magazines to become one of soapland's major names. Mrs. Carrington had always been a writer, even as a child. A native New York, she had collected a large stack of rejection slips before breaking into the big time with sales to *The Saturday Evening Post*, *Good Housekeeping*, and *Redbook*. From her home in New York, she wrote screenplays for a while, and had even done a Broadway play. Mrs. Carrington was established by 1932, when a rainstorm drove her into the NBC building. There she struck up a conversation with the network's head of program continuity, was asked to try a radio treatment, and returned later with the outline of a family drama.

The show was called *Red Adams*; the hero was a teenage boy, and the supporting characters were his parents and his sister. The network liked it. *Red Adams* went on the Blue Network October 2, 1932, as a sustaining drama.

Burgess Meredith played the title role, but for the first few years of the run, *Red Adams* had it problems. The hero lost his name twice, first becoming Red Davis when Beech Nut Gum agreed to sponsor. (Beech Nut didn't want its hero named after its top competitor.) Then Meredith left for bigger things, and the show did another turnaround. In 1935, the Davis family became the Young family, and the show was moved from its evening time slot into the afternoons. During this transitional period, it was called *Forever Young*.

Gradually the character of Red Davis became Larry "Pepper" Young. One day there he was, big as life; Pepper Young had found his niche, and *Pepper Young's Family* was on the air. The show was broadcasting under its final format by June 1936. Pepper's sister had become Peggy Young, and their parents were Sam and Mary. Sam was a sometime banker, a simple man of simple tastes and desires. Mary was a fine, old-fashioned housewife. Pepper wanted to be a writer; his childhood sweetheart was Linda Benton, who'd always thought he had had a flair for words. And Peggy was in love with young Carter Trent, the Chicago transplant who proposed one night in 1941, sitting there under the stars telling his future bride how great their lives would be *if only* he could get a job making as much as thirty-five dollars a week.

From those basic ingredients, Mrs. Carrington fashioned a high-quality soap whose primary appeal was rooted in characterization. Listeners fretted with the family over the simple things of life—dates, parties, and just making ends meet in a prewar depression. The Youngs were introduced as "your friends," and to the millions of housewives who listened daily, so it must have seemed. Though it ran for two decades on NBC, *Pepper Young's Family*—at the height of its popularity—was heard on Blue and Red Networks, and ran concurrently for one season each on Mutual (1937–38) and CBS (1942–43). Its longtime sponsor was Camay, "the soap of beautiful women."

As the serial grew, so did its characters. Pepper became a reporter for the *Free Press*, a local newspaper. He married Linda and settled down to raise their "Button." Peggy and Carter were married, but dark days lay in store for them. Late in the run, after serving for more than fifteen years as a leading *Pepper Young* character, Carter went off the deep end, ran away, and died a broken man.

It all came about with a huge oil strike on the Young property, where Pepper and Linda had retired to live the farm life. The oil well caught fire, burned out half the town, and killed Sam Young's best friend, Curt Bradley. Carter, asleep at the site when the fire broke out, blamed himself. Unable to face his family, he disappeared for more than a year, "moving from city to city" and living as a forgotten man.

Curtis Arnall, who had played Buck Rogers a few years before, played Red Davis from 1934 on, and initiated the role of Pepper Young. Lawson Zerbe took over after the first *Pepper* year, leaving in 1945. Then Mason Adams was Pepper until the end in 1959.

In other long-running performances, Betty Wragge went all the way as Peggy, and Marion Barney played the ever-patient Mrs. Young. The part of Sam Young was initiated by Jack Roseleigh, but was played for many years by Thomas Chalmers. Eunice Howard was Linda, and Curt Bradley was played by Edwin Wolfe. Chick Vincent was longtime director.

The success of *Pepper Young's Family* led Elaine Carrington to take on two new serials in the late 1930's. She dictated her scripts, playing out each role like Irna Phillips. She continued writing each episode, giving it that personal touch, until her death in 1958. In the final year, her children Bob and Pat wrote the scripts.

Perry Mason

Perry Mason came to CBS October 18, 1943, in a script written especially for radio by Erle Stanley Gardner. Gardner, a Southern California lawyer, had created Mason (a fictional alter-ego) in a series of mystery novels read by millions. So Perry Mason had a built-in audience when he made the jump to radio. Along with him came all the other Gardner regulars—secretary Della Street, legman Paul Drake, and crusty old Lieutenant Tragg of homicide. Mason trod heavily in the footsteps of *Mr. District Attorney;* he was billed as "defender of human rights, champion of all those who seek justice." But this was sheer soap opera, which ran in prime afternoon time, five days a week, 15 minutes per chapter, for Procter & Gamble. In one 1949 sequence, Mason and Tragg had a murderer pinned down in a ratty hotel. They argue like schoolboys over who should go in first.

(TRAGG: It's my job. MASON: Yeah, but you're the family man. TRAGG: Let me . . . MASON: No, let me . . .) While they're discussing it, the killer escapes through a window and takes a fire escape to the roof. Mason and Tragg finally push each other out of the way and stumble into the room, then begin arguing over who should go up the fire escape after Barker. Tragg wins ("We'll both go, but *I'll* go first"). Tragg takes a bullet in the leg and says the radio version of damn, double damn and hell; *now Mason will get all the credit!*

Bartlett Robinson played Mason when the series opened. Subsequent lead actors were Santos Ortega and Donald Briggs. By 1949, John Larkin was giving a short-tempered interpretation of the Gardner hero. Della was originated by Gertrude Warner, and was subsequently played by Jan Miner and Joan Alexander. Matt Crowley was Drake and Mandel Kramer was Tragg. Although Gardner started the scripting, he soon left it to Ruth Borden and Irving Vendig. The series ran until 1955, carried all the way on CBS for Procter & Gamble.

The Personal Column of the Air

The Personal Column of the Air was devised by Octavus Roy Cohen, a magazine writer, in 1935 London. Fascinated by the personals columns of *The London Times,* Cohen thought a radio show built around the same situations would have tremendous human interest. He wrote a script and the following year had an audition record made of the proposed show. It simply invited listeners to send in "messages you wish broadcast to people whom you have lost track of—friends or relatives and dear ones who have disappeared from your life." Cohen's faith was immediately justified: the show sold to Procter & Gamble for $4,000 a week, and soon was running 15 minutes a day, five times a week, on both NBC Red and Blue. It premièred nationally on November 16, 1936, after a short trail in selected cities. Inez Lopez (Mrs. Cohen) produced the show, sifting through hundreds of letters weekly to find the few to be dramatized by paid actors. It opened to the theme "L'Amour, Toujours L'Amour," and one of its first stories was of a long-lost turn-of-the-century love affair. After that, listeners were hooked, and *The Personal Column of the Air* had an extremely profitable, though brief year.

Pete Kelly's Blues

Pete Kelly's Blues took listeners to a smoke-filled Kansas City speakeasy of the 1920's. Prohibition was in, booze out, except at

George Lupo's place, 417 Cherry Street. There it was still tough to get a clear gin, but a lady liked the idea of a drink to match the color of her dress. "We start every night about 10 and play till the customers get that first frightening look at each other in the early light . . ."

Pete Kelly played cornet in Lupo's place, where bootlegged rotgut flowed freely and the customers came with personal hangups of all kinds. For Jack Webb, fresh from his first two years as Joe Friday of *Dragnet, Pete Kelly's Blues* was a half-step back to the tempo and pitch of *Pat Novak.* But only a half-step. Never again was Webb quite as hardboiled as Novak; as Pete Kelly of the Roaring Twenties he took on the Establishment and still managed to come out ahead.

Kelly's boss was a "fat, friendly little guy who wouldn't harm a fly—there's no money in harming flies." Under Lupo's watchful eye, Kelly headed a small combo (Pete Kelly's Big Seven) and belted out a brand of jazz that almost competed with the story.

Thirty musicians were auditioned before Webb picked Dick Cathcart to head up the combo on cornet. Other members of the Big Seven were Matty Matlock, clarinet; Elmer Schneider, trombone; Ray Schneider, piano; Bill Newman, guitar; Marty Carb, bass; and Nick Fatool, drums. Blues singer Meredith Howard played the part of Maggie Jackson, a speakeasy entertainer. The regular company of actors included William Conrad, Peggy Webber, Whitfield Connor, Vic Perrin, Herb Butterfield, and Jack Kruschen. The characters were created by Richard Breen of Webb's *Pat Novak* days. The writing by Jo Eisinger and James Moser was again a return to the *Novak* theme. Kelly's involvement with customers and show people of the era led quickly and surely to trouble, often to murder, and usually Pete Kelly was on the hook until he got himself off.

The program premièred on NBC July 4, 1951, and ran through the summer. It was one of Webb's best showings, and was the foundation for his 1955 movie of the same name.

ANNOUNCER: This one's about Pete Kelly . . .
(Music up, blues note, played in brass)
ANNOUNCER (Over music): It's about the world he goes around in . . .
It's about the big music . . .
And the big trouble . . .
In the big Twenties . . .
So when they ask you, tell them this one's about the blues . . .
Pete Kelly's Blues . . .

The Phil Baker Show

The Phil Baker Show was a comedy-variety series, long before Baker became quizmaster on Take It or Leave It. Backed by the Frank Shields orchestra and the singing of the Neil Sisters, Baker came to the Blue Network as The Armour Jester on March 17, 1933, for Armour Packing. In 1935, The Phil Baker Show moved to CBS for Gulf Oil and a Sunday format; in 1938 he took over a CBS Saturday time slot for Dole Pineapple, a show that co-starred the Andrews Sisters.

Baker's long career had begun on the stage of a neighborhood movie house, progressed through a variety of vaudeville acts, and culminated in his network radio show, which soon climbed into the magical top 10. An accomplished accordionist, he had toured in vaudeville with Ben Bernie, working up an accordion-violin act that was one of the headliners of the era. His show, written by Hal Block (at 21, Baker's head writer), Arthur Phillips, and Sam Perrin, featured skits with his butler, Bottle, a "veddy-veddy English chap" played by Harry McNaughton, and Beetle, a ghost who haunted, harassed, and goaded Baker unmercifully. Beetle was never seen, even by the studio audience; he spoke his lines from a loudspeaker offstage and posed for publicity stills in a mask. His intrusion into the first program was promoted by such ads in The New York Times as: MYSTERY RADIO VOICE BAFFLES PHIL BAKER. During the half-hour, Baker would do an accordion solo and the Seven G's offered a musical number; Baker then spent the rest of the show being persecuted by the persistent Beetle. Hank Ladd was the first Beetle; Ward Wilson and Sid Silvers also played the part. By 1939, Baker had thoroughly tired of this format, and so had the public. He dropped out of radio for two years, and re-emerged as Take It Or Leave It emcee in December 1941.

The Phil Harris–Alice Faye Show

The Phil Harris–Alice Faye Show grew out of the Fitch Bandwagon, premièring on the Bandwagon show of September 29, 1946.

Bandleader Phil Harris and his movie star wife Alice Faye met late in 1933, when she was singing with Rudy Vallee and Harris was leading his orchestra at New York's Lafayette. It wasn't a very memorable meeting: because of an accident, her face was wrapped in bandages, and conversation was limited to a few polite words. During the next eight years, Harris and Miss Faye went their separate ways. She married Tony Martin and became a top-flight singing movie star; he hooked up with Jack Benny in 1936 and began to bring out his brash character on the air. In the early 1940's, they got together again, in a meeting at Charlie Foy's Supper Club in Hollywood. Miss Faye's marriage to Martin was finished, and Harris liked her face much better with the bandages off. He overcame her initial resistance, and they were married after a brisk courtship.

In its *Fitch Bandwagon* days, the Harris–Faye show sometimes became just an extension of Benny's program. Benny would close with Harris saying, "S'long, Jackson," and the scenario would pick up from there on *The Fitch Bandwagon*, which followed immediately. The action centered on Phil's home life with Alice and his kids (Phyllis and Alice, Jr.), and on an incredible cast of wiseguys Harris would meet on the way home. Under Fitch sponsorship, Harris developed the basic format that followed when, on October 3, 1948, *The Phil Harris–Alice Faye Show* premièred for Rexall. It became radio's new leader in sarcastic comedy. The lines were punchy, riotously funny, and expanded the basic format created by Jack Benny. Harris had learned his comedy well during his long years as Benny's stooge.

As in its Fitch days, *The Harris–Faye Show* ran on NBC Sundays, just after Benny, whom Harris still served as bandleader. Benny by then had gone to CBS. But the *Harris–Faye Show* was established in its own right, and Harris' work with Benny was mentioned only occasionally. The format did continue in the time-tested Benny tradition, many of the situations revolving around Harris and Miss Faye in rehearsal, or in backstage bickering with their hard-headed sponsor. Each program contained two songs—a number by Miss Faye from her movie days and a novelty number by Harris. Like Benny, Harris built his show on character and well-defined personalities. His character—already well-established after a decade with Benny's troupe —was merely continued. He was the rough-cut, lovable egomaniac, of the curly hair and the flashy cars who abused the language mercilessly and always tried to bluff his way through a problem. When Harris crowed, "Oh, you dawwwwg!" liseners just knew he was looking at himself in the mirror.

Alice played herself—the movie star who had given up fame and glamor to be a wife and mother. Offstage, Harris has a reputation as a polite, almost shy man—a complete reversal of his radio image. On the air, he was a master of the crude quip, aided and abetted by the medium's best practitioners of the same. Elliott Lewis played Frankie Remley, the guitar player in Phil's band and "the worst musician in the world," if the judgment of Rexall boss Mr. Scott could be trusted. We never heard Frankie play. His sole function seemed to be getting

Harris ("Curly" to him) into one jam after another. Frankie's classic line, "I know a guy . . ." inevitably led Phil to some cut-rate "expert" in the problem of the week. Before the expert was finished, Phil had to pay through the nose, and sometimes even then he saved his hide only through his wife's diplomacy.

There really was a musician named Frankie Remley, and he really did play with the Harris band. The "Frank Remley gag," as it came to be known backstage, began around 1936, when Harris had just signed with Benny. Often Benny wisecracked about "Frankie the guitar player," and later, when the *Harris–Faye Show* was forming, it was decided to make him a character. At Remley's request, Elliott Lewis got the part.

Harris also had to contend with Julius Abbruzio, the most delightfully insufferable brat who ever came out of radio. Julius, the delivery boy with the thick Brooklyn accent, usually turned up in the last half of the show, thoroughly delighted to find Harris and Remley in hot water and more than willing to help them sink a little deeper. Julius was beautifully played by Walter Tetley, whose previous wiseguy credit as Leroy, the nephew of the Great Gildersleeve, was a mere rehearsal for this role. His best-remembered lines: "Are you kiddin'?" and "Get outta here!"

Robert North was fine as Willie, Alice's creampuff brother who roomed with the Harrises and drove Phil crazy. His weekly greeting, "Gooood morning, Philip," became one of the series' memorable phrases. The Harris children were played by Jeanine Roose and Anne Whitfield, who picked up their dad's mannerisms and had some brash, funny lines of their own. Once when Remley stole Phil's job, he tried to counter the little girls' weeping by reminding them that their father still worked for Jack Benny. To which Alice, Jr. replied, "You know there ain't no money connected with that job!"

Gale Gordon did his usual fine job as Mr. Scott, the harried sponsor. Playing a high-ranking officer of the Rexall Drug Company, Mr. Scott became a regular victim of Harris-Remley schemes. The sponsor's participation in the stories was one of the show's most unusual techniques. Other comedians had long used the device of incorporating the middle commercial into their situations, but Rexall played a major role in the stories as well. The company let itself in for some real ribbing. Frankie often expressed his dislike of the sponsor, and once asked Harris, "What's a Rexall?" Harris countered by suggesting that the company might make a fortune bottling and selling the Harris charm. It eliminated any need for a middle commercial, was far more effective, and Rexall came off as a company of good sports if nothing else.

The success of the series was due in great measure to the funny scripts by Ray Singer and Dick Chevillat. Walter Scharf composed and conducted, and the show was produced and directed by Paul Phillips. Bill Forman announced, opening each show with the famous slogan: "Good health to all from Rexall." Rexall carried the show until 1950, when it was sustained for a time by NBC. RCA became sponsor in 1951, and two years later the show moved to Fridays. *The Phil Harris–Alice Faye Show* was last heard in 1954.

The Philip Morris Playhouse

The Philip Morris Playhouse was a title given to several dramatic anthologies sponsored by Philip Morris. The first *Playhouse* ran on CBS Friday nights from 1939 through 1943. The basic format (same network, same night) was restored in 1948 for one season.

Generally, the show featured straight and crime drama; the 1948 run leaned toward murder mysteries under the eye of producer-director William Spier. He had directed *Suspense* in its salad days and brought to *The Philip Morris Playhouse* the same slick production he had developed for "radio's outstanding theatre of thrills." He enticed top name stars, used such writers as Morton Fine and David Friedkin, and wrapped the show up with a score by Lud Gluskin and announcing by Art Ballinger. Dan Dailey, Vincent Price, Marlene Dietrich, Howard Duff, and Harold (Great Gildersleeve) Peary were a few of the stars who worked for Spier.

A notable departure occurred in 1951 when the series moved to NBC Tuesday nights under the direction of Charles Martin. Then it was called *The Philip Morris Playhouse on Broadway*. But there were still name stars and murder stories, as in June 1951, when Gloria Swanson starred in *Double Indemnity* by James M. Cain. Music in this late version was by Alexander Semmler.

In all its forms, the most notable thing about *The Philip Morris Playhouse* was the commercial. Since 1933, when the first "Call for Philip Morrrraaiiss!" spot went over the air, millions of cigarettes had been sold by Johnny Roventini, a four-foot midget with an uncanny ability to hit a perfect B-flat every time. Early in 1933, he was a $15-a-week bellhop at the Hotel New Yorker. Milton Biow, head of the agency handling the Philip Morris account, came to the hotel one day, met Johnny, and was hit by a stroke of sheer inspiration. It was one of those ingenious pieces of advertising that come along a few times each decade, and Biow couldn't wait to get Johnny into a studio. He auditioned him right there in the New Yorker lobby. For several minutes, under Biow's direction, Johnny walked through the lobby paging Philip Morris. It was just too perfect.

That day saw a change in Johnny Roventini's lifestyle. His income went from $15 a week to $20,000 a year. As the ingenuity of the ads became apparent to all, Johnny was given a lifetime contract that still runs, more than two decades after the last "Call for Philip Morraaaiiisss" spot was heard on the air. He was a walking piece of public relations that reminded people of the product for twenty years. "Johnny" ads were used on billboards and magazines. Always in his crisp red bellhop's uniform, he was "stepping out of storefronts all over America" to remind smokers that "you get no cigarette hangover" with Philip Morris. When MGM's famed Leo the Lion died, Johnny was touted as the world's only living trademark.

Philip Morris was one of the big advertisers of radio, and Johnny was kept busy. In addition to the sporadic appearances of The Philip Morris Playhouse, the company offered the variety show Johnny Presents, and also for a time carried It Pays to Be Ignorant and Crime Doctor. Some of the shows originated in Hollywood, some in New York. Johnny Roventini couldn't be everywhere at once, so a group of understudies—"Johnny Juniors"—was recruited and trained by Roventini to stand in for him. Johnny Mirkin, one of the first, was lifted from a pageboy's job in Philadelphia.A quarter-century after its demise, the most memorable thing about The Philip Morris Playhouse is little Johnny, to the forlorn strains of "On The Trail" from The Grand Canyon Suite, reminding his listeners to "CALL FOR PHILIP MORRRAAAIIISSS!"

A final Philip Morris Playhouse was heard on CBS Wednesday nights in 1952–53.

Philo Vance

Philo Vance, based on the detective character created by S. S. Van Dine, was brought to NBC July 5, 1945, as a summertime replacement for the Bob Burns Show. José Ferrer played Vance, following Van Dine's formula of meticulous clue-gathering and last-minute revelation. Robert Shaw wrote the scripts, and the series was carried by Burns' sponsor, Lifebuoy. In 1948, a new Philo Vance was produced for syndication by the Frederic Ziv Company. Ziv was just bringing transcribed drama to the fore then, and Philo Vance was one of his weaker efforts. It featured Jackson Beck as Vance and George Petrie as Markham, the district attorney. Even the performance by Beck—one of radio's circle of established professionals—didn't save this one.

Phone Again, Finnegan

Phone Again, Finnegan, a rather weak effort of 1946, was first heard on NBC and moved to CBS for the summer. It starred Stuart Erwin as Fairchild Finnegan, a none-too-bright nice guy who managed the Welcome Arms Apartments and got himself into all kinds of problems with residents and fellow members of Gabby O'Brien's athletic club. Florence Lake played Miss Smith, the switchboard operator whose cheery "Phone again, Finnegan" became the show's catch phrase. Harry Stewart was Longfellow Larson and the show was directed by Hobart Donovan.

The Player

The Player was a syndicated series of the late 1940's, bringing to its 15-minute format "America's most versatile actor," Paul Frees. In *The Player* Frees was a "one-man theatre," doing all the characterizations. The stories were creepy and mysterious, and the Player was another of our all-knowing hosts; like the Whistler and the Mysterious Traveler, he knew all the answers but never appeared in any of the dramas. With his many voices, Frees helped pull it up to average marks on the radio rating chart. The only other voice heard on the show was the announcer, Gary Goodwin.

Plays for Americans

Plays for Americans was another in the series of Arch Oboler plays that created such an artistic stir during the years spanning 1938 and 1944. This was a short series, heard from February 1 through July 5, 1942, Sundays on NBC. As usual, it was written, produced, and directed by Oboler and featured such stars as Olivia De Havilland, Raymond Massey, Alla Nazimova, James Stewart, Bette Davis, Dick Powell, Robert Taylor, Joan Blondell, and Claude Rains.

Point Sublime

Point Sublime was a perfect setting for a radio drama. A fictitious little village somewhere on the Pacific coast, it had one newspaper, a golf course, a general store, 750 people, and a way of life all but lost in twentieth-century America.

There was a closed lighthouse on the point, and the town was split through the center by the coast highway, the principal thoroughfare. Here lived Ben Willet, storekeeper, town philosopher, man of great curiosity, and hero of Robert L. Redd's comedy-drama.

Redd—producer, director, and writer—brought *Point Sublime* to NBC in December 1940 as a Monday-night offering on NBC's West Coast stations. In the beginning, all life at Point Sublime revolved around Ben, town mayor and owner of the mercantile store and adjacent motel. The light of Ben's life was the widow Evelyn (Evy) Hanover, who frequently dropped into the store to share a bit of gossip.

Evy had come to Point Sublime to work for a paleontologist. He left, she stayed. Her conversations with Ben about the goings-on in Point Sublime always perked up his curiosity, leading inevitably to humor, sometimes to drama, and occasionally even to mystery.

Another relative newcomer was Howie MacBrayer, retired millionaire cattle baron. Like Evy, Howie drove into Point Sublime one day in 1940 and never drove out. He bought the golf and surf club, remodeled it, and settled there, becoming Ben Willet's friendly rival and the butt of all Ben's jokes about Texas.

Others in the cast were August Moon, the stuttering railway clerk who doubled as a helper in Ben's store; Hattie Hirsch, the native Point Sublimer whose fondness for gossip exceeded even that of Ben and Evy; Aaron Saul, the town jeweler; and "Monk" Rice, son of the local newsman.

Cliff Arquette, who gave up a map-making job as a young man to begin playing old men on the air, was Ben Willet. Arquette broke into radio in 1924, quitting a title insurance company to take a try at the new medium. It didn't take producers long to discover that Arquette had a perfect "old" voice, and he was tapped for old roles in many comedy and straight shows. He became an occasional player with Jack Benny, playing Benny's father. His best-remembered character was Charlie Weaver. Arquette's husky voice was just right for Ben. In character, his favorite expression of delight was, "Ain't we the ones?" Earle Ross, best known as Judge Hooker on *The Great Gildersleeve*, was Howie MacBrayer. Jane Morgan played Evy. Mel Blanc, using his best Porky Pig voice, was the stuttering August Moon. Verna Felton played Hattie Hirsch; Lou Merrill was Aaron Saul and Fred MacKaye was Monk.

The show was billed as "the human story of a fella named Ben Willet." After two years on NBC West, it moved to Mutual–Don Lee, where it continued on Monday nights through 1944.

On October 6, 1947, ABC resurrected *Point Sublime* for another West Coast run. By January 5, 1948, it had gone coast-to-coast. The original cast was assembled for this version, which was also heard Mondays for John Hancock Insurance. In the opening chapter, Ben Willet returned home to his friends after being away in Europe for many months. We assume he was home to stay, but *Point Sublime* disappeared after its initial season on ABC.

Popeye the Sailor

Popeye the Sailor was first heard on NBC September 10, 1935, in a three-a-week show for kiddies. It was almost an audio copy of the Paramount cartoons and the King Features Syndicate comic strip, begun in 1926 by Elzie Crisler Segar. The radio show featured the same cast of characters—Popeye, the gravel-voiced weakling who became a man of steel by downing a can of spinach; Olive Oyl, the sailorman's stringbean girl friend; Wimpy; and the young boy (called "Matey" and "Sonny" variously) adopted by Popeye in the first episode. The producers were hard-pressed to find a gravel voice that adapted to Popeye's "I yam what I yam" delivery; they tested some sixty people, including a group of Coney Island barkers, before settling on Detmar Poppen as the "whiskey baritone." Olive Lamoy played Olive Oyl; Charles Lawrence was Wimpy, and Jimmy Donnelly was Popeye's adopted son. Victor Irwin's Cartoonland Band (which also supplied the music for the Popeye cartoons) provided musical effects for everything from Popeye's bulging muscles to his rolling walk. The series ended in 1936, and a new version began August 31 that year on CBS. Floyd Buckley was a later Popeye. As in the first run, the sponsor was Wheatena. In a way, it was a cruel blow to fans everywhere. Now, instead of singing his old standby ("I'm strong to the finish, 'cause I eats me spinach"), there was Popeye, pushing another food:

> Wheatena's me diet,
> I ax ya ta try it,
> I'm Popeye the saiiilor man!
> Beep-Beep!

Portia Faces Life

Portia Faces Life opened on CBS October 7, 1940. Portia Blake was the wife of a handsome young attorney waging a relentless war against corruption in the small city of Parkerstown. His target: the town's most powerful political boss. But in the midst of this fight, Portia's husband was killed, leaving her to raise her young son Dickie alone.

That was the opening episode of this staunch soap. Portia Blake was a brilliant attorney in her own right, so she moved to NBC in 1941 and took up the campaign against the corruptors in her husband's memory. And for the next eleven years she thus faced life on NBC, for such General Foods as Bran and Post Toasties. Portia's rating was consistently high, far above the workaday world where most of her rivals lived.

This was "a story reflecting the courage, spirit, and integrity of American women everywhere." Later, following her marriage to the "brilliant, handsome" journalist Walter Manning, it became "a story taken from the heart of every woman who has ever dared to love completely."

Written by Mona Kent, *Portia* was based on the heroine of the same name in *The Merchant of Venice*. Miss Kent stubbornly tried to pull Portia out of her cliché-ridden world of soap, but whenever she began concentrating too much on characterization, a fresh batch of protest mail jarred her back to the well-worn themes. And so, into Portia's life came dashing Walter Manning; his chief function, from the mid-war years on, seemed to be to stir more grief into Portia's already curdled domestic porridge. At first, in the traditional formulas, all the forces of fate seemed to conspire against their marriage. Then, for a long time, they had to keep the union secret. Held behind enemy lines and later accused of being a dirty Nazi sympathizer, Walter finally emerged victorious through a brilliant piece of legal work by his wife. They married and settled in Parkersville, in a house on Peach Street. But all was not well at Manning House. Enter Clint Morley, stirring Portia's emotions with a devotion that later set town tongues wagging. Late in 1948, with Portia obviously pregnant and husband Walter nowhere to be found, speculation centered on Portia's "platonic" relationship with Clint.

Little did the townspeople know that, at that very moment, Walter lay desperately ill in a seedy Ankara hotel. Unaware that Portia was carrying his child (yes, his!), Walter was in hiding because his doctor had told him he had a fatal disease that would render him blind before finally killing him. The thought of Portia wasting her life on an invalid was too much to bear. Already blinded by the raging disease within his body, noble Walter sat in his room in Turkey while his longtime friend Eric Watson heaped praise on his new book and gave him one last ray of hope. Yes, there was one man who might yet save Walter's life—Dr. Peter Steinhart, long presumed dead in a Nazi concentration camp, but who at that moment was flying to Ankara from Tel Aviv on a mission of mercy.

That wasn't an easy decade for Portia. Even after daughter Sheilah was born, happiness was elusive and may in fact have been impossible. When last seen, Portia was being carted off to prison to face a phony sentence. Lucille Wall, who played Portia, confided to Richard Lamparski in one of his *Whatever Became Of . . .* books that the real purpose in having Portia convicted was to force the network —through a flood of angry letters—to reinstate the show. It didn't work.

Miss Wall went all the way as Portia, with the exception of a six-month period in 1948 when health problems forced her off the air. Anne Seymour took over until she returned. Bartlett Robinson originated the role of Walter Manning and played the part for many years. Portia's son Dickie was played by many child actors, including Alastair Kyle and Skip Homeier. John Larkin was Walter's old friend Eric Watson; Santos Ortega played the amorous Clint Morley. Portia's housekeeper and faithful friend Miss Daisy was played by Henrietta Tedro and Doris Rich. George Putnam announced.

Pot o' Gold

Pot o' Gold somehow got away with the networks' ban against lotteries for three seasons. It premièred on NBC for Tums September 26, 1939, giving away crisp $1,000 bills to people who answered their telephones when the *Pot o' Gold* maestro called. The contestants didn't even have to be listening to the show. All they had to be was home to answer the phone. Even if they weren't home, *Pot o' Gold* gave them $100 for being picked by its "Wheel of Fortune." The wheel was spun three times during each show. The first number selected indicated the volume to be plucked from the vast *Pot o' Gold* library of telephone books. The second spin gave the page number. The final spin gave the line number of the lucky person to be phoned. Interspersed between the spinnings was musical entertainment by Horace Heidt and His Musical Knights. When the party was finally reached by phone, host Ben Grauer shouted, "Stop Horace!" and informed the stunned person on the line that his $1,000 would be coming via Western Union. It was all very suspenseful to listeners who didn't consider the odds—about 80 million to one—against being called. But *Pot o' Gold* created a sensation in its early days, depleting movie houses so badly that some theatre owners offered $1,000 prizes to anyone who was called while attending the movie. This show was the unlikely creation of Ed Byron, who was getting *Mr. District Attorney* off the ground at the same time. It ran for Tums until 1941, and was revived October 2, 1946, for a season on ABC. In the new version, the entertainment between the spins was handled by comedian Happy Felton and by singers Very Holly and Jimmy Carroll.

Pretty Kitty Kelly

Pretty Kitty Kelly was the story of a "golden-haired Irish girl" who rode a 15-minute soap slot on CBS. The show premièred April 26, 1937, and ran for "slow-baked Wonder Bread and Hostess Cupcakes" until 1940. It followed the adventures of Kitty, who landed in New York from her native Dublin with no memory of her identity (again, the familiar soapland amnesia). On the ship, she had met two people from her native land, "Old" Patrick Conway, brother of New York police inspector Michael Conway, and an unscrupulous woman named Mrs. Meegram. Both disappeared upon arrival, and Kitty found herself alone, penniless, and on the receiving end of a murder charge. There was a lot of murder and intrigue for a show that opened to the lighthearted strains of "Kerry Dance." Over her three-year run, Kitty made friends with Michael Conway the younger, with Bunny Wilson, and with an older couple, Edward and Phyllis Welby. Their adventures ranged from kidnapping in the Everglades to murder in the big town. Arline Blackburn played Kitty; Clayton (Bud) Collyer was Michael Conway, and Helen Choate was Bunny. The Welbys were played by Dennis Hoey and Ethel Intropidi.

The Private Practice of Dr. Dana

The Private Practice of Dr. Dana was a Sunday-afternoon dramatic show, popularity known as *Dr. Dana*. It ran on CBS in 1947–48, and is notable as early exposure for Jeff Chandler, who was just a year away from *Michael Shayne* and *Our Miss Brooks*. *Dr. Dana* began as rather a grisly medical opera, but softened into the straight drama of Steve Dana, Nurse Gorcey, and their patients. Dana spent much time helping people with personal, as well as medical problems; the show was heard on CBS West Coast stations, and Mary Lansing played Gorcey. It was written by Adrian Gendot and produced by Sterling Tracy.

The Prudential Family Hour

The Prudential Family Hour was a popular series of concert music heard on CBS as a 45-minute Sunday-afternoon show from August 31, 1941, through 1945, and for 30 minutes from 1945 through 1947. In

1948, the concert format was dropped and the time slot became *The Prudential Family Hour of Stars*, shifting into a high-powered season of comedy-drama featuring the biggest names of Hollywood. In its early days, *Family Hour* was one of the most popular music shows of the air. Gladys Swarthout was its star, singing numbers from the operatic stage and the popular charts; she was supported by Ross Graham and critic Deems Taylor. José Ferrer served as host for a time, and the music was by Al Goodman's orchestra. In 1945 Patrice Munsel, then 19, became the prima donna of the show. The *Hour of Stars* format featured original dramas and comedies, performed by a distinguished company of stars. Gregory Peck, Bette Davis, Ginger Rogers, Humphrey Bogart, Robert Taylor, and Barbara Stanwyck were permanent members; among the "bonus stars" who appeared were Kirk Douglas and Ray Milland. Carmen Dragon handled the music for the new show; Truman Bradley announced; Ken Burton produced and Jack Johnstone directed. It ran through the 1948–49 season.

Pursuit

Pursuit was a high-quality suspense series that arrived on CBS Tuesday nights in 1949—too late in the game to make much of an impact. Its epigraph: "A criminal strikes, and fades quickly back into the shadows of his own dark world; and then, the man from Scotland Yard, the relentless, dangerous pursuit, when man hunts man!" The man from Scotland Yard was Inspector Peter Black, played initially by Ted de Corsia and in a 1951–52 CBS run by Ben Wright. The early run, 1949–50, was sponsored by Ford Motors, with music by Leith Stevens. Under Wright, Inspector Black usually closed his cases with the phrase, "Pursuit, and the pursuit is ended." Elliott Lewis produced and directed both series; Eddie Dunstedter provided music on the organ in the 1951–52 show, which was sponsored by Mollé Shave Cream and Dr. Lyon's Tooth Powder. Regular support through the run was by Bill Johnstone, John Dehner, Jeanette Nolan, Tudor Owen, Joseph Kearns, and Raymond Lawrence. Writers were from the front ranks of the medium, with scripting by Antony Ellis, E. Jack Neuman, and others.

The Pursuit of Happiness

The Pursuit of Happiness was one of Norman Corwin's early efforts at directing for CBS. It opened on October 22, 1939, and lasted less than a year. *Pursuit* featured dramatic and musical adaptations, by Corwin and writer George Faulkner, of such well-known writers as John Steinbeck, Stephen Vincent Benét, and Thomas Wolfe. Corwin drew Charles Laughton and Elsa Lanchester; he got Raymond Massey to read from *Abe Lincoln in Illinois,* and directed Ray Middleton in *How Can You Tell an American?* by Maxwell Anderson. Mark Warnow provided the music and Burgess Meredith was master of ceremonies, promoting weekly the oft-heard Corwin theme that "democracy is a good thing."

It was Americana at its best and most powerful. Far and away the most powerful thing in the show's short life was the November 5, 1939, appearance of the great black ballad singer Paul Robeson. The show was *Ballad for Americans,* based on an opera by Earl Robinson. Backed by a chorus, Robeson rocked the CBS studio for more than 10 minutes with a hard-hitting musical review of the nation's heritage. He sang of men, of machines, and of oppression. When it was over the studio audience of 600 persons burst into thunderous, unprompted ovation, continuing for more than 10 minutes after the show went off the air. It was one of radio's great moments and a great day for Robeson. Mail praising the show poured in for weeks; CBS telephone lines in New York and Hollywood were jammed with congratulatory callers.

That was the beginning for Corwin. *Time* called the *Pursuit of Happiness* a hit, but it died of malnutrition in the spring. Corwin, meanwhile, had stamped himself a man with a future. The good years were just ahead.

The Quality Twins

The Quality Twins were Ed East and Ralph Dumke, a pair of vaudevillians who turned to radio in 1926 with a parody of "advice to the housewife" shows. Also heard under the name Sisters of the Skillet, the pair broke in with WGN, Chicago, then moved to New York and began making the rounds of stations there around 1930. Their Skillet was on the Blue Network by 1931, sponsored for a time by Knox Gelatin; by 1937 a Quality Twins network (CBS) show was on for Kellogg's Corn Flakes. The show was 15 minutes of such tongue-in-cheek advice as (to farmers), "don't throw away your worn-out buttonholes; save 'em and use 'em for postholes." The boys, using such Bob-and-Ray-type impersonations as Gwendolyn, the Gorgeous Dishwasher and Pet Plenty, Love Expert Extraordinaire, told housewives how to stop hubby from snoring, how to save time in the kitchen, how to handle unruly young'uns. It was all in fun and, judging by their mail, well-received at home.

Queen for a Day

Queen for a Day was one of radio's most popular daytime interview shows. It was created in the glow of wartime victory, and lasted through the TV of the early 1970's. The show came to Mutual in the spring of 1945, formulated over lunch between a radio master of ceremonies and two ad men. The emcee was Dud Williamson, then being featured in another popular quiz, *What's the Name of That Song?* The ad men, Raymond R. Morgan and Robert Raisbeck, thought Williamson should have another show; Williamson suggested the format—an interview show in which women would be given whatever they asked for.

The show went on the air from New York April 30, 1945, as *Queen for Today,* with Williamson as host. The first *Queen* was Mrs. Evelyn Lane of Arcadia, California. Her shower of gifts cast the mold for all future queens: a new outfit, dinner, and a whirlwind tour of New York's hottest nightspots. In this early format, Williamson chatted with pre-selected women and was engaged in some give-and-take banter by stooge Bob Spence.

But it didn't last long in that form. Before the end of the year, the program had moved to Hollywood, where the host job was taken by Jack Bailey. A former vaudeville music man and once a barker at World's Fairs, Bailey made *Queen for a Day* a virtual career, following the show through a twelve-year radio run and into TV, where he became one of the best-known daytime personalities.

The Hollywood show, produced by Bud Ernst, operated in much the same manner as Williamson's show from New York. Before each broadcast, Bailey—accompanied by Ernst and announcer Mark Houston—canvassed the audience at the El Capitan Theatre (later the show moved to the Hawaii) for potential queens. Age and appearance didn't count on this show; Bailey once crowned 22-year-old and 70-year-old queens on successive days. What he was looking for was personality, and the ability to project it. The prospective queens would each try to pry open the hearts of the audience by telling in the interview what they would most like to have. Often the wishes were gestures of kindness toward others (they were the most likely winners), but the ladies also wished for such offbeat prizes as getting their footprints cast in cement at Grauman's Chinese Theatre, or having Bailey file the winner's fingernails for 24 hours. One woman wanted to switch roles with Bailey; she became the master of ceremonies, and he was "Queen for a Day."

After the initial interviews, a panel of judges—also from the audience—selected the Queen. The vote of this "Grand Council" was submitted for approval (by applause) of the audience. Also from the audience came two "jesters," allowed to tell one joke apiece. An "out-of-town queen" was selected by the spinning of a roulette wheel, marked with the names of the forty-eight states. One person from the state of the day was selected from the audience to select the out-of-town queen from her home town. That lucky woman got a box of stockings.

The show came in 30-minute doses, five times a week, to Bailey's dramatic cry: "Would *you* like to be *Queen for a Day?*"

The Quick and the Dead

The Quick and the Dead was a four-part documentary reflecting man's preoccupation with the Bomb in the early 1950's. Put together by writer and producer Fred Friendly, for airing on NBC on four consecutive Thursdays starting July 27, 1950, The Quick and the Dead was designed to show the average person the real facts behind atomic energy. Interviews were conducted with leading scientists, physicists, politicians, and laymen. The crew that dropped the first bomb was interviewed, and the script was laced with queries from the "average taxpayer." Bob Hope played taxpayer; Helen Hayes portrayed Dr. Lise Meitner, the Austrian-Swedish physicist whose work had contributed to the bomb's development; and Paul Lukas was Dr. Albert Einstein. It was a fast-paced, controversial show, written in common language and making print in national news magazines.

Quick As a Flash

Quick As a Flash was interesting, entertaining quiz fare, beginning on Mutual as a late-afternoon Sunday feature on July 16, 1944. Ken Roberts, first master of ceremonies, considered it the ultimate quiz, and a large listening audience agreed. Quick As a Flash was designed to provide entertainment in addition to serving as a quizzer. Questions were fashioned around music, history, news, and show business. Six panelists were assembled from the studio audience; each was placed at a desk containing a buzzer button connected to different-colored lighting flashes across the desk's face. When the buzzer was pressed, the question was stopped in progress and the contestant was given a chance to answer. The questions were posed as "races," and each was given the name of a famous racetrack ("The Belmont," "The Jamaica," etc.). They were designed to measure a contestant's reaction speed, with a $10 purse going to the winner of each. Contestants who gave a wrong answer dropped out of the running, and more clues were then given the others. Often the clues were elaborately staged and dramatized, or were illustrated musically by Ray Bloch's orchestra. The first race was a question on a current news event; the second was musical; the third was historical; the fourth was on entertainment or literature. Highlight of the show was the fifth race, the "Sponsor's Handicap." It usually featured a mystery play, fully dramatized by some of radio's top mystery stars, in character. Jay Jostyn, of Mr. District Attorney, was in the first Quick As a Flash mystery play. Others who appeared were Lon Clark of Nick

Carter, Master Detective, John Archer, then enjoying a brief stint on *The Shadow,* Victor Jory, hero of the short-lived *Dangerously Yours,* Santos Ortega of *Bulldog Drummond,* "Raymond" of *Inner Sanctum Mysteries,* and Ed Begley of *Charlie Chan.* Among the other shows represented: *Mr. and Mrs. North, Mr. Keen, Counterspy,* and *Crime Doctor.* At various times, contestants would stop the play and try to guess the solution. *Quick As a Flash* ran on Mutual from 1944 until 1949, always in its Sunday-afternoon slot, under Helbros Watch sponsorship. Win Elliot replaced Ken Roberts as emcee in 1947. The show was dropped from the Mutual lineup in 1949, but returned that fall as an ABC daytime show, three times a week for Quaker Oats. Bill Cullen served as host in this last version. In 1950–51, its last season, *Quick As a Flash* was heard each morning for Block Drugs.

Quiet, Please

Quiet, Please was an eerie little brew dreamed up by Willis Cooper, radio's best practitioner of an almost surrealistic dramatic form that read like poetry but contained all the elements of the play. One of radio's pioneers, Cooper had founded *Lights Out* in Chicago before moving on to the film pastures of the West Coast.

Quiet, Please opened on Mutual July 28, 1947. Cooper, writing and directing, unlocked his imagination and unrefined terror flowed out. His people had all stepped past the limits of reality into a fuzzy dream world where things were not always what they seemed. Cooper's world was far more terrifying than the melodrama of *Inner Sanctum.* Even when nothing particularly terrifying was happening, the element of menace was always there—abstract horror always just around the corner. In Cooper's hands, a field of lovely lilies could be deadly, a sunny field of trees touched with sinister implications.

Quiet, Please was cast in the *Lights Out* mold, but perfected in a subdivision of its own. Few of its happenings were explained or justified; things just occurred without reason or logic. In "Let the Lilies Consider," Cooper's flowers became thinking, talking beings with a full range of emotions and the means to murder. "The Thing on the Fourble Board" was unsurpassed in sheer horror, as oil-well drillers suddenly found their platform inhabited by an invisible spiderlike creature that had come up through the drilling hole from the bowels of the earth. Cooper was a master of mood and direction of voice; he took us to a dark side of life in a deceptively quiet way that held more terror than all the blood and gore of radio's "chop-'em-up" school.

Ernest Chappell was the host and star. It was his calm, strong voice that set the scene and told the stories, usually in first person, occasionally in present tense and often in flashback. Albert Berman provided an appropriately eerie musical score; the theme was a piano-organ rendition of the second movement of Franck's Symphony in D-Minor. After the play, Chappell signed off with a standard closing: "I'm quietly yours, Ernest Chappell."

The series ran on Mutual on various nights, then moved to ABC in 1948 for a second season as a late-afternoon Sunday show. Sustained for both years of its run, it was a fine, creative piece of radio that never enjoyed the success it should have had.

The Quiz Kids

The Quiz Kids, radio's juvenile answer to *Information, Please*, was first heard on NBC June 28, 1940, as a replacement for blind pianist Alec Templeton's show.

The hardest thing about staging such a show was finding the kids. Louis G. Cowan, a Chicago advertising–public relations man, got the idea early in 1940, but the right kids didn't grow on trees. Cowan knew that the show would rise or fall on the personalities of the little mental wizards he hoped to assemble as radio's newest answer to the surprisingly successful *Information, Please*.

Such shows were initially thought too highbrow for radio's mass market. In the end, the personalities on the *Information, Please* panel had helped put it across. What Cowan needed were half a dozen kids with those same qualities—humor, personality, and a good "mike sense." All this in addition to the essential genius.

Cowan got his first kid by reading the newspapers. A 6-year-old boy had just conducted a lecture on birds at a Chicago school. Little Gerard Darrow, it turned out, had known and identified 300 bird species by age 3. His knowledge of ornithology was fantastic, and he had an intimate, deepening knowledge of other areas of nature as well. At 6-going-on-7, Gerard was about to become radio's first Quiz Kid.

Only when he had a panel of five did Cowan put *The Quiz Kids* on the air. The format was classroom style: an adult quizmaster would challenge the Quiz Kids with questions submitted by the listening audience. The kids were awarded a $100 savings bond for each appearance, and the three best were brought back for successive appearances. Scores were tallied and points awarded, the final result taking into account the child's age as well as his raw score.

Finding the quizmaster was almost as difficult as finding the kids. The producers tested a humorless journalist and two wordy professors who were far more eager to display their own intellects than run an entertaining show. They tried a harried lecturer and many professional radio men. No one seemed to mesh as well with *The Quiz Kids* as Joe Kelly, a bald veteran of *The National Barn Dance* who had dropped out of school after the third grade.

Kelly's life came right out of storyland. As a child singer, he had gone on the road with a traveling stock company, and later he had sung in a minstrel show. Various players' groups followed, and for a time he quit show business. But it was in his blood, so he returned as a mikeman. Kelly had had a variety of radio acts around Chicago before landing at WLS with an early morning talk show, *Jolly Joe*.

After the first show with Kelly as quizmaster, Cowan didn't have to worry. Almost immediately, it won two major awards as best new show of the year. The program was flooded with teacher referrals, applicants from parents, and stories of bright children all over Chicago. Many came to take the tough oral and written examinations developed for "Kid" candidates; few made it. The five-member juvenile panel was dominated by regulars over the twelve-year run, and after being eliminated, the most popular kids were always given a chance to reinstate themselves by competing for one of the two guest chairs.

Early Quiz Kids were Joan Bishop, Cynthia Cline, Mary Ann Anderson, and Charles Schwartz. The questions they got were tough, many submitted by experts, and a large part of the show's fascination lay in the smooth, effortless way the kids answered them. The panelists ranged in age from 6 to 16, though exceptionally brilliant children as young as 4 were used. Their IQ scores ranged from 200-plus of Joel Kupperman to the "just above average" of Gerard Darrow. IQ's notwithstanding, all of the Quiz Kids had one outstanding specialty as well as a well-rounded storehouse of general information.

Thirteen-year-old Van Dyke Tiers, who had appeared on the first show, became the in-house expert in spelling, astronomy, and geography. Ruth Duskin was a Shakespeare authority at 7. Jack Lucal was the source of the Kids' political knowledge, and, until the arrival of Joel Kupperman, Richard Williams was almost unchallenged as a genius of figures. Harve Fischman joined the panel at 11, and finally was forced off after attaining the grand old age of 16. Claude Brenner was such an accomplished air personality at 13 that four times he filled in as the show's master of ceremonies when longtime quizmaster Joe Kelly couldn't make it.

Kelly's graduation to *The National Barn Dance* in the early 1930's had been right in character, but his selection as head man of *The Quiz Kids* was something entirely different. It terrified him at first, and the producers soon saw why. Kelly had virtually no defense against the vast bank of juvenile intellect he faced each week. There was virtually no way he could cover himself; his ignorance on all matters of book learning was bound to come through, and there he'd be—rendered a fool at the hands of a 7-year-old. Printed answers didn't help. No matter how well-researched a question was, there was usually at least one kid who had an answer not covered by the staff. And the kid's answer was usually equally correct.

After some initial stiffness that almost cost him the job, Kelly relaxed and learned to cope with the problem admirably. Having none of the conventions of academia, he also had none of its hangups. Kelly didn't mind admitting his ignorance. Acknowledging that a kid's answer "might be right" with a simple, "Well, I don't know about that," Kelly would then steer the conversation into the intended area without giving away the answer. The Quiz Kids was truly Joe Kelly's time in the sun, when an old trouper who had learned to add on his fingers came face to face with juveniles with minds like computers. The result was one of radio's brightest shows.

More than 135 kids had passed through the revolving seats by the time the show celebrated its third anniversary. Most just passed through, while the "stars" returned for encore after encore. The encore system started early, when Gerard Darrow was eliminated after his ninth week. Bales of letters begged his reinstatement, so the producers adopted the policy of bringing back the best kids after an absence of a few weeks. The regulars became nationally renowned, personally and as a group. They went into movies, made guest appearances with Jack Benny, visited the White House. Toys and novelty items bearing their names were common dime-store items, and the Kids themselves were constantly put to the knowledge test. They pinned the ears of older scholars with astonishing, embarrassing ease, defeating faculty members at the University of Chicago and professors at the University of Michigan in widely publicized contests.

Joel Kupperman came aboard in 1943 and was still appearing in 1949, mentally solving problems that had listeners doubting the show's credibility. He answered algebra problems almost instantly, with no pencil and paper. His toughest problem, submitted by a university expert, was to put an equilateral triangle inside an eight-inch circle, put another circle inside the triangle, and another triangle inside the circle. Joel was to give the area of the fifth circle in this progression. Kelly pronounced his answer wrong, but a deluge of mail from mathematicians convinced him otherwise, and he had to apologize the following week. In the end, the "expert" had blundered the answer to his own question, but Joel had rattled it off with precise accuracy.

For eleven years Quiz Kids was sponsored by Alka Seltzer, which followed through three changes of network. After its initial NBC Friday-night run, the show was heard from 1940 through 1942 Wednesday nights on the Blue Network. From 1942 through 1946, it ran Sunday nights on the Blue, which became ABC, and from 1946 through 1951 it was back on NBC, still on Sundays. In its final year, 1952–53, it was sustained by CBS on Sunday nights.

The Quiz of Two Cities

The Quiz of Two Cities was another innovative, interesting quiz show, adopted by Mutual from a spirited West Coast show of the early 1940's. In the original version, first heard locally in the spring of 1941, the show fanned the natural rivalry between Los Angeles and San Francisco. The L.A. part of the show was produced at KHJ; the San Francisco part at KFRC. Reid Kilpatrick in Los Angeles usually opened the show with some caustic remarks about San Francisco and drew four contestants from his studio audience for the quiz. In San Francisco, Mark Goodson (later Hale Sparks) asked his contestants the same questions and hurled some equally choice insults at L.A. The city with the highest number of correct answers was declared the winner of the broadcast, with the competition picked up the following week. A keen sense of competition developed among the listeners of both cities; the score was usually close, and later—to add to the competitive atmosphere—groups of people were pitted against each other; the Joneses of L.A. against the Smiths of San Francisco; a group of Earl Carroll glamor girls versus the businessmen of San Francisco. In this early format, it was produced by Jim Burton and score was kept by Tommy Dixon. By 1944, it had turned up in its brief run on Mutual. In this version, a rotating list of competing cities was used. Michael Fitzmaurice was overall master of ceremonies. Listerine sponsored the network show, which didn't seem to have that high school cheerleader atmosphere that sparked the original.

The Radio City Playhouse

The Radio City Playhouse was an NBC offering that premièred July 3, 1948, with a suspense tale called *Long Distance*. This story of a woman trying desperately to reach officials with new evidence before her husband was wrongly executed captured immediate attention, and was compared along Radio Row to the *Suspense* classic, *Sorry, Wrong Number*. It also gave a good preview of things to come. *The Radio City Playhouse* was heavy drama, usually turning on life-or death situations. For example, a woman and two men, trapped on an avalanche-prone mountain, faced a melodramatic situation with sticky social implications when part of their rope was lost and only two could go down. The guide could not remain behind, so the difficult choice was between the doctor with a possible cancer cure or the socialite whose major accomplishment was refined bitchery.

John Larkin and Jan Miner carried many of the roles, and the series was narrated and directed by Harry W. Junkin. It adapted the work of America's top writers—names like Paul Gallico, Cornell Woolrich, Ray Bradbury, John Galsworthy and Stephen Vincent Benét. Announcers included Fred Collins and Bob Warren; Richard P. McDonough supervised production for NBC. After running initially as a summer series, *The Radio City Playhouse* was booked into the regular lineup on November 8, 1948, and ran until January 1, 1950.

The Radio Guild

The Radio Guild was the air's first big, hour-long program devoted to experimental drama. It hit the NBC air in 1929, and soon had become a regular fixture. Directed by Vernon Radcliffe, The Radio Guild was unusual in another aspect: its entire ten-year run was mainly on weekdays, late in the afternoon, in what came to be known as prime soap time. The show was tried on virtually every day of the week, and for a time in 1935 it took the Sunday-afternoon place of The Lux Radio Theatre, which was departing for CBS, Hollywood, Monday nights, and fame. The Radio Guild never played in the Lux ballpark; it never used the superstar, became as famous, or attained the phenomenal ratings. But it was a solid forerunner to such highly regarded shows as The Columbia Workshop (though Radio Guild Dramas would seem rather straight today in comparison). The show offered such plays as John Galsworthy's Justice and Shakespeare's Midsummer Night's Dream. Early in the run, Radcliffe took his actors from Broadway; soon he had to abandon that and go with radio people. Those were the early years, when stage stars who still hadn't learned to act for the air were ever trying to project for the back row with the microphone just two feet away. Long before the phrase "theatre of the mind" became popular, Radcliffe understood its strengths and weaknesses. In 1935 he told Newsweek that "the ear is more important to emotional influences alone than when aided by the eye." The 60-minute version of Radio Guild Dramas folded in 1938; a half-hour version was tried on NBC in 1939–40.

The Radio Hall of Fame

The Radio Hall of Fame concept started tongues wagging right from the start. Variety, the trade paper of the entertainment world, proposed to do its own radio show. Time wondered aloud how a newspaper whose stock in trade was reviewing show business could now enter it. How could such a paper honestly review its own performers? One Variety reporter with fifteen years experience even quit in protest.

But on December 5, 1943, The Radio Hall of Fame went on the Blue Network as scheduled. Abel Green, Variety's spunky editor, reckoned he could handle the heat and put out a good paper and a good radio show all at once. Under Green's watchful eye, The Radio Hall of Fame would be a radio equivalent of a weekly Academy

Award. Those of the medium judged worthy that week would be invited to appear and do their thing in an all-star hour of music, comedy, drama, news, and views. They could, and did, feel honored.

Paul Whiteman served as maestro; master of ceremonies was composer, critic, and commentator, Deems Taylor. Philco was lined up as sponsor; Devere Joseph (Dee) Engelbach was director. And *The Radio Hall of Fame* went on the air, with the most spectacular variety show of its season.

Headlining the first show were Jimmy Durante and Bob Hope. In the weeks that followed *Fame* offered Fred Allen and his entire radio company, Groucho Marx, Metropolitan Opera star Lauritz Melchior, Sophie Tucker, Paul Muni, Eddie Cantor, Bing Crosby, George Burns and Gracie Allen, the Andrews Sisters, Frank Morgan, Gracie Fields and Tom Howard and George Shelton of *It Pays to Be Ignorant*. Such newsmen as Quentin Reynolds and Raymond Gram Swing gave impressions of the fighting fronts. For drama, Helen Hayes appeared in an adaptation of her stage play, *Harriet*. Jennifer Jones and Charles Bickford did *The Song of Bernadette*. In its last days, Agnes Moorehead was even invited in for a condensed version of her celebrated *Suspense* play, *Sorry, Wrong Number*.

It was a splash, produced in New York with elaborate cut-ins from Hollywood. *The Radio Hall of Fame* quickly shifted its focus away from strictly reviewing radio and toward the entire field of entertainment. The show was put into rough form each Monday, when director Engelbach met with *Variety* editors. The editors had the say on who would appear, then the talent was secured through a booking agency. Engelbach met next with the writers, George Faulkner and later Milton Geiger (who became the show's "executive writer"). A week of frenzied scurrying followed before, Sunday at 6 P.M., Whiteman struck up the band for the show's theme, and *Radio Hall of Fame* was on the air.

In its last year, the show changed slightly. Martha Tilton became a regular and the format was streamlined to 30 minutes in 1945. It was last heard in 1946, ending *Variety's* noble experiment and adding another high mark in the book of big-time radio.

The Radio Reader's Digest

The Radio Reader's Digest was the air edition of the popular national magazine, with true dramatic stories adapted from the *Digest's* pages and dramatized with leading film and stage stars in top roles. It came to CBS September 13, 1942, as a Sunday-night feature for Campbell Soups. Conrad Nagel, former master of ceremonies on *The Silver*

Theatre and out of job at the time, was hired as narrator. Lyn Murray provided the music, Robert Nolan directed, and the show was an accurate audio version of *Reader's Digest* content. The stories were dramatic in a soft way, always ending on the upbeat. It enjoyed a healthy rating and ran in this basic format until 1945. That year, Campbell dropped it and it was promptly picked up by Hallmark Cards, which continued the emcee format, bringing in Richard Kollmar to handle the job.

Les Tremayne became host in 1947. During the Hallmark years, the emcee also served as a narrator of sorts; the show was directed by Marx Loeb and scored by Jack Miller. A nice program, and durable, *The Radio Reader's Digest* ran for six years, the last two on Thursday nights. Hallmark dropped it in 1948 for *The Hallmark Playhouse.*

Raffles

Raffles was the B-grade summer adventures of a reformed burglar, safecracker, "gentleman adventurer and ace of knaves." Raffles had become a detective of sorts, spending a lot of time at Filipo's Restaurant and "devoting his time and talent to upholding law and order." This show came to radio in the summer of 1945, with Horace Braham as Raffles, under the direction of Jock MacGregor.

The Railroad Hour

The Railroad Hour was a blockbuster musical show, part of NBC's "Monday Night of Music," which also included *The Voice of Firestone, The Bell Telephone Hour,* and for a time, *Cities Service Band of America.* It was the best show of its kind since Jessica Dragonette had starred in the short-lived *Palmolive Beauty Box Theatre* during the spring of 1937.

The Railroad Hour actually began as an ABC show, premièring in an unusual 45-minute format October 4, 1948. By October 3, 1949, it had joined NBC's Monday-night schedule, trimmed to 30 minutes and offering the best operettas of the air. Gordon MacRae was host and star, the stories were adapted by Jerry Lawrence and Robert Lee, the music composed and conducted by Carmen Dragon, and the choir was under the direction of Norman Luboff. It opened with the blast of locomotive whistle and Marvin Miller's dramatic announcement: "Ladies and gentlemen, *The Railroad Hour!* . . ." More whistles and train noises; the hiss of escaping steam—"and here comes our star-studded show train!" Now the orchestra, up full with the theme, "I've Been Working On The Railroad."

The show had nothing to do with railroads, but took its name from the sponsor, the Association of American Railroads, "the same railroads that bring you most of the food you eat, the clothes you wear, the fuel you burn and all the other things you use in your daily life." The stories brought to life all the fantasy characters suggested by the music of Ira and George Gershwin, Victor Herbert, Franz Lehar, Jerome Kern, Rodgers and Hammerstein, Sigmund Romberg, and others. The Railroad Hour dramatized the lives of stormy German composer Robert Schumann and of waltz king Johann Strauss. It presented Gilbert and Sullivan in The Mikado and original scores based on the writings of Mark Twain. Show Boat, The Merry Widow, The Vagabond King, Swan Lake, Naughty Marietta, and Holiday Inn were among the musical offerings. All the top popular musical shows were heard on The Railroad Hour. And once a year, in December, the cast reviewed the old year in music and song.

MacRae always played the male lead. His leading ladies came from radio and from the Metropolitan Opera. Once he even got his star from the White House, when Margaret Truman appeared in the March 17, 1952, show, Sari. Lucille Norman, Dorothy Kirsten, and Dorothy Warenskjold appeared most often. Among the others who worked with MacRae were Nadine Conner, Marion Bell, Ginny Simms, Eileen Wilson, Irra Petina, Mimi Benzell, Annamary Dickey, and Gladys Swarthout.

It was a classy, popular production. After the show, MacRae always chatted briefly with the female lead, sketched in next week's show, and Marvin Miller finally chanted, "All aboard!" The train last pulled out on June 21, 1954, the end of a notable listening experience.

The Raleigh-Kool Program

The Raleigh-Kool Program was a half-hour musical-variety show, featuring Tommy Dorsey, "that sentimental gentleman of swing," his versatile orchestra, and assorted guest stars. The show was first heard on NBC Blue Saturday and later Friday nights, premièring November 13, 1937, but moved to Wednesdays on the Red for its final 1938–39 season. It was simply a musical showcase for Dorsey's orchestra, much like the Benny Goodman Swing School of the same era. In 1939, Dorsey staged an "amateur swing contest" and featured Dick Powell on cornet, Bing Crosby on drums, Shirley Ross on piano, Ken Murray on clarinet, and Jack Benny on violin. The producers went to all the trouble of setting up an audience applause device to determine the winner, then copped out and refused to choose between them. From strictly a layman's chair, it seemed that Dick Powell had had the best beat and Ken Murray got the most applause. But Dorsey wouldn't tell. Mumbling something about a meter malfunction (a likely story), he offered to split the $75 pot five ways. Instead, the contestants decided to give it to the Community Chest. Jack Leonard joined Dorsey as a regular, and Paul Stewart was master of ceremonies.

The Ray Bolger Show

The Ray Bolger Show was a summertime comedy-variety show on CBS, premièring July 6, 1945, as a vacation-time substitute for the comedy partnership of Jimmy Durante and Garry Moore. Backed by a cast that included Elvia Allman, Verna Felton, and singer Jeri Sullavan, Bolger—a screen actor most famous as the scarecrow in "The Wizard of Oz"—was assisted through the run by the Durante-Moore production staff: Roy Bargy led the band, Howard Petrie announced, and Phil Cohan directed. The sponsor was Rexall.

Red Ryder

Red Ryder was first heard on the Blue Network's West Coast stations early in 1942, but was released by the network soon after the Blue wrestled *The Lone Ranger* away from Mutual in May 1942. Mutual, stung by the loss of its top Western attraction, promptly picked up *Red Ryder* and programmed it in direct competition with "the masked rider of the plains." The result: Red gunned down the Ranger in early Hooper reports, and established enough following to hold his own through the 1940's as "America's famous fighting cowboy." The red-headed, red-shirted cowboy was created by Fred Harmon as an *L.A. Times*-syndicated comic strip, and was well-known to millions of kids long before his ratings duel began. As in the comic strip, Red was a two-fisted tornado who lived with his aunt, "The Duchess," his sidekick Buckskin, and his Indian ward Little Beaver, in the quiet Western settlement of Painted Valley. Mutual–Don Lee carried the series into the 1950's, and the long-time sponsor was Langendorf Bread. Reed Hadley, Carlton KaDell, and Brooke Temple all played Red, but Temple had the role longest, playing Ryder in 1945 and still in that role five years later. Little Beaver was played early in the run by Tommy Cook, a busy child actor who also appeared as Alexander on

Blondie. Henry Blair, the early Ricky Nelson on *Ozzie and Harriet,* took the Little Beaver role in February 1944, and it was subsequently handled by Johnny McGovern. Horace Murphy played Buckskin, and all Indian dialect (except Little Beaver's "You betchum, Red Ryder") was handled by Jim Mather. Paul Franklin, a writer of pulp Westerns who claimed he had never been west of Brooklyn before he took on *Red Ryder,* was writer-director. He passed the writing and producing chores to Albert Van Antwerp and Brad Brown in the mid-1940's, but returned after Van Antwerp's death just over a year later. For trivia fans, Red Ryder's horse was named Thunder, and the theme was an organ rendition of "The Dying Cowboy."

The Red Skelton Show

The Red Skelton Show, like Edgar Bergen's program, was a radio enigma. Bergen was a ventriloquist, Skelton a pantomimist. Neither art was particlarly adaptable to radio, but both shows were smash hits.

Like many of radio's big-name comics, Skelton came up the hard way. Born the son of a circus clown July 18, 1913, he eventually took up his dad's old life, with the same circus his father had worked in the 1890's. Skelton started his show business career at 10, hooking up with a traveling medicine show in his hometown, Vincennes, Indiana. Skelton played ukelele and ducked truant officers, traveling with the medicine show until a chance to earn $15 a week lured him into the tents. A minstrel show followed; soon Skelton had yet another job, playing on a show boat that sailed the Ohio and Missouri Rivers in the middle 1920's. His dreams of being a lion tamer vanished when he saw Clyde Beatty attacked by a circus lion. Ultimately he became a comic. For fifteen years he slugged along as an obscure, small-time entertainer.

By 1928, Skelton had broken into burlesque, playing cities through the Midwest with a standup routine of joke and pantomime. He was playing Kansas City one night in 1930 when he met young Edna Stillwell, an usher in the theatre where he was playing a fill-in spot. She thought his act was lousy; he didn't like her much either. But they grew on each other, and they were married in June 1931, the month before Skelton's eighteenth birthday. Together Red and Edna Skelton hit the road. She began playing his stooge, and soon she had begun to write his scripts. By 1935, they were ready for an assault on big-time vaudeville.

New York wasn't buying, so the Skeltons took to the "walk-athon" circuit, followed by another spell of "waiting for a break" that never came in New York. They were broke and were eventually thrown out of their apartment. A complete change of scene seemed necessary, so they struck out for Canada.

In Montreal, Edna really became his writer. They got a booking at Loew's Theatre, and there Skelton began polishing his pantomime routines. One evening, sitting in a café, Edna saw a man nervously dunking his doughnuts. He dunked, then looked around, then dunked again quickly. She wrote the scene as a pantomime for Skelton. It became a huge success and one of his best-remembered trademarks. Ultimately the skit led to a role in the Ginger Rogers film, *Having a Wonderful Time*, and brought Skelton to the forefront of cinema comics of the early 1940's. He was still in his mid-twenties.

By then, his radio career was well underway. Skelton's appearance on *The Rudy Vallee Show* August 12, 1937, led to several encores. He became a regular on *Avalon Time*, an obscure radio show of 1939. Although his appearances were successful, Skelton's main interest was in movies and vaudeville until October 7, 1941, when Raleigh Cigarettes brought him to NBC in his own long-running Tuesday-night show.

In a way, Skelton had the same disadvantage that Bergen faced when he first went on the air. Both were essentially visual artists. Skelton solved his problem by dragging out a character he had first used on stage in the 1930's. He became Junior, "the mean widdle kid" who spread carnage in a way that was most audible. His "I dood it again" became national slang in 1942. Other characters began to emerge from the Skelton closet: Clem Kadiddlehopper, the singing cab driver; Deadeye, the fastest gun in the West; Willie Lump-Lump; Bolivar Shagnasty. Skelton became a one-man theatre of the absurd; he was voted outstanding new radio star of 1941, and wife Edna —former Kansas City usher—was suddenly head writer on a big-time network radio program.

That it was big-time was unquestionable. In his first year, Skelton vaulted into the top dozen shows, and finished his second year with the second best rating in the nation. He also finished with a divorce. He and Edna remained friends; she still wrote for him (now aided by novelist Benedict Freedman) and managed his business affairs. Edna got custody of the massive Skelton gag file, painstakingly compiled by a large office staff and containing some 180,000 jokes. Both remarried in 1945.

Skelton's basic format changed little over the years. Junior, Deadeye, and Clem were the staples. When the show went on in 1941, Ozzie Nelson's band provided the music. Skelton got Ozzie's wife, Harriet Hilliard, as a fringe benefit of sorts. Though he paid for her services, he got a fine developing comedienne as well as a singing headliner. Harriet played Junior's fretful mother, and was also heard as Clem Kadiddlehopper's girl friend, Daisy June. Truman Bradley and then Pat McGeehan announced. Also aboard in those early days was Wonderful Smith, Skelton's chief antagonist, sometimes reviewed as "the Negro comedy find of the year." Skelton dropped out of radio soon after his draft notice arrived from the army in March 1944, losing Ozzie and Harriet. By the time he returned to the NBC air on December 4, 1945, after his discharge, they were going strong in their own comedy show. But it didn't take him long to regroup. Anita Ellis was hired as singer for the new show; Lurene Tuttle was brought in to play the comedy parts originated by Harriet; Verna Felton was added as Junior's grandmom, and the character of Daisy June was replaced by Sarah Dew. In the script, Daisy June had married while Clem was in the service. Sarah Dew was played by GeGe Pearson, who became one of the show's great regulars, appearing often as Skelton's wife in his roles as Bolivar Shagnasty and J. Newton Numskull.

For music, Skelton brought in David Forrester, whom he had heard and liked in the camps. Keith McLeod returned as director; Rod O'Connor became the announcer, and the new *Red Skelton Show* was ready to roll.

Within three weeks, Skelton had all of his old audience back. His Tuesday-night spot for Raleigh continued until 1948, when he moved to Fridays for Tide. In 1949, Tide followed him to CBS, where he was heard on Sundays for two years. In 1951, the show went to Wednesdays for Norge. Skelton's final season, 1952–53, found him in his original slot, Tuesdays on NBC, for a variety of sponsors. When TV came, most radio stars dropped like flies. But Skelton just dragged out his old pantomimes and laid 'em in the aisles again.

Renfrew of the Mounted

Renfrew of the Mounted premièred on CBS March 3, 1936, as a three-a-week thriller serial for Wonder Bread. It followed the adventures of Douglas Renfrew, inspector of the Royal Canadian Mounted Police, and was based on the stories by Laurie York Erskine. George Ludlum adapted the stories for the air, developing the noble redcoat in the finest "always get our man" tradition. House Jameson, best known later in the far different role of Henry Aldrich's father, was cast as the solemn Renfrew, something of an early Sergeant Preston. The show offered early training for many actors who would go on to long careers on the air, among them Carl Eastman, Joseph Curtin, and Robert Dryden. After a year as a 15-minute serial, *Renfrew* went to the Blue Network as a Saturday-night sustaining show. That lasted from

1938 through 1940. The show contained little or no music, leaving fade-outs to serve as time bridges. Brad Barker, noted radio animal imitator, did many of the sound effects, including the mournful howl of the wolf that opened the show. That's how *Renfrew* came at us, with the wind, a howling wolf, and a man shouting in an echo chamber:

RENNNNNNNNNNFREW! . . .
RENFREW OF THE MOUNTED!

Report to the Nation

Report to the Nation came to CBS in December 1940 as a documentary show of news remotes and dramatizations, much like *The March of Time*, but without that show's drum rolls and pomp. *Report to the Nation* focused on the top American developments of the week and since the United States wasn't yet in the war, many early shows revolved around domestic issues like unemployment and pending legislation. But soon enough *Report* took its listeners overseas on trips in flying fortresses and to battlefields, in stories of dramatic rescue. Albert Warner was anchorman in Washington, and the stories were dramatized by full-time government employees. Brewster Morgan, a *Columbia Workshop* veteran, was tapped as producer-director. Writers included Richard Hippelheuser, former editor of *Fortune* magazine, and Joseph Liss of the Library of Congress. The show was heard on Saturdays until 1941, when it moved to Tuesday. By 1943 Quentin Reynolds was anchorman-narrator. Then almost all dispatches were war-related. Reynolds, with the help of such field men as Eric Sevareid and Webley Edwards, gave first-hand accounts from the front, offered new war songs, and continued employing full dramatizations with sound effects. The new version, sponsored by united electric companies, was written by Peg Miller. It was produced by Paul White. *Report to the Nation* moved to Wednesday in the spring of 1944, and disappeared from the air later that year.

Results, Incorporated

Results, Incorporated was an interesting, short-lived comedy-mystery-adventure series first heard on Mutual October 7, 1944, as a Saturday-night sustainer. It starred Lloyd Nolan as Johnny Strange and Claire Trevor as his secretary, "the irrepressible" Theresa (Terry) Travers. Together they formed the agency, Results, Incorporated. Johnny started the agency in the initial broadcast by taking out two want ads: "Results, Inc.: your problem is our problem. Will locate your long-lost uncle, work your crossword puzzle, hold your baby. Where others fail, we succeed." and: "Secretary wanted; blonde, beautiful, between 22 and 28 years, unmarried, with the skin you love to touch and a heart you can't." Terry Travers answered the second ad and went to work for "25 percent commission, my hospital bills and bail money." Their first job: to locate a museum mummy that walked at night. It was a lively, fun series that vanished after its initial season. Lawrence E. Taylor created the characters, and Nolan and Miss Trevor played them well.

RFD America

RFD America was a very unusual quiz show whose contestants were all farmers from different states. It came to Mutual December 4, 1947, with Joe Kelly as quizmaster. Each show was a battle of rural wits between four farmers, and the winner was crowned "Master Farmer of the Week." He returned to defend the title, and kept coming back as long as he kept winning. One farmer, Ed Bottcher, won eight times in a row. When Kelly ran into a time conflict with his *Quiz Kids* show, Bottcher became the "RFD America" quizmaster. The show ran Thursdays on Mutual for one season, then in 1948 became NBC's summer replacement for *The Fred Allen Show*. When Allen returned, *RFD America* was shifted into a Saturday spot, and finished out the 1949 season as part of the regular NBC schedule.

Richard Diamond, Private Detective

Richard Diamond, Private Detective came to NBC April 24, 1949, representing the new Dick Powell image. Powell had gone almost full-circle, starting as a glamor-boy singer in the 1930's, graduating only through sheer stubbornness to the super hardboiled Philip Marlowe in the film *Murder, My Sweet*, and finally arriving at *Diamond*—a charming mix of slick sophistication and two-fisted action. As Diamond, Powell even managed to sing once in a while.

Movie producers had given Powell a hard time when he tried to break away from his babyfaced crooner image, and in *Murder, My Sweet* he had earned his stripes. So he relaxed with *Richard Diamond* and truly seemed to enjoy the part. Diamond was a happy-go-lucky dick, rather a lightweight who still managed to hold his own with Sam Spade, Johnny Dollar, and others of that ilk. He enjoyed the free life, enjoyed his girl friend Helen Asher, and—most of all—enjoyed ribbing the cops. Diamond tried to cooperate with frustrated Lieutenant Walt Levinson, but his special delight was badgering the incredibly dumb desk sergeant, Otis. Levinson was given a good ride by Ed Begley, who must have turned up on just about every radio series ever done. Otis was played by Wilms Herbert, who also doubled as Miss Asher's sheepish butler, Francis. Francis usually showed up at the end of the show, when Diamond would drop by Helen's Park Avenue home for a bit of song and fluff. It was a nice contrast to the rough-and-tumble body of the story, a time for Diamond and his girl to plunk out a song or two from one of Powell's early movies, share a piano stool, and maybe smooch a bit on the side. That was when Francis entered, fuming "You never warn me!" and rushing out of the room.

Helen was played by Virginia Gregg. Between this role, Brooksie on *Let George Do It*, and Betty Lewis on *Yours Truly, Johnny Dollar*, Miss Gregg spent a good part of her professional career trying to lead stubborn gumshoes to the altar. She never made it, but her failure was entertaining and believable.

That was all fringe action, back-and-forth sallies between the regulars to open and close each case. The middle 20 minutes was where the going got rough, with muggings, shootings, knifings, threats, and bombs that might or might not go off. These situations required all of Diamond's OSS training and most of his natural cunning. William P. Rousseau directed when the show opened as a Sunday-night sustainer. Blake Edwards was an early Diamond writer, and directed some episodes himself. Don Sharp produced, Jaime Del Valle later became producer-director. Music was by David Baskerville and later by Frank Worth.

Rexall picked up the show before its first year was up. In 1950, it moved to ABC for Camels on Friday nights. *Richard Diamond* lasted until 1952. Later it was revived on television, with David Janssen playing the lead. Janssen played it straight, as an almost humorless Diamond with strictly a cops-and-robbers theme. But this was really Powell's show and Powell's character.

The Right to Happiness

The Right to Happiness, one of Irna Phillips' four major daytime serials, first heard on NBC Blue October 16, 1939, evolved from *The Guiding Light* when Miss Phillips transplanted Rose Kransky from *Light* into the new format. But *The Right to Happiness* soon became the story of Carolyn Allen, a magazine editor's daughter whose search for a "God-given right to happiness" led her through four husbands, a prison sentence, and hours of anguish at the hands of her rebellious son Skip. Early in the run, Carolyn Allen became the wife of Bill Walker, a self-centered man who proved himself "capable of anything." She killed him with a pistol in an accident that police called murder, and endured four months of legal maneuvering and trial. Later, Carolyn Allen Walker married Dwight Kramer, a union foredoomed by the fickle nature of both. Son Skip, born while she was incarcerated in the state penitentiary, would become her greatest source of joy and pain, but that was still far in the future. Carolyn Allen Walker Kramer was to marry again, this time Governor Miles Nelson, who brought political intrigue into the plot. That marriage too gradually trickled downhill.

Finally Carolyn Allen Walker Kramer Nelson settled down with Lee MacDonald, a handsome, brilliant lawyer. With that marriage, her time was up. The serial expired November 25, 1960, before Carolyn could tire of Lee and move on to other marital pastures. It faded out with the two of them securely wrapped in each other's arms and Carolyn explaining her philosophy that "we are all born with the right to happiness." For twenty-one years this show came packaged to the theme, "Song of the Soul." Miss Phillips sold The Right to Happiness to an agency in 1942; it was moved from Chicago to New York, and John M. Young was selected to write it after a writing contest had been conducted by the agency to find Miss Phillips' successor. Eloise Kummer was the original Carolyn in Chicago; Claudia Morgan took over in New York and finished the role. Gary Merrill and John Larkin played Miles Nelson. Dick Wells and David Gothard were among those who played Dwight Kramer. Reese Taylor was the ill-tempered, ill-fated Bill Walker. Ruth Bailey played Rose Kransky, as she had on The Guiding Light. Procter & Gamble was the longtime sponsor. For the bulk of its run, The Right to Happiness was an NBC show; it moved to CBS in its final days.

Rin-Tin-Tin

Rin-Tin-Tin was one of the first and last adventure shows of the air, with a gap of two decades in between. The first Rin-Tin-Tin was heard on NBC Blue in 1930 as a 15-minute Saturday show for Ken-L Ration. That ran until 1934 (for CBS Sundays in its last year). It featured the exploits of the marvelous German shepherd wonder dog who battled badmen and the elements in the name of his master, and had been starred in movies as early as 1923. By January 2, 1955, three canine lifetimes had passed since the initial series, but Rinty was resurrected for another series, replacing The Shadow in a 30-minute Sunday format for Milk Bone and the Mutual Network. This time he was owned by a frontier lad named Rusty, who rode with the 101st Cavalry out of Fort Apache. It opened with a stiff bugle call and Rusty's pre-adolescent cry, "Yo, Rinty!" Near the story's end, Rusty put Rinty through his paces, inevitably ending with, "Okay, Rinty, you've earned your Milk Bone." This show ran one season.

Road of Life

Road of Life was the dynamic story of Dr. Jim Brent, who in the late 1930's and the early 1940's was paged into surgery five times a week for one of radio's most famous soap operas. "Dr. Brent . . . call surgery . . . Dr. Brent . . . call surgery. . . ."

By the mid-1940's, the filtered voice that opened those early shows had disappeared, but Dr. Brent endured. He had come a long way since September 13, 1937, when he first entered City Hospital, via NBC, as an intern.

Road of Life was the first major soap opera to invade the world of doctors and nurses; it marked Irna Phillips' dramatic departure from the "common hero" soaps of the early days. Miss Phillips' characters were always a cut or two above most other soaps in professional ability, common sense, and realistic dialogue. And Jim Brent, like most of her major creations, was durable. He lasted until January 2, 1959—a quiet, strong kind of hero, secret confessor to a cavalcade of characters across the twenty-two years of his radio life, and a man whose greatest battles were usually fought outside the walls of the hospital.

Following the Phillips tradition, Brent aged as the show aged. His internship soon passed and eventually he specialized in neuro-psychiatry. His early confrontations were with the evil Dr. Reginald Parsons, but even when Dr. Parsons had passed from the scene there was more than enough strife to carry the show. First Brent had to overcome many of his immature emotions. He was afraid of marriage; the preshow death of his childhood sweetheart had left him deeply scarred. For many years he was "just a friend" to the beautiful women who came across his path. In friendship, he helped Helen Gowan Stephenson through the woods when her former husband (Dr. Parsons) refused to divulge who had adopted their baby. He was a tower of strength to young Carol Evans, whose devotion went far deeper than the eye could see. And when Brent, early in the serial, adopted a young orphan boy, Carol Evans' concern for the youth drew them ever closer together.

The boy—named John Brent—never quite outgrew his nickname, "Butch." He eventually became a pediatrician who worked in the same Merrimac hospital as his father. During the war, Butch met a young girl named Francie in San Francisco; they were married after the Allied victory. Francie, a poor girl from across the tracks, became one of the show's most tempestuous, sympathetic characters. And Carol Evans eventually wore down the elder Dr. Brent's resistance and became Mrs. Brent.

Then the children and their problems figured more prominently in the story, and Jim Brent became truly a father figure. His marriage to Carol was not destined for happiness. Her head was turned by a glamorous career; time after time she left their little daughter Janie to attend her duties with the White Orchid Cosmetics Company. The marriage became a stormy series of quarrels as Carol blended more and more into the world of the international traveler. It came to a fiery climax when her plane crashed and she was reported killed.

Now Jim was free to marry the lovely Maggie Lowell, the woman he had come to love in these final months of agony. After a decent interval, a wedding date was set, and Jim seemed at last headed for true happiness. Then, on the very day of the wedding, Carol returned and threw Merrimac into turmoil. With hardly a whimper of protest, Jim turned away from true love Maggie and prepared "to do the right thing" by Carol.

Little did he know that the woman who had returned was not Carol, but actually Beth Lambert, a down-and-out actress. Through intense training and slight plastic surgery, Beth was able to carry off the deception beautifully, planted in Jim's house by the sinister Ed Cochran, who hoped to learn the details of Jim's current top-secret government experiments.

So went Road of Life. Dr. Brent eventually found happiness with another wife, Jocelyn McLeod, but trouble and discontent was ever ready to strike. Miss Phillips took her title from a piece of personal symbolism—that the doctor's road is the road of life. The show originated in Chicago's WBBM Air Theatre, and ran for most of its life on NBC for Procter & Gamble, moving to double network status in 1952, and to CBS in 1954, where it remained until the end.

Ken Griffin was the young Dr. Brent. By the late 1940's, a mature-sounding Don MacLaughlin had the role, and the part was also played by Matt Crowley and David Ellis. Young, innocent Carol was Lesley Woods; the older, not-so-innocent Carol was played by Louise Fitch and Marion Shockley. Muriel Bremner was Helen Gowan Stephenson, Reese Taylor the unscrupulous Dr. Parsons. Donald Kraatz played Butch Brent as a boy; others who had the role later were Lawson Zerbe and David Ellis. Elizabeth Lawrence was Francie, Barbara Becker played Jocelyn, and Maggie Lowell was played by Julie Stevens and Helen Lewis.

The show was sold as a package to the network, with Procter & Gamble spots already included. Miss Phillips wrote most of the early scripts, but later assigned the story to other writers under her supervision. The theme, Tchaikovsky's "Pathétique Symphony," was to housewives simply the music for "The DUZ program, *Road of Life.*"

The Road to Danger

The Road to Danger, a wartime adventure series on Saturday mornings on NBC during 1943–44, told of Stumpy and Cottonseed, two behind-the-lines American truck drivers who transported everything from munitions to prisoners and refugees. Based on a story by James Street, *The Road to Danger* told of their trips "on the unmarked highways of the world." In a bit of unusual casting, Stumpy was played by Curley Bradley (best known as Tom Mix) and Cottonseed was Clarence Hartzell (the Uncle Fletcher of *Vic and Sade*). It was directed by Jack Simpson. Its most forgettable catch phrase:

Stumpy, what are we waitin' for?
Not a durn thing, Cottonseed—let's go!

Rocking Horse Rhythms

Rocking Horse Rhythms came to Mutual in 1943. Its star was Bobby Hookey, a 5-year-old graduate of *The Horn and Hardart Children's Hour.* That's right, Bobby was 5 when he became master of ceremonies of this late-night (10:45 P.M.) Sunday-night show. He sang and mugged and even did guest interviews. Sometimes his singing (which he learned by ear, since he hadn't yet learned to read) was done on a rocking horse with a microphone attached to its head. Mort Howard accompanied the child wonder, who was described in *Newsweek* as "the youngest star ever to have his own weekly network program."

Rocky Fortune

Rocky Fortune had all the earmarks of a cheap production, except that its star was Frank Sinatra. But Sinatra was in a slump then. This was October 6, 1953; the bobby-soxers were gone forever, and the full impact of *From Here to Eternity* hadn't yet been felt. So Sinatra took this part, strictly from hunger and lasting only a year on NBC. Not surprisingly, it was sustained, so everybody came out losers except the sponsor who didn't take it. In the title role, Sinatra was a "footloose and fancy-free young man" who drifted from one adventurous job to another. It was put together by the same team responsible for the much better science fiction series, *X-Minus One*, a few years later. Fred Weihe and Andrew Love took turns at directing, and the scripts by Ernest Kinoy and George Lefferts got Fortune/Sinatra into all kinds of trouble. He worked at a museum and found a body in the sarcophagus. He worked as a truck driver and had to haul nitro over a bumpy road. He even took a job as bodyguard for a pro football player. Which proves, finally, that you could get away with anything on radio.

Rocky Jordan

Rocky Jordan was the resurrected 30-minute weekly version of *A Man Named Jordan*, which had run as a CBS 15-minute daily serial in 1945. The new show, also on CBS, (but on the West Coast only) was first heard in 1949–50 and was virtually a duplicate of the serial. It too starred Jack Moyles as Jordan, owner of the Cafe Tambourine, "where modern adventure and intrigue unfold against the backdrop of antiquity." The only real change was that the Tambourine was uprooted from Istanbul and plopped down in Cairo, "gateway to the ancient East." Moyles played the same hard-driving Rocky, a man always on the lookout for a loose buck and loose woman; his series was a solid feather in the CBS adventure cap. Jay Novello played Captain Sam Sabaaya of the Cairo police. For a time the show was sponsored by Del Monte Foods; it was directed by Cliff Howell, written by Larry Roman and Gomer Cool, and well-scored with original Oriental-sounding music by Richard Aurandt. Larry Thor announced. On July 18, 1951, still another *Rocky Jordan* came to CBS coast-to-coast. This time, though the production crew remained essentially the same, Moyles was replaced by George Raft. The change did nothing for Rocky's character, and in fact may have diminished it. Moyles had played the part since 1945; to listeners with long memories, he *was* Rocky Jordan. All Raft brought to the show was a glamor name. By 1952, even that was gone.

Roger Kilgore, Public Defender

Roger Kilgore, Public Defender operated on the opposite side of the justice scales from *Mr. District Attorney*, but came on with almost exactly the same pitch: that "justice, equal justice, is the sacred right of all people in a democracy," and that everyone has a God-given right to "life, liberty and the pursuit of happiness." *Kilgore* was an obscure 1948 Tuesday-night flash in the pan. Kilgore was played by Santos Ortega as a hard-fighting servant of the people, butting heads more than occasionally with D.A. Sam Howe, who was given a good stubborner-than-thou portrayal by Staats Cotsworth. Stedman Coles wrote the scripts; Jock MacGregor directed. The show never really had the appeal of the crime-busting *Mr. D.A.*, and was soon forgotten.

Rogue's Gallery

Rogue's Gallery was, in a sense, Dick Powell's rehearsal for *Richard Diamond*, coming to Mutual for Fitch Shampoo as a Tuesday-night feature September 27, 1945. Powell played private detective Richard Rogue, who trailed luscious blondes, protected witnesses, and did whatever else detectives do to make a living. It was a good series, though not destined to make much of a mark. Under the capable direction of Dee Englebach and accompanied by the music of Leith Stevens, Powell floated through his lines with the help of such competents as Lou Merrill, Gerald Mohr, Gloria Blondell, Tony Barrett, and Lurene Tuttle. Peter Leeds played Rogue's friend Eugor, an obscure play on names with Eugor spelling Rogue backwards. During the summer of 1946, the show was billed as *Bandwagon Mysteries*, with a tip of the hat to the sponsor. In the summer of 1947, it was again revived on NBC Sundays for Fitch, with Barry Sullivan in the title role. In 1950 the character again turned up in a two-year sustainer on the ABC Wednesday-night schedule. Chester Morris played the lead.

Romance

Romance reared its pretty head on CBS in 1947, a light summer series directed by Albert Ward and written by Charles S. Monroe. After several seasons as a summer show it went into the Thursday night CBS lineup for Jergens Lotion in 1952. It was a solid series of light romantic comedy produced during the middle 1950's by all the people who worked on the thriller *Escape*. Norman Macdonnell was producer-director; the scripts were by writers like Kathlene Hite and Antony Ellis. Top radio stars John Dehner, Shirley Mitchell, Jack Moyles, Virginia Gregg, Jack Kruschen, Lawrence Dobkin, Harry Bartell, and Ben Wright were featured. For most of the run, beginning in

1954, *Romance* was an early-afternoon Saturday show. Somehow, it held on until 1960.

The Romance of Helen Trent

The Romance of Helen Trent was first heard regionally July 24, 1933, and went into the CBS schedule October 30, 1933. It began in Chicago, in the depths of the Great Depression. Like *Ma Perkins, Myrt and Marge,* and other contemporaries, *The Romance of Helen Trent* developed as an endless struggle between Good and Evil, an audio simmering pot of primitive emotion, seasoned heavily with unrequited love, murder, tears, and madness, served up daily in 15-minute doses. A plunking banjo . . . the soft humming of "Juanita" . . . and the voice of Fielden Farrington:

> Time now for *The Romance of Helen Trent* . . . the real-life drama of Helen Trent, who—when life mocks her, breaks her hopes, dashes her against the rocks of despair—fights back bravely, successfully, to prove what so many women long to prove in their own lives: that because a woman is 35, and more, romance in life need not be over; that the romance of youth can extend into middle life, and even beyond . . .

The humming fades, the banjo plunks its last tinny note. It is just after noon, and the kitchens of 3 million women are electric with anticipation.

> Glamorous Helen Trent faces a desperate crisis in her deep love for the brilliant, handsome lawyer Gil Whitney. For within 48 hours, the beautiful but evil adventuress Fay Granville is announcing her intention of marrying Gil. As we heard Helen say: "Fay Granville has caught Gil in a trap. She pretended to be a secretary and Gil gave her a job. She pretended to be alone and penniless, and Gil showed her sympathy. He even took her out! And now Fay is claiming that Gil proposed to her, and she's threatening Gil with scandal. There's only one way to stop Fay Granville! That is to find some proof of her notorious past—to find someone who knows who Fay Granville really is—if it's not too late."

The plot thickens. At the root of all the trouble is Gil's wife ("in name only"), Cynthia Carter Swanson Whitney. Cynthia has one sole purpose in being on this earth—to hurt Helen Trent. For years she has refused to free Gil. But now that Fay apparently has Gil cornered, Cynthia can fly to Mexico, get her quickie divorce, let Fay marry Gil, and leave Helen Trent high, dry, and forever crushed.

But Gil has jumped into action. Last night, he offered Fay *one million dollars* to leave the country! Naturally, Gil doesn't have anything close to a million. He plans to raise the money on credit and pay it off for the rest of his life.

Of such stuff was *The Romance of Helen Trent* made. It stands today as the ultimate in high camp.

A long string of sponsors, including American Home Products and the Whitehall Drug Company, carried the show for twenty-seven years and 7,222 chapters. Like many of radio's famous soap operas, the cast, production crew, and writers were as faithful as the listeners. Director Blair Walliser stuck with the show for a decade, through its Chicago years. Les Mitchel directed briefly, then Ernest Ricca took over for a dozen years after the show moved (in June 1944) to New York. Only nine writers worked on the serial, an average of one every three years. The producers were (who else?) Frank and Anne Hummert. Only two men—Marvin Miller and David Gothard—played Gil Whitney on a regular basis. For more than a decade, the deliciously evil Cynthia was played by Mary Jane Higby. The part of Jeff Brady, owner of the motion-picture studio in Hollywood which employed Helen as its chief gown designer, was played by Kenneth Daigneau. Helene Dumas played Lydia Brady, Jeff's wife. Bess McCammon played Agatha Anthony, the "charming and sympathetic elderly woman who shares Helen Trent's attractive apartment" on Hollywood's Palm Drive. Gil Whitney's houseman Bugsy O'Toole was played by Ed Latimer.

As for Helen, that magnificent pillar of ice underwent only one permanent change of voice. Fill-ins were occasionally used but, as Gilbert Millstein wrote in 1956 in *The New York Times*, they could "be dismissed as, at most, Helen Trentlets." The real Helen came forth each noon in, first, the voice of Virginia Clark and later in the velvet tones of Julie Stevens. Both actresses led lives offstage that seemed to elude Helen, for all her adventures. Virginia Clark was a two-time divorcee, and Julie Stevens married a steel executive and bore two daughters during her sixteen years in the role.

What Helen really wanted was marriage, children, and a home. She was absolutely pure, nobly selfless, refusing to stoop to the tactics of her enemies until the last days of her run, when her purity became slightly ridiculous even to her loyal following. She never smoked or drank and seldom allowed herself even a minor show of temper. Only evil women like Helen's arch-rival, the insidious gossip columnist Daisy Parker, did those things. Housewives who went through three packs a day accepted that a woman who smoked or drank on *Helen Trent* was of questionable moral character.

Helen changed little in twenty-seven years. She was melodramatic even by soap opera standards, so intense that many faithful listeners caught up in her wildest adventures wrote letters of advice, remembered anniversaries, and sent gifts. At the height of her fame, Helen Trent (not Virginia Clark, nor Julie Stevens, but Helen) was getting 1,000 letters a week.

Her past was shrouded in mystery, unknown even to the scribes who pumped her lifeblood from their typewriters. Who her parents were was never known. The man of her past remained forever Helen's secret. She never talked about her late husband; all we know is that he was a fantastically lucky man. Helen was the goddess of all radio. No less than thirty suitors chased her through her twenty-seven years as a thirty-five-year-old; two dozen got close enough to propose marriage, but none got closer. One of the earliest was Dr. Reginald Travers (Pat Murphy), who begged three times a week for her hand, was rebuffed, and disappeared forever into the world of upper-class Vienna. Another—much later in the Stevens years—was millionaire Texan Brett Chapman, who chose South America as his place of exile after Helen had crushed his hopes.

They were the lucky ones. Oilman Dwight Swanson (Don MacLaughlin), after marrying Cynthia but still desperately in love with Helen, decided to end it all if he couldn't have her; he deliberately crashed his plane into a cliff. An artist once won her hand, but died of a heart attack the night before the wedding. Another doctor fell in love with her, but his wife came after Helen with murder in her heart. That was another disadvantage of being Helen Trent. People were always devising cruel and devious methods of doing her in.

Once she even became involved with a gangster. But listener response to that experiment was poor, and the guy was written out in a volley of bullets. Then in 1939, working on the set of a new motion picture, she met Gil Whitney. It was like Antony's first meeting with Cleopatra: Helen, the flashy dress designer with the mysterious past; Gil, the young lawyer and—to hear it on the air—the most incredibly handsome devil ever to live. We didn't know it then, but Gil would chase her through two decades of strife, refusing to give up even when his war wounds confined him to a wheelchair. Gil kept trying until 1958, when he married another woman and thumbed his nose at Helen's fickle nature.

The suitors broke down into two camps. The first group were the none-too-bright, basically decent guys like Whitney and Chapman. The second group were rebuffed suitors who, deciding that they could never have Helen for themselves, tried to kill her so nobody else could. A surprising number of men fell into this second grouping, but then, twenty-seven years is a long time.

People were constantly taking potshots at Helen. She was drugged, shot, framed, nearly pushed off a steep cliff, and once found herself at the mercy of a mad hypnotist (Alan Hewitt), who tried to have his way with her in a desolate mountain cabin. Kurt Bonine, an insanely jealous suitor, shot Gil as he sat helpless in his wheelchair, then tried to frame Helen for the dastardly deed. In one 1950 sequence, Helen was sent to jail on a murder rap and very nearly went to the gas chamber.

Indisputable queen of the soaps, Helen bade her final farewell on June 24, 1960. After twenty-seven years of such agony, did she find happiness? Gil Whitney was out of the way, and her new fiancé, Senate candidate John Cole (Leon Janney), looked like a solid contrast. But we could never be sure. Peter Bunzel, assistant editor of *Life* magazine, offered his readers a few possible solutions:

> When the word came down that *The Romance of Helen Trent* was over, the show's cast and production staff favored polishing the heroine off in the style of mayhem to which she had become accustomed. An assistant director wanted Helen and all her pals to be invited for dinner by Ma Perkins. That benevolent old busybody would serve roast turkey spiked with poison. The guests would successively clutch their throats and choke to death as Ma softly chuckled.
>
> But this was child's play compared with the finale plotted by Leon Janney, a veteran radio actor who played several of Helen's suitors including her last. Janney proposed a different agony for each of the five chief characters. During the final week of broadcasting, they would be disposed of one by one on a daily schedule. On Monday there would be a plane crash; on Tuesday an amnesia seizure; on Wednesday a landslide; on Thursday a lightning bolt. The worst would come last. Friday would be saved for Helen.
>
> After the music fades, Helen is discovered on a high balcony, soliloquizing about the week's carnage. Suddenly, with a resounding crash, the balcony topples into a deep gorge. Silence, long and ominous. Finally, a knock is heard on her door. Silence. More knocking, very frantic. Then comes a familiar pleading voice, the voice of the man she had loved the longest and hated to lose: "Helen! Helen!—it's Gil." Pause. "HELEN!"

Rosemary

Rosemary was Elaine Carrington's third major soap (the others were Pepper Young's Family and When a Girl Marries). It was first heard on NBC for Procter & Gamble October 2, 1944, but moved to CBS in 1946, where it remained until its demise in 1955. It told the story of Rosemary Dawson, a young (just 20 when the show opened) secretary who lived with her kindly mother and her teenage sister Patti. Rosemary supported the family on her meager secretarial earnings, and became its chief source of spiritual guidance as well. Early in the series there was some hint that Rosemary might become romantically involved with handsome and brilliant young lawyer Peter Harvey, but instead she married Bill Roberts, a shell-shocked war veteran, and by the time the show was ready for its June 1946 CBS première, it had become "her struggle to find happiness as the wife of a returned veteran." Bill's mind was a blank. The war had done that to him (though the blank mind was a general characteristic of most soap opera men); he could remember nothing of his life before. They lived in "a little white Cape Cod cottage outside Springdale" with Mother Dawson and sister Patti and might have gone on in blissful ignorance had not Rosemary's singing of "Night and Day" suddenly jarred his memory. Now he remembered former wife Audrey, and their little girl Jessica. Trouble was, in the remembering, he had lost the memory of his most recent four years, his marriage to Rosemary and all that went with it. "Are you someone I should know?" he asked blankly.

Dumbfounded but ever resourceful, Rosemary began to help him pick up the pieces. They found Audrey to be a typical soapy meanie, and the serial progressed from there. Later there was Bill's lengthy murder trial, another staple of daytime drama. Betty Winkler and George Keane played Rosemary and Bill through most of the run, and the roles were also done by Virginia Kaye and Robert Readick. The show sparked a real-life romance behind the scenes, culminating in wedding bells for Betty Winkler and George Keane, who had met at the studio. Marion Barney played Mother Dawson. Audrey was Lesley Woods and Joan Alexander; for a time Jone Allison played both Patti Dawson, and Audrey Roberts. Little Jessica was Joan Lazer. Sydney Smith played Peter Harvey. Joyce Miller, Rosemary's best friend, was played by Helen Choate and later Mary Jane Higby. The show was, during its formative years, under the direction of Theodora ("Dodie") Yates, one of the top female directors of daytime radio.

Roses and Drums

Roses and Drums was a major series of early historical dramas, premièring on CBS May 8, 1932, and featuring stars of stage and film. In its earliest forms, Roses and Drums drew its material from the entire scope of American history; its opening show starred Cecilia Loftus as Sarah Wright, in a drama of the 1676 Nathaniel Bacon Rebellion. Subsequent shows of that first year brought Fritz Leiber as James Madison; Henry Hull as Nathan Hale, and Glenn Hunter as a young British officer who defected to the Colonials after experiences at Valley Forge. Others who appeared on Roses and Drums that first year were William Faversham, June Walker, Geoffrey Kerr, Margaret Wycherly, and Margaret Sullavan. In the fall, the series dramatized "The Battle of the Alamo" with De Wolf Hopper, who became the star for the next three seasons. Roses and Drums moved to the Blue Network in 1934, where the emphasis eventually became deeply rooted in Civil War lore. Herschel Williams directed; United Central Life was the sponsor. Its final show, heard March 29, 1936, was appropriately titled, "Road's End."

Roxy and His Gang

Roxy and His Gang was one of radio's early variety hours. It was created by Samuel Lionel Rothafel, known throughout radio and filmdom as "Roxy." Born in Stillwater, Minnesota, on July 9, 1882, Rothafel had his greatest success as an innovator and entrepreneur in motion picture houses. During the turbulent 1920's, he became nationally known for his ability to transform neighborhood movie dives into palaces of the cinema; he was instrumental in bringing live vaudeville-type acts, entire concert symphonies, and spectacular lighting effects to houses that had formerly been used only for film. Throughout his professional career, he was known as "Roxy," a nickname he picked up in his youth, while playing second base in a northern Pennsylvania bush league. Roxy capped his career by becoming manager of Radio City Music Hall, a stint that was not successful; he also managed the Capitol, Strand, and Roxy theatres in New York. His radio career began around 1923 when, from the stage of the Capitol Theatre, he began broadcasting his Capitol Theatre Family shows, a Sunday morning variety hour that also featured Major Edward Bowes. In 1926, after receiving criticism from the

American Telephone and Telegraph Company for the "informality" of his announcing, Roxy quit the Capitol broadcasts and Bowes carried on with the show alone. It was a format that led ultimately to Bowes' highly successful *Original Amateur Hour*. Roxy, meanwhile, returned to the air on March 7, 1927, broadcasting the first of his *Roxy and His Gang* shows on NBC Blue. It was an elaborate, sweeping show for its day, heard Monday nights at 7:30, and featuring scores of soloists, musicians, and speakers. The "gang" for his opening show included: Maria Gambarelli, singer; Douglas Stanbury, baritone; Phil Ohman and Victor Arden, pianists; Adrian de Silva, tenor; Celia Branz, contralto; Geoffrey O'Hara, singer; Dorothy Miller, soprano; Gladys Rice, soprano; Beatrice Belkin, soprano; Anna Robinson soprano; Joseph Stopak, violinist; Jim Coombs, bass; Frank Moulan, comedian; Florence Mulholland, contralto; a "mixed chorus of 100 voices and a complete symphony orchestra of 110 instrumentalists." There was also a studio orchestra of 60 musicians, and four conductors were on hand to provide enough baton-waving for all the competition combined. It didn't matter much; Roxy snatched up the baton soon after announcer Milton Cross put the show on the air, and he led personally for most of the broadcast. Admitting that he was nervous "as a grasshopper," Roxy paced throughout the show, moving the soloists back and forth at the microphone to adjust for the strength of their voices. After the performances, he gave each artist a reassuring pat. For his second broadcast, Roxy introduced a new "gang" member, J. W. Roddenberry, who was said to have a "perfect" radio voice for those days of fragile tubes, when such things mattered. *Roxy and His Gang* held the Monday night Blue air for four years, and was last heard in 1931. Rothafel died January 13, 1936, a heart attack victim.

The Roy Rogers Show

The Roy Rogers Show came to radio November 21, 1944. Never in all his 80-odd Republic Pictures did Rogers face an owlhoot as frightening as that first Mutual microphone.

Just before his first broadcast, Rogers had a severe case of mike fright. Although he became a veteran of hundreds of radio shows between 1944 and 1955, he never quite lost the fear of the microphone.

Actually, his mike career began in 1931. But in those days his voice was part of a blend, when he sang on the air as a member of Uncle Tom Murray's Hollywood Hillbillies. He spent several of his early years organizing cowboy bands, worked for a time on a New

Mexico ranch, and traveled with Okies through Depression-era California. It wasn't until 1937 that he got his first big movie break, taking over as in-house star at Republic after former star Gene Autry had had a spat with the boss.

Soon Rogers was competing with Autry as the nation's top cowboy of the screen. His radio career, like his film career, followed Autry's by a few years, and the early shows followed the pattern set by Autry's *Melody Ranch*. Sponsored by Goodyear Tires, Rogers' show featured Roy and the Sons of the Pioneers in such fine Western favorites as "Tumbling Tumbleweeds," "Cool Waters," and "Don't Fence Me In." Much of the show was campfire banter and song, with Roy and songstress Pat Friday doing vocal solos, Perry Botkin leading the Goodyear orchestra and Verne Smith announcing. Dramatic skits were offered, but leaned to lighter material than what the show used in late years. Ultimately, it became primarily a Western thriller show.

The Sons of the Pioneers had strong personal ties to Rogers, and remained with him until 1948. Each member of the singing group claimed ancestry among the earliest pioneers, and Rogers had originally been part of the group. Then he was just Leonard Slye, a Cincinnati-born kid; they traveled to small-town engagements, sang on the radio, and shared hard times. Gradually their songs came into favor. Their famed recording, "The Last Roundup," pushed them into the ranks of the country's top Western performers. They were in demand for small singing roles in Republic Pictures, and when Rogers heard that the studio was looking for a new Western star, he donned his white hat and auditioned for the part. The Sons went with him into films, and Tim Spenser, Bob Nolan, Hugh Farr, and Ken Dawson of the original group sang on his first radio show.

Rogers' wife Arlene died in 1946. By then he and Dale Evans had teamed up as king and queen of the Old West; they were married on December 31, 1947. Dale also figured prominently on Rogers' radio show, playing the same girl friend–constant companion part she had had in the films. In 1946, the show went to NBC as a Saturday-night feature for Miles Laboratories; it returned in 1948 to Mutual on Sundays for Quaker Oats. Back it went to NBC for General Foods on Fridays in 1951. It moved to Thursdays in 1952. In its final season, *The Roy Rogers Show* was a Thursday-night NBC offering for Dodge.

Foy Willing and the Riders of the Purple Sage replaced the Sons of the Pioneers in 1948. Gabby Hayes was a regular then, and major musical numbers were done by Frank Worth's orchestra. Later Pat Brady (a froggy-voiced mixup with Autry's Pat Buttram) was Roy's sidekick. By the 1950's, the thriller element, featuring Roy, Dale, Pat, horse Trigger, and dog Bullet, was the backbone of the show. It closed in 1955, a memorable piece of juvenile radio, to the now-famous Rogers theme:

Happy trails to you
Until we meet again . . .

The Rudy Vallee Show

The Rudy Vallee Show opened on NBC October 24, 1929, for Standard Brands, the first major network variety hour.

Vallee was first heard on WABC, New York, in a February 1928 musical series sponsored by Herbert's Blue-White Diamonds.

He was born July 28, 1901, in Island Pond, Vermont. When he was a child, his family moved to Westbrook, Maine, where he was raised and cultivated his distinctive New England style. For a time Vallee thought he might follow his father in the pharmacy, but a growing interest in music led him in other directions. Vallee quit high school in 1917, lying about his age to get into the war with the Navy. The Navy found him out and kicked him out. At home, he continued his schooling and his music, eventually going to the University of Maine and then Yale. At Maine, he became an accomplished saxophonist, studying the records of Rudy Wiedoeft and practicing the Wiedoeft style until he could play professionally. At Yale he joined a group that played private engagements and third-rate vaudeville jobs. He borrowed Wiedoeft's first name, dropping his own Hubert Prior and becoming simply Rudy Vallee. Not yet out of school, he was already a rising semi-pro, making enough money from his music to fund his education.

Vallee went to London on tour, joined the Vincent Lopez orchestra, and quit after a year to head his own group. As the Connecticut Yankees they landed in New York's Heigh-Ho Club, where Vallee first began using the "Heigh-ho, everybody!" greeting that became his trademark. He continued using it even after the Yankees had outgrown the Heigh-Ho Club, and that didn't take long. By 1929, after a year on the air locally, NBC was strongly considering him for a national variety hour. The vote of the network programming board was tight; Bertha Brainard swung the decision in Vallee's favor. Only a woman, she reasoned, could understand the hypnotic power that the young crooner held in those days. The decision had been sound; Vallee was a smash.

Also popularly known as *The Fleischmann Hour* and *The Royal Gelatin Hour*, it was a natural showcase for new talent. Network radio was still a novelty; a show that projected big-time vaudeville right into the living room attracted huge audiences and made national reputations overnight. People had heard of Eddie Cantor, but few outside New York had been able to sample him until Vallee brought him into their homes. And Vallee himself was still riding a crest of personal popularity when his radio show went to NBC. He was the great heartthrob of the 1920's, the Vagabond Lover who sang through his nose and packed in the women wherever he played. His theme song, "My Time Is Your Time," became an immediately identifiable trademark.

Graham McNamee was Vallee's announcer, and guests booking into his show found skits tailored to their personalities and images by first-rate songsmiths. Composer Eliot Daniel joined Vallee around 1935, later working as a team with Joe Lilley to adapt popular songs and write original themes. Radio's best writers handled the dialogue. George Faulkner, Carroll Carroll, Sid Zelinka, and later Paul Henning, Mel Frank, Norman Panama, Jess Oppenheimer, Frank Galen, Charlie Isaacs, Ray Singer, and Dick Chevillat were among those who wrote for Vallee. Ole Olsen and Chick Johnson, team comics, were Vallee regulars in the 1930's. Guests included Noel Coward, Ed Wynn, Maurice Evans, and Helen Keller. By 1938, one of the best known regulars was Irving Caesar, "America's foremost safety man," whose safety songs were applauded by newspapers and rival radio personalities.

Both Eddie Cantor and Rudy Vallee loved their reputations for discovering new talent. Cantor claimed discovery of George Burns and Gracie Allen after Gracie alone appeared on his show. By that yardstick, Rudy Vallee could lay legitimate claim to the discovery of Cantor. Even though Cantor's stage antics were well-known before radio, it took his appearance on The Rudy Vallee Show to make him a national star, and to propel him into radio with his own program.

As a maker of stars, The Rudy Vallee Show won hands-down over all the competition combined. In the trade, Vallee's reputation as a talent scout was almost legendary. Reputation and fact fed each other; appearance became synonymous with "discovery," and Vallee was known to do strange things not normally done in the upper levels of show business.

He plucked Alice Faye out of the chorus in George White's Scandals and started her toward film stardom. He found Frances Langford singing on a small station in Florida. Beatrice Lillie, Milton Berle, and Phil Baker got their first major radio exposure on The Rudy Vallee Show. Tommy Riggs first introduced his character Betty Lou on Vallee's Fleischmann Hour. Joe Penner leaped from obscurity to fame, and Vallee was his vehicle. Bob Burns got his long-running job with Bing Crosby after a series of appearances on Vallee's show. The *Aldrich Family* and *We, the People* were first heard as skits on Vallee's program. But Vallee's greatest discovery came on December 17, 1936, when a previously unsung ventriloquist named Edgar Bergen first wisecracked on the air as Charlie McCarthy, starting a career that, for a time, was the hottest thing in radio. Ironically, though Vallee got widespread credit for "finding" Bergen, the ventriloquist was actually booked into the show by the agency handling the Fleischmann account.

For ten years to the month, Vallee held that slot and sponsor, doing the first seven years for Fleischmann's Yeast and the last three for Royal Gelatin. Vallee and Standard Brands parted company by mutual consent September 28, 1939. After a rest, he returned March 7, 1940, with a 30-minute musical-variety show, also on Thursday night NBC, for Sealtest. Vallee's rating, though always healthy, had begun to slip a bit in the late 1930's. The star and his sponsor decided to terminate their long partnership after ten years together. Vallee wanted a fresh approach. For Sealtest, he devised a format based on rehearsal scripts, which would be read in finished form as though the cast were still in rehearsal. The producers nixed this in favor of a Henning-written series of historical skits, which sent the ratings down thirteen points in three months. That was when Vallee reached into his grab bag, in one last attempt to save the floundering show, and selected Ed Gardner to replace departed producer-director Vic Knight.

It was Gardner who thought of dragging an aging John Barrymore out of theatrical mothballs and making him one of the accomplished comedic "finds" of 1940. He mixed borderline slapstick with heavy Shakespeare, and again the rating soared. Barrymore mugged shamelessly, taking his cues from director Dick Mack after Gardner had departed for *Duffy's Tavern*, and enjoying it immensely. Barrymore even took Mack's suggestions on Shakespeare, though the first time Mack offered them the cast braced for a confrontation. It never came. Barrymore simply said, "I think you're right," and did it Mack's way.

It was the twilight of Barrymore's career, and his health was a question mark all the way. Vallee knew he was hitting the bottle heavily, but felt that Gardner's judgment was sound. "When he is there, he'll be great," he said. When Barrymore wasn't there, his brother Lionel often came in as a last-minute replacement. Occasionally the writers even played upon Barrymore's weakness, in a mild way. For the show of May 14, 1942, a "farewell Barrymore" sketch was created. In dialogue with Vallee, Barrymore was to say, "This is my farewell appearance." "You mean you're leaving acting flat?" was Vallee's line. "Why not?" said Barrymore. "That's how it left me."

Backstage, there was talk of cutting the lines. The writers were afraid that because of Barrymore's health the skit might be in poor taste. Barrymore scoffed. "Leave it in," he said; "it's only a gag."

It turned out to be more than that. In rehearsal that Tuesday, Barrymore collapsed in pain and was rushed to the hospital. He died there May 29, 1942. The Vallee show had lost an irreplaceable asset, but Vallee continued for another year, until July 8, 1943, when he left for active duty with the Coast Guard. He turned the show over to Joan Davis, who had developed as a radio star on the series, and to newcomer Jack Haley. They turned it into The Sealtest Village Store.

There were other Vallee shows, but the age of the Vagabond Lover had come and gone. Vallee returned in 1944 starring with Monty Woolley in a Thursday-night NBC series for Drene, Villa Vallee. In 1946, he moved into a Tuesday-night slot for Philip Morris. In February 1950, he did a local show of records and talk for WOR, New York.

In the 1960's Vallee was pulled out of semiretirement to give a smash stage performance as J. B. Biggley in How to Succeed in Business Without Really Trying. But radio really died when he turned up on WOR, playing records, of all things, around his talk. Though Vallee would have hotly denied it, radio had found its ultimate disc jockey. Graham McNamee, his announcer from the great years, must have turned over in his grave.

The Sad Sack

The Sad Sack was strictly B-grade radio comedy, appearing on CBS June 12, 1946, as a summer replacement for vacationing Frank Sinatra. To assure continuity, Sinatra introduced the character on his show June 5. His sponsor (Old Gold) carried *The Sad Sack* through the summer, and that was the end of that. The show was developed from a cartoon feature created by George Baker for *Yank*, the army weekly newspaper. Baker, a former cartoonist with Walt Disney, had begun turning out the *Yank* panels in June 1942, depicting the adventures of "that beloved and eternal buck private" as he wept his way through KP and army life in general. But the radio show began with the Sack's discharge from the army and followed his adventures in the world of Back Home. There, he returned to an apartment run by crusty old Mrs. Flanagan, where he had shared a room with pal Chester Fenwick before the war. Chester, a prize con man in the best Kingfish tradition, was still there and was ever the accomplished four-flusher. The Sack also re-established contact with his girl friend, Lucy Twitchell; many of the shows concerned his bumbling attempts to impress Lucy and her unimpressible father. Herb Vigran, recently returned from the army himself, was given his first starring role as the Sad Sack. Jim Backus played Chester Fenwick, Sandra Gould was Lucy, Ken Christy was Mr. Twitchell, and Patsy Moran was Mrs. Flanagan. The scripts were by Charlie Isaacs. Dick Joy announced; Ted Sherdeman produced and directed.

The Saint

The Saint came to radio to the hollow footsteps on a lonely street and the forelorn whistle of a haunting tune, in a variety of formats built around a variety of stars. Based on the books by Leslie Charteris, *The Saint* was first heard as an NBC series January 6, 1945, with Edgar Barrier as Simon Templar, freelance sleuth.

Templar was known as the Saint, "a Robin Hood of modern crime" if the billing could be believed. But he was far too busy solving murders to indulge in any robbing from the rich. He was a clever devil with a smart mouth that almost rivaled Dick Powell's in *Richard Diamond*. The initial run, with Barrier supported by John Brown and Ken Christy was sponsored by Bromo Seltzer on Saturday nights.

On June 20, 1945, a new *Saint* opened for vacation time on CBS. This one starred Brian Aherne, noted screen star making his first appearance in a regular radio role. Backed by Louise Arthur as lovely Patricia Holmes, Aherne was right at home in the role of the debonaire Templar. But probably the best remembered *Saint* was the last series with Vincent Price in the title role. Price played Templar in a 1947 CBS summer series, and returned for a regular run two years later. It opened on Mutual in July 1949, ran for a time under Ford Motors sponsorship, and moved to NBC as a Sunday sustainer in 1950.

Price threw sarcastic barbs with reckless abandon; his Templar was a patron of the arts and a diner at restaurants superb. His all-time pet peeve was being interrupted while eating. He usually was; the interruptions led inevitably to jewel thieves, embezzlers, or murderers.

This show, a James L. Saphier production, was directed by Thomas A. McAvity and scored by Harry Zimmerman. Louis Vittes wrote many of the scripts. It petered out after two years, another of TV's notable victims.

Saturday Night Serenade

Saturday Night Serenade was a popular, long-running music show, sponsored by Pet Milk and heard on CBS for twelve years, beginning in 1936. It featured popular and light classical music, originally under the baton of Howard Barlow, but moving through a succession of maestros that also included Sammy Kaye and Gustave Haenschen. Singers included Hollace Shaw and Bill Perry; by 1944, Jessica

Dragonette was featured soloist. In 1948, the show was reorganized under the title The Pet Milk Show and was heard on NBC on Saturday nights again, but two hours earlier. Vic Damone starred in the new version, with backup by Kay Armen and the Emil Coty Singers. Warren Sweeney was host-narrator, and the theme was "You and the Night and the Music." In 1949, Bob Crosby's orchestra took over the music, and The Pet Milk Show was moved into NBC's Sunday linup. It ended in 1950, when Pet switched its advertising to Fibber McGee and Molly.

Saunders of the Circle X

Saunders of the Circle X was an outrageously corny Western serial, produced in San Francisco for airing on NBC's West Coast outlets. It premièred as a Thursday-night 30-minute continuation on October 2, 1941, and followed the adventures of "Singapore" Bill Saunders, foreman of the 90,000-acre Circle X Ranch. John Cuthbertson was starred as Singapore, Bert Horton was Hank Peffer the "tireless storyteller," Lou Tobin played ranch owner Thomas Mott, Bob Hudson was Pinto the happy cowboy, and Jack Kirkwood played ranch foreman Joe Williams. The show was written by Sam Dickson and scored with heavy Western organ music.

The Scarlet Pimpernel

The Scarlet Pimpernel was produced in London, syndicated in America in 1952, and picked up by NBC September 21, 1952, for its Sunday schedule. British actor Marius Goring starred as Sir Percy Blakeney, the London dandy who in moments of crisis became the infamous Scarlet Pimpernel, arch-foe of purveyors of terror during the French Revolution. With his companion Lord "Tony" Dewhurst, the Scarlet Pimpernel specialized in rescuing prospective victims of the guillotine during the reign of Louis XVI. Joel Murcott wrote the scripts, and the series was syndicated and produced by Harry A. Towers, whose Towers Of London Syndicate was at one time the world's top dealer in transcribed radio.

Scattergood Baines

Scattergood Baines enjoyed two runs on radio in two entirely differ-ent shows. It premièred February 22, 1937, broadcasting from Hollywood for CBS West Coast stations. By 1939 the show had moved to Chicago, and went on the national network for Wrigley's Gum as a five-a-week 15-minute serial. Though lighter than most of its competitors, *Scattergood Baines* did have its moments of gloom. Scattergood was a hardware merchant in the little town of Coldriver, a town philosopher of the David Harum–Papa David school. He had all the kindly, wise, and lovable traits bestowed upon him in the original magazine stories by Clarence Budington Kelland. Scattergood raised an adopted son, Jimmy, from infancy, only to have the boy's natural mother later turn up and claim custody. The mother, Mrs. Dodie Black, was unsuccessful, but she gave Scattergood some bad moments. Hippocrates Brown, a genial jack-of-all-trades known as "Hipp," was Scattergood's helper in the store. Pliny Pickett, a crusty man who distrusted anyone who traveled any other way, was conductor of the branch line. Clara Potts was a beautiful, nagging woman, a town activist who had married the garage mechanic, Ed Potts. J. Wellington Keats blew into town with a crooked carnival and stayed around to become manager of the hotel. And Harvey Fox was the man in black, the double-dealing four-flusher who promoted Mrs. Black's scheme to get Jimmy away from Scattergood. They were the main people of Coldriver.

Scattergood was played by Jess Pugh, Hipp by John Hearne, Pliny by Francis "Dink" Trout, Clara by Catherine McCune, J. Wellington Keats by Forrest Lewis, Jimmy by Charles Grant, Ed Potts by Arnold Robertson, Dodie Black by Eileen Palmer, and Harvey Fox by Boris Aplon. The serial was produced and directed by Walter Preston and was sponsored by Wrigley until 1942, when it left the air. *Scattergood Baines* returned in 1949 for a season as a 30-minute Mutual sustainer. This show was mainly situation comedy, with Wendell Holmes as Scattergood and a new set of characters. Gerald Holland wrote it; Herbert Rice produced. In the latter version, Scattergood was billed as "the best-loved, the most cussed at and by all odds the fattest man in the bustling, modern town of Coldriver."

Scramble

Scramble, a wartime series of adventure and aviation news for kids, was first heard on the Blue Network July 10, 1942, a joint project of the National Aeronautic Association and the armed forces to interest youngsters in aviation careers. The series dramatized the exploits of real-life warriors, often bringing them in person to the microphone for some after-show dialogue. *Scramble* also relayed the latest news from the world of the air. Robert Ripley was host for a time, and the scripts were written by Robert Monroe, who also directed.

Scramby Amby

Scramby Amby, a word-scrambling quiz show first heard on Cincinnati's WLW around 1941, proved so popular that it expanded to the West Coast, where in 1943 it was carried on some NBC stations from KFI, Los Angeles. In its KFI form, Perry Ward became master of ceremonies, Larry Keating was announcer, Paul Martin conducted the orchestra, and Anne Nagel was the songstress. The quiz was based on lists of scrambled words ("igoloanbit" is really "obligation") submitted by the listening audience. By stumping the contestant, the listener could win $5 to $50, depending on how many words were missed. The value of each word decreased as clues were given that made the translation easier. Some of the clues were verbal; others were musical, played by Martin's orchestra or sung by Keating. Listening clubs were formed and members had to "feed the kitty" as they missed words, with the winner taking home most of the pot. By July 26, 1944, *Scramby Amby* had become popular enough on the coast that it was put into a national Blue (ABC) Wednesday slot for Sweetheart Soap. Most of the West Coast cast made the transition. The music later was under direction of Charles Dant. Howard Blake was writer-producer. The series ran one season on ABC, but turned up again in 1946 as a Saturday-night Mutual sustainer.

The Screen Directors' Playhouse

The Screen Directors' Playhouse might have been a major series had it begun a little earlier in radio's life. It came to NBC January 9, 1949, a half-hour Sunday-night sustaining show. As the name implies, it was a Hollywood movietime extravanganza, following closely in the footsteps of the famous *Screen Guild Theatre* but containing the added element of director participation. The directors of the original films introduced the adaptations, which usually were done with the original stars. Afterward, the director and star reminisced briefly about the making of the film and about their respective careers since the film had been released. The show was the equal of any in its ability to draw the superstar and was much better than most of its adaptations of films. It opened as the *NBC Theatre,* featuring John Wayne in

Stagecoach, but soon changed its name to *Screen Directors' Playhouse.* By the first summer it had picked up Pabst Blue Ribbon as sponsor; later RCA began paying the bills. But the show was doomed to long stretches as a sustainer because of its late entry into the radio scene. Some of the famous movies done during the half-hour days were *Fort Apache* with John Wayne and Ward Bond, *Jezebel* with Bette Davis, *Whispering Smith* with Alan Ladd, *Pride of the Yankees* with Gary Cooper, and *Call Northside 777* with James Stewart. On November 9, 1950, *The Screen Directors' Playhouse* became a 60-minute show, running Thursday nights for several sponsors. Some of the hour-long shows were unquestionably great radio. They included *Spellbound* with Joseph Cotten, Mercedes McCambridge, and Alfred Hitchcock; *A Foreign Affair* with Marlene Dietrich, Lucille Ball, John Lund, and Billy Wilder; and *Lifeboat* with Tallulah Bankhead, Jeff Chandler, and Hitchcock. It was last heard August 30, 1951.

The Screen Guild Theatre

The Screen Guild Theatre was first heard for Gulf on CBS January 8, 1939. In all radio, no show succeeded in wooing more top Hollywood stars in the same timespan than this one. While *The Lux Radio Theatre* was paying up to $5,000 per appearance for its film stars, *Screen Guild* was a charity show, donating all star fees to the Motion Picture Relief Fund. By the end of its sponsorship in the summer of 1942, Gulf Oil had paid some $800,000 in star fees into the Fund. The money was used to build a home for aging and indigent screen stars.

Because of its mission, virtually every star in Hollywood was anxious to appear on *The Screen Guild Theatre.* When one star dropped out because of illness, producers were swamped with offers from others to take his place. And when the show was scheduled on Monday nights, back to back with the famous *Lux Radio Theatre,* the producers of both agreed in a rare display of cooperation to space out their heavy and light productions. When *Lux* ran a heavy, *Screen Guild* did a light comedy. The result was 90 minutes of top Hollywood action, and a vertiable corner for CBS on the cinema dramatics market.

But *The Screen Guild Theatre* got off to a shaky start. In the first year the stars' names were almost all the show had going for it; in many cases the material was second-rate, and in some cases just plain bad. Variety shows and revues were interspersed with dramas and comedies. After a few months of that, the variety was dropped, leaving the program simply a 30-minute comedy-drama show. Another casualty of those early months was Hollywood star and future politician George Murphy, who was signed as first host. He was replaced by Roger Pryor, a sometime actor then married to Ann Sothern, a frequent *Screen Guild* star. Oscar Bradley's orchestra provided the music, John Conte announced, and the series was directed on a revolving basis.

The *Screen Guild Theatre* always provided—once past its opening jitters—top Hollywood dramas on a consistently high level. Robert Taylor, Jeanette MacDonald, Judy Garland, Mickey Rooney, Clark Gable, Ginger Rogers, Gary Cooper, Bob Hope, Marlene Dietrich, George Burns and Gracie Allen, James Cagney, James Stewart, Loretta Young, Charles Laughton, Fred Allen, Helen Hayes, Fredric March, Basil Rathbone, Gene Autry, Eddie Cantor, Tyrone Power, Humphrey Bogart, Bette Davis, Jack Benny, and Joan Crawford were a few who appeared in the first year alone. Soon after turning down a reported $35,000 for a single radio appearance by Shirley Temple, her parents allowed her to go on *The Screen Guild Theatre* December 24, 1939, in the play *Bluebird*. Consistent with the *Screen Guild* doctrine, she was paid nothing.

In 1942, Gulf Oil dropped sponsorship because of the effect of the war on the oil industry. After a summer of frustration, the show was sold at the last minute to Lady Esther cosmetics, a new theme was added, and the time slot was moved from Sunday to Monday night. With the coming of Lady Esther in 1942, the show really settled into its own special niche. Bill Lawrence became producer-director, a job he held through one change of sponsors and two changes of network. He combed through *Box Office Digest* for leads to current films, always keeping an ear tuned to public taste. To Bill Hampton and later Harry Kronman fell the unenviable job of adapting two-hour movies into 22-minute air plays. With Lawrence, he viewed two or three movies a day in the constant search for material. Wilbur Hatch provided a fine musical score, and *The Screen Guild Theatre* was consistently nestled among radio's top fifteen shows. Lady Esther carried the *Screen Guild Theatre* until June 23, 1947; when the show returned on October 6, it was for Camel Cigarettes, still on Mondays.

There were few changes with the shift to Camels. Michael Roy became announcer. The show moved to NBC Thursdays (still for Camel) on October 7, 1948. The last show in this format was on June 29, 1950. On September 7, 1950, a new 60-minute *Screen Guild Theatre* began on ABC as a Thursday-night sustainer. Basil Adlam conducted the music. The 60-minute shows were outstanding. Notable among them were: Bing Crosby in *Birth of the Blues;* and Ronald Colman, Vincent Price, Art Linkletter, Barbara Britton, and Audrey Totter in a riotous spoof of early TV giveaway shows, *Champagne for Caesar.* That run ended May 31, 1951.

The Sea Hound

The Sea Hound, an adventure serial running on the Blue Network from June 29, 1942, through 1944, told of Captain Silver and his crew of the ship Sea Hound. Directed by Cyril Armbrister, the story focused on Silver's boy crewman Jerry, who traveled the primitive paths of the world, across the seven seas to jungle ports and desert outposts. Ken Daigneau played Silver; Bobby Hastings was Jerry. The serial also ran on Mutual in 1946–47, and a half-hour version played briefly on ABC around 1948. This one featured Barry Thomson as Silver, was directed by Charles Powers, and contained a complete story each Monday.

The Sealtest Village Store

The Sealtest Village Store was a gradual spinoff from NBC's Rudy Vallee Show. Although Vallee actually left the series July 8, 1943, it is difficult to know just where The Rudy Vallee Show began transforming itself into The Sealtest Village Store. Sometime in 1942, Vallee's radio work began conflicting with his duties in the Coast Guard, and it was decided that he would leave the show in the hands of Joan Davis. The shows began shifting focus, gradually moving away from Vallee and toward the new arrangement. By the time he departed, the fans were ready for it and the transition went almost unnoticed. The new focus was on Miss Davis as the proprietor of the Village Store. Vallee's old variety hour was completely swallowed by a situation comedy format. Shirley Mitchell came aboard as Shirley Anne; Gil Lamb played Homer Clinker, and Verna Felton was heard as Blossom Blimp. With Vallee's exit, Jack Haley was signed to carry what was viewed as an "essential" male lead, despite the opinions of some critics that Miss Davis was well-enough established to carry the lead alone. In the early shows, he played her helper in the store. Sharon Douglas played Penny Cartwright, Haley's girl friend, and music was provided by singer Dave Street, the Fountainaires Quartet, and the Eddie Paul orchestra. John Laing announced. Robert L. Redd continued as director, and the writers were Ray Singer and Dick Chevillat. In 1945, Joan Davis left and went into her own show. Jack Haley became the store proprietor, and Eve Arden was hired as his manager.

In 1947, Haley left the series and was replaced by Jack Carson. By that time it had gone through three complete changes of lead personnel. Various new writers were added, because Singer and Chevillat had by then joined Phil Harris. But consistent direction by Redd kept

The Village Store on a familiar track and healthy in the ratings wars. In its last year, music was by the Frank De Vol orchestra and Hy Averback announced. Carson and Miss Arden finished out The Village Store in 1948, when he returned to his own show and she went into Our Miss Brooks. That ended it.

The Second Mrs. Burton

The Second Mrs. Burton was the last soap opera of the air, bowing out under the CBS ax November 25, 1960, after a fifteen-year run. Mrs. Burton was the last of six remaining soaps chopped on the same day. It began as a Pacific Coast serial and went nationwide January 7, 1946. The show went all the way on CBS, most of the way under General Foods sponsorship. It told the story of a second wife and her search for happiness, and in fact evolved from an earlier West Coast show called Second Wife. Terry Burton and her husband Stan were the central characters, and the show was written on a lighter plane than most of its rivals. The Burtons lived in a small town, and were usually under the thumb of his domineering mother. It was one of the few real "family" serials, exploring character more than the traditional elements of plot and melodrama. Martha Alexander wrote the show until 1947, and Terry was played by Sharon Douglas, Claire Niesen, and Patsy Campbell. In the late 1940's, there was a shift toward melodrama, but that was reversed in the mid-1950's. John M. Young wrote the show during its years of strife. Hector Chevigny took over scripting in 1952, and brought the serial gradually back to its old, lighter themes. The last writer was Johanna Johnston. Ira Ashley was producer-director. Teri Keane played the title role for most of the later run, and Stan was played by Dwight Weist. Late in the serial, Stan's sister Marcia became one of the central characters. She and boyfriend Lew were married over the violent objections of Mother Burton. Alice Frost and then Arline Blackburn played Marcia; Larry Haines was playing Lew when the show ended. Ethel Owen was Mrs. Burton the elder. Doris Rich played Terry's wise old neighbor, Mrs. Miller, who shared many a cup of coffee and all the problems of raising her kids (Elizabeth and Ted). In all, this was an interesting soap, proving that life did not have to be all that miserable for afternoon survival.

Sergeant Preston of the Yukon

Sergeant Preston of the Yukon was the third major bigger-than-life character to come out of George W. Trendle's Detroit hero mill. The Lone Ranger had been rounding up owlhoots since 1933; the Green

Hornet since 1938. Now, on June 12, 1947, came the deep-voiced man of the great Northwest, complete with noble black horse Rex and wonder dog Yukon King.

Today the show is one of the best-remembered pieces of juvenile radio. Its opening was one of radio's classics:

Gunshot. Richochet
ANNOUNCER: Now, as gunshots echo across the windswept, snow-covered reaches of the wild northwest, Quaker Puffed Wheat . . .
Gunshot. Richochet
ANNOUNCER: and Quaker Puffed Rice . . .
Gunshot. Richochet
ANNOUNCER: the breakfast cereal shot from guns . . .
Two gunshots
ANNOUNCER: present, *The Challenge of the Yukon!*
YUKON KING: *Barks*
ANNOUNCER (Over Wind): It's Yukon King, swiftest and strongest lead dog in the Northwest, blazing the trail for Sergeant Preston of the Northwest Mounted Police, in his relentless pursuit of law-breakers!
PRESTON: On King! On, you huskies!
ANNOUNCER: Gold! Gold, discovered in the Yukon! A stampede to the Klondike in the wild race for riches! Back to the days of the gold rush, with Quaker Puffed Wheat and Quaker Puffed Rice bringing you the adventures of Sergeant Preston and his wonder dog Yukon King, as they meet the challenge of the Yukon!
Theme up

When Sergeant Preston came to ABC in 1947, his show was known as *The Challenge of the Yukon.* That title was gradually pushed into the background, and by 1953 the character had become the title. The series was also popularly known as *Yukon King* because the dog figured so prominently in the plot lines. Yukon King was forever mauling crooks and bushwhackers, chewing guns out of hands, hauling down one villain while Preston polished off the other. That's how he got to be "swiftest and strongest lead dog in the Northwest."

The joint stamp of Trendle and writer Fran Striker was all over *Sergeant Preston.* The show came packaged to classical music: the *Donna Diana* Overture theme, though not as well-known as the Ranger's *William Tell* Overture and the Hornet's "Flight of the Bumble Bee," was still perfect for the Canadian setting. It gave the illusion of Northwest backdrop without any plot or dialogue; its bouncy finale suggested the pomp and glory of the mounted police. The sergeant himself upheld the finest traditions of the mounties, always getting his man with the help of Yukon King.

And when it was over, the announcer always wished his young audience "goodbye, good luck, and good health"—a nice touch to a nice show.

Paul Sutton was Sergeant Preston for most of the run. Sutton had a deep, understanding voice, not unlike Brace Beemer of *The Lone Ranger*. Fred Foy was the early announcer, but he was too well identified with *The Lone Ranger* and was replaced by Jay Michael. Fred Flowerday directed and Charles D. Livingstone produced for Trendle Enterprises. The show was sustained on ABC until 1948, when it was picked up by Quaker Oats as a three-a-week 30-minute adventure. In 1950, *Sergeant Preston* went to Mutual, where it remained until it left the air in 1955. Brace Beemer took over the title role in the last year, and Fred Foy again became announcer. Why not? If you have *The Lone Ranger* as hero, might as well have his announcer too.

Seth Parker

Seth Parker, an intriguing mix of fact, fiction, and song, was the first radio creation of Phillips H. Lord, who became best known as the originator of such shoot-'em-up epics as *Gang Busters*. *Seth Parker* couldn't have been further from the violence themes of *Gang Busters*. It was the story of a kindly New England philosopher, played by Lord himself, and of his friends and neighbors in the little seatown of Jonesport, Maine. Billed for a time as *Sunday Evening at Seth Parker's*, the series featured a thin story line, heavy Yankee philosophy, and some gusty hymn singing. It came to be in 1929, when Lord and his wife Sophia quit their jobs at a Plainfield, Connecticut, high school and came to New York to crash Radio Row. Lord had the basic *Seth Parker* formula worked out, but ran into stiff resistance until the show was tried as a local sustainer in late 1929. By 1933 it was one of NBC's most prominent Sunday-night offerings, attracting a huge audience for the hymns and stories alike. More than 300 Seth Parker Clubs formed through the United States and Canada. The club members sang along with Seth, and many collected tons of food and clothes for the poor. In the story lines, Seth Parker was a married man with a snow-white beard. Ma Parker was played by Effie Palmer; Lord's wife Sophia played another character, Lizzie Peters. Lord had used his own grandfather as the model for Seth; the character evolved from something of a scamp into the kindly, strong hero later widely identified with the name.

The show brought Lord great financial success, and he moved on up the ladder with a new Blue Network Listerine show in 1932. In *The Country Doctor*, he also played a wise-old-man lead. His sudden wealth led to the next step in the Seth Parker epic, when Lord bought a 186-foot four-masted schooner and announced plans for an actual around-the-world cruise. The schooner was renamed the *Seth Parker* and the trip was made with great fanfare and publicity. The ship's original owner, one Captain C. Flink, was engaged to sail her, and Lord invited many friends and some of the *Seth Parker* cast along. The radio program continued as before, with Ma Parker remaining in Jonesport to lead the hymns in Seth's place. Each week during the show, there was a cable or a shortwave cutaway directly to the schooner, where Lord in character would relay some wisdom and perhaps tell a story of the sea. One week he persuaded four "lost" seamen, thought long dead by their families, to appear on the show. He preceded their talks with personal telegrams to each family, saying only that an event of "deeply personal significance" would take place, and urging them not to miss the broadcast. Songs were also done from the ship, and authentic sounds of ship's bells and sea wind were always present, via phonograph records. The schooner actually sailed along the coastal United States during the early months of 1934, then set sail for Morocco, Cairo, and points east. In February 1935, the *Seth Parker* was destroyed by a South Seas gale. Lord wired frantic SOS calls, and cast and crew were safetly evacuated. Newspapers leaped upon the story and denounced it as a publicity stunt. By 1936, in the wake of the bad publicity, *Seth Parker* had disappeared from the air. It would be revived by NBC in October 1938, but by then Lord's career had taken a gang-busting turn.

The Shadow

The Shadow made its radio debut in August 1930, on the CBS *Detective Story* program. The series grew out of the *Shadow* novels written by Walter Gibson and published in Street & Smith magazines. Jack LaCurto first played the role, when the Shadow was merely the narrator of stories on Blue Coal's *Detective Story* program. The character at that time simply hosted a story that had nothing to do with an invisible man . . .

LaCurto was followed by Frank Readick, who continued in the introductory-narrator role. The part was then passed to George Earle and Robert Hardy Andrews. The program ran until 1932, when it moved to NBC for Blue Coal. In 1934, it went back to CBS for Blue Coal, as a twice-a-week thriller. That lasted for two years.

Through this early period, 1932 through 1936, the Blue Coal people showed a mixture of fascination and dissatisfaction with the Shadow, dropping the show several times but always coming back for more. In 1937, they finally hit upon the right formula. Orson Welles, the 22-year-old audio magician, was tapped as the first Shadow in the new mold. Agnes Moorehead, who would go on to bigger things as a member of Welles' *Mercury Theatre*, became the first Margo Lane. *The Shadow* had arrived in his most famous format, the man of mystery who could "cloud men's minds so that they cannot see him."

In his heyday, Cranston and friends formed one of the hottest items on the Sunday air. He came our way with that eerie laugh, and the filtered voice to match: "Who knows . . . *what* evil . . . *lllllllurks* . . . in the hearts of men? *The Shadow Knows!*" The music came up—a chilling organ rendition of "Omphale's Spinning Wheel."

The Shadow, Lamont Cranston, a man of wealth, a student of science and a master of other people's minds, devotes his life to righting wrongs, protecting the innocent and punishing the guilty. Using advanced methods that may ultimately become available to all law enforcement agencies, Cranston is known to the underworld as the Shadow—never seen, only heard, as haunting to superstitious minds as a ghost, as inevitable as a guilty conscience . . .

Cranston, described as an amateur criminologist, stepped into cases that proved too tough for police. Especially in the early years, Police Commissioner Weston was depicted as a vain man who refused to listen to even the simplest advice, but could always be found basking in the glory after the Shadow had wrapped up his case for him. Weston seemed to hate Cranston passionately—probably because of Lamont's habit of stating the obvious—something Weston always overlooked.

Cranston, we were told, had learned his hypnotic power to cloud men's minds in the Orient. His "friend and constant companion, the lovely Margo Lane," was the only person who knew who the invisible Shadow was. Together, Lamont and Margo confronted the wildest assortment of lunatics, ghosts, and werewolves imaginable. Mad scientists—some frothing at the mouth—were to become standard *Shadow* villains. Evil doctors, corrupt politicians, and demented hypnotists plotting to Rule The World all got their just desserts.

Cranston had no mercy for those who stepped over the line. He got confessions from the guilty through methods that ranged from threats to mental torture, then cackled that electric laugh as the unlucky criminal was carted off to the Death House. "The weed of crime bears bitter fruit. Crime does not pay. The Shadow knows!"

That version was heard on Mutual, under sponsorship of Goodrich Tires, then again for Blue Coal. It became a Sunday tradition, running almost two decades for a variety of sponsors. Welles played the role until the fall of 1938, when The War of the Worlds made him a celebrity overnight. The producers of The Shadow, wanting their man of mystery to remain just that, went shopping for a new voice.

After auditioning forty-five actors, they bestowed the role upon Bill Johnstone. Miss Moorehead continued as Margo at least through the 1939 season. By 1941, the part of Margo had gone to Marjorie Anderson. Gertrude Warner played the part briefly.

Over the years, Cranston's relationship with Margo deepened from Lamont-Margo to darling-darling. By the time Bret Morrison and Grace Matthews came to the parts in the mid-1940's, the darlings were thicker than mad scientists; interesting, in the light of the many South Seas trips they shared. The role of Shrevie, the talkative cab driver, was played early in the run by Keenan Wynn; later it was handled by Alan Reed and Mandel Kramer. Many actors, including Dwight Weist, Kenny Delmar, Santos Ortega, and Ted de Corsia, played Commissioner Weston.

Johnstone left the title role in 1943 and was replaced briefly by John Archer. By mid-1945, Steve Courtleigh and Laura Mae Carpenter were Lamont and Margo. They were replaced in October 1945 by Bret Morrison and Lesley Woods. Morrison was the last Shadow; the part of Margo ultimately went to Grace Matthews.

John Barclay, Blue Coal's heating expert, appeared often with tips on home heating (usually based on the premise that Blue Coal in the furnace was the only way to go). Blue Coal had the show until the anthracite industry collapsed in 1949. Later sponsors included Grove Laboratories and Wildroot Cream Oil. The show ran until December 26, 1954, and was resyndicated with the coming of the nostalgia boom in the 1960's and 1970's. In its heyday, The Shadow was broadcast before a live audience, but the thunderous sound of applause after the last act seemed strangely out of place. After all, this wasn't The First Nighter Program. It was The Shadow, and the fate of the world—for 30 minutes each Sunday afternoon—hung in the balance.

Shafter Parker's Circus

Shafter Parker's Circus was an afternoon kiddie serial, first heard regionally around 1940 via Mutual–Don Lee. It revolved around circus life and the excitement of jungle safaris, and evolved from an earlier show, *The In-Laws*. Hal Berger, a baseball announcer in season and one of radio's earliest sportscasters, created *The In-Laws* for local Los Angeles radio in 1930. He played the part of General Shafter Parker when an actor failed to make an audition because of illness, and continued to play the role right through the 1930's and into its transition as a kids' show. Though *Shafter Parker* was a thriller, violence was kept to a minimum and no one was ever killed in the scripts. Berger maintained a balance between circus and safari stories, and kept the comedy element prominent throughout. Dale Nash (Mrs. Berger) played Shafter's sister Dolly.

Shell Chateau

Shell Chateau was the best-known of several radio programs built around Al Jolson. Billed for years as "the world's greatest entertainer," Jolson was primarily a stage performer, a blackface singer who popularized minstrel humor and the "Mammy" songs of the south.

Jolson—Asa Yoelson, the son of a rabbi—was born in Russia May 26, 1886, and filled his early life with thoughts of becoming a cantor. Somewhere along the line, greasepaint got into Jolson's blood; the greasepaint turned to burnt cork, and he ran away from home to live the life of a wandering minstrel. Eventually he became a specialist in blackface vaudeville skits and a down-on-one-knee delivery of Swanee River folksongs. Nobody could belt out a number like the young Jolson. But big-time theatre eluded him until 1909, when he first sang "Mammy" from a San Francisco stage.

After that his popularity grew quickly. Jolson starred in a long string of New York musical hits, and so enjoyed live performing that he often kept his captive audience overtime. Hollywood called in 1926; the following year Jolson starred in *The Jazz Singer*, a story based on his life that became famous as the world's first talkie. For a decade he turned out a film a year, supplementing his film work with irregular variety series on the networks.

Jolson had spoken on the air as early as 1928, but not until November 18, 1932, did he emerge on NBC with his own series. *Presenting Al Jolson* was a Friday-night variety program for Chevrolet, featuring Ted Fiorito and his band. It ran just under four months, but Jolson had returned to the NBC microphones by 1934 as host of the newly created *Kraft Music Hall*. His tenure with that program was equally brief. He shared billing there with Paul Whiteman and his musical revue, leaving *Kraft* to Bing Crosby after less than a year. He was back on the air in 1935 with *Shell Chateau*, a 60-minute Saturday-night NBC variety show.

Jolson's real métier was the stage. He had a natural charisma long before anyone had ever heard of the word. It was an undercurrent, running from performer to audience and back. Jolson loved performing before an audience like nothing else, and it was on stage that he made his greatest impact and enjoyed his greatest popularity.

But throughout his long career, Jolson was a formidable radio personality. He could project a large part of that dynamic, forceful nature over the air in a variety of formats for a variety of sponsors. If part of the personal undercurrent was missing, that may have been the fault of the medium. But with *Shell Chateau*, his radio took on extravaganza proportions. Jolson was billed as singer, comedian, and interviewer, trotting out such big stars as Lionel Barrymore, Ginger Rogers, Bette Davis, and Joe Penner. The new show, directed by Cal Kuhl, offered skits, playlets, and sports talks with such figures as "Slapsie" Maxie Rosenbloom.

The opening was boistrous as only Jolson could make it. Introduced calmly by an announcer offstage, the scene was shifted to Jolson "in Shell Chateau" for a musical welcome in his best style:

Gol-den Gate,
We're comin' through ya;
Shell Cha-teau,
Sez welcome to ya;
Each Saturday night
The stars you all know
Will shine at Shell Cha-teau!
We'll greet all you folks,
You sons and daughters;
That good old oil
For troubled waters.
Going strong now,
Won't be long now;
This is Al
In Shell Cha-teau!

There followed a few moments of opening banter with Jolson giving a bill o' fare and telling a few horrible jokes, generally at the expense of maestro Victor Young.

Shell Chateau was better than most of the big variety shows of that era—until Jolson left. Shell tried to keep it going with a series of less dynamic hosts, including Wallace Beery, but the show lost out in the ratings wars, indicating that Jolson's personality had been its greatest single attraction.

Jolson moved to CBS in 1936 for *The Lifebuoy Program*. Vastly inferior to *Shell Chateau*, *Lifebuoy* still gained a major share of the Tuesday-night audience. Martha Raye appeared regularly with Jolson. Both were musically fit, but the comedy was bad even by 1938 standards. The man responsible for much of the comic carnage was Harry Einstein, who had appeared with Eddie Cantor as an idiot named Parkyakarkus, and now burdened Jolson's show with dialect disaster as well. Again, Jolson carried it. *Lifebuoy* trickled off the air in 1939, just when ratings had begun to slip.

Jolson had another brief radio run in 1942–43, with a CBS Tuesday show for Colgate, produced by Bill Bacher and scored by Gordon Jenkins. Monty Wooley broke into radio on this show, and soon had equal billing at Jolson's insistence. By 1943, Jolson's career had begun to wane. Woolley had left the series, which was soon canceled anyway. Jolson began doing the guest circuit, appearing with George Burns and Gracie Allen, on Crosby's *Kraft Music Hall* and in other top-rated shows. In 1946, his career took another dramatic upward turn with the filming of *The Jolson Story*. Larry Parks played the young Jolson, but Jolson's voice was dubbed into the soundtrack, making "Mammy" famous all over again. The huge success of *The Jolson Story* led to guest appearances on every network. Once, asked by Crosby why he didn't settle down with a show of his own, Jolson replied, "What, and only be on once a week?" His last regular radio job was as master of ceremonies of *The Kraft Music Hall*, then an NBC Thursday-night feature. He got it when Crosby left Kraft in a dispute over transcribing his programs. Again, Jolson was a hot property. He had come full-circle back to the *Music Hall* he had left thirteen years before. Jolson held that job from 1947 through 1949.

The Jolson Story led to a sequel, *Jolson Sings Again*. Both stories were dramatized on *The Lux Radio Theatre*, with Jolson starring as himself. He died, still on top of it all, on October 23, 1950.

The Sheriff

The Sheriff came to ABC in 1945, when the sponsor of the long-running *Death Valley Days* gave up that show for a more modern view of the West. Originally called *Death Valley Sheriff*, it was sponsored by Pacific Borax, and brought to the air Sheriff Mark Chase, who had all the tools of modern criminology at his fingertips. Gone were chases on horseback; this sheriff patrolled his territory in a new car. And his flawless use of the language followed *The Lone Ranger* model. The one old-fashioned fly in the sheriff's ointment was his housekeeper, Cassandra Drinkwater, known everywhere as "Cousin Cassie." Cassie's first love was spreading gossip; her sworn duty (she thought) was protecting Sheriff Chase against the advances of anxious females. Chase, a former Marine who had come to California's Canyon County and become its sheriff, was played by Robert Haag and later by Don Briggs. In rather an odd bit of casting, Cousin Cassie was played by Olyn Landrick, a man who specialized in female impersonations. Landrick had been entertaining as a woman since his Navy days in World War I. The Sheriff was heard on Friday nights (with a final fling on Saturdays) for Borax throughout its six-year run. It left the air in 1951. For the entire run it continued the "morning bugle call" of the old wagon trains that had opened Death Valley Days throughout the 1930's.

Sherlock Holmes

Sherlock Holmes, the story of the world's most famous detective, came to radio October 20, 1930, as a Monday-night NBC thriller for George Washington Coffee. The remarkable hero of Sir Arthur Conan Doyle's classics of deduction was well-suited to radio drama, and no character enjoyed greater exposure at the hands of more artists. It seemed that almost everyone wanted to try Holmes; many got the chance. Holmes had the distinction of being the most revived major character of the airwaves. The character was good for several revivals on various networks, with many actors playing the lead. A breakdown:

1930–31 Holmes: William Gillette, later Clive Brooks. Watson: Leigh Lovell (through 1935)

1931–35 Holmes: Richard Gordon. Sponsorship continued under G. Washington Coffee. Show heard on NBC Blue Wednesdays until 1933, then Sundays.

1935–36 Holmes: Louis Hector. Watson: Harold West. Series heard on NBC Blue Sundays through May 1935. Moved to Mutual for Household Finance Saturday night in February 1936.

1936 Holmes: Richard Gordon. Watson: Harold West. Series continued as a Saturday-night Mutual show until October 1936, when it returned to NBC Blue as a Thursday-night sustainer. This early run ended December 24, 1936, and Sherlock Holmes disappeared from the air for three years.

1939–46 Holmes: Basil Rathbone. Watson: Nigel Bruce. The best-remembered Holmes of the air, this one premièred on the Blue October 2, 1939. Sponsored initially by Bromo Quinine, it was a Monday-night show. In September 1940 it moved to Sundays. It went to Mutual as a Friday-nighter for Petri Wine on May 7, 1943. On October 4, 1943, it moved again to Mondays, where it remained until May 27, 1946, the end of the run.

1946–47   Holmes: Tom Conway. Watson: Nigel Bruce. The Semler Company sponsored this version, which ran Saturdays on ABC, then moved to Mondays in January 1947.

1947–49   Holmes: John Stanley. Watson: Alfred Shirley, Ian Martin, George Stelden. A Mutual series, this was heard Sunday nights until January 1949, when it moved to Mondays. Sponsor: Trimount Clothing.

1949–50   Holmes: Ben Wright. Watson: Eric Snowden. This series began on ABC for Petri Wine September 21, 1949, and was heard Wednesdays. It ended March 8, 1950.

1955   NBC carried a sustaining Sherlock Holmes from January 2 through June 5, Sundays. This one was produced for the BBC in London; it starred Sir John Gielgud as Holmes and Ralph Richardson as Watson. Orson Welles played Moriarty, Holmes' arch-enemy.

The wheels for a Sherlock Holmes of the air began turning in 1929. Edith Meiser, a young actress turned radio writer, was doggedly trying to sell the networks on a series built around Conan Doyle's forty-year-old mastermind, but radio drama was then in its earliest development and no one would try it. In 1930, she finally persuaded NBC to take on a series she had adapted from the original stories. From then until the final days of network radio, Holmes was never off the air for more than three consecutive years.

Although the shows varied greatly in casting and production, the formats didn't stray far from that suggested so well by the Conan Doyle writings and established by Miss Meiser in that first run. Holmes' trusted assistant, Dr. Watson, always told the stories, answering questions put to him by staff announcers before and after the drama. In the early shows, Watson invited announcer Joseph Bell into his study, where there was usually "a blazing fire and a cup of George Washington Coffee" to ward off the cold. Watson (Leigh Lovell) then joined Bell in plugging the product with zesty "aaaahhhhs," frequently challenging Bell to find a better cup of coffee anywhere. Miss Meiser's scripts, especially the early ones, followed Conan Doyle carefully. She wrote at home, accompanied only by her Scotch terrier Doctor Watson, beginning with the short stories, then expanding into multi-part offerings of the novels. When the series outlasted the original material, she wrote new stories, using some incident from the master as a jumping-off point.

She wrote for Holmes through the late 1940's, tying together the isolated early runs with the consistency of her scripting. Many of her early scripts were redone in later runs. By the time announcer Knox Manning was interviewing a new Watson in 1939, the commercial plugs were gone from the story line, though the cheerful blaze was still crackling on the hearth.

The new Watson was of course Nigel Bruce, whose success with Basil Rathbone in the Sherlock Holmes films had prompted the return to the air. Rathbone, probably the best Holmes, is certainly best identified with the role. He was delightful as he reconstructed entire scenes with tiny scraps of detail, perused Watson's bewilderment with quiet mirth and stated, quite calmly, "Elementary, old chap, elementary!"

As in the movies, Watson was something of a disappointment. In the mass media he never approached Conan Doyle's intent—a man of high intelligence whose brain seemed small only in comparison with Holmes' deductive genius. The significance of the fragmentary clues were rightly overlooked by Watson and listeners alike. And when some listeners began complaining that the clues were too obscure, the producers had a problem. The try-to-guess-it crowd wanted an even chance with Holmes at solving the crime, and that could never have happened without reducing Watson (and the series) to Mike Clancy status.

But the films were hot, and the radio rating through the Rathbone-Bruce years hovered around 10. In 1943, with Owen Babbe doing the announcing, Edith Meiser was assisted in scripting by Leslie Charteris, author of The Saint, who did his Holmes work under the name Bruce Taylor. By 1945, Harry Bartell was interviewing Watson, and the bulk of the writing was done by the team of Denis Green and Anthony Boucher. Rathbone left the show in 1946 for an ill-advised fling at a silly series called Tales of Fatima, and new actors and writers worked in new Holmes runs. Max Ehrlich, Howard Merrill, and Leonard Lee wrote the later shows.

Louis Hector, who enjoyed a brief run as Holmes in 1935, played arch-rival Moriarty through most of the run. Orson Welles had that part in the BBC-produced series that ran on NBC in 1955. In the radio shows, far more than in the books, Moriarty became the all-evil enemy, the super-villain whose death clash with Holmes at Reichenbach Falls still fascinates Holmes buffs. But even after seventy years, the character of Holmes is what really turns the trick. He was truly a hero of the mind, a man who had no truck with invaders of unrefined concentration, including women. In the end, that was what pushed those weekly visits to fog-shrouded Baker Street among the high points of radio.

Shorty Bell

Shorty Bell came to CBS in the spring of 1948 as an audio vehicle for Mickey Rooney. Rooney fit the title role in stature and attitude. As Shorty Bell, cub reporter for the Capital City Times, he was always on the hustle for a major scoop that would send him scurrying up the journalistic ladder in his dad's footsteps. Shorty's dad was John Marshall Bell, once a great name in Capital City, who had started (just like Shorty) as a cub reporter and ended up as publisher of the whole paper. Shorty's quest for news pitted him against gangsters and hoods and, while each story was complete in 30 minutes, the series had enough loose thriller elements to carry it over to next week as a continuation—but unfortunately, not enough to sustain it on the air. The show was produced by William N. Robson and scripting was by Samuel W. Taylor. Two ex-newsmen, Frederick Hazlitt Brennan and Richard Carroll, were brought in to help write it. That didn't help, and soon Shorty Bell became just another faint echo.

Show Boat

Show Boat, one of the true giants of early radio, premièred on NBC October 6, 1932, and promptly became the nation's top variety hour. Within a year, the Maxwell House Show Boat had surpassed even Rudy Vallee's Fleischmann Hour, attaining an incredible 45-point rating and becoming must listening for Thursday-night dialers everywhere.

Bill Bacher was the first writer. The idea of using a show boat formula for radio had developed from the smash Jerome Kern musical of the late 1920's. Bacher, assigned to work up the continuity, went to Charles Winninger for advice. Winninger was a lifelong trouper; he had worked a real show boat, Captain Adams' Blossom Time, which sailed the Mississippi when the country was young, and later he had played Captain Andy in Ziegfeld's musical. In fact, Winninger proved perfect for the part of Captain Henry. He took the role from the first broadcast, stayed with the show through its first two years of glory, and left in late 1934 when backstage disputes and clashes of personality threatened to run the boat aground.

The format was elaborate and colorful: first the sounds of an excited crowd and a calliope playing; a carnival atmosphere, punctuated by Tiny Ruffner's excited description of the mooring of the boat. Then the chorus: "Here comes the show boat/here comes the show boat/puff-puff-Puff-Puff-PUFFIN'A-LONG!" Then Captain Henry, the genial skipper and host, took the microphone and welcomed listeners with a "Howdy, folks, howdy, howdy." Produced in New York, Show Boat thus gave the listener an illusion of perpetual movement, allegedly mooring at Portland, Maine, one week, Boston the next. Captain Henry gave a few colorful facts about the honor city, and the rest of the 60-minute show was a fast-moving mix of music, comedy and drama.

Winninger became Bacher's chief source of show boat lore. "Most people have the wrong idea about a show boat," he told Radioland in 1934. "It's just a theatre built on a scow. A steamboat hooks on behind with a paddle wheel and acts as the pilot boat. The captain of a show boat in reality knows very little about navigation. He is simply the manager of the theatrical troupe."

That's what Captain Henry was. His troupe included a stable of popular singers, many of whom had professional radio actors do their speaking parts. Top musical and comedic headliners from Bob Hope to Jessica Dragonette were brought to the Show Boat stage on a guest-star basis. The cast parodied Romeo and Juliet; they offered a light operatic treatment of The Red Mill, with Dragonette in the starring role; they sang the popular songs of the time and offered backstage dramatic sketches, further playing on the show boat theme. Irene Hubbard was featured as Captain Henry's sister Maria; Wright Kramer was her husband Water Jamison; Mark Smith was Uria Calwalder, and Pick Malone and Pat Padgett were Molasses and January.

Others included Conrad Thibault (Ned Wever handled his speaking lines for a time), Annette Hanshaw (who, in the opinion of Radio Stars Magazine, spoke "shyly for herself"), Jean Sothern, Jules Bledsoe, Winifred Cecil, and Louise Massey and the Westernaires. Music was by Donald Voorhees and Al Goodman and later by Gus Haenschen.

Early in the run, Lanny Ross was propelled to stardom by virtue of his boyish good looks and clear tenor voice. When Show Boat began, Ross was just another member of the cast; by the end of the first year, he was one of the sensations of radio and a prime factor behind that 45-point rating. Listeners speculated on Ross' real-life relationship with Mary Lou, the sweet young singer with whom he had so many duets and backstage dialogues. In reality, Mary Lou was a composite of many voices, with Rosaline Greene doing the speaking and Muriel Wilson handling the singing in the early days. With Miss Wilson's departure early in 1934, many young singers were tried on the air in the role, including Lois Bennett. Even Lanny Ross had two voices; for the first year Allyn Joslyn handled Ross' speaking lines. Ross began doing his own lines around 1934, when he moved to Hollywood for a brief film career and handled his *Show Boat* role in back-and-forth remotes between New York and California.

When differences of opinion with *Show Boat* producers culminated in Winninger's resignation, Ross became the most important man on the program, and probably saved it from going under then and there. Frank McIntire was signed as the new Captain Henry, but following an act as popular as Winninger's wasn't easy. He was criticized, probably unfairly, for his different approach to the part. By 1937 he too had walked the plank. It was obvious that *Show Boat* was foundering. The show had no sense of stability; scores of actors and singers were auditioned, used briefly, and discharged. Three-quarters of the audience had gone elsewhere. In a final gesture of confusion, Ross was yanked out of the cast and plopped down in a master of ceremonies role, which put him in the uncomfortable position of introducing his own songs. In the summer of 1937, Ross too announced his intention to quit.

There was talk of moving *Show Boat* to Hollywood, where Winninger had settled, and revamping it in the original format. Instead, Maxwell House dropped the show and settled on an even more elaborate, super-colossal filmland extravaganza, *Good News of 1938*. In a different way, *Good News* merely continued the confusion. Ultimately, Maxwell House chose the very simple Fanny Brice–Frank Morgan show. But the *Show Boat* formula remained a memorable one, and in 1940 NBC tried out a new version with Hugh Studebaker as Captain Barney, songs by Virginia Verrill and Dick Todd, and comedy routines by Marlin Hurt as Beulah.

The Silver Eagle

The Silver Eagle delighted kids of the early 1950's, bringing the untamed Northwest into living rooms twice a week just after suppertime. It premièred from Chicago July 5, 1951, with Jim Ameche starred as Jim West, the famed Silver Eagle whose eagle-feather arrow was his trademark. Sponsored by General Mills, *Silver Eagle* was cast in the *Sergeant Preston* mold, produced by James Jewell (longtime associate of *Preston* producer George W. Trendle) and is generally considered the last of the great juvenile shows. Like Preston, the Silver Eagle was a persistent tracker of criminals and lawbreakers. Widely known for never giving up on a case, Jim West was assisted by a giant sidekick, Joe Bideaux, who helped carry the show. To the vivid 10-year-old mind, Joe Bideaux was an unwashed Superman, a towering Canadian of French ancestry who ate three steaks at a sitting, who could batter down doors with his fists and crush a man's neck between his fingers. Joe slurred his words in realistic bursts of dialogue, mixing "sacre bleu" and "sonobagun" in the same sentence and constantly referring to West as "mon ami." Keeping with the image, Jack Lester, who played the role, was billed as "Jacques Lestair." The part was also played by Michael Romano. Bill O'Connor announced and narrated the stories. The series ran on ABC until March 10, 1955, opening to the howling wolves and winds of the wild north:

> A cry of the wild . . . a trail of danger . . . a scarlet rider of the Northwest Mounted, serving justice with the swiftness of an arrow . . . *The Silver Eagle!*

The Silver Theatre

The Silver Theatre came to CBS October 3, 1937, as a Sunday-afternoon series of "prestige drama." Thirty minutes long, the show, first billed as *Sunday Afternoon Theatre*, was sponsored by International Silver and featured Conrad Nagel—a movie star whose roots ran deep into the silent era—as host and director. *The Silver Theatre* offered heavy drama and comedy, serving as a springboard for newcomers while also using such top stars as James Stewart, Brian Donlevy, Olivia De Havilland, Loretta Young, Douglas Fairbanks, Jr., and Joan Crawford. Many of the scripts were written by True Boardman. After six years as a regular series, *The Silver Theatre* was reduced to summer status in 1945. In 1946, it was the vacation replacement for *Ozzie and Harriet*. Nagel was host through 1942, when he left Hollywood to do a New York play. John Loder was his replacement. Nagel returned to Hollywood and to *Silver Theatre* in 1945.

Singin' Sam

Singin' Sam was the popular name of Harry Frankel, who pounded the boards as a minstrel in the 1920's, turned to radio in 1930, and became nationally famous as a balladeer. Sam championed the old songs; he often stated that he had never introduced a new song in all his years on the air. His favorites came from "yesteryear," from the Gay Nineties through the Roaring Twenties. He plugged such favorites as "Darktown Strutter's Ball" and "Every Cloud Must Have a Silver Lining," carrying most of the 15-minute show alone. Sam's first show in 1930, for Barbasol on CBS, lasted until 1936, then went to the Blue for the 1937 season. He returned in 1941 with a syndicated show for Coca-Cola. By 1943, he had more than 170 independent stations and an income of $175,000 a year. The show was transcribed in New York, where he commuted by plane twice a month from his farm near Richmond, Indiana. In 1942, James Caesar Petrillo, head of the musicians' union, banned transcribed music. Coke—rather than go live —canceled the show. Sam rejoined Barbasol for a season on Mutual in 1943. He began another series of syndicated shows, *Reminiscin' with Singin' Sam*, in 1945. Singin' Sam died June 13, 1948.

The Singing Story Lady

The Singing Story Lady was first heard nationally on NBC Blue, January 11, 1932, in a story-song children's format for Kellogg cereals. Ireene Wicker, its star, writer, and producer, had originated the show on WGN Chicago about six months earlier. Miss Wicker told stories ranging from fairy tales to true skits about such people as Lily Pons. She used her natural voice as narrator, slipping into dialect and mood as she portrayed the voices of her characters. The stories were peppered throughout with songs. For a time her theme song, done in her natural voice, went like this:

    Chil-dren, you who wish to hear
    Songs and sto-ries, come draw near;
    Both young and old come hand-in-hand,
    And we'll be off to story-land.
    For sto-ries true from his-to-ry,
    And fairy tales and mys-ter-y;
    So come along on wings of song,
    Oh, come to story-land with me.

Miss Wicker came into radio with her first husband Walter, who was then writing, producing, and acting for the medium. She joined CBS in 1930, and about that time began her extensive collection of children's story reference books, which later formed the basis of her *Singing Lady* tales. Just before entering radio, she added the extra "e" to her first name on the advice of a numerologist, who told her the change would bring her great fortune. She went to NBC later in 1930, playing a variety of roles in straight radio dramas. Her own show was highly successful for two decades, winning almost every major award in the field. In 1937, she was doing four shows a week for NBC Blue and a 30-minute Sunday show on Mutual. She was especially popular with mothers, who waged a constant war against the blood and thunder of most juvenile fare. Her popularity with children was legendary. "I loved being a child myself," she told *Radio Stars* magazine in 1937. "I never wanted to grow up. That gives me a kinship with other children too."

The Six Shooter

The Six Shooter brought James Stewart to the NBC microphone on September 20, 1953, in a fine series of folksy Western adventures. Stewart was never better on the air than in this drama of Britt Ponset, frontier drifter created by Frank Burt. The epigraph set it up nicely: "The man in the saddle is angular and long-legged; his skin is sun-dyed brown. The gun in his holster is gray steel and rainbow mother-of-pearl. People call them both The Six Shooter." Ponset was a wanderer, an easy-going gentleman and—when he had to be—a gun-fighter. Stewart was right in character as the slow-talking maverick who usually blundered into other people's troubles and sometimes shot his way out. His experiences were broad, but *The Six Shooter* leaned more to comedy than other shows of its kind. Ponset took time out to play *Hamlet* with a crude road company. He ran for mayor *and* sheriff of the same town at the same time. He became involved in a delightful Western version of *Cinderella*, complete with grouchy stepmother, ugly sisters, and a shoe that didn't fit. And at Christmas he told a young runaway the story of *A Christmas Carol*, substituting the original Dickens characters with Western heavies. Britt even had time to fall in love, but it was the age-old story of people from different worlds, and the romance was foredoomed despite their valiant efforts to save it. So we got a cowboy-into-the-sunset ending for this series, truly one of the bright spots of radio. Unfortunately, it came too late, and lasted only one season. It was a transcribed show, sustained by NBC and directed by Jack Johnstone. Basil Adlam provided the music and Frank Burt wrote the scripts. Hal Gibney announced.

The Skippy Hollywood Theatre

The Skippy Hollywood Theatre was one of radio's most successful syndicated shows, beginning production in 1941 in the Hollywood studios of transcription tycoon C. P. MacGregor. MacGregor had been producing shows on disc since 1929, but throughout the early years there was widespread prejudice against "canned" entertainment. MacGregor used his most logical argument against the opposition: he believed that only a transcription enabled him to produce a flawless show. Stars could simply retake if a first effort wasn't up to par. For his *Skippy Hollywood Theatre*, he lined up top film stars, cast them in original dramas, and emerged with professional shows that equaled most live network offerings. He also lined up Skippy Peanut Butter as sponsor, and syndicated the series as a complete-with-commercials package to stations around the country. The show boosted Skippy from obscurity into a national product. The show's format was patterned after the great success of *The Lux Radio Theatre*—MacGregor was host, and after each play he interviewed his stars à la DeMille. The guests usually got in a plug for the product and everybody went home happy. Joan Bennett, Herbert Marshall, Anita Louise, Paulette Goddard, Jane Withers, Vincent Price, and Dana Andrews were a few of MacGregor's *Skippy* stars. The scripts were by True Boardman; Les Mitchel was director in the later run, with Budd Lesser serving as story editor; music was by Mahlon Merrick and later Del Castillo. The show was still going strong in 1950.

Sky Blazers

Sky Blazers premièred on CBS December 9, 1939, as a tribute to the glory of aviation. Each week producer-writer Phillips H. Lord offered a dramatization of some dramatic flight from the early days of the flying orange crates to the modern craft of prewar America. The show was hosted and narrated by Colonel Roscoe Turner, himself a World War I pilot, holder of many transcontinental speed records, and former operator of a flight school and flying circus. After each show, Turner interviewed the daredevil on whom the story was based. Sponsored by the Continental Baking Company, the series ran Saturday nights and lasted one season.

Sky King

Sky King featured "America's favorite flying cowboy," and first came zooming down through the 1946 ABC skies in his plane *The Songbird* for a quarter-hour of daily serialized action. The sustained serial version premiering October 28, 1946, didn't last long; by 1947 it had moved into a Tuesday-and-Thursday 30-minute, complete-in-each-episode format for Peter Pan Peanut Butter. Sky, played originally by Roy Engel and later by Earl Nightingale, flew into adventure from his Arizona ranch, usually accompanied by his young sidekicks Penny and Clipper. The plane took them to such remote, exotic locales as

France and South America, but many of the Sky King adventures were also set nearer home, in the modern American West. Beryl Vaughn played Penny, Jack Bivens was Clipper, and the announcer was Mike Wallace. Peter Pan stayed with Sky King through a network change in 1950. The show was heard for its last four years on Mutual, and ended in 1954. Sky King was also one of the successful transplants to early TV.

Smile Parade

Smile Parade was another Ransom Sherman effort, heard on NBC from Chicago in 1938–39. It was a Friday-morning series of music and talk, with Sherman handling interviews and monologues in his usual wacky style. He was backed by singers Fran Allison and Wayne Van Dine, the Our Serenaders quartet (Gale Watts, Gunther Decker, Earl Wilkie, and Burton Dole), and the music of Rex Maupin's orchestra.

Smilin' Ed's Buster Brown Gang

Smilin' Ed's Buster Brown Gang starred a gravel-voiced singer of sorts whose Saturday-morning Buster Brown Gang was must listening for kids 5 to 12. Using a cast of fantasy characters and a wildly cheering studio audience of children, Smilin' Ed McConnell worked his way into homes and hearts everywhere with an NBC show that began in 1944 and ran for eight years.

As a radio entertainer, Smilin' Ed went back a long way. A veteran of early vaudeville and the Chautauqua circuit, he first appeared on the air May 30, 1922, and soon became established locally as a one-man theatre of entertainment. Sometimes in those very early days, McConnell would entertain for hours on end with songs and a plunking banjo. Most of his early work was done off the cuff, without benefit of writers or any advance preparation. He went network in 1932, and by 1933 had become associated with longtime sponsor Acme Paint, which carried his 15-minute songfest on CBS through the mid-1930's. He was still doing an Acme show in 1940, then on Saturday morning NBC. At the same time, he had another show running daily on CBS for Taystee Bread.

Meanwhile, Buster Brown had been on radio as early as 1929 as a weekly CBS drama based on the Buster Brown comic strips. Buster was the boy who lived in a shoe; he came with dog Tige, who lived in there too. With the merging of Smilin' Ed and Buster Brown in 1944, a new kind of kiddie variety show began to take shape. McConnell told real, lusty stories of life on the frontier, in the jungles, and in the merry days of Robin Hood. The tales, complete in 15 minutes, were fully dramatized with music and sound effects, and were performed by a company that included Lou Merrill, June Foray, Joe Fields, Ken Christy, Wendell Noble, Tommy Cook, Conrad Binyon, and Tommy Bernard. Sound effects were by Bud Tollefson and Jack Robinson.

In addition, McConnell read letters from kiddies (many were submitted as "Brown Jug Jingles") and chatted away with his imaginary cast. The cast included Squeaky the Mouse, Midnight the Cat, Grandie the Piano, and Froggy the Gremlin. John Duffy provided organ music, and Ken Cameron was at the piano. One of the distinctive features of this show was the plunking of the piano (which, after all, was supposed to be a living creature) to each word emphasized by Smilin' Ed.

Froggy the Gremlin became the star. Supposedly an invisible imp whose "magic twanger" could bring him into view, Froggy delighted in badgering such "regular guests" as Algernon Archibald Percival Sharpfellow the poet, or Mr. Gymnasium the athletic instructor, or Alkali Pete the cowboy. The "guests" were always long-winded sorts who became tongue-tied at Froggy's incessant taunting, finally exploding and running offstage to the delight of the kids. Smilin' Ed's voice was ideal for the Froggy impersonation, though announcer Archie Presby doubled whenever Ed and Froggy sang a duet. Froggy's character was built on repetition: "Now I'll sing my song, I will, I will."

The show was produced by Frank Ferrin and directed by Hobart Donovan. It was a happy piece of juvenile radio, from the opening bar of Smilin' Ed's song:

I got shoes, you got shoes,
Why, everybody's got to have shoes!
And there's only one kind of shoes for me,
Good ole Buster Brown Shoes!

to the final thump of Grandie the Piano.

Smilin' Jack

Smilin' Jack was Jack Martin, the daredevil pilot of the Zack Mosley comic strip. Jack came to Mutual as a three-a-week serial for Tootsie Rolls on February 13, 1939. Despite a plot that was full of action and centered in the faraway places of the world, it never was big-time matinée drama and disappeared May 19, 1939.

Snow Village Sketches

Snow Village Sketches evolved from an early network show, Soconyland Sketches, sponsored by Socony Oil on NBC Tuesday nights between 1928 and 1930 and turning up under various names through the 1930's. It was a low-key comedy of life in rural New Hampshire, in a mythical town called Snow Village. All the various shows used the same basic characterizations and the same stars. A show called Snow Village was heard Saturday nights on NBC in 1936; another version showed up in 1943; still another ran on Mutual in 1946. It was a show that just wouldn't stay still. The 1946 version (like the others) starred Arthur Allen as Dan'l Dickey and Parker Fennelly as Hiram Neville. They played New England farmers who doubled as game warden and truant officer, respectively. Kate McComb played Dan'l's wife Hattie and Sarah Fussell, whose specialty was playing little boys, was young Herbie Pettingill. It was written by William Ford Manley and directed by Harold McGee.

Somebody Knows

Somebody Knows addressed itself to real-life murderers, and became another intriguing idea that never outgrew its summer status. It was based on a program originated at the Chicago Sun Times, and still in use by some newspapers. The idea was that no murder is ever perfect: "You out there, you who think you have committed the perfect crime, that there are no clues, no witnesses, listen—somebody knows!" The gimmick was to persuade someone to come forward with evidence leading to the arrest and conviction of the culprit. A $5,000 reward was offered by CBS for such information. Clues were to be submitted on plain sheets of paper, but in place of his signature, the tipster could put six numbers on the page, rip off the corner in a jagged tear, and write the same six numbers on his piece. After conviction, the bearer of the matching paper could walk out of CBS with $5,000, no questions asked. The show premièred July 6, 1950, as a replacement for Suspense, and left the air August 24 when the regular lineup was reinstated for the fall. The cases were fully dramatized and were narrated by Jack Johnstone, who also served as director. It was a James L. Saphier production, Frank Goss was the announcer and Sidney Marshall was writer. The last case dramatized was the brutal January 15, 1947, murder-mutilation of Elizabeth Short, known to police as

"The Black Dahlia." A quarter of a century later, police still hadn't found her killer. But if that "somebody" who knows is you, forget it. The date for submissions expired midnight September 13, 1950.

A Song Is Born

A Song Is Born was developed around 1934 by radio musician Richard Aurandt. But the show itself didn't get off the ground until February 21, 1944, when NBC and Langendorf Bread decided to give it a try. Each week, four composers were invited to sing their works, or have them sung by staffers Pat Kaye or Ronny Mansfield. Three of the composers were completely unknown—literally unsung amateurs who had never had a chance at network exposure. The fourth composer was a professional. After the song was performed, the story behind the song was told. Some of the stories were dramatized; others were just told straightaway. The composers got $25 in war bonds; the listeners got music and a story.

Space Patrol

Space Patrol was a latecomer to radio, but is fondly remembered by children of the 1950–55 era, when this 30-minute adventure of the future ran on ABC. It followed the universe-jumping exploits of Buzz Corey, commander-in-chief of the Space Patrol, and his unending quest to bring law and order to vast interplanetary space. Corey's companion on these missions was Cadet Happy, played by Lyn Osborn, whose strongest expression of emotion was "Smokin' rockets!" For a time the arch-enemy of the Space Patrol was Dr. Ryland Scarno, master criminal. The series was heard twice a week, sustained in 1950–51. Then it moved to Saturdays for a four-year run, sponsored by Ralston in 1951–54 and by Nestlés Chocolate in 1954–55. It was also seen on TV in the early 1950s. Ed Kemmer played Buzz, and the show was produced and directed by Larry Robertson. The opening was done to a singing, marching theme, and a shouting description right out of Mark Trail:

> High adventure in the wild, vast reaches of space!
> Missions of daring in the name of interplanetary justice!
> Travel into the future with Buzz Corey, commander-in-chief of the Space Patrol!

The Sparrow and the Hawk

The Sparrow and the Hawk was a well-produced CBS juvenile serial running from May 14, 1945, into 1946. Concentrating as much on character as plot, the series followed the adventures of a fictitious juvenile pilot named Barney Mallory. Sixteen-year-old Barney was called the Sparrow by his friends, a mark of admiration for his flying ability and for his relationship to the famous pilot, Colonel Spencer Mallory, formerly of the Army Air Corps. The colonel was Barney's uncle, known as the Hawk. Together they wove "a story of modern adventure, high in the sky, wherever planes can go." Don Buka and Michael Fitzmaurice were featured as the Sparrow and the Hawk; scripting was by Carl A. Buss, and Tony Marvin was announcer.

Speed Gibson of the International Secret Police

Speed Gibson of the International Secret Police was one of the corniest, most outrageously enjoyable serials of the 1930's. Now dated to the pinnacle of high camp, it followed Speed Gibson, ace 15-year-old flier, on the worldwide trail of yet another master criminal. Originally syndicated in 1937, Speed and his International Policemen hotly pursued the Octopus, enemy of all mankind, through Africa and the Orient. Speed's membership in the International Secret Police was secured by crack agent Clint Barlow, who just happened to be Speed's uncle. With their semi-comical, partially literate pilot Barney Dunlap, Speed and Clint utilized the latest miracles of the day (including shortwave radio) to track down the Octopus gang. Their airship, *The Flying Clipper*, took them to China, Tibet, and the Far East in the long quest. The opening contained the drone of an aircraft and the urgent voice of an air trafficker: "Ceiling zero! Ceiling zero! Ceiling zero!" The catch-phrase of the year-long serial was Barney's "Suffering whang-doodles."

The Spike Jones Show

The Spike Jones Show featured a delightfully insane band that played with cowbells, foghorns, and kitchen utensils. It roared into CBS on October 3, 1947, with a half-hour *Spotlight Revue* Friday nights for Coca-Cola. Music was never the same again. Spike and his City Slickers—including such memorable characters as Doodles Weaver,

Professor Frederick Gass, brothers Dick and Freddie Morgan, Horatio Q. Birdbath, and George Rock—clanged, hissed, hooted, and chugged their way through radio's greatest instrumental satire show, complete with long-suffering guest stars and Spike's "weekly musical round-table discussion."

For more than a dozen years, Jones had been one of the unsung musicians of Radio Row, serving as a drummer for many of the big-name bands of the air. Born Lindley Armstrong Jones, he took the name Spike from the railroad tracks where his father worked as a station agent. Jones started on drums when he was still in grammar school; he graduated to semi-pro dance bands even before high school, and emerged in the mid-1930's as an accomplished musician capable of playing with the best.

His first radio exposure came in Long Beach, when he organized a band of local kids and called it Spike and His Five Tacks. By 1938, he had joined Victor Young's orchestra and was playing for a nationwide radio audience. He went on to play in some of radio's top-rated shows—with Oscar Bradley on *The Screen Guild Theatre*, with Henry King on *Burns and Allen*, with Cookie Fairchild on *The Eddie Cantor Show*, with John Scott Trotter on Bing Crosby's *Kraft Music Hall*, and with Billy Mills on *Fibber McGee and Molly*. Jones was a man of great experience, but for several years he remained an unknown, one of the faceless, nameless men behind the scenes.

Most musicians never break out of that box, but Jones was different. By 1940, he had organized a band of musical satirists called the City Slickers. On weekends and at night, they got together and murdered the classics just for the hell of it. The early members were Don Anderson, John Stanley, Luther Roundtree, Country Washburn, Frank Leithner, Del Porter, Carl Grayson, and Willie Spicer. The group first appeared on the air in, of all things, a 1941 episode of *Point Sublime*, a situation comedy then airing only on a regional network. But their biggest break came in 1942, when they cut a novelty number called "Der Fuehrer's Face," a spoof of Hitler's antics that was due for release in a Walt Disney movie.

Jones' recording actually hit radio stations before the film's release, and soon it became a nationwide smash. He was signed for a regular stint on *The Bob Burns Show*, and appeared briefly in his own 1942 NBC radio shot. There were movies and more novelty recordings, and then Jones took the City Slickers on the road for the first of what would become regular "musical depreciation revues." New musical instruments began to creep into the language: the "annilaphone," the "anvilphone," finally, the "latrinophone," a toilet seat with strings.

Spotlight Revue, his best show, opened in 1947 and ran two years on CBS. The last year, it was called *The Spike Jones Show,* and was often done on the road, wherever the "Musical Depreciation Revue" was playing. Dorothy Shay (the Park Avenue hillbilly) was a regular in the first year; Michael Roy announced. Joe Bigelow was producer, and the routines were written by Jay Sommers.

The format was fairly rigid. Spike and the band opened with some zany ragtime or Dixieland number ("Charlie My Boy" was a favorite), then Jones shouted his standard greeting. His "Thank you, music lovers" never failed to draw a laugh. Then there would be a daft "round-table discussion" among band members and guest artists. People like Buddy Clark, Frankie Laine, Diana Lynn, and Don Ameche appeared with Spike; once Basil Rathbone joined the madness for a spoof of *Peter and the Wolf.* More music and a skit—often an operetta with soprano Eileen Gallagher—followed. Jones was best known for spoofing the classics, but he also took apart such moderns as Cole Porter and Rodgers and Hammerstein.

Despite their self-promoted image as musical incompetents, the City Slickers were all first-rate musicians. Their act was perfected through long rehearsals; Jones, who also conducted a "straight" band for the Frances Langford summer series in 1945, found his novelty act much tougher to pull off. But the result was one of radio's bright spots, a show that was completely original. It ended in June 1949. Jones remained popular through the 1950's, and died in 1965.

Spotlight Bands

Spotlight Bands was first heard on Mutual November 3, 1941, as a 15-minute nightly show for Coca-Cola. Its full name then was *The Victory Parade of Spotlight Bands,* and the idea was to take the best-loved bands in America to the scenes of wartime domestic activity. Each night the show traveled to a new location, appearing in camps, hospitals, and in plants and factories where war production was high. A different band was featured each night, and the most popular band in the nation (as determined by record sales) was invited to appear in the coveted Saturday-night slot. The first five shows featured Kay Kyser, Guy Lombardo, Sammy Kaye, Tommy Dorsey, and Eddie Duchin. The show was dropped after the 1941–42 season, but was revived in the fall on the Blue Network. In 1943 the Saturday show was eliminated, and *Spotlight Bands* ran as a five-a-week 30-minute show. It was dropped from the Blue in 1945, and went to Mutual three times a week for a final season in 1945–46.

Stagedoor Canteen

Stagedoor Canteen evolved from a live production created for servicemen at a theatre near Times Square. It was one of those very
special wartime shows that couldn't have been done in any other era.
The original Stagedoor Canteen was formed by the American Theatre
Wing, an organization of entertainers from every field. Each week the
group offered live entertainment to some 500 servicemen, and soon
became so popular that additional "canteens" were set up in remote
locations. At the New York Canteen, celebrities ad infinitum donated
their time to the entertaining, and many pulled KP duty as well. "It is
nothing to see Alfred Lunt emptying garbage pails, or Lynn Fontanne
presiding at the coffee pot," Radio Life wrote in 1942. "The waiters
and busboys are just as famous, with people like Brock Pemberton or
Ed Wynn scurrying around emptying ash trays or filling up coffee
cups for hungry men."

With that much talent floating around, it was only a matter of time
till radio grabbed the idea. That happened in 1942 when Helen Menken of American Theatre Wing proposed a series and Corn Products
Refining Company bought it. The show opened on CBS July 30 as a
Thursday-night variety entry, moved to Fridays in 1943, and ran for
most of the war's duration. Jane Froman, Orson Welles, Wendell
Willkie, Madeleine Carroll, Connie Boswell, Mary Martin, Rodgers
and Hammerstein, Helen Hayes, Merle Oberon, and George Burns and
Gracie Allen were a few who appeared. Bert Lytell was master of
ceremonies, opening the show with, "Curtain going up for victory!"
Raymond Paige provided the music, and the show was directed by
Earle McGill. It was actually broadcast from CBS, but the producers
strived for an authentic "at the canteen" format. The cast, decked out
in red, white, and blue, closed each broadcast with the singing of the
National Anthem.

The Stan Freberg Show

The Stan Freberg Show never really had a chance on radio,
premièring far, far too late on CBS July 14, 1957. It never was able to
attract a sponsor, exiting just fifteen weeks later. Too bad, because
Freberg was essentially a radio man, a shrewd, modern satirist who
thoroughly understood the possibilities of the medium. The sad thing

about *The Stan Freberg Show* is that it didn't happen ten years earlier, though then Freberg's comedy would have been ahead of its time and might have flopped anyway. Freberg had appeared in a starring role on the 1953 CBS comedy series *That's Rich*, playing a star-struck young man named Rich who came to Hollywood to break into the movies. His *Stan Freberg Show* better utilized the variety format. Within its fifteen-week spread, Freberg did many of the routines that later became classics—his "Wunnerful, Wunnerful" imitation of Lawrence Welk; his "Banana Boat Song" parody à la Harry Belafonte, complete with beatnik and tarantula; his frantic attempt to sing "Elderly Man River" while the "Citizen's Committee Censor" blipped out objectionable words. The bulk of the show was carried by Freberg, who also wrote most of his own material. Appearing in support were Peggy Taylor, Daws Butler, June Foray, Peter Leeds, and Jud Conlon's Rhythmaires. Music was by Billy May.

The Standard Hour

The Standard Hour was an early program of music that originated on the West Coast around 1925 and claimed the distinction of being the first Pacific network broadcast. It was heard from Hollywood and San Francisco (occasionally from Seattle) over an informal network, and with the formation of NBC in 1926 it was broadcast to that network's West Coast stations. It became a Sunday-evening fixture, sponsored for more than three decades by Standard Oil. The music ranged from popular to heavy symphonic, folk to light opera, and the show contained no commercials. Four times during the hour an announcer said simply, "This program is brought to you by the Standard Oil Company." The theme, which became very popular regionally, was "This Hour Is Yours."

Starr of Space

Starr of Space blasted out of Nova City Space Station twice a week during 1953–54 for another top-secret space mission. The adventures of Captain Starr, aided by comrades Gail Archer and Cadet Sergeant Stripes, were relayed by ABC in an undistinguished half-hour filled with hissing rockets, comets, countdowns, and other space trappings. John Larch played Starr, Jane Harlan was Gail, and creator-writer Tom Hubbard was Stripes. It was a totally forgettable show.

Stars Over Hollywood

Stars Over Hollywood came to radio in 1941 with people laying odds it wouldn't last. Radio had its prejudices, and one of the strongest in 1940 was against Saturday-morning programming. Saturday was the vast wasteland of radio, the ghetto of the schedule. So when Paul Pierce, a CBS production superintendent, announced plans to launch a star-packed show on Saturday mornings beginning May 31, people in the know began taking bets on how long it would last.

Later, with *Stars Over Hollywood* solidly established as a hit, Pierce liked to point to his show as the Saturday-morning pioneer. That wasn't quite true; a show called *Lincoln Highway* had preceded him by about a year. But long after *Lincoln Highway* had vanished, Pierce's show was hauling the stars out of bed for their 8 A.M. dress rehearsals and their 9:30 (Hollywood time) appointments with the microphones.

The show lasted thirteen years, going all the way in its ungodly Saturday-morning time slot. By 1942, when it was apparent that the show wasn't going to blow away, Dari-Rich had come aboard as sponsor, paying the bills until 1948. Armour & Company sponsored it for three years, and Carnation took over in 1951, carrying the program to the end of the road in 1954.

The stories were generally light comedies and giddy romances. Occasionally a suspense or mystery drama was used, but *Stars Over Hollywood* almost never did heavy drama. That would have been pushing luck a bit for Saturday morning. Instead, we got the college boy-meets-girl yarn, and the show business boy-meets-girl yarn, and the boy-meets-girl yarn dressed up with occasional new twists. To dish up these fictional slices of life, Pierce got such stars as Alan Ladd, Anita Louise, Mary Astor, Basil Rathbone, Bonita Granville, Phil Harris, and Merle Oberon.

The set was informal and loose, the clothes casual. Occasionally the stars arrived in robes and pajamas. But once on the air, it proceeded with all the precision of prime-time productions. Ivan Ditmars provided music in the early years, using organ, harp, and violin and sounding for all the world like a combo instead of a one-man operation. Art Gilmore was announcer, with Jim Bannon and Frank Goss also taking turns at the microphone. In addition to Pierce, Les Mitchel served as director (mid-1940's) and later visiting directors included such personalities as Hans Conried. A small group of about a dozen freelancers wrote most of the scripts, and the stars were backed by Hollywood's best professional radio actors. Pat McGeehan, Tom Collins, Lurene Tuttle, and Janet Waldo often appeared in support.

Stars Over Hollywood completely deflated the theories about Saturday-morning scheduling, and soon the air was full of big-time weekend drama, from Armstrong Theatre of Today to Grand Central Station. Stars Over Hollywood even made a jump into early TV, where the going was a little rougher than on Saturday-morning radio.

Stella Dallas

Stella Dallas had its origins in a turn-of-the-century novel by Olive Higgins Prouty, and first came to radio via WEAF October 25, 1937. By June 1938, the serial had gone on the entire NBC Network, where it became a 4:15 P.M. mainstay for Sterling Drugs and Phillips Milk of Magnesia. Its theme, "How Can I Leave Thee?" became one of soapland's greatest. "Memories" was used as the theme in the early 1940's in a sadder-than-thou version sung by a quartet.

In 1939, when this famous afternoon serial was only two years old, it was billed as "the true-to-life sequel, as written by us, to the world-famous drama of mother love and sacrifice." Sixteen years later, Stella had blossomed into middle age. Now it was "the later life of Stella Dallas," but the epigraph still summarized, in a classic of purple simplicity, the whole tear-stained run:

> Stella Dallas, a continuation on the air of the true-to-life story of mother love and sacrifice, in which Stella Dallas saw her own beloved daughter Laurel marry into wealth and society and, realizing the differences in their tastes and worlds, went out of Laurel's life . . .

Stella was a woman of little formal education who clipped her "g"s and used double negatives and "ain't" with gusto. What she lacked in school learnin' was more than offset by common sense, but even this quality couldn't save her from an endless array of tragedies. Only The Romance of Helen Trent rivaled Stella Dallas in the misery-per-episode quota, and both serials were from the sudsy pens of Frank and Anne Hummert.

Early in life, Stella married Stephen Dallas, an entrepreneur and adventurer, a man of the world, and the life of a Boston family man did not suit him. His divorce from Stella was a bitter pill; she was left to raise her Laurel ("Lolly-Baby" to Stell and to us) alone. In young womanhood, Lolly-Baby married Dick Grosvenor, a young banker on the way up, whose mother was a wealthy matron of Eastern Society. Realizing that her spellin' and readin' and maybe even her writin' weren't up to snuff, Stella made the supreme sacrifice. In Mrs. Grosvenor's eyes, Stell could never be more than a bumbling hick from the sticks, and she could see the conflict a-buildin' within Lolly-Baby's soft bosom over the differences in their tastes and worlds. So, rather than compromise one minute of Lolly's happiness, Stell choked back a sob and "went out of Laurel's life."

She didn't stay out for long, but her inherent conflict with the Grosvenors was always just beneath the surface. Despite her crude exterior, Stella was developed as a sharp judge of human behavior, and a pretty good amateur detective to boot. From the beginning, detecting was one skill she put to constant use. Her home and security were forever threatened by dark strangers with mysterious pasts, by thieves, kidnappers, and even murderers. Early in the run she fell in with a Middle East shiek, who led her through an incredible Suez Canal adventure in a submarine. In another cliffhanger, she braved the deserts and jungles of Africa. Her run-ins with the insane Ada Dexter added a tense element to the home front. Finally there was Raymond Wylie, an unscrupulous adventurer who had been Stephen Dallas' partner in Brazilian speculations—the evil Raymond had tried to kill both Stephen and Stella when he learned that Stephen had put all their South American holdings in her name.

Although she spent more time journeying than most heroines, Stella Dallas did have a home. After Stephen left her, she went to live in Minnie Grady's Boston rooming house. Minnie, sounding vaguely like Mrs. Davis of Our Miss Brooks, became Stella's closest friend and confidante. In Boston, Stella ostensibly worked as a seamstress. She never seemed to go hungry and always had enough pin money to get by, but at least during the 15-minute daily glimpses that radio took into her life, Stell took up needle and thread about as often as Jack Armstrong took up his schoolbooks.

Best-remembered announcers were Ford Bond, Howard Claney, and Frank Gallop. The show lasted until 1955. Anne Elstner played the whole run as Stella. Her husky voice made Stella Dallas the most distinctive character on daytime radio. In young womanhood, Miss Elstner married Jack Mathews, a former FBI man, and became a staunch defender of the American way and an arch foe of communism. They might have lived out their lives quietly on his Maryland tobacco plantation, but the Depression brought them back to New York to work. There, Miss Elstner began picking up the pieces of an acting career begun before her marriage. Radio seemed like logical, easy work. She played in such early radio shows as *Moonshine and Honeysuckle,* a light NBC weekly of 1930–33. She played Cracker Gaddis in the show of the same name, and there won her first major continuing radio part. Stints on *The March of Time, The Heinz Magazine of the Air,* and *Heartthrobs of the Hills* followed. Then came *Stella Dallas,* a role that completely absorbed her. With the collapse of radio, Miss Elstner opened a restaurant in New Jersey, obtained persmission to use the character's name, and began promoting "Stella Dallas' Restaurant" all along the banks of the Delaware. There, it is said, she could still be persuaded in the 1970's to bring Stell out of mothballs for an occasional bit of "Lolly-Baby" dialogue for admirers.

When the show opened in 1938, supporting players included Joy Hathaway as Lolly-Baby, Leo McCabe as Stephen Dallas, Grace Valentine as Minnie Grady, Carleton Young as Dick Grosvenor, and Arthur Vinton as Ed Munn. The part of Laurel later went to Vivian Smolen, who already had one juicy acting plum as *Our Gal Sunday.* Dick Grosvenor was also played by George Lambert, Michael Fitzmaurice, Macdonald Carey, and Spencer Bentley. Grace Valentine played Minnie Grady through the run, and Helen Claire was the batty Ada Dexter. Stuffy Mrs. Grosvenor was played by Jane Houston. Writing was credited to Anne Hummert, but as usual she sketched out the direction of the story line and left the dialogue to the Hummert assembly line.

Stepmother

Stepmother was the story of Kay Fairchild, who sought to answer the question, "Can a stepmother successfully raise another woman's children?" Kay, the young (under 30) daughter of a Chicago newspaperman, was herself embarking on a career in journalism when she gave it up to marry John Fairchild. John, a 40ish banker in the typical Midwestern town of Walnut Grove, had been a widower for years, and his kids Peggy and Bud had been virtually raised by their "faithful colored servant," Mattie. Kay encountered open warfare from Peggy from the moment she entered the house. But there was also another woman in John's life—the scheming divorcee Adella Winston, who would stop at nothing to attain her evil ends. John's infatuation with Adella caused him to lose his job at the bank, and Kay had to support the family by opening a dress shop in partnership with her friend Genevieve Porter. This drove John farther from her. When an opportunity arose for John to run for mayor, Kay encouraged it, hoping that a successful campaign would restore his self-respect and bring them together again. Little did she know that John was being manipulated by the evil Leonard Clark, crooked lawyer and the town financial power. But Kay turned detective, exposed the plot, and John won the election. All seemed headed for eternal bliss until the adventuress Adella was murdered by the evil Clark, who had mistaken her for Kay. Then Clark framed Kay for the murder, and misery began anew. No sooner was this resolved when John began brooding again over the difference in their ages. During the 1940 season, he took complete leave of his senses and went on a year-long tantrum. Convinced that Kay was falling in love with the young, dashing David Houseman, John ran away and was gone for weeks. Daughter Peggy, meanwhile, was having similar problems with her boyfriend Bert Weston. John returned and Peggy married Bert, then Peggy got pregnant. Bert followed John's example and ran away, then Peggy disappeared and Kay sent John away again and Bert came back, closely followed by John. Can a stepmother successfully raise another woman's children? You figure it out. You got little help from Sunda Love as Kay, Francis X. Bushman as John, Peggy Wall as Peggy, Cornelius Peeples as Bud, Ethel Owen as friend Genevieve, Cornelia Osgood as evil Adella, Ken Christy as Leonard Clark, Harry Elders as David Houseman, and Edith Davis as faithful Mattie. Roy Maypole wrote it; Les Weinrot was producer-director. The show was first heard on CBS January 17, 1938, and ran four years for Colgate.

Stoopnagle and Budd

Stoopnagle and Budd, two of radio's earliest satirists, came out of Buffalo in 1931 and unleashed unrefined havoc upon CBS. Frederick Chase Taylor and Budd Hulick came to radio from diverse backgrounds, and opened a field that would be developed even further by Bob Elliott and Ray Goulding almost two decades later.

Taylor had been in the lumber business as a young man. He gave that up to become a Buffalo broker. The events of 1929 convinced him that the brokerage house was no place for a human being, so he turned to radio. He landed with the Buffalo Broadcasting Corporation on Station WMAK, and there met a young announcer named Budd Hulick, a New Jersey native who arrived in western New York by way of Europe. While traveling on a steamer across the Atlantic, Hulick formed a small band, which accepted an engagement at Van Buren Bay; when the band broke up, Hulick took a job playing records on the radio.

The team of Stoopnagle and Budd was formed on the spot one day when Buffalo failed to receive a network show because of line problems. For 30 minutes, more or less, Taylor played the organ while Hulick engaged him in chatter and constantly referred to him as "Colonel Stoopnagle." The boys were a local sensation. It was a story not uncommon in the early days (*Easy Aces* started in much the same way).

They were brought to New York by CBS and offered a three-a-week 15-minute trial run in a format called *Gloom Chasers*. They had been given the royal buildup to the press, and the pressure was on to produce something really unusual or get out of town. Taylor and Budd arranged a banquet for the press, appearing as two waiters who dropped trays, engaged in violent fights, and spilled food into the laps of their journalistic guests. Soon they had the hall at the edge of a riot. Only then did they step forward and introduce themselves as Colonel Stoopnagle and Budd.

That was their introduction to New York. *Gloom Chasers* was first heard May 25, 1931. By 1932, they had a brief evening show for Ivory Soap. Pontiac sponsored them on CBS Thursday nights beginning in 1932 in a 30-minute program that featured Jeannie Lang, the cooing singer with the perpetual giggle at the end of each number; booming "Big Bill" O'Neal; announcer Louis Dean; and the music of the André Kostelanetz orchestra. Taylor had emerged as an expert double-talker and had taken the full name, Colonel Lemuel Q. Stoopnagle. The two chanted "We want a sponsor! We want a sponsor!" wildly on the air whenever sponsors dropped them. They began to mock radio with such skits as "No-Can-Do, the Magician," and around this time Taylor introduced the feature "Stoopnocracy"—simply a forum for listeners who wanted to air their pet peeves. Budd read the letters, which contained such suggestions as "eliminate the backward swing of hammocks" and "cut out the inside of soap, so that when the outside is used up, the inside won't be left for people to step on." They offered such premiums as the "both sides wrong" bed—"just tear off the top of the Empire State Building, mail it in and it's yours."

The show became a twice-a-week affair with Jacques Renard's orchestra in 1933. They were subsequently sponsored by Camel, Schlitz Beer, and Gulf Oil. In 1934 their CBS show featured Glen Gray's Casa Loma orchestra, singer Connie Boswell, and announcer Harry Von Zell. In another format, André Baruch announced and Mark Warnow handled the music. In 1935, the boys opened on the Blue Network with a 30-minute Sunday show featuring the music of Frank Black. Devoe & Reynolds, and later Ford Motors, carried the show that year. Don Voorhees became melodian in 1936. During the 1936–37 seasons they were semi-regulars on Fred Allen's *Town Hall Tonight*. In 1938, the team split. Hulick went into *What's My Name?* and Taylor hosted *Town Hall Tonight* for the summer.

In 1939, Stoopnagle began a two-year Friday quiz show, *Quixie Doodle*, on Mutual and later CBS, while Budd did a show called *Music and Manners*, heard on Mutual on the same night.

But their heyday had past. Stoopnagle was heard in a variety of summer replacement slots through the 1940's and eventually got a stint on the 1947 *Vaughn Monroe Show*, while Budd trickled back down the ladder into local radio.

Stop Me if You've Heard This One

Stop Me if You've Heard This One was first heard on NBC October 7, 1939, with Milton Berle as star, but is best remembered in its Saturday night 1947–48 Mutual time slot. In this version, highly reminiscent of *Can You Top This?*, it was billed as "the mirth of the nation, the program of laughs for the people, of the people, and by the people," in which "three gagbusters try to stop you, the people." In other words, listeners sent in their favorite jokes. If emcee Roger Bower read someone's joke on the air, that person received $5. If one of the three-member panel had heard the joke, he yelled "*Stop!*" and picked up Bower's narration to the punchline. If he missed the joke, the listener got $1 more, and an additional $1 for each time other members of the panel missed. If no one on the panel guessed the joke, the listener got $10. The show was also heard during the summer of 1948. Panelists over the run included Lew Lehr, Harry Hershfield, and Morey Amsterdam.

Stop the Music

Stop the Music is mainly remembered as the show that ended Fred Allen's long radio career. Allen was coasting along in 1947 with a rating in the high twenties. Just a year later, Louis G. Cowan, a radio executive responsible for the earlier *Quiz Kids*, cooked up a new batch of musical brew. Directed by Mark Goodson and announced by Don Hancock, the show offered bouncy, popular tunes, fabulous prizes unheard of in those days, and starred "*You*, the people of America!"

It had "hit" written all over it, even before the first broadcast. ABC booked it for a full 60 minutes, sold the time to a variety of sponsors, and ran it in one of the air's toughest time slots, Sunday nights, from 8 to 9 P.M. Its competition: Fred Allen and Charlie McCarthy. Variety announced it with a banner headline: WHO'S AFRAID OF FRED ALLEN? The optimism was well-founded. By January Bergen had taken his *Charlie McCarthy Show* off the air for a season and Allen had been dumped to thirty-eighth place on the Hooper charts, some seventeen points off his previous year's rating.

Stop the Music leaped into the top 10 and once got as high as number 2. Bert Parks, at his charismatic best, was master of ceremonies, moving the show along at a rapid pace. The overnight success of this program was based on suspense, a human inclination to root for the underdog, and the hope that the next call would be to your home. Phone calls were made at random to every part of America. Musical numbers were played by Harry Salter's orchestra and, as soon as the connection was made, a phonelike bell would ring and Parks would shout, "*Stop the Music!*"

The person on the line would be asked to name the melody being played. Naturally, he had to have been listening—another audience-building device. The melodies were usually popular hits of the day, and by naming them the listeners could win expensive gifts. But the gift was a mere prelude, for the contestant then became eligible to try the "Mystery Melody," a tougher quiz with a payoff averaging more than $20,000 (once in the first year it topped $30,000) in cash and prizes.

The melodies themselves were tantalizing and audience-boosting. Some were played by Salter's orchestra; others were sung by Dick Brown and Kay Armen, who hummed over the key words.

People from coast to cast swarmed to their radios, forgetting that the odds were at least 25 million to one against being called. Fred Allen pointed that out, and offered a $5,000 cash bounty to anyone who missed a call from *Stop the Music* by listening to his show. But the erosion had gone too far. Less than a year after *Stop the Music* began, *The Fred Allen Show* disappeared forever.

By then the popularity of the quiz was on the wane too. Bergen had returned to the air in his old time slot but on CBS, and was topping the ratings with 20-plus. *Stop the Music* began to sag, and never again would reach the peak of that first frantic year. It lost a little of its audience each year until 1952, when it too went the way of Fred Allen.

Stories of the Black Chamber

Stories of the Black Chamber was a brief serial for Forhan's Toothpaste, running on NBC in 1935. It dramatized the career of Major Herbert O. Yardley, former code expert with the War Department in World War I. Yardley was thinly disguised as "Bradley Drake," chief of the "Black Chamber," a sophisticated coding room where chemicals were used to decipher codes of allies and enemies alike. Jack

Arthur played Drake; Helen Claire was his secretary, Betty Andrews, and the scripting was by Tom Curtin.

The Story of Holly Sloan

The Story of Holly Sloan was a soap opera of short duration, built around the eternal triangle and adapted from the Rupert Hughes novel *Static*. It ran one season on NBC for General Mills beginning September 1, 1947. Holly was a small-town girl who came to New York to become a singing star of network radio. There she met dashing Johnny Starr, president of the station where she found work. The triangle evolved when Clay Brown, faithful boyfriend from back home, followed her to New York and vainly tried to persuade her to return to the sticks. The action shifted from home to New York and back again. Holly, motherless and insecure, had been raised by her kindly old Aunt Keturah, blind from birth. Her singing had developed on Keturah's front porch, where she spent many a summer evening entertaining the old woman. The serial, though it didn't last, got a respectable rating and the singing format was ideally suited to songstress Gale Page, who played Holly. Bob Bailey was Johnny Starr and Vic Perrin played Clay Brown. Georgia Backus was Aunt Keturah and Bob Griffin played Wilbur Ramage, head of the huge network where Holly found work. Louise Arthur played Sally Brown, a waitress who comforted Clay in his moments of despair and loneliness. The show was written by Ted Maxwell. Carl Wester was producer.

The Story of Mary Marlin

The Story of Mary Marlin appeared first on WMAQ, Chicago. Its characters, Joe and Mary Marlin, were married, and the road ahead had looked joyously ordinary. Joe was a young lawyer, in partnership with David Post in the little Iowa town of Cedar Springs. He was active in local politics, rather an unusual endeavor for a character of daytime radio drama.

That was October 1934. A few months later, Joe had been elected Iowa's junior senator, and was off to Washington and the heady world of hardball politics, with Mary and their little son Davey in tow. That brought them full focus into the coast-to-coast spotlight of NBC Red, beginning on January 1, 1935.

The Story of Mary Marlin first told how a woman coped with the glitter and swank of high political society. Mary wowed 'em, but she had her obstacles to overcome. First there was Bunny Mitchell,

Washington socialite who—dissatisfied with her own husband Frazier—put out her hooks for Joe. There was solid, faithful David Post, Joe's old partner—hiding his unrequited love for Mary behind a mask of platonic friendship. But the biggest problem of all came in 1939, when Joe disappeared on a diplomatic mission to Russia. This angle literally became the backbone of the serial, consuming a years-long search by Mary and her private detective, "Never Fail" Hendricks. Listeners knew that Joe was all right; that his plane had crashed on a rugged mountain slope; that even this moment he was wandering through Asia in a search for his identity, for the house on Main Street in Cedar Springs, and for the woman named Mary who haunted his dreams.

Rather than move back home to Cedar Springs and waste away pining for Joe, Mary filled Joe's political shoes, becoming Iowa's senator herself. Now *that* was an innovation for 1940 soap opera, but it worked so well that the drama was for a time carried on two networks and had one of the highest ratings in the afternoon. Housewives enjoyed the tales of the Washington atmosphere with its gay parties and the backstage interplay of personalities so far removed from the small-town settings of most soaps. Even presidential politics played a part, when *Marlin* character Rufus Kane was elected to the White House in 1940, Roosevelt notwithstanding. And Rufus, having attained his political goal, set about getting his personal goal—the beautiful, unattainable Mary.

Joe, meanwhile, still suffering the effects of total amnesia, had finally arrived in the United States with his Chinese friend, Oswald Ching. He had been traveling the world as "Mr. Ex," facing storm-tossed seas and rubbing elbows with gurus and generalissimos alike. Would he arrive and remember before Mary took that final step and became the First Lady? Listeners didn't know it then, but Joe and Mary were still a light-year apart. Thankfully, so were Mary and Rufus.

The show was packaged to the haunting melody of Debussy's "Clair de Lune," simply played on a piano. Listeners took the theme to their hearts; many wrote in asking for its origin. The show's writer-creator was Jane Crusinberry, a singer who turned to serial writing just after a vocal tour of Europe. Anne Seymour was the most famous voice of Mary; she played the part for more than six years. Other Marys were Betty Lou Gerson, Muriel Kirkland, Eloise Kummer, and Linda Carlon. The part was originated in Chicago by Joan Blaine, radio's original *Valiant Lady*.

Joe Marlin was played by Robert Griffin, Bunny Mitchell by Fran Carlon. Rupert LaBelle was Rufus Kane, Carlton Brickert played David Post, and Frank Dane was "Never Fail" Hendricks.

The serial ran on NBC for Procter & Gamble until 1943, when it was picked up by CBS for Tenderleaf Tea. It ran at midafternoon, "just before tea time," until 1945, when it was dropped from the air. A new version ran on ABC in 1951–52.

The Story of Myrt and Marge

The Story of Myrt and Marge was first heard on CBS November 2, 1931, as an early-evening serial drama for Wrigley's Gum. It was created and written by Myrtle Vail, then a 43-year-old vaudevillian and stage trouper whose own life had been a lot like that of her fictitious heroine. She had run away from home to go on stage at 15, and had soon landed in a road show as a back-row chorus girl. She fell in love with a tenor who sang in the show, and the following year she and George Damarel were wed. Their daughter Donna crashed their act at age 5 and couldn't be kept out afterward. For seven years they toured in *The Merry Widow*, and in 1917 Myrt had a son, George.

Donna Damarel was determined to follow her mother's path into show business, so she took the path of least resistance and they clashed head-on. Donna won, and soon she was doing the Charleston in her parents' act. Hard times came in the late 1920's; bookings were slim as vaudeville started into a decline. The Damarels quit show business and went into real estate in Chicago. The stock market crash ended that dream, and again they were faced with starting over. That was when Myrt thought of turning to radio.

She had never appeared at the microphone, but she scribbled off ten radio skits in longhand and prepared to sell her idea of two Broadway chorus girls to the Wrigley Gum Company. As an inducement, she gave Myrt the last name Spear and Margie was named Minter. Wrigley bought it, and *Myrt and Marge* was on the air.

Myrt and Marge was a story of Broadway; a story that went beyond the lights of the Great White Way into the lives of two chorus girls —two girls from the cast of that most glittering of all Broadway extravaganzas, *Hayfield's Pleasures*. In that long-ago first chapter, Myrt and Marge met for the first time. They didn't know it then, but they were actually long-lost sisters whom fate had ripped apart and cast on separate paths. Then, through thinnest coincidence, young Margie Minter wandered into Hayfield's Theatre, "just off Times Square," where the twenty-four-girl precision chorus was kicking in unison. These were the "chic-chicks," world-famous glamor girls who danced in the *Pleasures* of Francis Hayfield. And Hayfield, a thinly disguised Florenz Ziegfeld, charged the Broadway wolves as much as $25 a seat to see his "chic-chicks" in action.

Leading the troupe was Myrtle Spear, a seasoned veteran of the footlight wars. When young Margie fainted from hunger, Myrt's heart of gold came to the surface. She borrowed money and sent the girl out for a meal. Later Margie too became a *Pleasures* headliner, joining Myrt in a long series of adventures that, for a time, locked horns with *Amos and Andy* in a life-or-death battle of rating strength.

The show was an immediate hit, though gradually the sheer strength of *Amos and Andy* forced it into another time slot. As the story of Myrt and Marge unfolded, the characters developed more of a mother-daughter relationship. They were allowed to age, and their situations changed with the times.

When young Margie Minter first blundered into the Hayfield Theatre, she was 16 and Myrt 32. Six years later, when they settled into a daytime format, their ages were properly 22 and 38—quite a cry from Helen Trent's eternal 35. In the interim, Myrt had married Francis Hayfield, who had died in 1936. Marge had married a young lawyer, Jack Arnold, and in 1935 she became the mother of "baby Midgie." The death of Hayfield had closed the *Pleasures*, and Myrt and Marge had traveled through the Midwest and Hollywood, seeking new adventures. In 1937, having returned to New York, they were caught up again by theatre fever; their overpowering desire was to reopen Hayfield's and stage a new version of the *Pleasures*. Jack Arnold, meanwhile, had accepted a post with the New York district attorney, setting up new situations involving gangsters and racketeers. Actually the first major soap opera of the air, *Myrt and Marge* remained a nighttime feature for its first five years. On January 4, 1937, the show moved into an afternoon slot; that same year it became a daily morning drama for Super Suds.

By then the heyday of *Myrt and Marge* was over. The serial lost a little piece of its rating each year.

Jack Arnold was first played by Donna Damarel's husband, Gene Kretzinger. He was replaced when the marriage went on the rocks. In 1939, Donna won her divorce, and Vinton Hayworth took the role of Jack.

Clarence Tiffingtuffer, the costume designer with the farfetched moniker, was played by Ray Hedge; Little Midgie was Betty Jane Tyler; and, for a time, Francis Hayfield was played by Ed Begley.

On the afternoon of February 14, 1941, Donna—now remarried to swimmer Peter Fick—finished reading her lines and prepared to go to the hospital for the birth of her third child. She was in good condition as she checked in, but complications came on quickly. Her eight-pound boy was delivered just after midnight. Eighteen minutes later, with her mother at her side, Donna Damarel Fick died. Fans across the nation thought the tragedy would also be the end of *Myrt and Marge*. But Myrt, true to her breed, insisted that the show go on. Helen Mack was signed as Marge, to play out the year.

Myrt and Marge gradually faded away, and by 1942 held only a fraction of its original audience. In 1946, Myrtle dragged out her old scripts, did a rough rewrite, and a new version of *Myrt and Marge* was syndicated. In New York, it was first heard on WOR April 1, 1946, starring Alice Yourman as Myrt and Alice Goodkin as Marge. Vinton Hayworth recreated his Jack Arnold role, Ray Hedge returned as Tiffingtuffer, Richard Keith played Ray Hunt, and Helen Choate was cast as Billie Devere.

But the fever had cooled. At its network peak, the show was a giant, with an audience almost frantic in its devotion. Even today old-timers remember "Poor Butterfly" mainly as the theme of *The Story of Myrt and Marge*.

The Story of Sandra Martin

The Story of Sandra Martin, an obscure CBS soap, originated in Hollywood in 1945 and never made the big time. It told of a young girl reporter (Sandra) on the *Los Angeles Daily Courier*, and of her campaigns against such postwar rackets as the baby black market and real estate gyps. Gordon Hughes produced; Les Edgely wrote the scripts. Mary Jane Croft played Sandra, Grif Barnett was editor Wilson, Bob Latting was young reporter Eddie Dalton, Howard McNear was racketeer Steve Heywood, and Ivan Green was Sandra's love interest, Detective Hack Taggart.

Straight Arrow

Straight Arrow came to Mutual in early 1949 as a juvenile adventure show almost interchangeable with *Sky King*, *Bobby Benson*, or any of the other kiddie Westerns of the late 1940's. Like the others, *Straight Arrow* had its gimmick. Its hero, Steve Adams, was a young white man who had been raised among the Comanches.

To friends and neighbors alike, Steve Adams appeared to be nothing more than the young owner of the Broken Bow cattle spread. But when danger threatened innocent people, and when evil-doers plotted against justice, then Steve Adams, rancher, disappeared. And in his place came a mysterious, stalwart Indian, wearing the dress and warpaint of a Comanche, riding the great golden palomino Fury! Galloping out of the darkness to take up the cause of law and order throughout the West comes the legendary figure of *Straaaiiight Arrow*!

Howard Culver starred as Steve, who rode the Broken Bow plains with an old sidekick named Packy, and took up the tomahawk when things got too tough for local law. The series ran Mondays from 1949 until 1950, and twice a week in 1950–51. It was sponsored by Nabisco, whose ads were cleverly worked into the opening signature with tom-toms and Indian music:

N-A-B-I-S-C-O
Nabisco is the name to know;
For a breakfast you can't beat,
Try Nabisco Shredded Wheat!

The Strange Dr. Weird

The Strange Dr. Weird was a poor man's *Mysterious Traveler*, heard on Mutual in 1944–45. Played by the same Maurice Tarplin who brought the *Traveler* to life, *Dr. Weird* told grisly, fantastic tales compressed into 15 minutes. Except for the shorter format (and a corresponding loss of quality), the show was a virtual copy. Dr. Weird merely acted as narrator, relating the gore as it popped from the typewriter of Robert A. Arthur (also a *Traveler* scripter) and closing with the Traveler-like, "Oh, you have to leave now—too bad! But perhaps you'll drop in on me again soon. I'm always home. Just look for the house on the other side of the cemetery—the house of Dr. Weird!"

The Strange Romance of Evelyn Winters

The Strange Romance of Evelyn Winters was one of the better new soaps of the 1944 CBS schedule, premièring November 20 for Sweetheart Soap. It was "the story of Gary Bennett, playwright, who suddenly and unexpectedly finds himself the guardian of lovely Evelyn Winters." Gary, pushing 40, couldn't have been more thrilled, but he thought a man of his age was too old for a girl just out of finishing school—especially when the girl in question is his lovely new ward. Evelyn sounded plenty adult, but then . . .

The show opened by throwing the question to its listeners: "Do you think fifteen years is too great a difference for marriage?" They had a deep, mutual love, and although both stifled their feelings, the audience knew the longings of both hearts. Gary hid away in his Broadway office, pounding out smash hits under the eyes of manager Charlie Gleason and secretary Miss Bean. Evelyn hid away at home, protected by the ever-watchful Maggie, her "dearly adored house-keeper." Meanwhile, she had her hands full fending off the attention of young Ted Blades; she was also constantly worrying about young Jinny Roberts, her friend who was so vulnerable. Larry Elliott was the announcer, and the theme was an organ rendition of "Sweetheart" (remember that soap, ladies). Toni Darnay was Evelyn, Karl Weber and then Martin Blaine played Gary, Ralph Bell was Charlie Gleason, and Kate McComb was the adored Maggie. Mary Mason played Jinny Roberts; Stacy Harris was Ted Blades. The serial, a late-morning Hummert epic, ran until 1948.

Streamlined Shakespeare

Streamlined Shakespeare set off a furious "battle of the Bard" with its first broadcast over NBC Blue June 21, 1937. One month earlier, CBS had announced elaborate plans for a summertime Shakespeare festi-val, that would star the great actors of the stage and screen. Then the network sat back and let grass grow under its microphone while NBC quietly put into motion plans for its own Shakespeare series. The NBC show brought John Barrymore to the air in his own adaptations. Barrymore produced the series and, with the help of Forrest Barnes, wrote the scripts. The result was on the air while CBS was still daydreaming about its show.

Barrymore offered the Bard in an unusual format—a narrative sketch, punctuated by dramatized scenes, and streamlined to 45 min-utes each. Among the plays were *Hamlet* (with Barrymore playing both Hamlet and the ghost), *Richard III*, *Macbeth*, *King Lear*, and *Richard II*. CBS finally got its show off the ground on July 12, three weeks later, programmed it on the same night (Monday) but 30 min-utes earlier than Barrymore's show. CBS offered some of the same plays that Barrymore had done, bringing in such stars as Leslie How-ard, Walter Huston, Walter Abel, Edward G. Robinson, Tallulah Bank-head, Sir Cedric Hardwicke, Montagu Love, and Orson Welles. That show was directed by Brewster Morgan. NBC, meanwhile, finished up with Barrymore and continued through the summer with adaptations of Eugene O'Neill, featuring as stars Helen Hayes, Henry Hull, Peggy Wood, and Ian Keith. It was, in short, a time of heavies, and 1937 should long be remembered as Shakespeare's golden year.

The Street Singer

The Street Singer was Arthur Tracy, who became a national sensation soon after his appearance on CBS in 1931. Like Joe White, the "Silver Masked Tenor" who preceded him, Tracy was billed as a man of mystery, and for many weeks after his initial appearances his identity was a guarded secret. Tracy had broken into radio at WMCA, New York, in 1929, after a long singing apprenticeship begun as a child. He learned his craft studying the records of Enrico Caruso and later had a professional teacher at the Curtis Institute of Music. He sang in the Broadway and road shows *Blossom Time* and *The Student Prince*, and when CBS offered him a six-week trial in 1931, he decided to cloak his real identity à la White. Friends pointed out how White's popularity had waned once his identity was known. The "Silver Masked Tenor" had sung with the Goodrich Silvertown Orchestra on WEAF during the mid-1920's, and had gone to NBC in 1929. With his face always covered by a silver mask, he attracted a fanatical following in radio's earliest years. But the mystery element was the main attraction; once that was removed, White never again attained the same fierce devotion from his fans. Tracy's friends feared a replay, but the "Street Singer" opened on CBS as an unidentified voice anyway. Thousands of letters poured in demanding his identity. It was released in a flurry of publicity: newspapers carried stories, and thereafter he was billed as Arthur Tracy, the Street Singer. In 1932, he moved to Saturdays and a 15-minute CBS format; in 1933 he went to London, where he had also attracted a legion of fans. He returned to England in 1936 and stayed for several years. In America again, he tried a comeback with a three-a-week Blue Network show for Ex-Lax in 1941. It didn't last. Tracy's friends were probably right. The mystery element detracted from the real Tracy, as it had from White. It was like fool's gold; once the game was over, the real attraction—no matter how good—was just another voice.

Strike It Rich

Strike It Rich, radio's "show with a heart," came to CBS June 29, 1947, as a Sunday human interest quiz for Luden's. Todd Russell was the original host and Walt Framer was producer-director; by 1950, when the show went to NBC as a five-a-week daytimer for Colgate, Warren Hull had taken over. It was the one quiz that blatantly wanted to give away money; the contestants were all people with a worthy cause. Some needed money for operations, for trips to visit dying relatives, for great humanitarian fund drives. With few exceptions, the questions were easy and there were only enough misses to make it interesting. And if the contestant totally bombed on the quiz, there was a "heartline"—a special telephone onstage where people could call with offers from anywhere in America. Service organizations, businesses and individuals used the heartline, tossing $200, $500, or more into the contestant's kitty. *Strike It Rich* ran until the mid-1950's.

Studio One

Studio One came late to radio, first appearing on the CBS lineup April 29, 1947. It was a 60-minute presentation of novel and play adaptations directed by Fletcher Markle, produced by Robert J. Landry, and scored by Alexander Semmler. Markle, always something of a radio triple-threat man, also wrote and acted in some of the plays. The show was a high-quality Tuesday-night drama, and was sustained throughout the run. Starring roles were filled by seasoned radio professionals rather than by superstars of Broadway and Hollywood, so *Studio One* had no glamor to promote—just solid performers in solid stories. It relied somewhat on the fame of its plays—stories like *The Red Badge of Courage, Ah, Wilderness, Dodsworth, A Tree Grows in Brooklyn,* and *A Farewell to Arms* were standard *Studio One* offerings. Everett Sloane and Anne Burr appeared in many of the early shows, along with Paul McGrath, Robert Dryden, Joe Di Santis, Stefan Schnabel, and other fine radio actors. Later, the series did shift emphasis slightly and began using bigger names, but never to the extent of Markle's other show, *The Ford Theatre.* Robert Young, Charles Laughton, Geraldine Fitzgerald, Edward G. Robinson, and Madeleine Carroll were among those who appeared during this time. But *Studio One,* despite giving top stories and fine production, lasted only a year, bowing out in mid-1948.

Suspense

Suspense, "radio's outstanding theatre of thrills," was first heard on CBS June 17, 1942, starring Charlie Ruggles in "The Burning Court," by John Dickson Carr. It was on the air for the next twenty years, under many talented directors. Each brought his own mark to Suspense, making it one of the most diverse, unusually broad-based shows of the air. A breakdown:

June 17, 1942: Suspense premières as a 30-minute summer thrill show, Wednesday nights, CBS, sustaining. Charles Vanda, producer, then William Spier.

October 27, 1942: Becomes part of the regular CBS fall lineup, Tuesday nights. Spier is producer-director; scripting is by John Dickson Carr.

August 21, 1943: To Saturdays.

September 2, 1943: To Thursdays.

October 12, 1943: To Tuesdays.

December 2, 1943: To Thursdays. First show for Roma Wines. This basic format lasts for almost three years. The last Roma show is November 20, 1947.

November 28, 1947: To Fridays, sustaining.

January 3, 1948: Suspense goes into a 60-minute Saturday-night sustaining format. Robert Montgomery is host. William Spier continues as producer-director until February 21, 1948, when he is replaced by Anton M. Leader. The hour-long format lasts until May 22, 1948, when Suspense goes off for the summer.

July 8, 1948: Suspense returns to its old Thursday-night time slot, sponsored by Autolite and directed by Anton M. Leader. Leader leaves June 30, 1949, and Norman Macdonnell becomes director. (Spier is producer during the Macdonnell era). On August 31, 1950, Elliott Lewis becomes producer-director.

August 27, 1951: To Mondays, Autolite sponsor, Elliott Lewis, producer.

June 7, 1954: Last Autolite show. Moves to Tuesdays June 15, with Norman Macdonnell as director. Sustained.

September 30, 1954: To Thursday. Antony Ellis, director. Sustained.

February 22, 1955: To Tuesday.

July 11, 1956: To Wednesday.

September 25, 1956: To Tuesday.

November 4, 1956: To Sunday, with William N. Robson as director-host. Finishes its long run September 30, 1962, as a Sunday show. Bruno Zirato, Jr. takes over as director in 1959, leaving midway through the final year. Fred Hendrickson directs for the remainder of 1962.

In the early years of William Spier's reign, some unwritten rules were established that served as rough guidelines through the entire twenty-year run. Suspense dealt in life-or-death situations. That element was usually established within the first few minutes. Then, through characterization and audio coloring, little touches were added to heighten the sensation of impending doom. That was what suspense was all about: The slow tightening of the knot.

The thrill of the nighttime; the hushed voice and the prowling step. The crime that is almost committed. The finger of suspicion, pointing perhaps at the wrong man. The stir of nerves at the ticking of the clock. The rescue that might be too late, or the murderer who might get away . . . Mystery and intrigue and dangerous adventure . . .

Another of Spier's rules was that the murderer rarely got away. He also believed in staying close to home, with realistic themes and common-man heroes. No science fiction or ghost stories for him. *Suspense* featured tales of people in trouble. Human emotions were stretched to the breaking point, and the solutions were withheld until the last possible moment.

But Spier was also one of radio's most flexible directors, and he occasionally broke his own rules with great effect. The two-part Orson Welles show, "Donovan's Brain" was to become a classic of science fiction. Spier's "House In Cypress Canyon" was the story of a young couple who encountered a werewolf in their newly rented canyon home; today it ranks as one of radio's ultimate horror shows. "August Heat" propelled Ronald Colman into a date with fate and a madman with a knife—a chilling sequence foretold in an inscription on a tombstone. "The Dunwich Horror" retold H. P. Lovecraft's tale of an ancient race returned. The popularity of the dark side led Spier to try one or two such dramas a year. But, for the most part, he stayed with the tried and true everyday situations that had suddenly gotten out of hand and become extraordinary. Situations like Ernest Bowers' auto accident, sending him into a coma resembling death. This little piece of fiction became the show "Dead Ernest," and a race with time against an embalmer's knife.

By far the most famous of all *Suspense* plays was an exaggeration of everyday life. There was nothing supernatural about "Sorry, Wrong Number," except the intensity of Agnes Moorehead's performance. She played the invalid Mrs. Elbert Stevenson with such terrified emotion that it left her collapsed across the table at its conclusion. It horrified the nation when it was first heard May 25, 1943, and each of the seven additional times it was aired. And yes, Miss Moorehead admitted, it even scared her. It concerned Mrs. Stevenson's troubles with the telephone. Connected to a private number by mistake, she hears two killers plotting the murder of a bed-ridden woman. Her efforts to get help by phone are frustrated. Operators pass the buck; the cops seem unconcerned, and Mrs. Stevenson's mounting hysteria only adds to the problem. Too late she realizes that the murder being planned is her murder. A scream, a thud, and the phone drops to the floor. Mrs. Elbert Stevenson's final agony is lost in the wail of the 11 P.M. train passing just outside her window.

Even in "Sorry, Wrong Number," Spier broke a rule. The killers got away, adding the final wedge of horror to an already terrifying show.

"Sorry" became nationally known as radio's ultimate murder show. So intricate was the correlation between Miss Moorehead's lines and soundman Bernie Surrey's effects that a great bond of respect developed between them. Just before air time, they would clasp hands for good luck, and Miss Moorehead would organize the same battered, pencil-notated script she had used for the first broadcast. During one performance, she drank ten cups of water, yanked off her jewelry and shoes, and pulled out her blouse and collapsed on the table when it was over. The intensity of her performance led to her title "the first lady of Suspense."

Under Spier, Suspense was known as an "actor's theatre," and he built a reputation as "the Hitchcock of the air." There were usually only a few hours of rehearsal before shows; Spier liked to see the stars tense as they stepped before the microphone. People like Cary Grant, Fredric March, Charles Laughton, Humphrey Bogart, Lucille Ball, Olivia De Havilland, Gregory Peck, Peter Lorre, Henry Fonda, and Orson Welles headed the casts. Many top film stars asked to return for encore performances. Spier wasn't afraid to let people be creative, and it didn't matter whether they were highly paid film stars or staff musicians and sound men. Berne Surrey, Suspense sound effects artist during those days, was given a wide berth in creating the background for the exotic plays. He researched "Donovan's Brain" for almost three weeks before coming up with his impression of what a severed brain, kept alive in a tank and still experiencing powerful human emotions, would sound like. Surrey was also allowed to improvise on the spot if a suggested effect wasn't working or if something needed additional emphasis. Spier worked closely with musicians Bernard Herrmann, Lucien Moraweck, and Lud Gluskin, earning the latter's expressed admiration as a director who understood music, sometimes better than the musicians.

Early in the show, a general format was established and stuck throughout. Suspense opened to the ringing of soft churchbells intermingled with stinging music. By the fall of its first year, Joseph Kearns, a grim-voiced fellow known as "the man in black," was aboard as the narrator. That stuck through the Roma Wine years, with Truman Bradley (another of radio's most distinguished voices) doing the commercials. The man in black had disappeared by the time the show went to 60 minutes in 1948. Robert Montgomery, then the host, also acted occasionally in the dramas. During this time Anton M. Leader, a refugee from the syndicated *Murder at Midnight*, came on as director. The man in black never did return, though Kearns continued doing a variety of character parts. Harlow Wilcox became announcer with the shift to Autolite, and big-name guest stars continued to appear. Burt Lancaster made his first radio appearance in a *Suspense* show called "The Big Shot." Fibber McGee and Molly appeared out of character in "Back Seat Driver," a tight little tale about a ride with a killer. And James Stewart gave a powerful performance as a paralyzed war veteran whose sighting of a former Japanese torturer drove him back to health—and murder.

Suspense always had top directors. Norman Macdonnell, who followed Leader, was one of the best in the business, handling *Gunsmoke* and *Escape* as well. But perhaps the most distinctive *Suspense* work was done by Elliott Lewis. Under his hand, the program turned its emphasis to true material, to ultramodern themes and even to classics. Jack Benny, Red Skelton, and other comics were cast in serious roles. And Lewis, in what must have been a gutty decision, dramatized *Othello* on *Suspense* in two installments, using Shakespeare's original dialogue, casting himself in the title role, wife Cathy as Desdemona, and Richard Widmark as Iago (though none had ever played Shakespeare), and replacing the usual musical bridges with themes from Verdi operas.

Even in its old age, the show was good. William N. Robson, who took the helm in 1956, opened with a neat mixture of drama and rough-cut philosophy. He became known as "the master of mystery and adventure." The series kept the bells and a variation of the same music to the end. In its late years, the opening signature was breathed into the microphone in a menacing "And nowwwww . . . another tale well calculated . . ."

Sweeney and March

Sweeney and March came to CBS West Coast stations in 1946 as a Saturday-afternoon comedy feature. Sweeney was Bob Sweeney; March was Hal March, who would go on to host TV's *$64,000 Question* in the 1950's. The men had been doing a local radio show in Los Angeles when they were offered the network slot, and by 1947 their show was a coast-to-coast Wednesday sustaining feature. It began as a series of unrelated skits, written by Manny Mannheim, Jerry Brewer, and John Hayes. Within six months it had developed into a rough situation comedy format. The boys were supposed to be frustrated radio comedians who lived together in a trailer and occupied the smallest office at CBS. Mannheim produced and Sterling Tracy directed. The skits, later written by Frank Fox, Jack Crutcher, and William Davenport, gave March the "thinker" role and Sweeney the part of his immature, slightly addled partner. Sweeney's favorite recreation was reading *Outdoor Boy* magazine; the magazine's adventure stories often became Sweeney and March dramas. Wilbur Hatch provided the music when the show first went network; Lud Gluskin swung the stick later. Bob Lemond was announcer.

Sweet River

Sweet River was the "dramatic story of Willa McKay, who struggles and endures against the heartbreaks and trials that test our lives daily throughout America, in towns like Sweet River." It was first heard regionally around 1942, and came to ABC October 4, 1943. Sponsor was Stoy, "the new 100 percent soy flour." It was a flop and disappeared that year, its chief claim to fame being authorship by Charles Jackson, writer of *The Lost Weekend*.

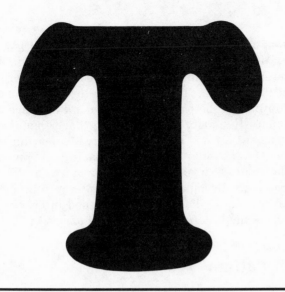

Take It or Leave It

Take It or Leave It, a typical quiz show with a top prize of $64, was first heard on CBS April 21, 1940. It became a long-running Sunday-night feature for Eversharp, outlasting five masters of ceremonies and casting the mold for that most famous of all TV quizzes, *The $64,000 Question*.

The big difference between the shows was that *Take It or Leave It* dealt in plain dollars, not *thousands* of dollars; thus, the producers could take themselves far less seriously. There was no isolation booth for contestants to stand in, and all the coaching was done onstage, in full view of the audience. The contestants were chosen from the studio audience by ticket stub numbers. Five women, five men, and two servicemen were called onstage; the emcee selected his contestants from that group. Bruce Dodge produced and directed; announcers included David Ross, Ken Niles, and Jay Stewart. Edith Oliver wrote the questions, which were arranged along a $1, $2, $4, $8, $16, $32, $64 progression and built around such categories as "Cards and Card Games," "First Names of People," "Titles in Literature," "Detectives," and the like.

There were few embellishments; questions were asked and answered and that was it. A major point of interest was the interviewing skill of the host, and the taunting "you'll be sorrr-eee" from the audience when contestants decided to risk their money and go for more. Although Miss Oliver tried to make the questions progressively difficult, it was widely believed that the $32 question was toughest.

Possibly that was why 75 percent of the contestants tried to go all the way. But it doesn't explain why only 20 percent made it.

The series began with Bob Hawk at the helm, but he gave it up in December 1941 after a salary dispute with Eversharp. Phil Baker, longest-running and best-remembered *Take It or Leave It* host, was often shamelessly blatant in his hinting. Baker handled the show until September 14, 1947. Then came Garry Moore, who had just split with Jimmy Durante after four years in their joint comedy show.

The show ran seven years on CBS, then moved to NBC in 1947 for its last three years. Eversharp took it all the way. Moore handled the job for two years; Jack Paar was sandwiched in briefly, and Eddie Cantor became the last *Take It or Leave It* emcee in 1949.

Tales of Fatima

Tales of Fatima was one of the shows Basil Rathbone took up after leaving *Sherlock Holmes* in 1946. The other was the equally brief *Scotland Yard*, which premièred on Mutual January 27, 1947, featuring Rathbone as Inspector Burke and Alfred Shirley as Sergeant Abernathy. Like *Scotland Yard*, *Tales of Fatima* was strictly from hunger, especially in the wake of Rathbone's fine seven-year stint as the genius of Baker Street. *Fatima* came to CBS January 8, 1949, and left October 1, 1949. Sponsored Saturday nights by Fatima Cigarettes, it was a strange show that had Rathbone playing Rathbone, getting himself into all manner of messy murder and moronic mayhem. Rathbone was aided in solving the mysteries by Fatima herself, a sultry-sounding dame who gave a veiled clue from her CBS echo chamber before the drama began. Armed with the clue, listeners were challenged to guess the killer before Rathbone did. Harry Ingram directed, Jack Miller added the music, and the announcer was Michael Fitzmaurice.

Tales of the Texas Rangers

Tales of the Texas Rangers brought cowboy star Joel McCrea to NBC July 8, 1950, for a two-year, initially Saturday, then Sunday, sustainer of the modern West. McCrea played Ranger Jase Pearson in "authentic re-enactments" of actual Ranger case histories. He covered Texas ("more than 260,000 square miles") with "fifty men who make up the most famous and oldest law enforcement body in North America." Only names, dates, and places were fictitious "for obvious reasons." The series was a respectable, if minor, part of the NBC lineup, and drew support from Tony Barrett, Peggy Webber, Ed Begley, Herb Vigran, Barney Phillips, Ken Christy, and the rest of Hollywood's "old pro" fraternity. Stacy Keach produced and directed; writer was Joel Murcott; Hal Gibney was announcer.

Tales of Tomorrow

Tales of Tomorrow, a science fiction thriller, was first a TV series (1951), then made the jump to radio, turning up on ABC January 1, 1953. It had a brief run, going only two months before moving to CBS. There, it lasted only six more weeks. The final show was April 9, 1953.

Tarzan

Tarzan came to radio in 1932, in what has generally come to be regarded as the earliest major syndicated series. This early version began with the initial novel by Edgar Rice Burroughs—*Tarzan of the Apes*. It followed the tragic end of Tarzan's British parents, Lord and Lady Greystoke. Stranded on a lonely African coast, mother and father were killed by apes; their infant son was taken alive to the den of the apes to be raised as one of them.

James Pierce, one of the early screen Tarzans, played the lord of the jungle in this 15-minute three-a-week serial. Joan Burroughs, the creator's daughter and Mrs. Pierce in private life, played Jane. With the conclusion of *Tarzan of the Apes*, new Burroughs stories were dramatized for the air—"Tarzan and the Diamond of Ashair" and "Tarzan and the Fire of Thor." In all, more than 350 chapters were produced, featuring such accomplished artists as Gale Gordon, John McIntire, and Jeanette Nolan in supporting roles. The serial was still running on some stations in 1935; by then Carlton KaDell had replaced Pierce in the title role.

Although the character was ideally suited for air drama, no other major attempt was made to bring *Tarzan* to radio until 1951. The new *Tarzan*, ironically enough, was a "canned" series like the first, syndicated by Commodore Productions. Lamont Johnson played the ape man, opening with the famous war cry that kids still associate with the shadowy figure of the jungle vines. "AAAAAAAAAaaa-aaahhhh-o-ahhhhhh-o-ahhhhhhh-o! From the heart of the jungle comes a savage cry of victory! This is Tarzan, lord of the jungle! . . . From the black core of dark Africa, land of enchantment, mystery, and violence, comes one of the most colorful figures of all time, transcribed from the immortal pen of Edgar Rice Burroughs—Tarzan, the bronzed white son of the jungle!"

Unlike the earlier version, this was complete in each 30-minute installment. It was produced by Walter White, Jr., and in 1952 was bought by CBS under sponsorship of General Foods. It ran one year on the network as a Saturday-night show, and enjoyed a healthy rating, especially considering the state of the industry then.

Tell It Again

Tell It Again was a good CBS adaptation of the classics starring Marvin Miller, running Sunday afternoons in 1948, and into 1949. Designed mainly to appeal to the young, the series offered tales so universally loved that the producers wanted to "tell them again." Bret Harte's *Luck of Roaring Camp*, Herman Melville's *Moby-Dick*, Charles Dickens' *A Tale of Two Cities*, Robert Louis Stevenson's *Kidnapped*, and Richard H. Dana's *Two Years Before the Mast* were some of the stories done on this summer show. Ralph Rose directed, and Del Castillo was at the organ.

Tena and Tim

Tena and Tim may have been one of the reasons radio died. It was a soap opera that tried to out-Lorenzo *Lorenzo Jones*, employing the elements of dialect humor that wasn't funny, a serial drama that wasn't gripping, and a cast of characters about as potent as last week's soapsuds. Tena, a maid with a thick Swedish accent who lived with a family called the Hutchinsons, talked too much, and the humor allegedly grew out of her efforts to "explain things." She was a chronic interrupter, earmarked as a loser the minute she began telling the kids, "Don't go around collecting your olders." CBS gets the blame for this one. Written by Peggy Beckmark, who also starred as Tena, it was first heard as a syndicated show, then was picked up by CBS August 7, 1944, for a long, long two-year run.

Tennessee Jed

Tennessee Jed was a 15-minute juvenile adventure serial broadcast daily on ABC for Tip Top Bread and Cakes from May 14, 1945, until 1947. Set in the years just after the Civil War, it told of a squirrel-gun marksman from the Old South anxious to forget the strife of war with a sojourn on the frontier. Tennessee Jed Sloan was an articulate gunman who could drill the eye out of a gnat at 500 yards. He did just that every night, in one of radio's celebrated opening signatures:

> There he goes, Tennessee! Get him!
> (Gunshot. Ricochet.)
> Got him! Deeeaaaad center!

Yes, it's Tennessee Jed, with his great horse Smoky and the two deadliest sixguns in all the West. He could ricochet a bullet and still get his prey five times a week. The serial was distinctive, scored by harmonica-accordion themes and bridges that suggested its Southern origin. But Tennessee the man was cast in the Lone Ranger mold. No slang for him. Played early in the run by Johnny Thomas and later in the best super-sophisticated *Counterspy* tones of Don MacLaughlin, Tennessee eventually became an agent of the White House, working directly for President Grant rounding up rustlers and badmen. Court Benson was narrator-announcer.

Terry and the Pirates

Terry and the Pirates, closely following Milton Caniff's strip, came to NBC Blue November 1, 1937, as a three-a-week show for Dari-Rich. This adventure serial told of the perils faced in the Orient by Terry Lee and his friends Pat Ryan, Flip Corkin, Connie-the-Coolie, Hotshot Charlie, and the ladies, Burma and the girl flier Eleta. They routed evildoers from Shanghai to Calcutta and provided a decade of juvenile listeners with daily doses of adventure by installment.

The series was dropped after two years, and the new Terry opened on the Blue in 1943, where it played for Quaker Oats until 1948. Like *Hop Harrigan*, the show attracted its biggest following and pursued its greatest adventures during the war years.

Listeners first heard the sound of a gong, then cymbals, then coolies jabbering in meaningless Chinese. It was easy to picture rickshaws dashing madly up a narrow alley, somewhere in the Far East. Again the cymbals and gong: "Terrr-eeee . . . and the Pirates! Quaker Puffed Wheat Sparkies present *Terry and the Pirates!*"

This was one of the first juvenile adventures to campaign against fascism, and was still warning that isolated pockets of enemy existed as late as 1946. Once war had been declared and battle lines drawn, writer Albert Barker lost no time casting Terry and his pals into the fray. Since he operated almost exclusively in the Orient, it is ironic that Terry's greatest wartime enemies were Nazis—brownshirts sent by Berlin to "oversee operations in the Pacific," or some such. In 1943, Terry teamed up with his old enemy the Dragon Lady (then supposedly working for the Chinese) to destroy a Japanese supply depot, hidden away on a Yellow River plantation under supervision of the evil Baron Von Krell. For Terry this was an uneasy alliance; he never knew when the infamous Dragon Lady might stab him in the back and cross over to the other side. In 1944, Pat Ryan and Terry were selected by British Secret Service to impersonate Nazi officers on a dangerous mission to Tokyo. As late as 1945, with Germany at its knees, they were still battling a ring of Nazis, this time working out of Calcutta.

Throughout the war years, Terry held its own with the best of them. Then in 1946 the rating drooped badly; the war elements faded into the past, and somehow Terry didn't seem quite so exciting without the Nazis and double agents to contend with. The Dragon Lady returned to her old bandit organization of international pirates, and for another two years Terry and his friends waged intermittent war with the evil organization throughout the Far East. Owen Jordan played Terry through this last run, and the part was carried earlier by Jackie Kelk and Cliff Carpenter. Bud Collyer, doing the voice of Superman at the same time, was one of several actors who played Pat Ryan. Flip Corkin was played by Ted de Corsia, Cameron Andrews was Hotshot Charlie, Frances Chaney was Burma, Gerta Rozan played Eleta, and Peter Donald was among the actors who played Connie. The Dragon Lady was played variously by Agnes Moorehead and Adelaide Klein.

The Dragon Lady was Terry's most formidable foe, but nothing quite rekindled the excitement of those war years, when announcer Douglas Browning wrapped his "Terrytales" around "Here comes Quaker with a bang-bang, rat-a-tat-tat-bang-bang" commercials. Browning threw around words like "robustitude" and "marvolious" and "cleverkins" (which all Terry listeners were). Like Jack Armstrong's Franklyn MacCormack, Browning pushed Quaker as the food "Uncle Sam wants you to eat to keep strong," and traded heavily on a "they're not rationed—no ration points" theme. Keeping the show's patriotic theme to the end, he closed with a daily "victogram," such as:

Paper is a mighty weapon
Haul it in, keep smartly steppin'.
Turn in every scrap you can,
To lick the Nazis and Japan.

Tex and Jinx

Tex and Jinx was the third of the major husband-wife breakfast shows. The stars were John Reagan (Tex) McCrary, newspaperman turned commentator, and his tennis player/swimmer/glamor-girl wife, Eugenia Lincoln (Jinx) Falkenburg. The breakfast boom began in the early 1940's with Ed and Pegeen Fitzgerald, expanded in 1945 with Dorothy and Dick Kollmar, and hit full stride in 1946 with the arrival of Tex and Jinx. Their first format, Hi, Jinx! was heard in New York on WEAF. Premièring April 22, it followed the McCrarys' June 10, 1945, wedding by less than a year. McCrary's influence over the show was obvious from the beginning; he kept it from slipping into the mindless chatter that often marked the others. Tex and Jinx talked about current events, brought in guest stars, and even discussed such mind-blowing subjects as venereal disease. They didn't clink china and pour coffee; they didn't even pretend to eat while running the show.

Jinx, who had been a model, movie star, and sportswoman of the late 1930's and early 1940's, was developed as a radio reporter in a series of on-the-air lessons by her husband. Tex had been with the New York Mirror, and supposedly knew the territory. He had met Jinx when sent by the paper to interview her. On their radio show, Tex played assignment editor, sending his wife out into the field with recording equipment. When she played the assigned interviews on the air the next day, he freely criticized her technique. They lured top guests, people like Bob Hope, Bernard Baruch, Esther Williams, Burgess Meredith, and Dorothy Lamour. In 1947, Meet Tex and Jinx was booked as a summer replacement for Duffy's Tavern, and so well-received that it was brought back in 1948. By 1950, the couple had a Tex and Jinx 60-minute morning show on New York radio. Here, Tex read the news from the front pages while Jinx discussed opening nights, films, and the lighter side.

The Texaco Star Theatre

The Texaco Star Theatre first rang its fire bells and siren on October 5, 1938, with an hour-long program of variety, drama, and music under the direction of Bill Bacher. It was a Wednesday-night extravaganza for CBS, opening with Adolphe Menjou as master of ceremonies, guest stars from Broadway and Hollywood, comic Ned Sparks, actress Una Merkel, announcer Jimmy Wallington, and the music of David

Broekman. In its 60-minute days, The Texaco Star Theatre offered full-length 30-minute dramas and 30 minutes of music and comedy, such as "The Jest," with John Barrymore, Elaine Barry, and Noah Beery. The dramatic stage was generally set to begin about 25 minutes into the show, with a little time left at the end for more variety. The emcee role was rotated among many big-name stars of the time, and finally settled on Ken Murray in 1939. In that year, the variety show came from Hollywood, while the drama was staged in New York. The Texaco Star Theatre as originally conceived ended in 1940; by fall it had become the Fred Allen program with Texaco Star Theatre logos. Texaco sponsored Allen's program for four years; by 1941, the time had been reduced to 30 minutes and it was settling into the format that Allen would use through the 1940's. The siren-and-bells opening was used until the show of December 10, 1941. But the sudden attack by Japan on Pearl Harbor raised the concern that a show opening with a siren might cause some alarm, so it was abandoned, to return after the war. Fred Allen dropped out of radio for a time in 1944, and The Texaco Star Theatre returned to a variety-concert format starring opera tenor James Melton. That show ran two seasons, with Melton accompanied in 1946 by Annamary Dickey, Broekman's orchestra, the Lyn Murray Singers, announcer John Reed King, and the old Texaco alumnus, Ed Wynn the "Fire Chief." In 1947 a new CBS Texaco Star Theatre featured Gordon MacRae, Evelyn Knight, the Jeff Alexander Chorus, comedian Alan Young, and the Victor Young orchestra. By 1948, that cast had moved with the show to ABC.

That Hammer Guy

That Hammer Guy starred Larry Haines as Mike Hammer, Mickey Spillane's tougher-than-nails private eye, in an undistinguished Mutual half-hour of 1953. It ran Tuesday nights for several sponsors.

That's a Good Idea

That's a Good Idea, a 1945 CBS Hollywood show, paid $5 to listeners who submitted usable, dramatizable ideas "for the benefit of mankind." The ideas ranged from the double-hooded umbrella (allowing two people to walk together in the rain) to the phosphorescent left-handed glove (for use by night drivers in hand signals). The ideas were dramatized by actors under the direction of creator-producer George Allen. Madelyn Pugh wrote the show and Del Castillo provided music on the organ. Dave Vaille was narrator and Jay Stewart announced.

Theatre Five

Theatre Five was ABC's attempt to bring back radio drama in the 1962–65 era. Even a top-flight radio production would have had a hard go in those days, and *Theatre Five* was little more than an echo of what radio had once been. Some 245 science fiction dramas were produced under this title, and the production was a far cry from NBC's fine *X-Minus One* of a few seasons before. Technique had sagged, dramatic muscles had grown old and flabby. ABC deserved an A for effort. Too bad the effort wasn't stronger than this.

The Theatre Guild on the Air

Although an earlier series, *Theatre Guild Dramas*, was heard on CBS in 1943, *The Theatre Guild on the Air* did not arrive until September 9, 1945, when it opened as a Sunday feature on ABC for United States Steel. This program differed from the earlier series in that its plays were produced by the Guild's top executives, and the productions also included a number of non-Guild plays.

The *Theatre Guild on the Air* had quite a different flavor than *The Lux Radio Theatre* and other Hollywood movie shows. The atmosphere of glamor was more subdued, with the emphasis shared equally by the production and the stars. The stage was a showcase for directors and authors as well. *Theatre Guild on the Air* did for Broadway what Lux had done for films. It became radio's most distinguished forum for legitimate drama. Following the Lux pattern, this show tried to obtain as stars the people who had played the roles on the stage. Occasionally a very adaptable book (such as John Steinbeck's *Of Mice and Men* or Ernest Hemingway's *A Farewell to Arms*) was dramatized, but for most of its run, the producers went for its material to the legitimate stage.

The Theatre Guild was formed just after World War I, when a group of theatre people met, pooled their money, and established a new production company on less than $500. Twenty years and 150 plays later, *The Theatre Guild on the Air* began bringing some of those plays to radio. Lawrence Langner, one of the original members and co-administrator of the Guild, supervised production with the help of Theresa Helburn. George Kondolf was producer and Homer

Fickett (whose directing credits included a long stint on the distinguished *Cavalcade of America*) became the show's director of long standing. Harold Levey wrote original themes and conducted the music, which was always low-key. Norman Brokenshire, one of the great early announcers of the air, introduced the plays; newsman George Hicks reported the latest developments in the steel industry for USS. Armina Marshall was executive producer; hosts in the later era included Roger Pryor and Elliott Reid.

For many years Langner served as host, a dramatic master of ceremonies of sorts. He introduced the stars and verbally set the stage. Stars weren't fawned over as they were on *Lux*; they weren't expected to peddle soap or steel. Some of the best names on Broadway made their first air performances on this show. Alfred Lunt and Lynn Fontanne appeared several times. The first production was *Wings Over Europe*, with Burgess Meredith. The producers had a liking for Eugene O'Neill, Maxwell Anderson, George Bernard Shaw, and William Shakespeare. Walter Huston appeared in *Ah, Wilderness*, Katharine Hepburn was in *Little Women*. In rather a strange bit of casting, Humphrey Bogart played *A Farewell to Arms*.

The Guild did musicals like *Brigadoon* and fantasies like *Dr. Jekyll and Mr. Hyde*, but pulled few punches. When Tennessee Williams' *Summer and Smoke* was run in 1949, it created an uproar because it depicted a girl turning to prostitution and was broadcast on Easter Sunday.

The ABC run lasted until June 5, 1949. *Theatre Guild on the Air* returned on September 11, 1949, as an NBC show. There it ran—still for U.S. Steel—until June 7, 1953. During the steel years, it was also billed as *The United States Steel Hour*.

On March 4, 1951, RCA joined USS to sponsor a 90-minute special of *Hamlet* with Sir John Gielgud. The shows were usually done from the Belasco Theatre in New York, though the producers, in the best tradition of live drama, often took the show on the road. Throughout the long run, USS maintained the admirable policy of keeping its fingers out of the dramatic pie. The program continued into 1954 as an NBC sustained show.

The Theatre of Famous Radio Players

The Theatre of Famous Radio Players was syndicated by producer Les Mitchel and was taken in by Mutual–Don Lee in 1945. Mitchel, long one of the most active producer-directors on Radio Row, created the series as a repertory of radio's best actors in plays written especially for them. Lou Merrill, Sharon Douglas, Barbara Fuller, David Ellis, Peggy Webber, Cathy Lewis, Lurene Tuttle, Forrest Lewis, Jack Edwards, Joseph Kearns, Gloria Blondell, and Marvin Miller were members of the group. The shows were produced at Mitchel's Universal Radio Productions studio in Hollywood.

Theatre of Romance

Theatre of Romance was another CBS show of superstar strength, broadcasting from New York in 1944 and moving the following year to Hollywood. The move came about after ratings had begun to drop. The sag was blamed on a shortage of top film stars available for service on the East Coast. *Theatre of Romance* didn't have that trouble in Hollywood, and soon featured the likes of Humphrey Bogart, Loretta Young, Alan Ladd, Cary Grant, Douglas Fairbanks, Jr., Errol Flynn, Shirley Temple, Van Johnson, and Herbert Marshall. The show was built around light, romantic stories and "stars of proven romantic appeal." Charles Vanda was producer-director; the show was carried by Colgate on Tuesday nights from 1944 through 1946.

Think

Think, also known as *The ABC Radio Workshop*, was a creative little show of the early 1950's. Like the later *CBS Radio Workshop*, it offered some experimental drama, but concentrated more on tales of imagination and science fiction. Some of the stories, such as Ray Bradbury's "Mars Is Heaven," had been done before on *Escape* and *Dimension X*, but the treatment on *Think* was changed completely by a new script and a different focus. It was a solid show, one of the better series of its time. Dave Ballard, host, was known as "the voice of Think."

The Third Man

The Third Man was the story of radio's all-time prince of knaves, Harry Lime, a character created by Graham Greene in his novel of intrigue. The novel became a film in 1950, and before the ink was dry on the reviews, Harry Lime was hanging out his shingle on Radio Row in a good series of syndicated shows.

Orson Welles had always seemed somewhat mischievous, ever

since that long-ago night when his men from Mars landed in the Jersey flats, so he was perfect as the voice of Harry Lime. Welles did about a year's worth of Lime shows, coming off as a double-dealing, conniving, covetous money-grubber, but somehow managing to make the character likable—at times even admirable—in his deceptions. No matter how straight Harry played it on the surface, he always had an angle somewhere. The kind of man who would dominate movies of the 1970's as the "anti-hero," he stole from the rich and gave to the poor. And Harry Lime was usually the poorest chap he knew. He thought nothing of double-crossing a partner, but the partners who associated with Harry Lime were just as likely to double-cross him if they thought of it first.

He flitted from continent to continent, drifting with the wind. Europe was generally his stamping ground. From Budapest to the Riviera, Harry Lime turned up wherever there was an easy heist. He charmed ladies out of their jewelry, and had even been known to break and enter when the situation demanded. The only real lines Harry drew were at murder and blackmail. That, plus the fact that his victims were usually blackhearts like himself, helped keep him on the good side of listeners.

Subtitled *The Lives of Harry Lime*, *The Third Man* was a well-done canned show. Welles again proved his mastery of the medium, in tight stories beautifully scored by the haunting "Third Man" theme of Anton Karas' zither.

The Thirteenth Juror

The Thirteenth Juror, a 1949 NBC summer series, told of great historical mysteries that have persisted through the ages and asked listeners to be "the Thirteenth Juror" and make up their own minds. The opening show pondered the question of John Wilkes Booth's alleged death after the assassination of Abraham Lincoln. History tells us that Booth was found hiding in a barn and was killed there while the barn burned. But the facts are obscure; some people claimed to have spoken with Booth much later. One legend had it that he died in 1903. Hans Conried and Vincent Price starred in the opener.

This Is Judy Jones

This Is Judy Jones was another NBC summer show, first heard in June, 1941. Mercedes McCambridge starred as Judy, a model and girl Friday for crotchety fashion designer Creighton Leighton. The show was light drama with strong elements of situation comedy, and provided early work for some of radio's top stars of later years. Ben Alexander was featured as Judy's great love, Junior Sheldon; Wally Maher was boss Creighton Leighton; Elliott Lewis played Mr. Peterson, the next-door neighbor in love with Judy's widowed mother (Betty Wilbur); and Marvel McInnis was Betz Bowman, Judy's best friend. Scripting was by Myron Dutton.

This Is My Best

This Is My Best, during its short life, was one of the most impressive CBS shows. Based on the book edited by Whit Burnett, it was billed immediately as prestige drama, and was unleashed with Edward Arnold as host on September 5, 1944, for a two-year Tuesday-night run for Cresta Blanca Wines.

Orson Welles became identified in a major way with the show very early in the run. Though originally produced by Homer Fickett and directed by Dave Titus, *This Is My Best* brought Welles to the microphone as star, reuniting him with two old graduates of his *Mercury Theatre*, Agnes Moorehead and Ray Collins. Welles and Collins recreated Norman Corwin's "best"—the delightful *Plot to Overthrow Christmas*. Both appeared with Miss Moorehead in *The Master of Ballantrae*, by Robert Louis Stevenson. Although some stories for *This Is My Best* were adapted from the classics, most were contemporary and had the personal approval of their living authors. Early shows included *Heaven Is My Destination* (Van Johnson) by Thornton Wilder, *The Secret Life of Walter Mitty* (Robert Benchley) by James Thurber, *Leader of the People* (Walter Brennan, Walter Abel, Agnes Moorehead) by John Steinbeck, and *Brighton Rock* (Ida Lupino) by Graham Greene. Sinclair Lewis' selection from *Babbitt* proved unsuitable for 30-minute radio presentation. The author agreed, and picked *Willow Walk* as his "second best," and Welles was cast in a dual role.

By 1945, Welles had ascended to the show's top spot—producer-director, occasional star, and narrator. He directed from a podium, puffing away on his eternal cigar and flashing directions with a specially designed cue box with colored lights (white = control room, red = sound effects, blue = orchestra, green = miscellaneous). By May 1945 he had left the show, and Don Clark later became producer. *This Is My Best* continued its established author-star policy, and became one of radio's prime testing grounds for unfilmed movie properties. The nation's top studios often worked closely with the show, testing their literary options on the air before making the commitment to film.

John McIntire was Cresta Blanca's host and announcer until the spring of 1945, when he and wife, Jeanette Nolan, dropped out of radio for a while. Miss Nolan was a perfect evil queen on the show's *Snow White*, in her last radio appearance of that period. Bernard Katz was conductor-composer and Robert Tallman adapted the books to sound. In all, this was a distinguished half-hour, last heard in 1946.

This Is My Story

This Is My Story ran on CBS in 1944–45, dramatizing true stories sent in by the listening audience. Hedda Hopper, Barbara Stanwyck, and Leo McCarey judged the stories, and the best one in each twelve-week period earned its author $1,000. As originally written, the stories were only 500 words long, and were judged mainly for dramatic content. Then they were dramatized for the air. One of the most publicized was the story of Louise Applewhite, the 13-year-old infantile paralysis victim. Louise couldn't get treatment locally because the hospitals were packed with polio victims. So she appealed directly to President Roosevelt; he immediately dispatched a plane and doctors to pick up the girl and enroll her in his Warm Springs Foundation. The poignant story was replayed on CBS the Saturday following Roosevelt's death.

This Is Nora Drake

This Is Nora Drake came to NBC October 27, 1947, another of the late-morning soaps exploiting the theme of a woman's career clashing with her personal happiness. Originally written by medical specialist Julian Funt, the show was later scripted by Milton Lewis.

Nora Drake was a nurse (later a departmental supervisor) on the staff of Page Memorial Hospital, in a medium-sized town. Nora, supposedly an orphan in the beginning, fell in love with Dr. Ken Martinson, and though he also loved her, he was burdened by many of the hangups of soap opera males. He dashed off and married Peg King, daughter of millionaire Andrew King and a girl of unbridled emotions. Soon realizing that he still loved Nora, Ken asked Peg for a divorce. In a fury, Peg confronted Nora, then roared away in a careening automobile and had an accident, rendering her a helpless cripple. Feeling that he couldn't possibly leave after that, Ken pined unabashedly for Nora, and the days passed in hopeless agony.

Meanwhile, Nora's long-lost father, Arthur Drake, turned up, proving himself a man of strong emotions and weak mind. After introducing his daughter to gambler Fred Molina, Drake turned a gun on Molina and seriously wounded him. For that he was sent to prison, adding more woe to Nora's already trauma-ridden life. Nora confided all to Rose Fuller, head nurse at Page, who became the serial's stock wise, matronly figure. Rose was always anxious to share the troubles of others despite knowing that she herself was the victim of a slow but fatal disease.

Nora was played originally by Charlotte Holland. By 1949, Joan Tompkins had the title role, and it was later played by Mary Jane Higby. Alan Hewitt, and later Leon Janney, played Ken Martinson, Ralph Bell was father Arthur Drake, Irene Hubbard was friend Rose Fuller, and Larry Haines was gambler Fred Molina. Lesley Woods, Joan Alexander, and Mercedes McCambridge had turns as crippled Peggy King Martinson; Roger De Koven played her father Andrew King. Grant Richards played Charles Dobbs, assistant district attorney who prosecuted Nora's father; Joan Lorring was Suzanne Turrie, his 18-year-old refugee ward, who loved him. Bill Cullen announced for Toni Home Permanent, which carried the show into the 1950's. *This Is Nora Drake* was last heard on January 2, 1959.

This Is Our Enemy

This Is Our Enemy was a government-sponsored and government-produced series that ran on Mutual as a late-night Sunday show in 1942–43. "We cannot win our war or make our peace unless we understand the character of the enemy we are fighting." That, in a nutshell, was the theme behind *This Is Our Enemy*. The shows, enacted by such top radio people as John Gibson, Lawson Zerbe, Roger De Koven, and Stefan Schnabel, depicted Nazi brutality in the starkest terms. The propaganda message came across loud and clear: "Nazis despise the common man . . . to have such people resist is an affront to them . . . it is not in their pattern of order and obey . . ." Each program promised to "add something to your knowledge of the enemy." One story told how the Nazis occupying France brainwashed a young boy into hating his father. Another dramatized the quiet resistance in Czechoslovakia. It was dramatically overdone, but historically fascinating today. Frank Telford directed.

This Is Your FBI

This Is Your FBI, the second long-running show using the FBI as thriller material, came to the Blue Network (ABC) April 6, 1945. *The FBI in Peace and War* had been running a little less than a year on CBS, and the appearance of a new G-Man thriller led to inevitable comparisons. In fact, there were striking similarities between the shows. The original music of *This Is Your FBI* had a bouncy, rousing rhythm much like the "Love for Three Oranges" march of *Peace and War*. Both shows used agent-heros of a rather faceless nature. Field Agent Sheppard of *Peace and War* probably could have filled in for Jim Taylor of *This Is Your FBI*, but in the all-important realm of entertainment, *This Is Your FBI* was better. The real differences were subtle, but just beneath the surface. While *Peace and War* took its material (or at least the inspiration) from a fictionalized book, *This Is Your FBI* got its cases from FBI filing cabinets. The result was a dramatic pace that *Peace and War*, for all its years on the air, never achieved.

This Is Your FBI was created, produced, and directed by Jerry Devine, a former comedy writer who had worked for Kate Smith before going straight and turning to thrillers. Devine saw his show as "the official story," the Bureau's own view of the criminal life. The FBI was glorified in the typical manner of the era, while criminals and racketeers were depicted as living the most lurid lives this side of hell. Crime might pay on the streets of New York, but not on *This Is Your FBI*. With its scientific tools and its worldwide communications system, the Bureau was infallible.

Devine prepared well for his show. He attended the FBI school for new agents, then got J. Edgar Hoover's permission to dramatize from old, closed cases, using only fictitious names, dates, and places. Hoover even gave the series a personal sendoff. Often in its first year, the show ran sensational, screaming stories of Nazi super-agents, of escaped Nazi prisoners of war, of saboteurs. Later, as the war faded into history, agent Taylor and his men came to grips with military frauds, juvenile delinquents, hijackers, bank robbers, and embezzlers. The stories were usually told from the inside out, from the viewpoint of the criminal or his victim. Taylor, played by Stacy Harris, had almost a supporting part during the entire eight years that the show was on the air.

Each episode was told in chronological form, with a harsh narrative overlay. Frank Lovejoy was the first narrator, and a good one. But he left within a year, and by 1947 Dean Carlton had the job. William Woodson came on as narrator in March 1948 and remained for several years. The show used freelance writers, mostly Lawrence MacArthur and Frank Phares, until Jerry D. Lewis came aboard as staff scripter in the late 1940's. Music was by Nathan Van Cleave and later by Frederick Steiner. Carl Frank was announcer. By 1948, Larry Keating —best remembered as George Burns' neighbor on early *Burns and Allen* TV shows—was announcing and doing spots for the Equitable Life Assurance Society. The show was carried by Equitable on Friday nights through 1952, and ran for another year as an ABC sustainer. The sponsor's well-remembered punchline was: "To your FBI you

look for national security, and to your Equitable Society for financial
security. These two great institutions are dedicated to the protection
of you, your home, and your country!"

This Is Your Life

This Is Your Life, first heard on NBC November 9, 1948, for Philip
Morris, was the second major human interest show created by Ralph
Edwards (the other was the long-running *Truth or Consequences*).
Edwards had long thought that a viable radio show could be built
around reconstructions of the lives of celebrities and common folk
alike. Edwards told the person's life chronologically, in the words of
the people who knew him best. Half-forgotten teachers, ministers,
lost relatives, and old Army buddies were located, flown in for the
show, and kept on ice backstage until the big moment. The subject
was unaware that his life was being eulogized until he was on the air.
Usually he or she was brought to the studio through some ruse, and
became aware of what was happening only when Edwards sang out
"This is your life!" (Some, such as newsman Lowell Thomas, got
rather huffy when they found out what was happening.) The stories
were done in a style that was painfully sentimental, with writing
designed to bring out the color of the person's background. "The
Story of Barney Ross" was told by Edwards in "rounds," with each
round representing another phase of the boxer's life. One of the most
successful stories was of Sam Canzona, a Chicago organ grinder
whose dream of bringing his wife's sister over from Italy became a
reality on *This Is Your Life.* The show was highly popular, but came at
the very end of network radio. It ran one year on Tuesday nights
and another year on Wednesday nights, then moved into TV, where it
became a great success for more than nine years.

This Life Is Mine

This Life Is Mine was the story of teacher Eden Channing and her
family as they met "our changing world with two conflicting points of
view." Betty Winkler starred as Eden, with Michael Fitzmaurice as
Captain Bob Hastings. Hastings was trying to cut Eden's fiancé, Paul,
out of her life while Paul was away fighting for his country. That was
dirty pool par excellence when this show premièred March 22, 1943.
But none of them would be around long enough to brood about it. *This
Life Is Mine* was a soap opera without soap, being sponsorless and
sustained by CBS. Sure enough, it had disappeared by the end of
1945.

Those We Love

Those We Love might have been a big show in the *One Man's Family* mold if sponsors and networks had had the good sense to leave it alone. But it had a very unstable run, shifted here and there, was dropped over the howls of its listeners, and was then reinstated months down the line. It came to the Blue Network January 4, 1938, as a 30-minute Tuesday-night show for Pond's Cold Cream. The following year it was moved to Monday. In 1939, it was picked up by Royal Gelatin for Thursday-night NBC. In 1940, it went to CBS on Mondays for Teel Soap. It replaced Eddie Cantor for the summer of 1942, and was Jack Benny's replacement in 1943. From 1943 through 1945 (the final season), *Those We Love* was heard regularly on Sundays for General Foods, at the ungodly hour of 11 A.M. on the West Coast. Even then, it was thrown back and forth between CBS and NBC like a hot potato. This would have been bad enough for a situation comedy or weekly drama; for a serial trying to maintain some continuity between episodes, it was disaster. Still, *Those We Love* consistently drew respectable ratings, peaking over 10 for two years running.

Written by Agnes Ridgway, it told the story of Kathy and Kit Marshall, young adult twins, and those they loved in the New England town of Westbridge. The loved included a father, John Marshall (Francis X. Bushman), an Aunt Emily (Alma Kruger) who had raised them like a mother, and a beloved housekeeper named Martha Newbury (Virginia Sale). Nan Grey played Kathy, whose romantic entanglements formed the backbone of the serial. Kit was played by Richard Cromwell, and by Bill Henry after 1942. Late in the run, Kathy settled down and became engaged to Dr. Leslie Foster (Donald Woods). Ann Todd played his little girl Amy; Mary Gordon was his Scottish housekeeper, Mrs. Emmett; Clarence Straight was Rags the dog. Nurse Lydia Dennison was played by Anne Stone, wife of producer-director Ted Sherdeman. In its first five years, *Those We Love* played only three years' total air time because of its insane scheduling. Some fans became so upset that they threatened to make it an issue with the FCC. Still, they followed *Those We Love* all over the dials for eight years. Its 1940 rating was 11-plus.

Those Websters

Those Websters was a giddy comedy about family life, set in the typical small town with the typical mom-dad-brother-sis combo. It originated in New York March 9, 1945, as a Friday-night feature for Quaker Oats, then moved to Chicago after a few months, and finally made the jump to Hollywood in the fall of 1946. In the interim, it switched days (to Sundays, 1946) and networks (from CBS to NBC) before winding up in 1947–48 as a Sunday show for Mutual. Quaker Oats stayed with the program, and for the most part, so did the cast. Willard Waterman was starred as George Webster, the slightly pompous father figure who was a fine preparation for Waterman's role of *The Great Gildersleeve* a few years later. Constance Crowder played his wife Jane, Gil Stratton, Jr. was son Billy, and Joan Alt was daughter Liz. Jane Webb played the Websters' neighbor, Belinda. *Vic and Sade* alumni Clarence Hartzell and Billy Idelson were cast as Mr. Watt and Emil respectively. Parley Baer played Emil's father, the grocery man Stulin. The Webster family lived at 46 River Road in the town of Spring City, where such mundane comedic adventures as visits by old classmates and matchmaking among friends revolved around them. It was billed as "our weekly reminder that families are fun," but it seemed that for old George Webster, frustration—not fun—was the byword. Joe Ainley produced and directed in 1946; Frank Worth scored the show, and the scripts were by Frank and Doris Hursley—a professor and a lawyer.

Three-Ring Time

Three-Ring Time claimed to be the first major transcontinental show offered by Mutual from the West Coast. It premièred September 12, 1941, and ran for a season under the sponsorship of Ballantine Ale on Friday nights. In a highly unusual casting mix, Milton Berle was teamed with Charles Laughton, but by January 1942 Berle had broken away for his own equally foredoomed show. It did give Laughton a chance to do some comedy—something he had always liked, but was usually denied—and featured songs by Shirley Ross and music by Bob Crosby.

Time for Women

Time for Women was an ABC news commentary show sponsored by Time magazine and premièring January 2, 1946. Written and edited each day by Time editors, it featured Shelley Mydans as commentator and was heard five times a week in the late afternoon. As the title suggests, its content was primarily of interest to women.

Today's Children

Today's Children was another of the sometimes-related Irna Phillips serials, first heard on NBC's Blue Network May 15, 1933, for Pillsbury Flour. The show grew out of another Phillips soap, *Painted Dreams*, owned by WGN, Chicago. When WGN refused to let Miss Phillips take it to the network, she quit the station and began an eight-year court fight to regain her rights to the show. She lost in the courts, but ultimately won on the air, bringing to *Today's Children* many of the same qualities—even the same thinly renamed characters—she had used on *Painted Dreams.*

The new serial, set in Chicago's Hester Street, told the stories of a cross-section of neighborhood families and their problems. It settled primarily on the Moran family. Miss Phillips herself played Mother Moran (she had been Mother Moynihan in *Painted Dreams*), a matriarch patterned after her own mother. Also in the early cast was Ireene Wicker (the Singing Lady), who played Mother Moran's daughter Eileen. Bess Johnson, who would later find unhappiness on *Hilltop House*, played Frances Moran. At the same time, Miss Phillips played the role of Kay Norton, Mother's adopted daughter.

By 1938, *Today's Children* was the top-rated serial on daytime radio. But when her mother died, Miss Phillips felt that her inspiration for the serial had died too. She dropped the program against the wishes of Pillsbury people, but immediately gave them *Woman in White*, which soon vaulted to the top. In a unique experiment, she had the cast of *Today's Children* tune in the new serial, *Woman in White*, and introduced the new show in a blending of both casts. *Today's Children* was absent for five years, returning December 13, 1943, as an NBC show for General Mills. That version ran strongly until 1950, and focused mainly on the Schultz family, still of Hester Street, Chicago. Though plotted by Miss Phillips, it was written by Virginia Cooke and promoted the same themes of family love and togetherness.

Mother and Papa Schultz were played by Virginia Payne and Murray Forbes, who made such a fine team on *Ma Perkins*. Their children were Bertha (Patricia Dunlap), Marilyn (Ruth Rau and Betty Lou Gerson), and Otto (Ernie Andrews). Marilyn had been born Maggie, but changed her name to Marilyn Larrimore to become a model. Otto returned from the war temporarily blinded. Maggie married lawyer John Murray (Kleve Kirby) and Otto married Jen Burton (Laurette Fillbrandt). Another of the Schultz children, Joseph, was killed in the war. But the family hadn't seen him in seventeen years anyway (he had been driven away by the impetuous Papa). Now comes Joseph's war buddy, Richard Stone (Art Hern), telling the family that he is Joe, that his war-torn face has been rebuilt by plastic surgery. The family, believing his story (though Ma Schultz knows in her heart), takes in the love-starved GI as one of them. And Richard, as he comes to know them, finds that his love for "sister" Bertha goes far deeper than sibling devotion. And so it went.

Tom Corbett, Space Cadet

Tom Corbett, Space Cadet came to ABC January 1, 1952, as a five-a-week connected 30-minute series of interplanetary juvenile adventure. By fall, the format had been trimmed to Tuesdays and Thursdays, with connecting elements between shows of the same week. Sponsored by Kellogg's Pep and announced by Jackson Beck, it had the same frantic sound as those other Kellogg-Beck serials, *Superman* and *Mark Trail*. With sounds of buzzers and countdowns, futuristic hisses and rumbles, Tom and his cadet friends Roger Manning and Astro (boys enrolled at Space Academy) blasted off for a loop around the universe in high pursuit of space pirates and hijackers. "Now, as roaring rockets blast off to distant planets and far-flung stars, we take you to the age of the conquest of space, with *Tom Corbett, Space Cadet!*" Tom was played by Frankie Thomas, Roger (the perennial wiseacre) by Jan Merlin, Astro was Al Markim, and their chief Captain Strong was played by Edward Bryce. Drex Hines directed. *Tom Corbett, Space Cadet* last saw Luna in 1952.

The Tom Mix Ralston Straightshooters

The Tom Mix Ralston Straightshooters was first heard on NBC as a three-a-week Western-mystery thriller on September 25, 1933. One of the true giants of juvenile adventure, this show was first based on the real-life experiences of the greatest Western film star of the silent era. Tom Mix really had lived a life of adventure as a turn-of-the-century soldier of fortune, serving with Teddy Roosevelt's Rough Riders in the Philippines and later seeing action in the Boer War and in China's Boxer Rebellion. Back in America, he signed on as a Kansas lawman, then joined the Texas Rangers. He was a champion rodeo performer; in 1906 he went on the road with the Miller Brothers Wild West Show. His movie career began in 1910, when he was 30. It swept him to national fame in silents of the 1920's, and made him a fortune. In 1933, after a few not-so-successful talkies, he retired from movies and bought a circus and Wild West show.

In 1935, when the serial was two years old, it was still relaying Mix's experiences in the Boer, Spanish-American, and Boxer wars. But soon Tom settled down, at least on the air, in the Texas country near the town of Dobie. There he established his TM-Bar Ranch and began his new reputation as hero of "radio's biggest Western-detective program."

As a serial character, Tom Mix was constantly involved in mysterious, "baffling" situations involving murder and mayhem to a far greater extent than was usual for juvenile thrillers.

The mystery element made the serial very popular in the late 1940's, pushing the rating past even the traditional leader, *Jack Armstrong*, whose murderless plots had by then begun to pale. While murder ran rampant, Tom tackled the mystery of a vanishing village and later tried to track down the origin of a mystery voice that appeared suddenly on his commercial records, defying all rational explanation. He went to Europe on a secret V-E Day mission, with saboteurs and agents snapping at his heels. And in one of the best-remembered wartime episodes, he tracked a giant to its lair, learning that it was merely a terrorist trick operated by the "Japs" (who else?) to disrupt the home front.

Harold Peary and Willard Waterman played Sheriff Mike Shaw in the late 1930's, discovering an ability to sound alike that would serve Waterman well on *The Great Gildersleeve* a decade later. Sheriff Mike was later played by Leo Curley. Wash was Vance McCune and then Forrest Lewis; Pecos Williams was played by Curley Bradley in those prewar years, long before he ever dreamed of being the lead.

By 1936, *Tom Mix* was heard five times a week. The serial was carried through its entire run by Ralston, except for the 1939 season, which was sponsored by Kellogg. In 1937, the show moved to the Blue Network, where it ran through 1942.

By 1940, most of the famous regulars were well-established in the *Tom Mix* dramas of the air. Tom's sidekick, the Old Wrangler, narrated the tales, opening each chapter with a friendly, "Howdy, Straightshooters, howdy!" The Wrangler had a solid role in the stories, too, serving as something of a solemn Gabby Hayes for comic relief. He rode a horse named Calico, and occasionally got kidnapped and had to be rescued. When he wasn't around, Sheriff Mike Shaw did just as well in that department. Their pal Wash was cook and the "man of all work" at Tom's TM-Bar Ranch. Pecos Williams was another of Tom's buddies; he was a singing sidekick who also had a penchant for trouble. Jimmy and Jane were the kids, young straightshooters who gave listeners of both sexes a sense of identity with the stories. Finally, there was miserly Amos Q. Snood, whose appearance in such a rip-roaring cowboy thriller always seemed slightly out of place.

After a brief absence in the early 1940's, the serial was revived on Mutual in 1944. There it ran as a daily show for Ralston until 1949. On September 26, 1949, it became a three-a-week, 30-minute, complete-in-each-episode thriller. With the Mutual run came a change of flavor.

The old Wrangler had been replaced by announcer Don Gordon, whose lead-ins were more direct. The character of Tom, which had been played by Artells Dickson, Jack Holden, and Russell Thorson, was now assumed by Joe (Curley) Bradley, a former Oklahoma cowboy and Hollywood stunt man who had really learned to sing around ranchhouse bonfires. Bradley's Tom was a singer as well as a fighter, his shows were marked by zippy singing commercials, formerly done by a Western quartet. He came galloping in with an organ crescendo, Wonder Horse Tony neighing and pawing the air, and the golden authority of his voice pushed Ralston right off Checkerboard Square:

> Shre-dd-ed Ralston for your breakfast
> Start the day off shinin' bright;
> Gives you lots of cowboy energy,
> With a flavor that's just right.
> It's delicious and nutritious,
> Bite-size and ready to eat.
> Take a tip from Tom,
> Go and tell your mom,
> Shredded Ralston can't be beat!

The serial was one of the top premium-givers of its time, offering such toys as a rocket parachute, a Sheriff Mike whistling badge, coded comic books, and a photo album "containing highly confidential information every straightshooter should know." All for a dime each and a few Ralston boxtops, sent without delay (remember, these offers are limited) to Ralston, Checkerboard Square, St. Louis, Missouri.

The show ended June 23, 1950.

While it ran, the real Tom Mix had nothing to do with the serial beyond lending it his name. Ironically, after all his dangerous adventures, Mix died in an automobile accident just outside Florence, Arizona, on October 12, 1940.

Tommy Riggs and Betty Lou

Tommy Riggs and Betty Lou grew out of the strange ability of Tommy Riggs to talk like a 7-year-old girl. Riggs wasn't a ventriloquist; yet deep in the world of Riggs' throat lived one of the most delightful characters of the air. Riggs had a condition that doctors at the Cornell

Medical Center, after X-raying his throat, once described as "bi-vocalism."

It simply meant that Riggs could talk in his normal voice or, on request, he could change to the voice of a little girl. This was no falsetto, hammed-up imitation of a little girl, but a voice so vivid that once, when he used it on a late-night local show in the Midwest, the child labor bureau threatened the station with action unless "that little girl" was taken off at such an ungodly hour.

Riggs first discovered Betty Lou hiding in his throat while he was a football player at Brown University. He uncorked her one day in the dressing room just to send his naked teammates scrambling for their clothes. Thereafter, Betty Lou was much in demand at parties and fraternity gatherings. In 1931, Riggs went to work as a singer and piano player with KDKA, in his hometown Pittsburgh. He brought out his character in an off-mike stream of blue dialogue, sending the station manager into hysterics and getting his first *Tom and Betty* show. It was an instant hit, and in the years that followed, Riggs used Betty on stations throughout the Midwest. They got their first national break on a 1937 *Rudy Vallee Show*. Before that, there had been a long string of local radio jobs; Betty Lou, with her charming good manners, had been a smash everywhere.

Riggs' appearance with Vallee was to have been for one show only, but Betty Lou was so popular that he was returned for a record forty-nine weeks. Critics, remembering that Edgar Bergen had also begun on Vallee's show, began to talk about similarities and contrasts between Betty Lou and Bergen's dummy, Charlie McCarthy. Charlie was funnier, but Betty Lou won hands down in all areas of charm and believability. Charlie was a scamp; Betty Lou was just a lovable little girl.

In fact, hundreds of listeners refused to believe that Riggs was doing both voices. Gifts poured into the network, all addressed to Betty Lou and containing little-girl toys, embroidered handkerchiefs, dolls. With his Vallee stint behind him, Riggs was a natural for his own series, so *Tommy Riggs and Betty Lou* came to NBC for Quaker Oats October 1, 1938. It lasted for two years, then Riggs began to slip into obscurity. He was almost a forgotten man when he was picked up in 1942 as a springtime regular on *The Kate Smith Hour*. That led to a new *Tommy Riggs and Betty Lou*, running during the summer of 1942 as a replacement for *Burns and Allen*. Betty Lou was a hit again. By the time George and Gracie returned in the fall, Riggs and his voice had wormed their way into the Swan Soap coffers. The sponsors decided to carry Riggs as well as Burns and Allen.

That summer Riggs first presented Betty Lou as his impish little niece. Wally Maher was tapped as her boyfriend, the sniffling, idiotic

Wilbur, and the show took on stronger aspects of situation comedy. Ken Christy played Wilbur's dim-witted father, Mr. Hutch. Verna Felton played Riggs' talkative housekeeper Mrs. McIntyre, and Bea Benaderet was Mrs. Wingate, the snooty neighbor. Other regulars were Mel Blanc, who played Uncle Petie and Rover the dog, Margaret Brayton, and Elvia Allman. Bill Goodwin announced until he returned to *Burns and Allen,* then Frank Graham took over. Writers were Sam Perrin, Jack Douglas, Bill Danch, George Balzer, and Al Lewin. Glenhall Taylor was the producer.

That basic format carried over into the regular series, which ran through the 1943 season as a Friday-nighter. Then Riggs dropped out of radio, joining the Navy and taking Betty Lou on a Far East entertainment swing through Allied camps. Eighteen months later, he returned to a Hollywood that had forgotten him again. Riggs had one more brief fling at radio, a summer job in 1946. Maher was restored as Wilbur, music was by Frank De Vol, and Don Wilson did the announcing honors. Then it was bedtime for Betty Lou, a charming moppet who once had all the personality of Charlie McCarthy, but couldn't quite hang in there.

Tonight at Hoagy's

Tonight at Hoagy's came to Mutual as a Sunday musical-comedy program in the fall of 1944. Hoagy Carmichael, one of the nation's foremost composers, developed the show around the idea of an old-fashioned jam session at home. Produced by Walter Snow, it featured such Carmichael favorites as "Stardust" and brought to the microphone as regulars singers Lulie-Jean Norman, Dave Marshall, and the Thrasher Sisters, musicians Opie Cates, Peewee Hunt, and Jimmy Briggs, and comedienne Ruby Dandridge as a character called Ella Rose. Larry Keating and Harry Evans (Hollywood columnist billed as "Hoagy's permanent house guest") were also featured.

Tonight at Hoagy's ran one season, and in February 1945, Carmichael opened on NBC in a Monday-night format called *Something New,* which ran into 1946. In this case, the "something new" was the orchestra—the Teenagers, an adolescent band headed by 19-year-old Jimmie Higson. Carmichael introduced Carol Stewart, Gale Robbins, comedian Pinky Lee (though Lee had been active in radio in a small way since the 1930's), and the comic team of Bob Sweeney and Hal March on the show. In 1946, a show of Carmichael's songs was heard Sundays on CBS for Luden's Cough Drops in a 15-minute format. It moved to Saturday as a sustainer in 1947–48.

Tony Wons' Scrapbook

Tony Wons' Scrapbook combined poetry, philosophy, and witty-humorous snatches of romantic dialogue; it became one of the great early successes of its kind. A self-made philosopher, Wons dropped out of school at 13 to work in a factory, but in the days before World War I he began to study on his own, beginning the scrapbook that would form the basis for his later radio shows. He memorized a lot of Shakespeare, and after the war took his material to WLS, Chicago, for an audition. The audition was a 40-minute reading of The Merchant of Venice, with Wons playing eight roles. It won him a staff job at $25 a week. Soon he began a Shakespeare series on WLS that ran for three years. His Tony Wons' Scrapbook began on CBS as a 15-minute, six-a-week sustained show in 1930. It featured Wons' own philosophizing and poetry, combined with that of the masters, and isolated bits and pieces that listeners sent in. It was an early-morning show, punctuated by his catch phrase, "Are yuh listenin'?" Wons was extremely popular with women; his appeal was built around a soft, direct approach, and listeners felt that he was talking right to them. His show ran four years on CBS, sponsored in 1932 by International Silver and in 1933 by Johnson's Wax. It moved to the Blue Network for Johnson's in 1934. Wons was off the air for several seasons, turning up again on CBS for Vicks in 1937. He also had a twice-a-week Hallmark show on NBC in 1940–41.

The Town Crier

The Town Crier was Alexander Woollcott, one of the most influential cultural figures of his time. Through his newspaper reviews, books, and acting, Woollcott had gained a great following by the late 1920's, and a legend was already growing around his name. Radio enhanced that, making Woollcott nationally known as the Town Crier. His first Crier broadcast was in 1929; his regular Town Crier format began on CBS September 13, 1933, and lasted intermittently for the next decade. In the twice-a-week 15-minute show, Woollcott interviewed people, plugged books, and discussed the issues of the day. His trademark was the ringing of a bell—town hall style—and the cry, "Hear ye, hear ye!" During his stint on the air, Woollcott became the most powerful literary critic in America; his endorsement could send a book soaring to the top of the best-seller list. He single-handedly plugged James Hilton's Goodbye, Mr. Chips until it became a financial blockbuster. Appropriately enough, Woollcott's career ended at the microphone. Appearing on a CBS *People's Platform* show on January 23, 1943, he was stricken by a heart attack, collapsed at the mike, and was carried out of the studio while the discussion continued uninterrupted. Woollcott died about four hours later.

Treasury Star Parade

Treasury Star Parade was syndicated by the government in the summer of 1942, and for the next two years brought forth Hollywood's brightest stars in 15-minute mini-dramas and variety shows, all designed to plug the Allied cause. Arch Oboler wrote many stories for this show; one of his most powerful was "Chicago, Germany," telling what America might expect from Hitler if the war was lost. Bette Davis starred; Joan Blondell later did a repeat. As with most of these *Treasury* programs, the stars and writers worked for nothing. Fanny Brice and Hanley Stafford, Gertrude Berg and company in a "Goldberg" skit, Edward G. Robinson, Vincent Price, Lionel Barrymore, and Carl Sandburg were a few of the well-knowns who appeared.

Troman Harper, Rumor Detective

Troman Harper, Rumor Detective was designed to spike Axis propaganda, much as Rex Stout had done with *Our Secret Weapon*. Harper's show, heard on Mutual for Grove's Bromo-Quinine in 1942–43, ripped into rumors with such convincing denials as "Pure malarkey!" or "Horsefeathers!" Then Harper countered the rumor with facts that sounded like War Department handouts. "If you repeat rumors, you're one of Hitler's best soldiers," he said. Was it true that Churchill really pulled punches with British bombs because he had financial holdings in Germany? Are all Chinese communists? What about the story that Allied parachutes are unsafe? What about reports that American GI's are being fed alfalfa? *Horsefeathers!* "I'll eat a bale of sawdust for every alfalfa leaf any American soldier finds on his plate—anytime, anyplace, anywhere," he snapped. Harper was colorful, and to our knowledge never had to eat any sawdust.

True Detective Mysteries

True Detective Mysteries, based on stories in *True Detective Magazine*, had several brief runs before emerging in 1944 as a durable

Sunday-afternoon Mutual feature. The earliest *True Detective* show ran on CBS Thursday nights in 1929–30; another was on Mutual Tuesdays in 1936–37. A third came to Mutual in 1938–39 as a 15-minute Tuesday-night show. But none of those had the cohesion or staying power of the show that premièred October 1, 1944. This time, *True Detective Mysteries* ran on Mutual for fifteen years. For eleven years it was a Sunday-afternoon favorite. O'Henry Candy was its best-remembered sponsor, carrying it from 1946 through 1953. It featured Richard Keith as John Shuttleworth, editor of *True Detective Magazine*. Keith narrated case histories of actual crimes, some of them twenty years old, but all proving the theory that crime doesn't pay. As Shuttleworth, he offered a $500 (later $1,000) reward for information leading to the capture of wanted criminals. Clues were given in *Gang Busters'* style at the end of each broadcast, and listeners were advised to get in touch with the real Shuttleworth for the reward, should their tip result in the criminal's capture.

Murray Burnett was writer-director and music was by Paul Taubman on the organ. Later the show was written, directed, and produced by Peter Irving; Shuttleworth's name was dropped and the unnamed "editor" was played by John Griggs. O'Henry, during the years of its sponsorship, developed a distinctive commercial, which became almost as famous as the stories:

(Phone Ringing.)
MAN: Hello? Hello?
WOMAN: O'Henry?
MAN: Hold the phone! Hold the phone! It's time for O'Henry, public energy number one!
ANNOUNCER: Yes, it's time for O'Henry, America's famous candy bar, to present, transcribed, *True Detective Mysteries* . . .

Truth or Consequences

Truth or Consequences opened on four CBS stations March 23, 1940. It was the most sensational hit of all radio quiz shows, vaulting into the top 10 and soon carried nationwide on NBC Saturday's for Ivory Soap.

Ralph Edwards had been in radio since 1935, working with several San Francisco stations before hitting the road in 1936 with $90 and a plan to get to New York, then the hotspot of network radio. He thumbed his way east, found a church to sleep in, and took his meals in a neighborhood greasy spoon. Soon he was hired as a CBS staff announcer, working on *Major Bowes' Original Amateur Hour* and a dozen other shows a week. Before long he knew announcing wasn't for him.

The *Truth or Consequences* show was built around man's age-old attraction to slapstick. Its conception occurred a few years before the war. The occasion: a party. Someone had dragged out the old parlor game, "Truth or Consequences," and the people were in hysterics over the antics of the losers, who were subjected to the wildest indignities that the partygoers could concoct. Edwards' assignment was to "scramble like an egg." Blessed with the mind of a radio man, he wondered why something that much fun hadn't been tried on the air. He tried it, and came up with the greatest success story of the 1940 season.

It combined lunacy with all the elements of the quiz, and soon had deposed *Information Please* as America's top question-and-answer show. It opened in the middle of an audience warmup, with people still in the throes of laughter. "Hello, there, we've been *waiting* for you! It's time to play *Truth* . . . (organ) . . . or *Consequences!*" Then the organ burst into the theme, a quick rendition of "Merrily We Roll Along."

People who offered themselves as contestants could win $15 by answering Edwards' question, but most missed intentionally and enjoyed a chance to ham it up onstage. "Beulah the Buzzer" indicated that a contestant had failed to answer, and now must pay the outlandish consequences. Contestants were required to wash elephants, talk like babies, squirm into girdles, howl like dogs. One man was asked to bark like a male seal looking for a mate, then was joined onstage by a female seal, compliments of *Truth or Consequences.* A soldier was required to call his girl and try to converse while an actress sat on his lap cooing into his ear. Once a couple had to feed each other blueberry pie—blindfolded—and talk normally as though they were sitting over a supper table at home.

Edwards thought up many of the gags himself, though he was usually aided by production manager Al Paschall, four gag writers, and a lawyer. Each Tuesday he met with the writers to toss around "consequences," and the show was roughly blocked out a month ahead. Edwards always appeared in full dress, keeping several extra tuxedos handy in case (as usual) one got spattered during a messy consequence.

Procter & Gamble, notably DUZ, sponsored *Truth or Consequences* from 1941 through 1950, Saturdays on NBC. In 1943, one of the most celebrated consequences of all time occurred, when Edwards asked listeners to each send one penny to a contestant, then required that she open each letter and count every penny received. The mail brought 330,000 pennies, but for Mrs. Dennis J. Mullane the consequence had a happy ending. She got to keep the $3,300.

On December 29, 1945, *Truth or Consequences* began what was intended as a spoof of the then-mushrooming giveaway shows. Each week "Mr. Hush" gave from offstage a veiled clue to his identity. The first person who guessed who Mr. Hush was would be awarded fabulous prizes. But the listeners took it quite seriously, and when ratings soared, Edwards felt compelled to continue it. After five weeks, Mr. Hush was identified as fighter Jack Dempsey, and the winner was given the then-unprecedented sum of $13,500 in prize money. The contest was so popular that a Mrs. Hush giveaway began soon afterward, with the winner hauling in $17,590 in prizes for correctly guessing Clara Bow. In 1947, a Miss Hush contest paid another $21,000-plus to the contestant who guessed a real toughie —dancer Martha Graham. The secret-identity craze culminated in 1948 with the "Walking Man" contest and $22,500 to the contestant who correctly guessed Jack Benny.

By then Edwards was thoroughly sick of it. What had started as a parody of giveaways had itself become the biggest giveaway on the air. The show moved to CBS Tuesdays for Philip Morris in 1950, but returned to NBC in 1952, for a three-year Thursday-night run for Pet Milk. By 1955, it had moved to Wednesdays, where it ran for several sponsors until 1957. The TV version was still going strong into the 1970's.

Twelve Players

Twelve Players was a 1945 summer show bringing to the CBS Saturday-night microphone a repertory of radio's best (though unheralded) professionals in plays of heavy drama. The players also selected the dramas, which were sustained. The twelve players were Cathy Lewis, Bea Benaderet, David Ellis, Jack Moyles, Edmond MacDonald, Mary Jane Croft, Jay Novello, Howard McNear, John Lake, Herbert Rawlinson, Lurene Tuttle, and Charlie Lung. Not a bad array of talent, even if the public didn't know their names. It was produced and directed by Ray Buffum (who with Moyles and MacDonald created the format) and scored by Wilbur Hatch. It never made a big splash, probably because of Hollywood's unfortunate prejudice that a show needed "big names" to put it across.

Twenty-First Precinct

Twenty-First Precinct, a CBS sustainer running from July 7, 1953, through 1956 on Tuesdays, then Wednesdays and the last year on Fridays, was one of many detective shows that followed *Dragnet* by letting "you the listener" follow a case from opening phone call until the final report was written. The Twenty-First Precinct was

"just lines on a map of the city of New York. Most of the 173,000 people wedged into the nine-tenths of a square mile between Fifth Avenue and the East River wouldn't know if you asked them that they lived or worked in the 21st. Whether they know it or not, the security of their homes, their persons and their property is the job of the men of the 21st Precinct."

This, then, was the behind-the-scenes story of the "160 patrolmen, 11 sergeants, 4 lieutenants, and the captain of the hotbox that is the 21st Precinct." Everett Sloane played the captain in command, with Ken Lynch and Harold Stone as lieutenant and sergeant, respectively. The show was written and directed by Stanley Niss, and done in cooperation with the Patrolman's Benevolent Association.

Twenty Questions

Twenty Questions was first heard on Mutual February 2, 1946, and continued for eight years, mostly for Ronson Lighters. It brought to the air the famous old animal, vegetable, or mineral parlor game, in which an unknown object had to be identified in twenty questions or less. The objects ranged from Ben-Hur's chariot to the Republican elephant, and a panel of questioning connoisseurs was assembled to do them justice. The regular panel consisted of Fred Van Deventer, Florence Rinard, Bobby McGuire, and producer Herb Polesie. One chair was reserved for rotating guests. In private life, Fred Van Deventer and Florence Rinard were husband and wife, and Bobby McGuire was their son. Mrs. Van Deventer decided to use her maiden name for radio, and Bobby took the maiden name of his maternal grandmother, to dispel the illusion that *Twenty Questions* was a one-family show—which it very nearly was.

The show was created at the Van Deventers' dinner table, where the family often engaged in mealtime quiz games. Van Deventer, a WOR newsman, had brought an announcer home as guest, and the discussion turned to radio quiz shows. Daughter Nancy, then 16, wondered how ideas were developed for the air. She suggested the old animal-vegetable-mineral game, and they were off. Nancy appeared occasionally on the show as a panelist, but was often away at school. The listening audience was told what the object was by a "mystery voice," an announcer in an offstage isolation booth. Sportscaster Bill Slater was master of ceremonies. The show was sponsored by Ronson until 1951. It ran on Mutual Saturdays, then Wednesdays (1946–47), then Saturdays (1947–50), then Sundays (1950–51). Ronson dropped it in 1951, and *Twenty Questions* was sustained for a year on Saturday nights. In 1952, it was picked up by Wildroot, and in 1953 it was again sustained, finishing as a Saturday-night show in 1954.

Twenty Thousand Years in Sing-Sing

Twenty Thousand Years in Sing-Sing was a dramatized series of prison stories told by Warden Lewis E. Lawes of Sing-Sing Prison and heard on the Blue Network for Sloan's Liniment from 1933 until 1939. Lawes, well-known as a lenient warden who ran a "loose ship," told human interest stories about men who had come back from life's knockdowns, overcome the obstacles of prison, and gone out to build new lives for themselves. Some stories weren't that positive. Lawes portrayed Sing-Sing as a city of intense emotion. From the 2,000-odd inmates—each in for a year or more—came the show's title. *Twenty Thousand Years in Sing-Sing* was heard on Wednesdays until 1936, on Mondays thereafter, and on Fridays in its last season, 1938–39.

Two Thousand Plus

Two Thousand Plus was a rather weak Mutual science fiction effort, first heard March 15, 1950, and running through the 1951 season as a Wednesday-night sustainer. Originally syndicated, it explored "the years beyond 2000 A.D.," promoting original and published stories in a melodramatic format. It was a Sherman H. Dryer production, with music by Emerson Buckley.

Uncle Don

Uncle Don might be described as the *Captain Kangaroo* of radio. His appeal was to children of preschool age, whom he fascinated for twenty years with his lively piano and pig Latin, his stories and poems, and his good-natured nonsense. He was Don Carney, whose voice for most of the twenty-year run was limited to the not-so-small seven-state area covered by Station WOR.

Carney had been born Howard Rice, coming out of St. Joseph, Michigan, with a rather unique talent—he could play piano standing on his head! With that he crashed vaudeville as Don Carney, trick pianist, and vaudeville was just a kiddie step from radio. Carney arrived at WMCA, New York, in December 1925 and joined WOR soon after. There, he was just a vocal handyman until a toy manufacturer came in on short notice looking for a kiddie show to sponsor. Carney was asked to come up with something, and he went on the air with a story about the toys the company was selling. Soon he was established as Uncle Don, and within a few years even his mother had almost forgotten that his real name was Howard.

The show usually opened with a bit of chatter and piano, and soon Don launched his famed "Hibbidy Gits" song:

Hello, nephews, nieces too,
Mothers and daddies, how are you?
This is Uncle Don all set to go

With a meeting on the ra-dio.
We'll start off with a little song;
To learn the words will not take long.
For they're as easy as easy can be,
So come on now and sing with me.
Hibbidy gits has-ha ring boree,
Sibonia skividy hi-lo-dee.
Honi-ko-doke with an ali-ka-zon,
Sing this song with your Uncle Don!

Carney's show set the pace for all other kiddie programs that followed: sing, tell a story, tell a joke, announce birthdays, scold misbehavers, pledge allegiance to the flag, and relay club news. He pushed spinach harder than Popeye, tied his various clubs shamelessly to his sponsors' financial interests, and filled the living room at suppertime with such new words as "crytearians," "leavearounders," "takechancers" and "scuffyheelers"—none of which Uncle Don wanted his little pals to be. Most of his clubs were unabashed commercial plugs—a listener could "belong" only if he or she supported Uncle Don's products; it is said that his Earnest Savers Club brought longtime sponsor Greenwich Savings Bank more than 40,000 new accounts.

Carney told tales of unruly kids and what happens to them. He scolded those who failed to brush teeth, cried at bedtime, and threw temper tantrums. His characters Willipus Wallipus (senior and junior) and Suzan Beduzin and her brother Huzen became almost as well-known (if not as enduring) as Jimmy Olsen and Lois Lane, who followed Uncle Don in *Superman* 15 minutes later. Carney's lectures were wrapped in story form; he told of germs boring holes in Suzan's teeth until Old Mr. Toothbrush routed them and chased them away. His birthday announcements were sometimes interrupted by startling news that Susie or Jimmy so-and-so had been good that month, and would find presents from Uncle Don behind their radio sets. Kids were delighted to find the presents, neatly wrapped, tucked in among the tubes. They never did learn of the not-so-startling collaboration between Uncle Don and the mothers of America.

For his efforts, Carney averaged $20,000 a year. He hit his peak in 1928–29, when his show was chosen one of radio's "blue-ribbon programs" and he hauled in a reported $75,000. But he spent most of his professional life denying a delightfully unsubstantiated story, that has become one of radio's classics. Carney, so the tale goes, was signing off one evening and, thinking the microphone was off, said, "There! I guess that'll hold the little bastards for another night."

Carney swore in every interview that it never happened, and once suggested that the story had been started by one of his rivals.

He worked seven days a week, reading Hearst comics on the air early Sundays. His show lasted until 1949, and was carried briefly on Mutual to five outlets in 1939 for Maltex Cereal.

Uncle Ezra's Radio Station

Uncle Ezra's Radio Station was a countrified variety show headed by Pat Barrett, the Uncle Ezra of The National Barn Dance. Supposedly it was broadcast from "Station E-Z-R-A, the powerful little five-watter down in Rosedale." Through his "radio station," Ezra brought to the air all manner of rural people who listened to the stories he had gathered squattin' around pot-bellied stoves in general stores around the country. Barrett, a real-life farmer in Illinois, came to radio from vaudeville, breaking in at WTMJ, Milwaukee, in 1930. There, he introduced Uncle Ezra to the air; soon his act was so popular that he was hired by WLS (Chicago), home of The National Barn Dance. Ezra's own show went on NBC in 1934, broadcasting as a three-a-week, 15-minute filler for Alka Seltzer. It ran in that format until 1938, when Barrett began doing two network shows (a 30-minute Sunday program, in addition to his 15-minute biweekly). His 30-minute show was also heard in 1940–41 on Saturdays for Camel Cigarettes. It featured Barrett's wife, Nora Cunneen, as Cecelia, singer Fran Allison; Cliff Soubier as Mayor Boggs; the Sons of the Pioneers; and the Rosedale Trio (Carolyn Montgomery, Betty Bennett, and Fran Allison).

Under Arrest

Under Arrest was an undistinguished Mutual show premièring June 8, 1947, as a summer replacement for The Shadow. It starred Craig McDonnell as Captain John Drake. After its summer run, a regular series opened on Mutual in 1948 and ran until 1954. By then it had become the story of Captain Jim Scott's fight against crime, of "criminals behind bars—under arrest," and opened with a ringing bell and a filtered voice barking, "Into your cells!" But often the stories were set outside the jail, centering on Scott's pursuit rather than later incarceration. Joe Di Santis was starred as Captain Scott; later the part was played by Ned Wever, the Bulldog Drummond of the 1940's.

The Unexpected

The Unexpected was a 15-minute syndicated terror show of the late 1940's, directed by Frank K. Danzig, and written by Frank Burt. It was very well done, especially considering the limitations of the 15-minute complete-in-each-sitting format. The Unexpected was based on fictional twists of fate and surprise endings. Somewhere, the show suggested, there was a "secret future, a hidden destiny, waiting for you . . . perhaps in just a moment you too will meet the unexpected!" Leads were handled by such fine players as Barry Sullivan, Lurene Tuttle, and Virginia Gregg.

The University of Chicago Round Table

The University of Chicago Round Table was first heard nationally on NBC in October 1933, and became—with The American Forum of the Air and America's Town Meeting—one of radio's major series of debate and public affairs. Its first local report, some two years before the national debut, set the tone, when three professors from the University discussed one of the hottest topics in the land, the Wickersham Report on Prohibition. Subsequent broadcasts were always fashioned around the most provocative and timely of national issues. John Howe directed for much of the early run; George Probst came out of the university debate team to take over around 1945. The show was the first to support its own weekly magazine; it won a coveted Peabody Award for radio excellence, and established an unusual format that sometimes found the three professors in spirited debate with such national figures as Eleanor Roosevelt, William Allen White, and Drew Pearson. Pearson sparked an uproar with his appearance in 1939, charging on the air that Herbert Hoover boosters were stumping throughout the South, trying to "buy up" delegates to the 1940 Republican national convention. When, on the following broadcast, university vice president Frederick Campbell Woodward apologized to Hoover for Pearson's remarks, Pearson threatened to sue. It was, in short, a spontaneous, completely unrehearsed forum, heard on NBC Sunday afternoons until June 12, 1955. Among the topics debated in the later years: The constitutionality of President Truman's seizure of the steel industry, the "problems of prosperity," and the continuing role of the United States in Southeast Asia. The "round table," by the way, was actually a triangle, collapsible for trips out of the Chicago area. It opened into a sloping pyramid, with a microphone at the top and time warning lights facing each speaker.

Unlimited Horizons

Unlimited Horizons was an NBC educational feature, starting on the West Coast around 1940 and expanding into a national program by 1943. Created by NBC public services chief Jennings Pierce, it told of the newest advances on the scientific front, using dramatizations after extensively interviewing the scientists making the news. The series was written and produced by Arnold Marquis.

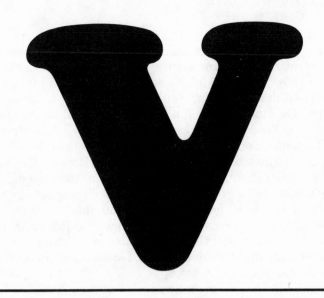

Valiant Lady

Valiant Lady was first heard on CBS for Gold Medal Flour March 7, 1938; by May 30 it had moved to NBC for General Mills. It was the story of Joan Barrett, soft-spoken heroine who married Dr. Truman (Tubby) Scott and tried to live a quiet life in the gossipy little town of Pine River. Joan, a talented actress, sacrificed career for family. But Tubby, a "brilliant plastic surgeon," was the typical soapy male figure and caused her grief no end. At first easy-going and kind, Tubby was nevertheless jealous throughout. As early as 1939—even before their marriage—Tubby had brawled with Joan's artist friend, "handsome, dashing" Paul Morrison, amidst growing speculation and scandal over the interrelationships between Joan, Tubby, Paul, and their friends. A baby was mixed up in it, and that kept tongues wagging even harder. Maybe he just didn't like to be called Tubby, but Joan's husband was established as a rather high-strung man early in the series. By 1941 he was undergoing a complete personality change, because a blood clot on the brain ("in whose existence he does not believe") began to sap away his life.

Now Tubby became coarse, hard, and arrogant, "an opportunist whose early ideals are peculiarly mingled with the savage lust for money. . . ." And while this is happening, a wealthy divorcee "whose fading youth has hardly touched her beauty" lies in the hospital and plots trouble for Joan. Highly melodramatic, *Valiant Lady* was one of radio's big shows when Chicago was the hub of serial activity in the

1930's. Joan Blaine, who originated the part of Joan, became one of the first real stars of the form, getting billing up front, before the title. When the show opened, Miss Blaine was supported by Francis X. Bushman, Judith Lowry, Olan Soule, and Sally Smith. Richard Gordon played her kindly father Jim Barrett, and Teddy Bergman, later known as Alan Reed, played a variety of roles. It was then directed by Gordon Grahame. Soon Bill Johnstone took over the role of Jim Barrett. Raymond Edward Johnson was Paul Morrison, and Tubby was played by Charles Carroll and Bartlett Robinson. Strictly a product of the 1930's, *Valiant Lady* suffered steadily declining ratings until it disappeared in 1946. Joan Banks played the title role in the mid-1940's; Florence Freeman was also heard as Joan. For the first four years, it was an NBC General Mills show; it moved to CBS in 1942. An ABC attempt to revive it in 1951–52 was not successful, and it finished after that season.

Vaughn de Leath

Vaughn de Leath was a singer and radio pioneer, sometimes known as "the first lady of radio" and "the original radio girl" because of the general agreement that she was the first woman ever to sing on the air. Miss de Leath was only nineteen in January 1920 when she went to Lee De Forest's studio in the World Tower Building and sang "Swanee River" into a primitive gramophone mike. The daughter of a windmill maker, she claimed to have learned to sing to the music of the spinning windmill blades. By age seventeen, she had made her professional singing debut on a Los Angeles concert stage. From her De Forest experiment, Miss de Leath rose through the ranks of pre-network radio to become the most popular star of her era. She pioneered a singing style that would later become known as "crooning," a necessity in those shaky days when high notes might shatter transmitter tubes. Miss de Leath was on hand for the opening in 1921 of WJZ, later the cornerstone of the Blue Network; she took over managership of WDT in 1923, and became one of the first American radio stars heard in Europe via transatlantic broadcasting. In 1930 she participated in one of the earliest major television experiments; by 1931 she was being featured in a twice-a-week songfest on CBS. Miss de Leath became widely identified with the theme, "Red Sails in the Sunset," which adapted ideally to her crooning style. She was heard intermittently through the 1930's; she died in Buffalo on May 28, 1943.

Vic and Sade

Vic and Sade was first heard on NBC June 29, 1932. It was a sustaining show until November 3, 1934, when it was picked up by Procter & Gamble for Crisco. One of radio's truly original products, it was created and written by Paul Rhymer and told of "radio's homefolks" who lived "in the little house halfway up in the next block." It is consistently rated by veterans of the medium, nostalgics, and collectors of radio shows as one of the greatest ever done on the air.

Rhymer's comedy was an absurd brand, drawing deeply from his own personality and playing on wild extensions of reality, quirks of character, and outrageous names. Rhymer, a Bloomington, Illinois, kid fresh out of college, went to work for NBC continuity in 1929. An ambition to do literature had been nagging at him for a long time, but continuity didn't give it much exercise. Rhymer filled his days scheduling and logging shows until one day in 1932 when a network production manager breezed in looking for a writer. He needed a family audition script as a test for a prospective actor. Rhymer worked Sunday, and came in Monday with a 10-minute opera about a homespun couple named Vic and Sade. He was asked to write more. Rhymer didn't want to do soap opera, but overcame his extreme reluctance, and Vic and Sade began to come to life.

Vic and Sade were the Gooks, a family who lived on Virginia Avenue in the town of Crooper, Illinois, where Vic worked as a bookkeeper for "Plant Number 14 of the Consolidated Kitchenware Company" and Sade was his naive homebody wife.

Vic was drawn as a normally quiet man with periodic bursts of temper; Sade was a whiney woman whose limited world was contained within the perimeter of her kitchen. With the casting of Vic and Sade, a strange magic began to brew. Art Van Harvey, who had been a grain dealer and an advertising man (but had limited experience as an actor) took the role of Vic. He brought with him an accent that cut a fine line between Indiana hoosier and second-generation German. Bernardine Flynn, a veteran of long stage experience, played Sade with a nasal twang that competed with the best moments of Jane Ace.

Broadcast initially in the middle of soap opera time, the show soon became (in the words of longtime announcer Bob Brown) "an island of delight in the sea of tears." During the heyday of the late 1930's, Vic and Sade was heard on NBC's Red and Blue Networks, and later on NBC and CBS simultaneously. It ran five times a week, 15 minutes per show, until September 29, 1944.

In those early days, the only other member of the cast was the Gooks' adopted son Rush (short for Russell), who had been explained somewhere as the son of Sade's sister, who couldn't afford to keep him. Cast as Rush was Billy Idelson.

With that, the stage was set. Each day, in a brief visit with the Gooks, the townspeople of Crooper began to come alive. Rhymer's genius made that crazy little town live without ever bringing anyone onstage but Vic, Sade, and Rush. They talked to people on the telephone; they talked about friends and neighbors; they read letters from Uncle Fletcher and Aunt Bess and other relatives. Piece by piece, Rhymer built character through one-sided phone conversations, through dialogue and episodes related second-hand through the eyes of Vic and Sade. And over the years, faithful listeners came to know the town and its eccentrics as if all had had leading speaking roles for years.

There were people like Ruthie Stembottom, Sade's friend who was always gossiping on the phone, and Godfrey Dimlok, who once invented a bicycle that could say "mama." Listeners knew Smelly Dave and Cora Bucksaddle, Ole Chinbunny and Ray Delfino, who could rub his feet together and make a flame hot enough to light a cigar. There was Mr. Gumpox the garbage man, whose old-fashioned wagon was pulled along Virginia Avenue by a horse named Howard; there were the twins, Robert and Slobbert Hink. Rush talked of his friends, Bluetooth Johnson and Orville Wheanie, and Vic grumbled about his boss, J. K. Rubich, who somehow came out as "Old Rubbish" most of the time. There was Rishigan Fishigan of Sishigan, Michigan, who married Jane Bane of Pane, Maine. The characters roll off the tongue like the names of old friends: Chuck and Dottie Brainfeeble; Willie Gutstop; Mr. Buller (Vic's business friend), and R. J. Konk (founder of Vic's lodge, the Drowsy Venus Chapter of the Sacred Stars of the Milky Way, of which Vic once attained the title Grand Exalted Big Dipper), L. J. Ghertner, the city water inspector, and Mervyn S. Spraul, the old man down the street who dearly loved "them peanuts with the chocolate smeared on the outside."

It was all done through dialogue; there were no props, few sound effects, and little music. In the beginning it had to be that way, since Vic and Sade was sustained and had a very small budget. Later, there wasn't any real need to change it. The originality of Rhymer (an avid practical joker who once named a group of jailbirds in his story after all the vice-presidents at NBC), combined with precisely the right stars to make it click and keep it the most creative comedy on the air for eight years.

In 1940 Van Harvey had a heart seizure, and Rhymer had to cope with the possibility of a new male lead. It was decided to bring in Uncle Fletcher, who until then had been only a letter-writing relative from afar. Auditions were scheduled, though it was assumed by the staff that the part would be offered to veteran character actor Sidney Ellstrom. But among those auditioning was Clarence Hartzell, a young man from Huntington, West Virginia. Hartzell, like Cliff Arquette, was destined to make a good part of his living playing old men on the air.

From the moment Hartzell opened his mouth, the part was his. Both Idelson and Miss Flynn saw at once that here, standing before them, was Uncle Fletcher in the flesh. They overcame the reluctance of everyone who had thought Ellstrom was a cinch; at the end of a long session, Hartzell was called in and given the job. As Uncle Fletcher, he became one of the best-known characters in all radio, a solid addition even after Van Harvey recovered and returned as Vic. Uncle Fletcher was the most absent-minded old cuss of the air, an eccentric who talked right through people, said "fine, fine" to everything without hearing one word of what was said, mused for hours about the "hyena grease" someone had made up at the Bright Kentucky Hotel, or followed the trek of some "half-wit fly" as it crawled lazily across the ceiling.

While Sade was relating the latest doings at the Little Tiny Petite Pheasant Feather Tearoom, Uncle Fletcher was lounging at the Bright Kentucky Hotel, where Smelly Clark's Uncle Strap was night clerk and the trains roared past on their way from Chicago to St. Louis. Uncle Fletcher could talk indefinitely about a particle of food wedged between his teeth (which "rooted him to the spot" until it was out). He could ramble on about friends who always seemed to be 38 years old, who had once lived in Dixon, Illinois, but then moved to Dismal Seepage, Ohio, by way of Sweet Esther, Wisconsin, and later died. Uncle Fletcher went on and on about a friend who was an armed guard at the Ohio State Home for the Tall.

That was the kind of humor Rhymer did. A simple situation was more than enough to kill a whole show: Rooster Davis opening a restaurant that would only serve bacon sandwiches . . . Uncle Fletcher bringing out a box of family heirlooms—letters from Aunt Bess and cards from a man who appreciated the peaches Fletch sent every ten years . . . Uncle Fletcher reading a letter from Aunt Bess, one he got last month but never opened . . . Vic coming home to find Rooster, Rotten, and Roper Davis sleeping upstairs . . . Uncle Fletcher's landlady going on a trip, and laying out all his meals in advance, all over the house . . .

Crisco was the longtime sponsor, and Procter & Gamble gets the all-time stupidity award for short-sightedly destroying its *Vic and Sade* transcriptions. Clarence Menser was the first director, holding rehearsals in those long-ago days in the NBC lobby. Other directors included Earl Ebi and Charles Rinehardt. Charlie Lyon was the first announcer; Clint Stanley was producer. Bill Idelson, who would grow up to produce such TV shows as *Bob Newhart*, played Rush until he joined the Navy in 1942. Johnny Coons and Sid Koss held the part while he was away. The show withered during Idelson's absence; it died on September 29, 1944.

A half-hour Thursday-night version was heard on Mutual in 1946, but though fully laced with Rhymer's distinctive wit, it was a flop. Rhymer's real genius lay in those daily little snatches of fantasy, requiring only the voices of Vic, Sade, Rush, and Uncle Fletcher. Johnny Coons and Cliff Soubier gave fine voice to Rhymer's other eccentrics, but for some reason it didn't click. It vanished from the air as suddenly as it had come.

The Victor Borge Show

The *Victor Borge Show* was first heard on July 3, 1945, as a three-month NBC summer substitute for *Fibber McGee and Molly*. Borge, the superstar of Danish entertainment before the Nazis invaded his homeland in April 1940, had been one of Hitler's biggest critics. Luckily for him, he was playing an engagement in Stockholm when the invasion came. He hopped a refugee ship for New York, arriving broke and in total ignorance of American custom and speech. He was joined by his wife, an American citizen, in August, then began a long program to learn the ways of the United States. He learned English by attending up to eight movies a day; when he was able to speak the tongue, he turned to entertainment as a way of life. New York's doors were closed, so Borge tried California. He was spotted by Rudy Vallee, and was booked as part of Vallee's pre-show warmup. There, he was seen by representatives of Bing Crosby's *Kraft Music Hall* and was signed for an appearance with Bing. That turned into an engagement of more than fifty weeks. Borge was unleashed upon radio as a free agent in 1943. He worked for two months on Nelson Eddy's show, then did a daily performance on Metro Goldwyn Mayer's Blue Network show, *The Lion Roars*. The *Fibber McGee* replacement was his first starring vehicle. It featured singer Pat Friday, McGee regulars Harlow Wilcox and Billy Mills, and spotlighted Borge's own special brand of piano comedy. Long one of Europe's best-known concert pianists, Borge's comedy revolved around verbal interpretations and introductions of his music. In September 1946, *The Victor Borge*

Show became a regular NBC Monday-night feature for Socony Oil. This one featured Benny Goodman's orchestra and ran for one season.

The Voice of Broadway

The Voice of Broadway was Dorothy Kilgallen's Broadway gossip show, first heard on CBS in mid-1941. Dorothy—writer, commentator, producer, and newspaper columnist—brought to the air all her knowledge of doings on the Great White Way. It ran a season for Johnson & Johnson, initially on Saturday, later on Tuesday, and was later heard on Mutual.

The Voice of Experience

The Voice of Experience belonged to Marion Sayle Taylor, a self-made sociologist who for more than ten years used radio as his chief tool. Taylor, son of a Louisville preacher, literally fell into his work. Early in life he wanted to be a surgeon, but an automobile accident left his hand partly disabled. He turned to social work and served in public health departments, helping prostitutes in West Coast cities and slowly gaining the experience he would later tout on the air. His radio career began in 1926. On September 11, 1933, he started a six-a-week advice show for CBS. Taylor distributed hundreds of thousands of dollars among the sick and poor—most of it contributions from his listeners—and he established an anonymous college scholarship fund. By 1934, 1,000 people were writing him daily; by 1939, the number was 6,000. His CBS show ended in 1936 and he went to NBC. In 1937, *The Voice of Experience* was picked up by Mutual, running there until 1940.

The Voice of Firestone

The Voice of Firestone, during more than twenty-seven years on network radio, became the nation's top musical prestige show. First heard on NBC December 3, 1928, it was one of radio's few untouchables, always heard on the same day (Monday) at the same time (8:30, EST) for the same sponsor. Might as well call it *The Voice of Woolworth* as disturb its position in the foundation of NBC's Monday Night of Music." After the show was dropped from the NBC lineup in 1954, ABC programmed *The Voice of Firestone* Mondays at 8:30. The network switch came about in a disagreement with NBC over that Monday-night time slot. The network wanted to change the time because of poor ratings by the *Firestone* television show; even though the radio show continued to thrive, it was locked in by being simulcast on TV.

The *Voice of Firestone* cut across all boundaries of musical taste, offering the classics, spirited marches, show tunes, and even popular songs. It began with a seventeen-piece orchestra under the direction of William Daly, and grew to eventually employ more than seventy musicians and soloists. Hugo Mariani took the baton briefly with Daly's death in 1936; that same year Alfred Wallenstein became conductor. For seven years he directed the Firestone Symphony Orchestra, leaving in 1943 to become musical director of the Los Angeles Symphony. Howard Barlow became the fourth conductor; by then the show was well-entrenched in its pattern of alternating guest artists with regular performers from the Metropolitan Opera. Lily Pons, Lawrence Tibbett, Igor Gorin, Lauritz Melchior, Gladys Swarthout, Ezio Pinza, Patrice Munsel, Nelson Eddy, Rose Bampton, and John Charles Thomas were a few of the guests. Richard Crooks came aboard around 1932 as regular soloist, later alternating with Margaret Speaks, who joined *The Voice of Firestone* in 1935. They held the major solo roles through the 1930's and into the middle 1940's. By 1947, Eleanor Steber and Christopher Lynch were the alternating stars. Hugh James was longtime announcer.

The *Voice of Firestone* was popular because its music was beautiful and familiar. Richard Rodgers' songs were mixed with *Carmen* and operetta numbers from Victor Herbert. John Philip Sousa's "Washington Post March" opened a program that included "The Maple Leaves Forever" and De Koven's "Recessional." Most familiar of all were the themes—"If I Could Tell You" and "In My Garden," composed by Mrs. Harvey Firestone, wife of the tire magnate.

Vox Pop

Vox Pop was a long running show originated by two ad salesmen from Houston radio. The title derives from *vox populi*, defined by Webster as "popular sentiment," "the voice of the people." In a nutshell, that was the premise of *Vox Pop*, which came out of local Houston radio to become one of the network's most popular interview shows.

It started a few days before the 1932 presidential election. Parks Johnson and Jerry Belcher took a portable microphone into the street to interview people on the Roosevelt-Hoover campaign. The answers they got were always spontaneous, sometimes humorous, and occasionally riotously funny.

This led to a series of sidewalk interviews and, when Standard Brands began looking for a summer replacement for Joe Penner, Johnson and Belcher were brought to New York. It premièred July 7, 1935. Again, the spontaneity of the show delighted listeners and sponsors alike. The talk ranged from national issues to personalities. One girl, asked by Johnson what she wanted for Christmas, leaned close to the microphone and breathed, "You."

Belcher soon left the show, and Wally Butterworth came aboard as Johnson's partner. This combination proved most popular and lasted longest. Johnson and Butterworth invented guessing contests (how many times a day does the average watch tick?), with prizes to the person whose guess came closest. They took their microphones to the New York World's Fair and traveled the United States seeking "the voice of the people." In 1941 they went to Central America, broadcasting from Mexico City, Puerto Rico, and Cuba.

Butterworth left the show in 1941 and was replaced briefly by Neil O'Malley, who in turn was replaced by young Warren Hull. In its later years, the show changed focus somewhat. While still a traveling "voice of the people," its guests were lined up in advance. Hull became master of ceremonies and Johnson's wife Louise was given $750 a week to buy gifts for the guests. During that era, more emphasis was placed on the gifts than the guests, and listeners often marveled at Mrs. Johnson's ability to buy hard-to-find items during those days of war shortages.

Vox Pop was heard on NBC from 1935 through 1938. Originally a Sunday show for Mollé, it moved to Tuesday in 1936 and to Saturday for Kentucky Club Tobacco in 1938. It went to CBS Thursday nights in 1939, still for Kentucky Club, and to Mondays in 1941. Bromo Seltzer was the sponsor from 1942 through 1946 in a long Monday run. Lipton Tea took it in 1946 for a season on Tuesdays. Vox Pop again jumped networks in 1947, doing a Wednesday-night ABC stint for American Express.

The Voyage of the Scarlet Queen

The Voyage of the Scarlet Queen, a Mutual series of high adventure, was first heard July 3, 1947, and ran for a season on Thursday nights. It starred Elliott Lewis as Philip Carney, master of the ketch Scarlet Queen, "proudest ship to plow the seas." Carney was a far cry from Lewis' comic Frankie Remley role, and he handled the skipper straight. The show opened with the rousing sounds of the sea, blending into a sharp cry of a lookout in the crow's nest. Then Carney made another verbal entry in the ship's log:

Log entry, the ketch *Scarlet Queen*, Philip Carney, master. Position: 3 dègrees, 7 minutes north, 104 degrees, 2 minutes east. Wind: fresh to moderate. Sky: fair. Remarks—departed Singapore after being guest at unsuccessful wedding. Reason for failure: "The Winchester Rifle and the Ambitious Groom."

It was a creative way to introduce the story's title. All *Scarlet Queen* stories had colorful titles: "The Bubble Dancer and the Buccaneer," "Ah, Sin and the Balinese Beaux Art Ball," "Rocky III and the Dead Man's Chest," "The Barefoot Nymph in the Mother Hubbard Jacket," and "The Pegleg Skipper and the Iberian Blade" were a few. Ed Max co-starred as Mr. Gallagher; frequent support came from William Conrad, Ben Wright, and John Dehner. The show was written by Gil Doud and Robert Tallman, scored by Richard Aurandt, and produced by James Burton. Like the opening, the closing was filled with the sound of the sea, creaks of the ship, and a final note in Carney's log: "Ship secured for night. Signed, Philip Carney, master."

Walter Winchell's Journal

Walter Winchell's Journal came to the Blue Network for Jergens Lotion December 4, 1932, broadcasting a Sunday night gossip show that would run for more than two decades. Winchell combined a nose for news with an almost flawless sense of showmanship to produce one of the most dynamic 15-minute shows ever heard. Though he broke many important news stories, his manner and delivery were rooted in the twelve-year vaudeville career he had vigorously pursued before he ever saw a big-time newsroom. Born April 7, 1897, Winchell was a product of old New York; a slang-spewing grammar school dropout who went into show business at 13 and soon joined Eddie Cantor and George Jessel in a singing usher act at the old Imperial Theatre. In 1910, all three were hired by Gus Edwards for his famous Newsboys' Sextet. Winchell originally spelled his name with one "l" until a printer's mistake made it "Winchell." "What the L?" he joked years later; it was easier that way anyhow. After a stint with the Navy in the first war, Winchell returned to vaudeville, but soon began to ease out of theatre and into journalism. He was hired by the *Vaudeville News* as a reporter-reviewer, and began to do occasional pieces for *Billboard*. Winchell's advance as a scribe was rapid; he went to the *New York Evening Graphic*, where he began to build a name. In 1929, he moved to the *New York Daily Mirror* with an audience estimated in the hundred-thousands.

Winchell was the best-read columnist of his time, and it was just a step from there to radio. From the beginning, his *Jergens Journal* was a show of a different cut. Drawing on an impeccable sense of timing gained in his years on the boards, Winchell began roasting, blasting, and praising the mightiest names in the land. He broadcast with his hat on, in the old newsman's tradition, script in left hand, operating with his right hand a set of telegraph keys that gave a distinctive "newsroom" ticker sound to his shows. His opening is one of the best-remembered of the era. Fiercely tapping his telegraph keys, Winchell barked, "Good evening Mr. and Mrs. North and South America and all ships at sea, let's go to press—FLASH!" Telegraph operators complained that Winchell's tappings were idiotic and meaningless, but an attempt to bring in a real telegraph operator failed. No one could keep up with Winchell's machine-gun pace, and tapping the keys personally made him more at ease on the air. His voice was harsh, uttering in staccato style a series of anecdotes, opinions, and one-liners. His 215 words a minute were reportedly the fastest in radio. Once, he claimed, he had been clocked at more than 220.

In those days, Winchell used no legmen, preferring to gather his information personally from his sources. There were scores of sources, from bank officials to Hollywood press agents. His specialty was the free-wheeling style; often he would throw out predictions of a very broad, general nature, then claim credit in specifics when his "scoop" panned out. He was a shrewd player of the law of averages; in fact, he was wrong about as often as he was right.

Winchell's items were often datelined, giving them a closer identification with journalism. He quoted liberally from newspapers, and frequently blamed a paper for his mistakes. But throughout his career, he put on a lively show and commanded a weekly audience of more than 20 million. At one point, his Hooper rating peaked over 33, generally translated at a million listeners a point.

His style was brash and nervy—once he started a "feud" with maestro Ben Bernie, lifting the bandleader from obscurity to national fame. In his first year he attacked Hitler, branding the Nazis "Ratzis." He was almost passionate in his defense of President Roosevelt, and freely lambasted the prewar isolationists who opposed the president strongly in the months just before Pearl Harbor. In 1947, Winchell added a new target—the communists. His admiration for Roosevelt didn't transfer to Harry Truman, and in his later years, Winchell became a staunch supporter of Red-hunting Senator Joseph McCarthy. He was always known for his crusades and strong political leanings.

A series of disputes with Jergens after Winchell's 1942 season led eventually to a new sponsor. When he gave up his exclusive turf on Broadway and took on politicians (he blasted the voters as "damn fools" in 1943), both the sponsor and the network began censoring his scripts.

For sixteen years the series ran in the same basic format, moving sponsorship to Kaiser-Fraser autos in 1948. In 1949, Richard Hudnut picked up the show, still on the Blue (which had become ABC), still on Sunday nights. Gruen Watches took over in 1952; various sponsors carried Winchell from 1953 through 1955, when his show went to Mutual for a final fling.

After his retirement from radio, Winchell narrated *The Untouchables*, an ABC-TV gangster series of 1959–63. He died in Los Angeles February 20, 1972.

The Warner Brothers Academy Theatre

The Warner Brothers Academy Theatre was a studio-syndicated series designed to push WB movies with dramatizations and prolific plugs. First heard in 1938, it featured developing movie stars enrolled in Warner's Academy of Acting. Developed in 1933, the Academy brought to the screen many actors and actresses who later became top-flight stars. The first-liners were often brought onstage after the production to chat with the audience during a curtain-call interview. Such newcomers as Ronald Reagan, Carole Landis, and Susan Hayward appeared on *The Warner Brothers Academy Theatre*. The production was sold to Gruen Watches and was packaged by the Trans-America Broadcasting System.

We Care

We Care was a 15-minute dramatic show heard in 1948 on ABC and sponsored by CARE, the nonprofit food agency. Douglas Fairbanks, Jr., then chairman of the Share Through Care Committee, was host. He delivered the CARE announcements, asking listeners to help hungry people in a war-torn Europe during the period of reconstruction. There was only one appeal, at the end of the show. The body of the program was a complete 15-minute drama,written by Milton Geiger and using various guest stars. The show was directed by William P. Rousseau, produced by Don Sharp, and scored by Rex Koury.

We Deliver the Goods

We Deliver the Goods, running on Sunday-night CBS in mid-1944, was a seaman's show produced by the men of the Merchant Marines.

With the exception of Howard Culver ("Your Maritime Narrator") and a few actors who dramatized stories of marine heroism, the entire cast of *We Deliver the Goods* was made up of seamen inexperienced in air techniques. Lieutenant Curt Roberts and his Maritime Service Band provided the music; the announcer was Bosun's Mate Second Class Sam Brandt. Vocalists were Chief Petty Officer Ray Buell and Ship's Cook Joe Sylva. Del Castillo was producer, and each show contained Culver's dramatic reading of the true adventure scripts. Often real-life heroes were brought to the microphone to tell their own stories.

We Love and Learn

We Love and Learn had a sporadic, unusual run beginning in 1941 as the syndicated serial *As the Twig is Bent*. On April 6, 1942, it premièred on CBS under its *We Love* title. Written by Don Becker and sponsored by General Foods, it told the story of Andrea Reynolds, a small-town girl who came to New York seeking fame and fortune and fell in love with "handsome, dashing" Bill Peters. Joan Banks starred as Andrea; she was replaced by Louise Fitch in mid-1944, just before the serial expired. Frank Lovejoy played Bill. *We Love and Learn* was revived by NBC for Manhattan Soap in 1949; Betty Worth played the lead. Again short-lived, it left the air in 1951. In 1955, the theme and scripts were again revived in a syndication featuring an all-black cast. The heroine's name was changed, the scene shifted to Harlem, and the show became *Ruby Valentine*.

We, the People

We, the People was first heard in 1936 as a skit on *The Rudy Vallee Show*. The show was created by Phillips H. Lord, whose popular *Seth Parker* had just gone under and whose equally popular *Gang Busters* was just getting started.

People was a strange mixture of humor, pathos, sentimental mishmash, and Hollywood glamor. Celebrities mingled with the common man, each coming before the microphones with a story of broad human interest and appeal.

We, the People, was really an audio potpourri, a museum of narrative curios designed for maximum dramatic impact. Some of the stories might have come right out of Ripley's *Believe-It-Or-Not;* others were so common that they instantly struck a universal emotion. Often the emotion was sympathy; a large percentage of the program's interviews related tragedy or misfortune. A young girl wanted to overcome the restrictions of her iron lung and dance again. The parents of a kidnapped 12-year-old boy appealed hopelessly for their son's safe return (a few months later, the headless body was washed ashore from the ocean). A 119-year-old woman from the Old South told of her days in slavery before the Civil War. And along with them came the famous: Jack Benny and Mary Livingstone, hamming it up on their twentieth anniversary, Joe Louis discussing pre-fight strategy; Mrs. Dutch Schultz, wife of the crime figure; Mrs. Eleanor Roosevelt; Lauritz Melchior; Grand Duchess Marie of Russia. Each had a stirring, funny or sad We, the People tale. Lord knew what the public wanted, and the program was extremely popular throughout its long run.

On October 4, 1936, it came to NBC as a Sunday-night show for Calumet Baking Soda. In 1937, it moved to CBS for Sanka Coffee, where it ran on Thursdays (1937–38), then Tuesdays (1938–42) before becoming a Gulf Oil show in 1942 (Sundays).

Probably the highest drama was attained with the unknowns. One of the most famous of all We, the People stories was that of "Mr. X," a man of about 70 who had had acute amnesia for about eight years and had been living at the Mississippi State Home near Jackson. His emotional appeal for identity drew more than 1,000 replies, and about a month later he was reunited with his Alabama kin.

But unknowns also were the greatest source of danger. More than once, We, the People was subjected to hucksters falsely representing themselves to get a shot at valuable network air time. That led the sponsor, in the late 1930's, to establish an elaborate double-checking system to verify the identity of each guest.

Newsman Gabriel Heatter was host and interviewer through the late 1930's and into the 1940's; his voice inflections showed him openly partisan to the causes brought before him. By 1944, Milo Boulton had replaced Heatter as host. In 1947 the show returned to Tuesdays; Boulton was replaced in 1948 by Dwight Weist. Others who carried the show were Eddie Dowling, Burgess Meredith, and Danny Seymour. Music was by Oscar Bradley's orchestra. It was a fine, entertaining half-hour, flawed only by the amateurish script-reading of the "People." The directors should have just let them talk their own language. In 1949 the program crossed networks, returning to NBC where it ran—still for Gulf—until 1951.

Welcome, Travelers

Welcome, Travelers, in contrast to We, the People, was entirely spontaneous and told its human interest stories in a much more natural manner. But it was virtually the same kind of show, an interview format during which people told their most dramatic experiences. This one was created by Les Lear and Tommy Bartlett in 1947, based on Bartlett's contention that travelers are more apt to "open up" than people at home. To prove his point he, Lear, and a staff of scouts began canvassing trains coming into Chicago. They searched diligently for interesting-looking people and soon developed keen eyes for dramatic possibilities. Welcome, Travelers went on ABC June 30, 1947, as a five-a-week noontime show. In 1948, it was bought by Procter & Gamble, and in 1949 it went to NBC, where it was heard daily at 10 A.M. (EST) until 1954. Bartlett was master of ceremonies, and the show was broadcast from the Hotel Sherman studio in downtown Chicago.

Once established, the train-riding routine proved time-consuming and unnecessary, and Bartlett and Lear developed teams of scouts to canvas airports, bus stations, and train depots for incoming people. Bartlett had no trouble filling the six or seven daily guest spots. In addition, the audience of about 1,000 was comprised entirely of travelers who obtained tickets at Welcome, Travelers booths set up in stations and airports. The guests told enduring love stories, tales of small-town life, agonizing separations from loved ones, and then were showered with gifts. Like We, the People, Welcome, Travelers occasionally had trouble with misrepresentation; one young boy who claimed he was an orphan on the way to visit a distant relative turned out to be a runaway. Bob Cunningham directed the show, and often the guests were introduced in train-barker style.

Wendy Warren and the News

WendyWarren and the News came to CBS June 23, 1947, in one of the most unusual soap opera formats ever devised. Played by Florence Freeman, Wendy was a news reporter for the Manhattan Gazette who also did a CBS newscast at noon. The show opened with three minutes of straight news, read by real-life newsman Douglas Edwards. The news flashes were read in bulletin style after a frenzied burst of telegraph-key noises. At the conclusion of the newscast, Edwards said something like, "And now, Wendy, what's the news today for the ladies?" Then Miss Freeman, in character, would give her "news reports from the women's world" (the "new cottons just in from St. Louis," or the like). This entire introduction took under four minutes and was described by one trade magazine as a "cunning trap" for people who hated soap operas. Following a commercial for Maxwell House Coffee, we rejoined Wendy, who was just stepping out of her control booth and into the drama written by Frank Provo and John Picard, Here Wendy, unburdened by Edwards and the news of the day, was just another bubbly heroine, her troubles compounded by two lovers, two "other women," and an endless array of villains. Lover number one was Mark Douglas (Lamont Johnson), who had been engaged to Wendy before the war separated them. That left an opening for lover number two—Gil Kendal, millionaire publisher and rather an insensitive clod to all but Wendy. Kendal (Les Tremayne) was being manipulated by Nona Marsh (Anne Burr), who swore that she alone would have him, and by the evil land developer Charles Lang (Horace Braham). Meanwhile, Lang's equally evil wife Adele (Jane Lauren) was flirting with Wendy's first love Mark, getting him irrevocably tangled in her web. Above it all was Wendy's father, Sam Warren (Rod Hendrickson) crusading editor of *The Clarion*, a newspaper in Elmdale, Connecticut. Home is where the heart is, and for Wendy, it was here, with father Sam and his matronly sister Dorrie (Tess Sheehan). But Wendy eventually married Gil and lived unhappily ever after—rather heavy stuff after such appetizers as Edwards' bulletins about Alger Hiss, the battle for Israel, and the current state of the Red probes. This show, which ran until 1958, surely didn't lack imagination. But, as *Radio Life* noted in review, "The combination of current events and drama is novel enough to attract attention without arriving in pulled-up collar and dark glasses."

What's Doin', Ladies?

What's Doin', Ladies? was a daily afternoon audience show, best described as *Breakfast At Sardi's* without Tom Breneman. Art Linkletter was the original host for this show, first heard from San Francisco on a West Coast Blue Network linkup around 1943. The early shows were done from Hale Brothers Department Store, where Linkletter browsed among the audience asking "What's doin'?", opening purses, and generally behaving his nosy best. Practical jokes were played on people in the audience, and several running gags were developed. On "Barter Day" (Tuesdays and Fridays), women could bring in useless items for trade. "Can You Take It?" pulled some unfortunate woman into the limelight, subjected her to head-to-toe criticism by beauty and fashion expert Dorothy Farrier, then gave her a free course in improvements most needed at Miss Farrier's school. By late 1943, *What's Doin', Ladies?* was originating in Hollywood (Linkletter had to be there Fridays for *People Are Funny*); with the arrival of Linkletter's *House Party* in 1945, a change of hosts was indicated. Perry Ward took the job in 1945; Jay Stewart became emcee in 1946.

What's My Name?

What's My Name? was one of the earliest cash giveaway shows, first heard on Mutual for Philip Morris in 1938. Arlene Francis was emcee chatting away with studio contestants while a male host asked the questions. The quiz was built around prominent people, with a cash prize to the contestant who could guess the subject's name from a series of clues. The prize was worth $100 for a correct guess on the first clue, $50 for a second-clue guess and $25 for third-clue. At the end of each show a jackpot question was asked, with the $500 prize going into the following week's pot if nobody won. Contestants were given two chances to win the jackpot, and jackpot questions included scrambled voices of the subjects. If the contestant didn't know, he was allowed to call anyone in his "old hometown" for help. The jackpot was then split between the contestant and his friend back home, if they coughed up the name between them. For a time, Miss Francis was supported in the show by Budd Hulick of "Stoopnagle and Budd" fame. In 1949, her partner was Ward Wilson and later Carl Frank, who had played her male lead on the 1940 soap, *Betty and Bob.* After its initial season, *What's My Name?* was heard on NBC Saturday nights for Oxydol, 1939–40, and on Mutual in 1941–42 for Fleischmann. It was off the air in the mid-1940's, while producer John Gibbs was in the Army, but returned to ABC in 1949 for another Saturday night stint.

What's the Name of that Song?

What's the Name of that Song? was a popular Mutual musical quiz running from 1944 through 1949. Dud Williamson was creator-emcee, and the show was based on an idea developed by him when managing a station in Seattle. Half a dozen contestants were brought onstage and were interviewed individually by Williamson. Then pianists Lou Maury and Frank Leithner played three numbers in quick succession. The contestants tried to guess the names—for one right answer, they collected $5; for two $15; for three $30. Williamson also took the show on the road, playing vaudeville-type between-film engagements at movie houses and broadcasting remote from wherever he was at the time. A vaudevillian before he entered radio, Williamson enjoyed the stage-show format. His show was popular, running its first year as a Sunday feature for Knox Gelatin. It was sustained on Sundays in 1945; on Wednesdays in 1946, and on Saturdays in 1947. When Williamson died in 1948, Bill Gwinn became emcee.

When a Girl Marries

When a Girl Marries was Elaine Carrington's third major soap opera, first heard on CBS May 29, 1939, under the direction of Kenneth MacGregor. Joan Field and Harry Davis, young marrieds from opposite sides of the tracks, overcame family strife, another woman, and even murder in their search for happiness. It was described as "the tender, human story of young married life, dedicated to everyone who has ever been in love." Harry eventually rose above his poverty to become a successful attorney, but in the beginning much of the strife centered around opposition to the marriage by family and friends. Joan and Harry partly solved this by moving early in the serial from Stanwood to Beechwood, a semi-rural community where they lived on Foxmeadow Lane. Harry's Mother Davis, a widow, became the show's philosopher-in-residence; his brother Tom had neither his brains nor his luck and remained a garage mechanic on the wrong side of the tracks. In Beechwood, Harry and Joan made friends with Irma Cameron, who with her second husband Steve had bought a farm and was in the process of going bankrupt. Much of the conflict revolved around Harry's feelings of inferiority and the aristocratic airs of Joan's old friends. Even though Harry once became romantically entangled with his secretary, he was generally a better soapmate than most of the men of daytime radio. Joan rewarded him by turning detective and finding the evidence that cleared him of a murder rap.

Noel Mills played Joan when the show opened, but her voice was wrong and MacGregor replaced her with Mary Jane Higby, who carried on until it ended in 1958. John Raby played Harry until he went to war in 1942; he was replaced by Robert Haag, and the part was later played by Whitfield Connor and Lyle Sudrow. Marion Barney added Mother Davis to her list of "mother" roles; William Quinn was Harry's brother Tom. Joan's sister Sylvia (Joan Tetzel, Toni Darnay, and Jone Allison) married Chick Norris (John Kane). Jeanette Dowling played friend Irma Cameron, Georgia Burke was Lily the Maid, and child impersonator Dolores Gillen was little Sammy, Joan's son. Throughout its nineteen-year run, When a Girl Marries was one of the most popular daytime shows of the air. It moved to NBC in 1941 after an initial two years at CBS, and ran there for General Foods until 1951 when it went to ABC for a variety of sponsors.

Which Is Which?

Which Is Which? was a novelty quiz first heard on CBS Wednesday nights for Old Gold October 25, 1944. Ken Murray, master of ceremonies, asked people from the audience to guess from the voices alone whether "celebrities" behind a curtain were real or were impersonators. A $50 prize was paid to winners; losers got $5, with the other $45 going to the National War Fund. The opener featured the real Basil Rathbone, the real Ted Lewis, the real Frank Morgan, and one Judie Manners, whose clever impersonation of Kate Smith fooled almost everyone. The show was produced by Mel Williamson and music was by Richard Himber. It ran one season.

Whispering Streets

Whispering Streets began on ABC March 3, 1952, as a five-a-week, 30-minute, complete-in-each-episode daytime show. It told stories of love, compliments of General Mills in the first two years, and was narrated by Hope Winslow, the fictional moniker of Gertrude Warner. The stories were written by Margaret E. Sangster, directed by Gordon Hughes, and produced by Ted Lloyd. In the mid-1950's, the show became a 15-minute anthology serial, doing complete stories each week. Cathy Lewis had a brief fling as Hope just before the changeover to the 15-minute format; Bette Davis even narrated for a time in 1958. She was followed by Anne Seymour and, again, Gertrude Warner. Bruno Zirato, Jr., who stayed with radio until the bloody end, directed in its last days. Whispering Streets was picked up by CBS in 1959 and went off on "the last day of soap opera," November 25, 1960.

The Whistler

The Whistler was big-league radio. With echoing footsteps and a haunting whistle, a new man of mystery flowed into the 1942 CBS night.

The whistle: thirteen notes destined to become one of the all-time lingering melodies of old-time radio, whistled softly at first, then louder as the Whistler steps close. That whistle could set a stage by itself: The stage of a narrow street, one dim streetlamp and a thin ground fog all around. A man steps into the street and walks toward us. He wears an overcoat belted around the middle, and leather gloves and a large-brimmed hat that keeps his face in the shadows. Closer he comes, closer, until he blots out the yellow light from the streetlamp in the distance.

> I am the Whistler, and I know many things, for I walk by night. I know many strange tales, many secrets hidden in the hearts of men and women who have stepped into the shadows. Yes, I know the nameless terrors of which they dare not speak . . .

In the melodramatic early years, The Whistler was written and produced by J. Donald Wilson, who occasionally had his character engage in dialogue with the people in the stories. Even then, it was all done on a subconscious level, the Whistler taking the role of conscience—arguing with the murderer, goading him on to his inevitable doom.

As the series matured, the Whistler stepped back and merely narrated. He was the first of the great omniscient storytellers (even though The Shadow started as a storyteller, he is best known as an invisible participant in the plot). More than a year after The Whistler premièred in the West, Mutual followed with The Mysterious Traveler, a show of the same type. Like the Traveler, the Whistler served up generous portions of ironic commentary with his stories. The tales were full of twists and surprises. Usually they contained a fine double twist at the end. In the early days, the Whistler sometimes summarized the surprise verbally, laughing like the Shadow as he doomed the killer with a few terse sentences from his well of infinite knowledge. Mercifully, this heavy-handed gimmick vanished as the show developed. By 1947 when The Whistler went coast to coast, the surprise was delivered in a fully dramatized scene, a brief epilogue that became widely anticipated as "the strange ending to tonight's story." That was when the Whistler turned the screws, when the killer who thought he'd gotten away after all trapped himself by some fatal flaw of character or deficiency in the master plan that was so obvious everyone except the Whistler had overlooked it.

When a newscaster decided to kill his wife, he had a perfect alibi. He had cut a recording of his 10 P.M. newscast, which would be played at exactly the moment he was choking the life out of her. The chief of police would be listening (he had seen to that), so he would automatically be eliminated from suspicion. Everything went as planned. With his wife's body still warm on the floor, the 10 P.M. newscast came on as scheduled. His voice filled the room, until the needle hit a flaw in the record, and skipped a groove. . . .

Despite the memorable nature of its format, The Whistler had rather a spotty record on the air. For most of the run, it was heard only regionally, billed over the Western CBS network through the mid 1940's as "the Pacific Coast's leading mystery show." By the time Signal Oil took sponsorship in 1944, George Allen had become producer-director. Berne Surrey, who created some of the most memorable sound effects for Suspense, worked on The Whistler as well. Head writer Harold Swanton and later Joel Malone bought the scripts from freelancers, then rewrote them to fit Whistler style. The finished script was given to Wilbur Hatch, veteran composer-conductor who had been with the show since the early Wilson days. Hatch created the special mood music that fit so well into the format.

The Whistler was played through most of the run by Bill Forman. Among the whistlers on the show was Owen James, who also whistled for The Saint. But for most of the run, the whistling was done by Dorothy Roberts. Wilbur Hatch, who composed the haunting theme, once estimated that only one person in twenty could come close to whistling the melody. The show was carried nationally in 1947–48, heard in the East for Household Finance and in the West for Signal Oil. It was still playing regionally in 1955.

The Wife Saver

The Wife Saver was a popular series of comic household hints, first heard on NBC Blue in 1932. Wife Saver Allen Prescott's hints ranged from spot removal to unsticking bureau drawers. He came to radio through newspapers, working first as a reporter for the New York Daily Mirror, then as a commentator for WMCA, New York, when such Mirror staffers as Walter Winchell made the transition in 1932. Later Prescott went to WINS as a reporter who sometimes gave household hints, and that format led directly to The Wife Saver. His show was on in early-morning time slots throughout the 1930's, and in the summer of 1941 he landed in Saturday-night prime time with a half-hour Blue Network variety show, Prescott Presents. Here, his hints were wrapped in a fully orchestrated format, featuring vocalists Diane Courtney and Joan Brooks and the quartet, Hi, Lo, Jack and the Dame.

Wild Bill Hickok

Wild Bill Hickok came to Mutual December 31, 1951, starring Guy Madison as Wild Bill and Andy Devine as his sidekick Jingles. It was basically the same show that went to early TV, with Wild Bill dusting off badmen with his fists and Jingles pounding them around with his gut. From 1951 through 1954, *Wild Bill Hickok* was a three-a-week half-hour for Kellogg. In 1955–56, it was sustained on Sunday.

The Witch's Tale

The Witch's Tale was the earliest significant horror show of the air, first heard on WOR on May 28, 1931.

The stories centered on ancient curses come true, native superstition and spirits that could not find rest, and of murder and the supernatural, told by Old Nancy, a cackling witch whose dialect was straight from the Middle Ages. By today's standards, her tales were crude and flat, but they were real chillers in 1934, when even the stilted sound effects and melodramatic music were audio novelties.

ANNOUNCER: *The Witch's Tale!*
Wind Up
Music Up
ANNOUNCER (over wind): The fascination of the eerie! Weird, blood-chilling tales, told by Old Nancy, the witch of Salem, and Satan, her wise black cat. They are waiting—waiting for you—now!
Wind Up
NANCY: Hee-hee-hee!
SATAN: *Howls*
NANCY: Hunner-an'-thirteen year old I be today, yes sir! hunner-an'-thirteen year old. Heh-heh-heh! Well, Satan . . .
SATAN: *Howls*
NANCY: We'll be gettin' down to our yarn-spinnin', if ye'll tell folks to douse all lights.
SATAN: *Howls*
NANCY: That's it—we want things nice an' cheerful fur our purty little tales. Now draw up to the fire an' gaze into the embers —*gaaaze into 'em deep*—an' soon ye'll be across the seas, in th' jungle land of Africa—British Africa, in what's called Tanganyika Territory. Hear that chantin' an' them savage drums?
Chants Up
Drums Up
NANCY: Then begins our story of "The Devil Mask!" Heh-heh-heh! "*The Devil Mask!*" HAHAHAHAHAHAHAHAHA!

Written and produced by Alonzo Deen Cole, the program originally starred Adelaide Fitzallen as Old Nancy, and was directed by Roger Bower. It also enjoyed a brief CBS run before settling into its long-running Mutual format on Tuesdays from 1935 to 1938.

The Woman in My House

The Woman in My House, a Carlton E. Morse soap opera premièring on NBC for Sweetheart Soap in 1951 and running until 1959, chronicled the saga of the Carter family, revealing many similarities of style and character to Morse's long-running One Man's Family. Each chapter began with the heady quotation: "Imperious man, look in your heart and dwell on this—without the woman in my house, what would I be?" Shades of the Barbours, even down to the later commercials for Miles Laboratories. The Carters lived in Miami and the serial again displayed Morse's fascination with the generation gap. Head of the house was the rather tight-laced and conservative James Carter (Forrest Lewis). With his wife Jessie (Janet Scott), he raised children Jeff (a 30-year-old writer cast in the Paul Barbour image and played by Les Tremayne), Sandy (Peggy Webber and later Anne Whitfield), Virginia (Alice Reinheart), Clay (Billy Idelson), and Peter (Jeff Silver) in a huge house on Elm Street. Morse produced the serial, which was written by Gil Faust and directed by George Fogle. Although the themes were similar, The Woman in My House never had the personal care that Morse gave his major serial.

Woman in White

Woman in White was first heard on NBC January 3, 1938, for Pillsbury. Broadcast from Chicago, it was Irna Phillips' replacement for her immensely popular Today's Children, which she had discontinued after her mother's death. Woman in White was patterned after Miss Phillips' successful, long-running Road of Life, and became one of the first radio shows to use doctors and nurses as chief characters. It followed the career of nurse Karen Adams, who had just graduated from training and was about to take her oath: "With loyalty will I endeavor to aid the physician in his work and devote myself to the welfare of those committed to my care." Naturally, keeping with the soap opera themes, Woman in White revolved mainly around Karen's romantic longings, which centered on one Dr. Kirk Harding. Eventually they were married, but Kirk got tangled up in some nasty business with the young wife of Karen's brother John. After a fiery scene, they separated.

Karen's problems were dominant through the first run of Woman in White which ended in 1942. The serial ran two years on NBC for Pillsbury, then moved to CBS where it was heard for Camay

Soap (1940–41) and Oxydol (1941–42). It was off the air for two seasons, and returned to NBC in 1944 with new characters. Now the show was part of Miss Phillips' General Mills Hour, when characters from *Today's Children* (which had been revived) interacted with those from *Woman in White* and *The Guiding Light*. The new lead was nurse Eileen Holmes, whose main romantic interest was Dr. Paul Burton. Some of the cast (such as Hugh Studebaker's Dr. Purdy) were continued from the old story line, but the central focus was now on Eileen and Paul. This version was carried by General Mills on NBC until 1948, when the show left the air. Like most of Miss Phillips' serials, this one was produced by Carl Wester from Chicago until Miss Phillips moved to the West Coast in the mid-1940's. In the early version, Luise Barclay and Betty Lou Gerson had longstanding parts as Karen Adams Harding; the role was also played by Betty Ruth Smith and Peggy Knudsen. Karl Weber and Arthur Jacobson played husband Dr. Kirk Harding. John Adams was played by Willard Farnum and Harry Elders, and Karen's sister Betty was Toni Gilman and Louise Fitch. In the new version, Eileen Holmes was played by an all-grown-up Sarajane Wells, who had been little Betty Fairfield of *Jack Armstrong* for thirteen years. Ken Griffin was the light of her romantic eye, Dr. Paul Burton.

Woman of America

Woman of America was first heard January 25, 1943, as a test on a limited East Coast NBC network of fourteen stations. The test period was eight months, and the serial premièred on the entire network for Procter & Gamble on September 27, 1943. *Woman of America* was highly unusual matinée fare. It told, in a soap opera format and time slot, of the trek along the Oregon Trail made by pioneers in 1865. The action centered on Prudence Dane, wagon train heroine, played by Anne Seymour. Each day the heroine's great-granddaughter Margaret (also played by Miss Seymour) relayed another chapter in the life of her homesteading ancestor. James Monks was featured as wagonmaster Wade Douglas. Probably because of its unusual afternoon nature, *Woman of America* got respectable ratings from the beginning and lasted three years. As the westward trek ended in the script, the action was shifted into a contemporary setting, following another great-granddaughter who had been named Prudence after the original heroine. This modern Prudence, a newspaperwoman, was played by Florence Freeman and was good preparation for her long-running role of *Wendy Warren*. *Woman of America* was last heard in 1946, carried all the way by Procter & Gamble for Ivory Snow.

Woman of Courage

Woman of Courage, the story of Martha Jackson and her troubled family allegedly proved that "if ye have faith, nothing shall be impossible." Billed as "the moving story of a wife and mother who is unafraid, because she knows that if you believe you can win, nothing in life can defeat you, and that what is right will be," it premièred on CBS January 1, 1940, for Octagon and Crystal Soap. Martha's problem-prone family included a crippled husband Jim and kids Lucy and Tommy, and the drama followed their lives in the little town of Farmington. Selena Royle played Martha, and the part was also handled by Alice Frost. Albert Hayes was Jim, Joan Tetzel was Lucy, and Larry Robinson played Tommy. Martha had a sister, Lillian Burke (played by Enid Markey), and so did Jim (his sister Cora was Tess Sheehan); the sisters tried to help them through their troubles but inevitably only added to the strife. Written by Carl Buss, Martha's biggest problem was husband Jim. In one chapter Jim wanted to show Martha how smart he was—so he paid $20,000 for a piece of desert that he had planned to get for $5,000 tops. While the crooks laughed and chortled, Jim planned to pay for it with Martha's new inheritance, which she hadn't even claimed yet. Helen Trent's Gil Whitney himself couldn't have done better. Jim, Martha, and company were gone before 1943.

Women in the Making of America

Women in the Making of America, a thirteen-week NBC series premièring on the Blue Network May 19, 1939, as a project of the Federal Radio Theatre, was created by Eva vom Baur Hansl, a longtime advocate of women's rights who had accumulated more than 17,000 articles on the subject over the years. *Women* was a dramatic series, moving through history to illustrate how long ago the women's movement had begun (as early as the seventeenth century) and how recently open acts of oppression had occurred. Jane Ashman wrote the scripts.

X-Minus One

X-Minus One was an extension of *Dimension X*, the fine NBC science fiction anthology that closed shop on September 29, 1951. Almost four years later, on April 24, 1955, *X-Minus One* opened on NBC, dramatizing many of the same tales previously heard on *Dimension X*, then striking out into deeper space with new adaptations and original stories.

Many of its stories came from *Galaxy Magazine*, featuring the work of such writers as Robert *(Psycho)* Bloch, Ray Bradbury, Isaac Asimov, Robert Silverberg, Robert Heinlein, Poul Anderson, and Theodore Sturgeon. Many of the old *Dimension X* production crew worked on the show. Scripts were adapted by Ernest Kinoy and George Lefferts; Fred Collins announced and Daniel Sutter was director. *X-Minus One* did more comedy than its predecessor; the stories ranged from amusing "Lifeboat Mutiny" to "Tunnel Under the World," about a public relations experiment so monstrous that it could be done only on radio.

The opening of *X-Minus One* was lively and active:

"Countdown for blastoff—X-minus five . . . four . . . three . . . two . . . X-minus one, fire" then the roar of a rocket as it ripped away from mother earth. "From the far horizons of the unknown come transcribed tales of new dimensions in time and space. These are stories of the future, adventures in which you'll live in a million could-be years on a thousand maybe worlds. The National Broadcasting Company, in cooperation with Galaxy Science Fiction Magazine, presents—X-X-X-X - MINUS - MINUS - MINUS - MINUS ONE ONE ONE one . . ."

Some of the best drama of the mid-1950's was heard on *X-Minus One*. It was one of the few remaining theatres of work for such old pros as Santos Ortega, Jack Grimes, Joseph Julian, Ted Osborne, Bob Hastings, John Gibson, Mason Adams, Raymond Edward Johnson, Bill Lipton, Reese Taylor, Luis Van Rooten, Leon Janney, Staats Cotsworth, Joseph Bell, Wendell Holmes, Ralph Camargo, Mandel Kramer, Guy Repp, John Larkin, and Joe Di Santis. Some did numerous encores. The series lasted three years, finally bowing out on January 9, 1958.

Then, with the nostalgia craze at its peak, NBC decided to use the old *X-Minus One* transcriptions in a test to see if radio drama could be supported in the 1970's. The old shows were aired once a month (an unwise bit of scheduling, with listeners forever trying to remember whether the show was running the third or fourth weekend of each month) beginning June 24, 1973. Announcers implored listeners to write in supporting the show and the idea, but *X-Minus One* died again in 1975.

You Are There

You Are There was unique in the realm of historical drama programming. Created for CBS by Goodman Ace, it blended modern technique with ancient drama, taking the entire CBS newsroom on a time trip to report the great events of history. "CBS asks you to imagine that our microphone is present at this unforgettable moment . . . all things are as they were then, except, when CBS is there, YOU are there!"

Based on "authentic fact and quotation," *You Are There* was 30 minutes of present-tense stream-of-consciousness drama, mixing on-the-spot interviews with "analysis" and dramatic running accounts of unfolding panoramas. Real-life newsmen with established reputations handled "remote" broadcasts, while anchorman Don Hollenbeck organized the field reports and summarized events for listeners as they came in from the correspondents.

The show opened just before some climactic event that was to change history. CBS asked its audience to believe that newsman John Daly was sitting in Ford Theatre with a microphone the night Lincoln was shot. The network placed its microphones inside the Alamo; in the "radio room" of the U.S. Senate for the 1805 impeachment of Justice Samuel Chase; on a grassy hillside for the fall of Troy. Hollenbeck or Daly usually opened the show, outlining the situation as it "stands now." In the show describing the battle of Gettysburg, Hollenbeck delivered a few crisp scene-setting sentences that clearly conveyed the electric atmosphere. It was the turning point in the Civil War . . . Lee's forces had been pushing relentlessly northward, with an unbroken chain of victories in their wake. Unless General Meade could hold the Confederates here, Lincoln would be forced to come to terms with the South, and the Union would be dissolved.

Hollenbeck's voice faded. Then came the booming, echoing signature: "July 3rd, 1863! Gettysburg! You . . . are there." The introduction was complete. Hollenbeck blended in again, and soon we heard John Daly in a short series of interviews with Yankee troops. Richard C. Hottelet was on hand, anlayzing the breaking story from the North's viewpoint. Suddenly Confederate cannon appeared in the distance, and we returned to John Daly for a description from the front lines.

Every kind of historical situation was handled, from the last days of Pompeii and the execution of Mary, Queen of Scots, to the exile of Napoleon and the assassination of Julius Caesar. The show originated as CBS Is There July 7, 1947, a Monday-night summer series. Produced and directed by Robert Lewis Shayon, the show then used—in addition to Daly—such well-known newsmen and announcers as Ken Roberts, Harry Marble, and Jackson Beck. Irve Tunick wrote the scripts. In 1948, in an attempt to create even greater listener involvement, the name was changed to You Are There. The show was a Sunday sustainer from the fall of 1947 through its demise in 1950, and was also one of the early shows of network television. The TV version featured Walter Cronkite as anchorman.

You Bet Your Life

You Bet Your Life opened a whole new field for Groucho Marx, who might otherwise have competed with Milton Berle as radio's most notable failure. By 1947, Marx had tried the air four times and bombed. His best show had been the ill-fated Blue Ribbon Town in 1943, and even that had folded after a season. Some of the top air personalities were even reluctant to use him as a guest.

It took a promoter like John Guedel to figure out what was wrong. Guedel happened to be in the wings one day when Marx teamed up with Bob Hope for a network guest skit. Hope dropped his script and Marx put his foot on it. Then Marx dropped his script and the two finished out the skit in a frantic session of ad-libbing. Guedel thought Groucho sensational.

Marx's greatest problem along Radio Row had been his reluctance to read "canned" material. It had always clashed with the reluctance of directors to put him on without a script, to let him do his thing in a natural, unrestricted way. Guedel proposed to do precisely that. "I figured he'd be great working with people out of an audience,"

Guedel recalled for *Radio Life*. "When the people were being funny, Groucho could be the perfect straight man; when the people played it straight, Groucho couldn't miss with his own comedy. With Groucho, I figured we'd be protected from both sides."

Guedel, then architect of two highly successful audience shows (*People Are Funny* and *House Party*) knew what he was talking about, but Groucho wasn't buying. Marx then was an almost legendary comic figure, the pivotal member of the screen's renowned Marx Brothers. He thought being relegated to a quizmaster's role would be a drastic comedown. Finally, in 1947, Guedel persuaded Marx to come to the studio after a *House Party* broadcast and cut an audition record. Thus armed, he went out to pitch the show to clients. It sold within five weeks. The show premièred October 27, 1947, on ABC, and was carried for two years by Elgin-American. George Fenneman introduced Marx at the beginning of the programs as "the one, the only . . ." and the audience finished the sentence with a thunderous "GROUCHO!"

You Bet Your Life differed from all other quiz shows in that the quiz was mere window dressing for the antics of the quizmaster. Each week Groucho, perched on his stool, was introduced to three couples. The couples were carefully selected by Guedel and henchmen Bob Dwan, Bernie Smith, Ed Tyler, and Hy Freedman. The producers combed through neighborhoods looking for people with unusual jobs, strange interests, and offbeat personalities to play against Groucho's wit. Some were actually taken from the studio audience, but Dwan and Smith (who became the show's co-directors) wanted a broader base than that. People were invited in, interviewed for more than an hour, and were either scheduled or dismissed on that basis. Opposites were deliberately paired, giving Marx two distinct targets for his questions. Even announcer Fenneman, the eternal straight man, was the ideal foil for Groucho.

Marx didn't meet the couples before they were brought before him; indeed, he hadn't gotten as much as a glimpse of their appearance or attire. Guedel wanted Marx to be absolutely spontaneous, and he was. Informed that a contestant was a used-car salesman, Marx might ask "How many times have you been indicted?" His wit was biting, his satire sharp. Marx was a shrewd interviewer who soon saw weaknesses and strengths of character, and wasted no time exploiting them. If people wanted to sing, he let them; sometimes he joined them in the chorus—and the worse the singing was, the better the comic effect. Groucho probed relentlessly, seeking anything that could be used for laughs. He loved beautiful blondes and people with funny names. A man with "Crumb" for a middle name didn't stand a chance.

The quiz portion was done straight; questions were asked and answered (or not answered) without surrounding gimmicks. Each couple was given $20 and told to bet as much as both wanted on each of four questions. If the questions were answered correctly ("only one answer between you"), the money would double with each successive step. Thus, it was possible for couples to win as much as $320 in the quiz or go broke on the first question. If they lost, Groucho asked a nonsense question for $25, grandly stating that "nobody leaves here broke." (A regular consolation question was "Who was buried in Grant's tomb?") The format allowed three couples to appear in the quiz; about 60 minutes of dialogue between Groucho and couples was taped, then Guedel edited it to 30 minutes for broadcast. The couple with the highest money total at the end got a chance at the giant jackpot, usually $1,000.

In addition, *You Bet Your Life* offered a "secret word" bonus prize, varying between $100 and $250 depending on the year. The word might be "table," or "air" or "water"—"It's a common word, something you see every day," Groucho reminded contestants. Guedel and Marx, co-owners of the show, paid all secret word winners out of their pockets, on the spot and in cash. The sponsor picked up the tab on contestant winnings and jackpots.

The critics reacted about as Marx figured. They cluck-clucked over what a comedown it must be for a famous film comedian to land on an audience show. But Groucho was doing what came naturally, and ratings began to climb. By its third year, the show had outgrown its original sponsor, arrived in radio's top 10, and won the Peabody Award, radio's equivalent of the Pulitzer, in the first award ever given to a comedian on a quiz show.

In 1949, *You Bet Your Life* moved to CBS and took on as longtime sponsor, the DeSoto-Plymouth dealers, who also carried the show on TV. The series ran until 1959, the last nine years as an NBC entry.

Young Dr. Malone

Young Dr. Malone was the long-running serial drama of Jerry Malone, young physician of Three Oaks. In his later years medical director of the Three Oaks Medical Center, Jerry was last seen heading toward the eternal happiness that had eluded him for so long. The time: November 25, 1960; *Young Dr. Malone* was the fifth of six soaps being cancelled on "the last day of radio soap opera." It had all begun November 20, 1939, when Jerry premièred on NBC Blue. In 1940, the serial moved to CBS, where it began a four-year run for Post Toasties and General Foods. After a year in mothballs, *Young Dr. Malone* was revived in 1945, running on CBS for Procter & Gamble until the mid-1950's.

The bulk of the action through the twenty-year run revolved around Jerry, his wife Ann (a later wife was named Tracy), their family and friends of Three Oaks. Family included Jerry's Mother Malone, a well-intended busybody whose efforts to aid Jerry's career and home life often resulted in embarrassment. There were the usual stock soapy situations: Jerry was shot down over Germany in World War II and presumed dead; while he was away, Ann took up with another man. Later, Jerry faced the inevitable murder trial, emerging victorious after months of strife. There was a crippling disease which Jerry overcame only after an eleventh-hour blood transfusion. Through it all were woven the longer threads: Ann's sometimes impetuous jealousy and Jerry's grand lifetime dream, the Three Oaks clinic, toward which end his professional life was dedicated. He realized the goal with the help of philanthropic Roger Dineen, Jerry's lawyer; Dineen's wife Lynne was Ann's best friend. Jerry's other close friend was Carl Ward, owner of the local newspaper. Jerry's daughter Jill grew up on the show and became a major character as the serial drew to a close.

Alan Bunce was the original Dr. Malone. Jerry was also played by Carl Frank, Charles Irving (late 1940's), and Sandy Becker, who carried the part throughout the 1950's, and bid fond farewell in 1960. Ann was played by Elizabeth Reller and later by Barbara Weeks. Evelyn Varden was Mother Malone; Jill was played by child impersonator Madeleine Pearce, and later as an adult was handled by Joan Lazer and Rosemary Rice. Larry Haines played newsman Carl Ward, Barry Thomson played philanthropist Roger Dineen, and Donna Keith played Roger's wife, Lynne. Tracy Malone, who came along later in the run, was played by Gertrude Warner, Joan Alexander, and Jone Allison. Medical specialist Julian Funt wrote the series; David Driscoll was the writer by the late 1940's.

Young Love

Young Love, a CBS situation comedy, premièring July 4, 1949, and sponsored by Ford Motors in 1950, starred Janet Waldo and Jimmy Lydon as a young married couple named, appropriately, Janet and Jimmy. Still in college, they were too poor to afford an apartment. Thus they lived apart—he in the Delta Phi Beta fraternity house, she in the girls' dorm—and had to meet on the Midwestern University bench overlooking Marble Lake. The comedy revolved around their frustrations and relationships with friends and faculty. Herb Butterfield as crusty Dean Ferguson, the grand old man who couldn't see without his glasses, was particularly hilarious. Shirley Mitchell played Molly Belle, Janet's roommate, resurrecting her Leila Ramsom voice from *The Great Gildersleeve* for such expressions as "matri-li'l-ole-mony" and "flippety-li'l-ole-flop." Others in the cast were Jerry Hausner and Hal March. Roy Rowan announced, and the series was written and produced by the *Railroad Hour* team of Jerry Lawrence and Bob Lee (Janet's husband in private life).

Young Widder Brown

Young Widder Brown rivaled *The Romance of Helen Trent* and *Stella Dallas* in sheer melodrama and agony. It came to NBC September 26, 1938, the story of "a woman as real as her friends who listen to her—the dramatic story of a very human mother's duty to her children, in conflict with the dictates of her heart." Later the story became one of "attractive Ellen Brown, with two fatherless children to support—the story of the age-old conflict between a mother's duty and a woman's heart."

Carried most of the way by Bayer Aspirin and Sterling Drugs, Ellen lasted on NBC until June 29, 1956. In that eighteen years lay some of the most excruciating radio torture ever devised by Frank and Anne Hummert. Ellen's troubles, typical of Hummert plots, started early in life. Still in her early 30's, still beautiful, she had been left alone by the death of her husband to raise their children Janie and Mark. Ellen settled in the typical Midwestern town of Simpsonville, where she opened a tearoom and began to charm the daylights out of every eligible bachelor in town. One of the most eligible in those early years was Dr. Peter Turner, who quickly became established as "the man Ellen loves." Lurking in the background, though, was Herbert Temple, Ellen's middle-aged admirer. Neither was to win her, of course. Though she was not pursued by nearly as many suitors as chased through *The Romance of Helen Trent*, Ellen Brown had a fickle nature that strongly resembled Helen's. By the early 1940's, Peter Turner was out, Dr. Anthony Loring was in. Anthony would become her most persistent admirer, this serial's version of Gil Whitney. For most of the two-decade run, he and Ellen were on the verge; their marriage plans were on again, off again, but somehow that ceremony never occurred.

Herbert Temple got wise fast; he gave up his dream of marrying Ellen and settled down with a simple, homey wife named Norine, who later became Ellen's best friend. Ellen, meanwhile, seemed forever doomed to raise those kids alone. With each drastic development, Anthony seemed to slip farther and farther away. The complications ran the gamut. Some were recalled by *Newsweek* as the magazine bid Ellen and friends adieu in 1956: "a false accusation of murder, amnesia, innumerable broken bones, addiction to a 'powder of forgetfulness' slipped into her (nonalcoholic, of course) drink by an unscrupulous painter, and blindness brought on by an allergy to chocolate cake (an affliction cured when a cake-flour advertiser complained)."

On April 25, 1949, Anthony thought Ellen had been killed in an airplane crash. Actually, she had only been badly injured, had lost her memory, and that very moment was being held prisoner in a lonely mountain hideaway by the confused David Blake. In the early 1950's, poor Anthony was tricked into believing a lie about her. Faced with the horrible possibility of finding happiness at last, Anthony chose agony instead; he cast Ellen out of his life and turned for consolation to an evil woman named Millicent. When they were married, Ellen's last hopes trickled away; she, in turn, agreed to marry dashing Michael Forsythe, who had been hounding her for months. But Anthony learned of Millicent's deceit and trickery and came crawling back to Ellen. For three years Millicent stood in their way. She became to Ellen what Cynthia Whitney was to Helen Trent—the enemy who lived only to cause her unhappiness. But late in 1955, Millicent Loring was brutally murdered, and Anthony, naturally, became the prime suspect. Ellen knew better; she knew that the kind Anthony could never kill, even for her. And we in the audience knew that the real murderer was the treacherous Ivan Mansfield, an artist whom Millicent had hired to break up the Anthony-Ellen romance.

It was a long haul, but happiness was almost theirs. They had but one murder rap to overcome; duck soup for most matinee heroines. Florence Freeman went almost all the way as Ellen; the part was finished by Millicent Brower. Ned Wever played Anthony. Ellen's children, Janie and Mark, were Marilyn Erskine and Tommy Donnelly. Bud Collyer was early suitor Dr. Peter Turner, Herbert Temple, who gave up early, was played over the years by House Jameson, Alexander Scourby, and Eric Dressler; his wife Norine was Joan Tompkins. Martha Atwell, who directed many soaps for the Hummerts, had a hand in this one too. George Ansbro announced for Phillips Milk of Magnesia, Haley's M-O and other products.

Anthony and Ellen beat the murder rap and still had time to get mixed up in another mess or two. First Millicent left Ellen $250,000 in her will, on condition that she never marry Anthony. For a time,

Anthony—silly man—actually thought she might take the money. Then Ellen's nasty cousin Isobel set her cap for Anthony. Isobel, in the process of shedding her current husband, named Ellen co-respondent in a messy divorce. Anthony wavered. Did he believe in Ellen or didn't he? The question lingered down to the last Friday of the last week, when at last they fell into each other's arms.

"Will you marry me, Ellen?"

"Yes, I will, Anthony!"

Then the organ was stilled; the final dust cover slipped over the NBC microphone.

Your All-Time Hit Parade

Your All-Time Hit Parade came to NBC February 12, 1943, as a Friday-night series of popular music for Lucky Strike. Tommy Dorsey, often the series maestro, offered such all-time favorites as "Wagon Wheels," "Chicago," and "Some of These Days," mixed with current favorites like "I'll Be Seeing You." Broadcast initially from Carnegie Hall, the program was plugged incessantly by Luckies in an extensive pre-show publicity campaign; the slogan "The best tunes of all have moved to Carnegie Hall" became for a time as well-known as Luckies' wartime ditty, "Lucky Strike green has gone to war." It was widely parodied by such comics as Fred Allen, Al Jolson, Colonel Stoopnagle, and Ed "Archie" Gardner. Your All-Time Hit Parade offered a pleasing mix of familiar tunes, done by Dorsey and such guests as Frances Langford, Frank Sinatra, and Sophie Tucker. Harry Von Zell announced. The show ran through 1944, serving as the summer replacement for The Jack Benny Program that year.

Your America

Your America, broadcast from Omaha, was first heard on the nationwide NBC network January 8, 1944, and ran through the season as a Saturday-afternoon Union Pacific Railroad show. UP had bought the half-hour variety format in observance of its seventy-fifth anniversary, and its theme was "America and American railroads." Each show was designed to tell, in words and music, the development of the American West. Josef Koestner was in charge of the music, composing and conducting over fifty-eight musicians and vocalists. Nelson Olmsted was chief storyteller until he went into the Army in mid-1944; then Elden Westley took over. Reporter Ray Clark conducted interviews with railroad people, and talks were lined up with governors of the eleven Western states served by Union Pacific. Much Omaha talent was used. Producer was Lyle DeMoss, program director of Omaha station WOW.

Your Hit Parade

Your Hit Parde came out of the 1935 NBC air with the top fifteen tunes of the week, served up by maestro Lennie Hayton, the Hit Paraders, and the Lucky Strike Orchestra. "Once again, the voice of the people has spoken," an announcer said, introducing a very early show: "New Yorkers and Californians, Northerners and Southerners, Republicans, Democrats, men, women and children—120 million of you have told us what songs you want to hear this Saturday night. You've told us by your purchases of sheet music and records, by your requests to orchestra leaders in the places you've danced, by the tunes you listen to on your favorite radio programs. That's why *The Hit Parade* is your own program."

It opened April 20, 1935, and officially closed shop in April 1959. But the real heyday of the program was in the early 1940's, when America's chief Saturday-night mania was to find out which song was number one, when people gathered around radio sets in cheering sections, pulling for musical favorites and sometimes putting stakes on the outcome.

In those days before disc jockeys and plastic radio formats, *Your Hit Parade* was the nation's only real authority in popular music. Batton, Barton, Durstine & Osburn, the ad agency handling the Lucky Strike account, kept the secret of its selection process under tight wraps, revealing only that a "large staff" was employed to check the statistics, that the system was "infallible," and (something listeners already knew) that it was based primarily on readings of radio requests, sheet-music sales, requests to orchestra leaders around the country, and juke-box tabulations.

The people believed it. By the late 1930s, *Your Hit Parade* had developed the natural formula of building to its suspenseful climax, saving the top three songs of the week for last. The others would be played randomly throughout the hour, 45 minutes or 30 minutes (the format varied greatly over the years). Intermingled with various "Lucky Strike Extras," the hit tunes were offered either musically by the orchestra or vocally by one of the show's regular or guest artists.

Hit Parade had a distinctive, bouncy style; the Lucky Strike themes floated over the furious tobacco chanting of former auctioneers L. A. (Speed) Riggs and F. E. Boone, while André Baruch peddled smokes and tried vainly to fend off the antics of W. C. Fields, who had managed to wrangle a comedy slot for himself during the 45-minute 1938 editions. By January 1943, listeners were chanting "Lucky Strike green has gone to war," a slogan inserted throughout the show whenever there was a 10-second pause for anything. They watched green go to war and never return, for the predominantly green Luckies package settled into its now-familiar red and white.

Probably no other program on the air ran as long with so many complete changes of format, character, and personnel. It went through more than a dozen top orchestra leaders and two score singers. Lennie Hayton's baton waving was followed by Al Goodman's in 1935; Goodman played through 1938, his two long stints broken by appearances of Peter Van Steeden, Ray Sinatra, Carl Hoff, Abe Lyman, Freddie Rich, Harry Salter, Harry Sosnick, Richard Himber, Leo Reisman, Scott Quintet, and Mark Warnow. Warnow led through the 1940's, with the exception of the two years (1947–49) when singer Frank Sinatra and his old friend from the Dorsey years, Axel Stordahl, were teamed. Raymond Scott conducted through most of the 1950's.

Vocalists of the early years included Gogo De Lys, Kay Thompson, Buddy Clark, Fredda Gibbson (Georgia Gibbs), Lanny Ross, Kay Lorraine, and Bea Wain. Barry Wood was the male lead in the era just before Sinatra, who roared into the show in February 1943 with a crowd of screaming bobby-soxers and left two years later for his own series. Joan Edwards became a regular in 1941, serving for six years and becoming the focal point of a nationwide Moan and Groan for Joan Club—the serviceman's answer to the inane female screams for Sinatra. Ethel Smith, red-headed and dynamic, was signed in 1942 as the show's organist. Metropolitan Opera star Lawrence Tibbett was tapped to replace Sinatra, a decision that caused a lot of talk in the music world. Tibbett's arrival marked an end of screaming and saw the overall rating of Your Hit Parade jump seven points.

Dick Todd, Johnny Mercer, Dinah Shore, Ginny Simms, Martha Tilton, Doris Day, and Dick Haymes served brief stints in the late 1940's. Andy Russell became a regular in 1946, Eileen Wilson came two years later. Sinatra and his legion of swooners returned in 1947 for two years. With the new decade came TV, and a roster of names like Snooky Lanson, Dorothy Collins, Russell Arms, Gisele MacKenzie.

The songs? There was no telling what might make Your Hit Parade. Novelty numbers, Christmas songs, rhythm and blues, jazz. Some songs flashed briefly onto the list, rising high into the top 5 and quickly dropping into oblivion. Others stayed for weeks. "Too Young," "Because of You," "Buttons and Bows," "Some Enchanted Evening," "A Tree in the Meadow," "Peg O' My Heart," "I Hear a Rhapsody," "Hey, There," "If," "I'll Be Seeing You," "Now Is the

Hour," and "You'll Never Know" were among the most-requested *Hit Parade* songs. "White Christmas" was a yearly favorite, riding high in the top 10 at Christmas for many consecutive years. Familiar to most Americans was the Saturday-night chant of the tobacco auctioneer:

> Hey twenty-nine nine nine nine nine nine nine, roundem roundem roundem roundem roundem, am I right at thirty thirty thirty thirty thirty thirty thirty thirty thirty thirty thirty thirty THIRTY one thirty one thirty one one one one one one one one one one one one TWO thirty two two two two two two two two two two two two two two two THREE thirty three three three three three three three three FOUR thirty four four four four four come along come along long long long four four thirty four four four FIVE thirty five five five five grab it grab it grab it five thirty five thirty five thirty five five five am I right am I right am I right at thirty five five five SIX six thirty six six six six six six six six six SEVEN seven seven seven thirty seven seven seven seven seven seven seven EIGHT eight eight eight eight thirty eight eight eight eight—sold A-merican!

And then:

> So long, for a while . . .
> That's all the songs, for a while . . .
> So long to "Your Hit Parade"
> And the tunes that you picked to be played . . .
> So long . . .

Your Hollywood Parade

Your Hollywood Parade came to NBC December 8, 1937, hot on the heels of *Good News of 1938*. The new show was a blatant *Good News* copy, using the same cooperative approach between network, sponsor, and major Hollywood studio. *Good News* had started the big Hollywood rush to the airwaves with the sensational announcement of a deal between Maxwell House Coffee and Metro-Goldwyn-Mayer, making any star on the MGM lot available to the broadcast. Now came Warner Brothers and Lucky Strike Cigarettes with essentially the same deal. Top movie stars would appear in lavish 60-minute variety acts, allowing for music, comedy, and mini-dramatizations of current Warner Brothers hits. The only difference between this and *Good News* was that George Washington Hill, head of American Tobacco, was calling the shots, not the studio. Dick Powell, fresh from his stint on *Hollywood Hotel*, was tapped as master of ceremonies; opening-night guests included Gary Cooper, Bette Davis, Basil Rathbone, and Olivia De Havilland. *Your Hollywood Parade* disappeared after its initial season.

Yours Truly, Johnny Dollar

Yours Truly, Johnny Dollar was first heard on CBS February 18, 1949, starring Charles Russell as the insurance investigator with the "action-packed expense account."

Dollar was a freelance insurance investigator, ever ready to hop away to the far corners of the earth for a client who would pay his expenses and fork over a cut of any goods recovered. He was equipped with a keen, analytical mind, a nose for murder, and more than enough brawn to take care of himself when the going got dirty—as it inevitably did.

Clients stood in line for his services. Whenever a big diamond heist or valuable stolen art brought about big insurance claims, Johnny Dollar was sent in for the probe. Often he worked through Universal Adjustment Bureau, a clearing-house for all client companies. Sometimes the assignment, on its face, was simple; perhaps Pat McCracken, Universal's head adjuster, merely wanted Dollar to play bodyguard for a wealthy client whose life had been threatened. But once a case began developing, the result was usually murder.

In its last days, *Yours Truly, Johnny Dollar* was one of the best detective shows on the air. The hero's character was as fully developed as 30-minute doses of radio would allow. Dollar was a shameless padder of his expense account. He was a confirmed bachelor, at least as long as he pursued "this crazy life," which probably meant forever. He had an in-bred streak of impatience, forever pleading with friends and clients to get to the point. More than once, Johnny charged ahead after hearing only part of what a person was telling him. Naturally, he had missed the most important part.

Playing against these characteristics were several semi-regular but well-developed supporting people. There was Betty Lewis, his best girl, plotting to get Johnny settled into the paper-and-slippers routine. There was Randy Singer, the cop, and Smoky Sullivan, the arsonist turned stoolie and one of Dollar's best tipsters. Finally, there was Alvin Peabody Cartwright, an eccentric client whose odd notions had a disturbing way of being at least partly right.

But mostly Johnny Dollar worked alone, dealing with new people each week. If the regulars appeared at all, it was only briefly; then Dollar would be away to a new locale. Dollar was the narrator of his adventures, and the stories always developed in terms of his expense account: "Expense account, item one," and we were off. It might be a buck fifty for cab fare across town or $200 airfare across the country. At the end of each case, the expenses were neatly totaled and signed, "Yours truly, Johnny Dollar."

The show thrived through five changes of lead. Edmond O'Brien became Dollar in 1950; John Lund in 1952; Bob Bailey in 1955; Robert Readick in 1960; and Mandel Kramer in late 1961. As originally played by Charles Russell, Dollar was a generous fellow who tossed silver dollars as tips to busboys and doormen. That corny trademark had vanished by the time O'Brien and Lund took the part. So stereotyped and hardboiled were these two that they were almost indistinguishable. In those early 1950's, some of the stories were about as dry as week-old biscuits. Paul Dudley and Gil Doud wrote for Russell, the music was by Mark Warnow, and Richard Sanville directed. Jaime Del Valle directed through the O'Brien-Lund years; writers included E. Jack Neuman, John Michael Hayes, Sidney Marshall, and Blake Edwards. Music was by Leith Stevens, Milton Charles, and Eddie Dunstedter. It ran as a five-a-week serial during the 1955–56 season; otherwise it was 30 minutes weekly.

With the coming of Bob Bailey and the 15-minute era, *Yours Truly, Johnny Dollar* began to take on life. Bailey was far and away the best Dollar, though Mandel Kramer ran him a close second. Both men projected real personality into the character, bringing insights that none of the others achieved. Bailey was a tougher Johnny, more the street-fighter than we had seen before. Kramer's interpretation was lighter; his Dollar developed a finely tuned, low-key sense of humor. Jack Johnstone became producer-director at the beginning of the Bailey era. Under his guidance, the serial was one of the brightest 15-minute shows on the air. Virginia Gregg, who appeared almost weekly during this period, played a variety of characters, from socialite to murderess; she was heard most often as girl friend Betty Lewis. In its last year, Johnstone took over the writing chores, leaving the directing to Fred Hendrickson and Bruno Zirato, Jr. Music was by Ethel Huber.

Yours Truly, Johnny Dollar used the acting talents of most of radio's old pros. Among those called back for repeat performances were Jim Boles, Bill Mason, Lawson Zerbe, Teri Keane, Ralph Bell, Larry Haines, William Redfield, Roger De Koven, Gertrude Warner, Jack Grimes, Elspeth Eric, Bob Dryden, Vic Perrin, John Dehner, Marvin Miller, Forrest Lewis, Bartlett Robinson, Russell Thorson, Sam Edwards and Harry Bartell.

Yours Truly, Johnny Dollar was the last major dramatic show on the network air, finally bowing out September 30, 1962.

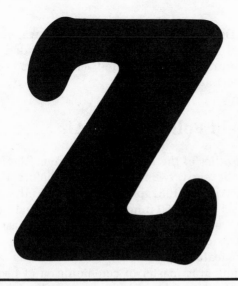

The Zane Grey Show

The Zane Grey Show premièred on Mutual September 11, 1947, and ran one season. It featured Vic Perrin and later Don MacLaughlin as Tex Thorne, Grey's even-tempered pony express rider, in tales of "the old West—rugged frontier of a young nation, where strong men lived by the strong law of personal justice." Director was Paul Franklin.

The Zero Hour

The Zero Hour began syndication in 1973, a highly potent thriller show brought about by the revival of interest in radio drama that came with the nostalgia craze. Like the contemporary *CBS Radio Mystery Theatre*, *The Zero Hour* featured many of radio's "old pro" fraternity, and also starred many "youngsters" who had come to the fore since TV. But while the *Mystery Theatre* was successful and is still running at this writing, *The Zero Hour* failed badly in its attempt at individual syndication. Also known as *The Hollywood Radio Theatre*, it was heard nightly, in five-chapter dramas featuring the best talent available. Rod Serling, whose unmistakable voice became famous through his *Twilight Zone* and *Night Gallery* TV shows, was host. Stars included Edgar Bergen, Richard Crenna, Howard Duff, George Maharis, Craig Stevens, Keenan Wynn, Joseph Campanella, John Astin, and Patty Duke. Elliott Lewis produced and directed, and theme music was by Ferrante and Teicher. There was only one problem: nobody bought it. By December 1973, *The Zero Hour* was reorganized and sold to Mutual, which changed the format, added new staff and booked too many commercials. It died, leaving *Mystery Theatre* alone to carry on a lost art.

The Ziegfeld Follies of the Air

The Ziegfeld Follies of the Air brought Florenz Ziegfeld, the master showman of the early twentieth century, before the CBS microphones for the April 3, 1932, première of his "Follies of the Air." As expected, it was a giant 60-minute musical-comedy splash.

The show was built around the stars of long-past Ziegfeld stage shows: Fanny Brice, Will Rogers, Billie Burke (Mrs. Ziegfeld), and Jack Pearl were featured performers. Eddie Dowling, a fair showman in his own right, was master of ceremonies and head writer. And leading the orchestra, as he had for so many Ziegfeld stage productions, was an old radio favorite, Al Goodman.

The original run lasted only a few months. Then Ziegfeld died and the name passed into legend. The show was revived on February 29, 1936, in another lavish 60-minute extravaganza over CBS. Written by Gertrude Berg of *Goldbergs* fame, this one followed the original in concept and intent, glamorizing the name with stars like Fanny Brice and James Melton. Al Goodman returned to lead the orchestra, and songs were by Benny Fields, Patti Chapin, and old, half-forgotten Follies headliners. Long-dead Follies stars who had enjoyed great popularity were impersonated, and musical numbers were introduced by a female trio, in rhyme. It was here, in the opening performance, that Miss Brice sang her famed "My Man," then introduced "Baby Snooks" to the world, with Jack Arthur playing the role of Daddy. Encouraged by good reviews, Arthur and Miss Brice continued the "Snooks" skits throughout the short summer run, and Miss Brice went on to Maxwell House, and a long career as radio's resident imp.

Revolving around the variety in this latter show was a bit of hokey backstage fluff, which Radio Guide for one found "hammy" and frivolous. This was the fictional story of Alice Moore, a girl from the sticks who was desperate to crack into big-time vaudeville. In the first show, she was forced to choose between love and the stage, threw away love and took a job as usher in the Follies. Now, hungry for any kind of break, she came to the dressing room of Fanny Brice herself, to plead for a chance. Fanny came off as something of a snob, but reluctantly agreed to give the drooling kid a shot.

The drama continued from week to week, with Alice edging ever closer to her goal. Will she make it? Will she become the Fanny Brice of the 1940's? It didn't last out the year, so we may never know. But it was a fascinating time to be alive. Values were different then and so were we. And that's what old-time radio was all about.

Index

Main alphabetical listings do not appear in this index except where there are cross references.